A WORLD PARLIAMENT

'This outstanding and comprehensive study by Jo Leinen and Andreas Bummel is now established as the standard work on the history, relevance and practical implementation of the idea of a world parliament, one that has been lacking for a long time. This book is a milestone in the debate on the democratisation of global governance. While the basic arguments remain valid, the second edition adds important material, in particular on current events.'

—**Frank Biermann**, Research Professor of Global Sustainability Governance at the University of Utrecht, founder and first chair of the Earth System Governance Project

'*A World Parliament* achieves several things. First, it shows how the campaign to create a people's assembly at the UN carries the baton forward in a long history of efforts to overcome nationalist and racist hatred, discrimination and oppression. Second, it demonstrates why the world's multiple challenges and crises cannot be addressed effectively and legitimately without a democratic body where everyone on the planet is represented as free and equal. Third, it offers a stirring vision of such a world parliament and a realistic plan of action for bringing it about. Each of these is a major accomplishment. Achieving them all in one book is a triumph.'

—**Mathias Koenig-Archibugi**, Associate Professor of Global Politics in the Departments of Government and International Relations, London School of Economics and Political Sciences

'Freedom in authoritarian countries has narrowed to the size of a prison cell. Even in developed democracies there are now setbacks. This important book shows that the struggle for freedom and democracy is a global struggle. In order to succeed, we need to build a global democratic order which offers no space to authoritarian regimes and puts the people first.'

—**Oleksandra Matviichuk**, Ukrainian human rights activist and Head of the Centre for Civil Liberties, recipient of the 2022 Nobel Peace Prize

'The authors of this 2nd edition of *A World Parliament* should be warmly congratulated for producing a highly readable and fascinating study. The new edition presents even more clearly ideas and vantage points that are urgently needed in rethinking the global order. The challenges we as a human species are confronted with are immense. This book explores the institutions and collective mechanisms, based on fairness, inclusivity and legitimacy, that are needed to ensure a safe and prosperous future for all.'

—**Maja Groff**, Esq., co-winner of the New Shape Prize, international lawyer, Senior Treaty Advisor, Integrity Initiatives International and Co-Founder, Global Governance Forum

'This wonderful book achieves the rare combination of realism and hope in charting a way forward for humanity. We simply need to reorient the global decision-making process from defending the national interest to serving the common good. This study explains why and shows how—by creating a Parliamentary Assembly to complement the General Assembly at the United Nations.'

—**John Vlasto**, Chair of the Board, World Federalist Movement-Institute for Global Policy

'In the 2nd edition of *A World Parliament*, Jo Leinen and Andreas Bummel strengthen the case for an approach to global governance commensurate with the needs of humanity today. They should be commended for producing a thoughtful and well-reasoned must-read.'

—**Daniel Perell**, Representative for the United Nations of the Baha'i International Community and Co-Chair, Coalition for the UN We Need

'This seminal work provides a comprehensive review of past measures to promote a world parliament and a guide to making the global parliamentary vision a reality. It is a vital resource for anyone interested in democratizing global governance.'

—**Andrew L. Strauss**, Professor of Law at the University of Dayton

'This book elaborates on how global governance must evolve based on humanity's centuries-old endeavour to create more democratic, just and peaceful societies. It shows that an international system built solely on relations between governments is no longer adequate. Creating a world parliamentary assembly to include citizens is long overdue. Essential reading for anyone who is concerned about our planet.'

—**Lysa John**, Secretary-General, CIVICUS: World Alliance for Citizen Participation

'The planetary crisis and the democratic deficit in global governance require humanity to establish and operationalize a world parliament. This timely book outlines a doable pathway towards this goal and addresses the persistent problem of achieving effective global cooperation. The second edition makes sure it is up to date in light of recent developments and adds new material throughout.'

—**Tim Murithi**, Institute for Justice and Reconciliation, Cape Town, and Extraordinary Professor of African Studies at the University of the Free State, Bloemfontein

'*A World Parliament* is an innovative and inspiring work. Its deep insights into the history, aspirations and, above all, the implementation of an elected universal assembly make it an indispensable resource for scholars, forward-thinking parliamentarians and decision-makers (yes, they do exist!) as well as anyone concerned with the future of democracy.'

—**George Katrougalos**, Professor of Public Law at the Democritus University of Thrace, UN Independent Expert on the promotion of a democratic and equitable international order, former Foreign Minister of Greece and former Member of the European Parliament

'Our globalized world is heading for disaster as long as it is based solely on national institutions. This extraordinary book is a valuable contribution to the literature on the global institutions we need to face the challenges of the 21st century.'

—**Fernando Iglesias**, Chair of the Foreign Affairs Commission of the Chamber of Deputies of Argentina and Co-President, World Federalist Movement-Institute for Global Policy

'In a time of dangerous and regressive political forces, Jo Leinen and Andreas Bummel have given us an outstanding atlas of hope—and a roadmap for the survival of humanity and democracy.'

—**William R. Pace**, former Executive Director, World Federalist Movement-Institute for Global Policy and Convenor, Coalition for the International Criminal Court

'The vision of a cosmopolitan world order as outlined in this recommendable book is vital for a world in which all people are closely connected and in which fundamental decisions are made for future generations.'

—**Heidemarie Wieczorek-Zeul**, former Federal Minister for Economic Cooperation and Development, Germany

'An excellent inspiration in the search for a sustainably better global governance.'

—**Yves Leterme**, former Prime Minister of Belgium and former Secretary-General of the International Institute for Democracy and Electoral Assistance

ABOUT THE AUTHORS

JO LEINEN served as a member of the European Parliament from 1999 to 2019. He chaired the environmental committee and the committee on constitutional affairs. From 2011 to 2017 he was president of the European Movement, an organization advocating for a democratic and enlarged European Union. From 1997 to 2005 he was presiding the Union of European Federalists that is dedicated to the promotion of European political unity. From 1985 to 1994 he was minister of the environment in the German state of Saarland. He graduated in law and was born in Bisten, Germany, in 1948.

ANDREAS BUMMEL is co-founder and director of Democracy Without Borders and of the Campaign for a United Nations Parliamentary Assembly. He has dedicated his career to the promotion of global democracy and world federalism. From 1998 to 2018 he was a Council member of the World Federalist Movement, an international NGO that promotes the rule of law, world peace, and federalism. He was trained in business administration, studied law and worked at a management consultancy firm. He was born in Cape Town, South Africa, in 1976.

A WORLD PARLIAMENT

Governance and Democracy
in the 21st Century

JO LEINEN
ANDREAS BUMMEL

*Second edition
expanded & updated*

A World Parliament
Governance and Democracy in the 21st Century
Jo Leinen and Andreas Bummel

© Democracy Without Borders, Berlin, 2024

Second edition
expanded & updated

The original English edition was published
in 2018 and was translated from the German edition
Das demokratische Weltparlament, Verlag J.H.W. Dietz Nachf., 2017
by Ray Cunningham

Cover design by Hermann Brandner, Cologne

Please contact us if you are interested in acquiring
foreign language or other rights to this publication

Paperback ISBN 978-3-942282-24-6
Hardcover ISBN 978-3-942282-26-0
Ebook ISBN 978-3-942282-25-3

Visit our website at
www.democracywithoutborders.org

Contents

Detailed Contents

PART III

Shaping the future: the design and realization of world democracy 474

Introduction

For the first time in history, people worldwide are linked together in a shared civilization that spans the entire Earth. Technological advances in communication, transportation, media, and information are driving planetary integration. The internet has become omnipresent and indispensable for society and business, connecting people and systems across the globe. Modern life relies on global trade, capital flows, services, and production chains. But the globalizing consumer society is unsustainable. Key natural resources are depleting and eventually will run out. Many renewable resources are at risk of collapse due to overuse. It is the age of the early Anthropocene. Human activities now affect the entire Earth system. Planetary boundaries that maintain a liveable environment and enable stable societies are being transgressed. Relentlessly increasing emissions from fossil fuels are exacerbating global warming which threatens to trigger multiple dangerous and irreversible tipping points. Meanwhile, the development of the political order is not keeping pace. Providing essential public goods such as climate protection, peace and security, health, food security, and financial stability relies heavily on the functioning of global structures and processes. But these, in turn, depend on the voluntary cooperation of two hundred states. The situation is paradoxical: while a shared civilization with a dense web of interdependencies has emerged, humanity remains politically divided and lacks collective agency.

This world is characterized by stark contrasts. Nuclear-armed states maintain thousands of missiles capable of annihilating population centers and the entire advanced civilization within less than thirty minutes. Dozens of intense violent conflicts rage around the world, some lasting for decades. Global military expenditures are staggering. Some states are unable to maintain basic public functions, leaving people to fend for themselves. Kleptocratic regimes, embedded into the global economy and finance, plunder their countries. Autocracies prevail, using modern methods and brute force if necessary to suppress freedom and dissent. They pursue a global program of autocracy promotion to undermine human rights and democracy beyond their borders. Whether a state is failed, autocratic, or democratic makes little difference on the international stage. All states are considered equal.

Never before in history has there been so much prosperity and abundance. The global economy is productive enough to enable all people on the planet to have a decent life with access to proper nutrition, social security, health care, education and other public services. But the instruments and conditions for this are lacking. Progress is difficult and inequality is extreme. While some people live in abject misery, others enjoy unprecedented wealth. Often it is only a simple fence that separates them. The accident of birth decides which side you are on. These dividing lines exist not only between countries but also within them. The promise of the global village is valid only for the rich. A global transnational class has emerged, able to go and stay wherever they want. But the age of territorial borders has not ended for those at the bottom. Free movement is not for them. Never before has the planet seen more border fortifications. The price of reaching the islands of prosperity, freedom, and democracy is steep and often deadly.

A global order must be established to ensure that all people on the planet are free and equal in dignity and rights, not only in theory but in reality. The benefits of globalization and growing productivity must be fairly distributed within societies and around the world. Just as slavery and colonialism were overcome, extreme poverty, economic exploitation, political despotism, and the institution of war must also be consigned to the history books. Achieving this requires more than just the right policies and good intentions. It necessitates creating the right political structures that enable their implementation. This book investigates the premises and functioning of international law, the United Nations, and other intergovernmental institutions and processes that constitute the system of global governance. We demonstrate that this system is inadequate. It preserves the status quo and can hardly go beyond it. This is morally and politically unacceptable—and a recipe for disaster. Driven by social, economic, environmental and political pressures, technological progress, changing identities, and dynamics beyond the control of any single actor, the evolution of the state and political order is continuing. In this book we trace elements of the global state formation process which appears to be heading towards a decisive moment. The model of the modern sovereign nation-state has outlived its time, yet powerful forces resist change. The inertia of economic and political elites is provoking the rise of nationalist, anti-modern, and counter-enlightenment forces, increasing the risk of global decline. If there is to be a common future, or perhaps any future at all, the sovereign nation-state will need to be merely an intermediate stage on humanity's journey toward a global polity.

In our vision, global governance will evolve into global government through a process of democratic revolution and political integration. This represents the third democratic transformation in human history, following the incomplete democratic beginnings in ancient times and the successive establishment of democracy in modern territorial states from the 18ᵗʰ century onwards. The most critical step in our view to strengthen and defend democracy is its expansion to the global scale. We explore why and how this can happen, with the development and goal of a world parliament at the center of attention. Universalism, cosmopolitanism, federalism, and democracy are among the concepts and principles that feature in our story. While a world parliament and a global constitutional order based on world law cannot be realized overnight, we argue that creating a global parliamentary assembly within the existing system is crucial and urgent to initiate the process. Some may be disappointed that we do not offer grand new blueprints to reinvent democracy. After all, the history of parliamentarism, for instance, spans over centuries. It is one of the most important mechanisms that has evolved to help govern human societies in a just, peaceful and democratic manner, and to hold power accountable. It needs to continue evolving and expand to the global scale. In this sense, we pursue a realistic utopia that builds seamlessly on past and present developments and experiences.

This book stems from our long-standing dedication to the vision of a world parliament and is based on over two decades of research, thought, and advocacy. Rather than offering a neutral analysis, this work serves as a passionate plea for this cause. As co-founders of the Campaign for a United Nations Parliamentary Assembly, we have actively pursued this project, driven by our conviction of its necessity. While the global risks and challenges of our time make a world parliament all the more imperative, the argument for it remains morally, conceptually, and politically valid even if existential threats and misery did not exist. In an interconnected global civilization, global decision-making and management are inherently necessary and all people need an equal opportunity to have a say. A world parliament is the institution that makes this possible.

This book also serves as a work of intellectual archaeology. It is good for proponents of this idea to see that they are part of a tradition stretching back centuries. The first part delves into historical and philosophical foundations, beginning with cosmopolitan thought in antiquity. For the first time in the literature, the book traces the evolution of the idea of a world parliament and the efforts to establish it from its origins in the French Revolution to the present day. We explore historical contributions and outline the project's impressive theoretical and practical underpinnings. In this regard, the book also functions as a comprehensive reference. We have made every effort to curate all possible sources related to a world parliament and to mention them, even if only briefly. It would have exceeded the scope of this work to contextualize each case. Certain regions and epochs have shown greater interest in this topic, providing richer source material than others. The historical narrative also touches upon related subjects such as the history of parliamentarism, democracy, and comprehensive peace plans.

The second part places the issue of a world parliament within the context of some of the most critical global challenges and long-term developments of our time. The coverage of policy areas is not exhaustive. Our starting point is the recognition of planetary boundaries, dealing with climate change, global public goods and the problem of growth. We address the instability of the global financial system as well as the race for deregulation and the need to stop global tax evasion. Transsovereign problems permeate all aspects of global society and we examine the fragility of world civilization, including the threat posed by pandemics. Advancements in bio- and nanotechnology, robotics, and artificial intelligence present profound questions for which humanity lacks institutional preparedness. This deficiency also extends to critical issues such as nuclear disarmament, collective security, safeguarding human rights, and combating global crime. As we point out, the construction of global democracy is also key for combating hunger, poverty and inequality, and for global water policy.

These issues are not tackled in isolation but are part of an overarching narrative that exposes the structural dysfunctions and deficiencies of the international system. Simultaneously, we delve into the foundations of a democratic world order and its underlying principles with increasing depth. The second part outlines the contours of a global state formation process that is already underway. We argue that currently, this process primarily benefits a transnational elite which requires global citizens to assert control through the establishment of a world parliament. Against the backdrop of global power structures dominated by this elite, we advocate for a new global social contract. Throughout our exploration, we critically examine the concept of national sovereignty and probe issues of hierarchical order, complexity, and the concept of world federalism. We touch on the development and universality of democracy, post-industrial value transformation, concepts of legitimacy and complementing representative democracy. The final chapter of the second part among other things explores the socio-political evolution of humanity within the context of long-term trends in cognitive, moral, and psychological development, tracing the emergence of a planetary consciousness.

Whenever possible, we let pertinent sources and relevant experts speak. Given the breadth of topics covered, we cannot delve into exhaustive academic or political debates. But we provide pointers and create connections that often receive little attention. This book showcases widespread support for a world parliament and critiques shortcomings in current discussions on global governance. At times, we outline policies that we believe a world parliament should implement, such as nuclear and conventional disarmament, a global basic income, or the regulation of global commodity markets. Throughout the book, we additionally examine proposals we believe should be part of democratic world governance under the oversight of a global parliamentary body. These include implementing unitary taxation for multinational corporations, establishing a global reserve currency and taxation system, creating a global anti-trust authority, enhancing the International Criminal Court's mandate, establishing a global criminal police force, forming a permanent UN peace-keeping force or setting up strategic global food reserves. The third part presents a possible evolutionary path toward implementing a world parliament and transitioning to a democratic global legal order. This includes how a UN Parliamentary Assembly can be put in place as an initial measure, how its membership could be selected and questions such as the apportionment of seats. We share reflections on a global constitution, compare principles of international law and world law, and explore outlines of the executive, legislative, and judicial branches of a new world organization. Finally, we discuss the underlying conditions and drivers for a transition toward global democracy, elaborating on a cosmopolitan movement and various other factors that likely will need to play a role.

We thank all colleagues, supporters, and partners, many of whom are mentioned or whose work has been quoted in this book, who have accompanied us on this long journey of endeavour. In the course of our activities, there have been countless encounters, discussions and events all over the world all of which have helped shape our thoughts and this book in one way or another. We are grateful to everyone who contributed to these exchanges and to the promotion of a world parliament. We hope you understand it is impossible to mention everyone individually. We wish to single out the Foundation for European Progressive Studies and The Workable World Trust (now discontinued) for their support in publishing the first English edition of this book, as well as Democracy Without Borders and all those involved in the organization. We hope this book will continue to facilitate serious debate and to provide a solid foundation for the ongoing efforts toward a world parliament. You are cordially invited to join this project. Share this book with friends, colleagues, and acquaintances. Support Democracy Without Borders which is leading this work. Become part of a new cosmopolitan movement!

Find out more at
www.democracywithoutborders.org

NOTE ON THE SECOND EDITION

While the fundamental arguments have remained unchanged, the second edition reflects significant developments since 2018, particularly the COVID-19 pandemic, autocratization, and the Russian war of aggression against Ukraine. This edition incorporates linguistic improvements, updated content, extensive revisions, and additions throughout the entire book, expanding its size by approximately one fifth. Hundreds of new articles, reports, and sources were analyzed, with over 450 included in this new edition. A few interviews were also conducted. New content was added in particular in Chapter 1, sections 'Cosmopolitanism in Medieval Baghdad' and 'Indigenous Concepts in the Americas and Africa'; in Chapter 3, 'Independence, Unification, and Division in Latin America', 'Parliamentarism and World Federalism in Japan', 'The "One World" Utopia of Kang Youwei' and the next three sections; in Chapter 5, 'The Moscow Declaration', 'Decolonization and World Order' and the next three sections; in Chapter 6, 'Uniting for Peace'; in Chapter 8, 'The "Political Trilemma of the World Economy"'; in Chapter 11, 'Planetary boundaries as a common concern' and 'Enforcement and its legitimacy'; in Chapter 12, 'Prosperity, happiness and democracy'; in Chapter 13, 'The financial crisis and national populism' and 'The role of a UN Parliamentary Assembly'; in Chapter 14, 'Building on the IMF's Special Drawing Rights', 'A global minimum corporate tax rate' and 'A UN Tax Organization'; in Chapter 16, 'Artificial intelligence', 'COVID-19, "Disease X" and the pandemic threat' and the next four sections; in Chapter 18, 'The terrorist threat and its impact'; in Chapter 20, 'The issue of multistakeholder governance'; in Chapter 24, 'The spectere of a global Leviathan', 'The principle of subsidiarity' and the next section; in Chapter 25, 'The issue of populism revisited', 'The historic beginnings of democracy' and 'Complementing representation'; in Chapter 26, 'Popular support for a world parliament'; in Chapter 29, 'The challenge of autocratization revisited' and 'A cosmopolitan movement'. Chapter 10 is new and most of Chapters 14, 27 and 28 is new or entirely rewritten.

NOTE ON TRANSLATION

The original English edition, on which this second edition is based, was translated from German by Ray Cunningham. All changes in this new edition were made by Andreas Bummel. Unless an English-language source is given for a quotation originally in a foreign language, translations are by the authors and/or the original translator. Some terms for political and legal concepts from the Germanophone world are difficult to translate into English, e.g. Rechtsstaat and its derivatives (such as *Rechtsstaatlichkeit*), or *Völkerstaat*. The original translator tried to signpost any important distinctive nuances in the text, but sometimes simply kept the German original where repeating such signposting would become a distraction.

PART I

The idea of a world parliament: its history and pioneers

The idea of a world parliament raises the question of the role played in the world order by each individual person. It is based on the conviction that all people, regardless of their many differences, are members of a single family of human beings encompassing the whole world. By virtue of their humanity alone they are, without exception, citizens of the world, with equal status and equal rights. As such, they share responsibility for the planetary community and its habitat, the Earth. The world parliament is the political institution in which all people will be directly represented by delegates whom they elect. The task of this institution is to stand guard over the wellbeing of all people and their common interest. It is a product and a symbol of the self-determination and sovereignty of humanity as a whole, and the foundation for a legitimate world state system.

The concept of global popular representation brings together historical and philosophical developments that can be traced back over many centuries. From at least the Enlightenment up to the present day, an important developing dynamic has been humanity's universal quest for emancipation, democracy, self-determination and peace. Given the number of autocratic regimes still in place today, the idea of a world parliament, because it is conceived as an institution whose members are elected by universal, equal and free votes, also represents a plea for continuing and progressive political emancipation and democratization. In this sense, the idea of a world parliament has its roots not only in universal values of the Enlightenment, which had the goal, in the words of Immanuel Kant, of freeing humankind from its 'self-imposed state of dependency', but it continues to further the cosmopolitan dimension of the Enlightenment programme. The establishment of a world parliament is the central goal of a *new global enlightenment*, because it would make every human being, without discrimination, an equal citizen of a world legal order. Building such an inclusive democratic global order is incompatible with hegemonic endeavours. It entails the goal of ending economic, political, social and racist oppression and dismantling imperialist structures and power. It is part of the universal project of including the excluded in a 'world in common' and recognizing the underlying principles of 'equal shares' and 'the fundamental unity of human beings' in the words of the historian and political theorist Achille Mbembe.[1]

As Edward Said (1935 to 2003), one of the founders of postcolonial studies, pointed out, narratives of emancipation and enlightenment are about *integration*, not separation.[2] Efforts toward political integration therefore play a key role in our considerations. The project challenges the centuries-old international law paradigm of territorial sovereignty which is a main obstacle to humanity's progress in practical and ideological terms. According to a standard account, its origins are to be found at the Peace of Westphalia of 1648 after almost a third of the population of central Europe had died in the Thirty Years' War and entire regions had been depopulated. Supposedly, agreement was reached by European powers on a 'law of nations' based on the reciprocal recognition of sovereign equality and independence of rulers, exclusive rule over a demarcated given territory, the principles of non-intervention, balance of power and the co-existence of differing confessions. This depiction of the treaty and its content is historically inaccurate, if not outright false.[3] What has become associated with Westphalia, the emergence of an international system of territorial sovereign states, is a development that took place gradually over the course of at least two more centuries. In practice, the Westphalian 'law of nations' was, to a considerable extent, a fictional construct. All states, in particular the powerful, adhered to those principles only to the extent that they found it necessary or convenient. They also shaped and interpreted them in their favour whenever possible. Of course, 'international societies were hardly the sole prerogative of Christian Europe', as political scientist Hendrik Spruyt noted in a book on the East Asian Sino-centric order, the Islamic empires and the polities of Southeast Asia from early modernity to the late 19th century. Their exclusion from the emerging 'Westphalian system', Spruyt observed, had primarily to do with the European powers establishing the idea of a 'civilized core', comprising themselves, as a stratagem to 'legitimate imperial practices' towards the 'uncivilized' rest of the world.[4] Antony Anghie showed how sovereignty doctrine, in particular, was crafted in a way in order to exclude the non-European in the colonial encounter and to legitimize subjugation of the

---

1   Mbembe, Achille. Critique of Black Reason. Durham: Combined Academic Publ., 2017, pp. 176-7.
2   Said, Edward W. 1994. Culture and Imperialism. Vintage, p. xxxiii.
3   See Osiander, Andreas. 2001. 'Sovereignty, International Relations, and the Westphalian Myth.' International Organization 55 (2): 251–87.
4   Spruyt, Hendrik. 2020. The World Imagined: Collective Beliefs and Political Order in the Sinocentric, Islamic and Southeast Asian International Societies. Cambridge University Press, pp. 6, 287. 8.

alleged 'non-civilized'.[5] While European expansionism stands out, Said aptly cautioned that in all 'nationally defined cultures' there probably is 'an aspiration to sovereignty, to sway and to dominate.'[6]

If sovereignty was initially a personal attribute of feudal lords and monarchical rulers, in the course of the American and French revolutions in the 18th century it metamorphosed into the sovereignty of the people in domestic affairs and that of the emerging modern state in foreign affairs. In this way the modern state seamlessly took over the legacy of the monarchies. The further continuation of the unfinished Enlightenment project in the global age must adopt as its objectives the overcoming of the arbitrary containment of human beings in territorial sovereign states, the establishment of global citizenship, the embedding of governance and democracy in clear global public structures, where necessary, and the successful achievement of the leap from international law (i.e. law between states) to a cosmopolitan world law. *World law*, in contrast to international law, will genuinely possess the characteristics of law: universally binding determination through legislation, the obligatory adjudication of disputes before courts, and the necessary means for enforcement. This will be the foundation of a truly post-Westphalian democratic order. Our focus is on the first of these aspects, and within that on the legislative institution.

The aim of establishing a world parliament is closely connected with contemporary problems and challenges. For an understanding it is essential to have a clear picture of the philosophical roots and historical dimension of the project. In this section, we provide a historical overview from its beginnings up to the present day.

5   Anghie, Antony. 2005. Imperialism, Sovereignty and the Making of International Law. Cambridge and New York: Cambridge University Press, pp. 29-30, 311-3.
6   Said, p. 16.

1.
From ancient times to Kant: cosmopolitanism, sovereignty, and the idea of a social contract

One of the founding principles on which the idea of a world parliament is based is that the entire Earth must be comprehended as the home of all human beings who enjoy equal rights as global citizens. It is an institutional reflection of cosmopolitanism, a worldview traces of which can be found in different manifestations across the world's regions and cultures deep into history. The core of a modern cosmopolitan view is an emphatic affinity with fellow human beings in all their diversity, the whole of humankind and life on Earth and an acknowledgement that they are part of a planetary unity. It is inclusive and does not build on an 'Us' vs. 'Them' distinction which is usually characteristic of group identity formation.[1]

Cosmopolitanism in ancient Greece

The origins of cosmopolitan thought in the West are usually traced back to the Greek philosopher Diogenes of Sinope (ca. 400 to 323 BCE), who, when asked about his home city, is supposed to have answered that he was a 'kosmopolitês'—a citizen of the world. It reflects the plurality and ambiguity of how the term was used in the course of history that scholars have offered different interpretations of this. In the Greek political culture at the time, a man instead would usually identify as a citizen of a particular polis or city.[2] According to Harold Carpane Baldry, a specialist in classic studies, rather than Diogenes declaring attachment to humanity, which is a common view, in the context of his Cynic worldview the quote needs to be understood as an expression of individual independence and *detachment* from any allegiances.[3] In a book

1   Cf. Bummel, Andreas. 2021. 'Towards a Planetary Polity: The Formation of Global Identity and State Structures.' In: Expanding Worldviews: Astrobiology, Big History and Cosmic Perspectives, ed. by Ian Crawford, 325–40. Cham: Springer.

2   Kleingeld, Pauline, and Eric Brown. 2019. 'Cosmopolitanism.' In: The Stanford Encyclopedia of Philosophy, ed. by Edward N. Zalta, Winter 2019 Ed. Stanford University. (plato.stanford.edu).

3   Baldry, H. C. 1965. The Unity of Mankind in Greek Thought. Cambridge University Press, p. 108-109. See also: Sellars, John. 2007. 'Stoic Cosmopolitanism and Zeno's Republic.' History of Political Thought 28 (1): 1–29, pp. 4-7.

on the subject Baldry stressed that tracing the idea of human unity in Greek ancient thought is not so simple. There is little literary evidence and often it is fragmented and second-hand, like in the case of Diogenes.[4]

An important, and no less ambiguous, role is accorded to Alexander the Great (356 to 323 BCE), who brought Persia, Asia Minor and Egypt under his rule, and extended it as far as the Indian subcontinent. Peter Coulmas wrote in an account of the history of cosmopolitanism that Alexander was the first to express the view that all people should be regarded as brothers and kin. He pursued the vision of an 'empire of the human race' encompassing many different peoples and countries.[5] He is supposed to have advanced the idea that 'the habitable Earth' was 'the common fatherland of all'. As the historian of antiquity Alexander Demandt recounted, Alexander, according to Plutarch (350 to 432), saw himself as the 'arbitrator and steward of humanity' whose task it was 'to merge all people together into a single body and to mix the peoples in a giant mixing bowl of friendship' and 'to unite them into a single family'. His philosophy was based on the idea that all people, Greeks as well as 'barbarians', were equal.[6] Although he may not have wanted to be regarded by Persians and other peoples as an alien ruler, the reality was different. Their incorporation into his empire was achieved by imperial and military force. According to Baldry, describing Alexander as 'the champion of human brotherhood and unity' rests on shaky grounds.[7]

It appears that in later Stoic philosophy, the idea of 'Cosmos' encompassing a natural community of humankind and the unity of all life was firmly established by around 300 BCE. This viewpoint was contrary to the prevailing particularism and parochialism of the ancient Greek world, which after the collapse of the Alexandrian empire was fragmented into rival city-states. In this situation, Zeno of Citium (334 to 262 BCE) published his work 'Republic' that did not survive but was commented on by others. Plutarch summarized that 'the much-admired Republic of Zeno' could be described by 'one main principle: that all the inhabitants of this world of ours should not live differentiated by their respective rules of justice into separate cities and communities, but that we should consider all men to be of one community and one polity'.[8] The idea that 'this whole universe should [be] thought to be one city in com-

---

4   Ibid., pp. 1-4.
5   Coulmas, Peter. 1990. Weltbürger. Geschichte einer Menschheitssehnsucht. Reinbek: Rowohlt, p. 90.
6   Demandt, Alexander. Alexander der Große. München: C.H. Beck, 2012. pp. 373, 378, 373.
7   Baldry, pp. 126, 128.
8   Plutarch. 1936. Plutarch's Moralia. Volume IV. Transl. by Frank Cole Babbitt. Cambridge: Harvard University Press, p. 397. On Zeno, see also: Wildberger, Jula. 2018. The Stoics and the State. Baden-Baden: Nomos, pp. 117-9 and Sellars, ibid.

mon between gods and human beings', as Cicero (106 to 43 BCE) put it later[9], had no explicit political intent, and was not necessarily meant to imply the idea of a world state. Nevertheless, as Coulmas observed, 'the secular and unique historic achievement of the Stoics was to project the community of citizens as realized in the Polis onto the community of humanity and thus to universalize it'.[10]

In one of Cicero's dialogues, the view is advanced that human solidarity and shared responsibility extend to the whole of humanity. A human being, it is argued, 'simply by reason of the fact that he is human, should not be considered a stranger by any other human being'. Every single person is connected to the human community. It is a natural duty 'to place the common interests of all people above our own'.[11] As the classical scholar Klaus Bartels remarked, the dialogue culminates in the concept of treason against humanity and in the astoundingly modern hypothesis that people have a duty not only towards the human community but also towards future generations. 'Whoever sacrifices the common interests or welfare of all for his own interests or welfare' deserves just as much censure as 'someone who betrays their fatherland'. And later on it is argued that steps must also be taken to ensure the welfare of 'those generations that will live in times to come'.[12]

The idea of a democratic world community was then formulated by Philo of Alexandria (ca. 15 BCE to 40 CE), one of the best-known representatives of Hellenic Jewry. There are two species of cities, he wrote in a treatise, and one of them is better than the other, namely the one 'which enjoys a democratic government, a constitution which honors equality, the rulers of which are law and justice'.[13] The ultimate purpose of the rise and fall of people and nations, he philosophized in another text, was 'in order that the whole world may become, as it were, one city, and enjoy the most excellent of constitutions, a democracy'.[14]

Cosmopolitan roots in the Asian region

Cosmopolitan thought is also found, and from very early on, beyond the cultural borders of ancient Greece. For example, in the collection of Old Tamil

9   Cicero. 2014. On the Republic and On the Laws. Transl. by David Fott. Ithaca and London: Cornell University Press, see: On the Laws, I.23, p. 138.
10   Coulmas, pp. 114-6.
11   Cit. from Bartels, Klaus. 2011. Jahrtausendworte in die Gegenwart gesprochen. Darmstadt/Mainz: Philipp von Zabern, p. 74.
12   Cit. from ibid., pp. 74-5.
13   On the Confusion of Tongues, Section XXIII (108), in: Philo Judaeus. 1993. The Works of Philo. Transl. by C.D. Yonge. New updated edition. Hendrickson Publishers. p. 243.
14   On the Unchangeableness of God, XXXVI (175), ibd., p. 172.

poetry 'Puṟanāṉūṟu', which is part of Sangam literature from the period between 100 BCE and the fifth century, it is said 'Yātum ūrē yāvarum kēḷir' in a poem by Kaṇiyaṉ Pūngunṟanār which expresses the view that all places are the common home of all, literally translated as 'every city is your city, everyone is your kin'.[15]

The Hindu Upanishads, which are in part much older, and other ancient Indian Sanskrit texts contain the philosophical concept 'Vasudhaiva Kutumbakam', which in Sanskrit means 'the whole world is one family'.[16] Most prominently, two verses in the Maha Upanishads note that 'only small men discriminate saying: One is a relative; the other is a stranger. For those who live magnanimously the entire world constitutes but a family.'[17] The ancient Indian political order nonetheless was fragmented into hundreds of small dynastic states whose relationship was characterized by enmity. The dynamics of these inter-state relations and questions of sovereignty were a subject of ancient Hindu political thought. According to the international legal scholar Charles Henry Alexandrowicz (1902 to 1975), the polymath Kauṭilya (375 to 283 BCE) in his treatise 'Arthashastra' described an anarchic 'concert of sovereigns in the circle of states', called 'mandala', which remains unstable and 'outside the orbit of law' until a ruler emerges who manages to subjugate all others as the supreme suzerain 'and replace decentralization by a universal empire'.[18] The Indian sociologist Benoy Kumar Sarkar (1887 to 1949) pointed out that Hindu political thought produced 'several categories to express the same idea of the world state or universal sovereignty.'[19] Basically, they all rested on the notion that the strongest ruler will impose imperial order on the others as vassals and thus, similarly to Alexander the Great's empire, do not reflect cosmopolitan inclusiveness despite their universal aspiration.

Turning to China, in the 'Book of Rites', one of the five classics of the Confucian canon, which are derived from the teachings of the Chinese philoso-

---

15   There are many translations of this line indifferent variations.For this one see: The Four Hundred Songs of War and Wisdom. An Anthology of Poems from Classical Tamil. 1999. Ed. and transl. by George L. Hart and Hank Heifetz. New York: Columbia University Press, p. 124.

16   See e.g. the fable 'The Brahman and his weasel' in the Hitopadesha; see also Śarman, Lakshmīnarayaṇa. 1830. The Hitopadesha: A collection of fables and tales in Sanskrit by Vishnusarmá. Calcutta: Shástra Prakásha Press, pp. 508-509 (Ch. 4, Fable 13).

17   The Sāmānya Vedānta Upaniṣad-s. 1991. Ed. and transl. by A.G. Krishna Warrier. Madras: Adyar Library and Research Centre, pp. 206-7. For a different translation see Joshi, K.L., et al., eds. 2016. 112 Upaniṣads. Vol. 2. Transl. by Board of Scholars. 5th Reprint Ed. Parimal Publications, p. 264.

18   Alexandrowicz, C.H. 2017. 'Kautilyan Principles and the Law of Nations (1965-1966).' In: The Law of Nations in Global History, id., ed. by David Armitage and Jennifer Pitts, 35–52. Oxford University Press, p. 40 and id., 1967. An Introduction to the History of the Law of Nations in the East Indies. Oxford: Clarendon Press, p. 226.

19   Sarkar, Benoy Kumar. 1919. 'Hindu Theory of International Relations.' American Political Science Review 13 (3): 400–414, p. 409.

pher Confucius (551 to 470 BCE), can be found the idea of Dadong or the 'Great Unity', according to which the world should be shared equally and harmoniously by all.[20] Still older is the concept of Tianxia, which means roughly 'everything under heaven' or 'nothing outside'. This rose to importance in the Zhou dynasty, around 1046 to 256 BCE and includes the idea that the Chinese Emperor unites and rules the world as the Son of Heaven. In the Zhou dynasty, according to the Chinese philosopher Zhao Tingyang, the starting point of all political thinking was the world as a whole. It was regarded as the 'uppermost political entity', to which all other political entities should be subordinate. According to the theory of Tianxia, which is undergoing a modern re-interpretation, a political system can only claim to be in a state of peace 'when the notion of externality no longer exists; in other words, when nothing and nobody is excluded', as Tingyang explains. The philosopher pointed out that the Tao Te Ching, for example in chapter 54, has a global perspective, too.[21] Interestingly, in a comparison of the classic concepts of Cosmos and Tianxia, Yudan Chen of Fudan University concluded that they are 'quite similar', share 'some significant points' and provide an inclusive perspective that has been too long ignored in the contemporary world.[22]

A people-centred and inclusive cosmopolitan philosophy is part of the founding myth of Korea that dates back to 2333 BCE when the 'grandson of heaven' Dangun established the kingdom of Gojoseon and the first Korean dynasty. It is said that this was done under the guiding principle of 'Hongik Ingan' which means that Koreans shall 'live and work for the benefit of all humanity'.[23] As Nobel Peace laureate Kim Dae-jung argued, this principle contains a fundamentally democratic idea that can be traced throughout Korean history: people, not rulers, are the most important subjects of government.[24] 'Independent of the social transformations that would come in Europe during the Reformation, Renaissance and Enlightenment eras many centuries later, Hongik Inan ideals allowed Koreans to have an enlightened view of humanity and its relation to heaven', Hyun Jin Moon, founder of the Global Peace Foundation, explained.[25]

20   On Tianxia, see also pp. 530f.

21   Zhao, Tingyang. 2009. 'A Political World Philosophy in terms of All-under-heaven (Tian-xia)'. Diogenes (56) 221: 5–18. pp. 8-10.

22   Chen, Yudan. 2016. 'Two Roads to a World Community: Comparing Stoic and Confucian Cosmopolitanism.' Chinese Political Science Review 1 (2): 322–35, pp. 332-3.

23   See Korean Spirit and Culture Promotion Project. 2011. The Practice of Hongik Ingan. Lives of Queen Seondeok, Shin Saimdang and Yi Yulgok. Seoul: Diamond Sutra Recitation Group, p. 7.

24   Kim, Dae-jung, and Lee Hee-ho. 2018. Conscience in Action: The Autobiography of Kim Dae-Jung. Translated by Jeon Seung-hee. New York, NY: Palgrave Macmillan, p. 300.

25   Moon, Hyun Jin Preston. 2020. Korean Dream: A Vision For a Unified Korea. New York London Nashville Melbourne Vancouver: Morgan James Publishing, p. 119.

In Japan, the traditional concept of kyōsei represents the cosmopolitan idea best according to sociologist Yoshio Sugimoto. The term literally means 'living together' and has ecological and biological connotations. Sugimoto argued that it captures transnational and multicultural cosmopolitan orientations in particular. First, a 'value system in which individuals or groups regard themselves as citizens of a global community' and second, 'an endeavor to dispel ethnic prejudice and stereotypes, guarantee equal rights to foreigners and minority groups and promote harmonious co-existence with mutual respect for cultural heritage, across socio-cultural divisions'.[26]

Cosmopolitanism in medieval Baghdad

Following the conquests of the Muslim caliphates that by the 7th century created a vast empire stretching from the Spanish peninsula in the West and the Indus river in the East, political fragmentation set in with the rise of regional Muslim dynasties. In the 10th century, Baghdad became the centre of a renewed interest in the 'intellectual legacy of Greek antiquity' in an environment 'permeated by a spirit of scepticism and secularism' according to Joel Kraemer, a scholar of Islamic philosophy.[27] One of the best known philosophers of this time is Abū Nasr al-Fārābī, or Alfarabi (872 to 950), who in the Islamic tradition was called the 'Second Teacher', following Aristotle as the first. Among other things, Alfarabi touches in his works on the notion of a universal human community that encompasses the entire 'inhabited world'. His writings appear to leave room for conflicting interpretations, though. While some scholars think he had a worldwide and secular cosmopolitan political association in mind, others believe it is 'very plausible' that he was rather referring to 'the promised universal Muslim world state under the rule of Imam Mahdi' who is believed to appear at the end of times.[28] Clearly, cosmopolitanism was in the air though. The Syriac Jacobite Christian philosopher, theologian and translator Abū Zakarīyā' Yaḥyá ibn 'Adī, or Yahya ibn Adi (893 to 974), who had the same teacher as Alfarabi, argued that the universality of reason implies the ultimate unity of humankind. One who loves perfec-

26 Sugimoto, Yoshio. 2012. 'Kyōsei. Japan's Cosmopolitanism.' In: Routledge Handbook of Cosmopolitanism Studies, ed. by Gerard Delanty, 452–62. Taylor and Francis.

27 Kraemer, Joel L. 1992. Humanism in the Renaissance of Islam: The Cultural Revival During the Buyid Age. 2nd rev. ed. Leiden et al.: Brill, p. vii.

28 Hayes, Josh. 2022. 'Cosmopolitanism in the Medieval Arabic and Islamic World.' In: The Edinburgh Critical History of Middle Ages and Renaissance Philosophy, ed. by Andrew LaZella and Richard A. Lee Jr., 217–33. Edinburgh University Press; and Ali, Ishraq, and Mingli Qin. 2019. 'Distinguishing the Virtuous City of Alfarabi from That of Plato in Light of His Unique Historical Context.' HTS Teologiese Studies/Theological Studies 75 (4).

tion, he wrote, should thus 'train his soul to harbor friendship toward all men' for 'men are one tribe, related to one another, joined together by humanity.'[29]

Indigenous concepts in the Americas and Africa

There are indigenous ancestral concepts, learned and passed down culturally over generations, which express cosmopolitan thinking as well. In the rituals of the Lakota people, who belong to the Native American plains tribes, the formula of 'mitákuye oyás'iŋ' has an important role.[30] At the conclusion of the pipe ceremony, for instance, all participants in turn state these words which mean 'all my relatives, all of us, everyone', as Lame Deer (1903 to 1976) explained. According to the Lakota holy man, the expression includes 'all human beings upon this earth, all living things down to the tiniest insect, the tiniest plant'.[31] It is a statement of 'profound implication' for the Lakota and an 'affirmation of the mysterious interrelatedness of all that is', wrote anthropologist Joseph Epes Brown.[32]

In the case of the concepts of Ubuntu in Sub-Saharan Africa and Sumak Kawsay in the Andean and Amazonian regions there are also no historical writings to draw upon. Their meaning and relevance are subject of vivid scholarly debates.[33] In a modern interpretation, many see them as indigenous contributions to a global inclusive cosmopolitanism.

The term Ubuntu belongs to the South African Nguni language family which includes Zulu and Xhosa, among others. Variants exist in languages spoken in Kenya, Tanzania, Mozambique, Congo and Angola. Nigerian scholar Michael O. Eze reported that most often it is simply translated as 'humanism'.[34] According to South African human rights activist and Anglican cleric Desmond Tutu (1931 to 2021), Ubuntu encapsulates the notion that no human being can exist in isolation: 'A person is a person through other persons'. All individual action thus must be seen in relation to others and 'affects the whole world'. A person 'with ubuntu', said Tutu, is 'affirming of others' and knows he or she belongs to a 'greater whole' and is diminished when others

---

29 Cit. from Kraemer, p. 115.
30 Powers, William K. 1982. Oglala Religion. University of Nebraska Press, pp. 154-5.
31 Lame Deer, John (Fire), and Richard Erdoes. 1972. Lame Deer: Seeker of Visions. Simon & Schuster, p. 197.
32 Epes Brown, Joseph. 2007. The Spiritual Legacy of the American Indian. Bloomington, Indiana: World Wisdom, Inc., pp. xv, 39-40.
33 See, for instance, Matolino, Bernard, and Wenceslaus Kwindingwi. 2013. 'The End of Ubuntu.' South African Journal of Philosophy 32 (2): 197–205; and Cubillo-Guevara, Ana Patricia, and Antonio Luis Hidalgo-Capitán. 2015. 'El sumak kawsay genuino como fenómeno social amazónico ecuatoriano.' OBETS. Revista de Ciencias Sociales 10 (2): 301–33.
34 Eze, Michael Onyebuchi. 2010. Intellectual History in Contemporary South Africa. New York: Palgrave Macmillan, pp. 93, 90.

are humiliated, tortured or oppressed.[35] Ubuntu thus stresses a relational feature of cosmopolitanism.[36] In the formation of a new post-apartheid South Africa, the notion of Ubuntu helped build an inclusive national imaginary of a 'rainbow nation' that integrated heterogenous cultures, races, memories and perspectives.[37] In the view of South African professor and founder of the Ubuntu Global Network, John Volmink, the concept has 'moved us away from narrow nationalistic ideologies and towards a broad and humanistic universalism' that can be applied as a global ethic.[38] As a normative ethical concept, Ubuntu implies and calls for a 'global institutional order' that 'promotes the interests of the global community of all human beings', argued Peter Mwipikeni, a lecturer at the University of Zululand.[39]

In terms of Sumak Kawsay, researchers point out that the expression was used by the Amazonian Kichwas people, among others, long before it began to be popularized in the early 1990s. The first to do so was Kichwan intellectual and politician Carlos Viteri who translated it as 'buen vivir' or 'good living'. He explained that in the holistic 'cosmovision' of indigenous societies there is no conception of linear progress or development that is paramount in Western thinking. Rather, they seek to establish and maintain the material and spiritual conditions for good or 'harmonious living'.[40] The concept of 'buen vivir' or 'vivir bien' respectively, was included in the constitutions of Ecuador in 2008 and Bolivia in 2009. According to María Fernanda Espinosa, who was a social researcher in the Amazon before starting a steep career in Ecuadorian and international politics, it is now 'a common denominator' of these 'plurinational countries'. She said that vivir bien 'includes an alternative notion of development that is not tied to growth. Increasing gross domestic product and over-consumption does not equal increasing happiness.' The former Ecuadorian foreign minister and president of the UN General Assembly explained that vivir bien 'is not a monolithic concept' and that 'indigenous communities across the Andean and Amazon region have different understandings and different challenges applying it.' However, she believes that the 'core principles of Sumak Kawsay such as harmony, empathy and kindness, not only be-

---

35 See interview in: Schnall, Marianne. 2010. 'The Elders Speak: Desmond Tutu, Jimmy Carter And Mary Robinson.' Huffington Post. May 4, 2010. (huffpost.com) and Tutu, Desmond. 2000. No Future Without Forgiveness. New York: Image, p. 31.

36 Graness, Anke. 2018. 'Ubuntu and the Concept of Cosmopolitanism.' Human Affairs 28 (4): 395–405, p. 404.

37 Eze, pp. 106, 112, 128, 181.

38 Volmink, John D. 2019. 'UBUNTU: Philosophy of Life and Social Ethics.' In Building Bridges - Ubuntu and Servant Leadership. Ubuntu Leaders Academy, p. 53.

39 Mwipikeni, Peter. 2018. 'Ubuntu and the Modern Society.' South African Journal of Philosophy 37 (3): 322–34, p. 332.

40 Cubillo-Guevara, pp. 312-3, 316-7.

tween humans but also towards the natural environment, need to be applied universally, at the global scale' and can 'underpin the idea of a global parliament' which she 'fully supports'.[41] Bolivia's former UN ambassador Pablo Solón confirmed that 'it is not possible to enact vivir bien in a single country' due to global interdependence. In his view, the notion entails a 'continual struggle for decolonization', in particular 'liberating our minds and souls, which have been captured by false and alien concepts.'[42]

Vitoria's 'republic of the whole world'

The first detailed formulation of the idea of the whole of humanity as a state-like community appeared at the start of the European colonization of Central and South America. It was in stark contrast to the unchecked inhumanity of the Spanish Conquista which was protested against from early on but to no avail. According to Bartolomé de Las Casas (1484 to 1566), a Dominican priest who chronicled and spoke up against the atrocities, they were at a magnitude of barbarism that threatened 'to bring a collapse of civilization' and presaged 'the end of the world'.[43] In his view, all human beings, including the Indians, were basically equal and 'thus the entire human race is one', he wrote.[44] In a similar spirit, Pope Paul III in 1537 declared in the bull 'Sublimis Deus' that even if they were outside the Christian faith, 'Indians and all other people who may later be discovered' are 'by no means to be deprived of their liberty or the possession of their property' which they 'freely and legitimately' enjoy as 'true men'. This had little effect though, if any.

The Dominican theologian Francisco de Vitoria (1483 to 1546), who from 1526 onwards gave lectures at the University of Salamanca, developed the concept of a 'res publica totus orbis', a community spanning the entire globe. There had been other sketches for a world state, notably that for a tiered universal monarchy developed by Dante Alighieri (1265 to 1321). The latter was conceived around an imperialist Christian Roman empire under an unrestricted ruler.[45] While Dante argued that church and state power were to be independent from each other, thus paving the way for secular political theory,

---

41   Interview on 24 May 2022.

42   Solón, Pablo. 26 March 2018. 'Vivir Bien: Old Cosmovisions and New Paradigms.' Great Transition Initiative. (greattransition.org).

43   Las Casas, Bartolomé de. 1992 [1552]. A Short Account of the Destruction of the Indies. Translated by Nigel Griffin. Penguin Classics, p. 128.

44   In ch. 48 of his Apologetic History published around 1560. Excerpts in: id. 1992. Witness: Writings of Bartolomé de Las Casas. Ed. by Gustavo Gutiérrez. Maryknoll, New York: Orbis Books, pp. 174-5.

45   Sullivan, Mary Elizabeth. 2018. 'Is Dante a Cosmopolitan?' Postmedieval 9 (4): 511–23.

he ultimately accepted the supremacy of the pope.[46] The term 'cosmopolitan' resurfaced in early modern Europe in the 16th century but first in such imperial contexts.[47]'In contrast to the universal monarchy,' wrote the Vitoria scholar Johannes Thumfart, 'Vitoria appears as the champion of a concrete, democratically legitimated and pluralistically structured global polity.'[48]

For us, accustomed as we are to the division of the world into states, Vitoria's conceptual approach is not very easy to grasp. As Josef Soder explained, the community imagined by Vitoria is 'neither a state like other states, nor a super-state, but simply the summation of the whole of humanity, whether divided into states or not'.[49] In Vitoria's conception, the global state community of the 'totus orbis' is aboriginal. It precedes the formation of separate individual polities and is therefore also not annulled by their emergence. Indeed, the 'totus orbis' can issue laws that are binding on all people and all states. Remarkably, this requires only the assent of a majority in his conception. Vitoria, to be sure, did not explain exactly how such decisions on the part of 'the whole globe' were to be reached in practice. At any rate, the goal or purpose of what he believes to be this naturally occurring community is the wellbeing of all people.

The aboriginal community of all human beings in Vitoria's conception is the starting point for state organization, and every individual is by nature a subject of international law entitled under certain conditions to certain rights. Vitoria assumed in all of this that all people are essentially equal, regardless of their religion or other characteristics. He formulated this view at the beginning of the era of globalization, just as Europeans were coming across peoples who had until then been entirely unknown to them. According to Vitoria's doctrine of international law, non-Christian communities such as those found in the 'New World' also had a right to self-governance and property. Their subjugation was therefore wrong, and at the very least required justification.[50] Rolf Grawert commented: 'at a time when Spaniards are murdering Aztecs and overthrowing their rule, and when Francis I of France forms an alliance

---

46   Davis, Derek. 1991. 'Seeds of the Secular State: Dante's Political Philosophy as Seen in the De Monarchia.' Journal of Church and State 33 (2): 327–46, pp. 344, 340.

47   Penman, Leigh T.I. 2022. The Lost History of Cosmopolitanism. The Earyl Modern Origins of the Intellectual Ideal. 1st paperback ed. London et al.: Bloomsbury Academic, p. 16.

48   Thumfart, Johannes. 2011. Francisco de Vitorias Philsophie: globalpolitisch, nicht kosmopolitisch. In: Die Normativität des Rechts bei Francisco de Vitoria, ed. by Kirstin Bunge, Anselm Spindler and Andreas Wagner, 229-254. Stuttgart-Bad Cannstatt: frommann-holzboog Verlag, p. 249.

49   Soder, Josef. 1955. Die Idee der Völkergemeinschaft. Francisco de Vitoria und die philosophischen Grundlagen des Völkerrechts. Frankfurt am Main: Alfred Metzner Verlag, pp. 53-5.

50   Although Vitoria disapproved of the atrocities of the Conquista, he did offer one argument for the justification of the Spanish campaign. He argued that the Spaniards had a right to intervene in the Indian communities in order to provide protection against the practice of human sacrifice.

against Charles V with Suleiman the Magnificent and Moors as well as Jews are being persecuted, this appeal to a universal human nature is of extreme political significance, and has remained so up to the present day'.[51] The agreement between Francis I and the Ottoman empire of 1535 actually was a turning point in the history of international treaty-making as Alexandrowicz noted.[52] For mutual military and geopolitical gain, primarily in their struggle against the House of Habsburg and the Holy Roman Empire, this major alliance simply left aside Christian-Islamic enmity. In an apologetic note to Pope Paul III, the King of France remarked that all human beings shared 'the same origin' and the Turks, too, were part of an all-embracing 'natural association of mankind' which was not affected by 'differences of religious and cultural tradition' or the separation into different states.[53]

Conceptions of peace under the 'sovereign power of the state'

Vitoria's reflections on a cosmopolitan human community, which in his view afforded every individual the right of freedom of movement, remained an exception until the 18th century Enlightenment. Already in Dante's time, 'the actual development of history had begun to move away from the idea of a supra-national political unity. At the start of the 14th century it was no longer possible to imagine that the Emperor or the Pope could once again become a universal power. The cohesion of the Christian world was being increasingly broken down by the claims of the territorial rulers to independence', wrote Maja Brauer in her history of world federalism.[54] The Islamic world, too, became fragmented and one of its most important cultural centres, Baghdad, was devastated by the Mongols in 1258. In the course of the transition from the Middle Ages to the modern era, the princes and the other rulers, in a development that spanned generations, fought ever harder to bring geographical territories that were as homogeneous as possible under their sole control. The French political theorist Jean Bodin (ca. 1529 to 1596) formulated the concept of sovereignty as the most important political objective of the new power of the state. According to Bodin, the sovereign ruler is the owner of all armed force within his territory, is independent of others, especially of the Emperor and the Pope, and recognizes only God alone above him. 'The principal characteristic of sovereign majesty and absolute power,' wrote Bodin in 1583, lies

51   Grawert, Rolf. 2000. 'Francisco de Vitoria. Naturrecht - Herrschaftsordnung – Völkerrecht'. Der Staat 39: 110-125, p. 117.
52   Alexandrowicz, p. 77.
53   Ibid. and 'Francisci Christianiss. Francorum Regis Ad Caroli V. Imp. Calumnias Epistola Apologetica Ad Paulum III Pont. Max. Scripta.' 1542. Hispanic Digital Library. (bdh.bne.es).
54   Brauer, Maja. 1994. Weltföderation - Modell globaler Gesellschaftsordnung. Frankfurt a. M. et al.: Peter Lang, p. 26.

in the power 'to impose laws on all subjects without their consent.'[55] This idea, together with the development and proliferation of administrative institutions, led to the gradual formation of discrete, 'sovereign' territorial states.

The nature of sovereignty and who held it became an important subject of debate. Bodin's understanding was opposed early on by the Calvinist legal philosopher Johannes Althusius (1557 to 1638) who by some is considered the most important federalist thinker of his century.[56] In his main work 'Politica' of 1603 he argued that there is no such thing as absolute and indivisible sovereignty vested in a single ruler. Rather, politics was based on associations of people who formed through an explicit or tacit agreement 'for the purpose of establishing, cultivating, and preserving a communal life among them'. The 'so-called rights of sovereignty' in Althusius view belong to the ultimate 'universal association' which origins in the people and members of the commonwealth, in particular cities and provinces. They are not a property of the king but conferred to and exercised by him merely 'on certain conditions and terms', Althusius argued.[57] His approach that sovereignty can rest in a supreme political entity made up of constituent parts and that this entity can delegate parts of its sovereign rights to the latter and other bodies was a major conceptual breakthrough at the time. In particular, it helped scholars to better understand the complex layers and relationships of authority in the Holy Roman Empire which was divided into hundreds of imperial estates.[58] While Althusius' theory, in principle, does not seem to rule out a universal association encompassing the entire globe, it appears that this is not something he contemplated.

'For centuries, the model of a great community of peoples was replaced by the model of the association of sovereign monarchs who agreed rules for the peaceful resolution of disputes and common responses to violent acts committed by individual members', as Brauer summarized the period following Dante.[59] In the face of the continuing Ottoman expansion into Europe since the 15th century and of the sieges of Vienna in the years 1529 and 1683, the idea of a pooling of Christian forces against the 'Turkish threat' was an important aspect of the peace plans of this period, one that often gave them an imperialist orientation. One example of this is the plan for 'a perpetual and general peace among all the peoples of Europe' put forward from 1711 onwards, piecemeal and in

---

55 Bodin, Jean. 1976 [1583]. Über den Staat. Stuttgart: Reclam, p. 31-2, see also p. 42.
56 Elazar, Daniel J. 1995. 'Althusius' Grand Design for a Federal Commonwealth.' In: Politica, by Johannes Althusius, edited and transl. By Frederick S. Carney, pp. xxxv–xlvi. Indianapolis: Liberty Fund.
57 Quoted in Osiander, Andreas. 2007. Before the State: Systemic Political Change in the West from the Greeks to the French Revolution. Oxford: Oxford Univ. Press, p. 436-7. See also Althusius, ibid., pp. 7, 17, 24, 67, 70-72.
58 Dickmann, Fritz. 1998. Der Westfälische Frieden. 7th ed. Münster: Aschendorff, pp. 131-134.
59 Brauer, p. 27.

several versions, by the French diplomat the Abbé Castel de Saint-Pierre (1658 to 1743). His proposed Christian-European alliance of states, which would have a court of arbitration and a common army, did not include the Ottoman Empire as a full member. On the contrary: in a third volume about the project in 1716 he described the 'expulsion of the Turks' as an 'urgent necessity'.[60]

The proposals for international peace alliances usually envisaged congresses and assemblies meeting on a regular basis. They had little to do with a world parliament in the sense of cosmopolitan and democratic popular representation by independent delegates. What was envisaged as a rule was assemblies made up of delegates of the aristocratic rulers bound by their instructions; such was the case with Saint-Pierre, and also with the peace concept of Émeric Crucé (1590 to 1648), which distinguishes itself by virtue of its ecumenical approach, notably including the Islamic world. It was often assumed, for example by Saint-Pierre and Crucé, that these rulers' congresses should be able to come to binding decisions for safeguarding peace between states, right up to determining common sanctions against peace-breakers. It had nothing at all to do with representation for the 'subjects' of their rule in international law. If there is a reference within these peace plans to a parliament, then it is generally in the pre-modern sense of a simple council of representatives of interested parties, and in this case of the sovereign rulers in particular. The term parliament derives from the Old French 'parlement', which literally means parley or interlocution.

The idea of the social contract in Hobbes and Locke

The founder of Pennsylvania, William Penn (1644 to 1718), argued in 1693 in an essay on a peace model for Europe that the sovereignty of the rulers would not be constrained by a guarantee of collective assistance, but on the contrary would be strengthened by increased security against reciprocal attacks. Penn regarded the concept of the 'sovereign equality' of rulers as naïve. In the assembly of representatives of the sovereigns which he proposed, he envisaged that votes would be weighted according to economic strength in order to mirror in the assembly the 'inequality between the rulers and between the states' and to make participation more attractive to the greater powers. In 1710, John Bellers (1654 to 1725), a friend of Penn's and like him a Quaker, also put forward a peace model envisaging weighted votes. However, he uses population as his weighting basis. Bellers is one of the first to address the rights of the subjects in the context of the consideration of a federation of states: 'by consent of the General Council' of the alliance of states 'there should be established an order

60   Borner, Wilhelm. 1913. Das Weltstaatsprojekt des Abbé de Saint-Pierre. Diss. Berlin, Leipzig, pp. 31-3.

and regulation, between sovereigns and subjects, to hinder on one side, the oppression and tyranny of princes; and on the other side, the tumults and rebellion of subjects'.[61] One had to accept a tyrannical prince, wrote Crucé almost a hundred years earlier, in the same way 'one accepts a year with a poor harvest, in the hope of better times to come.'[62]

With 'De Cive' in 1642 and 'Leviathan' in 1651, Thomas Hobbes heralded the end, in political philosophy, of the legitimation of political rule by divine right. In its place came the theoretical concept of contractual self-commitment by the individual, the idea of the social contract. Hobbes constructed a hypothetical state of nature in which, because of what he believed to be the competitive attitude inherent in man's lupine nature, and because of mutual distrust, selfishness and fear in the absence of a general power capable of imposing justice and law, an anarchic 'war of all against all' prevails. In order to escape this general condition of insecurity, a state, with an absolute ruler and a monopoly on force, is established by means of a reciprocal contract between each and every individual. This contract comes into general force as soon as a majority gives assent. It is a unique and irreversible hypothetical act, from which Hobbes derives the unlimited power of an absolute sovereign, who should be as invincible as the Leviathan, the sea monster of the Old Testament.

In the year 1649, the English Civil War between the parliamentary forces around Oliver Cromwell and the Royalists around Charles I ended with the execution of the King and the abolition of the English monarchy (which was restored in 1660). The so-called Levellers, who represented a new interpretation of democracy, formed a strong grass-roots political movement within the revolutionary camp. 'The Levellers were convinced that political rule derived from the rational will of originally free and equal men by way of a contract of each with all,' wrote the political scientist Richard Saage.[63] Similar to Johannes Althusius' thinking, they had recognized that relations between rulers and subjects were designed and maintained by human beings and not 'natural', as Aristotle had argued. Hobbes used the same insight to justify a rigorous absolutism. But the theory of the social contract which underpinned this also made possible a radical reappraisal of the question of legitimate state rule and its relation to the individual. 'The history of the modern state is the history of the taming of the Leviathan—by human rights and rational law, by the rule of law in the state, by

---

61 Bellers, John. 1710. Some Reasons for an European State. London, p. 19. Nb this citation: ed. of 1723, in: Alan P.F. Sell, et al. (eds.). 'Protestant Nonconformist Texts Volume 2: The Eighteenth Century'.
62 Crucé, Émeric. 1953 [1623]. Der neue Kineas. In: Ewiger Friede. Friedensrufe und Friedenspläne seit der Renaissance, ed. by Kurt von Raumer, transl. by Walther Neft, 289-320. Freiburg: Verl. Karl Alber, p. 314.
63 Saage, Richard. 2005. Demokratietheorien. Wiesbaden: VS Verlag für Sozialwissenschaften, p. 82.

Rechtsstaatlichkeit and constitutionalism, by the separation of powers and democracy,' wrote Wolfgang Kersting, professor of philosophy at Kiel.[64]

The model of the state proposed by John Locke (1632 to 1704) represented one milestone in this process. In his 'Two Treatises of Government', published anonymously in 1689, this English philosopher took up the idea of the social contract and used it as a starting point for the deconstruction of the concept of absolute monarchy. He argued that in the hypothetical state of nature human beings were completely free, equal and independent. His underlying view of human nature, in contrast to Hobbes, is positive. The purpose of the community created by the social contract was the maintenance of order and the protection of the natural rights of the individual, especially the right to life, liberty and property. The state's powers were limited to serving 'the public good of the society'. 'It is a power, that ... can never have a right to destroy, enslave, or designedly to impoverish the subjects' wrote Locke.[65] This is followed by ruminations on how the social contract might be designed to control political power. An elected legislature is envisaged as sovereign, 'made up of representatives chosen for that time by the people'[66]; its laws, passed by majority, are universally binding, including on the lawmakers and on the state itself. Here Locke formulated a system of popular rule via elected representatives and the principle of the rule of law. In arguing for separating law enforcement, or the exercise of the monopoly on force, from the legislative function, in order to prevent abuses of power, Locke is also emphasizing for the first time the need for the separation of powers. Should the legislature betray the people's trust and act against the state interest, then sovereignty is forfeited and returns to the people, who can renew the social contract and replace the legislature.

The idea of the social contract in Hobbes and Locke was particularistic rather than universal and applied to specific communities rather than to the foundation of a world state. But Hobbes showed how the individual sovereigns, too, could be understood to be in an anarchic state of nature, without law and order. 'Concerning the Offices of one Soveraign to another, which are comprehended in that Law, which is commonly called the Law of Nations, I need not say any thing in this place; because the Law of Nations, and the Law of Nature, is the same thing', wrote Hobbes.[67] Thus the original 'war of all against all', a hypothetical relationship between individuals in the state of nature, becomes a reality between sovereigns in the international sphere. In this view, to ensure the preservation of their capacity to act, indeed of their exist-

---

64   Kersting, Wolfgang. 2002. Thomas Hobbes zur Einführung. 2nd ed. Hamburg: Junius, pp. 12-3.
65   Locke, John. 1689. Two Treatises of Government, § 135, p. 103.
66   Ibid., § 154, p. 118.
67   Hobbes, Thomas. 1651. Leviathan. Ch. XXX.

ence, under these conditions, states must make the greatest possible efforts for their own security and must prevent the development of excessive power imbalances. The consequence is a perpetual increase in alliance-building and in expenditure on armed forces, which in turn simply increase insecurity yet further. This gives rise to what the German-American scholar of international law John H. Herz described as the 'security dilemma'.

A similar understanding of international relations underlay most conceptions of peace under international law and remains influential today. 'Let us admit then' as Saint-Pierre wrote in his plea for a federal Europe at the beginning of the 18th century, 'that the Powers of Europe stand to each other strictly in a state of war, and that all the separate treaties between them are in the nature of a temporary truce rather than a real peace.'[68] A lasting general peace through a balance of powers was 'a mere figment of the imagination' wrote Kant in 1793.

The social contract and Wolff's 'Völkerstaat'

In a subsequent logical step, the idea of the social contract then offers an escape route out of the international 'state of nature' by way of a sovereign common polity encompassing all states. In his noteworthy study of cosmopolitan models for a global state, the Zürich philosophy professor Francis Cheneval identified Christian Wolff (1679 to 1754) as the first person to use the theory of the social contract as the foundational rationale for a world state (a 'Völkerstaat', or 'peoples' state'), and therefore as the person who heralded 'a shift to the supranational in the philosophy of international law'.[69] Following Cheneval's analysis, the philosophical concept put forward by Wolff in 1749 and 1750 must indeed be seen as a significant milestone in the evolution of cosmopolitan models of world order. In Wolff's abstract conception of the social contract, which is extended to include all levels of human social interaction, he outlines (according to Cheneval) a universal community of cooperation between people, a 'civitas maxima', which has as its goal and purpose the wellbeing of all people, and which ultimately leads to a democratically constituted 'Völkerstaat'. Wolff not only transformed the theory of the social contract, and thereby superseded the theory of divine right, but—as probably the first person since Vitoria—in his model of international law he resurrected the idea of a community of the human race, comprising all individuals. This 'societas magna' of all people,

---

68 Rousseau, Jean Jacques. 1953. Auszug aus dem Plan des Ewigen Friedens des Herrn Abbé de Saint-Pierre. In: Ewiger Friede. Friedensrufe und Friedenspläne seit der Renaissance, ed. by Kurt von Raumer, transl. by Gertrud von Raumer, 343-368. Freiburg, München: Verlag Karl Alber, p. 348.
69 Cheneval, Francis. 2002. Philosophie in weltbürgerlicher Bedeutung. Über die Entstehung und die philosophischen Grundlagen des supranationalen und kosmopolitischen Denkens der Moderne. Basel: Schwabe & Co, pp. 132-5.

and the human rights embedded within it, are the foundation of all further social development, according to Wolff.[70]

As Cheneval explained, Wolff's argument for a 'Völkerstaat' follows the logic of social contract theory and attempts to derive from this a general validity for a universal legal system. Wolff showed that the justification for government in social contract theory cannot logically be restricted to the nation state level only to disappear beyond that in a reversion to the 'state of nature' at the international level. 'A contractualism limited to the national level is therefore incoherent, because at the level of international law it turns against its own principles' wrote Cheneval.[71] The theory logically requires that states bind themselves together in a superordinate 'Völkerstaat', or superstate. 'Wolff argued for a federal superstate, one which comes into being through an originating contract between the individual state and the group and the group with the individual state, one in which an assembly of state representatives, a senate of the peoples, passes binding laws on the principle of majority rule, laws on which limits are set by the acknowledgement of a community of mankind based on principles of natural law and of certain basic laws', Cheneval summarized.[72] Yet this would not give rise to a global Leviathan, precisely because Wolff underpinned this with a tiered and functionally differentiated conception of sovereignty under which the resulting superstate has only those powers that are assigned to it by the states and necessary for the fulfilment of its responsibilities. For Wolff it was clear that this 'Völkerstaat' does not yet exist. The conception is rather an ideal of a rational, social world order to be aspired to over the course of history.

Kant's cosmopolitan project

Cosmopolitan thinking reached a highpoint in the philosophical work of Immanuel Kant (1724 to 1804). In the essay 'Idea for a Universal History from a Cosmopolitan Point of View', published in 1784, Kant outlined, following social contract theory, how world history was leading to 'the civic union of the human race' under a 'lawful constitution'.[73] In his famous essay 'Perpetual Peace' of 1795, Kant wrote that from a universalist perspective the state of nature could only be overcome if three elements of a civic constitution are combined: namely, citizenship rights within a nation, international law between states, and cosmopolitan rights, where 'individuals and states ... may be regarded as citizens of

---

70   Ibid., p. 172.
71   Ibid., p. 202.
72   Ibid., p. 135.
73   Kant, Immanuel. 1963 [1784]. Idea for a Universal History from a Cosmopolitan Point of View, in: On History, ed. by Lewis White Beck, The Bobbs-Merrill Co., 7th and 9th theses.

one world-state (jus cosmopoliticum)'.[74] Similarly, Kant's conception of a world republic by no means abolishes the states, but rather makes them into constituent parts, into 'citizens', of a superordinate world constitutional order.

However, Kant recognized several different impediments which meant that the ideal 'Völkerstaat', with its three specified elements for the overcoming of the state of war, could not be established immediately, but only step by step, by 'a continuous approximation' through 'gradual reform'.[75] For one thing, he believed that 'with the too great extension of such a Union of States over vast regions any government of it ... must at last become impossible'.[76] For another, he cited the potential risk of despotism,[77] given that most states were still autocratic themselves. But what was decisive was his judgement that the states, that is the rulers of his day, would not be prepared to abandon the international 'state of nature' for the establishment of a shared republican 'Völkerstaat'. As a first practical step, therefore, and as the only one possible, only a league of states came into question for him. 'For states, in their relation to one another, there can be, according to reason, no other way of advancing from that lawless condition which unceasing war implies, than by giving up their savage lawless freedom, just as individual men have done, and yielding to the coercion of public laws. Thus, they can form a State of nations (*civitas gentium*), one, too, which will be ever increasing and would finally embrace all the peoples of the earth. States, however, in accordance with their understanding of the law of nations, by no means desire this, and therefore reject *in hypothesi* what is correct *in thesi*. Hence, instead of the positive idea of a world-republic, if all is not to be lost, only the negative substitute for it, a federation averting war, maintaining its ground and ever extending over the world may stop the current of this tendency to war and shrinking from the control of law. But even then there will be a constant danger that this propensity may break out.'[78] The federation of states proposed here has no sovereignty in the way that a civil constitution does and is therefore incomplete. In contemporary terms it would be more accurate to speak of confederation. The limitation of cosmopolitan rights to a right to visit foreign countries should be understood, in line with Kant's philosophy of history, as a concession to the reality that the rulers would not be willing to allow more. He compared the unwillingness of the states to subject themselves to legal and self-drafted binding powers to the

74 Id. 1903 [1795]. Perpetual Peace, transl. by M. Campbell Smith. London: George Allen & Unwin, p. 119.
75 Ibid, 3rd definitive article; and id., The Metaphysics of Morals, § 61 and conclusion.
76 Ibid., § 61.
77 Id. 1798 [1793]. On the Popular Judgment: That may be Right in Theory, but does not Hold Good in the Praxis, in: Essays and Treatises, Vol. I., transl. by John Richardson, London: Richardson, p. 188.
78 Id., Perpetual Peace, ibid., 2nd definitive article.

'attachment of savages to their lawless liberty', which should be regarded 'with profound contempt as barbarism and uncivilisation and the brutal degradation of humanity'.[79]

The confederation of states outlined by Kant as a minimal solution is in line with traditional international peace conceptions and is not innovative. As the Dutch professor for philosophy Pauline Kleingeld rightfully noted, Kant's views today are often misunderstood and misrepresented.[80] For his contemporaries there was no mistake, though, that the proposed league was only to be a first intermediate step as a review by Johann Gottlieb Fichte shows.[81] If a loose confederation was all Kant had to offer, his peace theory by now would be obsolete and even reactionary, not worthy of much discussion.[82] However, a new way forward is suggested by the notion of a cosmopolitan programme envisaging a development from this confederation of states to a world republic, one in which not only the states but also the people would be subjects of a community of humanity. The dogma of absolute sovereignty within international law was thus broken in two ways simultaneously. On the one hand, by the partition of sovereignty between individual states and the world republic; and on the other hand, by the participation of the individual alongside the states in the sovereignty of humanity. Kant said nothing about the specific institutional shape to be taken by the 'state of nations' as the incorporation of perpetual peace, the greatest political good. But as Kant 'made the idea of representation the defining characteristic of the republic, the representation of the citizens of a state by its government or by directly elected delegates at the supra-national level was not a problem for him,' reasoned Cheneval.[83] Thus, the idea of a world parliament was at least implied in Kant's philosophy even if he did not spell it out.

79   Ibid.
80   Kleingeld, Pauline. 2013. Kant and Cosmopolitanism: The Philosophical Ideal of World Citizenship. Cambridge University Press.
81   Fichte, Johann Gottlieb. 1796. 'Rezension von Zum Ewigen Frieden', in: Philos. Journal Bd. IV. S. 81-92. In: Johann Gottlieb Fichte's Sämmtliche Werke, ed. by I.H. Fichte, Vol. 8, 1846, pp. 427–36. Berlin: Verlag von Veit und Comp, p. 433. See also Kleingeld, p. 58.
82   Kleingeld, ibid., p. 192.
83   Cheneval, p. 620.

2.
The 18th century: enlightenment, revolutions, and parliamentarism

The American federal state and representative democracy

From the middle of the 18th century onwards, the spirit of Enlightenment and an urge for freedom spread over four continents.[1] Diogenes' claim that he was a citizen of the world became a programmatic statement of the era, repeated by Thomas Paine, David Hume, Voltaire and Gotthold Ephraim Lessing among others. Of course, the monarchs pursued their dynastic and geopolitical interests just as ever before, by means of war if necessary, but the spirit was blowing in a new direction.[2] 'The barriers that separated states and nations in their antagonistic pursuit of self-interest have been breached. All thinking minds are linked together now by a cosmopolitan bond,' Friedrich Schiller (1759 to 1805) enthused in his inaugural lecture in Jena in May 1789.[3] For a short period, intellectual forces saw themselves as united in the spirit of enlightenment and cosmopolitanism. From this crucible there emerged for the first time the explicit idea, indeed the concrete political demand, for a world parliament. The cosmopolitan ideal combined together with the theories of representation and of democracy, which had just burst through into practice in such spectacular and historic fashion in North America, and joined forces with the French Revolution.

In the American Declaration of Independence of 1776, the equality and liberty of all people, at least in theory, was for the first time proclaimed and made the foundation of a new state order. Following the British victory in the war with France for domination in North America, from 1763 onwards the tension between London and the colonists mounted. 'No taxation without representation' became the slogan for their unsuccessful demand for representation in the English parliament. They argued that when a government infringed unalienable human rights, as King George III of England (1738 to 1820) had done, a right of resistance was thereby created. In the war of independence which followed, the colonists threw off English rule and ushered in a new era, a

1   Polasky, Janet. 2015. Revolutions without Borders. Yale University Press.
2   Ibid., pp. 333-5.
3   Schiller, Friedrich. 1789. 'Was heißt und zu welchem Ende studiert man Universalgeschichte?'

'novus ordo seclorum'. In this they had one great advantage: they could make a clean start. 'We have every opportunity and every encouragement before us, to form the noblest purest constitution on the face of the earth. We have it in our power to begin the world over again,' declared Thomas Paine.[4] With the Articles of Confederation of 1777, the thirteen former colonies at first established a loose confederation which did not impinge on the sovereignty of the individual states, not even with respect to foreign or trade policy. Common resolutions were hardly implemented at all, and were therefore ineffective. It proved impossible, for example, to create a common economic area. In the pursuit of their individual interests, the states divided and came into conflict. Eventually the federalists prevailed. The United States of America was established as a genuinely federal state with the Constitution of 17 September 1787. Legislative power in this new, geographically extensive federal state, whose citizens mainly originated from all over Europe, was in the hands of a Congress consisting of two chambers: the House of Representatives, directly elected (initially by male census suffrage) to represent the people, and the Senate, made up of representatives of the individual federal states elected by their parliaments (and from 1913 also directly). The new republic suffered of a critical inconsistency, though. All thirteen states continued to allow slavery. A strong condemnation of slavery as a 'cruel war against human nature itself' included in Thomas Jefferson's 'original rough draft' of the Declaration of Independence did not make it into the final document. Even at the time a would-be nation of slaveholding revolutionaries, including Jefferson himself, faced a dilemma when evoking moral principles and abolitionists insisted it could not serve the world as a model of freedom.[5]

The early slave-holding proto-democracies in the Greek city states (up to about 300 BCE) and in the Roman Republic (up to the beginning of the principate in 27 BCE) were based on assemblies of the (male) electorate, and were limited to comparatively small city states. Referring to these early models, Jean Jacques Rousseau (1712 to 1778) was still saying in 'The Social Contract' of 1762 that only an assembly of the whole people could constitute a sovereign legislature expressing the common will. As popular sovereignty could neither be subdivided nor delegated to representatives, a republican system could only ever be realized in small states. The political scientist Robert Dahl (1915 to 2014) described the gradual shift in the interpretation of democracy, away from its historical roots in the city states to the more extensive areas of rule of a nation, a

---

4   Paine, Thomas. 1995 [1776]. Common Sense. In: Rights of Man, Common Sense and Other Political Writings. Oxford University Press.
5   Davis, David Brion. 1999. The Problem of Slavery in the Age of Revolution, 1770-1823. 2nd ed. New York: Oxford University Press, pp. 10-2, 285-6, 307, 326-8.

country or a nation state, as 'the second democratic transformation' of history.[6] The example of the USA showed that democracy, understood as representative democracy, could be organized not only in a large territory but also in the innovative political form of a federal state. Benjamin Franklin, for example, expressed the idea in 1787 already that the new American federal constitution might function as a model for a 'federal union' in Europe.[7]

The historical roots of modern parliamentarism

The United States of America heralded a new epoch in the history of representative democracy. The founding fathers of the USA regarded their system as unique, on account of its embedding of popular sovereignty in a written constitution, of its republicanism and federalism. 'Yet it is also clear,' according to the historian Colin Bonwick, 'that the state constitutions as well as the United States Constitution (which were all drafted during the revolutionary era and must be taken together) owe much to the experiences of other countries—and especially to the British constitutionalism from which Americans were escaping.'[8] The development of parliamentarism, which reached its zenith up to that point in the US Constitution, can be traced back over many centuries to the societies of the Middle Ages and the early modern period, with their hierarchical estates of the realm. Representatives of the nobility, the clergy, and later also of the higher classes from the cities were able to achieve some rights to political participation or consultation vis-à-vis their rulers. Membership of the assemblies of the estates which then developed was exclusive, and usually based on personal privilege, public office, property or guild or trade membership, often itself in turn based on birth. The members of the assemblies of the estates represented only their own interests, and not those of the subjects in general at all. The rulers were often dependent on their cooperation and assent, especially for raising taxes. The development of the representation of the estates and of parliamentarism followed complex paths, with interruptions and with peculiarities specific to every region.

The first assembly of the estates to be established on a long-term basis and with some powers over the king, and which moreover included representatives not only of the nobility and the clergy but of the cities, was convened in 1188 as the Cortes by Alfonso IX (1171 to 1230), King of León in the Spanish peninsu-

---

6   Dahl, Robert. 1989. Democracy and its critics. New Haven: Yale University Press, pp. 213-5.
7   Letter of Benjamin Franklin to Rodolphe-Ferdinand Grand, 22 Oct. 1787, in: Benjamin Franklin Papers, ed. by The American Philosophical Society and Yale University, digital ed. by The Packard Humanities Institute.
8   Bonwick, Colin. 1999. The United States Constitution and its Roots in British Political Thought and Tradition. In: Foundations of democracy in the European Union. From the genesis of parliamentary democracy to the European Parliament, ed. by John Pinder, pp. 41-58. Basingstoke: MacMillan Press. p. 41.

la.[9] In return for their support, in particular raising funds for war, the king promised protection and that from now on he would consult and accept the advice of the Cortes 'in matters of war and peace, pacts and treaties', political theorist John Keane reports in a history of democracy. It was agreed further, among other things, that guidance would be taken from general laws inherited from earlier times, in particular the Visigothic code. The León assembly managed to survive for several hundred years and its example was copied in neighbouring kingdoms such as Aragon, Catalonia and Valencia even though they 'never became democratic institutions, even in the minimal sense that the estates and the monarch were equal debating and deciding partners'.[10] In the Visigothic kingdom, the bishops, assembled in the Council of Toledo between the 5th and 7th century CE, already attempted to limit the authority of the monarch, declaring that his power was received from God.[11] The Visigothic code, published in 645, only survived in fragments. It included elements of the rule of law. For instance, one of its laws said that 'the royal power' should 'be subject to the majesty of the law' and another addressed 'how the avarice of the king should be restrained.'[12]

The development of parliamentarism in England was a special case. For England, according to the political scientist Klaus von Beyme, 'was the only country in the world to develop parliamentary government with no significant break in continuity in the constitutional development from a system based on the estates of the realm from the late Middle Ages onwards'.[13] Following his conquest of England in the year 1066, William I (1027 to 1087) introduced regular consultations with the clergy and the landed nobility in order to ensure their assent on important questions and thus to make them into supporting props for his rule. After the 'Magna Carta' was successfully pushed through in 1215, the English King was for the first time obliged to obtain the assent of an assembly of the landed nobility in order to introduce new taxes. From 1295 onwards, representatives from the towns and boroughs also took part in the English parliament. And from 1341, the 'commons' assembled separately from the nobility and the clergy. The English parliament thus developed into a two-chamber system. In the 15th century a general census suffrage was introduced for the lower chamber, the 'House of Commons'. By 1619, twelve years after

---

9   Zanden, Jan Luiten van, Eltjo Buringh, and Maarten Bosker. 2012. 'The rise and decline of European parliaments, 1188–1789'. The Economic History Review, 65 (3), pp. 835–861.

10 Keane, John. 2010. The Life and Death of Democracy. London: Pocket Books, pp. 169-72, 175, 187.

11 O'Callaghan, Joseph F. 1983. A History of Medieval Spain. Ithaca and London: Cornell University Press, p. 57.

12 See Book II, Title I, Law II and V: The Visigothic Code (Forum Judicum). 1920. Transl. and ed. by Samuel Parsons Scott. The Boston Book Company, pp. 12, 14.

13 Beyme, Klaus von. 1999. Die parlamentarische Demokratie. 3rd ed. Opladen/Wiesbaden: Westdeutscher Verlag, p. 21.

the founding of Jamestown as the first permanent settlement of English colonists in the 'New World', the first assembly of elected political representatives of the colonists in North America was formed in the province of Virginia, and valuable experience of democracy began to be gained.

The long evolution of 'sovereign' territorial states produced a 'tendency among the monarchs and princes, who had occupied the pinnacle of the medieval feudal pyramid, to claim the new sovereignty for themselves alone, and to exclude the estates, which had developed in the medieval state into co-holders of public political power,' according to the historian Heinz Schilling.[14] The conflicts over power and privilege between monarchs and representatives of the estates during the three centuries from 1500 onwards were a central aspect of all great socio-political confrontations of the epoch.[15] Often, kings would simply refuse from the outset to convene the assembly of the estates, as for example Charles I did in the decade prior to the outbreak of the English Civil War in the year 1642. Eventually, in the Revolution of 1688/89, the English parliament made itself the bearer of the sovereignty of the state by means of the 'Bill of Rights'. Even if the monarch continued to determine the overarching political questions, and in particular to decide on war and peace, from now on he had to win a majority in the newly independent parliament for the government budget.

Cosmopolitanism in the French Revolution

Developments in England, and the ideas of John Locke, did not fail to have an impact in France, the centre of the Ancien régime. In the course of the 18th century they slowly but surely undermined the authority of the monarchy. When Louis XVI found himself forced to convene the Estates General of France in 1789, for the first time since 1614, in order to legitimate and implement tax reforms, it was a signal that electrified people far beyond the borders of France. Following the elections to the Estates General, in the so-called Tennis Court Oath of 20 June 1789 the Third Estate, representing around 98 per cent of the population, declared itself to be a National Assembly for the creation of a constitution. The storming of the Bastille on 14 July is regarded as the symbolic moment of birth of the Revolution. The Declaration of the Rights of Man and of the Citizen was issued on 26 August, beginning with the declaration of the equality and liberty of all and of the sovereignty of the people, and identifying the principles on which the new order would be based.

---

14 Schilling, Heinz. 1994. Aufbruch and Krise: Deutschland 1517-1648. Vol. 5. Siedler Deutsche Geschichte. Berlin: Siedler Verlag, p. 20.
15 See Zanden, ibid.

In the turmoil of the Revolution, one of the issues at stake was whether the establishment of a republican system beyond France for those other peoples of Europe still under monarchical rule should be among the aims. Republicanism 'at that time of upheaval and at the historical birth of modern European democracy was not yet particularist but rather European and cosmopolitan', Cheneval emphasized. The concept of the 'nation' was not necessarily synonymous with the nation-state during the first few years of revolution.[16] The external situation was decisive at this point. In May 1790 the National Assembly declared its renunciation of wars of conquest, but revolutionary fever, sparked by the proclamation of the right of peoples to self-determination, was spreading, and increasingly unsettling the European monarchies. Louis XVI discussed with them the possibility of armed intervention 'in order to put a stop to the agitators'.[17] In April 1792 military conflicts began between France and an alliance led by Austria and Prussia which continued until 1797, in the course of which France would occupy the Southern Netherlands and the Dutch Republic.

It was an expression of the cosmopolitan revolutionary spirit of the time when, on 26 August 1792, the National Assembly awarded French citizenship to seventeen foreigners who had rendered outstanding service to the Revolution, including Jeremy Bentham, Alexander Hamilton, James Madison, Thomas Paine, Johann Heinrich Pestalozzi, Friedrich Schiller and George Washington. Among those honoured was Johann Baptist Baron de Cloots, also known as Anacharsis Cloots (1755 to 1794), born in Kleve in Prussia but with Dutch family roots. Like Paine, Cloots lived in Paris, and had been an active member of the Jacobin Club since 1789. In September 1792, again like Paine, he was elected to the National Assembly, and was called on from time to time to help draft the Constitution. It is remarkable that Cloots, the first person to explicitly formulate the idea of a world parliament, was not a philosopher but a revolutionary.

Cloots' 'republic of humanity'

For Cloots, the Revolution had a universal character and mission. He was emphatically of the view that a world republic should be established, starting with France. In his work 'Bases constitutionelles de la République du genre humain' of 1793, Cloots argued for a radically individualistic interpretation of sovereignty. From human rights he derived the 'mutually supportive and in-

---

16   Cheneval, Francis. 2004. 'Der kosmopolitische Republikanismus - erläutert am Beispiel Anacharsis Cloots'. Zeitschrift für philosophische Forschung 58 (3): 373-396, pp. 376, 378.

17   Tulard, Jean. 1989. Frankreich im Zeitalter der Revolutionen 1789-1851. Geschichte Frankreichs. Vol. 4. Stuttgart: DVA, pp. 90-2.

divisible sovereignty of the human race'.[18] Nations that were in any kind of reciprocal contact, or even simply knew about each other, could not both be sovereign simultaneously. In Cloots' view, autonomous self-determination is then no longer possible, and the foundations for conflict are given. In contrast, 'the Republic of Humankind' would 'never be in dispute with anyone, for there is no communication between the planets', argued Cloots.[19] Thus he rejected at the same time the idea developed by his colleague Paine in the book 'Rights of Man' from 1791/92 that universal peace and prosperity could be achieved when all countries had established representative democracy as their form of government (thereby founding the 'democratic peace theory' still debated today). Sovereignty requires that all people are unified in a universal community based on human rights. And this is achievable, given that all share the same goals of liberty, equality, security, justice and the protection of property and peace and from oppression.[20] According to Cloots, the constituent subjects of the world republic could only be individual persons, on account of the indivisibility of sovereignty. Women were naturally included in his conception of *genre humain*.[21] At the centre of the world republic he promoted stood a directly elected parliament as legislature. *Départements* were envisaged as subsidiary administrative units, at the same time serving as the electoral constituencies for the parliamentary representatives. In accordance with his design, Cloots proposed that France, with its new constitution, should be a universal republic to which all nations liberated from monarchy should accede as *départements*. His goal was a 'united, free, and peaceful world without slavery'. But according to the historian Frank Ejby Poulsen he made political calculations. In June 1791, Cloots argued that it would be 'politically damaging' for the interests of France 'to free the colonies immediately' and that slavery had to be accepted temporarily. This approach 'appears cynical and unusual to his, otherwise fervent, idealism', Poulsen observed.[22]

The end of cosmopolitanism

To Cloots' great joy, the parliament brought into being by the first experiment in democracy in German history, the 'Rheinisch-German National Convention' elected under French occupation in Rhine-Hesse and the Palatinate in February

18 Cloots, Anacharsis. 1793. Bases constitutionnelles de la république du genre humain. Paris: L'Imprimerie Nationale, p. 3.
19 Ibid., p. 14.
20 Ibid., pp. 35-6.
21 Poulsen, Frank Ejby. 2023. The Political Thought of Anacharsis Cloots: A Proponent of Cosmopolitan Republicanism in the French Revolution. De Gruyter, p. 152.
22 Ibid., p. 165.

1793, voted for the 'Republic of Mainz' which it had proclaimed to accede to France. However, only one month later the territory of the Republic west of the Rhine was retaken by troops of the Prussian-Austrian alliance. When the offensive pushed forward into French territory and the French National Convention felt compelled to introduce general conscription, the Levée en masse, the revolutionary mood turned. Prompted by Maximilien Robespierre, Cloots and other foreigners were arrested as saboteurs of the Revolution, tried and found guilty, and executed by guillotine on 24 March 1794. During the 1970s, the renowned German performance artist Joseph Beuys (1921 to 1986) would sometimes use the name 'Josephanacharsis Clootsbeuys' in memory of Cloots, his ideas and his fate.[23] Thomas Paine escaped the guillotine by sheer good fortune. Poulsen believed that Cloots name has wrongly been forgotten as he was a 'significant political thinker' whose ideas 'deserve serious consideration'.[24]

Republicanism joined forces with xenophobia and French nationalism.[25] In July 1793, Schiller was already lamenting the failure of the Enlightenment in forceful terms. 'The attempt by the French people to claim their sacred human rights and to win their political freedom' has 'cast not only that people, but with them a substantial part of Europe and a whole century back into barbarism and slavery ... So it was not free people who were being oppressed by the state, no, it was only wild animals, which it held in benevolent chains.'[26]

23   Guido de Werd. 1988. Vorwort. In: Anarchasis Cloots - Der Redner des Menschengeschlechts, ed. by Städtisches Museum Haus Koekkoek. Kleve: Boss-Verlag, p. 7.
24   Poulsen, p. 3.
25   See Cheneval, 2004, pp. 377-9.
26   Letter from Friedrich Schiller to Herzog Friedrich Christian von Augustenburg, 13 July 1793, in: Schillers Werke. Bd. 26, ed. by Edith Nahler and Horst Nahler. Weimar: Verlag Hermann Böhlaus Nachf., 1992, pp. 257-268, p. 262.

3.
From Vienna to The Hague:
the dynamics of integration and
the inter-parliamentary movement

In the nascent nation states of Europe, the transition from monarchical regimes to parliamentary forms of government was a long drawn-out process that oscillated between revolution and restoration. In France, for example, the Constitution of 1799 practically abolished general elections again and prepared the ground for the military imperialist dictatorship of Napoleon Bonaparte. Following Napoleon's military defeat in the 'Battle of the Nations' at Leipzig in 1813, the Congress of Vienna of 1814/15 established a new balance of power in Europe and set itself the goal of restoring monarchical authority. In the course of the century, a system of 'sovereign states' emerged in Europe and Latin-America at the same time.[1]

Independence, unification and division in Latin-America

When Napoleon occupied the Iberian Peninsular in 1808 and forced the Spanish King to abdicate the throne, the vacuum helped spark open revolt in the colonies. At the same time delegates from across Spain and its overseas territories were convened as a Cortes assembly and in the Cádiz Constitution of 1812 they declared that sovereignty resides in the parliament, and not the King, since it is the former that represents the people. The constitution established a constitutional monarchy with a parliamentary system based on universal male suffrage and opened the door towards 'a sort of Federal government in the Spanish Empire, with the American Viceroyalties attaining equal status, rights and representation to those of the Kingdom of Spain'.[2] But only one year later, after the defeat of Napoleon, Spanish absolutism was back and the constitution was abolished. The colonies successfully fought for independence. Initially this went along with unifying efforts and the creation of republican systems of government. In the southern part of the continent, the United Provinces of the Río de

---

1 See also Vergerio, Claire. 2021. 'Beyond the Nation-State.' Boston Review. May 27. (bostonreview.net).
2 Gurmendi, Alonso. 2022. 'Latin Lieber: Uncovering the History of the Treaty on the Regularisation of War.' Opinio Juris (blog). June 10, 2022. (opiniojuris.org).

la Plata emerged in 1816. Much of the northern part of South America in 1819 was united in the centralist state of Gran Colombia under the leadership of its founding President Simón Bolívar (1783 to 1830). In 1823, two years after their independence, Central American nations merged in the Federal Republic of Central America. Bolívar in 1826 organized the Congress of Panama which aimed at creating a confederal league of the new Latin-American republics. This did not include the notion of a continent-wide elected parliament, however. According to Bolívar, a federation of the 'New World' was 'not possible, because America is divided by remote climates, diverse geographies, conflicting interests, and dissimilar characteristics.'[3] The meeting in Panama was not successful and on top, Gran Colombia, the United Provinces and the Central American state failed and broke up into smaller independent countries by 1831 and 1841, respectively, Nevertheless, parliamentary bodies were regularly considered in the intellectual debate over peace plans for Europe and the world as a whole.

Sartorius' 'peoples' republic'

For example, in an article published in 1837, the political scientist Johann Baptist Sartorius (1774 to 1844), born in Lorraine in France, put forward a plan for a representative popular republic of the human race in which legislative power was vested in a senate to be elected by global popular vote—indirectly, via electoral colleges, 'in order to make the election quick and easy to oversee and run'.[4] Every six years, one third of the Senate (the seats of the longest-serving members) would be elected anew. This would ensure continuity. The right of initiative would lie with a regent, also elected by popular vote. There is no provision for the representation of individual states in this world state, which is to be founded by a voluntary treaty between the states. Like Cloots, Sartorius too argued that there can only be one sovereignty and that this must lie with the collective, that is, with the world state. Within their own 'spheres of authority', however, the nations would have 'free rein'. Limits would be set on the power of this peoples' state by 'positive constitutional norms'.

Pecqueur's concept of worldwide integration

One of the most important contributions to the thinking about a world parliament in the first half of the 19th century came from the French social and economic theorist Constantin Pecqueur (1801 to 1887). In his work 'De la Paix' in 1842 he presented detailed reflections on how a democratic federal world state

---

3   Bolívar, Simón. 2003. El Libertador: Writings of Simón Bolívar. Ed. by David Bushnell. Transl. by Frederick H. Fornoff. Oxford University Press. See 'The Jamaica Letter', pp. 27-8.

4   Sartorius, Johann Baptist. 1837. Organon des vollkommenen Friedens. Zürich: S. Höhr, p. 272.

could be established. The division of humanity into nations, he argued, was a 'relic of barbarism', and meant—entirely in line with the tradition of social contract theory—that the states were in a state of nature which entailed regular outbreaks of armed conflict. In Pecqueur's work, the peace question is strongly linked to what was called the social question. This must also be understood in context, at a time when industrialization and urbanization, together with the incipient population explosion, were bringing increasing immiseration of the hired labour force. According to Pecqueur, global prosperity was directly related to the duration and continuity of peace. Ever closer economic exchange between nations served not only to promote more peaceful relations but also to increase prosperity. Pecqueur developed a programme for a step by step integration which is to begin with trade and customs unions. He took as his model the German Customs Union established in 1834, which in turn grew out of a merger of the Prussia-Hesse Customs Union, the Central German Trade Union and the South German Customs Union. 'These partial mergers,' wrote Pecqueur, 'can be understood as preparations for a comprehensive union, first European, then cosmopolitan.'[5] By means of a gradual dismantling of trade barriers, complete global free trade is to be achieved incrementally; the path to that point requires avoiding national trade imbalances while occasionally allowing protectionist measures as an exception. With his support for the idea of free trade, Pecqueur set himself against the dogma of mercantilism, which had been the prevailing practice and theory since the 16th century, and according to which governments should use public policy to try to promote exports and obstruct imports. Friedrich List, who also spoke out in favour of global free trade, described the mercantilist system in 1819 as an 'unfortunate delusion' which fed 'a perpetual war for wealth'. 'I am convinced,' wrote List, 'that humanity will only be able to achieve the highest peak of physical wellbeing, as well as of intellectual perfection, when over the entire surface of the Earth civilized peoples are able to extract from Nature her treasures and to exchange the surplus of their products in mutual free trade.'[6]

But economic convergence was not sufficient for Pecqueur. It was also intended to set in train the political integration of the states. Economic integration would 'inevitably' be followed by 'political convergence'.[7] This perspective, one we would like to term the dynamics of integration, and one which Pecqueur was the first to use as the foundation for a project to establish a federal world state, was not the arcane opinion of an outsider. The project for a

5   Pecqueur, Constantin. 1842. De la Paix. De son Principe et de sa Réalisation. Paris: Capelle, p. 212.
6   Friedrich List. 1929. Schriften, Reden, Briefe. Ed. by Erwin von Beckerath et al., Vol. 1, Berlin, p. 571.
7   Pecqueur, p. 320. See also pp. 189-92.

German customs union, for example, which had been under discussion at various political levels since 1820, also derived from an 'unambiguously grand political perspective' from a Prussian point of view, as Thomas Nipperdey writes.[8] Thus, the Prussian finance minister Friedrich von Motz wrote in a memorandum of 1829 to King Frederick William III that 'if it is accepted in political science that import, export and transit duties are simply the consequence of the political divisions between states (and this is true), then by the same token it must also be accepted that the unification of those states into a customs and trade union will lead at the same time to unification into one common political system. And the more natural is the combination into *one* commercial customs and trade system ... so the closer and stronger will be the combination of those states into *one* political system'.[9]

Pecqueur's world federation and world parliament

In contrast to the Prussian finance minister, who was dreaming of a unification of the German states, including Austria, under the leadership of Prussia, Pecqueur had in mind a 'complete union' of the entire globe. All nations and peoples, beginning with Europe, should be gradually joined together into a world state with world institutions, without however having to forfeit their own statehood. The federal constitution of the USA served as his model. Sovereignty was to be tiered between the individual states and the common federal state envisaged. Pecqueur emphasized that, in addition to customs and trade issues, defence, foreign policy and policing were to be the province of the federal state. This would involve the establishment of a federal diplomatic service, while the foreign ministries of the individual states would be abolished. Once the federal state had become universal, the entire service could be disbanded. The same applied to national armies. Within the federal state, a common 'cosmopolitan police' would ensure security and law enforcement. Supra-national authority would be based on the principle of justice, which for Pecqueur meant equality, fraternity and liberty. Disputes would be resolved in court on the basis of world law. The organs of the world federal state would have to be established by direct elections. If the best form of government for the individual nations was representative (that is, democratic), then this applied to their union, too. Pecqueur regarded as the ideal legislative organ a congress directly elected by popular vote. 'The members of this European or cosmopolitan Con-

---

8   Nipperdey, Thomas. 1998. Deutsche Geschichte 1800-1866: Bürgerwelt und starker Staat. München: C.H. Beck, p. 359.

9   Eisenhart, Wilfried von and Ant Ritthaler (ed.) 1934. Vorgeschichte und Begründung des Deutschen Zollvereins 1815-1834. Vol. 2. Berlin: Verlag R. Hobbing, p. 534.

gress can be elected neither by the legislative nor by the executive branches of the states they are to represent,' Pecqueur wrote in order to underline the necessity for direct elections. If this is not possible to begin with, then at the very least the appointed members have to be 'absolutely independent'.[10] It would be absurd to believe that the congress would be able to operate as a higher authority if its members were dependent on the individual states.

Pecqueur saw the monarchical regimes as being the greatest problem and obstacle for the project of integration. In the year 1842, when Pecqueur published his work, there was—in today's terms—hardly any democracy in the entire world. Dynastic rule in the individual states, in particular, was incompatible with the establishment of a supranational authority. As long as it was not possible for a federal state congress to be freely elected by popular vote, then the fear must be that its decisions would do the people more harm than good. For the congress, as an assembly of aristocrats, would continually make decisions in the interests of the governments and against the interests of the governed. In which case the project of achieving universal peace through the agency of a universal congress would find itself jeopardized by 'a renewal of the alliance of the kings against the people'.[11] In any event, monarchical regimes would be very concerned about their sovereignty and not at all inclined to subordinate themselves to a supranational authority.

Pecqueur saw the ideal solution as starting the project in the form of a merger between a small group of states with democratic forms of government. All states, however, regardless of their form of government, should be invited to join. However, it must be a condition of membership that, at a minimum, the representatives of the individual states in the federation should be elected by 'more or less' general suffrage. This would doubtless apply initially more often to small countries, as these had an interest in strengthening their protection against the great powers. The growing union would then gradually become of more interest for the larger countries. As the autocratic regimes would not want to find themselves isolated, Pecqueur thought they would eventually agree to the clause concerning representation in the common congress in order to be allowed to join. 'This Congress would be a school of liberty and of cosmopolitan representation, an advanced course in politics for the enlightened masses of all countries,' wrote Pecqueur.[12] The initial aim would be a step-by-step unification of Europe, in the form of a confederation of states on the model of the first US constitution. As civilization progressed, so

10 Pecqueur, p. 290.
11 Ibid., p. 333.
12 Ibid., p. 381.

competences and functions could be developed further to the point where cooperation would eventually lead to a federal state whose congressional delegates were all directly elected.

Each country would send an equal number of deputies. Proportionality according to population size would contradict the principle of the equality of the states and could provoke mistrust on the part of countries with smaller numbers of seats. However, if the great powers would not agree to equal numbers for all, it might still be acceptable. For the great powers favoured the pursuit of their own conflicting interests over the idea of uniting against the small countries. Consequently, small numbers of seats could be of great significance in determining majorities in particular circumstances. The interests of smaller countries would therefore have to be considered if they were to be won over.

Tennyson's 'Parliament of Man'

The poem 'Locksley Hall', written in 1837 by the English poet Alfred Tennyson (1809 to 1892), was published in the same year as Pecqueur's book. It is about a soldier who comes upon a place familiar from his childhood and is moved to mixed emotions. In the course of a utopian dream of the future, he sees 'the vision of the world, and all the wonder that would be'. Among the peoples and nations, war prevails, until a world parliament and world federation, with universal law, bring peace:

> Till the war-drum throbbed no longer, and the battle-flags were furl'd
> In the Parliament of man, the Federation of the world.
> There the common sense of most shall hold a fretful realm in awe,
> And the kindly earth shall slumber, lapt in universal law.[13]

The poem had considerable influence, especially in the Anglo-American world, and the lines quoted above are still often quoted today. The British historian and political scientist Paul Kennedy (born 1945), for example, inspired by this poem, titled his 2006 book on the United Nations 'The Parliament of Man'. Kennedy wrote that US President Truman (1884 to 1972) often fished out and read aloud a copy of these lines.[14]

---

13 Tennyson, Alfred. 1842. 'Locksley Hall', in: Poems. Boston: W. D. Ticknor, lines 127-130.
14 Kennedy, Paul. 2006. The Parliament of Man. The Past, Present, and Future of the United Nations. New York: Random House, pp. xi-xii.

The long struggle to extend the right to vote

The period in which Pecqueur and Tennyson published these two works was turbulent. In many states, forms of popular representation were slowly but surely evolving. The disintegration of the hierarchical medieval order which accompanied the growth of industrialization, and the so-called 'social question', placed monarchical ruling structures in Europe under relentless pressure to change. A key issue was the inclusion of the power-hungry bourgeoisie in political decision-making. The American Revolutionary slogan 'no taxation without representation' now came to be seen as relevant and significant in this context too. As a rule, what emerged initially was a plutocratic parliament based on male census suffrage. The balance of power vis-à-vis the crown varied, and was another source of conflict. For most reformers and revolutionaries, the goal was universal male suffrage, though the demand to extend the right to vote to women as well was heard as early as 1791 during the French Revolution. The revolutionary activist Olympe de Gouges (1748 to 1793) protested against the fact that the National Assembly's Declaration of the Rights of Man and of the Citizen in practice applied only to men, and she drew up a 'Declaration of the Rights of Woman and of the *Citoyenne*'. In 1793 she too was executed. It was only from the end of the 19th century onwards that the right to vote among the world's states was gradually freed from conditions such as property ownership and the payment of taxes and also extended to women.

In the USA, too, where the right to vote was a matter for the federal states, there were restrictions in some states until around 1865 on the basis of tax payments, property or race. Following the Civil War and the end of slavery, the Fifteenth Amendment of 1870 constitutionally prohibited a denial of the right to vote on account of race or colour. Former confederate Southern states however enacted so-called 'Jim Crow' laws enforcing racial segregation and effectively disenfranchised African American citizens until the Voting Rights Act of 1965 prohibited racial discrimination in voting. The first examples of the permanent introduction of universal male suffrage occurred in Europe, for instance in the revolution of 1848 in France and in Switzerland. Otto von Bismarck (1815 to 1898) introduced it in the North German Confederation in 1867, and in 1871 it was adopted in the new German Empire. At the time, Bismarck probably calculated that the poorer rural population would be more inclined than the urban bourgeoisie to vote for the monarchist camp, which is why the abolition of restrictions on suffrage would favour that party.

The research programme 'Polity' has analysed all countries with more than 500,000 inhabitants from 1800 to today and classified them by year and form of government. According to the latest data of this programme, of the 57 states analysed for the year 1871, five were considered democratic under their criteria: Greece, Colombia, New Zealand, Switzerland and the USA. 36 were classified as incoherent mixed forms between democracy and autocracy, or 'anocratic', and 16 as autocratic.[15]

Parliamentarism and world federalism in Japan

Japan was one of the so-called 'anocracies' according to this classification. A milestone was taken when the Meiji constitution of 1889 established the Imperial Diet as the first elected legislature not only in Japan, but in the whole Asian region, albeit initially only enfranchising males who paid above a certain amount of national taxes. One of the activists 'at the forefront of the democratic movement'[16] and 'the only man' at the time to promote equal rights of men and women[17] was Ueki Emori (1857 to 1892) who also became a member of the first Diet. Although he did not elaborate specifically on a popularly elected global parliament, he did advocate the notions of a world government, a world constitution and world law. According to historian Amin Ghadimi, it 'was not just within Japan's borders that Ueki sought a federative system. He called, too, for a global federation under the helm of a supreme world governmental and legal system.'[18] In a history of pacifism in Japan, historian Klaus Schlichtmann showed that over time the idea of world federalism continued to gather prominent support in the country. He pointed out, for instance, that the 'father of Japanese parliamentarism', Yukio Ozaki (1858 to 1954), is remembered in a memorial behind the Diet building as 'a zealous proponent of world federation' in his later years.[19]

The birth of the inter-parliamentary movement

With the advance of parliamentarism and of universal voting rights, the concept of a world parliament, too, began to develop. 'Naturally, over the course of time,' according to Claudia Kissling, 'the thinking about international parliamentarism adopted the democratic principle being enacted at the nation state

---

15 Available at: Center for Systemic Peace. Polity5 Project, Political Regime Characteristics and Transitions, 1800-2018. (www.systemicpeace.org/inscrdata.html).

16 Ghadimi, Amin. 2017. 'The Federalist Papers of Ueki Emori: Liberalism and Empire in the Japanese Enlightenment.' Global Intellectual History 2 (2): 196–229, p. 201.

17 Anderson, Marnie S. 2011. A Place in Public: Women's Rights in Meiji Japan. Harvard University Asia Center, p. 81. Anderson cautions, though, that Ueki still based the right to vote on paying taxes, a primary duty of men.

18 Ghadimi, pp. 207-8.

19 Schlichtmann, Klaus. 2009. Japan in the World: Shidehara Kijuro, Pacifism, and the Abolition of War. Volume I. Lexington Books, pp. 41-2. We are grateful to Klaus Schlichtmann for important references.

level and transposed this to the international level.'[20] For example, in the public law teaching of Georg Jellinek (1851 to 1911), the concept of parliamentary representation is already integrated quite naturally into the institutional framework of a federation of states. Jellinek wrote in 1882 that, for a federation of states, it was not out of the question 'that for the purposes of agreeing common standards the representatives of the governments might be joined by representatives of the people, such as parliamentarians from the contracting states'.[21] He differentiated thereby between a federation of states and a federal state. The nature of the latter namely required 'a parliament elected by direct popular vote, whose members conceive of themselves not as agents of the individual states but as direct agents of the collective state'.[22] One of the intellectual pathbreakers of the Argentinian constitution of 1853, the lawyer and later diplomat Juan Bautista Alberdi (1810 to 1884), stressed in 1870 in his book 'El Crimen de La Guerra' that the human being as an individual is ultimately the basic unit of every human community. A world community would therefore be based not only on states but also on the people themselves. On the road to a political world union, the sovereignty of the individual states would have to gradually give way in favour of the sovereignty of the human race, he argued.[23]

From the 1830s onwards, the idea slowly took root and grew that the delegates to the various popular representative bodies should work directly together in order to promote international understanding and the establishment of a permanent peace. The paramount issue of foreign policy, namely that of war and peace, should not—this was the idea of interparliamentarism—remain solely in the hands of the cabinets and heads of government.

A Constituent Assembly for a global Magna Charta

The erstwhile Spanish parliamentarian Don Arturo de Marcoartu stressed in an essay of 1876 the necessity of finally codifying the relationship between the states, and their rights, by means of general treaties. In the future he envisaged an international congress being held for this purpose at which not only representatives of the executive branch of government would take part; a full and proper reflection of the representative system required that other political forces at the state level also needed to be represented. Marcoartu proposed a 'Constituent Assembly' to establish a 'Magna Charta' of 'the constituent rights of nations

---

20   Kissling, Claudia. 14 February 2005. 'Repräsentativ-parlamentarische Entwürfe globaler Demokratiegestaltung im Laufe der Zeit'. forum historiae, no. 5.

21   Jellinek, Georg. 1882. Die Lehre von den Staatenverbindungen. Wien: Alfred Hölder, p. 186.

22   Ibid., p. 283.

23   Alberdi, Juan B. 1900. El Crimen de la Guerra. Buenos Aires: Talleres Gráficos Argentinos, ch. 10.

in peace, in war, and in cases of dispute'.[24] This assembly, which he saw as the inception of an international parliament, should include representatives of the executive, legislative and judicial branches from the individual states, all equal in status: in each case, one delegate appointed by the government, two members or former members elected by the parliament (one each from the majority and minority groups), and one magistrate nominated by the highest court and the universities. In order to implement and enforce the laws passed by this assembly, an international tribunal of arbitration would be needed—an old idea, whose roots Marcoartu traces back as far as the assembly of the Greek city states convened by the Athenian King Amphictyon around 1497 BCE. If no existing government were to demonstrate its willingness to convene such an assembly in the foreseeable future, then the delegates of the national popular representative bodies should prepare the ground with their own parliamentary conferences. 'To encourage parliamentarians to cooperate on promoting international understanding as representatives of the people rather than of their governments was a logical consequence of the movement for the emancipation of the bourgeoisie, which over the course of the 19th century had advanced into the margins of political power' wrote Ralph Uhlig in his history of the early interparliamentary peace movement.[25]

The establishment of the IPU

Under the slogan 'Peace through arbitration', the 'Inter-Parliamentary Union' was founded in 1889 in Paris, initially with the name 'inter-parliamentary conference on arbitration'. It was the first international union of national parliamentary delegates. Very soon it was working on models for a standing international tribunal of arbitration. An early highpoint was the annual conference in Budapest in 1896, when 250 parliamentarians took part and approved proposals for submission to the European governments by the administrative office of the organization. The aim was to press the governments to hold a diplomatic conference for the establishment of a tribunal. The members of the IPU supported these efforts in their national parliaments. The idea was to create parliamentary majorities for peace policies, and especially for the principle of international arbitration, in the individual popular representative assemblies, and thereby to exert influence on the governments. Russian diplomats, too, took part in the conference in Budapest. 'It appears that the Rus-

---

24   Marcoartu, Don Arturo de. 1876. Internationalism and Prize Essays on International Law. In: id., A.P. Sprague and Paul Lacombe. Internationalism. London, New York: Stevens and Sons, E. Stanford, Baker Voorhis and Co, 6-55, pp. 17-8.
25   Uhlig, Ralph. 1988. Die Interparlamentarische Union 1889-1914. Wiesbaden: Franz Steiner Verlag, p. 3.

sian observers in Budapest were impressed by the arguments of the friends of peace' wrote Uhlig.[26] In order to avoid the expense of having to modernize the Russian artillery, the idea arose in Moscow to conclude an agreement with the Austro-Hungarian Empire on mutual limits on such weapons. Tsar Nicholas II eventually proposed a general peace conference, which then did indeed take place in The Hague in 1899, with representatives from 30 states.

The Hague Peace Conferences as a catalyst

At the first Hague Peace Conference, it was agreed that a court of arbitration should be established for the voluntary resolution of international disputes, and the Hague Convention with respect to the Laws and Customs of War on Land was issued. This document stipulates, among other things, that in the event of war, civilians and civilian establishments are to be spared to the greatest extent possible; and in an annex it forbids the use of chemical weapons. The court of arbitration is not a standing court for the judgement of cases, but an administrative bureaucracy which is available when needed to enable temporary tribunals or investigative commissions to be set up quickly and easily. Overall, the Hague Peace Conference and its outcome were judged a success by the interparliamentary movement. As a next step, it hoped to develop the court of arbitration into a full court. The IPU and the wider peace movement also saw the need for further action in the area of arms control, where no progress had been made, and in the development of standards of international law. From 1903 onwards, the calls grew louder for a second Hague Conference, and in general for regular meetings of a world congress, in order to achieve these goals. These calls were linked once more, in the USA especially, to the idea of a world parliament.

Internationalism in the USA

As Warren F. Kuehl related in his history of internationalism in the USA, the year 1903 marked 'the beginning of the modern movement for an international organisation'.[27] For example, the two chambers of the Massachusetts legislature, prompted by a citizens' petition initiated by the journalist Raymond L. Bridgman (1849 to 1925), sent a resolution to the US Congress requesting the US President to launch an initiative for 'the governments of the world' to establish 'a regular international congress'. This idea received a great deal of attention in the press, and was supported by the iron and steel magnate Andrew Carnegie (1835 to 1919) among others. Bridgman expanded on the proposal in his book

---

26 Ibid., p. 245.
27 Kuehl, Warren F. 1969. *Seeking World Order. The United States and International Organization to 1920.* Nashville: Vanderbilt University Press, pp. 62-3.

'World Organization' from 1905. He undertook a critical analysis of the concept of sovereignty and concluded that it made sense only at the global level, and not for nation states. The time had come to acknowledge this, and to organize humanity into one common polity. This would need to have legislative, executive and judicial branches. Business necessities, and not political theories, demanded speedy action. 'Already the necessity is upon us for world legislation, because business transactions now extend all over the world and no national legislature will be adequate to protect the people from world monopolies,' Bridgman adduced by way of example.[28] The USA, whose own constitution was the model for the proposed world organization, should take the lead in establishing it. This idea was not unique to Bridgman. The New York lawyer Hayne Davis (1868 to 1942) also saw the constitution of the USA as the model for the global level. Beginning in 1903, and independently of Bridgman, he promulgated in numerous articles the idea of an international organization which in fact was already under construction. The Hague tribunal, he argued, had already endowed humanity with 'the united nations' (which made Davis in all probability the first person to use this term).[29] Following the creation of the Hague tribunal, an executive and a legislature were now needed. With regard to the last, he added that all laws passed by the world congress should become binding on all parties when they had been ratified by four-fifths of all countries, representing four-fifths of the world's population.[30]

Davis eventually joined forces with Congressman Richard Bartholdt (1855 to 1932) from Missouri in order to work on this internationalist project. Bartholdt, who was originally from Germany and had emigrated to the USA in 1872, established an IPU group within the US Congress in 1904 and in that same year, with the support of the Congress, organized the first annual meeting of the IPU outside Europe, in St Louis. There, at his instigation, a resolution was passed calling on US President Theodore Roosevelt (1858 to 1919) to convene a second Hague conference. The request was delivered to Roosevelt in person at a reception at the White House. One month later, Secretary of State John Hay took the matter up on behalf of the President. However, it was not until September 1905, after the conclusion of the Russo-Japanese War in which Roosevelt had acted as a mediator between the parties, that the time seemed propitious. The USA left it to the Tsar to officially launch the initiative to convene the second Hague Peace Conference.

28   Bridgman, Raymond L. 1905. World Organization. Boston: Ginn & Company, pp. 46-7.
29   Davis, Hayne. 12 February 1903. 'The Perpetuation of the Union of Nations'. The Independent (Boston), vol. 55, pp. 384-386.
30   Davis, Hayne. 7 July 1904. 'A World's Congress'. The Independent (Boston), vol. 57, pp. 11-19.

The 'One World' utopia of Kang Youwei

According to Kang Youwei[31] (1858 to 1927), the first Hague peace conference convened at the turn of the century reflected an initial manifestation of the evolution of the political system 'into a single world government' based on an elected 'public parliament'. As he wrote in his work 'Datong Shu'[32] or 'The Book of Great Unity', this would happen 'inevitably' within 'two or three hundred years' and political union would be achieved within one century.[33]

Kang was a Chinese scholar and political activist who challenged the orthodox view, which had prevailed for two millennia, that Confucianism stood for a static society. As a book by Wen-Shun Chi on China's leading modern intellectuals noted, Kang was 'the first major Chinese thinker to theorize that change was the fundamental rule of human history'.[34] Referring to a description of what he claimed to be three unfolding epochs of disorder, gradual peace and great peace in the classic Confucian 'Gongyang Commentary'[35], among other things, he argued that social and political evolution was indeed ingrained in Confucian thinking and needed to be embraced. It was noted that his ideas, underpinned by a re-evaluation of the Confucian classics, had 'explosive force' and 'shocking effects' at the time.[36]

Kang's book 'Datong Shu', put into final form in 1902, describes three similar successive stages in humanity's development towards an age of 'complete peace and equality'. It is at the same time historical analysis of the past, a political program for the present and an utopian vision of the distant future. The utopian vision consists of a harmonious and united world characterized by equality of all people and the absence of material needs that has managed to resolve the main causes of human suffering by overcoming divisions by territorial frontiers and sovereign states, descent, social class and private property, ethnicity, language, gender, sexual orientation or family. As historian and political scientist Kung-Chuan Hsiao pointed out in a major study of Kang, it is clear that the process of transformation towards this vision was to be one of 'piecemeal utopian

---

31   Also K'ang Yu-wie, Chinese: 康有為.

32   Also Ta-t'ung shu, Chinese: 大同書

33   Kang, Youwei. 1958. Ta T'ung Shu: The One-World Philosophy of K'ang Yu-Wei. Edited and translated by Laurence G. Thompson. London: George Allen & Unwin Ltd., pp. 90-1.

34   Chi, Wen-Shun. 1986. Ideological Conflicts in Modern China: Democracy and Authoritarianism. New Brunswick and Oxford: Transaction Books, pp. 12, 15, 39.

35   This classic was transmitted by oral tradition and was first written down by Humu Sheng during the early Han dynasty (206 BCE–220 CE), see Miller, Harry, ed. 2015. The Gongyang Commentary on The Spring and Autumn Annals: A Full Translation. Palgrave Macmillan US, p. 2.

36   Chi, pp. 16-8.

engineering' in the sense of Karl Popper.[37] This means that little incremental changes should be made step by step. At the time, Kang was careful not to unleash the entirety of his utopian ideas on the public, fully aware of their far-reaching implications and their potential political impact. He did not feel that the time was ripe. While the first two parts of the book, around one third, appeared in 1913, the full work containing all ideas was published posthumously in 1935.[38]

Consequently, in his political activism, too, Kang was a reformer and not a revolutionary. At student protests instigated in 1895 Kang became the leader of 'the first generation of Chinese to claim that government should be regularly supervised by the people' and figurehead of a pivotal historic moment to set China 'on the path of democracy', as political scientist Andrew Nathan put it.[39] Among other things, Kang pressed for the creation of a national parliament and constitution.[40] He advocated setting up a constitutional monarchy first and believed that an immediate leap to full democracy will not work and backfire. However, for the old guard even this reformist approach was too far-reaching. Three years after the initial protests, in the 'Hundred Days of Reform', the Guangxu Emperor implemented many of the protesters' proposals but was stopped by a coup of Empress Dowager Cixi. Kang in turn had to flee the country and live abroad for the next fifteen years. To this day, memories of this 'shattering event for an abortive Chinese modernity' have survived and keep inspiring democratic activists in China.[41]

From division to union and from autocracy to democracy

As a general principle, Kang observed, human affairs are characterized by a progression 'from division to union': family clans were formed from individual people, accumulating family clans coalesced to form tribes which in turn coalesced to form nations, and 'accumulating nations coalesced to form large unified states'. This 'coalescing to become larger', he wrote, was 'accomplished by numberless wars.' In China, the process of unification into a single state had required two thousand years, Kang explained. According to his description, starting from the time of Huangdi, Yao and Shun in the 'legendary period' in the centuries before 2200 BCE, there were ten thousand states in the region. By

37 Hsiao, Kung-Chuan. 1975. A Modern China and a New World. K'ang Yu-Wei, Reformer and Utopian, 1858-1927. Seattle and London: University of Washington Press, p. 480.
38 Kang, pp. 26-7.; Hsiao, p. 411.
39 Nathan, Andrew J. 1986. Chinese Democracy. First Paperback Ed. Berkeley and Los Angeles: University of California Press, pp. 45-6.
40 Chi, p. 13.
41 Interview of Peter Zarrow with Evans Chan. 2011. 'Late Qing Dreams of Modernity.' China Beat Archive. (digitalcommons.unl.edu/chinabeatarchive/7/).

the time of Cheng Tang, the founder of the Shang dynasty at around 1700 BCE, the number had decreased to three thousand, only to shrink further to 800 by the time of King Wu, the founder of the Chou dynasty at about 1100 BCE, and to reach around 200 by the Spring and Autumn Period approximately from 770 to 476 BCE. These coalesced to seven states in the Warring States period (403 to 221 BCE) which then, in 221 BCE, united into one under the Qin dynasty.[42]

Kang saw similar trends of amalgamation happening everywhere across the world, providing the formation of Persia, India, Greece, Germany, France or Italy as examples. The advancement of colonialism to him seemed to confirm that overall 'natural selection' was at play in this process with ever stronger and larger states swallowing up the 'weak and small'. Aggressive conquest of this kind, though observable, wasn't in line with Kang's vision. He noted that 'the way in which Germany and America have established large states through uniting their small federated states is a better method of uniting states'. As a step towards 'the complete unity of the whole world' he considered it likely that continental alliances would emerge.[43] According to Kang, there are three typologies of alliances which cannot be achieved by the use of force: treaties between equal sovereign nations (like the Treaty of Vienna), federations of nations which imply the delegation of power to a superior governmental structure (like the Three Dynasties) and finally full unions in which states merge under a new common government (like the United States).[44]

The scholar identified several 'difficulties in uniting states', including their 'conflicting self-interest' and unwillingness 'to surrender their sovereignty'. According to Kang, 'the progress of democracy from less to more' was a 'natural principle', too, that influenced the process. Expressing a view similar to that of Constantin Pecqueur before, that's because 'when states are autocracies, it is natural that they are self-centred, and it is difficult to unite them with other states'. However, 'if there are democracies, then federation is easy', Kang wrote. Thus, the 'arising of democracy' and the 'flourishing of constitutions' across the world were 'first signs' of One World. He was convinced, however, that each community would get there on its own pace. Eventually, he wrote, monarchy 'will certainly be abolished and discarded' in all states, paving the way for peaceful federation. When all states have become democracies, he noted, 'mutual aggression will automatically be eased.' The door would then be open for the creation of a global 'universal legislature' with disarmament as a

---

42 Kang, pp. 79, 84-5.
43 Ibid., pp. 85, 89.
44 See Brusadelli, Federico. 2020. Confucian Concord: Reform, Utopia and Global Teleology in Kang Youwei's *Datong Shu*. Confucian Concord. Brill, p. 60-2. Under contemporary terms, these could be called intergovernmental treaties, confederation and federation.

main objective. In Kang's opinion, the desire for peace cannot be accomplished without disarmament, but disarmament in turn 'cannot be accomplished without abolishing sovereign states' whichever government type they may have.[45]

Initially, the powers of individual states would still be 'very great'. At some point, however, even though large and strong states would continue to exist, these would no longer be able 'to create disorder or swallow up other states' as they would become part of the global federative system. As the world moves from the 'Age of Disorder' towards the 'Age of Increasing Peace-and-Equality', a 'centralization of authority' would occur gradually as it happened in the United States, Kang explained.[46]

Kang's conception of a global 'public parliament'

In Kang's view, the creation of a global 'public parliament' was the first and most important step on the path towards world unification. In his book he elaborates in some detail on the design and functioning of this parliamentary body and how it would develop over time. Kang was ahead of his time. In broad strokes, the ideas he expressed in this regard are echoed in the thinking of many later proponents of a world parliament, although most were and likely still are unfamiliar with him. Initially vested with deliberative functions only, the parliament's power and scope would grow step by step. Mid-way in the 'Age of Increasing Peace-and-Equality' it would turn into a proper legislative body made up of two chambers according to Kang: an upper house composed of government officials who represent their own states and a lower house composed of elected members who represent the world. In the former each state would have two delegates and in the latter, the number of members 'is according to the size of the population'. For a bill to be enacted, it would have to be passed by both houses and 'perhaps' would need to be approved by individual states. By all means, the latter requirement would vanish later. The parliament would command 'public joint military forces composed of troops of the individual states' in order to enforce international law. Troops of individual states as well as those under the parliament's command would be reduced year by year until they are 'done away with entirely'.[47]

The distant future

In Kang's 'Age of Complete Peace and Equality' sovereign states and all military forces cease to exist. Instead of states there would be three thousand local

---

45 Kang, pp. 86f., 88, 96, 83.
46 Ibid., pp. 92, 97.
47 Ibid., pp. 111, 94, 98.

self-governing political and administrative units. None of them would be sovereign, however, but part of the global federation. At all levels, all matters 'will be decided by public vote' based on 'universal public discussion'. Public order will be maintained by police only although Kang envisaged that eventually 'crime and punishments will have been abolished' just as severe illness and material needs would disappear. These latter points are a reminder of the utopian nature of this final stage in Kang's book. Killing of all kind, including of animals, will be a thing of the past, too. In the end, all causes of suffering will be overcome and there will be 'utmost happiness'. In the distant future, ages from now, Kang envisaged that humankind will attain full spiritual enlightenment, 'abandon the human sphere and enter the sphere of immortals and buddhas'.[48] In an analysis Peter Zarrow noted that this ultimate vision 'has embarrassed most scholars of Kang'. However, the historian pointed out that interest in Kang and his cosmopolitan ideas was reviving in the Chinese speaking world. Even his final mystical imagination is 'not entirely incompatible with today's posthumanism', Zarrow observed.[49]

As Wen-Shun Chi reported, the founder of the People's Republic of China and first autocratic ruler of the Chinese Communist Party, Mao Zedong (1893 to 1976), made a short remark to the effect that although Kang had written about the Great Unity, he didn't find a way how to achieve it. The Chinese Communist Party branded Kang and his democratic thinking as counterrevolutionary. After all, as Chi notes, the Communist's 'dictatorship of the proletariat' in actual practice was much farther from democratic rule than even a constitutional monarchy. Further, in Chi's assessment, Kang basically 'did not think it right to launch a revolution at the expense of sacrificing thousands of lives' and in this 'remained a soft-hearted pacifist'.[50]

An initiative at the IPU

Meanwhile, in the United States, Richard Bartholdt was working hard to try and make the establishment of a world parliament a central aim of the IPU. '[I]n order to perfect the peace machinery there lacked only, first, an international parliament or a World Congress, and second, a general arbitration treaty to guide the court as well as the ruling powers', as Bartholdt recalled.[51] The US American delegation to the IPU submitted a proposal to this effect at the

---

48 Ibid., pp. 120, 235, 39, 275.

49 Zarrow, Peter. 2021. Abolishing Boundaries: Global Utopias in the Formation of Modern Chinese Political Thought, 1880–1940. State University of New York Press, p. 24.

50 Chi, pp. 42, 37-8; see also Brusadelli, pp. 162-4.

51 Bartholdt, Richard. 1930. From Steerage to Congress. Reminiscences and Reflections. Philadelphia: Dorrance & Company Inc, p. 261.

annual conference in Brussels in 1905. The proposal included the suggestion that the IPU should lobby for the establishment of a standing 'international congress', consisting of a senate and a chamber of deputies. In fact, the proposal was for each nation to be given two seats in the senate, while seats in the chamber of deputies would be allocated in proportion to the respective share of world trade, though this was not spelt out in more detail. Every member would receive one vote. Any decision passed by a majority vote in both chambers would be legally binding unless an as yet unspecified number of national parliaments were to reject it. The competence of the congress was restricted to international matters, and decisions would have to respect the 'territorial and political integrity' of every nation represented there. The proposal also invoked equal treatment with respect to trade issues as a matter of principle. Finally, the states represented in the congress should have a duty to place their armies at its disposal for the enforcement of the decisions made by the Hague court.[52]

The proposal was not put to a vote, but passed on to a study commission. There, the American proposal met with 'some surprising counter-arguments' from the more conservative Europeans, as Uhlig reported.[53] It was objected that the prospects for success were small in view of the prevailing international tensions, and that the efforts of the IPU should be focused on the issue of ensuring that the Hague conference became a recurring event. An 'academic discussion over the purely hypothetical organisational structure of a world parliament' would add nothing to this. But the Italian delegate Beniamino Pandolfi brought the discussion to a point. He made a blunt plea that no parliamentarians should take part in the proposed congress. This 'untypical viewpoint' for an IPU parliamentarian, as Uhlig writes, was based on his judgement of the 'essential and foundational interests of interparliamentarism', for Pandolfi believed that the American plan put the existence of the IPU itself in jeopardy. 'The incorporation of a parliamentary element into the Congress, elected by the local parliaments, would leave the Interparliamentary Union no other option but dissolution. So we are voting not only on a dangerous and anarchic institution but at the same time on our own suicide,' in the words of Pandolfi's own submission.[54] By the end of the next IPU Conference in London in 1906, nothing was left of the original proposal from the US American group. The call for an international parliament was not included in the IPU's programme for the second Hague Peace Conference. The Confer-

---

52 Lange, Christian (ed.). 1911. Un Congrès International, Conférence de Bruxelles, 1905. In: Union interparlementaire. Résolutions des Conférences et Décisions principales du Conseil, 93-94. 2nd ed. Brussels: Misch & Thron.
53 Uhlig, pp. 413-4.
54 Citation from ibid., p. 413.

ence took place in October 1907 but saw no notable progress made. The introduction of obligatory arbitration failed, in large part because of its rejection by the delegation from the German Empire.

Once the project of a world parliament had effectively been stalled within the IPU, enthusiasm among the early activists in the USA slowly began to ebb away over the next few years. In France, the socialist deputy Francois Fournier (1866 to 1941) instigated an attempt in parliament in July 1913 to prompt the French government into a diplomatic initiative for a world parliament. The government resisted, and Fournier's proposal was roundly defeated in the National Assembly.

Arguments emerging out of the German peace movement

In Germany, powerful supporting voices emerged in the shape of the historian and later Nobel Peace Prize winner Ludwig Quidde (1858 to 1941) and the international law specialist Walther Schücking (1875 to 1935), both leading members of the German Peace Society founded by Bertha von Suttner (1843 to 1914) in 1892. Suttner herself promulgated the 'vision of a united congress of all states, working for a new international federation and international co-operation' on the model of the USA.[55] Schücking argued, in a book published in 1908, for a world federation of states with a world parliament, and criticized 'Germany's reactionary position' at the Hague, much to the annoyance of the Kaiser's government. Referring to already extant shared administrative bodies under international law such as the Universal Postal Union, founded in 1874, Schücking wrote that it would be a 'pointless waste of time, energy and money' if 'as happens today, the same group of states sets up a new union of states for each new international purpose because no general international organisation yet exists'.[56] Such ad hoc unions should be superseded by the general federation of states. In a study of the Hague Conferences, which concluded that they had 'if not *expressis verbis*, then implicitly and *ipso facto*, created a world federation of states',[57] Schücking explained in more detail that the world parliament, alongside the congress of states, should initially have only an advisory role and should be made up of delegates from the individual member states of the federation. He illustrated the advantages offered by the involvement of such a world parliament in international negotiations and in the setting of interna-

---

55　Citation from Walker, Barbara (ed.). 1993. Uniting the Peoples and Nations. Readings in World Federalism. Washington D.C. and New York: World Federalist Movement & World Federalist Association, p. 97 ('A Message to American Women' in: The Women Voter, Vol. V., October 1914).

56　Schücking, Walther. 1908. Die Organisation der Welt. Tübingen: J.C.B. Mohr, pp. 610-1.

57　Id. 1912. Der Staatenverband der Haager Konferenzen. Ed. by Walther Schücking. Vol. 1. München, Leipzig: Duncker & Humblot, p. 6.

tional laws by means of two examples of possible constellations arising 'in the struggle between national and international law' (Jellinek). In the first, it is postulated that the world parliament might help overcome government resistance in the course of negotiations if a majority within the world parliament—and within that a majority within the respective national parliamentary delegation—were to take a position different from that of the government. At the second Hague Conference, for example, it would have been possible to get the obligatory recourse to arbitration adopted, at least with respect to some matters. 'For if this had revealed that the implacable resistance of the German government did not even have the backing of their own parliament, then it would probably have given way', according to Schücking.[58] In the second example, it was possible to imagine a case where there was resistance in a national parliament to agreement to an international norm negotiated by the national government. In such a case, the world parliament could help avoid a dispute between the executive and the legislature over the ratification of treaties, because its existence would mean that a delegation from the national parliament took part from the very beginning in the 'legislative tasks of the world federation of states'. Such participation would make it easier to persuade a possibly sceptical national parliament of the argument for ratification, especially in states such as the USA where the powers are rigorously separated.

The idea of a world parliament was taken up repeatedly over the following years. For example, the lawyer and former German Reichstag deputy Ernst Harmening (1854 to 1913) highlighted in a lecture given in the year 1910 that 'national economic and governmental interests' were now international, and 'could not be adequately safeguarded without the help of other nations'. The concept of sovereignty needed to be revised. It was 'no longer a guarantee for the unlimited self-determination of a polity', and even less so for the welfare of the population. Instead, people were adopting 'a new belief in the solidarity of the interests of the entire civilized world, and ultimately of humanity'. The need for 'self-government by the peoples' in the framework of a 'federal community of nations' would in his view be met by a world parliament. The IPU represented the beginning of this process, he argued, citing its influence on the Hague Conferences.[59]

In the Christmas edition of the 'Berliner Tageblatt' of 1912, the renowned social critic, author and dramatist Frank Wedekind (1864 to 1918) complained that the 'edifice of missions, legations and embassies' of international

---

58 Ibid., p. 302.
59 Harmening, Ernst. 1910. Das Weltparlament. Vortrag gehalten in der Staatswissenschaftlichen Gesellschaft zu Jena. Jena: Bernhard Vopelius, pp. 6-7, 11, 31, 25.

diplomacy was 'a completely medieval apparatus' that operated 'without taking any account of either the rotary press or wireless telegraphy'. The best Christmas present he could imagine would be the establishment of a world parliament. 'The world parliament would of its nature be a permanently open peace conference, with all the instruments of power of the entire world at its disposal, unlike the peace congresses to date, which were a convocation of dilettantes and notorious business opportunists', wrote Wedekind in a deliberate provocation of the diplomatic establishment.[60] He had come to this idea in tandem with the anarchist and anti-militarist writer Erich Mühsam (1878 to 1934), who also reported on their collaboration shortly afterwards in his 'Magazine for Humanity'. Mühsam wrote that despite their differing views on the state they had quickly agreed that 'currently the most serious danger for the people of the world lies in the lack of control over those persons to whom are entrusted humanity's most effective instruments of power'. What was frightening was above all the 'shadowy secrecy' in which 'these people' habitually consorted. Overnight, an argument could break out between the foreign ministries of the great powers, and a war could begin. 'The world parliament for which we call', wrote Mühsam, 'has as its purpose the constant public supervision of international diplomacy.' All the factors affecting relations between nations were by their nature public affairs, and would indeed be public affairs were it not for the pathological secretiveness of the intermediaries. 'When we know that peace is no longer threatened by any diplomat or by any international quarrel, then we will have fulfilled our task', he wrote.[61] There were many other lesser-known proponents of a world state and an elected world parliament at the time.[62]

60 Wedekind, Frank. 25 Dec. 1912. 'Weihnachtsgedanken'. Berliner Tageblatt, no. 656, 1. Beiblatt, p.1/2. Also printed in: id. 1920. 'Weihnachtsgedanken (1912)'. Schweizerland Vol. 2 (2nd half-year): 849–854.
61 Mühsam, Erich. 1913. 'Das Weltparlament'. Kain. Zeitschrift für Menschlichkeit (2) 10: 145–163., pp. 150-1, 163.
62 E.g. Eduard Loewenthal or Kurt Wolzendorff, see Riehle, Bert. 2009. Eine neue Ordnung der Welt: föderative Friedenstheorien im deutschsprachigen Raum zwischen 1892 und 1932. V&R unipress, pp. 81-3, 112.

4.

World War and the League of Nations

The programme of the 'Round Table' group

Beginning in 1909, an international network was formed of people concerned for the future of the British Empire, which was felt to be losing its grip on its predominant position in world affairs. The group, called the 'Round Table', can be traced back to the influence of Cecil Rhodes (1853 to 1902), the South African politician and co-founder of the diamond company De Beers. All his life, this British imperialist dreamed passionately, albeit without concerning himself with detail, of an Anglo-American federation that would ensure that 'the peace of the world would be secured for all eternity'.[1] After Rhodes' death, his fortune was left to the Rhodes Trust, which not only established one of the most prestigious scholarship programmes in the world but was created with the additional purpose of pursuing this goal.[2] With the support of the Rhodes Trust, the 'Round Table' developed a plan for the transformation of the British Empire into a federal state, a 'Commonwealth of Nations'. This would entail the end of the dominance of the Empire by the United Kingdom. Like its former colonial possessions, it would become just a member state of the new federation. At the centre of this federation there would be 'a central sovereign imperial authority directly elected by the people of the Empire to conduct foreign policy and control the armed services, raising taxation through its own officers'.[3] This programme accorded with the proposals made by Lionel Curtis (1872 to 1955), one of the leading members of the group, who was committed to the cause of international integration and who had played a role in the setting up of the Union of South Africa in 1910. The Empire Parliamentary Association of 1911 was the world's second international network of parliamentarians (after the IPU). The purpose of this association was to improve contacts and information flows between the parliamentarians of the Domin-

1   Rotberg, Robert I, and Miles F Shore. 1988. The founder: Cecil Rhodes and the pursuit of power. Oxford University Press, p. 666, see also pp. 102, 281, 316.
2   On the plans for a secret society see Bummel, Andreas. 8 October 2003. 'Kritische Anmerkungen zur Urlegende moderner Verschwörungstheorien'. Telepolis.
3   Lavin, Deborah. 1995. From Empire to Commonwealth. A Biography of Lionel Curtis. Oxford: Clarendon Press, p. 108.

ions (the self-governing colonial territories of the United Kingdom) and the British Parliament. After the end of the First World War, consideration was given to the idea of transforming the association into a genuine common parliament in the context of an institutional reformation of the Empire.[4]

The theory of sociocultural evolution and a world federation

The outbreak of the First World War in 1914 destroyed all hopes for a third Hague conference. On account of its hitherto unimaginable, monstrous scale, the War was experienced, not only by pacifists and internationalists, as an apocalyptic rift. The 'great edifice of nineteenth-century civilization', wrote Eric Hobsbawm, 'crumpled in the flames of world war, as its pillars collapsed'.[5] The members of the 'Round Table' were alarmed. Some of them now began to think beyond the original plan. The historian Carroll Quigley, who studied the group, described their fear 'that all culture and civilization would go down to destruction because of our inability to construct some kind of political unit larger than the national state, just as Greek culture and civilization in the fourth century B.C. went down to destruction because of the Greeks' inability to construct some kind of political unit larger than the city-state'.[6] The original hope for a 'Commonwealth of Nations' and a British-American Union was seen from then on as a part of the project of a universal federation of nations.

The idea of establishing a worldwide organization for peace began to receive mass support. All over the world, peace associations and societies sprang up and campaigned for a league of nations. The 'League of Nations Union', established in England by the writer H.G. Wells (1866 to 1946) among others, grew into the largest group in the British peace movement and in 1931 could count over 400,000 members.[7] Wells, Curtis and others joined together in order to argue, based on their reading of world history and against the backdrop of total war, the essential necessity of a world federation if civilization was to have any future. World history showed human affairs to be a story of 'the oscillating action of separatist and unifying forces', and the time had now come for the unification of the whole world.[8] At the root of their argument lay the theory of sociocultural evolution, which by 1912—on account of an influ-

---

4   Hall, H. Duncan. 1920. The British Commonwealth of Nations. A Study of its Past and Future Developments. London: Methuen & Co., pp. 306-8.

5   Hobsbawm, Eric. 1995. Age of Extremes. London: Abacus, p. 22.

6   Quigley, Carroll. 1981. The Anglo-American Establishment. New York: Books In Focus, p. 137.

7   Baratta, Joseph Preston. 2004. The Politics of World Federation. United Nations, UN Reform, Atomic Control. Vol. 1. Westport, Connecticut; London: Praeger Publishers, p. 74.

8   Wells, H. G., et al. 1919. 'The idea of a League of Nations'. The Atlantic Monthly 123: 106-115, 265-275, p. 106.

ential essay by the anthropologist Franz Boas (1858 to 1942)—had become closely associated with the peace issue, and which now became a fixed basic element of the ideology of world federalism. 'The history of mankind,' wrote Boas, 'shows us the grand spectacle of the grouping of man in units of ever increasing size that live together in peace, and that are ready to go to war only with other groups outside of their own limits.'[9] Notwithstanding all temporary revolutions and the provisional collapse of larger units, the progress towards unification had been so regular and so marked that the only possible conclusion was that this tendency would continue to govern history in the future. Units of the size of modern nation states would have been inconceivable earlier, just as now the idea of the unification of the whole world seemed to exceed the power of imagination. But the assumption that this development would now halt at the nation state could not be justified. In his observations, Boas agreed with other early theorists of sociocultural evolution such as Herbert Spencer (1820 to 1903) and Lewis Henry Morgan (1818 to 1881), although he disagreed with and strongly criticized them on other aspects, especially as regards their belief in a teleological development of human civilization. His approach was developed and extended by social scientists such as Norbert Elias (1897 to 1990) and Gerhard Lenski (1924 to 2015) within a 'neo-evolutionary' framework which rejects any element of determinism.

A world parliament on the Versailles agenda

After 17 million deaths, the greatest massacre in the history of the world to that point was brought to an end with a ceasefire in November 1918. In February 1919, the Paris Peace Conference, under the leadership of Great Britain, France, Italy and the USA, approved the establishment of a League of Nations, as proposed one year earlier by US President Woodrow Wilson (1856 to 1924) in the last of the 'Fourteen Points' of his peace plan. During the negotiations over the statutory rules for the planned League of Nations, the idea of including a parliamentary body was proposed from various quarters. An important member of the 'Round Table' group was appointed as one of the British negotiators in the person of Lord Robert Cecil (1864 to 1958), later President of the League and a Nobel Peace Prize winner. In his proposals for the setting up of the League of Nations he raised the idea of a 'periodical congress of delegates of the Parliaments of the states belonging to the League, as a development out of the existing inter-Parliamentary Union'. This interparliamentary congress could discuss the reports from the inter-state conference and other interna-

---

9   Boas, Franz. 1912. 'An Anthropologist's View of War'. The Advocate of Peace 74 (4) (April): 93-95, p. 94; First published in: International Conciliation, no. 52 (March 1912).

tional bodies and thus 'cover the ground that is at present occupied by the periodical Hague Conference'.[10] However, the only committed supporter of this idea was the second leading member of the British delegation, the South African politician Jan Christiaan Smuts (1870 to 1950) (who, incidentally, had for a short period been Rhodes's legal adviser at De Beers in 1895). On 12 February 1919, at his insistence, the British delegation submitted a proposal to the drafting committee to add to the organizational infrastructure of the League 'a Representative Assembly elected by the legislative bodies of all States members of the League'.[11] This assembly of parliamentarians would provide advice for the work of the assembly of government representatives and the Executive Council envisaged in the current draft. Further details of its operations could be left to the Executive Council. At the ninth session of the drafting committee on the following day, Smuts amended the proposal in a much less ambitious direction. Now the draft Covenant should include only the stipulation that 'at least once in every four years, an extraordinary meeting of the Body of Delegates shall be held, which shall include representatives of national parliaments and other bodies representative of public opinion'. In the discussion that followed, Cecil was given the first word. Surprisingly, he rejected the proposal, on the grounds that the time was not yet ripe. Smuts' initiative was not supported by any of the other 18 participants in the session. It was objected that such a provision was unnecessary, as states were already free to appoint parliamentarians as their delegates. In the opinion of the French negotiator Léon Bourgeois, delegates chosen by a government represented the majority views of the citizens anyway, and, as Wilson said, would without doubt 'be true representatives of the people at large'. The leader of the Belgian delegation, Paul Hymans, expressed fundamental reservations. If a beginning was made of giving representation to 'social groups', it would end up with an international parliament holding yearly meetings. Such a body might lay before the League all sorts of questions, and its scope of action would be too widely extended. Ultimately, elections would take place, and 'the international parliament would no longer bear any relation to the present conception of the Body of Delegates'.[12] With that, the proposal was off the table.

The intention to constitute the League as an exclusive space for governments did not meet with the approval of the peace movement. In March 1919 over 60 organizations from 22 countries gathered in the Swiss capital Bern for the international conference of 'League of Nations Societies', among them

---

10   Miller, David Hunter. 1928. The Drafting of the Covenant, vol. 2. New York: G.P. Putnam's Sons, p. 62.
11   Ibid., vol. 1, pp. 218, 273.
12   This and previous citations from ibid, vol. 2, pp. 299-301.

H.G. Wells' English group, to consult on the constitution drafted in Paris, which had now been published. The first of 26 amendments they proposed was for the establishment of a world parliament as the principal body of the League. 'An international parliament elected by the peoples should replace the assembly of delegates proposed in the Paris text. This parliament should have full prerogatives and legislative powers, each country electing one member for each million inhabitants.'[13] This was similar to a proposal approved by a Swiss 'Committee for the Preparation of the League of Nations' in June 1918. This group of around three dozen individuals, about one third of them members of the Swiss parliament, suggested that the league should be run by a popularly elected 'World Council' at the centre, stressing that no representation of member state governments was desirable.[14] Magnus Hirschfeld (1868 to 1935), the German doctor and sexologist who is regarded as a global pioneer for gay rights and the emancipation of sexual minorities, was another who spoke out for a world parliament. In a speech in front of the Berlin Reichstag he declared on 10 November 1918 that the slogan of the future should no longer be 'workers' but *people* of the world unite'. 'We want people's tribunals and a world parliament', Hirschfeld proclaimed to a crowd of several thousands.[15]

The 'German Plan' for the constitution of the League

The German Empire, as one of the parties responsible for war and one of the losers, was not able to take a direct part in the Paris negotiations, nor to bring about any changes to the work carried out by the Allies on the treaty. But following the November Revolution of 1918 and the forced abdication of William II (1859 to 1941), who fled into exile in Holland, Germany was on the path to a republic, with a new government in charge. The elections of January 1919, which took place for the first time on the basis of a universal, equal, secret and direct franchise (for women, too), resulted in the appointment of Philipp Scheidemann (1865 to 1939) as Prime Minister. In order to give their own ideas for a league of nations concrete form, Scheidemann's cabinet issued a 'German plan' on 23 April 1919 for the constitution of the league, drawn up in the foreign ministry with Schücking's participation. One of the key features of the plan, alongside other organs such as a congress of states (i.e. an assembly of representatives of the member states) and a permanent international

13   'Berne Conferees Suggest Amendments'. New York Times, 19 March 1919.

14   Schweizer Komitee für Vorbereitung des Völkerbundes. 1918. Vor-Entwurf mit Erläuterung für eine Verfassung des Welt-Völkerbundes. Bern: Verlag Paul Haupt. See section B of the draft, in particular §§ 55-62, pp. 17-9 and comments on pp. 72-3.

15   Hirschfeld, Magnus. 'Ansprache vom 10. Nov. 1918'. Vierteljahresberichte des Wissenschaftlich-humanitären Komitees während der Kriegszeit hg. statt des Jahrbuch für sexuelle Zwischenstufen (18) 4: 165–166, p. 166.

court, was a 'first world parliament', made up of representatives of the individual parliaments of the member states. The Scheidemann cabinet was therefore the first government ever to support and call for the establishment of a world parliament, and to the best of our knowledge remains the only one to have done so to date. In this plan, the assent of the world parliament would be required for 'a) changes to the constitution of the federation; b) the creation of universal international legal standards; c) the creation of new administrative organs for the federation; d) the determination of its budget'.[16] The individual parliaments should be entitled to one representative per one million inhabitants, up to a maximum of ten. These were regarded as provisional regulations for a first world parliament, which would then—with the assent of the congress of the states—determine its own future composition itself. Other regulations were also discussed within the foreign ministry, such as direct elections and sliding scales for the allocation of seats. However, according to Gottfried Knoll in a study of 1931, the aim was to keep the regulations pragmatic, simple and clear, so that ordinary people would be able to understand them, and in order to avoid creating unnecessary obstacles to this first step. In Knoll's view, the German proposal for a world parliament was intended perfectly seriously. The government saw the world parliament as a potential 'counterweight against the megalomania of the Allied governments', and hoped that it might exert a moderating influence and bring 'a breath of the spirit of cosmopolitanism' into the League of Nations.[17] If the League were constructed only on the basis of states, there was a danger that 'the old politics' would infiltrate it by way of its various corporate organs. There was also the consideration that a world parliament might generate positive feedback for the democratic parliamentary system of the new German Republic. In this vein, Foreign Minister Ulrich Graf Brockdorff-Rantzau (1869 to 1928) said that German democracy could not be secure 'unless and until the necessary measure of democracy exists in the League of Nations'.[18]

Disappointment over the League of Nations

The German position was irrelevant to what was going on in Paris. The agreed constitution was signed by the negotiating parties as part of the Versailles Treaty on 28 June 1919. Although the League of Nations project had been driven principally by US President Wilson, in March 1920 the US Senate refused to

---

16 Knoll, Gottfried. 1931. Der Deutsche Regierungsentwurf zu einer Völkerbundssatzung vom April 1919. Leipziger rechtswissenschaftliche Studien 61. Leipzig: Verlag von Theodor Weicher, p. 87.
17 Ibid., pp. 22, 25.
18 Citation from ibid., p. 21 (Daily News, 25 February 1919).

ratify it. The reason for this was not only, as is usually claimed, American isolationism. On the contrary: Kuehl's study, for example, reports a striking level of popular support for the idea of a league of nations in the US. But the specific form this idea was given in the Versailles Treaty did not stir any enthusiasm. 'The court has almost disappeared international law, I think, is hardly mentioned; and the thing has turned into a plain political alliance', the Senate majority leader Henry Cabot Lodge complained in a letter.[19] Above all, the Senate felt itself ignored by Wilson, who had only belatedly and grudgingly consulted that body.

It was not only in the USA that the majority of internationalists and pacifists, for various reasons, were disappointed by the League of Nations. Hadn't the democratic countries prevailed over the autocratic regimes? The Romanov, Habsburg and Hohenzollern dynasties, like the Ottomans, had vanished from the political screen. Still, colonial rule had emerged relatively unscathed from the war as the empires of Great Britain, France, the Netherlands, Belgium and Portugal made no losses or even territorial gains. Anticolonial protest and unrest developed new momentum across the globe. Self-determination and democracy, after all, had been one of the war aims declared by Wilson.[20] The civic rights activist W.E.B. Du Bois (1868 to 1963) noted that no true 'federation of the world' can exclude 'the black and brown and yellow races from its counsels. They must equally and according to number act and be heard at the world's council.' In addition, the writer made it clear that a democracy is only worth its name if all citizens are enfranchised.[21] While he expressed doubts over the political possibility of a world parliament that could 'dictate a world policy to the United States, France and the British Empire' and stressed the need of the development of a spiritual 'sense of human oneness', the Indian philosopher, yogi and journalist Sri Aurobindo (1872 to 1950) complained that the constitution of the League did not even recognize 'the principles of the progress to be made'. In particular, he commented that the principle of self-determination was 'ruthlessly thrown overboard'.[22] In 'The Outline of History', in the last section of which he argued for a democratic world state, H.G. Wells expressed his outrage over the absence of democracy in the League of Nations. This League of Nations, he wrote, 'was not a

19 Kuehl, Warren F. 1969. Seeking World Order. The United States and International Organization to 1920. Nashville: Vanderbilt University Press, p. 335.
20 Jansen, Jan C., and Jürgen Osterhammel. 2017. Decolonization: A Short History. Princeton University Press, pp. 36-9, 42-5.
21 Du Bois, W.E. Burghardt. 1920. Darkwater: Voices from Within the Veil. Harcourt Brace & Howe, p. 146.
22 Ghose, Sri Aurobindo. 1997 [1915-20]. The Human Cycle: The Ideal of Human Unity, War, and Self-Determination. Sri Aurobindo Ashram Publication Department, pp. 576-8, 647-8.

league of peoples at all; it was a league of "states, dominions, or colonies".' There 'was no bar to a limited franchise and no provision for any direct control by the people of any state. ... An autocracy would no doubt have been admissible as a "fully self-governing" democracy with a franchise limited to one person. The League of the Covenant of 1919 was, in fact, a league of "representatives" of foreign offices.'[23]

In his novels and non-fiction books, Wells regularly touched on the need and rise of a world state. According to historian Warren Wagar, this was perhaps the essence 'of every book Wells ever wrote', whether he called it 'federation, confederation, world state, system of world controls, scientific world commonweal, cosmopolis, modern utopia, world directorate'—it was 'always much the same thing'.[24] In his 1921 non-fiction book on 'The Salvaging of Civilization' Wells wrote that a world state should be based on a directly elected assembly as 'a real gathering of representatives, a fair sample of the thought and will of mankind at large'.[25] Seven years later in 'The Open Conspiracy' Wells promoted the idea of a 'world movement for the supercession or enlargement or fusion of existing political, economic, and social institutions' and took a more pragmatic and vague approach, shifting his focus away from the institutions of a possible future world state and emphasizing the realization of practical 'systems of world control' that would promote peace, freedom and wellbeing. In this connection he now argued that in 'a polyglot world a parliament of mankind or any sort of council that meets and talks is an inconceivable instrument of government'.[26]

Gerhart Hauptmann (1862 to 1946), winner of the Nobel prize for literature in 1912, regarded America as the 'great shining model for Europe', and for the world. The League of Nations was not even worth mentioning. 'We all long for a world parliament. We need a real league of peoples,' was how Hauptmann described the feelings of many intellectuals in the midst of German hyperinflation and the heightened conflict over reparations.[27] The debate over a world parliament at first continued unabated following the foundation of the League of Nations. Quidde called for a revision of the Covenant of the

23 Wells, Herbert George. 1920. The Outline of History. Being a Plain History of Life and Mankind. Vol. 2. New York: The MacMillan Company, p. 558.

24 Wells, H. G., and W. Warren Wagar. 2001. The Open Conspiracy: H.G. Wells on World Revolution. Westport, Conn: Praeger, p. 8.

25 Wells, Herbert George. 1921. The Salvaging of Civilization. London et al.: Cassell and Company, p. 85-6; an elected world council is also a subject in his 1914 novel 'The World Set Free'. See Wagar, W. Warren. 1961. H. G. Wells and the World State. New Haven: Yale University Press, pp. 212-3.

26 Wells, H. G. 1928. The Open Conspiracy. London: Victor Gollancz Ltd., p. 32.

27 Citation from Tschörtner, Heinz Dieter (ed.). 1994. Gespräche and Interviews mit Gerhart Hauptmann. Berlin: Erich Schmidt Verlag, p. 79 (New York Times, 10 September 1923).

League to introduce a world parliament, among other things. However, the structure of the parliament must not be based 1:1 on population, 'for that would condemn the whole of Europe to impotence in the face of the gigantic empires of East Asia'.[28] He rejected the measures put forward in the German government plan as being too undifferentiated. There would have to be a sliding scale between small and large states in order to take full account of both population size on the one hand and the principle of equivalence of the states on the other. The Austrian-born sociologist Rudolf Broda (1880 to 1932), who had made a detailed study of this issue, drew attention in 1920 to an important argument for a world parliament. Delegates to a peoples' parliament would regard themselves 'to a much greater degree as representatives of humanity in general or as members of an international party crossing national borders' than as representatives of their country.[29] The parliamentary history of the German Empire, he argued, had demonstrated that the Reichstag deputies had regarded themselves as representatives of the people as a whole, and that this had suppressed potential conflict between the constituent states. In a world parliament, it would no longer be countries that stood in opposition to one another but ideas. The danger of inter-state conflict would be reduced by the parliament. It was clear that the prospects for structural reform of the League of Nations were poor. But sooner or later, in the view of Quidde among others, this idea would prevail, because people would grasp 'that the security of their vital interests would only be made possible by the construction of something over and above the nations, something which would prevent these nations from raping one another in their brutal egotism; by establishing the sovereignty of humanity over and above the individual states, the sovereignty of the League of Nations'.[30]

28   Quidde, Ludwig. 1922. Völkerbund and Demokratie. 2nd ed. Berlin: Verlag Neuer Staat, p. 16.
29   Broda, Rudolf. 1920. 'Das kommende Weltparlament'. Der Völkerbund: 347-358, p. 348.
30   Quidde, p. 27.

5.

The Second World War and the atomic bomb: world federalism in the early years of the UN

Federalism under pressure from fascism

The time between the beginning of the First and the end of the Second World Wars was regarded by historians such as Eric Hobsbawm or Arnold J. Mayer as one continuous world conflict lasting thirty-one years. The sociologist and political scientist Sigmund Neumann spoke in 1946 already of a 'second Thirty Years' War'.[1] Democracy and the parliamentary system came under pressure in many places. Fascist regimes sprang up. In the years between 1911 and 1929, according to the Polity programme, there were consistently more democracies than autocracies in the world of states (the rest were hybrid forms). But from 1930 the proportions were reversed. The Inter-Parliamentary Union, despite its dogged work on international issues such as disarmament or the strengthening of international law, sank slowly into political irrelevance. By the end of the Second World War at the latest, the IPU was 'out of the race', as Kissling wrote.[2] The 'Round Table' group's aim of transforming the British Empire into a federation of states foundered on the will to independence in the dominions. Their sovereignty was finally sealed by the Statute of Westminster of 1931. The British Commonwealth became a loose association of independent states.

The federal idea reappeared in a new form as a response to the rise of National Socialism and fascism. In the 1939 book 'Union Now', Clarence Streit (1896 to 1986), originally from the German Palatinate but an emigrant to the USA in 1911, bemoaned the lack of cooperation between the democratic countries, who in the international political sphere behaved like autocracies, and proposed a political union of democracies as a counterweight to the fascist dictatorships. This would begin with the USA, Great Britain, Canada, Australia, New Zealand, South Africa, Ireland, France, Belgium, the Netherlands, Switzerland, Denmark, Norway, Sweden and Finland, and with the gradual accession of new members would ultimately grow to a universal world organization. As

1   Neumann, Sigmund. 1946. The Future in Perspective. New York: G.P. Putnam's Sons, pp. 6-8.
2   Kissling, Claudia. 2006. Die Interparlamentarische Union im Wandel. Frankfurt: Peter Lang, p. 145.

Geneva foreign correspondent of the *New York Times*, Streit, who was in contact with Curtis and greatly admired him, had observed at close quarters the agony of the League of Nations. 'The Union's existing and potential power from the outset would be so gigantic, its bulk so vast, its vital centres so scattered, that Germany, Italy and Japan even together could no more dream of attacking it than Mexico dreams of invading the American Union now,' wrote Streit, who had been a Rhodes Scholar at Oxford.[3] At the centre of his plan for a Union was a congress directly elected by popular vote in the member states, consisting of a house of representatives and a senate. The federal union, based on guaranteed human rights and Union citizenship, would among other things have sole responsibility for foreign and defence policy as well as currency and trade issues, and would guarantee a democratic form of government in the member states.

The growth of world federalism

Streit's book became a bestseller, translated into many languages, which gave new impetus to the idea of a supra-national federal union. In many free countries, new groups were established to press for the idea of supranational integration. In 1939, the organization 'Federal Union' was founded in the USA, with Streit as its chair; it advocated as a first step a union between the western democracies, and it is still active today under the name 'Streit Council for a Union of Democracies'. Alongside Brauer, the historian Joseph Preston Baratta has been especially active in researching the history of world federalism and the multifaceted world federal movement, in a two-volume study published in 2004. The 'campaign for a world government', established in 1937 by the feminists and peace campaigners Rosika Schwimmer (1877 to 1948) and Lola Maverick Lloyd (1875 to 1944), is regarded as one of the earliest world federalist organizations. They published a pamphlet calling for a worldwide constitutional convention and sketching out their ideas for a directly elected world parliament as the basis for a future democratic world federation.[4] As Megan Threlkeld showed in a historical account, women in the US were strongly involved in promoting world government. For instance, she reported on a commission of the Women's Centennial Congress in New York in 1940. Chaired by Louise Laidlaw Backus (1906 to 1973), the group recommended curtailing national sovereignty and creating a global executive carrying out the will of a global bicameral legislature, the lower house of which should be di-

---

3   Streit, Clarence K. 1939. Union Now. A Proposal for a Federal Union of the Democracies of the North
    Atlantic. London: Jonathan Cape, p. 25.
4   Schwimmer, Rosika, and Lola Maverick Lloyd. 1942. Choas, War, or a New World Order. 4th ed.

rectly elected.[5] This idea also emerged in Sweden. Although historians noted that 'references to a United Nations' were sparse in the neutral country during the war, a merger of peace organizations, that later became the UN Association of Sweden, in 1944 advocated 'that international relations undergo a world-federalist transformation'. In particular, it was suggested that an 'assembly of elected representatives of the people in a bicameral world parliament, similar to the United States Congress' should be set up.[6]

The issue of a world parliament was now inseparably commingled with the discourse of the federalists. World federalism without a democratic world parliament is logically not possible, even if this institutional aspect was often not foregrounded or explicitly articulated. The issue of federalism had long played an important role in some resistance movements. In Italy there had been a tradition of federalist thinking since the First World War. In the 'Ventotene Manifesto' of 1941, which was to prove very influential, the Italian anti-fascists Altiero Spinelli (1907 to 1986) and Ernesto Rossi (1897 to 1967) set out the goal and ideal of a federal European state. They denounced the 'ideology of national independence' as the root of the formation of totalitarian states and the outbreak of wars. The principle of non-intervention as adopted by the League of Nations had proved absurd, leaving each nation 'free to choose the despotic government it thought best'. And they were already looking beyond Europe. '[O]nce the horizon of the Old Continent is passed beyond,' runs the text of the Manifesto, written during their imprisonment, 'and all the peoples who make up humanity embrace in a grand vision of their common participation, it will have to be recognized that the European Federation is the single conceivable guarantee that relationships with American and Asiatic peoples can exist on the basis of peace cooperation; this while awaiting a more distant future, when the political unity of the entire globe becomes a possibility.'[7]

The idea of a world federation was to be found in other regions of the world as well, for example among the opponents of British rule in India. 'While [we] must primarily be concerned with the independence and defence of India in this hour of danger, the Committee is of opinion that the future peace, security and ordered progress of the world demand a world federation of free nations, and on no other basis can the problems of the modern world be solved', read the text of the famous 'Quit India' resolution adopted by the All-India Congress Committee in 1942, supported by the future Indian Prime

---

5   Threlkeld, Megan. 2022. Citizens of the World. U.S. Women and Global Government. University of Pennsylvania Press, pp. 119-20.

6   Götz, Norbert. 2016. 'From Neutrality to Membership: Sweden and the United Nations, 1941–1946.' Contemporary European History 25 (February): 75–95, p. 79.

7   Spinelli, Altiero, and Ernesto Rossi. 1941. 'The Manifesto of Ventotene'.

Minister Jawaharlal Nehru (1889 to 1964) and by Mohandas Gandhi (1869 to 1948) among others.[8] As the historian Manu Bhagavan writes, the idea of 'One World' that Nehru and other politicians advocated 'had become a common euphemism for a global parliament'. 'A global parliament is exactly what Nehru had in mind,' he pointed out.[9] The Indian politician (and defence minister 1957 to 1962) and UN Ambassador Krishna Menon (1896 to 1974) described a world government and a world parliament in a speech to a committee of the UN General Assembly in 1954 as 'very desirable'.[10] According to Bhagavan, this reflected the official position of Nehru and of the Indian government.

The Guardian of the Bahá'í Faith, Shoghi Effendi (1897 to 1957) from near Haifa, a great-grandson of the Founder of the Faith Bahá'u'lláh (1817 to 1892), also spoke in 1938 about the necessity of a world state that curtails national sovereignty and includes a world parliament whose members would be elected by the people of all countries. He added, though, that their election 'shall be confirmed by their respective governments'.[11]

In his 1940 book 'The Jewish War Front', Wladimir Zeev Jabotinsky (1880 to 1940), a Russian Jew who developed the ideology of revisionist Zionism, noted that national sovereignty tended to be incompatible with an effective enforcement of minority rights, pointing out that 'no outside supervision can permanently prevent a sovereign nation from doing exactly what it likes inside its own frontiers' and that the 'unlimited sovereignty of nations will have to go by the board, at least in Europe, if civilization hopes to survive'.[12] Earlier he expressed in a personal letter his opinion that no Hebrew-Arab federation in the Middle East needed to be pursued in connection with creating a Jewish state because the states concerned in the region would become part of a world federation anyway. He wrote that he was 'passionately hopeful' that this would happen within the next decades.[13] At a UN hearing in 1947 Israel's founding father David Ben-Gurion (1886 to 1973) said that if the world was to 'abolish separate sovereignties, we will bless it' but so long they would ask for the same

8   All-India Congress Committee. 1942. 'Quit India Resolution'.
9   Bhagavan, Manu. 2013. India and the Quest for One World: The Peacemakers. Houndmills, Basingstoke, Hampshire: Palgrave Macmillan, p. 66.
10   Official Records of the General Assembly, Ninth Session, First Committee, 26 October 1954, p. 215-25. Citation from Reddy, E.S., and A.K. Damodaran (ed.). 1994. Krishna Menon on Disarmament. Speeches at the United Nations. New Delhi: Sanchar Publishing House, p. 12.
11   Effendi, Shoghi. 1938. The World Order of Bahá'u'lláh. (bahai.org)
12   Jabotinsky, V. 1940. The Jewish War Front. London: George Allen & Unwin Ltd., pp. 85, 250. See also pp. 25-6, 39-40.
13   Gorny, Yosef. 2006. From Binational Society to Jewish State: Federal Concepts in: Zionist Political Thought, 1920-1990, and the Jewish People. Leiden and Boston: Brill, p. 34.

status as 'any other free nation'.[14] According to the Israeli writer, journalist and activist Uri Avnery (1923 to 2018), in spring 1949 a group was formed in Israel 'to advocate the setting up of a Palestinian state next to Israel, and the signing of a covenant between the two nations' that would establish some kind of federation. Recalling this later, Avnery argued that peace would have to be built 'floor after floor from the bottom up'. The first floor was a two-state solution, the second was close collaboration of both states and the third then was a regional union. But 'the crown of a new order', he wrote, was a new kind of world governance that involved humankind electing a world parliament.[15]

In the aftermath of the Second World War, the debate about world federalism was dominated by three questions. Should the aim be to create a world federation step by step, via a union initially involving only a limited number of states, or in one great universal step encompassing all of them? Should it be restricted to certain narrowly defined core policy areas, i.e. minimalist in scope, or should it be given much more wide-ranging powers? After the founding of the UN, the additional question arose of whether the aim should be to establish a world federation as a new organization or as the outcome of a reform of the UN. A substantial stream of thought within the federalist movement supported the idea of an international convention tasked with drafting a constitution for a world federation, which would then be submitted to the individual countries for ratification. One early outcome of these efforts was the 'Declaration of the Federation of the World' passed by the House of Representatives and Senate of North Carolina in 1941 which supported this goal and which in the ensuing period up until 1950 was adopted in nineteen other US federal states.

Planning the post-war order

However, the establishment of a world parliament and of a federal world order was not given serious consideration by the Allies either during the war or afterwards. In December 1941, US President Franklin D. Roosevelt (1882 to 1945) had a team set up within the US foreign ministry, the State Department, to work on political plans for after the war. Although there was some initial discussion in the planning team of a federal structure for a future world organization, it was adjudged to be politically impossible and therefore abandoned. 'The various governments and peoples are not believed to be ready for an international federal government even if it were theoretically desirable', ran

---

14　United Nations. 1947. 'Hearings of the Representatives of the Jewish Agency - UNSCOP 21st Meeting – Verbatim Record.' UN doc. A/AC.13/PV.21, p. 60. Thanks to Oded Gilad for this and the previous source.

15　Avnery, Uri. 10 Aug. 2013. 'A Federation - Why Not?' Arab News. (arabnews.com).

the minutes of a planning meeting.[16] A solution was required that would be acceptable to all governments, and particularly to the Soviet Union.

Indeed, the notion that a democratic world federation with a freely elected global parliament could have been established with the totalitarian USSR participating was fundamentally flawed. Political repression and gross human rights violations in the USSR were known. Soviet elections from 1937 to the mid-1980s, for instance, were 'elections without choice' and 'a demonstration of the subordination of the whole people under an almighty ruler'. In 1937 alone, over 380,000 people were executed and a similar number sentenced to forced labour under the order of Joseph Stalin (1878 to 1953) so they could not spoil the desired voting outcomes.[17] Under Stalin's rule, many millions were shot, deliberately starved to death, detained and deported. In a genocidal famine known as the Holodomor, three to five million people died in the Ukrainian Soviet Socialist Republic in 1932-33. Western governments were in the picture. While overshadowed by heavy USSR propaganda and regime-friendly coverage even by Western journalists, there were public reports on these realities, too, already at the time. At the end of 1942, the Soviet Union went on the offensive in the Battle of Stalingrad, and the Battle of El Alamein ushered in the end of the German-Italian presence in North Africa. The Allies declared their war aim to be the unconditional surrender of the Axis powers. Looking ahead to the post-war order, the founder of the Ford Motor Company, Henry Ford (1863 to 1947), called for the creation of a world parliament directly elected by worldwide vote 'to put the world on a peace basis'.[18] The Governor of Minnesota, Harold Edward Stassen (1907 to 2001), also took up the theme. He urged in January 1943 that the Allies begin planning for a world organization. The most important body of the organization, according to Stassen, should be a parliament consisting of only one chamber, which would elect the chairperson of the executive, which in turn would take the form of a world council. The representatives of each country in the parliament should be appointed on the same basis used for the respective national legislature. In the face of such calls, the team in the US foreign ministry considered the possibility of a world legislature empowered to create binding law as the basis of a new world organization. 'Unless a broadly federal scheme of international organization is adopted, which is unlikely, it would be difficult to secure sup-

---

16 Citation from Baratta, Joseph Preston. 2004. The Politics of World Federation. United Nations, UN Reform, Atomic Control. Vol. 1. Westport, Connecticut; London: Praeger Publishers, p. 97.

17 Merl, Stephan. 2011. 'Elections in the Soviet Union, 1937–1989: A View into a Paternalistic World from Below.' In: Voting for Hitler and Stalin: Elections under 20th Century Dictatorships, edited by Ralph Jessen and Hedwig Richter, 276–308. Frankfurt/New York: Campus Verlag, pp. 276, 283.

18 'World Parliament is Predicted by Ford'. New York Times, 2 January 1943.

port for this proposal, particularly in the United States. This proposal would create a serious constitutional problem in the majority of states', opined the State Department.[19]

The Moscow Declaration

In the UK, a former official of the League of Nations, Konni Zilliacus (1894 to 1967), who later got elected to the House of Commons, tried to build support for a post-war 'international authority' with a directly elected world parliament. However, the matter was settled with the Moscow Declaration of 30 October 1943, in which the allied 'Big Four' -the US, the UK, the Soviet Union, and China—declared that the post-war international organization, just as the League, shall be based on the principle of national sovereignty. This was the end to any far-reaching proposals.[20] In the 1944 book 'Peace Through Law', for instance, which received strong attention in the legal community, Hans Kelsen (1881 to 1973) concluded that the best way to secure international peace was 'self-evident', namely 'to unite all individual States' into 'a World State, to concentrate all their means of power, their armed forces, and put them at the disposal of a world government under laws created by a world parliament.' He also concluded, however, that the idea of a 'universal world federal state' at least 'at present' was confronted with 'insurmountable difficulties'. Among other things Kelsen noted that the 'center of a democratic World State must be a world parliament' but in this legislative body 'India and China would have approximately three times as many deputies as the United States of America and Great Britain together', indicating the latter would find that unacceptable. He believed that 'a long and slow development equalizing cultural differences between the nations of the world' was first necessary. Most importantly, Kelsen pointed out that 'the government of a sovereign State is by its very nature inclined to resist any restriction upon its independence'. Thus, the idea was 'not within the scope of political reality' as it was incompatible with the principle of sovereign equality expressed in the Moscow Declaration. The declaration had made it clear, Kelsen wrote, that the governments concerned do not wish to establish an 'international agency endowed with legislative or executive power'. The prominent Austrian legal scholar who had fled Europe for the United States in 1940 argued that the 'desirable aim' of a world state 'can be reached only by a series of stages'. In his opinion, the creation of an 'international court endowed with compulsory jurisdiction'

19　Citation from Baratta, vol. 1, p. 99.
20　Birn, Donald S. 1984. 'Konni Zilliacus.' Peace Research 16 (3): 28–38, p. 31 and id., 1981. The League of Nations Union 1918-1945. Oxford: Clarendon Press, pp. 218-9.

to settle disputes between states was a necessary and possible next step. He believed that even the Soviet Union could be expected to join such an arrangement.[21]

Fundamental criticism of the UN, and the shock of the atom bomb

At the conference of the United Nations in San Francisco from 25 April to 26 June 1945, representatives from fifty states finally came together to discuss and adopt the charter of the coming world organization.[22] Beginning in August 1944, the piecemeal liberation of the German concentration camps brought the industrialized mass murder of over six million Jews and further persecuted groups in the Holocaust to the attention of the global public in all its horror. On 8 May, Nazi Germany surrendered. In the Pacific the war continued. On 6 and 9 August 1945, the USA dropped atomic bombs on Hiroshima and Nagasaki on the orders of President Truman. About 200,000 people were killed instantaneously. Estimates set the total number of deaths in the Second World War at up to 70 million.

The most important cornerstones of the Charter of the UN, which came into force on 24 October 1945, are the principles of national sovereignty and of non-intervention in internal affairs. The organization took the form of an association of sovereign states. According to the provisions of Chapter VII of the Charter, however, the Security Council can decide on universally binding coercive measures 'to maintain or restore international peace and security'. The five victorious powers of the World War secured for themselves permanent seats, with a right of veto, on this body, the most important one. In the event of the use of armed force by the UN, a Military Staff Committee should take over the command of the forces provided by the members. However, this provision has never been implemented. In the General Assembly, which cannot pass any universally binding resolutions, all states are equally represented with one vote. Further, the International Court of Justice was created as one of the UN's principle organs. Unlike what Kelsen and others had hoped, however, the court's jurisdiction was designed to be fully optional.

Internationalists criticized the structural principles behind the new world organization, and evoked the failure of the American confederation and of the League of Nations. The logical conclusions had not been drawn from the lessons of the past. 'The League of Nations, which had failed in [its] task,' wrote Curtis for example, 'was reconstructed as the United Nations Organization. Both were based on the same principle as the Articles of Confederation, that is

---

21   Kelsen, Hans. 1944. Peace Through Law. Chapel Hill: The University of North Carolina Press, pp. 5, 10, 12, 42, 15.
22   Poland was one of the UN's founding members, too, but wasn't present in San Francisco.

to say on a compact between sovereign States, which in terms maintained their sovereignty.'[23] This view was shared in Canada and the United States by a broad cross-section of the population. The polling institute Roper, for example, in 1946 conducted a survey in the US which included the following question: 'If every other country in the world would elect representatives to a world congress and let all problems between countries be decided by this congress, with a strict provision that all countries have to abide by the decisions whether they like them or not, would you be willing to have the United States go along on this?' Of those questioned, 62.8 per cent answered 'yes' and only 19.8 per cent 'no'.[24] In Canada, 59 per cent of respondents in the same year approved of Canada turning over 'control of all her armed forces and munitions, including atomic bomb materials, to a world parliament, providing other nations did the same' according to the Canadian Institute of Public Opinion.[25]

Prominent support for a federal world order

The dropping of the atom bomb came as a great shock, and led to an even more urgent prioritization of the problem of 'international anarchy'. Leading atomic scientists such as Robert Oppenheimer or Philip Morrison, who had themselves worked on the Manhattan project for the development of the bomb, condemned its use, and issued urgent warnings against a nuclear arms race and nuclear war, which would mean the destruction of human civilization. In a volume of essays entitled 'One World or None', Leó Szilárd wrote in 1946 that the problem could only be contained by a world government. Twenty prominent figures, including the Nobel Prize winners Albert Einstein (1879 to 1955) and Thomas Mann (1875 to 1955), the philosopher and author Mortimer J. Adler (1902 to 2001), the former US Supreme Court Judge Owen J. Roberts (1875 to 1955) and US Senator William Fulbright (1905 to 1995), published a joint statement on 10 October 1945 making the same point. 'The first atomic bomb destroyed more than the city of Hiroshima,' they wrote. 'It also exploded our inherited, outdated political ideas.' Since the San Francisco Charter upheld the absolute sovereignty of rival nation states, it was similar in spirit to the Articles of Confederation of the thirteen original American republics. 'How long will the United Nations Charter endure? With luck, a generation? A century?', they asked. But it was not enough to rely on luck. 'We

23   Curtis, Lionel. 1949. World Revolution in the Cause of Peace. New York: Macmillan, p. 33.
24   See Guma, Greg. 11 Sep. 2013. 'Waking Up from World Order Amnesia'. Global Research (globalresearch.ca).
25   See Wittner, Lawrence S. 2009. Confronting the Bomb. Stanford University Press, p. 16.

must aim at a Federal Constitution of the world, a working world-wide legal order, if we hope to prevent an atomic war.'[26]

Reves' critique of democracy, the nation state and sovereignty

With this statement, the prominent signatories were at the same time also expressing support for the recently published book 'The Anatomy of Peace' by the Hungarian-born American journalist Emery Reves (1904 to 1981), in which he made a powerful attack on the concept of the sovereignty of nation states and a plea for world democracy. The book sold in tens of thousands of copies in several translations, and can be seen as a modern update on cosmopolitanism. Just as in the transition from the Ptolemaic to the Copernican worldview, it argued, a revolution in thinking was required. Currently, the only point of reference and starting-point for all political analysis was one's own 'sovereign' nation state. But the nation state system was like the era of feudalism, as there was still no recognition of any higher legal authority. In the highly integrated world of the industrial age, this perspective was 'bankrupt'. The principle of national self-determination propounded by President Wilson was already an anachronism by then, and had laid the groundwork for the Second World War. Peace was not a question of a static international mechanism which would maintain the status quo and suppress aggression between states; rather, it had to be understood as a dynamic social system with the capacity to react to the changes and developments in human society and to steer them. This could only be achieved through a universal legal order—something that was not even conceivable on the basis of the Ptolemaic ideology of nation states. 'The modern Bastille', wrote Reves, 'is the nation-state, no matter whether the jailers are conservative, liberal or socialist. That symbol of our enslavement must be destroyed if we ever want to be free again.'[27] By this, Reves meant not the abolition of the nation states but a radical reorientation of our understanding of democracy, one that would no longer have the nation state as its point of reference. 'We cannot have democracy in a world of interdependent, sovereign nation-states, because democracy means the sovereignty of the people. The nation-state structure strangulates and exterminates the sovereignty of the people, that sovereignty which, instead of being vested in institutions of the community, is vested in ... separate sets of sovereign nation-state institutions.'[28] He concluded, as had Cloots and others before him, that

---

26 Citation from Nathan, Otto, and Heinz Norden (ed.). 1960. Einstein on Peace. New York: Simon and Schuster, pp. 340-1.

27 Reves, Emery. 1946. The Anatomy of Peace. 10th ed. New York, London: Harper and Brothers, p. 270.

28 Ibid., p. 162.

popular sovereignty and democracy could now only be achieved within the framework of a universal and worldwide legal order.

Albert Einstein and Albert Camus as advocates

One of the internationally best-known advocates of a world federation and world parliament after the war was Albert Einstein. From 1933 onwards, he lived in exile, and in 1939 he warned US President Roosevelt of a possible German atom bomb programme. He had long since adopted the peace question as a cause. Along with many other prominent figures, such as John Boyd Orr (1880 to 1971), the Scottish Nobel Prize winner and founding Director of the UN Food and Agriculture Organization, and Brock Chisholm (1896 to 1971) from Canada, the first Director-General of the World Health Organization, he was a supporter of the international umbrella organization of world federalists known today as the World Federalist Movement, WFM, founded in August 1947 in Montreux in Switzerland. Einstein intervened time and again in the public debate. In October 1947, for example, he published a widely-admired open letter to the UN General Assembly. In this, he lamented the fact that the member states had failed to transfer any of their competences upwards to the supra-national level of the United Nations, and he made three suggestions for the future development of the organization. Firstly, the UN General Assembly needed to be strengthened, and the Security Council made subordinate to the Assembly. Secondly, the method of representation had to be substantially changed. 'The present method of selection by government appointment,' Einstein wrote, 'does not leave any real freedom to the appointee. Furthermore, selection by governments cannot give the peoples of the world the feeling of being fairly and proportionately represented. The moral authority of the United Nations would be considerably enhanced if the delegates were elected directly by the people. Were they responsible to an electorate, they would have much more freedom to follow their consciences.'[29] Thirdly, the General Assembly should remain in permanent session, and should take the initiative in the construction of a 'supra-national order'. If necessary, the other countries should proceed without Russia, as long as it was made clear that the door remained open and that the 'partial world Government' would never be misused as an alliance against others.

The philosopher Albert Camus (1913 to 1960), who had joined the Résistance during the war and who received the Nobel Prize for literature in 1957, also spoke out for a world parliament. In November 1946 he wrote that de-

---

29   Einstein, Albert. 'Open Letter to the General Assembly of the United Nations, October 1947'. In: Einstein on Peace, Otto Nathan and Heinz Norden (ed.), 440–443. New York: Simon and Schuster, 1960, p. 442.

mocracy was 'a form of society in which the law is above those who govern, the law being the expression of the will of all, represented by a legislative body'. International law, however, according to Camus, 'is made and unmade by governments, that is, by the executive. We are therefore in a regime of international dictatorship. The only way out is to place international law above governments, which means that this law must be made, that there must be a parliament for making it, and that parliament must be constituted by means of worldwide elections in which all nations will take part.' Until such a parliament existed, the only option was resistance against the 'international dictatorship'.[30] The writer stressed that this parliament needed to include the 'colonized civilizations from the four corners of the earth' so that 'its law will truly become universal law.'[31] Camus later became a member of the international council of the WFM, and alongside Abbé Groués-Pierre (who was also active in the WFM), André Breton, Georges Altman, Robert Sarrazac-Soulage and other French intellectuals was in the solidarity committee supporting the former US Air Force bomber pilot Garry Davis (1921 to 2013). In 1948, Davis had generated considerable publicity by handing in his US passport at the US Embassy in Paris as a protest against nationalism and declaring himself 'the first citizen of the world'. He then camped illegally on the 'world territory' set aside for the UN General Assembly, which was holding its third meeting there, thereby creating an international furore and launching a mass movement for world citizenship. Interrupting a session of the assembly in November, he called on delegates to convene a 'world constituent assembly' or otherwise, he pointed out, a 'People's World Assembly will arise from our own ranks'. Five years later he stated his belief that 'as human beings, we are all world sovereigns' and as such he proclaimed for himself a world government that 'for the moment only exists in my person', calling on others to join him.[32]

The position of the Catholic Church

During the fourth world congress of the WFM in Rome in 1951, Pope Pius XII agreed to receive a delegation from the movement in the Vatican. In an address to the delegation, the Pope declared that the aim of a federal political world organization with 'effective authority' was in accordance with the 'traditional teachings of the Church'. 'Nothing is more in concurrence with its proclamation on just and unjust war, particularly under today's circumstanc-

30 Camus, Albert. 2007. Camus at 'Combat': Writing 1944-1947. Ed. by Jacqueline Levi-Valensi. Transl. by Arthur Goldhammer. Princeton University Press, p. 268.

31 Ibid., p. 269.

32 Davis, Garry. 2003. World Government, Ready or Not. Reprint of 1st ed. Burlington, Vermont: World Government House, pp. 32-5.

es', he said. Whoever was engaged in trying to realize a 'comprehensive political organisation', for example in the form of a world parliament, should be thinking about it precisely from a federalist standpoint.[33] Following Pius XII, the call for an 'effective political organization of the world' has become a fixed component of papal teaching. In 1963, for example, it was expressed by John XXIII, in 1967 by Paul VI, in 2009 by Benedict XVI, and by Pope Francis in the encyclicals 'Laudato Si'' in 2015 and 'Fratelli tutti' in 2020. 'The creation of a parliamentary world legislature that supervises a global executive branch and that allows for the participation of the world's citizens in global political affairs', wrote Maja Brauer and Andreas Bummel in a study of 2016, is set out in Catholic doctrine and is 'fully in conformity with papal teaching.'[34]

The British initiative of November 1945

One important government politician of the post-war period who spoke out explicitly in support of a world parliament was the Labour politician and British foreign minister Ernest Bevin (1881 to 1951). Curtis, one of the co-founders of the Royal Institute of International Affairs in 1920 and a prominent figure in London foreign policy circles, had met with Bevin (whom he had known for a long time already) in October 1945 and put to him the idea of an international assembly.[35] In a parliamentary speech one month later, Bevin said that a new study was needed 'for the purpose of creating a world assembly elected directly from the people of the world, as a whole, to whom the Governments who form the United Nations are responsible and who, in fact, make the world law which they, the people, will then accept and be morally bound and willing to carry out.' He would be willing to sit down with anyone, regardless of their party or nation, in order to work on the constitution of such a world assembly. International law presupposed conflict between nations; it would be replaced by world law, with a world judiciary to interpret it, with a world police to enforce it, created by a sovereign world authority elected by the people themselves.[36] These arguments were not without impact. The Canadian foreign ministry, for example, considered supporting Bevin's initiative if it were to be officially proposed by the British government. In his speech to the first UN General Assembly, the Canadian foreign minister Louis St. Laurent (1882 to

33 Reprinted in Brauer, Maja. 1994. Weltföderation - Modell globaler Gesellschaftsordnung. Frankfurt: Peter Lang, pp. 332-3.

34 Brauer, Maja, and Andreas Bummel. 2016. 'The Federalist Principle in the Catholic Social Doctrine and the Question of a World Parliament'. Committee for a Democratic UN, p. 8.

35 Lavin, Deborah. 1995. From Empire to Commonwealth. A Biography of Lionel Curtis. Oxford: Clarendon Press, pp. 301-2.

36 Hansard Debate, House of Commons. Series 5, Vol. 416, 23 November 1945, 759-846, pp. 786-7.

1973) spoke of the transformation of the UN into a world government. In an internal memo for the Canadian delegation to the third session of the Economic and Social Council of the UN, the Canadian foreign ministry outlined that 'the direction in which Canada would wish to see the United Nations develop is towards a world government with the Assembly presumably evolving towards a democratic world parliament directly representative of peoples on a geographic basis and with direct authority.'[37] All democratic countries had incorporated this principle of representation in their constitution.

But only six months after his statement in the House of Commons, Baratta reports, Bevin had backed away from it entirely. A speech in Moscow's Bolshoi Theatre by the Soviet dictator and mass murderer Joseph Stalin was interpreted as a hidden threat of war against the West. In Fulton, Missouri, in March 1946, the former British Prime Minister Winston Churchill (1874 to 1965) coined the term 'Iron Curtain' for the sealing-off of Soviet-controlled Eastern Europe. As early as June 1945, out of fear of Soviet expansion, he had as Prime Minister authorized an examination of the 'purely hypothetical contingency' of a preventive Anglo-American strike on the Soviet zone in order to drive Stalin back out of Eastern Europe.[38] The looming Cold War was beginning to determine the political agenda.

The issue of a Charter review conference

The elements of the Charter that came in for particular criticism following the San Francisco conference were the right of veto in the Security Council, the principle of the sovereign equality of all states, and the weakness of the General Assembly. Many governments, too, were especially unhappy from the beginning with the right of veto in the Security Council. World federalists complained that even though the Charter opens with the words 'We the peoples', there was no place in the bodies of the UN for delegates elected by popular vote—a fact that has been pointed out time and again since then. On the other hand, it was noted that at least all of the great powers had joined the new organization, in contrast to the League of Nations. Stassen, as a member of the US delegation, had urged strongly in San Francisco that the Charter should at the least be regularly reviewed. In Article 109 of the Charter, it was duly prescribed that after ten years at the latest a proposal for a conference for the

---

37 Ministry on Foreign Affairs and International Trade Canada (ed.). 1946. 'Extracts from the Draft Commentary for the Delegation to the Third Session of the Economic and Social Council of the United Nations, DEA-FAH/7-1946/1, September 1946 (doc. 534)'. In: Documents on Canadian External Relations: 1977. Vol. 12.

38 It has only been known since 1998 that this scenario was explored. See Hastings, Max. 2009. 'Operation unthinkable: How Churchill wanted to recruit defeated Nazi troops and drive Russia out of Eastern Europe'. Mail Online, 26 August 2009 (www.dailymail.co.uk).

purpose of reviewing the Charter had to be on the agenda of the next General Assembly. Thus, the year 1955 became a 'magical date' (Brauer) for world federalists and other advocates of a reform of the UN.

At the urging of the US American lawyer and world federalist Grenville Clark (1882 to 1967), Cuba—at this time under President Ramón Grau—brought a proposal to the second UN General Assembly in 1946 to hold a review conference in 1947. The proposal was rejected by a majority vote, with numerous non-votes and abstentions. In the course of the debate, an issue arose that was to feature repeatedly up to 1955 and beyond, namely that of weighted votes in the General Assembly. The UN Ambassador of the Philippines, Carlos P. Rómulo (1899 to 1985), a 1942 Pulitzer Prize winner who had served as a colonel in the US Army in the Pacific and would later be his country's foreign minister for almost two decades, not only spoke out against the right of veto and in favour of a review conference in 1947 but explained why he would support the introduction of weighted voting in the General Assembly. The principle of 'one nation, one vote' namely served to dissuade the great powers from equipping the General Assembly with 'any power to enact binding world law'. '[M]y nation would be very happy indeed', Rómulo said, 'to trade the fiction of equality in a powerless Assembly for the reality of a vote equal to our actual position in the world in an Assembly endowed with real power.' What was needed was 'a narrowly limited World Federal Government'.[39] In fact, the Philippine's delegation in San Francisco had not only objected to the veto but also had put forward an amendment, that only got their own vote, to the effect that the General Assembly 'should be vested with the legislative authority to enact rules of international law which should become binding upon members after such rules shall have been approved by the Security Council.'[40] Ecuador had suggested that rules adopted by a two-thirds majority of the General Assembly and subsequently ratified by the same number of states should 'come into compulsory effect for all members'.[41] Great Britain's UN representative Hartley Shawcross (1902 to 2003), the leading British prosecutor at the Nuremberg trials, at least agreed on the point that 'some day it might be necessary to devise a weighted form of voting which gave each member State a voting strength in the Assembly consonant with its real influence in world affairs'.[42] But despite this, Great Britain too voted against a

---

39 Citation from Baratta, vol. 1, p. 205 (Statement before Committee I, 16 November 1946)
40 Documents of the United Nations Conference on International Organization, San Francisco, 1945, Vol. III, pp. 536. and Vol. IX., p. 70.
41 Ibid., Vol. III, p. 427, see also pp. 403-4.
42 Citation from Rusett, Alan de. 1954. 'Large and Small States in International Organization. Present Attitudes to the Problem of Weighted Voting'. Intl. Affairs 30 (4): 463–474, p. 464 (The Times, 12 December 1949).

Charter review conference. The issue was endlessly deferred from one General Assembly to the next. In a thesis presented in 2016, Shar-yar Sharei makes the point that the core provisions of the UN Charter, in particular the veto right in the Security Council, were being dictated by the future five permanent members on a majority of states gathered in San Francisco. He argued that they accepted the arrangement not least in return for the promise of a review conference, a promise that to this day was not kept.[43]

The foundation of the Council of Europe

The goal of political integration in Western Europe, as a contribution to the creation of an anti-Soviet bloc, was supported by the American Committee for a United Europe, whose founding President was Senator Fulbright, and which in turn was financed in part by the Ford Foundation set up by Ford in 1936. At the European Conference on Federation, possible pathways towards a United States of Europe were examined. In 1949 the Council of Europe was established, initially comprising ten members, with the constitutional aim of achieving 'a greater unity between its members'. Within the structure of this new intergovernmental organization, the idea of an international parliamentary assembly was actually made concrete for the first time in history. Alongside the Committee of Ministers, in which the governments of the member states are represented, the constitution requires an advisory parliamentary assembly whose members are not government diplomats but delegates sent by the member state parliaments. The allocation of seats in the parliamentary assembly is tiered according to population size. The Union of European Federalists, an umbrella organization for federalist movements in Europe founded in December 1946, pressed for the advisory assembly of the Council of Europe to work on drafting a European constitution to be put forward for ratification by the member states.

Sohn's proposal for a parliamentary assembly at the UN

The creation of this new form of assembly was seized upon as a potential precedent for international organizations in general. 'There is no reason for limiting this interesting development to the countries of Western Europe', wrote the world federalist and lawyer Louis B. Sohn (1914 to 2006), who in 1939 had fled Lemberg in today's Ukraine for the USA, had taken part as a US delegate in the San Francisco conference, and later became a Professor at Harvard University. Using the example of the advisory assembly of the Council of

---

43   Sharei, Shahr-Yar. 2016. Reconstructing Article 109(3) of the UN Charter: Towards Constitutionalisation of the United Nations and International Law. PhD Thesis, Kent Law School, University of Kent.

Europe, Sohn proposed in 1949 the establishment of a parliamentary assembly within the United Nations too. Sohn argued that such an assembly, reflecting 'the various shades of world opinion', would increase global public support for the UN and thus contribute to strengthening it. If real statesmen were to emerge in the assembly, capable of representing a global perspective beyond national ambitions, then its decisions, although only advisory in nature, 'might have more effect than the recommendations of the General Assembly or of the Security Council', thought Sohn. As the instrument of international law needed for the creation of this parliamentary assembly, he recommended using a resolution of the General Assembly under Article 22 of the UN Charter which allows the establishment of 'such subsidiary organs as it deems necessary for the performance of its functions'. An alternative would be an international treaty, as long as it were clearly contained within the framework of the UN. These remain today the two options most often cited and debated, and they will be examined in more detail at a later point in this study. In Sohn's view, the allocation of seats should be in line with each country's relative proportion of the world population. For example, one seat could be allocated for each five million inhabitants, albeit no fewer than three for any country and no more than thirty. Altogether, his model at that point produced fewer than 500 seats.[44] At this time, the efforts of world federalists were focused as a rule on radical change, and consequently the proposal to institute a purely advisory assembly within the UN received comparatively little attention. The WFM, for example, principally supported the idea of organising a world constituent assembly.

The Chicago draft of a world constitution

In order to lend weight to the calls for a world government, which had been increasing at an accelerated pace since the dropping of the atomic bomb, a number of people at the University of Chicago and across the country led by the Italian literary scholar and historian Giuseppe Antonio Borgese (1882 to 1952), who had gone into exile to the USA in 1931 as an anti-fascist and later took on American citizenship, formed a study group to draft a world constitution. It was chaired by the Chancellor of the University, the educationalist Robert M. Hutchins (who left to become Director of the Ford Foundation in 1951). It was one of the first such initiatives. Elisabeth Mann Borgese (1918 to 2002), the youngest daughter of Thomas Mann, was one of those who promoted the 'Preliminary draft for a world constitution' published in 1948; she

---

44 Citations from Sohn, Louis B. 1949. 'The Development of International Law'. American Bar Association Journal 35 (October): 860–862.

was married to Borgese, and for two years, up to 1950, was Chair of the executive committee of the WFM. Later she was an active supporter of the concept of a 'Common Heritage of Mankind' and contributed substantially to the genesis of the Convention on the Law of the Sea in 1982. G.A. Borgese was a friend of Mann's (who had gone into exile in 1933 and moved to Princeton in the USA in 1938). Together with the theologian Reinhold Niebuhr (1892 to 1971), the philosopher of technology Lewis Mumford (1895 to 1990) and fourteen other prominent figures, they had stated already in 1940 in the jointly written essay 'City of Man' that the fundamental prerequisite for world-structure today was a 'constitutional order'.[45] The draft of 1948 now contained concrete proposals for a federal world government with responsibility for peacekeeping, the implementation of human rights, arms control, worldwide taxes, currency and credit issues and other areas. The right of legislative initiative and the capacity to pass laws would lie with a council comprised of 99 members appointed by a federal convention, in turn made up of 'delegates elected directly by the people of all states and nations, one delegate for each million of population or fraction thereof above one-half million'.[46] In her 2017 book 'The Emergence of Globalism', covering Britan and the USA from 1939 to 1950, Or Rosenboim, a lecturer at City, University of London, discussed the Chicago draft and how it came about. She pointed out that the 'people's direct political influence was therefore limited to electing a large and ineffective body of representatives, whose main mission was to elect other representatives.' Further, a council-elected president in charge of the global executive power would be able to veto any council-initiated legislation. The 'limited democracy of the world federation is evident', Rosenboim noted and in fact, the study group did not manage to reach a consensus for this and other various reasons. Two members, James Landis and Richard McKeon, refused to approve of and sign the draft.

The French Catholic philosopher Jacques Maritain (1882 to 1973) according to Rosenboim suggested that a 'clearly defined supranational status of citizenship' needed to be added to the draft.[47] Maritain, who had some influence on the drafting of the Universal Declaration of Human Rights through a brief involvement as French representative at UNESCO, in his work 'Man and the

45 Agar, Herbert, Frank Aydelotte, Giuseppe Antonio Borgese, Hermann Broch, Van Wyck Brooks, Ada L. Comstock, William Yandell Elliott, et al. 1941. The City of Man. A Declaration on World Democracy. New York: The Viking Press, p. 94.

46 Committee to Frame a World Constitution. 1948. The Preliminary Draft of a World Constitution. Chicago: The University of Chicago Press.

47 Rosenboim, Or. 2017. The Emergence of Globalism: Visions of World Order in Britain and the United States, 1939-1950. Princeton University Press, pp. 197-8, 200, 204.

State', published in 1951, concluded that a world federation needed to be universal and based on the will of all peoples. Thus, it 'can only occur after a long time'. As a first step, he entertained the idea of a directly elected 'kind of world council' composed of members 'previously proposed by the highest institutions and the governments of every State' who would be given 'world citizenship' and by its moral authority this council would influence world public opinion.[48]

Apart from the Chicago draft, other model constitutions, which naturally also dealt with the issues of the structure of a world parliament and the procedures of global legislation, were drawn up over time and published by many other groups and individuals. One prominent example is the 'Earth Constitution' originally drafted by the World Constitution and Parliament Association at sessions held in 1968 and 1977. The Swiss international lawyer Max Habicht (1899 to 1986), who had opened the founding conference of the WFM in Montreux, counted 13 such texts in the years 1939 to 1971, beginning with Streit's 'Union Now'.[49]

The Clark and Sohn model

The proposals for a comprehensive revision of the UN Charter published (together with a commentary) by Clark and Sohn in the book 'World Peace Through World Law' constituted the model which attracted the most attention. Clark—inspired by Streit—had concerned himself with the subject since 1939, and then joined forces with Sohn. Their book appeared in different versions in the years 1958, 1960 and 1966.[50] 'Of all the twentieth-century proposals for world constitutionalism, however,' wrote the political scientist Samuel S. Kim, "World Peace Through World Law", by Grenville Clark and Louis Sohn, remains the most comprehensive, detailed, rigorous model of world constitutionalism.'[51]

What did this model for the decision-making organs of a reformed UN look like in outline? For a start, the draft Charter proposed that the citizens of all UN member states should automatically receive an additional and automatic citizenship of the United Nations, thus creating a direct relationship between the UN and the individual. Gradually, following a three-stage plan over 24 years, the members of the General Assembly would be directly elected:

---

48 Maritain, Jacques. 1998 [1951]. Man and State. Washington D.C.: The Catholic University of America Press, p. 214.

49 Habicht, Max. 1980. 'Le droit de l'homme à la paix'. Transnational Associations (2): 84–88, pp. 85-6.

50 In the following we only refer to the latest edition: Clark, Grenville, and Louis B. Sohn. 1966. World Peace Through World Law. Two Alternative Plans. 3rd ed. enlarged. Cambridge: Harvard University Press.

51 Kim, Samuel S. 1993. 'In Search of Global Constitutionalism'. In: The Constitutional Foundations of World Peace, Richard Falk, Robert C. Johansen, and Samuel S. Kim (eds.), 55–81. Albany: State University of New York Press, p. 57.

by the national parliaments in the first stage; half of them by the parliaments and half directly in the second stage; and from the third stage onwards, entirely by direct election. The allocation of seats would be roughly in line with each country's proportion of the world population, in six tiered categories, whereby none of the then 99 countries would have more than 30 seats, and each at least one. Clark and Sohn wrote that they had also examined proposals for two-chamber and three-chamber systems, but had rejected them. A world legislature consisting of only one chamber was the simplest and most effective option. In their model, the reformed General Assembly would be given the power to pass binding world laws on issues regarding the maintenance and enforcement of peace, disarmament, and the control of nuclear energy. Resolutions in other policy areas would continue to have only the status of recommendations. The former Security Council, now transformed into an executive council without permanent members or a right of veto (it is not possible to go into the full detail of its proposed structure and procedures here), would be subordinate to the General Assembly and would implement its decisions. Clark and Sohn went into considerable detail in their model on plans for disarmament and for the establishment of a permanent UN peacekeeping force, together with a reserve force, which could be mobilized for peacekeeping and when enforcement measures were required. The reasoning behind this model was that general and extensive disarmament can only be achieved through the creation of a supranational armed force, under a shared command, with a monopoly on the use of such force. This is the focus of Clark and Sohn's plan. The Chicago group, by contrast, had supported a 'maximal' option, arguing that a restriction to policing functions only made no sense because it meant that the world organization would have no effective way of dealing with or resolving the social and economic injustice which lay at the root of many conflicts, and which it would then in fact tend to consolidate.[52]

CURE's deliberations and conclusions

The US-based 'Conference Upon Research and Education in world government' (CURE) which since around 1953 organized an ongoing exchange of a wide range of 'students of world affairs' eventually came forward with a set of charter revisions to illustrate 'that it is possible to strengthen the present Charter so that the United Nations can function as a true federal government in world affairs'. According to CURE's proposal the General Assembly was to be composed of an 'Assembly of Nations', representing governments, and an

52 Brauer, p. 133.

'Assembly of Peoples', representing world citizens. This bicameral body was to be vested with the power to 'ratify or revise international conventions', among other things. In a book that summarized CURE's debates and elaborated strongly on the issue of citizen representation at the UN, it was noted that by contrast to Clark and Sohn's idea 'most federalists recognize' the 'necessity for at least a bicameral legislature'. CURE's participant and prolific world federalist lecturer Vernon Nash is quoted saying that two houses will be created 'since all federal systems have adopted that compromise after long struggle in constitutional convention'. Even if the powers of the UN wouldn't be increased, CURE participants had 'a strong feeling' that the peoples should be more directly represented. 'A popularly elected chamber without power, but with capacity to voice world public opinion,' said renowned political scientist Quincy Wright, 'might assist in the emergence of a world public opinion and a world legislative body.' Still, the report asserted that such an assembly of peoples 'will enable the world to entrust more responsibilities to the United Nations.' In terms of how seats should be allocated, an overwhelming majority of CURE's participants recommended 'some modification of straight population ratios' at least initially.[53]

Parliamentary cooperation for a world federation

In the years following the Second World War, world federalist parliamentary groups arose in numerous countries. In some parliaments, hearings took place on the question of a world government—for example in the US Congress, where up until 1950 a number of proposals for resolutions on world federalism were considered. Indeed, one of these proposals was supported by 111 Congress members, including the future US Presidents John F. Kennedy and Gerald Ford.[54] None of them passed through the relevant Committees and got adopted though. Speaking on behalf of the State Department, Assistant Secretary of State John. D. Hickerson expressed opposition to each of them. 'We cannot afford to risk jeopardizing or losing what we have without some real assurance that we are getting something better in its place,' he said at a hearing of the Senate's Committee on Foreign Relations, adding that proponents of a world government 'have a burden to show specifically that what they pro-

---

53 Millard, Everett Lee. 1966. Freedom in a Federal World. Rev. 4th ed. Dobbs Ferry, NY: Oceana Publications, pp. 206, 209-10, 63-4, 65, 74, 58.

54 See H. Con. Res. 64, printed in: U.S. Congress. 1949. To Seek Development of the United Nations Into a World Federation. Hearings before the Committee on Foreign Affairs, House of Representatives, 81st Congress, 1st Session. Washington: United States Government Printing Office, p. 1 and S. Con. Res. 56, printed in: id. 1950. Revision of the United Nations Charter. Hearings before a Subcommittee of the Committee on Foreign Relations, United States Senate, 81st Congress, 2d Session. Washington: United States Government Printing Office, p. 73. See also S. Con. Res. 66, ibid., p. 317.

pose offers a better chance of attaining our objectives and has a real chance of a general acceptance.'[55] In his opinion, they were unable to do so.

With the help of the British parliamentary group founded by Labour Party member Henry Usborne (1909 to 1996), an international umbrella association was founded in London in 1951, the World Association of Parliamentarians for World Government. The former British Prime Minister Clement Attlee (1883 to 1967) acted as honorary President. Prime Minister Shigeru Yoshida (1878 to 1967) belonged to the Japanese national group. The purpose of these groups, which existed in more than ten countries, and in some cases—such as Japan—continue to exist, was to provide support for world federalism through the national parliaments. Their activities were closely coordinated with the WFM, which at that time had a presence in over 50 countries. In a strategy supported by the WFM, it was envisaged that an international committee of parliamentarians would set to work on drafting a world constitution if and when the time came.[56] A highpoint of the movement's international parliamentary activities was the third global conference of the World Association of Parliamentarians for World Government, which took place in the Danish Parliament in Copenhagen, with over 400 delegates participating. A year earlier, the question of whether the IPU should transform itself into a world parliament, or indeed whether it should be pressing for a world parliament at all, had once again petered out in inconclusive internal debates.[57] Looking ahead to the hoped-for UN Charter revision conference in 1955, the conference in Copenhagen passed fourteen revision proposals, including one for the transformation of the UN General Assembly into a world legislature made up of a senate and a chamber of deputies. With respect to the proposed powers for this world legislature, the proposal was 'minimalist', like the later one from Clark and Sohn. Only resolutions passed by both chambers for peacekeeping purposes were to be binding. The concept of UN world citizenship can also be found already in the Copenhagen proposals. 'To ensure that world law can be enforced by the means of the United Nations against individuals breaking the law,' it reads there, 'every citizen of a member state shall be a citizen of the U.N., as well as of his own country. The Charter and the laws enacted thereunder shall bind each individual citizen of the U.N.'[58] Additionally, the conference proposed that the world legislature should have the power 'to raise

---

55 Ibid., p. 429.

56 On the parliamentary activities of world federalists see Brauer, pp. 171-7.

57 See Kissling, p. 213.

58 World Association of Parliamentarians for World Government (ed.). 1954. Report of the Third World Parliamentary Conference on World Government held at the Parliament House, Christiansborg, Copenhagen, August 22-29, 1953, p. 132.

revenue for UN purposes', whereby a maximum global rate would be fixed in the Charter and levied from the member states proportionately according to their national income. In the Clark and Sohn proposal, the member states would raise specific taxes themselves following a similar model and transfer the sums raised direct to a local UN finance office.

Decolonization and world order

The view of many Black Atlantic activists at the end of the Second World War was captured in a resolution adopted at the 5th Pan-African Congress that was held in Manchester in October 1945. Participants included the prominent civic rights advocate W.E.B. DuBois as well as Jomo Kenyatta (1897 to 1978) and Kwame Nkrumah (1909 to 1972) who later were to become the first Prime Ministers and Presidents of Kenya and Ghana, respectively. The document stated that 'We demand for Black Africa autonomy and independence, so far and no further than it is possible in this "One World" for groups and peoples to rule themselves subject to inevitable world unity and federation.'[59]

The UN Charter that entered into force that same month stated that the UN should develop international relations based on the principles of equality and 'self-determination of peoples.' This helped open the floodgates for anti-colonial activism. At this historical moment, though, the UN's other proclaimed bedrock, state sovereignty, was met with scepticism in Black Atlantic circles. Alain LeRoy Locke (1886 to 1954), a philosopher and one of the fathers of the Harlem Renaissance in the 1920s, held the view that the 'ancient political idol of the sovereign, essentially irresponsible nation' must be repudiated, 'politically sacred as though it be'. Some of it had to be given up, he wrote, in order 'to prevent war, to get fellowship among nations' and 'to erase conflict boundaries'. In addition, like DuBois, he pointed out that the alleged democracies had to practice what they preach, alluding not only to the colonial empires still in place at the time, but also to the ongoing racial oppression in the United States. This was the price to be paid in order to reach the 'necessary goal of world democracy', Locke noted.[60]

As the statement of the Pan-African Congress and the earlier 'Quit India' resolution illustrate, there was a wide-spread understanding among anti-colonial activists at this time that the world order should move beyond being a collection of sovereign states. Achieving sovereignty as separate states, as

59   The Challenge to the Colonial Powers. 1945. In: Padmore, George, ed. 1947. Colonial and Coloured Unity: A Programme of Action. History of the Pan-African Congress. London: The Hammersmith Bookshop. p. 5.
60   Locke, Alain, and Charles Molesworth (ed.). 2012. The Works of Alain Locke. Oxford University Press, pp. 544, 555-6, 540.

promoted by the UN, was not perceived as the obvious or best route towards self-determination. The 1940s and 1950s in this regard were 'a phase of intense political imagination'.[61] Independence, it was argued, could be achieved in the shape of federal unions at different levels and with layered sovereignty, all encompassed by a world federation. The case was made that postcolonial states would be weak on their own. Their 'balkanization' in a Westphalian framework thus would make it hard to achieve nondomination and development. This approach marked 'a radical break from the Eurocentric model of international society' dominated by a 'Westphalian regime of sovereignty', argued the political scientist Adom Getachew in a book on the subject.[62]

Attempts at postcolonial integration

The long efforts of the 'Round Table' group had failed to achieve a transformation of the British Empire into a federation. Instead, the Commonwealth materialized more and more as a lose and insignificant association of independent states. In the two years following independence in 1947, India under Prime Minister Jawaharlal Nehru pursued the goal of establishing a common citizenship for all citizens of the Commonwealth but to no avail. While the idea was not to turn the Commonwealth into a 'Super-state', as a diplomatic memorandum pointed out, it was suggested to 'strive for the federal ideal of having a common citizenship with no arbitrary discrimination between the citizens of one unit and those of another'.[63] As Raphaëlle Khan of the Harvard University Asia Center wrote, the ambitious concept would have allowed Commonwealth citizens to move freely across the association's member states, among other things. According to the political scientist, the proposal represented a flexible postcolonial imagination of sovereignty and contradicts the mainstream narrative that the newly decolonized states from the outset 'simply assimilated already existing Western norms'.[64] It is rather the case that the former colonizers resisted and rejected alternative approaches.

In the French Empire, in turn, federal integration was pushed forward in the discussions on the Fourth Republic's constitution following the liberation from Nazi rule in 1944. One of the leading proponents was the Senegalese poet and politician Léopold Senghor (1906 to 2001) who was also instrumen-

61   Jansen and Osterhammel, pp. 160, 47.
62   Getachew, Adom. 2019. Worldmaking after Empire: The Rise and Fall of Self-Determination. Princeton University Press, p. 11.
63   Rau, B. N. India's Constitution in the Making. Ed. by B. Shiva Rao. Bombay: Allied Publishers, 1963, p. 361.
64   Khan, Raphaëlle. 2021. 'Sovereignty After the Empire and the Search for a New Order: India's Attempt to Negotiate a Common Citizenship in the Commonwealth (1947–1949).' The Journal of Imperial and Commonwealth History 49 (6): 1141–74, pp. 1141-2, 1144.

tal in the Négritude movement of the African diaspora. At the time, Senegal was part of French West Africa and one of over twenty French colonial entities around the world. According to this scheme, all people in the French overseas départements, territories and perhaps the associated states, as well as those of the metropole, would become equal citizens of a federal French Union with a common legislature. Integration through universal enfranchisement at a supranational federal level, not political separation, was seen as a key vector for decolonization. In Paris, this notion of equality provoked pushback. 'Citizens of the overseas territories will be more numerous than citizens of the metropole', the influential politician Édouard Herriot of the Radical Party declared, adding that 'France would thereby become the colony of her former colonies.'[65] This fear prevailed in the end. While the constitution of the Fourth Republic that entered into force in October 1946 actually created a French Union, its institutions were far from being 'egalitarian, multinational, or federal', the historian Frederick Cooper summarized. There was no universal suffrage and the influence of the numerous overseas entities was limited. In the National Assembly, for instance, overseas deputies were a small minority. The Assembly of the French Union, in turn, was designed as a consultative body with no power.[66]

In addition, as the historians Jan C. Jansen and Jürgen Osterhammel reported, building on 'larger imperial traditions, schemes for federal units popped up in various parts of the disintegrating British, Dutch and French empires—in places such as Indonesia, Malaysia, South Arabia, French West Africa, the French-controlled parts of the Sahara, the British West Indies, or the Dutch Antilles.' In those cases where they succeeded, these projects remained small-scale and short-lived.[67] The Caribbean West Indian Federation lasted for only four years until 1962, for instance. The Arab League, already established in March 1945, was no federation at all. Some argued it was deliberately designed to enhance state sovereignty instead of Arab unity.[68] A Pan-African federation, promoted by Nkrumah, among others, did not materialize. The Organization of African States, formed in 1963, was a typical intergovernmental organization.

---

65 Quoted in: Duong, Kevin. 2021. 'Universal Suffrage as Decolonization.' American Political Science Review 115 (2): 412–28, p. 425. See also: Cooper, Frederick. 2016. Citizenship between Empire and Nation: Remaking France and French Africa, 1945-1960. Reprint Edition. Princeton Oxford: Princeton University Press, pp. 105-7.

66 Cooper, pp. 85, 102-4, 122-3.

67 Jansen and Osterhammel, pp. 161-2.

68 Acharya, Amitav, and Alastair Iain Johnston, eds. 2007. 'Designed to Fail or Failure of Design? The Origins and Legacy of the Arab League.' In: Crafting Cooperation: Regional International Institutions in Comparative Perspective. Cambridge: Cambridge University Press.

By the mid-1950s, the momentum had shifted towards sovereignty and the Westphalian model. Dreams of federation, a world federation in particular, did not vanish completely, but had little relevance. This was apparent at the first Afro-Asian conference of twenty-nine non-aligned states in Bandung, Indonesia, in 1955. Issues such as the creation of a world parliament were not on the official agenda. But at least it appears to have been on the mind of some participants. A leading Indonesian educator, politician and freedom fighter, who remains anonymous, told African American activist and author Richard Wright in the margins of the congress that he believed 'true planning is possible only on a world basis' and that for this 'a superparliament' was needed. 'The insistence upon state sovereignty', he added, 'is what blocks world planning'. In Bandung this was a fringe view though. Wright later commented that it was 'unthinkable' that African and Asian nations 'so recently freed from color and class domination of the West, would voluntarily surrender their sovereignty'.[69]

One year after becoming the first President of Senegal in 1960, Léopold Senghor explained in a message to a congress of WFM in Vienna, that 'federalism must be both internal and international. It represents essentially the search for unity in diversity.' He pointed out that he has 'always been in favor' of the movement's proposals for UN reform and added that it was 'particularly necessary' to complete the UN 'with an assembly of the peoples'.[70] To our knowledge, though, his government did not take action in this regard.

Serial production of sovereignty

Eventually, decolonization became 'an apparatus for the serial production of sovereignty', as Jansen and Osterhammel aptly put it, a 'sovereignty machine that produces political units, standardized according to templates of international law'.[71] Of course, those who found themselves in these units had no part in the original shaping of this law or the design of the UN in particular. One of the key issues, for instance, was gaining national control over natural resources. Foreign companies insisted on the concessions granted by the previous colonial authorities and proper compensation under customary international law.[72]

Once such a unit was born, it developed its own dynamics of self-preservation. Attention shifted towards capturing the power these new units prom-

---

69   Wright, Richard. 2008. Black Power. Harper Perennial, pp. 468, 724.
70   Quoted in: Billion, Jean-Francis. 2001. World Federalism, European Federalism, and International Democracy. A New History of Supranational Federalist Movements. New York/Ventotene: World Federalist Movement-Institute for Global Policy/Altiero Spinelli Institute for Federalist Studies, p. 82.
71   Jansen and Osterhammel, pp. 9-10.
72   See Anghie, Antony. 2019. 'Inequality, Human Rights, and the New International Economic Order.' Humanity 10 (3): 429–42, p. 432.

ised. With few exceptions, like India or Botswana, postcolonial states ended up under autocratic rule. The new states inherited a culture of colonial authoritarianism, low levels of general education and development, and had little, if any, experience with democracy. In fact, Olúfẹ́mi Táíwò, chair of Cornell University's Africana Studies Center, argued that colonialists had aborted 'the modern project in Africa' instead of facilitating it.[73] Foreign interference, in particular by the USA, USSR and the former colonial powers, came on top following independence. In the end, as legal historian Samuel Moyn at Yale University explained, anticolonialists in their respective localities were more interested in 'collective liberation from empire, not individual rights.'[74] Thus started the 'second struggle for freedom' in the postcolonial states according to Táíwò.[75]

In the period from 1945 to 1965 alone, the UN's membership more than doubled from the original 51 founding members to a number of 120. The vast majority were new states which emerged from decolonization. By 1975, roughly the end of its main period, UN membership had almost tripled to 144. Data from the Polity programme indicates that most were autocratic. According to their assessment, 24 per cent of the states they rated in 1945 overall could be seen as democratic. 50 per cent were rated as hybrid regimes and 26 as autocracies. By 1975, the scales had turned against democracy. While a similar number of 25 per cent was considered democratic, the share of autocratic states had risen to 59 per cent.[76]

Support in Ghana

In 1957 Ghana was the first Sub-Saharan African country to gain independence. Its descent under the Pan-Africanist Nkrumah into a despotic one-party state was particularly discouraging.[77] The idea of world federalism and a global parliament attracted Ghanian politicians at the time. One of them was Komla Agbeli Gbedemah (1912 to 1998), a close ally of Nkrumah and long-time finance minister, among other things. From 1957 to 1961 Gbedemah served as President of the WFM. Another was Joseph Boakye Danquah (1895 to 1965) who had fallen out with Nkrumah long before independence. According to Danquah, the 'only adequate machinery for ensuring the maintenance of uni-

73　Táíwò, Olúfẹ́mi. 2022. Against Decolonization: Taking African Agency Seriously. 1st ed. London: C Hurst & Co Publishers Ltd, pp. 193-199, 204.

74　Moyn, Samuel. 2010. The Last Utopia: Human Rights in History. The Belknap Press of Harvard University Press, pp. 85-7, 117.

75　Táíwò, Olúfẹ́mi. 2009. How Colonialism Preempted Modernity in Africa. Indiana University Press, p. 25.

76　Data available at Center for Systemic Peace. Polity5 Project, Political Regime Characteristics and Transitions, 1800-2018 (www.systemicpeace.org/inscrdata.html).

77　See James, C.L.R. 2022. Nkrumah and the Ghana Revolution. Ed. by Leslie James. Duke University Press.

versal peace' was 'a world government with a world parliament'.[78] In 1958 Nkrumah pushed through the Preventive Detention Act which empowered him to detain anyone without trial. Everybody who disagreed with him was thus threatened and silenced, if not actually imprisoned. Gbedemah fled the country in 1961 to escape this fate. Danquah was incarcerated several times and died in prison in February 1965.

78 Danquah, Joseph Boakye. 1997. The Ghanaian Establishment. Accra: Ghana Universities Press, p. 138.

6.

Bloc confrontation and
the rise of the NGOs

World federalism caught between the fronts in the Cold War

The authors of the Chicago draft constitution of 1948 were convinced of the rightness of their cause, but at the same time they were not under the illusion that the preconditions for the establishment of a world republic were actually in place. 'Yet World Government shall come', wrote Hutchins and G.A. Borgese, 'whether within five years or fifty, whether without a conflagration or after it.' Their draft should be seen, they said, as 'a proposal to history'.[1] The transfer of sovereignty was rejected not only by the Soviet Union; moreover, internationalism, and more especially world federalism, was slowly but surely being ground between the two fronts of the East-West conflict. In the USA, anti-communist hysteria broke out, personified in the figure of Senator Joseph McCarthy (1908 to 1957). World federalists were suspected by those who succumbed to this hysteria of being communists in disguise. Conversely, in the Eastern bloc they were seen as agents of capitalism. The reaction to Einstein on the Soviet side, for example, was that his idea for a 'world super-state' was 'nothing but a flamboyant signboard for the world supremacy of the capitalist monopolies'.[2] After the IPU put the issue of a world parliament on its agenda in 1949, a number of the 'peoples' republics of Eastern Europe' decided to boycott their conferences and the subject fizzled out inconclusively.[3] The change of mind of the influential commentator and theologian Reinhold Niehbur is an illustrative case for this period. As the retired professor of philosophy of religion and theology David Ray Griffin explained, Niebuhr in 1943 made 'his most passionate statements' about the need for some form of democratic world government but by 1946 the idea 'even as a possibility for the distant future seems to have disappeared' from his mind and two additional years later he even started attacking it. According to Griffin, the bestselling author and public intellectual had come to the conclu-

---

1   Committee to Frame a World Constitution. 1948. The Preliminary Draft of a World Constitution. Chicago: The University of Chicago Press, p. vii.

2   Citation from Nathan, Otto, and Heinz Norden (ed.). 1960. Einstein on Peace. New York: Simon and Schuster, p. 445.

3   Kissling, Claudia. 2006. Die Interparlamentarische Union im Wandel. Frankfurt: Peter Lang, p. 212.

sion, among other things, that establishing a common global community was an illusion in view of the enmity between the USA and the USSR and that world-government utopianism was a distraction from the immediate task of defeating communism.[4]

The federalist movement and the founding of NATO

The Soviet blockade of West Berlin in June 1948 represented the first dramatic crisis of the Cold War. It was not least as a reaction to this escalation that NATO was founded in April 1949, as a military alliance between the Western European countries, the USA and Canada. As the historian and political scientist Ira Straus noted, it is not widely recognized how decisive the influence of federal thinking originally was on the architects of the Atlantic alliance.[5] 'If it hadn't been for Union Now', wrote the then Director of the Office of Western European Affairs at the State Department, Theodore Achilles, 'I don't think there would have been a NATO Treaty.'[6] The decisive impulse for the creation of the NATO Parliamentary Assembly also came out of the federalist movement. This conference for parliamentarians from the NATO partner countries has been coming together since 1955, and although not a constitutional organ of NATO has been informally recognized since 1967. With the help of Federal Union, the Atlantic Union Committee was set up in New York in 1949, under the leadership of former US Supreme Court judge Roberts, to further the cause of a 'Federal Union of the Democracies'. Numerous prominent figures in the USA joined the committee, including former US President Truman and George C. Marshall (1880 to 1959), who during the war from 1939 to 1945 was chief of staff of the US Army and who received the Nobel Peace Prize in 1953 for the Marshall Plan he devised for European reconstruction. The transatlantic federalists thought that NATO should be more than just a military alliance. The proposal for an Atlantic parliamentary assembly, wrote John A. Matthews, a member of Federal Union, 'stemmed from a more fundamental proposal to create a comprehensive government of democratic nations—most of which have gradually come to be thought of as the Atlantic Community'.[7] In this view, the NATO Parliamentary Assembly was to become the core and the motor of a transatlantic integration project. The renowned British historian Arnold Toynbee (1889 to 1975) argued in an article

---

4   Griffin, David Ray. 2021. Reinhold Niebuhr and the Question of Global Democracy. Annoka, Minnesota: Process Century Press, pp. 71-3, 86, 90-1.

5   Straus, Ira. 1999. 'Atlantic Federalism and the expanding Atlantic Nucleus'. Peace & Change 24 (3): 277–328.

6   Citation from ibid., p. 291 (interview of Achilles by Straus on 18 March 1983).

7   Matthews, John A. 1962. 'Evolution of an Atlantic Assembly', Repr. in: U.S. Congress, Congressional Record, Proceedings and Debates of the 99th Congress, 2nd Sess., Jan. 28, 1986. Ed. by. U.S. Congress, p. 3.

of 1952 that the assembly ultimately had to become a directly elected common legislature for the western community.[8]

Uniting for Peace

From January 1950, the USSR in a boycott stayed away from meetings of the UN Security Council assuming that due to their absence no decisions could be made. The Soviets demanded that the Chinese permanent seat should be occupied by the mainland government of the Chinese Communist Party instead of the Taiwanese Republic of China led by the Kuomintang. When North Korea invaded South Korea in June 1950, the Council, unimpressed by the Soviets' nonattendance, seized the opportunity and adopted a resolution mandating the United Nations Command, a multinational military force to assist the South. The USSR returned and blocked further resolutions related to the Korean war. This resulted in the General Assembly adopting a landmark resolution on 3 November 1950 titled 'Uniting for Peace'. According to this document, the General Assembly can assume subsidiary responsibility on matters of international peace and security if the Security Council, because of lack of unanimity of the permanent members, fails to exercise its primary role. In theory, this shifted the power balance in favor of the assembly. Observers noted that the creation of NATO and the adoption of the 'Uniting for Peace' instrument compensated some of the deficiencies of the UN that had already become apparent.[9]

The declining popularity of world federalism and a world parliament

But from 1950 and 1951, the political climate – against the backdrop of the Korean War, which is estimated to have claimed three million lives – grew ever more difficult for more fundamental change. This was the first of numerous so-called proxy wars, including those in Vietnam and Afghanistan, in which the two superpowers and their respective blocs stood on opposing sides as political adversaries, de facto if not officially. The 'Declaration of the Federation of the World' alluded to earlier was actually revoked in thirteen of the US states which had adopted it. And the UN Charter revision conference provided for in Article 109 failed to take place in the key year of 1955 as anticipated. Instead, the General Assembly passed a resolution to the effect that it should take place 'at an appropriate time' and appointed a committee to rec-

---

8   Toynbee, Arnold J. 1952. 'Union of Free Inevitable'. Freedom & Union 7 (10): 19–23.
9   Finkelstein, Lawrence S. 1952. 'National Policies and Attitudes Toward the United Nations.' World Politics 5 (1): 129–32.

ommend when that time might be, but which in practice never did so. After 1967 the issue disappeared from the UN agenda for good.

In an influential *New York Times* essay, Soviet dissident and later Nobel Peace Prize laureate Andreï Sakharov (1921 to 1989) in 1968 expressed the view that the dangers humanity was facing made 'any action increasing the division of mankind' a crime and only 'universal cooperation' would 'preserve civilization'. He outlined his vision of democratic changes in the Soviet Union and social progress in the United States which eventually would pave the way for a 'convergence' and 'the creation of a world government'.[10] He did not elaborate on the latter's design but remarked that 'economic, social, and ideological convergence should bring about a scientifically governed, democratic, pluralistic society free of intolerance and dogmatism, a humanitarian society which would care for the Earth and its future, and would embody the positive features of both systems.'[11] Three years later Sakharov called for the creation of an international consultative 'Council of Experts' on 'the Problems of Peace, Disarmament, Economic Aid to Needy Countries, the Defense of Human Rights, and the Protection of the Environment' composed of 'authoritative and impartial individuals' who have 'maximum independence' from 'the interests of particular states and groups of states'. An international agreement should oblige national legislatures and governments to consider this Council's recommendations.[12]

The question of a world parliament now arose only infrequently until the early 1980s. When the IPU decided in 1965 to review its relations with the apparently indifferent UN, Kissling reported that the British IPU group proposed 'a transformation of the IPU into an advisory parliamentary assembly of the UN by means of simple resolutions of both organisations', but that this met with no support.[13] In 1970, on the 25th anniversary of the founding of the UN, the US American Commission to Study the Organization of Peace (founded in 1939, and influential during the war) submitted a detailed report on the future of the world organization. Sohn was now Chair of the Commission. This report also recommended, as an element of a wider programme to strengthen the General Assembly, the establishment of a UN parliamentary assembly. This was to be the next step in the evolution of international parliamentary institutions. The report also pointed to the examples of the IPU and the NATO Parliamentary Assembly. However, the Commission had

---

10   Sakharov, Andreï. 22 July 1968. 'Thoughts on Progress, Peaceful Coexistence and Intellectual Freedom.' The New York Times.
11   Sakharov, Andreï. 1990. Memoirs. New York: Alfred A. Knopf, p. 282.
12   Reprinted in ibid., p. 643-649, quoting p. 645.
13   Kissling, p. 217.

passed its zenith and attracted little attention any more, and in 1972 it was quietly wound up.

While world federalism was no longer on the agenda in the Eastern or Western blocs, in India—which had played a leading role in the establishment of the Non-Aligned Movement—it remained a live issue. It is no accident that the sixteenth world congress of the WFM in 1975 took place in New Delhi, with the support of the Indian Prime Minister Indira Gandhi and the Indian President Fakhruddin Ali Ahmed, and that 'virtually the entire political leadership of India' took part, as an observer noted.[14]

The World Order Models Project

From 1968 onwards, a new catalyst for world order studies emerged in the form of the academically-oriented World Order Models Project, led by the legal scientist Saul Mendlovitz (b. 1925) of Rutgers University. WOMP served to help build up a transnational framework for the study of issues of world order and of 'preferred future models' oriented on four goals: the minimization of the extensive use of collective force; the maximization of social and economic wellbeing; the implementation of basic human rights and political justice; and the restoration and preservation of ecological stability. The contributors were by no means all committed to the programme of global constitutionalism as advocated by Mendlovitz and his colleague Richard Falk (b. 1930) from Princeton University. In 'A Study of Future Worlds', published in 1975, Falk presented a comprehensive model of a preferred world system at the institutional centre of which was a 'world assembly' with special responsibility for setting standards in the areas of the four WOMP goals. The assembly would consist of three chambers, each with 200 votes, representing respectively the governments, the peoples and civil society organizations. The model does not make clear how the seats are allocated, nor how or by whom the representatives are appointed. This is 'a complicated task of institutional design'.[15] However, it is proposed that decisions endorsed by all three chambers with a four-fifths majority would have binding status, and those endorsed with only a two-thirds majority would have recommendatory status. A world court would be able to subject the decisions to legal scrutiny. Each chamber would elect seven representatives to an executive council charged with implementing the decisions of the assembly and able to call on the services of a coordinating council, whose members would also be elected by the three

14　Logue, John. 'One World, One Family. A Report on WAWF's New Delhi Congress'. Transnational Perspectives 2, no. 1 (1975): 4–8, p. 4.
15　Falk, Richard. 1975. A Study of Future Worlds. Amsterdam: North-Holland Publishing Company, p. 238.

chambers. So the creation of a broadly-based world legislature was regarded as indispensable within the WOMP, too.

The growing importance of NGOs

A particularly interesting feature of Falk's model is the third 'chamber of organisations'. Other academics working at WOMP were also involved in this initiative. The peace researcher Johan Galtung (1930 to 2024), for example, recommended not only transforming the General Assembly into a directly elected world parliament but also the establishment of a UN chamber for 'nonterritorial actors'.[16] Such proposals reflected the growing significance on the international stage of civil society organizations independent of governments. Anti-Slavery International was one of the first internationally active associations of this kind to be founded, in 1839. They were concerned with the abolition of slavery, with votes for women, with workers' rights and with peace. The International Labour Organization, founded in 1919 and since 1945 continuing under the aegis of the UN, can be regarded as setting the precedent for their inclusion within inter-state organizations. In the structural bodies of the ILO, employees' and employers' associations are represented alongside the governments of the member states, by delegates with equal status. At the annual International Labour Conference, for example, each country has two government representatives and one each representing employees and employers.

After the World Wars, the number of international civil society organizations grew rapidly. Article 71 of the UN Charter stipulated that ECOSOC, the United Nations Economic and Social Council, 'may make suitable arrangements for consultation with non-governmental organizations'. This is the reason for the use since then of the term 'non-governmental organizations', or NGOs. Up to 1975, 650 NGOs had been registered as having consultative status with ECOSOC; today there are more than 3,500, and their exact categorization is a science in itself. Not only did their numbers grow, but the range of topics they address also grew ever broader. Of particular significance was environmental protection. The biologist Rachel Carson (1907 to 1964) stimulated environmental awareness and helped its breakthrough into the popular consciousness with her 1962 book 'Silent Spring', in which she drew attention to the catastrophic impact of chemical toxins like DDT. 'Along with the possibility of the extinction of mankind by nuclear war, the central problem of our

---

16 See e.g. Galtung, Johan. 1975. 'Nonterritorial Actors and the Problem of Peace'. In: On the Creation of a Just World Order. Preferred Worlds for the 1990's, ed. by Saul H. Mendlovitz, 151–188. New York: The Free Press; and id., 1986. 'International organizations and world decision-making'. Transnational Associations (4): 220–224.

age has therefore become the contamination of man's total environment with such substances of incredible potential for harm', she wrote.[17]

In the human rights sector, Amnesty International, founded in 1961, quickly became a prominent and influential group. One of Amnesty's co-founders and international chairs was the Irish politician, former foreign minister and lawyer Seán MacBride (1904 to 1988), who received the Nobel Peace Prize in 1974. In his acceptance speech in Oslo he pointed out that ultimately a world parliament and a world government were needed to achieve world peace. 'Of course, it will be difficult', he said, 'but what is the alternative? The nearly certain destruction of the human race.'[18]

In 1972, the first UN conference on the environment took place in Stockholm, led by the Canadian Maurice Strong (1929 to 2015). It was shadowed by a parallel gathering of NGOs—a practice repeated at many subsequent UN conferences. Parliamentary associations like the IPU or the Parliamentarians for Global Action, founded in 1978 by the New Zealander Nicholas Dunlop (b. 1956), initially under the umbrella of the WFM, were—in the perspective of the UN—just NGOs like all the others. The Stockholm conference led to the establishment of the United Nations Environment Programme, UNEP, with Strong as its first Director until 1975. In a speech in New York in 1984 Strong advocated a bicameral system for the UN 'in which peoples' directly elected representatives sit in one chamber and representatives of governments in the other'.[19]

The idea of a 'second chamber'

A closer integration of NGOs in the work of the UN was also advocated by the Medical Association for the Prevention of War (now, under the name Medact, the British branch of International Physicians for the Prevention of Nuclear War, IPPNW), set up by the genetic scientist Lionel Penrose (1898 to 1972) and others. At the second special session of the UN General Assembly on disarmament in 1982, this Association proposed the establishment of a 'second chamber' alongside the General Assembly. As one of the initiators, the British doctor Jeffrey Segall (1924 to 2010), explained, this body would concern itself with fundamental global problems, would consist of delegates who were independent of government and not attached to political parties, and would help

17 Carson, Rachel. 2000. Silent Spring. New edition. London et al.: Penguin Classics, p. 25.
18 MacBride, Seán. 12 December 1974. 'Nobel Lecture: The Imperatives of Survival'.
19 Citation from Nerfin, Marc. 1993. 'United Nations: Prince and Citizen?' In: The Constitutional Foundations of World Peace, ed. by Richard Falk, Robert C. Johansen and Samuel S. Kim, 147–165. Albany: State University of New York Press, p. 156 (Maurice F. Strong, 'Some Thoughts on the Future of the UN', remarks at a meeting of the New York Chapter, Society for International Development, November 29, 1984).

to give expression to 'world public opinion' within the UN.[20] In the course of the following year the Medical Association formed an international network of NGOs to press for such a chamber—the International Network for a UN Second Assembly, INFUSA. On the 40th anniversary of the UN in 1985, the network appealed to the General Assembly to set up an expert group to examine this proposal. INFUSA's idea had been for an assembly of NGO representatives, but it proposed that each UN member state should itself decide how to select its representatives. It identified some options, such as direct election by the entire electorate, or a vote taken by electors who had registered specifically for that purpose, or indirect election by an electoral college which might be made up of representatives of selected NGOs, trade unions, academic establishments and members of national UN societies. At any event, the spirit of the proposal would exclude the option of nomination by government. A formula developed by Penrose in 1946 was proposed as the method for calculating the number of seats per country, namely representation proportional to the square root of the country's population in millions. This formula would automatically result in a graduated distribution.[21]

The issue of weighted voting in the UN General Assembly

Weighted voting in the UN General Assembly remained an issue. As the Canadian peace researcher Hanna Newcombe (1922 to 2011) reported in 1971, the US State Department carried out a confidential study to calculate the impact that different systems of weighted voting would have had on past votes in the General Assembly. The question was which system would have given the best results for the interests of the United States. The investigation concluded that 'the U.S. does best under the present one-nation, one-vote scheme, because so many small nations habitually vote in the Western bloc led by the U.S.'[22] The State Department therefore decided against supporting any form of weighted voting. For organizations such as the Center for War/Peace Studies, reorganized by the journalist Richard Hudson (1925 to 2006) in New York, however, the introduction of weighted voting remained an indispensable requirement for a strengthening of the General Assembly. Hudson later wrote that the General Assembly 'with its absurd one nation, one vote deci-

20   Segall, Jeffrey J. 1982. 'A UN Second Assembly'. Reconciliation Quarterly (June): 35–37.
21   International Network for a UN Second Assembly. 1987. 'Appeal to the United Nations General Assembly to consider the proposal for a UN Second Assembly'.
22   Newcombe, Hanna. 1971. 'Weighted Voting Formulas for the UN'. Security Dialogue (2): 92–94, p. 92.

sion-making system' has 'no chance to make global laws'.[23] The Center developed its own proposal, the so-called 'Binding Triad'. In this, the voting weight of a country would be determined by three factors: one nation, one vote (as previously); population size; and the contribution to the regular UN budget (for which a ceiling would be fixed). Decisions of the Assembly would have to achieve specified qualified majorities in all three of these areas in order to acquire binding status.

In August 1985, the US Congress then did call for the introduction of weighted voting in the General Assembly. In order to add weight to its call, the Congress held back a portion of the US contribution to the UN budget, and moreover cut it by 20 per cent, thereby drastically aggravating the UN's funding crisis. It took issue both with mismanagement within the UN administration and with what it saw as unacceptable anti-western politicization of the organization by developing countries, who formed a majority. Clearly, the voting arithmetic in the UN bodies had changed. The ruling was brought in by Senator Nancy Kassebaum and Gerald Solomon, a member of the House of Representatives. Voting rights for the member states on issues relevant to the budget of the UN and its specialized agencies, it was argued, should be in proportion to the budget contribution made by each member state.[24] Agreement was then reached with the other member state governments that budget issues would be decided by consensus in order to ensure the assent of the biggest budget contributors without having to formally change the official procedures.

Bertrand's report

Funding crisis, management reform and budget issues were at the very top of the agenda in the UN's 40th anniversary year. The 'Joint Inspection Unit of the United Nations', an independent subsidiary body of the General Assembly established in 1966 to examine the working efficiency of the UN and its specialized agencies, took the opportunity to instruct the outgoing Inspector, Maurice Bertrand (1922 to 2015) from France, to prepare a report with suggestions for reform. The report, delivered in December 1985, turned into a wide-ranging critique. Bertrand lamented the 'extreme fragmentation' of UN activities and their 'extraordinary and unnecessary ... institutional complexity'. Most of the organization's problems had structural causes. Resistance to any attempt at improvement was strong. The member states were not interested

23 Hudson, Richard. 1991. 'Should There Be a Global Parliament? What Is the Binding Triad?' In: A New World Order. Can It Bring Security to the World's People? Walter Hoffmann (ed.), 32–36. Washington D.C.: World Federalist Association, p. 34.
24 United States Foreign Relations Authorization Act, Section 143, Fiscal Year 1986-1987, H.R. 2068, P.L. 99-93, August 17, 1985, Reprinted in: International Legal Material, vol. 25 (1986), pp. 17-43.

primarily in efficiency but in political control of the administration. With regard to the allocation of posts, for example, the principal aim was not to find the best qualified person, but rather to get one's own nationals selected if at all possible. Considerations for reform of the UN had to focus 'following the two unfinished experiments of the League of Nations and the United Nations, on a third generation World Organization'. At the conclusion of the report Bertrand recommended, amongst other things, examining proposals for opening up the UN to more non-state actors. However, 'the time had not yet come to think in terms of a "World Parliament"'. Over the next few decades, the world organization 'should remain an intergovernmental organization'.[25] The Inspection Unit rushed to distance itself from this devastating report. Bertrand, it stated, had gone beyond his remit and his powers. The Administrative Committee on Co-ordination, which brings together the heads of all the UN specialized agencies, declined for the same reasons to comment on the report at all.

Perestroika and Gorbachev's initiative

The policy of perestroika introduced by Mikhail Gorbachev (1931 to 2022) from 1986 onwards, involving a step by step democratization and market economy reforms in the Soviet Union, also ushered in the end of the era of bloc confrontation. Since the Cuba crisis of 1962 at the latest, it had been clear to the governments of the nuclear powers that any dispute could potentially spiral out of control and quite possibly lead to an exchange of nuclear strikes and mutual annihilation. War, understood in the terms of the Prussian General Carl von Clausewitz (1780 to 1831) as a political instrument for the achievement of one's aims with physical force ('the continuation of politics by other means'), was no longer a realistic option. In his book on Perestroika, in which his stated aim was to 'talk without intermediaries to the citizens of the whole world about things that, without exception, concern us all', Gorbachev described the importance of 'the new way of thinking' for Soviet foreign policy. The core of this new way of thinking lay in the realization that, in view of the dangers of a nuclear war, 'humankind's survival' had to take priority over national interests. All of humankind was in the same boat, and would sink or swim together. Transparency, dialogue and the willingness to cooperate were the maxims required for foreign policy.

In this connection, Gorbachev argued that 'the new style in international relations implies extending their framework far beyond the limits of the diplomatic process proper. Parliaments, along with governments, are becoming

---

25   Bertrand, Maurice. 1985. 'Some reflections on reform of the United Nations, Report of the Joint Inspection Unit'. JIU/REP/85/9; A/40/988, pp. 1, 5-6, 65-6.

increasingly active participants in international contacts, and this is an encouraging development. It points to a trend toward greater democracy in international relations'. The increasing role of public opinion and of NGOs in the domain of international politics was a sign of the times, and should be welcomed.[26] In a pathbreaking newspaper article in *Pravda* on disarmament and collective security among other topics, Gorbachev wrote in September 1987 that a 'world consultative council' should be established within the UN to bring together the world's intellectual elite. Scientists, politicians, public figures, representatives of civil society and the churches, writers, artists and others would be able to 'seriously enrich the spiritual and ethical potential of contemporary world politics'.[27] The proposed body is reminiscent not only of the council proposed by Andreï Sakharov in 1971 but also of a 'universal council' already envisaged by the philosopher Johann Amos Comenius (1592 to 1670) in the 17th century which he described as a gathering of enlightened 'philosophers, churchmen and politicians of outstanding eminence in wisdom, piety and prudence pledged to introduce plans at long last full enough to secure, establish, and increase the safety of all mankind'.[28]

However, it is likely that the four important, independent, international expert commissions of the 1980s will have served Gorbachev as model and inspiration. The Brandt Commission, set up in 1977 and chaired by the former West German Federal Chancellor and Nobel Peace Prize winner Willy Brandt (1913 to 1992), set itself the task 'to study the grave global issues arising from the economic and social disparities of the world community',[29] and it published reports on the 'world crisis' in 1980 and 1982. In 1982 a report also appeared from the Independent Commission for Disarmament and Security chaired by the former Swedish Prime Minister Olof Palme (1927 to 1986). In addition, the following year the UN General Assembly set up an independent World Commission on Environment and Development, chaired by the Norwegian politician Gro Harlem Brundtland (b. 1939). After deliberations taking up several years, at the end of 1987 this body published its concluding report, 'Our Common Future', in which the concepts of sustainable development and intergenerational justice were set out and developed. Finally, in July 1987, the International South Commission was established under the chairmanship of the

---

26   Gorbachev, Mikhail. 1987. Perestroika. Collins, pp. 9, 146, 158.

27   Id. 1987. 'Reality and Guarantees for a Secure World'. International Affairs: A Russian Journal of World Politics, Diplomacy and International Relations 33 (11): 3–11, p. 10 (Pravda, 17 September 1987).

28   Comenius, Johann Amos. 1671. Panorthosia Or Universal Reform, Chapters 19 to 26. Transl. by Archie Dobbie. Sheffield: JSOT Press, p. 129.

29   Independent Commission on International Development Issues. 1980. North/South: A Programme for Survival. London: MacMillan, p. 12.

former President of Tanzania, Julius K. Nyerere (1922 to 1999). Its concluding report was published in 1990, and it later gave rise to the South Centre, a joint think tank today involving fifty governments from the global South.

Gorbachev did not set out his proposal for a 'world consultative council' in detail. But the simple fact that the idea of a permanent advisory body within the UN was now being supported at the very highest political level was seen by advocates of a world parliament as an important development, particularly because Gorbachev welcomed the idea of a role for parliaments in international relations. But the proposal for a consultative body was not met with unalloyed enthusiasm. At a conference of the United Nations Institute for Training and Research in Moscow in September 1988 attended by 100 people, for example, the topic was discussed with great interest, but there was no agreement in its favour.[30] In a speech to the UN General Assembly on 7 December 1988, Gorbachev affirmed once more, this time in a slightly different formulation, 'that the idea of convening on a regular basis, under the auspices of the United Nations, an assembly of public organizations deserves attention'.[31] However, as far as we know, there followed no concrete diplomatic initiatives for the establishment of such an assembly or of a consultative council. Many other pressing problems and tasks were given higher priority on the political agenda.

Five months after the official dissolution of the Soviet Union in December 1991, its former and last President spoke in Fulton, Missouri. Gorbachev noted that humanity was at a 'major turning point' as the world was now characterized by 'all-encompassing interdependence'. The 'prospect of catastrophic climate changes' as well as the need to control nuclear and chemical weapons, to guarantee a peaceful use of nuclear energy, to stop the export of conventional weapons 'by the year 2000', and to enforce adherence to human rights worldwide, among other things, would require 'means of collective action' of a 'democratically organized world community'. Democracy, he said, 'must move from the national to the international arena.'[32] At this point, however, Gorbachev was a retired statesman who had lost all political power.

30   Kingué, Michel Doo. 1989. 'Report of the Chairman'. In: The Future Role of the United Nations in an Interdependent World. Papers of the International Roundtable in Moscow, 5-9 September 1988, sponsored by the USSR Association for the UN and UNITAR, ed. by John P. Renninger, 257–265. Dordrecht: Martinus Nijhoff, p. 264.

31   Citation from Gorbachev, Mikhail. 2006. The Road We Traveled. The Challenges We Face. Ed. by Izdatelstvo Ves Mir. Moscow: Gorbachev Foundation, p. 44.

32   Gorbachev, Mikhail. 1992. 'The River of Time and the Imperative of Action.' Westminster College, Fulton, Missouri, May 6 (www.nationalchurchillmuseum.org).

7.

The end of the Cold War:
the democratization wave and
the revitalization of the debate

The democratization wave

The political turnaround in the Soviet Union, and the accompanying end to bloc confrontation, led to a worldwide wave of democratization. At the beginning of 1989, free elections took place for the first time in the Soviet Union. In Eastern Europe and elsewhere, the yoke of autocratic regimes and their feared security apparatuses was thrown off after decades of oppression. The inhuman apartheid regime in South Africa was peacefully overcome by negotiation, and Nelson Mandela (1918 to 2013) was freed after 27 years in prison. From 1991 onwards, according to the data of the Polity research programme, for the first time since 1930 there were more democracies than autocracies in the world again. Between 1987 and 1992 the proportion of autocratic regimes in the world halved. Democracy and peoples' right to self-determination seemed to be prevailing at last. The American philosopher Francis Fukuyama announced in 1989 in a widely-read essay, followed shortly by a book with the same title of 'The End of History', that the 'end point of mankind's ideological evolution and the universalization of Western liberal democracy as the final form of human government' had come.[1] An extraordinary summit meeting of the Conference on Security and Cooperation in Europe, which had been meeting since 1973, declared in the 'Charter of Paris' of 21 November 1990 that the division of Europe was over. The 32 signatory countries pledged, among other things, 'to build, consolidate and strengthen democracy as the only system of government of our nations'. To mark the beginning of Operation Desert Storm for the liberation of Kuwait from occupation by the Iraqi troops who had invaded five months earlier, on 16 January 1991 US President George Bush welcomed 'the opportunity to forge for ourselves and for future generations a new world order—a world where the rule of law, not the law of the jungle, governs the conduct of nations'.[2]

1   Fukuyama, Francis. Summer 1989. 'The End of History?' The National Interest: 3–18.
2   Bush, George. 16 January 1991. 'Speech Announcing Commencement of Operation Desert Storm'.

The revitalization of the debate

On the initiative of Brandt, who had invited the members of his North-South Commission and those of the Commission on Disarmament and Security, the World Commission on Environment and Development and the International South Commission to a joint meeting, and with the support of the Swedish Prime Minister Ingvar Carlsson (b. 1934), the Stockholm Initiative on Global Security and Governance was formed. A year later it published a memorandum. 'We need a new world order, based on justice and peace, democracy and development, human rights and international law', it read. The optimism of the period is reflected in the ambitious proposal to convene 'a World Summit on Global Governance ... similar to the meetings in San Francisco and at Bretton Woods in the 1940s' at which the United Nations and the international financial institutions were established.[3] Brandt, Brundtland and Nyerere then asked Carlsson and the Guyanese Shridath Ramphal (b. 1928), who had been Secretary General of the Commonwealth from 1975 to 1990, to instigate a 'Commission on Global Governance' to develop its own set of proposals.

Meanwhile, motivated especially by Gorbachev's statements regarding a meeting of NGOs and a 'world consultative council', participants in the INFUSA network organized three conferences on the democratization of the UN in the years 1990 to 1992, the so-called Conferences on a More Democratic United Nations, CAMDUN. The first of these, in New York, was the most important. It was documented and edited commendably by the nuclear physicist Frank Barnaby (b. 1927), Director of the Stockholm International Peace Research Institute SIPRI from 1971 to 1981.[4] Around one hundred expert participants, including Stassen, Hudson and Newcombe, debated the proposals for a 'second chamber' and a parliamentary assembly in the UN in great detail, and also addressed other topics such as reform and strengthening of the General Assembly, the possibility of worldwide referenda and the role of NGOs in the UN system in general.

A UN parliamentary assembly as a strategic concept

The various proposals for a 'second chamber', a citizens' chamber, a world parliament and other models—as also debated within CAMDUN—'circulated like flies around the margins of the world federalist movement', wrote the

---

3   Stockholm Initiative. 1991. Gemeinsame Verantwortung in den 90er Jahren. Die Stockholmer Initiative zu globaler Sicherheit und Verantwortung / Common Responsibility in the 1990's. The Stockholm Initiative on Global Security and Governance. Ed. by Stiftung Entwicklung and Frieden. Bonn, pp. 13, 70.
4   Barnaby, Frank (ed.). 1991. Building a More Democratic United Nations. Proceedings of the First International Conference On A More Democratic UN. London/Portland: Frank Cass.

Canadian Dieter Heinrich (b. 1954), then head of the political committee of the WFM.[5] The WFM, whose President from 1991 was the actor Peter Ustinov (1921 to 2004), eventually developed a strategy set out by Heinrich in the 1992 pamphlet 'The Case for a United Nations Parliamentary Assembly'. The chances of successfully establishing a directly elected world parliament from a standing start were regarded as very slim. Such a world parliament, capable of creating world law, should therefore remain the ultimate goal, but it should now be pursued in stages, in a long-term evolutionary development. The European Parliament provided the inspiration, having evolved over decades in the course of European integration from a purely advisory assembly of national parliamentarians into a directly elected legislature. The first stage within the UN would therefore be an advisory assembly comprised of national delegates, a 'United Nations Parliamentary Assembly', UNPA. Sohn had already argued for such a body in 1949, but had been unable to arouse much enthusiasm. Now, however, it would no longer be seen as the ultimate destination, but rather as the starting point on the road to that destination. 'What shifted for me', wrote Heinrich, 'was seeing a possible parliamentary body not as a final tree but as something able to be begun from a small seed with the most modest of steps. This made it achievable even in a time of low political will. Once established, it could be its own best advocate, generating its own creative force from within as it all the while drove the process of UN reform itself.'[6]

The prospect that the proposal for a UNPA would fall on fertile ground now looked good. In comparison to a world parliament, the proposal was not overly ambitious. The European Parliament in its early phase and the Parliamentary Assembly of the Council of Europe served as reference points. Moreover, in the 'Charter of Paris', the heads of state and government of Europe, Canada, the USA and the Soviet Union had spoken out in support of the establishment of a parliamentary assembly at the CSCE. No doubt this was due to the fact that, on the initiative of the IPU, the CSCE process had been accompanied at the interparliamentary level from the beginning. Between 1973 and 1991, seven CSCE parliamentarians' conferences took place independent of the government conferences, contributing to the thaw between East and West. The interest shown by the governments and the UN in the IPU altogether increased dramatically after the very first of these conferences in Janu-

---

5   Heinrich, Dieter. 2010. The Case for a United Nations Parliamentary Assembly. Extended reprint, originally published 1992. Berlin: Committee for a Democratic UN, p. 42.
6   Ibid.

ary 1973, according to Kissling.[7] The long slumber into which the IPU had fallen as a result of being perceived as just one more NGO among many was now coming to an end. And in July 1992 in Budapest, the first meeting took place of the new CSCE parliamentary assembly, with delegates from all the countries of the northern hemisphere from Vancouver to Vladivostok, among them four of the five permanent members of the UN Security Council (i.e. all of them apart from China). The parliamentary assembly became a formal organ of what from 1995 was re-badged as the Organization (formerly Conference) for Security and Co-operation in Europe. If a parliamentary assembly made sense as a structural element of the OSCE (or the CSCE), asked Heinrich, then why not of the United Nations? The Cold War was over. Democracy was on the march. In the past, Heinrich argued, the idea of a world parliament had foundered on the existence of so many countries with undemocratic governments. As was seen earlier, Pecqueur had identified this problem as early as 1842. But Heinrich argued that countries with credible parliaments were now increasingly forming the majority. It would therefore be 'a terrible and unjustifiable surrender to these dictatorships if they were allowed to stand as an obstacle to the formation of a UN parliamentary body'.[8]

Support for a world parliament and a UNPA

A committee of the Liberal International (the worldwide federation of liberal parties) led by the then Finnish foreign minister Paavo Väyrynen (b. 1946) seemed to be thinking along the same lines and expressed its support for the long-term goal of a directly-elected world parliament in a report on the federation's ideas for strengthening the UN. This would introduce a 'democratic ingredient' into the UN. In December 1992, this report was presented to UN Secretary-General Boutros Boutros-Ghali (1922 to 2016), who had then been in office for only a year, by the LI President and Chair of the German FDP party Otto Graf Lambsdorff (1926 to 2009).[9]

In Heinrich's analysis, the WFM had published for the first time a detailed description of the concept of a UNPA. The basic approach taken remains relevant today, as do many of the arguments put forward. It will therefore be examined in more detail later on rather than here, in the historical exposition section of the book. The work done by Heinrich and the WFM certainly had some impact. A report from the Standing Committee on External Affairs and Interna-

---

7   See Kissling, Claudia. 2006. Die Interparlamentarische Union im Wandel. Frankfurt: Peter Lang, pp. 219, 289-91, 341-3.

8   Heinrich, p. 15.

9   Liberal International. 1992. Strengthening of the United Nations. Report produced by a Committee headed by Paavo Vayrynen, Foreign Minister of Finland, pp. 11-2.

tional Trade of the Canadian House of Commons, chaired by John Bosley (1947 to 2022), recommended in the spring of 1993, citing Heinrich's text, 'that Canada support the development of a United Nations Parliamentary Assembly' and 'offer to host the preparatory meeting of the Assembly in the Parliament Buildings as the centrepiece in [its] celebration of the 50th anniversary of the United Nations in 1995'.[10] In addition, the Committee commissioned PGA in New York (to which 900 deputies from all over the world now belonged) to carry out a study on the establishment of a UNPA. The study was led by PGA Secretary-General Kennedy Graham (b. 1946) from New Zealand. The report, which appeared in September, concluded that existing international parliamentary institutions, and especially the IPU, were not sufficient 'for the purpose of parliamentary deliberation of UN issues'.[11] Almost all of the PGA members surveyed for the report were in favour of the establishment of a UNPA. However, October 1993 brought a change of government in Canada, and the report was not followed up directly either by the Canadian Parliament or by PGA.

In February 1994, the European Parliament declared in a resolution on reform of the UN that the possibility of establishing a parliamentary advisory assembly at the UN should be given serious consideration. This was the first time that any parliament had expressed support for the idea. In May, the InterAction Council, an association of former heads of state and government founded in 1983, carried out a consultation on the future of 'global multilateral organizations'. In the report, written under the joint leadership of Andries van Agt (b. 1931) from the Netherlands, Olusegun Obasanjo (b. 1937) from Nigeria and Ola Ullsten (1931 to 2018) from Sweden, it was stated that 'the feasibility of a parliamentary chamber or assembly complementing the present intergovernmental structure should be seriously explored, as it might enhance the political legitimacy of the organizations and strengthen accountability of organizations and governments'.[12] In an extended study with the title 'The Capacity to Govern', which was accepted as a Report by the Club of Rome, the Israeli political scientist Yehezkel Dror (b. 1928) suggested that a 'global advisory assembly, composed of from one to six representatives of each country, either directly elected or elected from the parliaments', should be formed. By this means not only 'the direct links between the citizens and the coming

---

10 House of Commons. 1993. Canada's role in the United Nations. 8th Report of the Standing Committee on External Affairs and International Trade. Parliament of Canada. Penultimate para.
11 Parliamentarians for Global Action (ed.). 1993. 'A United Nations Parliamentary Assembly - Analysis and Parliamentarian Opinion. A Briefing Paper Prepared for the Standing Committee on External Affairs and Trade of the Canadian House of Commons'.
12 InterAction Council. 1994. Report on the Conclusions and Recommendations of a High-level Expert Group on 'The Future Role of the Global Multilateral Organisations'. Chair: Andries van Agt. The Hague, para. 16.

world government' but also 'an identification of each individual with the whole of humanity' could be furthered.[13] This last point had also been a substantial consideration for Heinrich.

The establishment of a UNPA was then investigated and urgently recommended by Erskine Childers (1929 to 1996) and Brian Urquhart (1919 to 2021) in their widely-discussed study 'Renewing the United Nations System'. They cited Heinrich's study, among others, and also referred to the recent proposals from Canada and the European Parliament. They came out in favour of a directly elected UNPA and emphasized that the proposal did not constitute a 'supranational government'. Both had expert inside knowledge of the UN system, which meant that their initiative could not simply be dismissed. Urquhart had been working on the development of the UN since 1945, and had been one of the advisers to UN Secretary General Dag Hammarskjöld (1905 to 1961). Childers, too, had worked for 22 years in various capacities at the UN. Another who was convinced by Heinrich's arguments was the Belgian-born Robert Muller (1923 to 2010). From July 1994 onwards he spoke out frequently in support. Muller had served the UN for 38 years before settling in Costa Rica in retirement and taking on the role of honorary Chancellor of the UN's University for Peace. The establishment of a UNPA was one of numerous reform proposals set out in a dialogue (published as a paperback) between Muller and the Canadian Douglas Roche (b. 1929), a long-serving parliamentarian, founding President of the PGA and Chair of the UN commission on disarmament.[14]

A radical restructuring of the world organization was discussed at an expert panel meeting organized by the Graduate Institute of International and Development Studies in Geneva in the spring of 1995. The starting point was a draft constitution, drawn up by Bertrand, for a 'world security organization' to replace the UN. The issue of a parliamentary body was also debated. Bertrand's draft included a directly elected world parliament as one of eight proposed main bodies; it would comprise a maximum of 800 delegates, with seats allocated on the basis of population and GDP of the member states. In the context of the existing system, it was argued, democratic popular representation—for example, by means of an advisory UNPA on the basis of Article 22—would be of very little practical significance. The key issue was that of competences, and this could only be satisfactorily resolved in the framework of a

---

13   Dror, Yehezkel. 1995. Ist die Erde noch regierbar? Ein Bericht an den Club of Rome. Transl. by Hans-Jürgen Baron von Koskull. 1st ed. C. Bertelsmann, pp. 271-2.

14   Muller, Robert, and Douglas Roche. 1995. Safe Passage into the Twenty-First Century. New York: Continuum, p. 119.

fundamental transformation of the procedures and structures of the UN. Not until such a transformation was on the agenda would the time be right for it.[15]

The report by the Commission on Global Governance

The Commission on Global Governance under the joint chairmanship of Carlsson and Ramphal published its report—entitled 'Our Global Neighborhood', and, following three years' work, extending to several hundred pages—on the fiftieth anniversary of the founding of the UN. The optimism of 1990 was gone, it found. The United Nations and the members of the Security Council had proved incapable of effectively countering extreme abuses of human rights and genocide, in Bosnia from 1992 and in Rwanda between April and July 1994. The UN-mandated US-led 'Operation Restore Hope' in Somalia had been a disaster. The UN and international law were not up to the challenges they faced. '[T]here is deepening disquiet over the actions--and in some cases the inaction--of governments and of the United Nations', wrote the Commission in its report.[16] US President Bush's proclamation of a 'new world order' had proved an empty slogan, masking what was essentially a continuation of US American great power politics in the new global political conditions. 'It is remarkable how quickly the idealistic formulations of the "transition period" from 1989-1991 were replaced by the classical terminology of power politics once America's position as the sole superpower had gradually become clear and then been consolidated', was the analysis of the Innsbruck philosopher Hans Köchler, co-organizer of the second CAMDUN conference.[17] Unlike after the two World Wars, when the United States took the lead in establishing the League of Nations and the United Nations, now the USA was making no effort at a fundamental restructuring of international relations by means of a reform and strengthening of the world organization. Köchler argued that a new world order as a radical alternative to a simple shift in the power relations between the states required the application of democracy to transnational relations. 'Anyone pressing for a new world order', continued Köchler, 'would have to begin with an amendment to the UN Charter to remove the voting privileges of the permanent members and to institute a second chamber of deputies.'[18]

---

15 Bertrand, Maurice, and Daniel Warner (ed.). 1997. A New Charter for a Worldwide Organisation? Nijhoff Law Specials 22. The Hague et al.: Kluwer Law International, p. 25. See also p. 217.
16 Commission on Global Governance. 1995. Our Global Neighborhood. Oxford University Press, p. 2.
17 Köchler, Hans. 1998. Neue Wege der Demokratie. Demokratie im globalen Spannungsfeld von Machtpolitik und Rechtsstaatlichkeit. Wien: Springer-Verlag, p. 38.
18 Ibid., p. 54.

Alongside other recommendations too numerous to go into here, the Commission on Global Governance recommended exactly that. The drive for reform should find its culmination in a review conference as proposed in Article 109 of the UN Charter. 'Our recommendation is that the General Assembly should agree to hold a World Conference on Governance in 1998, with its decisions to be ratified and put into effect by 2000.' The right of veto in the Security Council should be gradually abolished. Proposals for a UN parliamentary body should also be discussed further. 'When the time comes, we believe that starting with an assembly of parliamentarians as a constituent assembly for a more popular body is the right approach. But care would need to be taken to ensure that the assembly of parliamentarians is the starting point of a journey and does not become the terminal station.' It must not become a substitute for a revitalization of the General Assembly, and a start could be made in the meantime by means of an 'annual Forum of Civil Society'.[19] This approach reveals a fundamental problem with the Commission. 'Its proposals and orientation are too reformist, humanist and populist', Falk commented, 'to be acceptable either to leading states or to the new elites of globalization.' At the same time, however, they were not radical enough to enthuse or even to satisfy civil society.[20] At any event, for world federalists the report was a disappointment. Its categorical rejection of the idea of world government, without even having considered the extensive relevant literature, was downright insulting according to one response—from the economist James A. Yunker, in the foreword to a collection of essays on the topic.[21] For the Commission dismissed the idea in its report with the short and simple remark that global governance did not imply 'world government or world federalism'.[22]

The report by the World Commission on Culture and Development

The World Commission on Culture and Development also delivered its concluding report in 1995. It had started its work three years earlier following resolutions by the UNESCO General Conference and the UN General Assembly. It was chaired by the Peruvian Javier Pérez de Cuéllar (1920 to 2020), who from 1982 to 1991 had been Secretary-General of the UN. International democracy featured prominently in the report. Democracy, it declared, was 'an

---

19 Commission on Global Governance, pp. 258, 351-2.
20 Falk, Richard. 1995. 'Liberalism at the Global Level: The Last of the Independent Commissions?' Millennium - Journal of International Studies 24 (3): 563–576, p. 574.
21 Harris, Errol E., and James A. Yunker (ed.). 1999. Toward Genuine Global Governance. Critical Reactions to 'Our Global Neighborhood'. Praeger Publishers, p. ix.
22 Commission on Global Governance, p. 336, see also p. xvi.

indispensable principle of a global ethics' and must be universally implement-ed—in global governance and in the United Nations, too.[23] An international system based solely on relations between governments was no longer adequate for the 21st century. 'The global community should start with a fresh vision that inspires many new generations in the twenty-first century. One bold step could be a General Assembly directly elected by the people of all nations, learning some lessons from the experience of the European Parliament.' The United Nations and all institutions of global governance must become focused on the citizens. The whole range of diverse cultures, and especially marginal-ized groups, minorities and indigenous peoples, must be given a voice in the international forums. Since a directly elected popular assembly remained only an aspiration at this time, the establishment of a UN world forum of NGOs accredited by the UN seemed a sensible first step in the right direction.[24] In this respect the positions taken by the Commission on Culture and Develop-ment and the Commission on Global Governance were very similar. But the issue was given much higher priority in the report of the Commission on Cul-ture and Development: two of the ten concluding recommendations related to this issue.

23   United Nations Educational, Scientific and Cultural Organization. 1995. *Our Creative Diversity*. Report of the World Commission on Culture and Development, pp. 38, 284-6.
24   Ibid., p. 286.

8.
Democracy in the era of globalization

Globalization and the nation state

The question of whether, or to what degree, increasing international interdependence was taking the traditional nation states beyond the control of politics became an important topic of public debate from at least the middle of the 1990s onwards. The idea that the existing forms of government were incapable of meeting the challenges posed by contemporary global change and therefore had to be transformed was the starting point, for example, of the report by Dror to the Club of Rome cited above. Globalization was undermining 'the effectiveness of territorially-defined democratic control mechanisms', agreed the political scientist Karl Kaiser, Director of the German Council on Foreign Relations.[1] The worldwide bestseller 'The Global Trap: Civilization and the Assault on Democracy and Prosperity' by the *Spiegel* journalists Harald Schumann and Hans-Peter Martin perhaps best expressed the popular perception that governments were increasingly being driven by the inescapable hard realities of international politics and that the democratic state was losing its legitimation. At the national convention of German historians in Munich, President Roman Herzog declared that the nation state 'and the conception of sovereignty associated with it' had outlived its day.[2] The future lay in European integration—a conclusion shared by Schumann and Martin. The influential Egyptian intellectual Samir Amin, writing from a global perspective, said in 1992 that there was 'no solution' to the problems raised by the decoupling of the world economy from the nation states because 'no supranational state is visible on the horizon'.[3] The 'chaos which defines the present situation', according to Amin, was in part a result of the fact that 'new forms of political and social organization transgressing the nation-state' had not been developed. Since then, the idea of a world parliament has surfaced in his writings on several occasions, even if only as a catchphrase. 'In many ways, the creation

---

1   Kaiser, Karl. 1998. 'Globalisierung als Problem der Demokratie'. Internationale Politik (4): 4–11, p. 4.
2   Herzog, Roman. 17 Sept. 1996. Speech at the 41st Historikertag in Munich.
3   Amin, Samir. 1992. The Empire of Chaos. Transl. by W.H. Locke Anderson. New York: Monthly Review Press, pp. 10-1.

of such a "world parliament" would go beyond the present concept of inter-state institutions.'[4]

As UN Secretary-General, Boutros-Ghali took up some bold positions. For example, he said in a statement of January 1996 that the democratization of international relations was a fundamental requirement in today's world. He understood this to mean the opening up of the UN to new global actors like NGOs, national parliaments and private companies, but also to 'each and every man and woman who feels he or she is a full member of the big human family'. This not only applied to the UN but meant 'the democratization of all places where authority is exercised at the world level'.[5] Boutros-Ghali became the first UN Secretary-General to be denied a second term of office. The USA was the only government against a renewal, and used its veto. In December 1996, in the last week before the expiry of his term of office, and without an explicit mandate to do so, Boutros-Ghali arranged for a report he had written on national and international democratization to be distributed to the members of the UN General Assembly. In it he stressed how, on account of globalization, a growing number of decisions now had to be taken at international level, and how this was hollowing out national democracy. 'Democracy within the State will diminish in importance if the process of democratization does not move forward at the international level', declared Boutros-Ghali.[6] The following year, in the journal *Le Monde Diplomatique*, the French journalist Ignacio Ramonet wrote in an article echoed by many others that the globalization of financial capital 'makes a mockery of national boundaries and diminishes the power of states to uphold democracy and guarantee the wealth and prosperity of their peoples'. The financial markets had long since 'established a separate supranational state with its own administrative apparatus, its own spheres of influence, its own means of action'. This world state was a power with no base in society. 'It is answerable instead to the financial markets and the mammoth business undertakings that are its masters. The result is that the real states in the real world are becoming societies with no power base.' He advocated a Tobin tax on financial transactions and the power to tax unearned income, which was 'a sine qua non of democracy'.[7] Ramonet's specific call for the creation of an NGO entitled 'Attac' (an abbreviation for 'Action pour une taxe Tobin d'aide aux citoyens') to pursue on a broad base the estab-

---

4   Id. 1993. 'The Future of Global Polarization'. Africa Today 40, no. 4: 75–86, pp. 76, 80.
5   United Nations, 1996. 'Secretary-General says democratization of international relations fundamental requirement for today's world'. Press Release SG/SM/5883.
6   Boutros-Ghali, Boutros. 1996. Supplement to reports on democratization. Report to the 51st Session of the United Nations General Assembly, pp. 19-20.
7   Ramonet, Ignacio. 12 December 1997. 'Disarming the markets', Le Monde Diplomatique.

lishment of an international tax on currency transactions was followed up in a number of countries.

The theory of 'cosmopolitan democracy'

In the search for a fundamental answer to these problems, work had been going on already for some time on the theory of 'cosmopolitan democracy', which was also explicitly intended to investigate the possibility of a middle way between the confederal and federal models for an international order. 'The attainment of democracy at the international level requires us to steer between the Scylla of a mass of independent autonomous states and the Charybdis of a planetary Leviathan. To achieve this goal, a new concept of world citizenship must be formulated', wrote the Italian academic Daniele Archibugi (b. 1958) in 1993. A worldwide body representing the interests of individuals as citizens of the world would be a significant step towards overcoming the confederal structure of the global system, Archibugi argued, and in contemplating such an assembly he built on the work of Segall and the CAMDUN conferences.[8] Traditionally, theories of democracy had started from the assumption that there was a direct connection, forged principally through elections, between political decision makers and the people affected by their decisions. 'But the problem is', wrote the British political scientist David Held (1951 to 2019) in 1992, 'that regional and global interconnectedness contests the traditional national resolutions of the key questions of democratic theory and practice.'[9] Political decisions increasingly affected people across borders who had no power to influence those decisions. He cited as examples the setting of interest rates by a central bank and the economic effects this has on other countries, and the decision to build a nuclear power station near a border with another country.

In an essay from 1992, the philosopher Thomas Pogge (b. 1953), who has also concerned himself with cosmopolitanism, argued along similar lines. Sovereignty, anchored in the nation state, has to be divided vertically between several political decision-making levels through decentralization and centralization. The justification for this is in part democratic. '[P]ersons have a right to an institutional order under which those significantly and legitimately affected by a political decision have a roughly equal opportunity to influence the making of

8   Archibugi, Daniele. 1993. 'The Reform of the UN and Cosmopolitan Democracy: A Critical Review'. Journal of Peace Research 30 (3): 301–315, p. 306, 307-9. His overall discussion of cosmopolitan democracy is included in Archibugi, Daniele. 2008. The Global Commonwealth of Citizens. Princeton University Press.
9   Held, David. 1992. 'Democracy: From City-states to a Cosmopolitan Order?' Political Studies 40 (Special Issue): 10–39, p. 31.

this decision—directly or through elected delegates or representatives.'[10] Growing global interdependence also requires a 'democratic centralization of decision making'.[11]

The sociologist Ulrich Beck (1944 to 2015) pointed out the transnational character of the risks associated with modernity in 1986 already in his widely admired book on the evolution of the 'risk society'. These risks went together with the industrial system of production and—like the international intertwining of markets and capital—exceeded the reach and powers of the nation state. They had an immanent tendency towards globalization'.[12] A dramatic historical event that seemed to confirm this finding was the meltdown and explosion in the nuclear power plant at Chernobyl, shortly after the book's publication, which led to a massive release of radioactive material into the atmosphere. The contamination fallout spread across Europe and ultimately across the entire northern hemisphere. With the coining of the term 'second modernity', Beck later sought to identify the characteristics of an epochal change driven in part by processes of globalization. The institutions established in the course of modernization, above all that of industrial society organized in nation states, were being dissolved and supplanted by a second modernity.[13] A core challenge for theory and praxis in all of this was the change of perspective from 'nation state centrism' to cosmopolitanism. On the occasion of the 150th anniversary of the 1848 revolution, Beck said that what had been going on then, in the Paulskirche in Frankfurt, was 'the transformation of the religiously-based feudal order into the nation state democracy'. 'Today', he continued, 'what is going on is the transition from the nation state democracy to the transnational, indeed the cosmopolitan democracy. This entails fundamental institutional innovations, indeed a detailed working out of the principles of democracy for a world which has become a danger to itself.'[14]

In his 1995 book 'Democracy and the Global Order', now a standard in the field, Held explained that the democratic setting of regulatory standards has to be internationalized in order to remain effective: 'the implementation of a cosmopolitan democratic law and the establishment of a cosmopolitan community' must 'become an obligation for democrats, an obligation to build a

10 Pogge, Thomas. 1992. 'Cosmopolitanism and Sovereignty'. Ethics 103 (1) (October): 48–75, pp. 63-4.
11 Ibid., p. 66.
12 Beck, Ulrich. 1986. Risikogesellschaft. Auf dem Weg in eine andere Moderne. Frankfurt: Suhrkamp, pp. 48, 310.
13 Id. 1996. 'Das Zeitalter der Nebenfolgen und die Politisierung der Moderne'. In: Reflexive Modernisierung, ed. by Ulrich Beck, Anthony Giddens, and Scott Lash, 19–112. Frankfurt am Main: Suhrkamp, p. 27. See also id., 1994. Reflexive Modernization. Polity Press.
14 Beck, Ulrich. 1999. 'Wie wird Demokratie im Zeitalter der Globalisierung möglich?' (Speech at Paulskirche, 05 May 1998. In: Ende des Staates - Anfang der Bürgergesellschaft. Über die Zukunft der sozialen Demokratie in Zeiten der Globalisierung, ed. by Hans Eichel and Hilmar Hoffmann. Reinbek: Rowohlt, pp. 41-2.

transnational, common structure of political action which alone, ultimately, can support the politics of self-determination.'[15] The cosmopolitan model seeks 'the creation of an effective transnational legislative and executive, at regional and global levels, bound by and operating within the terms of the basic democratic law.' Transnational referenda should be enabled. Regional parliaments should be created, for example for Africa and Latin America, and should take part in the setting of regulatory standards. The functional organizations of the international system should be democratized, which could 'perhaps' be done on the basis of 'elected supervisory boards'. 'But the full implementation of cosmopolitan democracy would also require the formation of an authoritative assembly of all the democratic states and agencies—a reformed General Assembly of the United Nations, or a complement to it', Held wrote. As a long-term goal he identified among other things a global parliament with limited taxation powers.[16] The need of cosmopolitan democracy featured strongly in Anthony Gidden's (b. 1938) promotion of a 'third way' between the 'old left' and neoliberalism. 'Globalizing processes', the sociologist wrote, 'have transferred powers away from nations and into depoliticized global space' and this new space required regulation. 'The expansion of cosmopolitan democracy is a condition for effectively regulating the world economy, attacking global economic inequalities and controlling ecological risks', he argued, noting that 'what currently is the UN could be divided into a parliament and a council'.[17]

The question of a world parliament was also taken up by Jürgen Habermas (b. 1929). The key feature of the right of world citizenship sketched by Kant, he argued, was that it transcended the nation states as subjects of international law and directly endowed the individual legal subject with 'unmediated membership in the association of free and equal world citizens'. A contemporary reformulation of Kant's idea that cosmopolitanism could pacify the warlike 'state of nature' between the states, Habermas argued in an essay of 1995, 'would inspire on the one side energetic efforts for the reform of the United Nations, and more generally for the further development of supranational capacity for action in the various regions of the world.'[18] Referring to Archibugi, Habermas wrote that proposals for reform of the UN focused on three points: the establishment of a world parliament, the further development of a world justice system, and the reorganization of the Security Council. If the UN is to cast off its status as a 'permanent congress of states', then the General

15 Held, David. 1995. Democracy and the Global Order. 1st ed. Cambridge: Polity Press, p. 232.

16 Ibid., pp. 272-4.

17 Giddens, Anthony. 1998. The Third Way: The Renewal of Social Democracy. Cambridge: Polity Press, pp. 141, 145.

18 Habermas, Jürgen. 1999. Die Einbeziehung des Anderen: Studien zur politischen Theorie. 1st ed. Frankfurt am Main: Suhrkamp, pp. 192-236, pp. 210, 217-8.

Assembly will need to be transformed into a kind of federal senate and to share its powers with a second chamber. 'In this parliament', according to Habermas, 'people would not be represented by their governments but by elected representatives, as the sum of the citizens of the world.' States that did not allow democratic elections should be represented by 'non-state organizations appointed by the world parliament itself as representatives of the oppressed population'.[19]

The Falk and Strauss essays

In September 1997, Ted Turner (b. 1938), the US American media entrepreneur and founder of the news channel CNN, announced that he would donate 100 million US dollars each year for the next ten years in support of UN activities. This prompted the first in a series (which still continues today) of joint articles advocating the establishment of a global parliament written by Falk together with Andrew Strauss (b. 1958), an international law specialist, at the time based at the private Widener University near Philadelphia in the US state of Pennsylvania.[20] In the first of these contributions, which appeared in the *International Herald Tribune,* they wrote that it was only due to globalization that philanthropists like Turner and George Soros (b. 1930) had been able to amass such extraordinary wealth in the first place. Soros is a US American investor of Hungarian extraction who came to international attention in 1992 when he speculated against the British currency and thereby allegedly amassed a billion pounds (the pound crisis cost the British taxpayer 3.3 billion).[21] Soros had been engaged, via his own foundations, in the promotion of an open society in the sense defined by the philosopher Karl Popper (1902 to 1994) since 1984. His Open Society Institute is now active in over 50 countries. In any event, Falk and Strauss suggested that billionaires like Turner and Soros should promote a democratization of the global order and should directly provide money for the creation of a global peoples' assembly elected by universal direct vote, since the governments were reluctant to take this on themselves. The citizens of the world would then have, for the first time, 'a forum to express their planetary aspirations and grievances outside the traditional nation-state context'.[22]

---

19 Ibid., p. 218.
20 Collected in the following volume: Falk, Richard, and Andrew Strauss. 2011. A Global Parliament: Essays and Articles. Berlin: Committee for a Democratic UN.
21 Tempest, Matthew. 9 February 2005. 'Treasury papers reveal cost of Black Wednesday'. Guardian (www.guardian.co.uk).
22 Strauss, Andrew, and Richard Falk. 1997. 'For a Global Peoples' Assembly'. International Herald Tribune, November 14. Reprinted in: Falk/Strauss, pp. 177-8.

Falk and Strauss proposed a new option for bringing about such an assembly. They suggested that the elections to the global citizens' parliament should be organized independently by worldwide civil society through the agency of an international committee of citizens created for the purpose. This assembly would have only the legal status of an NGO to begin with, but on account of the election process it could claim to speak in the name of the global population and would therefore have considerable moral legitimacy. Formal recognition of this body by governments and the United Nations would then follow sooner or later. It would acquire its own socio-political momentum, leading to an ever more significant role for it in world politics. It is not clear whether Turner or Soros ever became aware of this proposal, but the latter certainly concerned himself seriously with the problems of globalization in his book 'The Crisis of Global Capitalism', and he concluded that the global capital system was on the brink of collapse. The evolution of a global economy had not been accompanied by the evolution of a global society; the necessary regulatory and political framework was lacking. Although it was therefore possible to speak of a global regime for economics and finance, there was no such global regime for politics. Money and credit were intimately bound up with issues of sovereignty, which no country was willing to sacrifice.[23] Yet international law was based on a presumption of the voluntary self-limitation of state sovereignty. A permanent solution, he later wrote, was dependent on a single worldwide currency and a world central bank. But to call for these things was unrealistic.[24]

A community of the democracies?

Soros wanted the democratic countries in the United Nations to join together in an alliance which he hoped would constitute a majority and be able to take over the leadership of the world organization. Thus the UN could be reformed and conduct its business by majority vote. The General Assembly should become 'more like a legislature in charge of making laws for our global society'. At the moment it was no more than a talking shop. Any laws would have validity only in those countries which ratified them, so they would not be directly binding. However, the members of this 'open society coalition', as Soros called it, would be free to commit themselves to the automatic adoption of these laws, subject to their being adopted by a specified majority. As a potential model, Soros pointed to Hudson's 'binding triad', which, as mentioned previously, entails three conditions: two thirds of the countries, two thirds of the population and two-thirds of the UN budget. Coalition member states that did

---

23   Soros, George. 1998. The Crisis of Global Capitalism. New York: PublicAffairs, pp. 103, 109, 120.
24   Id. 2005. George Soros on Globalization. New ed. New York: PublicAffairs, p. 130.

not accept decisions passed under these conditions would have to leave the alliance. 'In that way', said Soros, 'a body of international law could be developed without infringing on the principle of national sovereignty. The General Assembly could decide what laws are needed and how to enforce them.'[25] An open world society, he argued, could not be created by individuals or by independent citizens' organizations; it required cooperation between the states.

Soros was by no means a lone figure in advocating closer cooperation between the democratic countries within the UN. For example, considerable interest was attracted by the book 'Pax Democratica', published by the former US diplomat James R. Huntley in 1998 and firmly in the tradition of Clarence Streit. It argued in some detail for the incremental establishment of an 'intercontinental community of democracies' in which NATO, the OECD, the EU, the Council of Europe and the G7 could gradually be subsumed. This organization would not be set up in opposition to the UN; rather, using the UN delegations of the member states, it could operate within the UN structure. This was perhaps the first and the easiest step of the whole project.[26] One important organ of the community would have to be a parliamentary assembly of the democracies. At the appropriate time, this body could replace other assemblies of parliamentarians such as the NATO assembly or that of the Council of Europe. In June 2000, on the initiative of Madeleine Albright (1937 to 2022) and Bronisław Geremek (1932 to 2008), at that time foreign ministers of the USA and Poland respectively, a community of democracies was indeed established as an inter-state organization in Warsaw, and in 2010 an associated forum of parliamentarians was formed. However, the community is active only in promoting democracy, and has no brief with respect to integration. Dieter Heinrich argued that world federalists should seek to strengthen this community, with the goal of supra-national integration in mind. 'Instead of taking a universal organization, the UN, and trying to democratize it, we can now also propose a democratic organization which can be universalized.'[27] The debate around a 'league of democracies' reached a highpoint when the Republican US Presidential candidate John McCain lent his support to this proposal and announced that within a year of taking office he would convene a summit of the democracies to explore practical steps towards this

25 Soros, 1998, p. 287.
26 Huntley, James Robert. 1998. Pax Democratica: A Strategy for the 21st Century. New York: St. Martin's Press. See in particular pp. 109, 153.
27 Heinrich, Dieter. June 2006. 'Uniting the democracies: Let's imagine'. Ed. by World Federalists of Canada. Mondial, 8–9, p. 9.

goal. This league was not intended to supplant the UN, but 'could act where the UN fails to act'.[28]

Höffe's federal world republic

Another important contribution to the debate about a world state was made by Otfried Höffe (b. 1943), professor of philosophy at Tübingen, with his 1999 book, first published in German, 'Democracy in the age of globalization'. In this, as in numerous newspaper articles, he argued for an incremental development towards the ideal of a federal world republic based on subsidiarity and with a 'graduated cosmopolitanism'. Höffe basically followed the theory of the 'state of nature', and argued that every individual possessed a fundamental moral status which took precedence over any statehood. But this relativization applied not only to individual nation states but also and even to the world state; for that reason, the world state must not be accorded the status of an absolute, and must not be allowed to abrogate the nation states. If, and to the degree that, the nation state served the interests of the individual, and acknowledged and accepted the worldwide moral authority of the complementary world republic, then it too had moral status. It follows, according to Höffe, that a 'dual world societal contract' is required as a foundation for a world republic, a contract that encompasses both the wishes and interests of the individual states and those of the global populace. 'The world republic', wrote Höffe, 'acquires its democratic legitimacy through a combination of popular legitimation and legitimation by the states.' In order to reflect these two elements in institutional terms, the supreme body of the federal world state, the global legislature, would therefore have to consist of two chambers, a world council representing the states and a world parliament representing the citizens. While the first would be primarily responsible for issues of international law and inter-state relations, the citizens' chamber would have priority with regard to 'world society' issues. Höffe didn't only touch on the issue of a world legislature at the margin, but was in fact the first person in a long time to consider a little more thoroughly the options for its structure and procedures. He saw the question of how to include both the mini-states and the giant states as a significant area of potential difficulty, and regarded a voting system weighted by population size as being absolutely essential. He brought into the discussion the idea that other, intermediate—regional, continental or sub-continental—political entities positioned between the world republic and the existing nation states might come into play; but he concluded nevertheless

---

28   McCain, John. 1 May 2007. 'Address at the Hoover Institution'. Council on Foreign Relations (www.cfr.org).

that the 'primary states' should in any event be directly represented in the world legislature. He, too, supported the development of a citizens' chamber on the model of the European Parliament as a concrete proposal for reform of the UN.[29]

The call for a WTO parliament and the role of the IPU

Meanwhile, the protests against the third ministerial conference of the World Trade Organization (WTO, founded 1995) in Seattle in late 1999 turned into the birth of the worldwide anti-globalization movement as a media phenomenon. 'No Globalization without representation' was one of the slogans used. It was not only the trade unions and other groups protesting on the streets who felt excluded and marginalized. On the initiative of the US American Senator William V. Roth (1921 to 2003), around 150 parliamentarians who were present in Seattle issued a statement calling for the establishment of a permanent committee of parliamentarians within the WTO by February 2001 in order to improve its transparency and democratic legitimacy. 'Not only have we a crucial role to play in interacting with the citizens and representative organizations of our respective countries to address their concerns', the statement ran, 'but also to approve or legislate on the agreements negotiated under the auspices of the WTO.' The call for a parliamentary assembly within the WTO was then taken up and promoted with particular energy by the European Parliament. However, the proposal quickly ran into the sand, mainly because of the requirement for unanimity at the WTO, which gives every government a veto over all decisions, even though it was supported in principle by the then WTO Director Mike Moore, a New Zealand Labour Party politician, and the Italian Foreign Trade Minister Piero Fassino, among others.

Furthermore, the efforts of the European Parliament and others in support of a parliamentary assembly at the WTO were opposed by the IPU. Its position was that new structures were neither wanted nor needed, explained Anders Johnsson (b. 1948), the Swede who was Secretary-General of the IPU from 1998 to 2014. 'The legislative function at the WTO', argued Johnsson, 'is undertaken by government negotiators who are held to account in their national governments and parliaments. Providing a parliamentary dimension to the WTO that seeks to mirror the constitutional role that parliaments play at the national level does not make sense.'[30] Eventually, the IPU and the European

29 Höffe, Otfried. 2002. Demokratie im Zeitalter der Globalisierung. New ed. Munich: C.H. Beck, pp. 304-5, 308-10, 333-4.

30 Johnsson, Anders. 2003. 'A Parliamentary Dimension to International Cooperation'. In: A Reader on Second Assembly & Parliamentary Proposals, ed. by Saul H. Mendlovitz and Barbara Walker, 20–29. Wayne, NJ: Center for UN Reform Education, p. 28.

Parliament agreed to hold regular joint conferences on world trade issues, the first one taking place in 2003. This compromise still remains a matter of regret within the European Parliament today. In 2008, for example, the Parliament continued to stress in a resolution 'the need to create a WTO parliamentary assembly with consultative powers, given the WTO's lack of democratic accountability and legitimacy'.[31]

The IPU had at least succeeded in reaching a symbolic agreement on cooperation with the UN in 1996 (it was then awarded observer status at the UN in 2002, since when it has been allowed to distribute its documents at the UN General Assembly). In its own view, the IPU should be the principal forum for all interparliamentary work. In the concluding document of the first world conference of presiding officers of national parliaments in September 2000, it was stated that the so-called 'parliamentary dimension of international cooperation' must be carried out by the IPU, albeit principally by the national parliaments and at the national level. This accords with the definition of the IPU in its Statutes as 'the international organization of the Parliaments of sovereign States'. However, the French parliamentary president Raymond Forni (1941 to 2008) went even further at this world summit. The agreement reached in 1996 could be only a first step, he said. 'The Inter-Parliamentary Union could eventually become a genuine parliamentary assembly of the United Nations, consulted by the General Assembly, the Security Council and the Economic and Social Council and able to make proposals to them.'[32] The Speaker of the Canadian Senate, Gildas Molgat (1927 to 2001), said that the IPU deserved to be recognized as a world parliament and that its status at the UN should be altered accordingly.[33] But in expressing these ideas it is clear that Forni and Molgat represented only a minority within the IPU.

Other initiatives towards a world parliament and a UNPA

The European Parliament declared in the spring of 1999, in a resolution on global governance, that 'transnational economic power' is 'beyond all democratic scrutiny' and that there was therefore an 'urgent need to create a more consistent institutional structure at world level that is capable of coping with the problems of globalization'. The institutions needed to become both more representative and more democratic. A parliamentary dimension could be

---

31 European Parliament. 24 April 2008. 'Towards a reform of the World Trade Organization'. Resolution P6_TA(2008)0180.

32 Forni, Raymond. 30 August 2000. 'Discours au Conférence des Présidents des Parlements nationaux organisée par l'Union interparlementaire du 30 août au 1er septembre 2000 au siège des Nations Unies à New York', New York.

33 Molgat, Gil. 2000. 'A Parliamentary Vision for International Co-operation'. Canadian Parl. Review 23 (4).

introduced to the democratization of the UN system 'by creating parliamentary bodies composed of the chairmen of parliamentary committees of national and regional parliaments, starting e.g. with Environment and Foreign Affairs'.[34] The tenth Human Development Report of the United Nations Development Programme (UNDP), the flagship of its publications programme, also focused on globalization and its impacts. Like the European Parliament, the Report urged the development of a 'a more coherent and more democratic architecture for global governance'. It recommended 'a two-chamber General Assembly to allow for civil society representation' as one of seven key institutions needed for the 21st century. What exactly was meant by that was not set out in detail, however.[35] As has already been seen, the term 'second chamber' is not very precise and can encompass many variants, from an assembly of NGOs to a directly elected body.

On the initiative of the French politician and entrepreneur Olivier Giscard d'Estaing (1927 to 2021), a committee was formed in Paris in the year 2000, the 'Comité pour un parlement mondial' (COPAM). This committee was able within a short time to attract a number of prominent personalities as honorary members. They included the former heads of state or government Andreas van Agt from the Netherlands, Felipe Gonzales from Spain, Prince Hassan of Jordan, the Nobel Peace Prize winners Nelson Mandela from South Africa and Shimon Peres from Israel, Mario Soares from Portugal, Gaston Thorn from Luxembourg and from France Raymond Barre, Michel Rocard and Valéry Giscard d'Estaing, Olivier Giscard d'Estaing's brother. Other supporters included the former UN Secretaries-General Pérez de Cuéllar and Boutros-Ghali as well as Jacques Delors, former President of the European Commission, Sonia Gandhi, the Chair of the Indian Congress party, and the Nobel Prize winner for economics Amartya Sen. It proposed the establishment of an advisory body set up on the basis of a separate intergovernmental treaty and with its members initially elected by the national parliaments, though not necessarily themselves parliamentarians. Like Forni, COPAM originally thought that the IPU could form the starting point for global parliamentary assembly. COPAM's operations were very limited but d'Estaing sought to enter into a dialogue with the IPU about this idea, but in vain. 'After several meetings', he told us, 'our idea of transforming this institution met with a categorical rejection.'

---

34 European Parliament. 23 March 1999. 'Resolution on the challenges of global governance and the reform of the United Nations'. A4-0077/1999, points T, U and 10.

35 United Nations Development Programme. 1999. Human Development Report 1999. Oxford University Press, pp. 12, 111.

Outside the IPU, there were other significant initiatives towards the establishment of a UNPA or world parliament. Thus, the Parliamentary Assembly of the Council of Europe declared in a resolution of September 2000 that the UN should develop, in cooperation with the IPU, a 'parliamentary dimension' with 'competencies similar to that of the Parliamentary Assembly of the Council of Europe'.[36] Such a body could contribute to finding solutions to problems where inter-governmental politics had stalled. In May 2000, the Millennium Forum, a body made up of representatives of over a thousand international civil society organizations which had come together at the UN headquarters in New York at the invitation of UN Secretary-General Kofi Annan, had already urged in its concluding declaration, among numerous other recommendations, 'that the UN should consider 'the creation of a UN parliamentary body related to the UN General Assembly'.[37]

At the United Nations Millennium Summit in New York—which, with over 150 heads of state and government participating, was the largest summit meeting in history up to that point—some of the required foundations were laid, above all the agreement of the eight so-called Millennium Development Goals for the year 2015. However, there was no notable progress on UN reform. At the conference of presiding officers of national parliaments which took place shortly beforehand, Annan stressed the importance of integrating the parliaments into the work of the UN. 'In the age of globalization', Annan said, 'the ancient challenges of poverty and conflict can no longer be met simply by governments working together. Whole societies are affected by international relations, and are playing their part in it. They need to be represented in many different ways.' The national parliaments had a unique role to play in bringing global institutions such as the United Nations 'closer to the peoples they are meant to serve'. Seattle had shown how dangerous it can be when local people are alienated from international organizations.[38] With regard to this issue, however, the concluding declaration of the Millennium Summit contained only a formulaic call for better cooperation between the UN and the national parliaments through the intermediation of the IPU.

But the question of a world parliament was addressed at the world summit. The Czech President Václav Havel (1936 to 2011), a central figure in the Velvet Revolution of 1989, devoted his speech to this issue, which had long con-

---

36 Council of Europe Parliamentary Assembly. 27 September 2000. 'The United Nations at the turn of the new century'. Recommendation 1476 (2000).

37 Millennium Forum. 26 May 2000. 'Declaration and Agenda for Action: Strengthening the United Nations for the 21st Century'. A/54/959 of 8 August 2000, see section F, point 6.

38 Annan, Kofi. 2000. 'Parliamentary Voices Must Be Heard If Global Democracy Is to Thrive'. Address to the Conference of Presiding Officers of National Parliaments. UNIS/SG/2641.

cerned him. He argued that the UN should develop from a community of governments and diplomats into a joint institution belonging to all the inhabitants of the planet, not only for the protection of their individual security but for the pursuit of a lasting wellbeing and genuine quality of life for all humanity. 'Such a United Nations', said Havel, 'would probably have to rest on two pillars: one constituted by an assembly of equal executive representatives of individual countries, resembling the present plenary, and the other consisting of a group elected directly by the globe's population in which the number of delegates representing individual nations would, thus, roughly correspond to the size of the nations.'[39] These two bodies, he explained, would create global laws, and a reformed Security Council would be accountable to them. The UN of the future would have its own military and police forces to enforce its laws and decisions. Lech Wałęsa (b. 1943), the former Polish State President and Nobel Peace Prize winner, chair of the trade union Solidarność from 1980 to 1990, later expressed similar ideas. 'Our great grandfathers invented the bicycle, and suddenly the village was too small for them', Wałęsa said for example in one newspaper interview. 'Now we have aeroplanes, and suddenly the nations are too small for us: a jet can cross them in minutes. That's why we have to think globally today. We need a global parliament, a global government, maybe a global ministry of security.'[40]

Finally, the US American humanist and philosopher Paul Kurtz (1925 to 2012) published the 'Humanist Manifesto 2000', which revolved around a worldview guided by secular and philosophical principles, in the tradition of the two humanist manifestoes of 1933 and 1973 (another was to follow in 2003). The Manifesto 2000 explored the need for, and content of, a so-called '*post*-postmodern planetary humanism'. The question of a world parliament was of crucial importance in this. More than ever before, it was argued, a world organization was needed that represented human beings and not just national states. An effective, directly elected parliament should be established for the passing of global laws, perhaps together with the existing General Assembly as a bicameral system. The details were to be worked out by a Charter revision conference, which the Manifesto called for. The document was supported by 140 prominent figures from over 30 countries. The signatories included the British author Arthur C. Clarke (1917 to 2008), who became famous through the film of his science fiction novel '2001: A Space Odyssey'; the biologist Edward O. Wilson (1929 to 2021); and the British evolutionary biol-

---

39 Havel, Vaclav. 8 September 2000. Address of the President of the Czech Republic at the Millennium Summit of the United Nations in New York.

40 Walesa, Lech. 27 August 2005. 'Unser Sieg ist uns teuer zu stehen gekommen' Interview by Konrad Schuller. Frankfurter Allgemeine Zeitung.

ogist Richard Dawkins (b. 1941), the author of the popular science books 'The God Delusion' and 'The Greatest Show on Earth'. Most of the signatories were scientists, among them ten Nobel Prize winners.[41]

The 'political trilemma of the world economy'

In an article published in 2000, the economist and Harvard professor Dani Rodrik (b. 1957), started making an argument that got more and more attention, especially when it became a key point of his popular book 'The Globalization Paradox' published eleven years later. In brief, Rodrik argued that global markets undermine national democracy and that this leads to a 'fundamental trilemma of the world economy' because it was not possible to have 'hyperglobalization, democracy, and national self-determination all at once'. At most two of the three were available. In order to attain globalization and democracy, it becomes necessary to relinquish the significance of the nation state. On the other hand, if the nation state is to be preserved alongside the pursuit of international economic integration, democracy must be abandoned. Finally, the coexistence of democracy and the nation state would entail the abandonment of 'deep globalization'.[42] The option Rodrik 'liked best' when he initially presented the concept, and which he considered possible in 'the next 100 years or so', was 'a model of global federalism' that aligns jurisdictions with the market. This would be achieved by 'supranational legislative, executive, and judicial authorities' which include, in particular, 'an elected global legislative body' and a 'global fiscal authority'. Politics, he wrote, would not shrink but 'relocate to the global level'.[43] But in the 2011 book he revised his preference and voiced strong scepticism of the global governance option 'mostly on substantive rather than practical grounds'. Rodrik went as far as saying that 'global standards and regulations are not just impractical; they are undesirable'. The only option was to 'sacrifice hyperglobalization'. A global legislature, he wrote, was 'too much of a fantasy'.[44] Still it is not entirely clear what made him change his mind.

41   Barju Benacerraf, Paul D. Boyer, Herbert A. Hauptmann, Harold W. Kroto, Jean-Marie Lehn, Mario Molina, Ferid Murad, José Saramago, Jens C. Skou and Jack Steinberger. A full list of signatories is printed in: Kurtz, Paul. 2000. Humanist Manifesto 2000. A Call For A New Planetary Humanism. Amherst, New York: Prometheus Books.

42   Rodrik, Dani. 2011. The Globalization Paradox: Democracy and the Future of the World Economy. Oxford University Press, p. 200.

43   Id. 2000. 'How Far Will International Economic Integration Go?' The Journal of Economic Perspectives 14, no. 1: 177–86, pp. 181-3, 185.

44   Rodrik. 2011, ibid., pp. 203-4, 208.

9.

The 'War on Terror', the role of the IPU, and the campaign for a UNPA

The ban on landmines, the International Criminal Court and the World Social Forum

The beginning of the new century saw some initially very promising developments. A new and successful means of achieving progress in international law seemed to be establishing itself, in the form of cooperation between international NGOs and sympathetic governments. The Ottawa Treaty prohibiting the use of anti-personnel mines came into force in March 1999. The International Campaign to Ban Landmines, founded in 1992 by a group of NGOs and awarded the Nobel Peace Prize in 1997, had contributed substantially to the development of the treaty. Additionally, at a historic United Nations conference in Rome in July 1998, the statute of the International Criminal Court was negotiated and adopted, with 120 votes in favour, nine against and 21 abstentions. The necessary number of 60 ratifications for the statute to enter into force was reached on 1 July 2002. The Coalition for the International Criminal Court, founded by Amnesty International, Human Rights Watch and other big human rights organizations and led by the WFM, played a decisive part in the success in Rome and in the swift ratification of the treaty. The project had long been dismissed as 'unrealistic'. In addition, criticism of globalization was ubiquitous after Seattle. Under the motto 'another world is possible', thousands of initiatives, unionists, activists and NGOs from all over the world gathered in Porto Alegre in Brazil in January 2001 for the first World Social Forum, which has met every year since. Public interest in this counter-event to the elite World Economic Forum in Davos was (initially at least) extraordinarily high. From the very beginning, there has also always been a meeting of the parliamentarians who take part in the World Social Forum. The 'World Parliamentary Forum', it was stated in the first declaration issued by the deputies (who are usually from the left and Green end of the political spectrum), aims to support the movements coming together at the Social Forum in their resistance to the 'inhuman neo-liberal order' and to ensure that their concerns are fed into the national parliaments. According to *Zeit* magazine, the French

European Parliament member Harlem Désir, one of the initiators of the parliamentary forum and party leader of the French socialists for two years from 2012, saw it as 'a preliminary stage for its long-term goal, a world parliament'.[1]

New contributions on the idea of a global parliament

Falk and Strauss were encouraged by these developments. Globalization and democratization, they thought, were the two dominant themes of the post-Cold War world. With the aid of a coalition of NGOs and open-minded governments, a global parliament could be established that would bring these two phenomena together and into balance. Alongside the possibility that such a parliament might be organized by civil society itself, they now brought into the discussion the additional option of a new inter-state treaty. An article they wrote in the journal *Foreign Affairs* in early 2001 taking this line of argument attracted considerable attention and probably still remains the most frequently cited publication on this topic.[2] Inspired by Schumann and Martin's critique of globalization, the Australian parliamentarian Duncan Kerr, Australian Justice Minister from 1993 to 1996, then argued in his book 'Elect the Ambassador', also published in 2001, that the process of globalization and the global markets could definitely be brought under political control, namely by democratising and then strengthening the international system. Among the ten proposals he put forward to this end was the establishment of a UNPA. Kerr emphasized that the procedure by which deputies were elected should not be uniformly prescribed. He was sure, though, that it would be the directly elected deputies who would dominate the evolution of the 'second chamber'.[3]

The British journalist and environmentalist George Monbiot, on the other hand, argued in his weekly column in the *Guardian* that 'democracy is meaningless unless ultimate power resides in a directly elected assembly'.[4] Monbiot at the time contributed a great deal, particularly with his 2003 book 'The Age of Consent', to the growing interest within the anti-globalization movement in the idea of a global parliament. 'As everything has been globalized except democracy', Monbiot wrote, 'the rulers of the world can go about their business without reference to ourselves.' 'If we wish to be represented', he continued, 'then let us be represented, and let us no longer accept the evasions, half-measures, impediments, intermediaries and arbiters whose installation mas-

1   Greve, Christiane. 'Der Internationale'. Die Zeit, no. 06/2002 (www.zeit.de).
2   Falk, Richard, and Andrew Strauss. 2001. 'Toward Global Parliament'. in: Foreign Affairs 80 (1): 212–220. Repr.
     in id.: 2011. A Global Parliament: Essays and Articles. Berlin: Committee for a Democratic UN, pp. 21-28.
3   Kerr, Duncan. 2001. Elect the Ambassador! Building Democracy in a Globalised World. Annandale: Pluto
     Press, pp. 144-6.
4   Monbiot, George. 17 July 2001. 'How to rule the world'. The Guardian (www.guardian.co.uk).

querades as global democratization. The only genuinely representative forum is a directly representative one, by which, of course, I mean a world parliament.'[5] Anybody working and hoping for a fairer world, he thought, must in all logic speak out in favour of equal rights for all. It was therefore indispensable for everyone to have an equal vote in any election to a world parliament. This could be achieved by having, for the purposes of such elections, 600 roughly equal electoral districts across the world, cutting across national frontiers. Initially, the principal role of the parliament would lie in monitoring the activities of other international organizations and holding them to account. The parliament would derive its power from its moral authority. If it were to lose the support of the people, its authority would decline in proportion. Thus there would emerge a self-regulating system of legitimate exercise of power.

The option of a global assembly as an electronic network, although cost-efficient, could only be in Monbiot's eyes 'a poor substitute for a real debating chamber'.[6] The 'e-Parliament' set up in 2004 by Nicholas Dunlop, the former Secretary-General of the PGA, together with William Ury, the co-founder of the Harvard Program on Negotiation, the then MEP Anders Wijkman and others serves only to link parliamentarians from all over the world via the internet and to support their political communication. Since 2012 the initiative has concentrated on climate policy. The German political scientist and negotiations expert Rasmus Tenbergen, meanwhile, pursued the idea of a global internet parliament organized by civil society, whose decisions and votes could be participated in by everybody, as an exercise of direct democracy, and which could acquire more than merely moral authority once it reached a critical mass of individual supporters. Tenbergen hopes to demonstrate the validity of this approach through the online project 'World Parliament Experiment', which also involves representative features.

The Lucknow conferences

In 2000, the first 'International Conference of Chief Justices of the World' was held in Lucknow, the capital of the Indian federal state of Uttar Pradesh. The conference has been held there every year since, hosted and organized by the City Montessori School and its founder Jagdish Gandhi (1936 to 2024), with over 60,000 pupils the biggest school in the world. This private institution regards itself as the 'self-appointed guardian of the two billion children worldwide and of future generations'. The object of the conference is the strengthening of international law and global governance. Reference is being

5   Id. 2004. The Age of Consent. Manifesto for a New World Order. London: Harper Perennial, p. 83.
6   Ibid., p. 91.

made to Article 51 of the Indian constitution which says that the state shall 'promote international peace and security' and 'foster respect for international law', among other things. The establishment of a world parliament able to pass binding world laws has been called for in every one of the conference's concluding declarations. According to the school, around 700 judges from highest national courts have taken part in the twenty-four conferences held up to 2023, as well as other judges from over 100 countries. Engagement of the participants with the students is a key focus of the event.

9/11 and global democracy

Following the attacks of 11 September 2001, the 'war on terror' ('You are either with us or you are against us', said US President George W. Bush) became the USA's highest priority. Terrorism emerged as the new perceived enemy. The prospect of success for international democratization dwindled rapidly. On the other hand, it was argued that building up a global community based on the rule of law was essential in order over the long term to deprive terrorism of its breeding grounds. Friedrich Merz, leader of the German CDU/CSU parliamentary group at the time and again since 2022, said for example in a keynote speech in October 2001, referring to Höffe, that a world state based on subsidiarity and with a federal constitution was a prerequisite for peace and security, human rights and a fair world economic order. This would entail the creation of a sense of world citizenship, of a cosmopolitan ethos and of democratic institutions such as a world parliament and world courts.[7] It fits with this line of thinking that the conservative German CDU/CSU group in the European Parliament indicated as early as 1999 its willingness to cooperate constructively towards the establishment of a UNPA (a position the group still maintains), as announced on behalf of the group by the MEP Elmar Brok. This notwithstanding, as Brok wrote, a solution still had to be found to the problem of how to deal with dictatorships.[8]

In his book 'Power in the Global Age', Beck warned, in the light of the hegemonic undertones of the war on terror and the accompanying growth of state surveillance, against a 'global anti-democratic populism based on threat prevention' and against a related 'cosmopolitan despotism'—an ostensible worldwide defence of human rights, democracy and peace which has itself been decoupled from those values and thus in reality serves to undermine them. The September 11 attacks, Beck thought, had made it clear for the first time in 50

---

7   Merz, Friedrich. 10 October 2001. 'Gedanken zur Politik im 21. Jahrhundert'. Speech at the Konrad-Adenauer-Stiftung. Pressedienst der CDU/CSU-Bundestagsfraktion. Mitteilung 1630, pp. 17-8.

8   Letter from Elmar Brok to Andreas Bummel, 27 September 1999.

years that the peace and security of the West were not compatible with the continued existence of armed conflicts, and of their root causes, in other areas of the world. In that sense, cosmopolitanism was the appropriate response to the terrorist threat. To be sure, the 'cosmopolitan regime' would have to be conceptually and institutionally conjoined with human rights and democracy and promoted and supported as a reform project at the level of global politics. Among the features that would serve as guarantors of the legitimacy of such a regime, Beck lists making the case for and establishing a world parliament—even if, he writes, an initiative to that end undertaken by sympathetic governments might realistically include initially only a small fraction of the existing states, and even if such a parliament might initially control the levers of symbolic power only.[9]

The report by the German Bundestag's Enquete Commission

The report of the German Bundestag's Enquete Commission inquiry into economic globalization, delivered in the middle of 2002 at over 600 pages long, proved less progressive in outlook. Although it identified the democratization of international institutions as an important task, it did not come out in support of the establishment of a UNPA; rather, it described the proposal as controversial. The initiative met with scepticism, the report said, 'as agreement on the composition of such a parliament presents problems (of demography, for example) that are almost impossible to resolve'.[10] The only recommendations for action in this area were for support for a stronger representation of the global regions in the UN Security Council. Additionally, it was proposed that the right of veto should be subject to a duty to justify its use to the General Assembly. The report did also express the view that the delegates should be given some powers of supervision and influence with regard to processes of globalization, especially in negotiations over agreements under international law. The process of international policy formulation should be monitored and influenced more effectively through the building up and development of interparliamentary networks. To this end, the IPU should be developed and strengthened, and the parliament was encouraged to pursue this. Thilo Bode, the director of Greenpeace International for six years up until 2001, thought it regrettable that there was very little interest in the report even within parliament. He thought Germany had no policy at all on globalization. But, he said,

---

9   Beck, Ulrich. 2009 [2002]. Macht und Gegenmacht im globalen Zeitalter. Frankfurt am Main: Suhrkamp, pp. 425-7, 426, 444, 446.

10   Deutscher Bundestag. 2002. Final Report of the Enquete Commission 'Globalisierung der Weltwirtschaft - Herausforderungen und Antworten', p. 430.

the idea that the nation states were being marginalized by globalization was a myth. All too often, it served national governments as a way of hiding vested interests or their own mistakes. But it was certainly true, he argued, that the nation states had recklessly delegated powers to international bodies without ensuring the maintenance of the necessary democratic controls over those powers. In order to overcome this democratic deficit, Europe should instigate a convention for the creation of a world parliament to take over this supervisory and monitoring role.[11]

The World Commission on the Social Dimension of Globalization

In a resolution on relations between the EU and the UN passed in January 2004, the European Parliament renewed its efforts to this end and called for the creation of a consultative parliamentary assembly in the UN. The following month, the 'World Commission on the Social Dimension of Globalization', set up by the ILO two years earlier under the joint chairmanship of the Finnish President Tarja Halonen and the Tanzanian President Benjamin William Mkapa, delivered its detailed and comprehensive concluding report. The conclusions of the Commission, made up of over twenty prominent international figures, included the following. 'Parliamentary oversight of the multilateral system at the global level should be progressively expanded. We propose the creation of a Parliamentary Group concerned with the coherence and consistency between global economic, social and environmental policies, which should develop an integrated oversight of major international organizations.'[12] The governments of Finland and Tanzania were especially engaged in promoting the report and ensured that it was discussed in the General Assembly. The two governments had already, in early 2003, jointly started the 'Helsinki Process on Globalization and Democracy'. This initiative brought together representatives of government with experts and prominent figures from politics, academia and the NGOs for a dialogue on global problems and possible solutions, and was designed to push forward, in a second phase (running until 2008), the implementation of selected proposals.

The Ubuntu Forum campaign

Momentum was building within civil society, too. In April 2001 a world forum of civil society networks, a 'network of networks', had formed in response to a call from the Spaniard Federico Mayor, Director-General of UNESCO

11 Bode, Thilo. 2003. Die Demokratie verrät ihre Kinder. Stuttgart, München: DVA, pp. 11, 205, 192-4.
12 International Labour Organization. 2004. 'A fair globalization: Creating opportunities for all'. Report of the World Commission on the Social Dimension of Globalization. Geneva, p. xiv, see also p. 121.

from 1987 to 1999, in order to press for a more humane, more just and fairer world. One of its goals was the democratization of decision-making and institutions at all levels, including the global. The name of this forum, Ubuntu, is an African term describing a particular philosophy of life based on togetherness, charity and community. The roll-call of organizations involved in this initiative, which was based in Barcelona and had also participated in the Helsinki Process from the beginning, included Oxfam, WFM, the South Centre, CIVICUS: World Alliance for Citizen Participation, the Grameen Bank, IPPNW, the International Peace Bureau IPB, the Third World Network and the London School of Economics. The international associations Caritas, Greenpeace, the Red Cross and Médecins Sans Frontières were among the organizations with observer status. In 2002, under the aegis of the Ubuntu Forum, a 'World Campaign for In-Depth Reform of the System of International Institutions' was initiated. The Campaign's London Declaration of April 2004 included a call for comprehensive democratization. 'It is necessary for the world's citizens to be directly represented in the international institutions', it read. To this end, work should go forward on the creation of a parliamentary assembly 'which could play a role in establishing international law, put forward recommendations and exercise control over the other institutions forming part of the system'.[13] The Campaign Declaration was signed by over fifty prominent public figures including Mayor, Soares, Boutros-Ghali, Pérez de Cuéllar, the Nobel Peace laureates Rigoberta Menchú, Adolfo Pérez Esquivel and Joseph Rotblat, Nobel Literature laureates Gabriel García Márquez and José Saramago as well as the future Nobel Peace laureate Muhammad Yunus and Danielle Mitterand, wife of François Mitterrand, French President from 1981 to 1995. The campaign continued, but slowly lost steam, not least due to a lack of funding. One of the last activities before it quietly died down was the publication of a book in 2009.[14] The Ubuntu Forum itself was only able to keep going for a few more years.

The Cardoso panel report

A report from an independent body of experts on the relationship between the UN and civil society was scheduled for June 2004. The panel had been set up by UN Secretary-General Annan as part of his reform drive, and had worked under the chairmanship of the former Brazilian President Fernando Henrique

---

13 World Campaign for In-Depth Reform of the System of International Institutions, and UBUNTU Forum Ad Hoc Secretariat. 2004. 'Reforms of the System of International Institutions to Make Another World Possible'. London Declaration of 1 April 2004, p. 2.

14 Ubuntu Forum Secretariat, Unbuntu Forum, ed. 2009. Reforming International Institutions: Another World Is Possible.

Cardoso. In addition to investigating how NGOs and other actors could be better integrated into the work of the UN, the panel was also tasked to throw light on the interaction between the UN and parliamentarians and to make recommendations for its improvement. The IPU was also consulted on this issue. However, it was very far from agreeing with the conclusions. In early May, IPU Secretary-General Johnsson went so far as to contact Annan directly to set out the IPU's 'serious misgivings' with regard to the report and to urgently request fresh consultations between the parties involved before the Cardoso report was published.[15] But his request was in vain. The recommendations in this area, drawn up principally by panel member Birgitta Dahl, former President of the Swedish Parliament, were supplemented by a further reference to the IPU but otherwise not amended at all. What was at issue here?

The Cardoso Report found that democracy was coming under pressure, since the substance of politics was globalising rapidly while the most important political institutions such as elections, parties and parliaments remained rooted at the national level. A major factor in the increasing disenchantment with politics was 'the perception that traditional forms of representation are less relevant in this age of globalization. Elected legislators and parliaments', the report continued, 'seem to have little impact on decisions made intergovernmentally or in the supervision and regulation of international markets ... Given that national parliaments are formal and powerful institutions of democracy, the Panel considers it important to link them more structurally with the international intergovernmental process and to explore international parliamentary mechanisms to do so.'[16] Conversely, it is possible to infer an implied criticism of the IPU here. The panel clearly did not believe that the IPU was fulfilling this task, as it would otherwise not be necessary to set up new mechanisms.

The Cardoso Report specifically recommended the establishment—as an experiment initially—of so-called 'Global Public Policy Committees'. These should be organized under the aegis of the UN secretariat ('in consultation with' national parliaments, the IPU and other specialized organizations) and should be made up, in each case, of two to four members from different political parties from up to 30 parliaments for all regions. The idea, just as in the 1999 proposal from the European Parliament, was that the members would be selected from the relevant specialist committees of the national parliaments. The global committees would hold public debates and hearings involving

---

15   Letter from Anders B. Johnsson to Kofi Annan, 4 May 2004.

16   United Nations. 2004. We the Peoples: Civil society, the United Nations and Global Governance. Report of the Panel of Eminent Persons on United Nations–Civil Society Relations. A/58/817. Points 8, 106.

experts from academia, civil society, business and government agencies. The broader aim of the Cardoso panel was to build up overarching participative policy networks, of which these committees would form a substantial constituent part. Gradually, it was hoped, a formalized process could emerge out of these committees. For example, they could be given the right to make recommendations to the UN. The panel stressed that this proposal should be seen by the IPU as an opportunity for closer cooperation with the UN, and expressed scepticism towards the IPU's claim to an exclusive right of representation. Not all parliaments, claimed the report, wanted to be represented exclusively through the IPU, and indeed some were not even members of the organization. This last point was in reference principally to the US Congress. Since the early 1990s, practically no US representatives had taken part in IPU conferences, and in fact the US Congress formally cancelled its membership of the IPU in 1999. Unofficially, the IPU was increasingly seen as a 'talking shop', and moreover as being hostile to the USA.[17]

At a debate in the UN General Assembly in October, Johnsson made it clear that the IPU did not think much of the Cardoso proposals. The report, he said, causes concern 'because it suggests that the United Nations, an intergovernmental institution, should create its own inter-parliamentary structures'. This would duplicate the work of the IPU, and moreover, in Johnsson's view, 'runs contrary to the principle of separation of powers between the legislative and the executive branch of government'.[18] The Cardoso panel, by contrast, had argued that the principle of the separation of powers did not apply so clearly to international intergovernmental institutions as there was no legislative body of elected representatives 'to supervise and oversee the executive function'.[19]

The branch of the Helsinki Process dealing with 'New Approaches to Global Problem Solving' declared itself in agreement with the proposals of the Cardoso panel and the ILO World Commission. The Helsinki Process should support 'the establishment of Global Public Policy Committees (proposed by the Cardoso panel)' and 'the development of a Global Parliamentary Group (proposed by the ILO Commission). In order to address these questions, a meeting of representatives from the IPU, other apex bodies of parliaments and parliamentarians,

17 Turner, Fred, and Zlatko Šabič. 2011. 'The US Congress' Participation in NATO and the Organization for Security and Cooperation in Europe (OSCE) Assemblies'. Paper presented at the International Studies Association Annual Conference 'Global Governance: Political Authority in Transition', Montreal, p. 12 (according to an interview of the authors with a high-ranking staff member of the US Congress).
18 Johnsson, Anders. 4 October 2004. 'Statement at the United Nations General Assembly joint debate, agenda items 52 and 54.'
19 United Nations, 2004, point 8.

as well as regional parliaments, should be organised.'[20] However, the IPU had no interest in such consultations. The idea was allowed to fizzle out.

Growing support for a UNPA

Meanwhile, the voices going beyond such moderate proposals and calling for the establishment of a UNPA were growing more numerous. At the 22nd Congress of the Socialist International in São Paulo in October 2003, for example, the worldwide gathering of over 150 social democratic parties and organizations (including the German SPD) declared that 'the time has come to build up efficient democratic structures of global governance'. The text was drawn up by a committee headed by Christoph Zöpel, an SPD member of parliament for many years and former minister of state in the German foreign ministry. 'The goal of the SI must be to parliamentarise the global political system.' At some point, it read, consideration would need to be given to a UN Parliamentary Assembly.[21] At that time, the President of the SI was António Guterres, former Prime Minister of Portugal, who took office as UN Secretary-General in 2017.

With the support of the authors, the Committee for a Democratic UN, or KDUN, was formed in Germany in 2003, a cross-party association whose sole purpose was to lobby for the creation of a UNPA (in 2017, KDUN was turned into Democracy Without Borders). In a strategy paper by Andreas Bummel, the group aligned itself broadly with the argument set out by Heinrich. UN Secretary-General Annan sent a message to let the Committee know that the paper was 'very welcome' at a time when the UN was considering reform options.[22] Among the Committee members was Remo Gysin, a member of the Swiss National Council and one of the initiators of the successful national referendum that led to the accession of Switzerland to the UN in March 2002. With the help of the Committee and of the Society for Threatened Peoples, Gysin organized a cross-party open letter to UN Secretary-General Annan by 108 members of Swiss federal councils, including a majority of the National Council. It stated that Switzerland 'has always promoted international law, democracy and respect for human rights' and that 'on the basis of this tradition' the signatories were asking Annan 'to introduce the idea of a Parliamentary Assembly at the UN into the reform debate and to forward this sugges-

20 Helsinki Process. 2005. 'Governing Globalization - Globalizing Governance. New Approaches to Global Problem Solving'. Finish Ministry for Foreign Affairs, p. 6.
21 Socialist International. 29 October 2003. Governance in a Global Society – The Social Democratic Approach. Report adopted at the XII. Congress, São Paulo. Chapter III.0.a), and 3.3.
22 Letter from Marta Maurás, Director of the Executive Office of the Secretary-General, to Andreas Bummel, 27 October 2004.

tion to the governments of the UN member states for further discussion'.[23] The letter aroused considerable interest and comment in the Swiss media. In an interview Switzerland's UN ambassador Peter Maurer, who later became President of the International Committee of the Red Cross, stated that the proposal was 'in line with Swiss foreign policy'.[24] Micheline Calmy-Rey, Head of the Federal Department of Foreign Affairs, later agreed that the creation of a parliamentary body within the UN would strengthen its democratic credentials and its proximity to the citizens. However, she claimed it would be difficult to realize this aim, given that an amendment of the UN Charter would require a two-thirds majority of all member states and the assent of all five permanent members of the Security Council. For this reason, other options were also being considered, such as strengthening the role of the IPU within the UN.[25]

In May 2005, the world congress of Liberal International in Sofia declared its support for a UNPA in a resolution, linking back to the LI report of 1992 and a more recent report prepared by the LI committee on UN reform which recommended 'forming a World Parliament to represent the people of member countries'.[26] The resolution pointed out that a UNPA could be established without amending the Charter either as a new body on the basis of Article 22 of the UN Charter or—assuming its agreement—through a transformation of the IPU.[27] The South Centre, whose Chairman from 2003 to 2006 was Boutros-Ghali, also drew attention to the proposal for a UNPA. The reference came in a paper, dating from one year earlier but now made public, submitted to the High Level Panel on Threats, Challenges and Change (another panel initiated by Annan). Subsequently, so this think tank for the developing countries of the global South argued, a World Parliament, directly elected by the people in the style of the European Parliament, could be created.[28]

The issue was also taken up again—for the fourth time now, and more decisively than ever before—by the European Parliament itself. In a resolution on reform of the UN put forward by Armin Laschet, CDU member of the European Parliament and later Prime Minister of North-Rhine Westphalia, the European Parliament called in June 2005 'for the establishment of a Unit-

23 Gysin, Remo, Josef Lang, Christa Markwalder Bär, Heiner Studer, and Rosmarie Zapfl. 8 February 2005. 'Establishment of a Parliamentary Assembly at the UN. Open letter of 108 Members of Parliament to the UN Secretary-General'. Swiss National Council.

24 Interview with Peter Maurer. 14 Feb. 2005. 'Schweiz muss auf faire Spielregeln achten'. Tages-Anzeiger.

25 Schweizerischer Bundesrat. 18 May 2005. 'Bericht 2005 über das Verhältnis zur UNO und zu den internationalen Organisationen mit Sitz in der Schweiz', pp. 11-2.

26 Liberal International, Dec. 2002. 'From Globalisation to Global Governance. The UN in the 21 Century.' Report of the Committee on UN Reform chaired by Paavo Vayrynen.

27 Liberal International. 14 May 2005. 'Strengthening citizens representation on international level through an UN Parliamentary Assembly'. Resolution adopted by the 53rd Congress in Sofia, Bulgaria.

28 South Centre. 2005. What UN for the 21st Century? A New North-South Divide. Geneva, pp. 38-9.

ed Nations Parliamentary Assembly (UNPA) within the UN system, which would increase the democratic profile and internal democratic process of the organization and allow world civil society to be directly associated in the decision-making process'. This assembly 'should be vested with genuine rights of information, participation and control, and should be able to adopt recommendations directed at the UN General Assembly'.[29]

One week later, with the votes of the SPD and the Green Party, the German Bundestag passed a resolution on 'parliamentary involvement in the United Nations system'. Over the preceding six months, following publication of the Cardoso report, the Bundestag had been one of the first national parliaments to investigate the issue in any detail. The text was compiled for the foreign affairs committee by the sub-committee on UN affairs, led by Zöpel, in cooperation with the IPU delegation. There was consensus in the subsidiary committee that the addition of a 'parliamentary dimension' to the UN system was needed, and that its institutional form (and this was the wording in the text then passed by the Bundestag) 'could perhaps be described as a "parliamentary assembly"'. In any event, the delegates thought that the IPU was preferable to alternatives such as 'forming a new parliamentary body within or outside the United Nations, with the IPU remaining in its existing form'.[30] The KDUN by contrast had recommended not putting all of the eggs in one basket and therefore continuing to keep alternative options open in case the further development of the IPU proved impossible. A reference to Article 22 of the UN Charter as a potential vehicle for the construction of a parliamentary assembly was removed from the text at the request of the foreign ministry. The Greens had made it a condition of their assent that an 'agreement' had to be reached with the foreign ministry, at that time headed by Joschka Fischer. Zöpel lamented that it had not proved possible to get the foreign ministry to accept a 'genuine parliamentarization of global politics on the basis of a separation of powers'. The ministry also insisted on the removal of core responsibilities and competences that the lower chamber had proposed should be given to the parliamentary UN assembly, for example participation in the deliberations on multilateral treaties and their ratification, participation in setting and monitoring the budget, a so-called 'right to implement transparency' and the involvement of NGOs. 'There is still a long way to go', Zöpel summed up, 'before the Bundestag understands its role to be that of the German part of a global democratic separation of powers which includes an effective global

29 European Parliament. 6 June 2005. Resolution on the reform of the United Nations, P6_TA(2005). See point 39.
30 Deutscher Bundestag. 15 June 2005. Für eine parlamentarische Mitwirkung im System der Vereinten Nationen. 15/5690, p. 3.

parliamentarism.'[31] The Green Party manifesto for the Bundestag elections of July 2005 then included the following sentence: 'We also support the establishment of a parliamentary assembly as an advisory body at the United Nations'.[32] The fact that the route through the IPU was a dead end was confirmed shortly afterwards. At the UN summit meeting Millennium+5 in September 2005, the occasion for the second worldwide meeting of presiding officers of national parliaments, Johnsson—who was not unaware of the growing support for a UNPA—affirmed once more that the IPU was not in favour of 'the creation of any parliamentary assembly at the United Nations or elsewhere'.[33] Nor was there any indication of a possible reform of the IPU in this direction.

This characteristic stance of the IPU failed to convince the Parliamentary Assembly of the Council of Europe. The Italian delegate Tana de Zulueta explained this as resulting in part from the fact that the IPU was not contemplating 'any structured or systematic participation by parliamentarians in the work of the UN', nor did it plan to establish links between the parliamentarians and the functioning of the UN institutions and bodies. To only offer a platform was not sufficient.[34] Her proposal for a resolution was unanimously accepted in the relevant committee, and subsequently passed by the assembly. In it, the UN General Assembly was called upon to develop, together with the IPU, an incremental strategy for the creation of a parliamentary dimension within the UN. This could include, on a trial basis, the establishment of parliamentary committees that could ultimately lead to the creation of a UNPA. The General Assembly was to institute a panel to work up proposals regarding the exact size, constitution and procedures of a UN assembly of parliamentarians.[35] In October 2006, Andreas Gross, a Swiss parliamentarian and member of the Council of Europe who had also been one of the instigators of the Swiss referendum on accession to the UN, also spoke out in favour of a UN parliamentary chamber in a speech to the UN General Assembly. Annan welcomed the idea at a meeting with the foreign affairs committee of the Swiss National Council. However, at the same time he doubted whether the governments of the UN member states would show any interest in it.[36] It was probably this, as well as the negative stance of the IPU, which explains why Annan never took up the proposal in his official reports.

---

31 Zöpel, Christoph. 2005. 'Die Vereinten Nationen and die Parlamente (II)'. Vereinte Nationen (4): 145–148, p. 148.

32 Bündnis 90 / Die Grünen. 10 July 2005. 'Eines für alle. Das Grüne Wahlprogramm 2005', p. 107.

33 Johnsson, Anders. 16 Sep. 2005. 'Statement at the High-level Plenary Meeting of the UN General Assembly'.

34 Zulueta, Tana de. 2005. 'Parliamentary dimension of the United Nations'. Report to the Political Affairs Committee of the Parliamentary Assembly of the Council of Europe. Doc. 10771, pp. 8-9.

35 Council of Europe Parliamentary Assembly. 23 Jan. 2006. 'Parliamentary dimension of the United Nations'. Resolution 1476 (2006).

36 'Forderung nach UNO-Parlament'. 21 October 2006. sda wire news.

The international campaign for a UNPA

The open letter from Switzerland was seen by many world federalists and supporters of a UNPA as a milestone. Shortly afterwards, the Committee for a Democratic UN—together with the Society for Threatened Peoples, Ubuntu, WFM and other partners—began planning an international campaign. The time seemed to have come to join together the various international strands of support for a UNPA in order to make them more effective. In 1996, in one of his first speeches as the new Secretary-General of WFUNA, the worldwide umbrella organization for national UN societies, Childers had encouraged the creation of a coordinated campaign.[37] Now, ten years after his sudden death in 1996, the WFUNA world congress meeting in Buenos Aires passed a resolution officially committing it to support for a UNPA. It called on 'the governments of the United Nations member states, parliamentarians and civil society representatives to jointly examine possible steps and options to create a United Nations Parliamentary Assembly'.[38]

With the publication in April 2007 of an 'Appeal for the establishment of a Parliamentary Assembly at the United Nations', addressed to the UN and the governments of its member states, the international campaign for a UNPA was launched simultaneously in a number of world capitals, including Berlin, Brussels, Berne, Buenos Aires, Dar es Salaam, London, Madrid, Ottawa and Rome. It was an informal network on the model of the campaign for the International Criminal Court. The Appeal created a common political denominator which made it possible to bring together most of the supporters of a UNPA to speak with one voice in a single campaign. 'To ensure international cooperation, secure the acceptance and to enhance the legitimacy of the United Nations and strengthen its capacity to act,' it read, 'people must be more effectively and directly included into the activities of the United Nations and its international organizations. They must be allowed to participate better in the UN's activities. We therefore recommend a gradual implementation of democratic participation and representation on the global level.' The statement saw the establishment of a UNPA as a first and indispensable step in this direction. The assembly 'could initially be composed of national parliamentarians'. But '[s]tep by step, it should be provided with genuine rights of infor-

37 Childers, Erskine. 16 March 1996. 'The United Nations and Global Institutions'. Speech delivered at the 'Conference on The Fate of Democracy In The Era of Globalisation', Wellesley College, Massachusetts.
38 World Federation of United Nations Associations. 10 November 2006. 'A United Nations Parliamentary Assembly'. Resolution adopted at the 38th Plenary Assembly, Buenos Aires, Argentina.

mation, participation and control vis-à-vis the UN and the organizations of the UN system. In a later stage, the assembly could be directly elected.'[39]

Boutros-Ghali, who had encouraged the KDUN to undertake the campaign early on, wrote in a message to all its supporters that 'we need to promote the democratization of globalization, before globalization destroys the foundations of national and international democracy' and that a UNPA was 'an indispensable step to achieve democratic control of globalization'.[40] An international meeting took place in Geneva in October 2007 under the patronage of Boutros-Ghali. It agreed that representatives of regional parliaments such as the European Parliament could also be members of a UNPA, and that the process of parliamentarization must also encompass the Bretton Woods institutions, i.e. the World Bank and the International Monetary Fund. In addition, it was agreed to support regulations that would allow states participating in a UNPA 'to opt for direct elections of their delegates if they wish to do so' from the beginning. Direct elections of the UNPA's delegates were to be regarded as a precondition for vesting the body with legislative rights.[41] It was decided to build up the network further and to continue the campaign by means of the Appeal. The Swiss government, which had been an observer at the meeting, voiced 'sympathy' for the proposal of a UNPA, but emphasized in an official report of the Federal Council that the UN was an inter-state organization.[42] In the following years up to 2015, there were four further international meetings, in the European Parliament in Brussels, in New York and in the Argentinian Senate in Buenos Aires. A particular topic of discussion in Brussels in 2008 was the relationship between the proposed UNPA and the IPU—a topic which kept recurring and for that reason seemed to require a common policy statement. The conclusion was that a UNPA 'would not replace or duplicate the IPU's functions. Quite the contrary, a UNPA would provide a response to the democratic deficit in global governance which the IPU in its current structure is unable to offer'.[43]

The campaign receives international support across all ideological and party political divides. As per 2022, the campaign's appeal has been signed by over 1,700 members of parliament and several thousands of other people from

---

39 Campaign for a UN Parliamentary Assembly. 20 April 2007. Appeal for the Establishment of a United Nations Parliamentary Assembly (www.unpacampaign.org).

40 Boutros-Ghali, Boutros. 16 May 2007. 'Message to the Campaign for a UN Parliamentary Assembly'.

41 Campaign for a UN Parliamentary Assembly. November 2007. 'Conclusions regarding policies of the Campaign for a UN Parliamentary Assembly'.

42 Schweizerischer Bundesrat. 21 May 2008. 'Bericht 2008 über das Verhältnis der Schweiz zur UNO und zu den internationalen Organisationen mit Sitz in der Schweiz', p. 39.

43 Campaign for a UN Parliamentary Assembly. November 2008. 'The establishment of a United Nations Parliamentary Assembly and the Inter-Parliamentary Union'.

150 countries, including many hundreds of prominent figures from politics, academia and civil society. Only a few can be listed here by name, even if all would deserve to be. They include serving and former heads and ministers of state and government, some presiding officers of parliaments, over 300 university professors, and around twenty winners of Nobel and alternative Nobel Prizes (or 'Right Livelihood Awards'), among them the Nobel Peace Prize laureates the Dalai Lama and John Hume. Among the supporters already named in this section of the book are Daniele Archibugi, Boutros Boutros-Ghali, Elmar Brok, Arthur C. Clarke, Harlem Désir, Richard Falk, Johan Galtung, Bronisław Geremek, Olivier Giscard d'Estaing, Andreas Gross, Remo Gysin, Václav Havel, Dieter Heinrich, David Held, Otfried Höffe, Karl Kaiser, Hans Köchler, Armin Laschet, Federico Mayor, Saul Mendlovitz, Mike Moore, Thomas Pogge, Michel Rocard, Douglas Roche, Harald Schumann, Andrew Strauss, Brian Urquhart, Anders Wijkman, Christoph Zöpel and Tana de Zulueta. In India, important supporters include Shashi Tharoor, an acclaimed writer, parliamentarian and former diplomat as well as Najma Heptulla, a long-time member of parliament and President of the Inter-Parliamentary Union from 1999 to 2002.

Calls for a UNPA following the campaign's launch

The campaign helped to maintain the call for a UNPA as an issue for discussion. In Canada, the committee for foreign affairs of the House of Commons recommended in a June 2007 report on the global development of democracy that favourable consideration should be given to the establishment of a UNPA. The Pan-African Parliament, on the initiative of the Mauritian delegate Mokshanand Sunil Dowarkasing, passed a resolution on 24 October 2007 dealing in detail with a UNPA. The first President of the PAP, Gertrude Mongella from Tanzania, who had extensive experience with the UN (for example as head of the UN World Conference on Women in Beijing in 1995), had long been an outspoken supporter of a UNPA. The PAP called on the African Union, which in 2002 succeeded the Organization of African Unity, to develop a common position on the issue. Apparently, though, the resolution was never officially presented to the AU and the request was ignored. The PAP was founded in March 2004 as an advisory body to the African Union and is made up of 235 national parliamentarians from the member states. According to its founding Protocol it is intended to become a directly elected legislative body for the entire African continent. A UNPA, its resolution stated, could similarly develop step by step. Ultimately, the PAP thought, it would need to be endowed with rights of participation and oversight, and in particular with the right 'to send fully participating parliamentary delegations or representatives to international governmental fora and negotiations'. A UNPA would not run counter to the valuable and highly regarded work of the IPU in any way at all.[44] Almost ten years later, in May 2016, PAP reaffirmed its support in another resolution that was initiated by Ivone Soares from Mozambique and called on the African Union and its member states to support a UNPA.

When representatives of the European Parliament and the PAP met in South Africa in May 2008, a common statement of support for a UNPA was removed from the agenda at the urging of the Spanish MEP and honorary President of the IPU Miguel Angel Martínez. The year before, a small advisory group of the IPU Committee on United Nations Affairs had affirmed once more that the IPU should not support the establishment of 'some form of world parliament'. A world parliament, it was put on record, 'would only ever make sense if there was a world government'.[45]

In May 2008, the second Global Congress of all Green parties in São Paulo in Brazil passed the so-called '21 Commitments for the 21st Century', which included the establishment of a UNPA in the section on strengthening democracy. The third Global Green Congress in Dakar, Senegal, in April 2012 passed a resolution calling on 'Greens around the world' to participate in the campaign for a UNPA. The federal board of the German Greens (Bündnis 90/Die Grünen) had decided on the same step two years earlier. 'A global parliament would be well suited to make the United Nations more democratic and more transparent,' commented party chair Claudia Roth at the time.[46]

In Latin America, the call for a UNPA was initially principally carried forward by two Argentinians, the parliamentary delegate Fernando Iglesias from the Coalición Cívica and the Senator Sonia Escudero from the Peronist party. In the book 'Globalizar la democracia: por un Parlamento Mundial', published in Spanish in 2006, Iglesias had dealt in some detail with the question of a world parliament.[47] Argentina had come through a severe economic and financial crisis, including a deep recession, during which the country had descended at some points into chaos and had had to declare itself bankrupt in 2001. There was great controversy over the conditions imposed by the International Monetary Fund, which had been involved as a creditor in determin-

44 Adopted on 24 October 2007, repr. in: Brauer, Maja, and Andreas Bummel. 2020. A United Nations Parliamentary Assembly: A Policy Review of Democracy Without Borders. Berlin: Democracy Without Borders, pp. 141-143.

45 Inter-Parliamentary Union (ed.). 2007. 'Meeting of the Advisory Group of the IPU Committee on United Nations Affairs, 12-13 July 2007, Summary Report', p. 2.

46 'Grüne unterstützen Kampagne für ein UNO-Parlament', 2 July 2010 (www.unpacampaign.org).

47 Iglesias, Fernando. Globalizar la democracia: por un Parlamento Mundial. Buenos Aires: Manantial, 2006.

ing the country's fiscal policy since the early 1990s, and which therefore was regarded as sharing the blame for the 1999—2002 crisis. The IMF seemed to many to be a faceless and undemocratic bureaucracy which was subject to no effective external controls and could not be held to account for its failed policies. A democratization of the international institutions therefore seemed extremely important, and a UNPA was seen as a potential starting point. Iglesias and Escudero took a first step in this direction in the Latin American Parliament, where Escudero held the office of General-Secretary from 2006 to 2010. The 'Parlatino' is a deliberative assembly founded in 1964 with delegates from 23 national parliaments. The assembly has hopes of becoming the legislative organ of the Community of Latin American and Caribbean States (CELAC) but there was little progress in this regard in the decade following the bloc's establishment in 2011. In December 2008 the Parlatino declared its 'support to efforts towards the creation and establishment of a Parliamentary Assembly of the United Nations Organization'.[48] Similar resolutions followed from the Argentinian Senate and Chamber of Deputies and in December 2011 in the Mercosur parliament, comprising delegates from the Mercosur member states of Argentina, Brazil, Paraguay and Uruguay. If evidence were still required that the call for a UNPA is not a Western but a global project, then it will have been provided by these declarations from Africa and Latin America.

During the global financial crisis, half a year after the collapse of the US American investment bank Lehman Brothers, the leaders of the G20 met in London in April 2009 to discuss what measures could be taken. The campaign took the opportunity to publish a 'Call for global democratic oversight of international financial and economic institutions', which attracted support from many individuals, including the former German finance minister Hans Eichel. 'At this critical juncture we urge the United Nations and the governments of its member states to support the establishment of a United Nations Parliamentary Assembly in their deliberations on the reform of international monetary, financial and economic institutions', said Boutros-Ghali.[49] The assembly could take on a supervisory role vis-à-vis the Bretton Woods institutions, could provide a voice for citizens and could be given a consultative role in the appointment of the executive directors of the institutions.

The Parliamentary Assembly of the Council of Europe, in a resolution drawn up by Gross, emphasized that 'the incorporation of a democratic element in the United Nations system has become even more necessary in re-

---

48　Reprinted in: Brauer and Bummel, p. 149.
49　'Call on world leaders: Global parliament to exert oversight of international system', 30 March 2009 (www.unpacampaign.org).

sponse to the process of globalization'. The members regretted that there had been no reform proposal among the many officially brought forward within the UN in recent years 'aimed at improving the democratic character of the United Nations'. Their proposal was for a parliamentary assembly within the UN 'composed either by representatives of international regional parliamentary assemblies or directly elected representatives'.[50] But an amendment was also accepted acknowledging that, besides a new assembly, the IPU was 'one of the potential options to be considered as the parliamentary branch of the UN'.[51]

The third World Conference of Speakers of Parliament

At the IPU itself, preparations were under way for the third World Conference of Speakers of Parliament, due to take place in Geneva in July 2010. A key question for the further development of the IPU's role within the UN would be the issue of its legal status. Three options were under discussion: maintaining the status quo, aiming for an amendment of the Charter to transform the IPU into an organ of the UN, or putting the IPU onto a different footing through a new intergovernmental treaty. It seems that the Secretariat favoured the third option. But there was unanimity on the point that there should be no additional institution independent of the IPU. The preparatory committee therefore confirmed its rejection of the idea of a UNPA, as such a body, it argued, would be 'incompatible with the strategy for parliamentary interaction with the United Nations'.[52] At the World Conference the differing views within the IPU came out into the open. Abdirahin Abdi, Kenyan Speaker of the East African Legislative Assembly EALA proposed that the parliaments should be formally integrated into the decision-making processes of the UN (the President of the Kenyan Parliament, Kenneth Marende, who was not in Geneva, supported a UNPA). 'It can be made a requirement', said Abdi, 'that every decision of the UN General Assembly or the UN Security Council is subjected to some form of a parliamentary process before it becomes binding. We can do this by strengthening the existing international parliamentary forums like the Inter-Parliamentary Union to co-determine with the UN General Assembly or Security Council the shape of world policies.'[53] Norbert

---

50   Council of Europe Parliamentary Assembly. 1 October 2009. 'United Nations reform and the Council of Europe member states'. Resolution 1688 (2009).

51   'PACE: Global governance must be based on democratic principles, debate on UN's parliamentary dimension', 1 October 2009 (www.unpacampaign.org).

52   Inter-Parliamentary Union. 15 February 2010. '122nd Assembly and related meetings: Governing Council Item 13, Preparations for the 3rd World Conference of Speakers of Parliament, Annex I: Summary of decisions of the Second Meeting of the Preparatory Committee'. Document CL/186/13-R.1, p. 2.

53   Abdi, Abdirahin H. 20 July 2010. 'Address of the Speaker of the East African Legislative Assembly on the occassion of the 3rd Conference of World Speakers', Geneva.

Lammert, President of the German Bundestag, took an opposing position defending the status quo. In his speech he argued that the IPU was 'neither a world parliament nor a subsidiary organization of the UN', and nor should it become either.[54] In contradiction to the resolution of the Bundestag itself, he spoke out against a structural reform. Under Lammert's aegis, an alliance between Arab and European parliamentary Presidents was successful in maintaining this position (this was still before the Arab Spring). 'The World Conference of Speakers of Parliament', wrote the *Neue Zürcher Zeitung*, 'passed a sober resolution in which Western pressure curtailed the ambitious plan to create a world parliament to realistic dimensions.'[55] However, Abdul Aziz Al Ghurair, the billionaire Speaker of the House of the Federal National Council (FNC) of the United Arab Emirates, spoke out at the same time in favour of IPU support for the creation of a new institution, 'an international independent body representing peoples of the world to act as a parliamentary arm for the United Nations (UN) and hold any country—whatever be big or small—accountable democratically if it flouts its international responsibilities as per principles of international law and legitimacy'. This, he said, would not replace the IPU but complement it.[56] In January 2013, the East African Legislative Assembly passed an official resolution lamenting 'the insufficient formal involvement of elected representatives in the work of the United Nations' and supporting the establishment of a UNPA.[57] In the overview of the report of the World Economic Forum's Global Redesign Initiative, Richard Samans, Klaus Schwab and Mark Malloch Brown explained that a consultative UN Parliamentary Assembly was 'a necessary means for advancing democratic participation'.[58]

The European Parliament resolution of 2011

Meanwhile, in the European Parliament it was now a delegate from the German FDP, Alexander Graf Lambsdorff, who was responsible for UN issues. Before his election as an MEP in 2004 he had worked in the German foreign office. Lambsdorff did not think a UNPA was a good idea. The strongest argument against it, in his view, was that the issue of how to involve undemocratic countries was an insoluble problem. This meant that the drafts drawn

54 Lammert, Norbert. 20 July 2010. 'Rede des Präsidenten des Deutschen Bundestages, Prof. Dr. Norbert Lammert, auf der 3. Weltkonferenz der Parlamentspräsidenten in Genf'.
55 Neue Zürcher Zeitung. 22 July 2010. 'Idee für ein Weltparlament gestutzt'.
56 Emirates News Agency (WAM). 20 July 2010. 'UAE calls for world body for democratic accountability'.
57 East African Legislative Assembly. 29 January 2013. 'Resolution of the East African Legislative Assembly on the establishment of a United Nations Parliamentary Assembly'.
58 World Economic Forum. Everybody's Business: Strengthening International Cooperation in a More Interdependent World Report of the Global Redesign Initiative. Cologny/Geneva, 2010, pp. 34-5.

up by Lambsdorff for recommendations by the European Parliament to the Council on UN policy always excluded the issue of a UNPA. Its supporters in the Parliament were obliged to propose amendments. In 2011, such a proposal, drawn up by Jo Leinen, Elmar Brok and the two liberal MEPs Alexander Alvaro from Germany and Andrew Duff from Great Britain, was adopted. So the resolution passed by the European Parliament on 8 June 2011 included the following recommendation addressed to the Council: 'to advocate the establishment of a UNPA within the UN system in order to increase the democratic nature, the democratic accountability and the transparency of global governance and to allow for greater public participation in the activities of the UN, acknowledging that a UNPA would be complementary to existing bodies, including the Inter-Parliamentary Union'.[59] This resulted in about 40 societies and associations in Germany as well as over 150 prominent public figures writing an open letter to Federal Chancellor Merkel and Federal Foreign Minister Westerwelle asking them to act on this recommendation and to press for the establishment of a UNPA at the UN General Assembly. The signatory associations included Attac, BUND (Friends of the Earth Germany), the United Nations Association of Germany, the Society for Threatened Peoples, Mehr Demokratie e.V., and World Vision Germany. Individual signatories included 40 professors, around 70 Members of the Bundestag and of the European Parliament, from all parties, Chair of the SPD Sigmar Gabriel, former State Premiers Hans Eichel and Erwin Teufel, numerous former Federal Ministers, the former President of the Bundestag Rita Süssmuth and the former CDU Secretary-General Heiner Geißler. No response to the letter was received.

In November 2011, in response to a formal parliamentary question in the European Parliament, the European Council replied succinctly that it '[did] not have a position on this matter'.[60] A little over two years later, the Belgian Foreign Minister Didier Reynders listed some familiar arguments in a letter to the Campaign. Following extensive discussions at the level of the EU Council Working Group on the United Nations in the course of 2012, the conclusion had been reached that the establishment of a UNPA 'could, for the time being, not be retained as a priority for the EU'. Reynders pointed to the cooperation between the UN and the IPU as a reason. Besides, the UN was an intergovernmental organization whose members were accountable to their national parliaments. In addition, he claimed that a modification of the UN Charter would be

---

59 European Parliament. 8 June 2011. '66th Session of the United Nations General Assembly'. Resolution P7_TA (2011) 0255. Points (be) and (bf).

60 EU Council/European Parliament. 28 November 2011. 'Reply to a question for written answer. Subject: United Nations Parliamentary Assembly'. Doc. P-008768/2011.

necessary, and that this was 'for the moment, unrealistic'. Finally, the establishment of a UNPA would entail a high cost that could not be absorbed.[61]

In June 2012, a group of intellectuals from over ten countries led by Fernando Iglesias, who one month later was elected to the chair of the international council of the WFM, published a joint manifesto 'for a global democracy'. Only a few days after the UN conference on sustainable development in Rio de Janeiro and the G20 meeting in Los Cabos, Mexico, the 25 initial signatories emphasized that the challenges of globalization called for 'the rapid implementation of forms of democratic global governance on all the issues that current intergovernmental summits are evidently incapable of solving'. 'The existing national-state organizations', the manifesto continues, 'have to be part of a wider and much better coordinated structure, which involves democratic regional institutions on all the continents, the reform of the International Court of Justice, a fairer and more balanced International Criminal Court and a United Nations Parliamentary Assembly as the embryo of a future World Parliament.' The signatories included Jacques Attali, Zygmunt Bauman, Ulrich Beck, Noam Chomsky, Susan George, Saskia Sassen and Vandana Shiva.[62] A proposal for support for a parliamentary assembly at the UN brought into the chamber of deputies of the Italian Parliament in November 2013 referred to this manifesto in its rationale. It was initiated by the MP Federica Mogherini of the Democratic Party. Three months later she was appointed Italian Foreign Minister and left the parliament. From 2014 to 2019 she then served as High Representative of the EU for Foreign Affairs and Security Policy. Her hands were tied on this subject, though, since it was not brought up and supported by any EU member state government.

The de Zayas recommendations

The proposal for a parliamentary assembly was now also raised in an official context at the UN for the first time. On the initiative of Cuba, a one-party state that severely restricts political and civic rights, the UN Human Rights Council had passed a resolution for the 'Promotion of a democratic and equitable international order' and had mandated an independent expert under UN special procedures to report on this task. The resolution, passed by 29 votes in favour with 12 votes against and 5 abstentions, included detailed consideration of the preconditions for 'a democratic and equitable international order'. Among them were 'the right to equitable participation of all, without any dis-

---

61   Letter from Didier Reynders. 26 February 2014. 'Objet: United Nations Parliamentary Assembly'.
62   'Intellectuals call for rapid implementation of forms of democratic global governance'. 26 June 2012 (www.unpacampaign.org).

crimination, in domestic and global decision-making'.[63] The same wording has been used in various resolutions at the UN General Assembly on this topic since 2004, which have been regularly adopted by a two-thirds majority.[64] To date, votes against have come predominantly from Europe and the USA and their closest allies. Considering it originally was a Cuban initiative, they see the mandate as not much more than a tool for political propaganda. Nonetheless, according to the UN Human Rights Council, the newly-appointed independent expert was to 'identify possible obstacles to the promotion and protection of a democratic and equitable international order, and to submit proposals and/or recommendations to the Human Rights Council on possible actions in that regard'. The person elected to carry out this task was Alfred de Zayas, a US American born in Cuba who had worked for over twenty years as a high-ranking UN official in the area of human rights. This expert in international law, who taught in Geneva, announced that he would be looking at the proposal for a parliamentary assembly at the UN. And in a report presented to the UN Human Rights Council on 10 September 2013 he described this proposal as a 'promising initiative' and recommended that the Council commission a study on it. A representative from Egypt, where the democratically elected president had been removed in a coup d'état only a few months earlier, said during the debate that his country viewed 'in positive regard the reference to the proposed United Nations Parliamentary Assembly as one instrument of involving the global public opinion in the global decision-making process'.[65] One month later, on 28 October 2013, de Zayas recommended in a report to the UN General Assembly that the UN should hold a conference to discuss proposals such as those for a worldwide assembly of parliamentarians and for a new world court of human rights. At a press conference for the presentation of the report at the UN headquarters in New York, the international law expert said that the establishment of a worldwide assembly of parliamentarians was 'indispensable' if global decision-making was to be made truly representative.

Week of Action, Malta and Schwartzberg

Following the fifth international conference on a UNPA, held in the European Parliament in Brussels in October 2013 and including a consultation with de Zayas, the latter declared in a press release that the time was ripe for a world-

63   United Nations. 13 October 2011. 'Resolution adopted by the Human Rights Council: Promotion of a democratic and equitable international order'. A/HRC/RES/18/6, point 6 (h).

64   See for example United Nations. 19 December 2016. 'Promotion of a Democratic and Equitable International Order'. A/RES/71/190., point 6 (h).

65   Roshdy, Hussein O. 10 September 2013. 'Statement at the 24th Session of the Human Rights Council'. Permanent Mission of the Arab Republic of Egypt.

wide assembly of parliamentarians. The Brussels conference was hosted by the MEPs Elmar Brok, Jo Leinen, Isabella Lövin and Graham Watson, from the four largest political groups: the European People's Party, the Progressive Alliance of Socialists and Democrats, the Greens and the Liberals. The meeting of the international campaign signalled at the same time the launch of the first 'Global Week of Action for a World Parliament'. Activists had organized events in more than fifty cities around the world calling for the establishment of a democratically-elected world parliament. In their call to action they expressed their fear 'that our current political system is inadequate to deal with growing global challenges'. They argued that the primary concern of governments was to defend what they consider to be in their national interests and not 'the common good of humanity and the environment'. By contrast, a world parliament would be 'an instrument to find and implement solutions that are democratic, accountable and serve the best interest of humanity'.[66] It was decided that the week of action should be held every year in October. In 2014, actions calling for a world parliament were organized in 40 locations around the world. The aim of the global action week is to increase knowledge of the call and international publicity for it. The week was intended to inspire widespread grassroots action and to complement the UNPA campaign's perceived diplomatic approach with more radical public action. As yet, this did not work out as some had hoped. Each year less activities were held and the COVID-19 pandemic disrupted the little momentum that was left. In 2022, the Young World Federalists, an international youth organization created three years earlier, organized a few events to revive the initiative.

The UNPA proposal, however, continued to attract steady support. At the Commonwealth summit meeting in Sri Lanka in November 2013, the Maltese Foreign Minister George Vella, who in 2019 became Malta's President, called on the governments of the Commonwealth member states and the Commonwealth Parliamentary Association to support the international campaign for a UNPA. Pointing out that the Commonwealth includes 54 members, Vella said that it could play a major role in bringing about the adoption of an assembly at the UN to strengthen 'representation and parliamentary diplomacy'.[67] To the best of our knowledge, Vella was the first foreign minister in office to speak out in support of the proposal since Ernest Bevin in 1945. With its support for the concept of a 'common heritage of humanity' during the negotiations that led to the Law of the Sea Treaty, Malta had already demonstrated its

---

66 Global Week of Action for a World Parliament. 2013 'Let the People Decide - World Parliament Now!'
67 'Vella calls on Commonwealth to support creation of UN Parliamentary Assembly'. 16 November 2014 (www.maltatoday.com.mt).

openness to progressive ideas before. The Maltese UN mission in New York was looking into the matter but eventually did not take action. It appears they were expecting to receive instruction from the capital but none was forthcoming at the time.

In a number of papers and monographs published in the last decades, Joseph E. Schwartzberg (1928 to 2018), a Professor of geography at the University of Minnesota until his retirement in 2000, put forward various proposals for weighted voting in the UN General Assembly, a World Parliamentary Assembly and other organs of the UN system. Most of these involved the use of simple mathematical formulas. The most comprehensive of these works, 'Transforming the United Nations System: Designs for a Workable World', was published by the United Nations University Press in November 2013 with a warm endorsement of Boutros Boutros-Ghali, among others. A year later Schwartzberg established the Workable World Trust to promote the recommendations included in his book that was translated into seven languages.

In terms of a World Parliamentary Assembly he envisaged three stages of development in his 2013 book, the first two of which were largely in line with the UNPA campaign's approach which indeed he had helped shape and endorsed from the beginning. Thus, at first there would be in his view a consultative assembly made up of representatives of national parliaments which later, in a second step, would be transformed into a popularly elected body with increasing legislative competence. Schwartzberg suggested specific formulas for the apportionment of seats, though, something the UNPA campaign deliberately did not do. In his opinion, in the first stage seats should be distributed per country based on respective population numbers, economic weight and the principle of equality. In the second stage he suggests that the method should be changed in a way so the *number of seats* per country is equivalent to the square root of its population size, thus applying the Penrose formula mentioned before. However, on top he proposed that each seat should have a different *voting weight* based on the square root of the total number of seats assigned to a given country. He believed that this would be 'one possible and reasonable solution' to achieve a system 'politically acceptable to the demographically larger powers' and still making sure the smaller ones were adequately represented. In a third stage then, to achieve full proportional representation, the planet would be divided into a set of roughly equal 'electoral fields', in demographic terms. If possible this would be done in line with nation-state borders and existing subnational divisions but often not so, in particular as many small countries would have to be grouped together. This was a long-term scenario Schwartzberg did not believe was likely to come into being 'before the end of the present century.'[68]

The report by the Albright-Gambari Commission

In 2014, under the co-chairmanship of the former US Secretary of State Madeleine Albright and the former Nigerian Foreign Minister Ibrahim Gambari, and in the tradition of the Commission on Global Governance, a 'Commission on Global Security, Justice, and Governance' was formed. Among the members of the 16-person Commission, whose work was supported by The Hague Institute for Global Justice and the Stimson Center in Washington D.C., was the former Canadian Foreign Minister and President of the WFM Lloyd Axworthy. In the run-up to the 70th anniversary of the founding of the UN, the Commission published a report in June 2015 containing 80 recommendations designed to counter the current 'crisis of global governance'. The recommendations include the establishment of 'a UN parliamentary network'. 'Adopting a pragmatic approach toward strengthening UN-citizen relations and overcoming the world body's democratic deficit, a United Nations Parliamentary Network established under UN Charter Article 22 could wield tremendous potential for expanding public knowledge of and participation in the work of the preeminent global institution', the report stated. A UN parliamentary network made up of deputies from the national parliaments 'would complement the work of the Inter-Parliamentary Union and the longer-term efforts of civil society organizations to develop a transnational democratic culture'.[69] One passage in the report goes into more detail to emphasize the different purposes of the IPU. Whereas the latter concerns itself principally with national issues, the network would focus on the UN and on decision-making at the global level. The report points to the parliamentary conference of the WTO and to the parliamentary network of the World Bank and the IMF, founded in 2000, as models. In contrast with these, however, the UN parliamentary network would be formally linked to the UN. Experts in the field have questioned where exactly the difference would lie between the parliamentary network proposed in this report and the proposal for a parliamentary assembly already on the table for some time.

Unlike with previous panels of this kind, this work was not expected to finish with the publication of the report. Bearing in mind the successful examples

---

68   Schwartzberg, Joseph. 2013. Transforming the United Nations System. Designs for a Workable World. Tokyo, New York, Paris: United Nations University Press, pp. 52, 59.

69   Commission on Global Security, Justice & Governance. 'Confronting the Crisis of Global Governance'. The Hague Institute for Global Justice and The Stimson Center, Juni 2015, pp. xv, 84.

of the International Campaign to Ban Landmines and the Coalition for the International Criminal Court, the Commission aimed to promote the creation of new coalitions for the implementation of its recommendations involving different actors such as governments, NGOs and businesses. The Commission was thus pursuing a dual strategy. On the one side it suggested simultaneous work on several specific proposals. For example, the report said that 'specific UN task forces' made up of permanent representatives from all major world regions could deliberate on reform of the organs of the UN, including the establishment of a UN parliamentary network. At the same time, it was promoting the organization of a 'World Conference on Global Institutions' to mark the 75th anniversary of the UN in 2020, with the purpose of introducing institutional reforms in the system of global governance. This could include the consideration of amendments to the UN Charter, as the report explained.[70]

---

70   Ibid., pp. 109-10.

10. Autocratization, the UN at 75, and the global polycrisis

The election of Trump and autocratization

In a surprise result, Donald Trump won the US election on November 8, 2016, and became 45th President of the United States. He received 304 of the 538 electoral votes, the distribution of which favors states with smaller populations. In the popular vote Hillary Clinton was ahead by 2.1%, causing many to doubt the fairness of the electoral college system. This result was a blow to the Albright-Gambari Commission, which had probably anticipated that they would be able to work with a Democratic administration under Clinton to push their plan of a UN reform summit in 2020. Instead, there was now a nationalist president in the White House who under the slogan of 'America First' undermined his own State Department's influence, shattered US relations across the world, announced cuts in US contributions to the UN, and in a symbolic step withdrew US support for the Paris climate agreement, among other things. At the same time, Trump did not hold back with his admiration of authoritarian leaders such as Russian's President Putin or Xi Jinping, Chinese President and the leader of the Chinese Communist Party.

Trump's presidency was perceived by many, and rightfully so, as a threat to democracy, multilateralism, and indeed to world peace. It represented a tentative climax of national populism that was gaining ground in many countries. One such example was the referendum on the UK's continued EU membership in June 2016 when by a margin of 3.78 per cent voters decided in favour of Brexit. Scholars warned that national populism was part of a 'wave of autocratization' that reminded of the breakdown of democracies in the 1930s. According to their analysis, since around 2010, each year more countries were now on record that moved toward autocracy compared to such that made progress in democratization.[1] This trend did not stop from established democracies. Trump's disdain of democracy and the US constitution, for instance, reached a high point when he led a criminal conspiracy to overturn the results of the 2020 Presidential elections and incited a right-wing mob to storm the US

---

1   Lührmann, Anna, and Staffan I. Lindberg. 2019. 'A Third Wave of Autocratization Is Here: What Is New about It?' Democratization 26 (7): 1095–1113.

Capitol on 6 January 2021.[2] Similar scenes unfolded almost exactly two years later when a mob of disappointed supporters of ousted right-wing ex-president Jair Bolsonaro of Brazil rioted in Brasilía's government district. In 2016, the United States was downgraded from a 'full democracy' to 'flawed democracy' in the Economist Intelligence Unit's annual global democracy assessment.

Democracy Without Borders

It became apparent that the vision of a world parliament, and a UNPA as a first step, had to be pursued as part of a larger strategy of defending and strengthening democracy. A success of democracy at the national level is a major precondition for global democracy. A slowdown of democratization and threats to democracy across the world's states undermined the goal of a global parliament and thus needed to be addressed. The Committee for a Democratic U.N., which had been steering the UNPA campaign for ten years since its launch in 2007, decided to reinvent itself as a group that promotes democracy at all levels, albeit with a focus on global governance. It became part of the new international civil society organization Democracy Without Borders, or DWB in short, which was continued to be led by Andreas Bummel as Executive Director.

'Democratization at the national and global levels is strongly connected. As democracy comes under pressure worldwide, a holistic approach is needed that recognizes this relationship', the group announced, stressing in its mission statement, among other things, that it promotes a 'strong collaboration between all forces that support the establishment and strengthening of democratic principles at the national, regional, and international levels.'[3]

In the meantime, the DWB-led UNPA campaign continued. In November 2016, it was announced that six current UN-appointed independent experts recently expressed their support of a UNPA in addition to four former ones and numerous former UN officials. The UN's special rapporteur on rights to freedom of peaceful assembly and of association, Maina Kiai from Kenya, noted on this occasion that 'one weakness of the United Nations is that its member states are represented solely through the executive branch. The involvement of additional actors such as parliamentarians and civil society is critical to democratizing the UN.'[4]

---

2   This is well documented in: U.S. House of Representatives. 2022. Final Report of the Select Committee to Investigate the January 6th Attack on the United States Capitol. Washington D.C.: U.S. Government Publishing Office.
3   See www.democracywithoutborders.org.
4   UNPA Campaign. 3 Nov. 2016. 'United Nations experts endorse the creation of a UN Parliamentary Assembly'. (www.unpacampaign.org).

In May 2017 the campaign brought together representatives of twelve governments at an off-the-record briefing on the UNPA proposal in New York, hosted by Canada's UN mission. Although the meeting was not official, DWB saw this as an important step in engaging with open-minded governments, with a view to eventually persuading one or more of them to take the initiative. A summary of an international roundtable organized by Parliamentarians for Global Action in the same month in the Dutch parliament in The Hague highlighted 'the necessity of parliamentary representation in the form of a decision making or advisory body to the UN.'[5]

The first English edition of this book was published a year later and over time a number of DWB chapters emerged across the world. The first among them were in Sweden, led by Petter Ölmunger, a minister in the Evangelical Lutheran Church of Sweden, and another in Kenya. For several years, the group was supported primarily by the Workable World Trust, which continued after Joseph Schwartzberg's death in 2018, managing part of his estate. The trust was wound up four years later, as planned, after all its funds had been distributed to various initiatives.

A low point of inter-parliamentarism

In a low point in the history of inter-parliamentarism, the IPU turned out to be much less progressive than even the UN. At the UN Human Rights Council, historic progress had been made on LGBT rights since in 2011 a resolution had been adopted, led by South Africa, that requested a report 'on discriminatory laws and practices and acts of violence against individuals based on their sexual orientation and gender identity'. According to retired Archbishop and South African Nobel peace laureate Desmond Tutu, 'the fight against homophobia was similar to the campaign waged against racial apartheid in South Africa.'[6] The report was presented six months later by the UN's High Commissioner for Human Rights and was updated subsequently based on another resolution on the subject. In 2016, the Human Rights Council created the mandate of an Independent Expert 'on protection against violence and discrimination based on sexual orientation and gender identity'.

A wave of outrage went through the LGBT community and beyond when the IPU Assembly convened in Geneva in March 2018 voted to ban a debate at the IPU on the 'role of parliaments in ending discrimination based on sexual

---

5   PGA. 20 June 2017. 'Roundtable on Strategies to Strengthen the United Nations by Increasing Democratic Representation.'

6   Frymann, Abigail. 27 July 2013. 'I'd Rather Go to Hell than Worship a Homophobic God': Desmond Tutu Speaks out as He Compares Gay Rights to the Struggle against Apartheid in South Africa.' The Daily Mail. (www.dailymail.co.uk).

orientation and gender identity, and ensuring respect for the human rights of LGBTI persons'. It would have been the first time for the IPU to discuss LGBT issues. Around 50 per cent of votes were recorded in favour of the ban, 39 per cent disagreed, and 10 per cent abstained.[7] The Ugandan Speaker of Parliament who led the effort, supported by the delegations of China, Iran, Russia, Saudi Arabia and others, declared that '[t]oday, we have made a final vote that will prohibit the issue of LGBT from appearing on the IPU agenda.'[8] According to the Swedish IPU delegate Teres Lindberg, 'it felt like the assembly was filled with hatred' and the vote was 'a major setback in the history of the IPU.'[9]

The IPU's Twelve Plus group, composed of countries from Europe as well as Australia, Canada and New Zealand, subsequently organized an unofficial side event on LGBT issues in the following year. Speaking at this event, Indian parliamentarian Shashi Tharoor cautioned that the IPU's refusal to even discuss LGBT rights was a confirmation of the fact that 'parliaments are not always in the vanguard of social change'. In India, too, he recalled, it was not the parliament that took action but it was the Supreme Court that in 2018 declared section 377 of the Indian Penal Code unconstitutional and thus decriminalized homosexuality in the country.[10] The IPU thus became a warning that the powers of a global parliament must be limited by a global constitution that grants basic human rights that are not at the discretion of parliament.

The IPU reviews its 'political project' at the UN

In the run-up to the fifth World Conference of Speakers of Parliament, which the IPU planned to convene in 2020, the organisation launched a review of its UN-related activities, which ended up revealing serious issues. The records of the first preparatory meeting already noted that 'formally, the institutional relationship between the IPU and the United Nations has gone as far as it can in terms of having identified and utilized all processes and venues that are normally granted to observer entities.' Among a number of challenges, the document listed a lack of capacity 'to follow UN negotiations in depth' and to 'advance specific parliamentary input'.[11] In October 2019, the results of a survey of member parliaments were presented at the IPU's gathering in Belgrade.

7   IPU. 2018. 'Results of the Roll-Call Vote on the Unfinished Business of the 138th Assembly.' In Summary Records of the Proceedings of the 139th Assembly, 39 (www.ipu.org).

8   Daily Monitor. 18 Oct. 2018. 'Gay Agenda Permanently Banned from IPU Assemblies.' (monitor.co.ug).

9   Video recording of the side-event organized by the IPU's 12 Plus Group at the 141st IPU Assembly in Belgrade, Serbia, on Leaving No-One behind: LGBTI Inclusion and the SDGs. October 16, 2019. (www.youtube.com).

10 Ibid.

11 IPU. 2019. 'Fifth World Conference of Speakers of Parliament. First Meeting of the Preparatory Committee (Geneva, 8-9 February 2019).' CONF-2020/PrepCom1/4-R.1, p. 4.

It was the first survey of its kind on the subject. According to the IPU, the low response rate of 27.9 per cent suggested that 'many parliaments are either not engaged with the United Nations in a significant way or do not see the need to involve themselves in UN affairs'.[12] At a meeting of the IPU's UN Committee, a member of the IPU's staff noted that there 'were two overarching conclusions from the survey. Firstly, parliaments were mostly absent from key UN processes. Secondly, parliaments were not using their full oversight potential'. In response, Pakistani Senator Farooq Hamid Naek outlined the UNPA proposal and urged the IPU to support it as a means that allows 'elected representatives to exercise a parliamentary function directly at international level'. The former Minister of Justice's plea was blocked by a staff member of the IPU Secretariat who claimed that governments would never support a UNPA, that it would require UN Charter reform, that selecting UNPA members would be hugely difficult, and that it was doubtful whether citizens would feel represented by this global body. The IPU staffer closed the debate before it even started by saying that 'after holding many discussions on whether to establish a UN Parliamentary Assembly, it was overwhelmingly clear that there was no appetite for one'.[13] If anything, this episode highlighted that the IPU administration is opposed to setting up a UNPA, while at least some IPU delegates are open to the idea, if not outright supportive, and wish to discuss it.

A similar dynamic could be observed in the context of a panel discussion at the in-person segment of the fifth world conference of speakers of parliament, which took place in 2021. In this case, the former Dutch Senator, Member of the IPU Executive Committee and international law expert Nico Schrijver, a Professor at Leiden University, pointed out that creating a consultative UNPA of national parliamentarians was an opportunity 'for national parliaments and the IPU' to exercise control of global governance. 'To exert maximum parliamentary influence', he said, 'it is better to be within and part of the UN than remaining outside its institutional structure', implicating that a UNPA would need to exist in conjunction with the IPU. Describing a win-win scenario, he added that the IPU 'could serve as the de facto mother organ and Secretariat of the UNPA'.[14] By contrast, however, the IPU's official conference report prepared by the IPU Secretariat claimed that there was 'overall agreement'

---

12 Id. 2019. 'Reporting by Members on IPU-Related Activities: Survey Report on the Engagement of Parliaments with the United Nations.' CL/205/12-R.2, p. 1.

13 Id. 2019. 'Summary Records of the Proceedings of the 141st IPU Assembly', pp. 120-2.

14 Schrijver, Nico. 2021. 'Panel Contribution to IPU World Conference of Speakers of Parliament, Panel 5 on Parliaments and Global Governance: The Unfinished Agenda.'

that the 'lack of parliamentary inclusion in UN processes would be better solved using existing structures, notably the IPU'.[15]

This approach was challenged by an evaluation of the IPU's so-called 'political project at the United Nations' carried out on its own behalf by Global Partners Governance, a London-based consultancy firm, in the course of 2020. Their report, presented at an IPU assembly in Indonesia in early 2022, showed that existing arrangements were insufficient to achieve even minimal goals, and that the IPU's influence at the UN was questionable. In blunt language, the study pointed out that the UN was not keen 'to strengthen parliaments' ability to contribute to UN decision-making processes or call the UN to account for its policies and decisions'. This was not possible to start with because the IPU had 'no formal role in the UN policy process'. Its observer status at the UN, the assessment highlighted, 'does not cover the ability to participate in negotiations, table papers or motions within the UN, and does not even entitle it to distribute its own resolutions through the UN system'. Further, there was no recognition 'that the IPU might perform a unique role in bringing the parliamentary voice to UN deliberations'. All in all, the IPU had no 'clear central strategy' with regard to its role at the UN and for sure it had no role and authority to oversee UN activities or to participate in UN decision-making.[16] These are features, of course, a UNPA is supposed to have.

The IPU's approach did not change as a result of this devastating assessment. A document approved by its Governing Council in Kigali in October 2022 stated, among other things, that '[o]pening up UN processes to parliamentary scrutiny and input is best done through the intervention of national parliaments vis-à-vis their respective governments (national level intervention) as opposed to the IPU's intervention as the representative of the world's parliamentary community at the UN (global level intervention)'. It further elaborated that 'the IPU's political work at the UN should aim, in the first instance, at strengthening the capacities of parliaments to hold their governments to account for what they say or do at the UN.'[17] Thus, the IPU once again dismissed the idea of establishing a meaningful parliamentary role in UN processes and also ignored its own findings that action by national parliaments cannot fill this gap.

---

15   IPU. 2021. 'Fifth World Conference of Speakers of Parliament. Report on the Conference, Vienna, Austria, 7-8 September 2021', pp. 17-8.
16   Global Partners Governance. December 2020. 'Analysis of the IPU's Political Project', pp. 6-9.
17   IPU. 2022. 'The IPU Political Project at the United Nations. Implementation Roadmap. Endorsed by the IPU Governing Council at Its 210th Session.'

The Swiss government's report

More than a year before the outbreak of the COVID-19 pandemic, Daniel Jositsch, a member of the Swiss parliament's upper house representing the canton of Zürich, submitted a motion calling on the government to present a report on whether it believes there is a democratic deficit at the United Nations and how it should be remedied. The motion, which was unanimously adopted in March 2019, additionally asked the government to state whether a UN Parliamentary Assembly 'in the sense of a second chamber representing the population' was considered a useful model.[18]

The request was forwarded to the Swiss foreign ministry which presented a report 1.5 years later. The document revealed a sceptic stance that stood in contrast to the open-mindedness in Switzerland on the subject in the past. The foreign ministry claimed that since there was no universally accepted definition of democracy, it was *per se* impossible to determine a democratic deficit. It argued that the UN as an intergovernmental organization could only be judged by its own Charter which did not include provisions concerning democracy. The report said that the government thus could not recognize 'a general democratic deficit at the UN' and in turn there was no starting point for examining how such a deficit might be addressed.

The report devoted three of its 19 pages on the UNPA proposal. If something more than a consultative body was to be established, it claimed, the UN's Charter would have to be amended. 'However, such a renegotiation of the UN Charter is not in Switzerland's interest, as many of its achievements would probably no longer be reached to the same extent in the current world situation', the document stated, adding that 'a growing number' of UN members would insist on continuing the exclusive representation of states through governments. This group of member states would tend to oppose any effort towards democratization. There would be no agreement on Charter review to start with. The assessment outlined further obstacles and concluded that implementing a UNPA at present was not a realistic project. Due to a possible disadvantage of small states in the allocation of seats it was also 'not fully in Switzerland's interest'.[19]

Jositsch himself, who was President of DWB's new chapter in Switzerland for two years until mid-2021, had a different view. An article the criminal law professor co-authored in August 2020 stated that the 'world's people need an

---

18 Schweizer Parlament. 2018. Postulat 18.4111 von Daniel Jositsch eingereicht am 27.11.2018: 'Demokratisierung der Vereinten Nationen.' (www.parlament.ch).
19 Schweizerische Eidgenossenschaft. 2020. 'Demokratisierung der Vereinten Nationen.' Bericht des Bundesrates in Erfüllung des Postulates 18.4111 Jositsch vom 27.11.2018 (www.admin.ch).

actual say in global affairs that is not intermediated by national governments
and their diplomats. The key ingredient of a new UN should be a democratically elected world parliament'.[20] He moved on to become chair of the Swiss
parliament's IPU delegation. At the IPU's assembly in Kigali in Rwanda in
October 2022, the social democrat pushed for an analysis to be done as to how
implementation of IPU resolutions could be made more effective.

Runup to the UN's 75th anniversary

Unimpressed by the setback represented by Trump's election, a group of NGOs,
among them the Stimson Center, WFM, and the Workable World Trust, in
early 2017 started to promote the idea of a UN 2020 reform summit which
had been suggested in the Albright-Gambari Commission's report. The initiative's long-term thinking did not match the aspirations of UN member states,
though. A draft General Assembly resolution put forward in connection with
the working group on the assembly's revitalization in August 2018 failed to
achieve consensus on a call for 'timely preparations for the seventy-fifth anniversary of the United Nations.' As the UN 2020 initiative's coordinator Fergus
Watt from Canada reported, 'opposition came from Algeria, Indonesia and
some other members of the non-aligned group of states'.[21]

The goal of a 2020 UN summit, pushed forward by civil society, was closely
connected to the proposal for a UNPA. In terms of the latter, an important
step was achieved when the European Parliament in July 2017 passed its annual resolution on the European Union's policy at the UN. The new rapporteur, Andrey Kovatchev from Bulgaria, supported an amendment introduced
by European parliamentarians Jo Leinen, Elmar Brok and Soraya Post. For the
first time since 2011, the EP once again referred to a UNPA and called on the
Council of the EU to foster a debate at the UN 'on the topic of establishing a
United Nations Parliamentary Assembly with a view to increasing the democratic profile and internal democratic process of the organisation and to allow
world civil society to be directly associated in the decision-making process.'[22]
In a reply to a parliamentary question, the EU's foreign affairs representative
Federica Mogherini previously had told the deputies on behalf of the Commission that the EU 'continues to promote reform of the UN system and of its
main bodies and organs', but also that there was still 'no formal position' as

20 Jositsch, Daniel, and Andreas Bummel. 28 Aug. 2020. 'It Is Time for a Democratic Global Revolution.'
    (www.democracywithoutborders.org).
21 Watt, Fergus. 4 April 2019. 'A United Nations summit in 2020: Landing pad or launch pad?' (www.demo-
    cracywithoutborders.org).
22 European Parliament. 5 July 2017. 'Recommendation to the Council on the 72nd Session of the United
    Nations General Assembly'. P8_TA-PROV(2017)0304. See point 1 (bm).

regards the creation of a UNPA.[23] In a response to a question put forward in the Irish parliament, Irish foreign minister Simon Coveney noted that 'Ireland remains open minded' on the concept of a UNPA but no action followed.[24]

In July 2018 the EP took up the issue of a UN 2020 summit. A resolution recommended to the EU Council 'to support the establishment of an open and inclusive intergovernmental preparatory process under the auspices of the UN General Assembly for a UN 2020 summit, on the occasion of the UN's 75th anniversary, that will consider comprehensive reform measures for a renewal and strengthening of the United Nations.' The parliament added that this should go along with advocacy of 'the establishment of a United Nations Parliamentary Assembly within the UN system in order to increase the democratic character, the democratic accountability and the transparency of global governance and to allow for better citizen participation in the activities of the UN.'[25]

A resolution adopted by the 42nd plenary assembly of the World Federation of United Nations Associations convened in the Dominican Republic in October 2018 in almost the same words called for 'a UN 2020 summit that considers comprehensive reform measures, including the creation of a UN Parliamentary Assembly.' One month later, a group of over thirty sitting and former members of parliament, among them the former foreign ministers of Germany and Malta, Sigmar Gabriel and George Vella respectively, warned that 'the UN, the multilateral order and democracy are under attack'. In a joint statement, later printed in the *Guardian* newspaper, they said that a UNPA was needed to 'confront democratic deficits in intergovernmental affairs' and expressed their belief that 'the 75th anniversary of the UN in 2020 must be used as an opportunity to take stock and initiate far-reaching reforms, including the establishment of a UNPA.'[26] In a similar spirit, Amre Moussa, former foreign minister of Egypt and former Secretary-General of the Arab League stated that he was 'delighted' to support a UNPA. 'The rise of the extreme right in some countries and the lack of diplomatic ability is undermining international collaboration. In this situation', he said, a 'UN Parliamentary

---

23 Id. 16 January 2017. 'Answer to a written question - VP/HR - United Nations Parliamentary Assembly', E-006879/2016.

24 Oireachtas. 2018. Dáil Éireann Debate, Thursday, 10 May 2018, written answer to question 67 by Deputy Thomas P. Broughan.

25 European Parliament. 2018. 'Recommendation to the Council on the 73rd Session of the UN General Assembly.' P8_TA(2018)0312.

26 Iglesias, Fernando, Daniel Jositsch, Jo Leinen, Florence Mutua, Syed Naveed Qamar, Ivone Soares, et al. 2019. 'Call to Action on the Creation of a UN Parliamentary Assembly.' The Guardian, March 6, 2019 (www.theguardian.com).

Assembly can help mobilize citizens and parliaments in support of the UN and help strengthen multilateralism and the international system.'[27]

In December 2018, Spanish Foreign Minister Josep Borrell, who previously served as President of the EP, wrote in *El País* that in '2020 the UN turns 75 years old. That may be a good time to discuss at a summit some institutional changes needed to enhance the legitimacy and effectiveness, such as Security Council reform, to make it more representative and to limit the use of the vetoes of the great powers, or the establishment of a Parliamentary Assembly, thereby strengthening the role of civil society and the democratic dimension of the multilateral system.'[28]

Together with CIVICUS and Democracy International, a Cologne-based group primarily focused on promoting direct democracy, DWB co-hosted an informal briefing with the Canadian, Malaysian and Swiss UN missions in New York. With a view of the upcoming 75th anniversary of the UN, the meeting discussed not only a potential UNPA but also a new proposal, a World Citizens' Initiative. While the UNPA belongs to the sphere of democratic representation, citizens' initiatives are participatory instruments which allow groups of citizens to put proposals on the agenda of political bodies. In this case, the idea is that the UN General Assembly or the UN Security Council would have to consider citizen proposals that are formally registered and reach a certain threshold of global support.[29] As was the case two years ago, the meeting was off the record. Representatives from ten governments attended, and some of the questions and concerns they raised seemed to indicate that, overall, they hadn't seriously studied the proposals on the agenda. Civil society and activists, though, continued to do so. The outcome document of an alternative 'People's Assembly' hosted by Global Call to Action Against Poverty together with dozens of other groups in September 2019 in New York endorsed the UNPA proposal and the creation of a World Citizens' Initiative 'to ensure that the citizens of the world have a greater voice in global affairs'.[30]

27　UNPA Campaign. 13 May 2019. 'Amre Moussa: Parliamentary Assembly can help support UN and multilateralism' (www.unpacampaign.org)

28　Borrell, Josep. 2018. 'Reformar, reforzar y, sí, reivindicar las Naciones Unidas.' El País, December 10, 2018, sec. Opinion (elpais.com).

29　Organ, James, and Ben Murphy. 2019. A Voice for Global Citizens: A UN World Citizens' Initiative. Democracy Without Borders, Democracy International, CIVICUS: World Alliance for Citizen Participation (www.worldcitizensinitiative.org).

30　'People's Assembly Resolution.' New York, 24-25 September 2019. (gcap.global).

Public consultations, COVID-19, and the UN75 declaration

UN Secretary-General António Guterres saw the UN's upcoming 75th anniversary as an opportunity for the organization to learn about people's priorities and expectations of international cooperation. For this purpose, he launched the UN's most ambitious effort thus far to gather input from the global public through public consultations, dialogues and surveys throughout 2020. The outbreak of COVID-19, declared a public health emergency of international concern by the World Health Organization on 30 January 2020 and a global pandemic some six weeks later, changed the situation dramatically as health systems came to the brink of collapse. Public life and international travel got disrupted and in many places came to a complete halt. Due to the pandemic, however, 'the number of people who joined the initiative multiplied', the UN reported. According to the final report of the UN75 office, more than 1.5 million people ended up participating online and in other ways.

The report wrote that 'hundreds of thousands of participants in more than 3,000 UN75 dialogues held across the world called on the United Nations to innovate and change the way it works'. It pointed out that some of the most frequently shared and key ideas put forward in the consultations to renew the UN included 'establishing a UN parliamentary assembly as a subsidiary body of the General Assembly under article 22 of the Charter, or introducing a "citizen proposal initiative" to the UN General Assembly', among other items.[31]

The UN2020 coalition with Together First in May 2020 organized a virtual conference that adopted a 'UN75 People's Declaration and Plan for Global Action'. For now, this was the culmination of years of civil society efforts to push for ambitious UN reforms. However, it was already clear that there would be no UN summit on the occasion of the 75th anniversary that could serve as a platform for this. Some governments like Russia had actually been pushing against the idea of having an anniversary summit at all and any dedicated process leading to it. Thus, as a priority, the document called on UN member states to establish 'a mandated post-2020 follow-up mechanism to enhance global governance'. Among the numerous substantive proposals was a UNPA as a medium-term goal. It was stressed that the assembly could be directly elected.[32]

Together First was an initiative of several civil society groups, run by the UN Association of the UK and supported by the Stockholm-based Global Challenges Foundation, that had conducted its own consultations on best ideas for improving the global system. Its origins go back to a conference held

---

31   United Nations. 2021. 'Shaping Our Future Together: Listening to People's Priorities for the Future and Their Ideas for Action. Concluding Report of the UN75 Office' (un75.online), pp. 8, 66.

32   UN2020, and Together First. 2020. 'UN75 People's Declaration and Plan for Action.' (un.org).

by the foundation in 2017, where three papers on global governance reform, selected from over 2,700 submissions, were awarded. One of the winning papers co-authored by Augusto Lopez-Claros, Arthur Dahl and Maja Groff described a framework of enhanced international cooperation and was inspired by Grenville Clarke and Louis Sohn's work in the 1950s and '60s mentioned in an earlier chapter. Based on this, in January 2020, Lopez-Claros and his co-authors published a 540-pages book titled 'Global Governance and the Emergence of Global Institutions for the 21st Century' which includes a chapter on a World Parliamentary Assembly, a term they used synonymously for a UN-PA. In addition, Lopez-Claros, an international economist and former senior official at the World Bank, together with Groff and others established the Global Governance Forum to promote their proposals further.

A statement of the Bahá'í International Community released on the occasion of the UN's 75th anniversary emphasized that 'a second chamber of the General Assembly of the United Nations, where representatives are directly elected' was a proposal 'worthy of further deliberation' as it could 'do much to strengthen the legitimacy and connection people have to that global body'.[33] At the same time, the Stimson Center's Global Governance, Justice and Security Program led by Richard Ponzio continued to emphasize the need of a 'UN Parliamentary Network' as a first step to address the UN's 'democracy and legitimacy deficits'. For instance, the Stimson Center highlighted this proposal, originally put forward by the Albright-Gambari Commission, as one of ten selected 'innovations to renew the UN system' in a report published in June 2020.[34]

At the UN's headquarters in New York, too, in-person conferences were cancelled, restricted and avoided due to the COVID-19 pandemic from April 2020. At the high-level segment of the 75th General Assembly in September, mostly New York-based ambassadors participated, instead of heads of state as usual, and over 100 governments provided pre-recorded video statements. A declaration was adopted calling the pandemic 'the largest global challenge in the history of the United Nations'. It stated that the world, in addition, was plagued by growing inequality, poverty, hunger, armed conflicts, terrorism, insecurity, and climate change, all of which could only be addressed 'through reinvigorated multilateralism'. Despite official rhetoric such as this, the response to the COVID-19 pandemic was characterized by nationalist approaches. The pandemic, with millions of dead and infected, did not usher in a new era of collaboration as world federalists might have hoped and ex-

---

33 Bahá'í International Community. 2020. 'A Governance Befitting: Humanity and the Path Toward a Just Global Order', p. 7.
34 Stimson Center. 2020. UN 2.0: Ten Innovations for Global Governance - 75 Years beyond San Francisco, p. 42-3.

pected. Quite the contrary. 'Coordinated, global leadership was absent', a panel of the World Health Organization found later, stating that 'global tensions undermined multilateral institutions and cooperative action'.[35] The UN declaration did not offer solutions or address specific global reforms, but rather set out twelve general commitments in a variety of fields. Most importantly, as civil society had hoped, it requested the UN Secretary-General to make recommendations on how to advance 'our common agenda and to respond to current and future challenges'.[36] Subsequently, the UN2020 NGO initiative decided to keep pushing for results and continued its work as 'Coalition for the UN We Need', in short C4UN.

The 'We The Peoples' campaign

Working on his report in response to the resolution's request, the UN chief launched another consultation which took place in April and May 2021 via an online platform set up for this purpose. An official summary of the outcome failed to acknowledge that the UNPA proposal was one of the three most popular out of over 500 that were submitted and voted on by the participants. Moreover, it ignored the fact that a UNPA was even a distinct proposal, stating only that 'other proposals that attracted support were various forms of parliamentary assembly/network, youth assemblies'.[37] The consultation coincided with the publication of a civil society statement 'for inclusive global governance' which became the platform of a new campaign.

Led by DWB, CIVICUS and Democracy International and called 'We The Peoples' as a reference to the opening words of the UN Charter, the campaign insisted that the UN's high-flying rhetoric be followed by action. Among other things, UN Secretary-General Guterres had noted in a speech that 'a new model for global governance' was needed, one that must be 'based on full, inclusive and equal participation in global institutions'.[38] With this in mind, the statement called on the UN and its member states to implement 'three specific institutional changes to strengthen the inclusive and democratic character of the UN': the instrument of a World Citizens' Initiative, a UN Parliamentary Assembly and a UN Civil Society Envoy. The number of endorsing

35 Independent Panel for Pandemic Preparedness and Response. 2021. COVID-19: Make It the Last Pandemic. A Summary. (theindependentpanel.org).

36 United Nations. 21 Sep. 2020. 'Declaration on the Commemoration of the Seventy-Fifth Anniversary of the United Nations.' UN Doc. A/75/L.1.

37 Igarapé Institute. 2021. 'Accelerating Inclusive Global Collaboration: Summary of the We the Peoples Digital Consultation.' (igarape.org.br), p. 9, see also pp. 34, 36. The UNPA proposal had around 80 votes, over 90% of them in favour.

38 Guterres, António. 2020. 'Tackling the Inequality Pandemic: A New Social Contract for a New Era.' Nelson Mandela Annual Lecture 2020. July 18, 2020.

civil society groups and networks grew to over 200. These included Action-Aid, Avaaz, the Coalition for the UN We Need, Global Call to Action Against Poverty, Global Challenges Foundation, Global Governance Forum, Greenpeace, Open Society Foundations, Together 2030, Together First, WFM or Forus International, an alliance of over 60 national NGO platforms representing more than 22,000 organizations, to name but a few. This was making it one of the best supported civil society initiatives in this field in a long time. It was telling though, that a number of NGOs and groups invited to join were unable or unwilling to do, for instance because of slow and cumbersome internal procedures or because they felt that the campaign was outside their mandate and didn't grasp how the proposed changes at the UN could help advance their own causes, too.

The Executive Office of the UN Secretary-General assured the campaign that its three proposals were 'greatly appreciated' and would be considered alongside others. There was agreement 'with the underlying premise that global governance needs to be underpinned by more inclusive and representative models of participation'.[39] In a report published in August 2021, Livingstone Sewanyana, who three years earlier had taken over the mandate of UN Independent Expert 'on the promotion of a democratic and equitable international order', endorsed the proposals of the 'We The Peoples' campaign and called on UN member states to do the same.[40]

Breakdown or breakthrough

In his September 2021 report 'Our Common Agenda' UN Secretary-General António Guterres wrote that the 'best projections show that a stark choice confronts us: to continue with business as usual and risk significant breakdown and perpetual crisis, or to make concerted efforts to break through and achieve an international system that delivers for people and the planet'. Held together by the idea of a 'new social contract' and a 'new global deal' the complex document includes a variety of more than 90 proposals across the twelve commitments of the high-level declaration of heads of state and government adopted on the occasion of the UN's 75th anniversary. According to the report, one of the strongest calls emanating from the UN's public consultations 'was to strengthen the governance of our global commons and global public goods'. The document noted that this 'does not require new institutions' and the way

---

39   Letter from Volker Türk, Assistant Secretary-General for Strategic Coordination, 7 July 2021.
40   Sewanyana, Livingstone. 9 Aug. 2021. 'In Defence of a Renewed Multilateralism to Address the Coronavirus Disease (COVID-19) Pandemic and Other Global Challenges. Report of the Independent Expert on the Promotion of a Democratic and Equitable International Order.' UN Doc. A/HRC/48/58.

forward was 'ultimately in the hands of Member States'. Conceptually, the document limits the UN to a supporting role and it did not make suggestions on institutional UN reform. While 'any social contract' also had 'a global dimension' it originates 'at the subnational and national levels', up to each society to determine, the report pointed out. Trust, inclusion and participation were highlighted but the need and possibility of better citizens' representation through a UN parliamentary body was not discussed. Parliaments and parliamentarians, the most direct representatives of the people, were treated as part of a range of 'non-state actors' that needed to be included 'in a form of multilateralism that is more networked'. The document said that the 'United Nations system, including the Secretariat, will also take further steps to become more inclusive. For certain constituencies, such as parliamentarians, the private sector, and cities and subnational authorities, which are crucial and innovative drivers of global change today, we have been asked to consider standing mechanisms for engagement and consultation, consistent with the sovereignty of Member States and provisions of the Charter on membership of the United Nations.' In line with this, options to 'enhance parliamentary inputs at the United Nations' would be explored further 'working with our existing partners'.[41] The latter remark seemed to indicate that the UN was intending to listen primarily to the IPU, arguably its most important 'existing partner' in this field, which would radically limit the scope and creativity of options to be considered. The report suggested that the 'listening exercise' of the UN75 public consultations was the model the UN would follow in the future. As CIVICUS' 2022 State of Civil Society report pointed out, the proposals of the 'We the Peoples' campaign were 'broadly ignored' despite 'extensive civil society engagement with the consultation processes that fed into Our Common Agenda' and although they actually only constituted 'fairly modest steps'. The alternative was for the UN 'to drift into irrelevance', the group wrote.[42] A 'parliamentary statement for inclusive global governance' that supported the 'We The Peoples' campaign, published in January 2022, noted that 'ad hoc consultations and existing mechanisms' were no longer sufficient to satisfy the need of greater participation and inclusion at the UN. Over 120 parliamentarians from all world regions said in the joint statement they were 'convinced that the UN is overdue to implement institutional changes that strengthen its democratic and participatory character'. A 'Group of Friends for Inclusive Global Governance' should be established by UN member states to advance

41   United Nations. 2021. 'Our Common Agenda: Report of the Secretary-General', paras. 5, 62, 19, 104, 119
42   CIVICUS: World Alliance for Citizen Participation. 2022. '2022 State of Civil Society Report.' (civicus.org), p. 48.

the proposals of the 'We The Peoples' platform and perhaps others.[43] Among the signatories was Anthony Giddens, a member of the UK House of Lords and one of the most prominent modern sociologists.

Following the publication of 'Our Common Agenda', the Bahá'í International Community and C4UN under the co-leadership of Daniel Perell organized a series of events in New York and online, bringing together representatives of civil society and UN member states to discuss various dimensions of the report. One of these events was held in September 2022 in collaboration with DWB with a focus on participation and representation at the UN. Malaysia's Foreign Minister Saifuddin bin Abdullah, a member of the Malaysian United Indigenous Party, announced his personal support for a UNPA. Subsequently, he shared his view on Twitter, later renamed "X", and in an article published in the newspaper *Sinar Harian*. In the latter he pointed out, among other things, that the need for a UNPA stems 'from the dissatisfaction of the people and their elected representatives who are disconnected from and denied a real role in intergovernmental platforms and institutions' to the extent that their legitimacy is questioned and they, in turn, become ineffective.[44] Two months later Malaysia held a snap election and Saifuddin was replaced as foreign minister, giving him no opportunity to make this official government policy. At the same time, however, a signatory of the parliamentary statement joined the government as the new minister on the environment and the climate, Nik Nazmi bin Nik Ahmad of the Parti Keadilan Rakyat.

Russia's attack on Ukraine and the global polycrisis

Russia's full-scale invasion of Ukraine, which began on 24 February 2022, met with fierce resistance. Russia failed in its immediate goal of capturing the Ukrainian capital, Kyiv, and overthrowing the government led by Volodymyr Zelenskyy in order to reverse the country's democratic development and stop its Western EU orientation. But Russia continued its attack, including on civilian targets, and tried to occupy as much territory as possible. There was no doubt that this was a blatant violation of the UN Charter and international law which undermined the whole idea of a 'rules-based international order' and put a spotlight on the UN's weakness. According to Democracy Without Borders, the attack was an escalation of the 'covert and open global war of autocratic regimes against democracy' and it confirmed the need of 'a major reform of the UN' that would enable the world organization 'to maintain in-

---

43   See wethepeoples.org/mpstatement/.
44   DWB. 14 Oct. 2022. 'Malaysian foreign minister supports a new UN Parliamentary Assembly.' (democracywithoutborders.org).

ternational peace and security and to deal with global challenges such as climate change or pandemics.'[45] Following Russia's veto in the Security Council which prevented the body from condemning the Russian illegal war of aggression, a special emergency session of the General Assembly was called under the 'Uniting for Peace' mechanism.[46] The assembly adopted a resolution with 141 votes in favor, 5 against and 35 abstentions, demanding, inter alia, that the Russian Federation cease its use of force and 'immediately, completely and unconditionally withdraw all of its military forces from the territory of Ukraine'. But abstentions included China, India and South Africa, which, like most countries in Latin America and Africa, did not impose sanctions as the United States, the European Union and other countries did. At the time, there were 17 high-intensity violent conflicts in the world, including, with most fatalities, in Afghanistan, Yemen and Syria.[47] The Russian war became the most violent and exacerbated global geopolitical rifts and tensions, including the perception of a New Cold War that included China as a major adversary who aligned with Russia. Russian President Vladimir Putin appeared to be making a nuclear threat against the United States and the European Union when he announced on 27 February 2022 that Russia's nuclear forces had been placed on high alert, a status that observers said was the standard anyway. The war disrupted international food and energy supply as Ukraine was a major producer of agricultural products such as grain and Russia the largest gas exporter. Resulting shortages and price shocks affected many parts of the world. In the wake of COVID-19, the UN measured a global decline in the Human Development Index which affected 9 out of 10 countries. It was the first time this occurred for two years in a row since calculations started 32 years ago. 'Global crises have piled up: the global financial crisis, the ongoing global climate crisis and Covid-19 pandemic, a looming global food crisis', the report stated, adding that these 'acute crises are giving way to chronic, layered, interacting uncertainties at a global scale'. It pointed out that the COVID-19 pandemic and the war against Ukraine were 'devastating manifestations' of this new 'uncertainty complex'. Each exposed 'limits of—and cracks in—current global governance' which was operating in a geopolitical order 'creaking under the weight of naked national interests'.[48] Researchers increasingly spoke of a 'global polycrisis' which means 'a single, macro-crisis of interconnected, runaway failures of Earth's vital natural and social

45   DWB. 27 Feb. 2022. 'Russian attack on Ukraine escalates "global war" on democracy, group says.' (democracywithoutborders.org)
46   On Uniting for Peace, see p. 97.
47   Escola de Cultura de Pau. 2022. Alert 2022! Report on Conflicts, Human Rights and Peacebuilding (escolapau.uab.cat), p. 26.
48   UNDP. 2022. Human Development Report 2021/2022, pp. 3-5.

systems that irreversibly degrades humanity's prospects'.[49] Already in 1999, Edgar Morin and Anne Brigitte Kern wrote that 'one is at a loss to single out a-number one problem to which all others would be subordinated. There is no "single vital problem," but many vital problems, and it is this complex intersolidarity of problems, antagonisms, crises, uncontrolled processes, and the general crisis of the planet that constitutes the number one vital problem' and this they characterized as the polycrisis.[50]

In the hope of achieving global governance reforms, civil society was now anticipating a 'Summit of the Future' proposed by Guterres in his 'Our Common Agenda' report which originally was supposed to be held in 2023 but was moved to September in the next year. C4UN in collaboration with a number of groups in March 2023 convened a civil society forum in New York, the first of its kind since the COVID-19 pandemic had broken out, which resulted in 'interim' recommendations across seven thematic fields addressed to UN member states. These included, for instance, setting up an 'environmental governance agency' with 'binding supranational authority' and ideas for global taxation. The document endorsed the 'We The Peoples' campaign proposals.[51] The need of creating a UNPA came up separately in the forum's discussions on human rights and participation, in connection with environmental governance as well as in the track on 'UN and global governance innovation'. Despite the tense global situation, or perhaps because of it, some thought that a review of the UN Charter needed to be discussed, if only to be prepared should an unexpected window of opportunity open up. Already in the margins of the 2022 annual meeting of the Academic Council on the UN System, an independent association of scholars and practitioners studying the UN, a meeting was held that looked at a number of scenarios. A year later, the Global Governance Forum's Augusto Lopez-Claros, with the support of the Global Challenges Foundation, started gathering an international group of around twenty individuals, among them Nobel peace laureate Jody Williams, the former President of the UN General Assembly María Fernanda Espinosa, and the authors of this book. The group explored how the UN Charter could be renewed and refreshed. One of the items the group agreed on was to propose a bicameral decision-making system at the center of a revised Charter that included a parliamentary assembly, the other chamber being composed of representatives appointed by member states. Together, these two chambers at

49 Homer-Dixon, Thomas, Ortwin Renn, Johan Rockström, Jonathan F. Donges, and Scott Janzwood. 2022. A Call for an International Research Program on the Risk of a Global Polycrisis. Cascade Institute.
50 Morin, Edgar, and Anne Brigitte Kern. 1999. Homeland Earth. Cresskill, NJ: Hampton Press, p. 73-4.
51 Coalition for the UN We Need. May 2023. 'Interim People's Pact for the Future. 2023 Civil Society Perspectives on the Summit of the Future.'

some point could become a global legislature empowered with adopting bind-ing world law 'within the limits provided for in a revised Charter'. The Securi-ty Council, or rather its successor body, should be made subordinate to these two assemblies.[52] Ahead of the 28th round of the UN's climate talks, held in Dubai in November 2023, a report of the Climate Governance Commission said that 'empowered with new authorities and capabilities, current and new international governance institutions must exert competent crisis leadership, developing and deploying emergency plans, disaster preparedness, and a new generation of effective policies'. In the field of 'citizen participation in global governance', the report, among other things, referred to the proposals put forward by the 'We the Peoples' campaign.[53] 'Given the global polycrisis and systemic failures of global governance in particular in the field of climate poli-cy we need to improve the efficacy, credibility, and legitimacy of the interna-tional governance systems in a number of respects. The consideration of the creation of a global parliamentary consultative body is one important element of this', commented the Commission's convenor and international lawyer, Maja Groff.[54] The Commission—co-chaired by María Fernanda Espinosa, Mary Robinson, former President of Ireland, and Johan Rockström, Director of the Potsdam Institute for Climate Impact Research—noted that a 'world parliamentary body' composed of a UNPA and the General Assembly over time could provide an 'integrated approach to global governance' as well as accountability to the people.[55] In March 2024, the Climate Governance Com-mission together with the World Federalist Movement and the US-based group Citizens for Global Solutions launched a new platform called Mobiliz-ing an Earth Governance Alliance in order to facilitate implementation of proposals aimed at strengthening global environmental governance, among them a UN Parliamentary Assembly. As WFM's Board Chair John Vlasto argued, under a federal model, 'the UN would still have a General Assembly representing the interests of nations. But it would also have a parliamentary assembly, representing the people, making decisions to serve the common good of humanity.'[56]

52   Global Governance Forum. 2023. 'A Second Charter: Imagining a Renewed United Nations', pp. 26-7.
53   Climate Governance Commission. 2023. 'Governing Our Planetary Emergency.' (stimson.org), pp. 10-1.
54   DWB. 30 Nov. 2023. 'Planetary Crisis Requires Urgent and Bold International Changes: Report.' Democra-cy Without Borders (blog). (democracywithoutborders.org).
55   Climate Governance Commission, p. 77.
56   Interview with Vlasto, John. 2 Dec. 2023. 'Global Governance: "It may take a crisis as big as the one that originated the system to produce the reform it needs"' CIVICUS. (civicus.org).

PART II

Governance and democracy in the 21st century

The phenomenon of industrialization, which began in England in the second half of the 18th century, brought in a period of rapid economic growth, technological innovation and social upheaval which has continued until today and has encompassed the entire globe. These developments could not have been imagined when the calls for a world parliament first arose around the time of the French Revolution. 'The evolution of western industrial society', according to the sociologist Georg W. Oesterdiekhoff, 'represents probably the biggest single event in the history of human culture since the emergence of the species, or since the Neolithic era.'[1] Compared with the industrial dynamism of the last two hundred years, he wrote, the thousand-year history of Neolithic agriculture is 'a slow and boring affair'. Modernity is the story of a continuous striving for ever faster production, mobility, transport and communications. The empirically observable globalization of modernity and industry has meant 'that at no point in the history of the world have the living conditions of so many people undergone such drastic changes in such a short space of time.'[2] A periodical visitor from outer space', wrote the British diplomat and scientist Crispin Tickell, 'would find more change in the last 200 years than in the preceding 2000, and more change in the last 20 years than in the preceding 200.'[3] The sense that this development is accelerating is not new: H. G. Wells made a similar observation in 1902. 'In the past century', he wrote, 'there was more change in the conditions of human life than there had been in the previous thousand years.'[4]

The development of human civilization since industrialization can be gauged with the aid of a few key global statistics. The anthropologist Leslie A.

1   Oesterdiekhoff, Georg W. 2005. Entwicklung der Weltgesellschaft: Von der Steinzeit zur Moderne. Münster: LIT, p. 7.

2   Ibid., p. 55.

3   Tickell, Crispin. 2005. 'Are We Pushing Gaia Too Hard?' The 46th Annual Bennett Lecture for the 50th Anniversary of Geology, University of Leicester.

4   Wells, Herbert George. 1913 [1902]. The Discovery of the Future. New York: B.W. Huebsch, p. 58.

White (1900 to 1975), a neoevolutionist in the tradition of Lewis Henry Morgan, emphasized the fundamental role of energy availability in the development of a system. 'Culture', as he put it in his 'basic law of cultural evolution', 'evolves as the amount of energy harnessed per capita per year is increased, or as the efficiency of the instrumental means of putting the energy to work is increased.'[5] The upheavals of the industrial revolution were literally fuelled by the mechanical exploitation of the energy stored in coal, and later in oil and gas. From 1820 to 2018, the *annual* worldwide consumption of primary energy grew by a factor of over 40, from 389 million tons of oil equivalent to 16 billion (a ton of oil equivalent is the sum of energy released by the burning of one ton of crude oil). From 2008 to 2018, the increase was almost 20 per cent and since 1998 almost 60.[6] World population has grown from about one billion people in 1800 to over 8.1 billion in 2024. It has doubled since 1975. Finally, *annual* global economic output has increased by a factor of over 70 since 1820. The scale of this increase is clearer if we look at *cumulative* economic output over the whole of human history. Using the data gathered by the economist Angus Maddison, it is possible to observe for example that roughly a quarter of the goods and services ever produced in the history of human activity were produced in this century, i.e. since the year 2000. The proportion produced in the 20th century is around 55 per cent, and that in the 19th century already as little as around 5 per cent.[7] In view of such escalating figures, scientists are speaking of 'The Great Acceleration', calling it the most anomalous period in the history of the human species that began 200,000 years ago.[8]

The rapid rise in world population alone gives us some idea of the concomitant rise in the complexity of the human world and of the world system. For if history is made by people, and if currently there are seven times more people alive than two hundred years ago, then today seven times as much history is being made.[9] In 1965, the futurologist Alvin Toffler diagnosed a 'future shock', meaning the 'dizzying disorientation brought on by the premature arrival of the future' that makes human beings 'progressively incompetent to deal rationally with their environments'. Future shock was 'a time phe-

5   White, Leslie A. 1969. The Science of Culture. A Study of Man and Civilization. 2nd ed. New York: Farrar, Straus and Giroux, pp. 368-9.

6   Malanima, Paolo. 2014. 'Energy in History.' In: The Basic Environmental History, 1–29. Heidelberg et al.: Springer, p.17 and: id., World Energy Consumption. A Database. 1820-2018 (2020 Revision) (histecon.fas.harvard.edu).

7   See Maddison, Angus. 2010. 'Statistics on World Population, GDP and Per Capita GDP, 1-2008 AD'; The Economist Online, 28 June 2011 'Quantifying history: Two thousand years in one chart' (www.economist.com). The percentage share before our time is negligible.

8   McNeill, J. R., and Peter Engelke. 2014. The Great Acceleration: An Environmental History of the Anthropocene since 1945. Cambridge, Massachusetts: The Belknap Press, p. 5.

9   The Economist Online, ibid.

nomenon, a product of the greatly accelerated rate of change in society'.[10] As the sociologist Norbert Elias explained over 75 years ago, this acceleration is also a characteristic of an ever-thickening, ever-spreading global mesh of interdependence. 'This "tempo"' he wrote, 'is in fact nothing other than a manifestation of the multitude of intertwining chains of interdependence which run through every single social function that people have to perform, and of the competitive pressure that permeates this densely populated network, affecting directly or indirectly every single individual act.'[11]

A large proportion of the world's population today enjoys historically unprecedented material prosperity. Although there are of course large regional disparities, average global life expectancy is higher than ever. According to UN data it has risen from 47 years in 1955 to 72.6 years in 2019. Nevertheless, the confident faith in progress of earlier times has for an increasing number of people given way to fear of the future and disorientation in the face of continual warfare, genocide, nuclear weapons, terrorism, environmental destruction, the climate crisis, dwindling resources, industrial catastrophes, extreme inequality, hunger, misery, poverty, unemployment and the growing mountain of public debt. Jürgen Habermas spoke of a 'new obscurity' and of the helpless confusion of the intellectual class.[12] The French philosopher Jean-François Lyotard, in his 1979 book 'La Condition postmoderne', announced the total failure of modernity and the beginning of 'postmodernity'. In the modern era, a very condensed version of his argument might say, there was always an overarching vision of the future, an 'idea yet to be realised', which served as orientation and legitimation. Lyotard meant by this the 'grand narratives' such as progress, enlightenment or socialism. The crime of the Holocaust, he argued, had made it clear in the most tragic terms that such grand legitimating narratives had lost their credibility. The downfall of the meta-narratives, as he also called them, meant the simultaneous destruction of the project of modernity. This left 'capitalist techno-science' as the victor, continuing the process of deligitimation in the name of modernity but in doing so actually furthering its destruction.[13]

The continuing crisis of modernity provides the wider context in which the project of a world parliament, of a world legal system and a new global enlightenment, must be seen. Although the idea of a world parliament goes back

---

10   Toffler, Alvin. 1984. Future Shock. Reissue. New York: Bantam, p. 11

11   Elias, Norbert. The Civilizing Process: Sociogenetic and Psychogenetic Investigations. Transl. by Edmund Jephcott. Revised edition. Oxford; Malden, MA: Blackwell, 2000. p. 379

12   Habermas, Jürgen. 1985. Die neue Unübersichtlichkeit. Frankfurt am Main: Suhrkamp, pp. 141, 145.

13   Lyotard, Jean-Francois. 1990 [1984]. 'Randbemerkungen zu den Erzählungen'. In: Postmoderne and Dekonstruktion, ed. by Peter Engelmann and Jean-Francois Lyotard. Stuttgart: Reclam., pp. 49-51.

hundreds of years, it is not obsolete, but on the contrary has become ever more topical and more urgent. It is no longer merely about ensuring world peace. Rather, the question being posed is the much wider one of *world government*, one which reveals at the same time a profound intellectual crisis. The starting point of our deliberations is the influence exerted by human activity on the Earth's ecological balances, which provide the existential basis for the survival of today's global civilization.

11.

**The Anthropocene, planetary boundaries
and the tragedy of the commons**

The era of humankind

In the earth sciences it has become accepted that humanity's impact on the planet is now on a geological scale. The introduction of a new geological era was under consideration, to succeed the Holocene, which began twelve thousand years ago.[1] The intended purpose of such a decision was to put the spotlight on the influence exerted by humankind. The Dutch meteorologist Paul J. Crutzen, who received the Nobel Prize for chemistry for his contribution to research on the ozone hole, argued in *Nature* magazine that the impact of human activity on the global environment had become so significant that the new epoch would have to be called the 'Anthropocene', meaning roughly 'the era of humankind'. The Italian geologist Antonio Stoppani recognized the huge influence of humanity on the environment as early as 1873, and spoke of an 'anthropozoic era'. 'The Anthropocene', Crutzen wrote, 'could be said to have started in the latter part of the eighteenth century, when analyses of air trapped in polar ice showed the beginning of growing global concentrations of carbon dioxide and methane.'[2] The proportion of CO_2 in the atmosphere has risen by more than a third compared with pre-industrial times, and is higher than at any time in the last 2.1 million years.[3] The main cause is the use of fossil energy which was stored up over hundreds of millions of years from the remains of prehistoric organisms and is now being released. It will probably still be possible to find the traces of industrial civilization millions of years from now in sediments and fossils. It is likely, too, that from our time forward, many species will rarely be found in fossil form, or even not at all, which represents another marker. The Harvard biologist Edward O. Wilson, one of the first to use the term 'biodiversity', spoke in 1992 in his book 'The Diversity of Life' of the sixth great extinction in Earth history, brought about by human

---

1 A formal recommendation was made at the 35th International Geological Congress in August 2016, see Zalasiewicz, Jan, et al. 2017. 'The Working Group on the Anthropocene: Summary of evidence and interim recommendations'. Anthropocene 19 (Supplement C):55–60.

2 Crutzen, Paul J. January 2002. 'Geology of mankind'. Nature 415: p. 23.

3 Measured according to boron isotopes in planktic foraminifer shells, see: Bärbel Hönisch et al. 2009. Atmospheric Carbon Dioxide Concentration Across the Mid-Pleistocene Transition, in: Science 324 (5934), pp. 1551–1554.

beings.[4] Researchers believe that some of the plastic waste now spread all over the planet will, under certain conditions, be deposited and geologically preserved. One likely example is the mix of materials referred to as 'plastiglomerate', first found on Hawaii.[5] A study found that plastics 'are already present in sufficient numbers to be considered as one of the most important types of "technofossil" that will form a permanent record of human presence on Earth' in geological sediments.[6] In addition, according to Crutzen, the world's strata from 1945 onwards contain tiny but measurable amounts of artificial radionuclides produced by the detonation of atomic bombs. Up to 1996 over two thousand atomic bombs had been detonated, more than five hundred of them above ground in the atmosphere. Crutzen and others believe that these artificial radionuclides could also constitute a geological marker for the beginning of the Anthropocene.[7] The formal determination of geological epochs is governed by the International Union of Geological Sciences. Identifying exact start dates is part of the exercise. After nearly 15 years of debate, a relevant committee in early 2024 felt it was not possible to single out one particular start date for the Anthropocene across the planet and thus could not formally elevate it to the status of a new epoch. For the time being, the Anthropocene will be treated as a geological 'event', a category that is less rigorous.[8] Whatever the formal geological categorization may be, the concept of the Anthropocene is a means of highlighting the now epochal influence of human activity on the Earth's natural balancing systems. Its significance lies not in an anthropocentric approach interested only in the needs and concerns of human beings; on the contrary, what it acknowledges and emphasizes is the effects of human activity *on all of life on Earth and on the Earth system as a whole*. Human beings and their civilization are inseparably embedded in nature and in the Earth system. According to the political scientist Frederic Hanusch at Gießen University in Germany, the notion of the Anthropocene has not only 'diminished the separation between nature and culture' but also 'opened an entry point into deep time that brought the distant past and the far away future into the present'.[9]

4   Wilson, Edward O. 1992. The Diversity of Life. Cambridge: Belknap Press of Harvard Univ. Press, pp. 32, 278-80.

5   Corcoran, Patricia L., Charles J. Moore, and Kelly Jazvac. June 2014. 'An anthropogenic marker horizon in the future rock record'. GSA Today 24, no. 6 (www.geosociety.org).

6   Zalasiewicz, Jan, et al. 2016. 'The Geological Cycle of Plastics and Their Use as a Stratigraphic Indicator of the Anthropocene.' Anthropocene 13 (March): 4–17, p. 15.

7   Zalasiewicz, Jan, Mark Williams, Will Steffen, and Paul Crutzen. 2010. 'The New World of the Anthropocene'. Environmental Science and Technology 44 (7): 2228–31, p. 2230.

8   Zhong, Raymond. 5 March 2024. 'Are We in the "Anthropocene," the Human Age? Nope, Scientists Say.' The New York Times, (nytimes.com).

9   Hanusch, Frederic. 2023. The Politics of Deep Time. Cambridge Univ. Press, p. 13.

Earth system boundaries

The idea that life on Earth is based on a self-regulating and highly complex integrated system was articulated and popularized by the British scientist James Lovelock (1919 to 2022) in 1979 in his 'Gaia hypothesis'. In Greek mythology, Gaia was the name of the primeval goddess of the Earth from whom all life came. This systems-based perspective has found broad acceptance. Thus, for example, the path-breaking Amsterdam Declaration on Global Change, issued in 2001 by four leading international research networks, spoke of the Earth system behaving 'as a single, self-regulating system comprised of physical, chemical, biological and human components'. The scientists from the participating programmes pointed out in the declaration that Earth system dynamics are not linear but characterized by critical thresholds and abrupt changes. 'Human activities', they wrote, 'have the potential to switch the Earth System to alternative modes of operation that may prove irreversible and less hospitable to humans and other life.'[10] To put it another way: the self-regulating life support system named 'Gaia' could collapse because of human intervention.

Earth system science represents an interdisciplinary research area focused directly on these issues. It aims to create an understanding of the Earth as an integrated system and to evaluate anthropogenic influences. One important topic of research is planetary boundaries. 'These boundaries', wrote the Swedish researcher Johan Rockström and his 27 colleagues in 2009, 'define the safe operating space for humanity with respect to the Earth system.' If these boundaries are crossed, then humans could be faced with 'deleterious or potentially even disastrous consequences'. Over the course of the Holocene, lasting more than ten thousand years, the Earth system had been in an exceptionally stable state, they wrote, without which the development of agriculture and complex societies would not have been possible. The aim had to be to preserve this stable state. So far, critical boundaries have been defined in nine areas. They measure climate change (using the concentration of CO_2 in the atmosphere and changes in radiative forcing); biodiversity loss; interference with the nitrogen and phosphorus cycles; stratospheric ozone depletion; ocean acidification; global freshwater use; change in land use; pollution by chemical and other 'novel entities'; and atmospheric aerosol loading.[11] In a popular book titled 'Breaking Boundaries' that was turned into a Netflix documentary, Rockström and Owen Gaffney, a global sustainability analyst, highlighted that

10 International Geosphere-Biosphere Programme (IGBP), International Human Dimensions Programme on Global Environmental Change (IHDP), World Climate Research Programme (WCRP), and DIVERSITAS. 13 July 2001. 'The Amsterdam Declaration on Global Change'.
11 Rockström, Johan et al. September 2009. 'A safe operating space for humanity'. Nature 461: 472–75.

these boundaries have already been exceeded with respect to climate change, biodiversity loss, land use and the nitrogen cycle. Climate and biodiversity are core boundaries, they explain, that on their own 'can push Earth into a new state'. Parts of the Earth system like the Amazon rainforest, the Greenland ice sheet or the Atlantic jet stream have tipping points that may be crossed. This could result in a cascading and irreversible domino effect.[12] Recent research suggests that freshwater use and environmental pollution boundaries have by now also been crossed.[13]

Carbon emissions and global warming

Especially worrying is the concentration of CO_2 in the atmosphere, for which the critical threshold had until recently been regarded by the Intergovernmental Panel on Climate Change, IPCC, as 450 ppm (parts per million), but which in the opinion of Rockström and other scientists such as James Hansen, the former lead climate researcher at NASA, should be seen at 350 ppm. Measurements taken at the Mauna Loa Observatory on Hawaii on 9 May 2013 exceeded 400 ppm for the first time ever, and will probably remain above this level for generations to come. The upward trend continues and accelerates, with new highs being recorded each year. In May 2024, the concentration reached a new peak of 426.9 ppm.[14] Over the past 800,000 years that are covered by ice core data, levels have fluctuated between 172 and 300 ppm.[15] The IPCC believes that with increasing cumulative CO_2 emissions, the forests and oceans are losing their efficacy as carbon dioxide sinks which will exacerbate the situation as an ever higher proportion of CO_2 will remain in the atmosphere.[16]

In its very first report, in 1990, the IPCC came to the firm conclusion that the emission of anthropogenic greenhouse gases like CO_2 was increasing the greenhouse effect. Over the course of the last one hundred years, an increase in worldwide *average* air and water temperatures of 0.74 °C has been measured, of which according to NASA two-thirds has taken place since 1975. The global mean temperature for 2023 was 1.45°C above the preindustrial baseline calculated for 1850 to 1900, making it the hottest ever recorded by now. All

---

12   Rockström, Johan, and Owen Gaffney. 2021. Breaking Boundaries: The Science of Our Planet. London: Penguin Random House, pp. 74-6, 93.
13   Wang-Erlandsson, Lan, et al. 2022. 'A Planetary Boundary for Green Water.' Nature Reviews Earth & Environment 3 (6): 380–92; Persson, Linn, et al. 2022. 'Outside the Safe Operating Space of the Planetary Boundary for Novel Entities.' Environmental Science & Technology 56 (3): 1510–21.
14   Data from the NOAA Global Monitoring Laboratory (gml.noaa.gov/ccgg/trends/).
15   Lüthi, Dieter, et al. 2008. 'High-Resolution Carbon Dioxide Concentration Record 650,000–800,000 Years before Present.' Nature 453 (7193): 379–82.
16   Intergovernmental Panel on Climate Change (IPCC). 2021. Climate Change 2021. The Physical Science Basis. Summary for Policymakers, point B.4, p. 25 (www.ipcc.ch).

years since 2015 have been over 1°C above pre-industrial levels and are the warmest on record thus far.[17] One of the consequences of global warming is a rise in sea level due to melting ice which affects all coastal areas. A rise of 19.5 centimetres has been measured over the period from 1870 to 2004.[18] According to IPCC scenarios, relative to 1995-2014 figures, a further rise of between 28 and 101 centimetres can be expected by 2100 and an increase of up to 2 meters under a very high emission scenario cannot be ruled out.[19] Indeed, melting of ice sheets has accelerated to a degree that is in line with worst-case scenarios, scientists pointed out.[20] Due to a lag effect, warming and ice melting will continue for centuries to come even if emissions were stopped right now. The overall consequences of the rise in temperature for the stability of the Earth system—because of shifts in ocean currents, for example—are uncertain.

A 2022 IPCC report described impacts of climate change on human societies and elaborated on 127 risks 'which are becoming increasingly complex and more difficult to manage'. According to this assessment, many of them are already 'unavoidable' and potentially irreversible if certain thresholds are exceeded even if global warming slows down later. Mid-term and long-term impacts, including from heat, drought, wildfires, floods, storms and rising seas, will be 'up to multiple times higher than currently observed' and will make parts of the planet uninhabitable.[21] The extent depends primarily on the degree of warming.

Planetary boundaries as a common concern

The identification and observance of planetary boundaries is a central and ongoing task for humankind in the Anthropocene. Avoiding the destabilization of the Earth system by human influence is a fundamental prerequisite for the long-term flourishing of human civilization. This task is in the interests of humanity as a whole. Those goods whose exploitation brings us up against planetary boundaries are therefore to be regarded as part of the 'common heritage of humankind'. According to Rockström and Gaffney, 'all parts of the Earth system that protect Earth's ability to remain in a Holocene-like stability—the planetary boundaries—must be viewed as global commons. Every child's birthright', they pointed out, 'is, after all, a stable and resilient planet.' While the

---

17   WMO. 2024. State of the Global Climate 2023, p. 3. (wmo.int).

18   Church, John A. and Neil J. White. 2006. A 20th century acceleration in global sea-level rise, Geophysical Research Letters, Vol. 33, L01602.

19   IPCC, 2021, point B.53., p. 28.

20   Slater, Thomas, et al. 2021. 'Review Article: Earth's Ice Imbalance.' The Cryosphere 15 (1): 233–46.

21   Intergovernmental Panel on Climate Change. 2022. Climate Change 2022. Impacts, Adaptation and Vulnerability. Summary for Policymakers, p. 15-6., 20. (www.ipcc.ch).

researchers contend that their focus is the 'physical and biological reality of the planet', they also noted that 'this is a challenging idea for a planet organized by nation states.' Today's global institutions, they add, 'were not designed to deal with the speed, scale, and surprise of the Anthropocene, though. So, perhaps now is the time to reopen discussions about adopting more democratic principles at the global level—everyone might one day vote in a world parliament.'[22] In an article published together with an interdisciplinary group of 21 co-authors, Rockström argued that the approach of 'global commons' should be replaced by a new framework of 'planetary commons' that includes 'not only globally shared geographic regions but also critical biophysical systems that regulate the resilience and state, and therefore liveability, on Earth', irrespective of where they are located. Governing planetary commons 'will require an overarching global institution that is responsible for the entire Earth system', the group wrote. While the UN's General Assembly may be a starting point, 'novel arrangements' such as weighted voting and a UN Parliamentary Assembly 'might be needed to make governance at the planetary scale more representative, legitimate, just, effective, and reflective'.[23] Indeed, the responsibility for the management and use of these commons is shared by the whole of humanity. How they are used is everybody's concern. Humankind must wake up, grow up and take responsibility for itself and for all life on earth. This is the deeper meaning of the Anthropocene. However, the appropriate instruments and institutions do not yet exist. And in the current framework of international law it is very unlikely that they can be created.

The problem of voluntarism

The principle of state sovereignty in international law excludes the possibility of a higher authority above the state—not even humankind itself. States take on commitments only on a voluntary basis. A state can evade its common responsibilities simply by refusing to enter into a treaty, or by withdrawing from one previously entered into. Reference is occasionally made in international law to the common interests of humankind, but the inherent contradiction with the principle of state sovereignty is impossible to resolve.

The United Nations Framework Convention on Climate Change, which was adopted at the Rio Conference of 1992 and which entered into force two years later, states in its opening sentence that 'change in the Earth's climate and its adverse effects are a common concern of humankind'. This wording

---

22 Rockström and Gaffney, pp. 113-4., 203.
23 Rockström, Johan, et al. 2024. 'The Planetary Commons: A New Paradigm for Safeguarding Earth-Regulating Systems in the Anthropocene.' Proceedings of the National Academy of Sciences 121 (5), pp. 1, 5-7.

links back to a resolution of the UN General Assembly in 1988 in which climate change was already described as a 'common concern of mankind'. 'Mankind' (or 'humankind', as would generally be preferred today), however, has remained an abstract concept. The Climate Change Convention in fact reaffirms 'the principle of sovereignty of States in international cooperation to address climate change' and is constructed accordingly. It took five years for the Kyoto Protocol for the reduction of greenhouse gas emissions to be passed in 1997. Eight years later it finally entered into force. It has not been ratified by the USA – before Kyoto, the US Senate had already passed a unanimous resolution that the USA would not adopt any resolution which did not include reduction targets for developing countries. And indeed reduction targets were included for only 37 countries in the Kyoto Protocol, for which the first commitment period ended in 2012. China, with roughly a quarter of all emissions and the world's biggest emitter today in absolute terms, was one of those not included. Moreover, any country that wishes to withdraw can simply do so. This is what Canada did in 2011 in order to avoid penalty payments for missing reduction targets.

At the Paris Climate Conference in December 2015, an agreement was finally reached which all the states in the world were willing to adopt. The Paris Agreement includes a new target for international climate policy, that of reducing emissions so as to limit the worldwide temperature rise to a maximum of 1.5°C compared to the pre-industrialization baseline. At the climate conference in Copenhagen in 2009 an initial target of 2°C had been agreed. The Paris Agreement was celebrated as a breakthrough in international climate policy. However, the agreement does not include any binding reduction targets for individual states. Instead, they are required to report on so-called 'nationally determined contributions' (NDCs), to the global reduction of emissions every five years. There is an understanding and expectation that these targets will be progressively more ambitious. In fact, a 2023 study that quantifies 'safe and just' Earth system boundaries, carried out by over 50 experts led by Rockström, concluded that a just 'no significant harm' boundary would need to be set 'at or below 1.0 °C' of warming. At 1.5 °C, hundreds of millions of people, now and in the future, would be significantly harmed which they say is incompatible with 'the widely accepted "leave no one behind" principle'. In this assessment, seven of eight 'quantified safe and just Earth System Boundaries' are already exceeded.[24]

---

24 Rockström, Johan, Joyeeta Gupta, Dahe Qin, Steven J. Lade, Jesse F. Abrams, Lauren S. Andersen, et al. 2023. 'Safe and Just Earth System Boundaries.' Nature, published online May 31, 2023.

In terms of global warming, it is questionable whether a system of voluntary commitment can achieve the reductions required, A UN report in 2022 which made an assessment of NDCs declared to date concluded that taken together they imply an increase of about 10 per cent in global greenhouse gas emissions by 2030 compared to 2010. Subject to 'significant uncertainty', it was estimated that this would lead to a temperature increase between 2.1 and 2.9°C by the end of the century.[25] One indicator for lack of progress is the share of fossil fuels in total final energy consumption. This effectively did not change from 2009 to 2019.[26] The share remained steady at 82 per cent of global supply in 2022 despite the largest ever increase in renewable energy capacity.[27] According to an IPCC report, global greenhouse gas emissions between 2010 and 2019 were higher than in any previous decade. In terms of declared NDCs, the IPCC identified an implementation gap.[28] UN Secretary-General António Guterres concluded that the world was on a pathway to global warming of more than double the 1.5°C limit that was agreed in Paris. He described the report as 'a litany of broken climate promises' which revealed a 'yawning gap between climate pledges, and reality'.[29] Indeed, since 2021 annual carbon emissions reached new all-time highs after a pandemic-related decrease, suggesting that 'permissible emissions could be depleted within 2-7 years' with a view of the 1.5°C limit.[30] At a warming of 2.7°C by the end of this century, researchers estimate that 22 to 39 per cent of the world's population will live outside the 'climate niche' to which humans are adapted physiologically and culturally.[31] States remain free to evade the limitations and costs of regulatory frameworks such as the Paris agreement, and to reap the benefits of being free riders, if they so wish. Economists speak of 'negative externalities' if third parties suffer negative consequences whose costs are not borne by the party causing them. The 2006 report by the economist Nicholas Stern, commissioned by the British government, on the economic consequences of climate change looks at greenhouse gases from this perspective. 'Those who produce greenhouse gas emissions', the report states, 'are bringing about climate

---

25 UN Climate Change. 2022. 'Climate Plans Remain Insufficient: More Ambitious Action Needed Now | UNFCCC.' October 26, 2022 (unfccc.int).

26 REN21. 2021. Renewables 2021: Global Status Report, p. 33 (www.ren21.net).

27 Energy Institute. 2023. Statistical Review of World Energy. (energyinst.org).

28 Intergovernmental Panel on Climate Change. 2022. Climate Change 2022. Mitigation of Climate Change. Summary for Policymakers (www.ipcc.ch).

29 'UN Climate Report: It's "Now or Never" to Limit Global Warming to 1.5 Degrees.' 2022. UN News. April 4, 2022. (news.un.org).

30 Zhu Liu et al., 'Monitoring Global Carbon Emissions in 2022,' Nature Reviews Earth & Environment 4, no. 4 (April 2023): 205–6.

31 Lenton, Timothy M., et al. 2023. 'Quantifying the Human Cost of Global Warming.' Nature Sustainability, May 22, 1–11.

change, thereby imposing costs on the world and on future generations, but they do not face directly, neither via markets nor in other ways, the full consequences of the costs of their actions.'[32] As the emitter doesn't bear the costs, they have no economic incentive to reduce them. But the economic consequences are enormous. Although the Stern report stressed the difficulty of producing an economic estimate, it calculated the costs of stabilising the concentration of greenhouse gases in the atmosphere at 500 to 550 ppm CO_2 equivalent by 2050, subject to certain conditions, at around one per cent of global economic output per year.[33] To this must be added the costs of the damage actually caused by climate change. Stern estimated that in economic terms these costs could lie in a range between five and twenty per cent of annual global GDP. Climate change, the report stated, 'must be regarded as market failure on the greatest scale the world has seen'.[34]

The 'tragedy of the commons'

The state is able to counteract the negative effects of emissions, and to create an economic incentive to reduce them, by means of taxation, emissions trading systems and other forms of regulation which set an appropriate price on them. However, the difficulty lies in the fact that the atmosphere is a *global* common good. Regulation at the level of the individual state or the region, for example through the EU, leads to distortion of competition. Experts speak of 'carbon leakage' when higher emissions costs in one country lead to the displacement of emissions to another country where those costs are lower. One study concluded that although countries with Kyoto commitments reduced their emissions on average by seven per cent, no commensurate reduction in their 'carbon footprint' could be observed. The 'carbon footprint' captures the CO_2 emissions of a country on the basis of the goods consumed there, regardless of where they were produced. The study found that the fact that emissions were reduced while the footprint was not implied a rise in net CO_2 imports. The conclusion to be drawn from the phenomenon of 'carbon leakage' was that unilateral climate policy was not effective in a globalized world. Rather, it argued that effective climate policy required all countries to be bound by a global climate treaty.[35]This treaty should not only include binding reduction requirements but also an agreed global carbon tariff system that is harmo-

32 Stern, Nicholas. 2006. The Economics of Climate Change. The Stern Review, pp. 24 6.
33 Ibid., p. 212-4; two years later, Stern spoke of two per cent, see Jowit, Juliette, and Patrick Wintour. 26 June 2008. 'Cost of tackling global climate change has doubled, warns Stern'. The Guardian (www.guardian.co.uk).
34 Ibid., pp. 1, 25.
35 Aichele, Rahel, and Gabriel Felbermayr. 2011. 'Auswirkungen der Kyoto-Verpflichtungen auf Emissionen and Carbon Footprints'. ifo Schnelldienst, no. 22: 23–26, p. 26.

nized with global trade rules. In 2023, for instance, the EU started implementing a unilateral carbon levy on imported carbon-intensive goods that effectively adjusts their carbon price to that of domestic EU products, thus discouraging carbon leakage from an economic point of view. But India and other countries consider the measure a protectionist trade barrier that contradicts the WTO principle of non discrimination.

The problem is a form of the 'tragedy of the commons' as originally described by the biologist Garrett Hardin (1915 to 2003), in an influential article, as a widely-observed phenomenon. The model shows how the 'rational' users of a limited common resource, in seeking to maximize their short-term utility, thereby exhaust the common resource over the longer term, with the result of ruin for all. Despite the fact that everyone wants to maintain the resource, they are all trapped by the inherent dynamics of the situation. One of the examples is common grazing land on which the individual herds are continuously increasing in numbers. In order to escape the dilemma, Hardin suggested either the transformation of the common goods into private property or setting limits to their common use—that is, managing them.[36] 'Socialism or the privatism of free enterprise', as he later put it, were by this account the alternatives for their management.[37] In the area of environmental pollution, according to Hardin, comprehensive state regulation is the only possible answer. '[T]he air and waters surrounding us cannot readily be fenced,' he emphasized, 'and so the tragedy of the commons as a cesspool must be prevented by different means, by coercive laws or taxing devices that make it cheaper for the polluter to treat his pollutants than to discharge them untreated.'[38]

According to Mary Wood, the founder of the University of Oregon's Environmental and Natural Resources Law Center, '[r]anking among the most essential purposes of government is the necessity of protecting natural assets for the common benefit of the people and their society.' She argued that the doctrine of 'public trust' that is to be found in legal systems around the world expands to the atmosphere.[39] In the absence of a global legislature as a primary trustee and a global government that can act as its agent, there is no other way than to make national governments accountable relative to their duty to enforce a reduction of atmospheric emissions. In 2022, less than 4 per cent of

---

36   Hardin, Garrett. 13 December 1968. 'The Tragedy of the Commons'. Science 162 (3859): 1243–1248

37   Id. 1 May 1998. 'Extension of The Tragedy of the Commons'. Science 280 (5364): 682–683.

38   Hardin (1968), ibid.

39   Wood, Mary. 2012. 'Atmospheric Trust Litigation Around the World'. In: Fiduciary Duty and the Atmospheric Trust, ed. by Ken Coghill, Charles Sampford, and Tim Smith, 99–163. Ashgate Publishing, pp. 106-7, 126-8.

global emissions were covered by a direct carbon price implemented by national jurisdictions to the extent needed to stay within a 1.5°C limit.[40]

The management of global common goods

Many instances have been pointed out where the common use of limited resources, at local as well as regional levels, has not led to exhaustion because of a system of self-organization among the users, demonstrating the existence of additional alternatives. Moreover, both state management and privatization are also equally capable of failing. This relativizes the model, and the suggested solutions. The US American political scientist Elinor Ostrom (1933 to 2012) was awarded the Nobel Prize in economics in 2009 for her groundbreaking research in this area. '[T]ragedies of the commons are real, but not inevitable', was how she and four colleagues summarized this finding in the magazine *Science*.[41] However, they expressed themselves more cautiously with regard to *global* common goods, and spoke of the necessity for global institutions. The lessons to be drawn from local and regional examples of self-organization were encouraging, 'yet humanity now faces new challenges to establish global institutions to manage biodiversity, climate change, and other ecosystem services'.[42] It seems that the potential benefits of the kinds of self-organization studied by Ostrom cannot be fully realized in respect of global common goods. In the *Science* article, six reasons were listed why management seemed to be especially problematic in such cases. Firstly it is the scale. The huge number of users of global common goods—ultimately, all of humanity—increases the difficulty of organizing, agreeing on rules, and enforcing rules. Then there is cultural diversity, along with the differences between industrialized and less-industrialized countries, which make it less likely that shared interests and understandings can be found easily. Compared with the management of local grazing land or woodland, for instance, the systems of global common goods furthermore are more complex, including in terms of how they intermesh with each other, and it is more difficult to grasp where the common interests in their management lie. Another factor is a continuing acceleration of the rate of change. Ecological thresholds are being exceeded before they are even noticed. 'Learning by doing' is increasingly difficult, as past lessons are increasingly less relevant to current problems. The principle of voluntarism is highlighted as a reason here as well. The fundamental prin-

40   World Bank. 2022. 'State and Trends of Carbon Pricing 2022', p. 9.
19   Ostrom, Elinor, Joanna Burger, Christopher B. Field, Richard B. Norgaard, and David Policansky. 9 April 1999. 'Revisiting the Commons: Local Lessons, Global Challenges'. Science 284 (5412): 278–282, p. 281.
42   Ibid.

ciple of global resource management is that of voluntary assent to international treaties. National governments can demand special privileges as a price for joining regulatory agreements, 'thus strongly affecting the kinds of resource management policies that can be adopted at this level.' Finally, there is no room for experiment. In earlier times, people could migrate to other resources if they made a major error in managing a local resource. In the management of global common goods there is no room for failed experiments.[43]

The problem of the generations

The US American philosophy professor Stephen M. Gardiner has pointed out an additional problematic issue. It is linked to the fact that the *cumulative* effects of greenhouse gases build up over a very long time period. In his view, these delayed effects create an even worse form of the tragedy of the commons. '[C]ontrol of the situation', he wrote, 'rests completely with the current generation.' Future generations have no influence whatever on whether the current generation chooses to act as quasi-free riders or not. Normally, all parties in principle have an interest in cooperation. But if the consequences of over-exploitation are not experienced by the current generation, Gardiner asks, why should it forego the benefits? Perhaps the worst aspect of this is that the situation is repeated from generation to generation. Each new generation will find itself in the same situation with regard to the generations to come.[44]

A solution to the problem of the generations lies in a world legal system based on democratic majority decisions. A team of researchers at Harvard University has simulated the use of common resources over several generations using a game theory model. In this, the resource is almost always over-exploited and exhausted when the decisions on its use are made on an individual basis. This is because a minority of users always decides to exploit the resource without regard to coming generations. However, when use decisions are made by democratic majority vote, then the usage is always sustainable, and the resource is maintained. What is decisive is that all users have to be bound by the vote. 'Votes that are only partially binding, such as the international Kyoto protocol, have little power', the researchers wrote in *Nature* magazine.[45]

43 Ibid., pp. 281-2.

44 Gardiner, Stephen M. 2004. 'The Global Warming Tragedy and the Dangerous Illusion of the Kyoto Protocol'. Ethics & International Affairs 18 (1): 23–39, pp. 30-2.

45 Hauser, Oliver P., David G. Rand, Alexander Peysakhovich, and Martin A. Nowak. 10 July 2014 'Cooperating with the Future'. Nature 511 (7508): 220–23, pp. 221-2.

Global majority decision-making

With respect to global common goods, it is our view that the 'tragedy of the commons' model still provides the best picture of what is happening at the international level. Alongside the central problem of greenhouse gas emissions, many other unresolved examples of the tragedy of the commons can be adduced. In a critically-acclaimed book on the drastic overfishing of the seas, for example, the Swedish politician Isabella Lövin wrote that the condition of 'most of the world's fisheries are nothing but a shining example of how this theory works in practice'.[46] Withegard to forest governance the Brazilian social scientist and policy expert Adriana Abdenur contended that the intergovernmental discussions in various successive formats over decades 'brought to light some of the limitations in inter-State, consensus-based negotiations over forests'. One of the most important barrier the efforts have run up against in the Amazon region is governments invoking sovereignty over their territories. While deforestation continues at 'breakneck speed', a binding Global Forest Convention, one of the major proposals already on the table at the Rio Summit in 1992, has yet to be agreed.[47]

It needs to be emphasized here that regulation which aims to break the dilemma of over-exploitation can only work if it binds all users equally and if there are no free riders to undermine it. For us, therefore, the principle of voluntarism in international law is among the most serious of the problems identified by Elinor Ostrom for global resource management. The effective management of *global* common goods like the atmosphere and the oceans, or of resources as complex as biodiversity or forests, is not possible on the basis of international law 'à la carte'. The answer lies in a framework provided by a *world legal system*. 'The logic that leads to regulation of the commons is compelling', the world federalist Dieter Heinrich wrote, 'and is one of the main forces driving global political integration at a time of increasing interdependence.'[48] As the Turkish international law specialist Kemal Beslar wrote in 1998, in a study on the concept of the 'common heritage of mankind', 'effective implementation' can 'only be achieved by setting up a supranational authority whose power surpasses those of nation-states' and which can 'represent mankind as a whole'.[49]

---

46   Lövin, Isabella. 2012. Silent Seas: The Fish Race to the Bottom. Rothersthorpe: Paragon Publishing, p. 72.

47   Abdenur, Adriana Erthal. 2022. 'What Can Global Governance Do for Forests? Cooperation and Sovereignty in the Amazon.' United Nations University Centre for Policy Research, pp. 9-11.

48   Heinrich, Dieter. 2010. The Case for a United Nations Parliamentary Assembly. Extended reprint, originally published 1992. Berlin: Committee for a Democratic UN, p. 16.

49   Baslar, Kemal. 1998. The Concept of the Common Heritage of Mankind in International Law. The Hague et al.: Martinus Nijhoff, pp. 92, 94.

An international Earth systems research project has been under way with a specific focus on Earth systems governance, that is, on issues concerning the institutional and regulatory management of the Earth system. In 2012, a group of around 30 researchers led by Frank Biermann at Utrecht University, presented a list of what they consider to be the most important building blocks for a more effective institutional framework. In an article in *Science* magazine, they wrote that 'structural change', a 'major transformative shift' and a 'constitutional moment' were needed in global governance and world politics today—just as in 1945 when the UN was founded. They stressed that the prevailing consensus-based decision-making mechanisms at the international level 'limit decisions to the preferences of the least ambitious country'. International standards setting needed to be based much more on qualified majority decisions and linked weighted voting mechanisms. Governance systems based on majority decision-making, they argued, are quicker to arrive at far-reaching decisions.[50] According to Biermann, we 'could think about different majority and voting rules for different issue areas. We can think about multiple, complex, combined, or layered majorities. And surely, we need to clearly define institutional guarantees that protect smaller countries', he added.[51]

The negotiations around the UN Framework Convention on Climate Change, for example, are based on consensus, as the governments have been unable since the first Conference of the Parties in 1995 to agree on another system. This is why, for example, the concluding document from the climate conference in Copenhagen in 2009 was only 'to be taken note of' rather than binding. According to a report in the *Observer* newspaper, Bolivia, Venezuela, Nicaragua, Sudan and Saudi Arabia had threatened up until the last minute to use their veto to block a formal deal.[52] Nor has the Paris Agreement changed anything with respect to the consensus principle in climate negotiations.

'Though consent does indeed protect the interests of states and support notions of sovereign equality, it also functions as a barrier to effective cooperation in a world of vastly divergent priorities and concerns', wrote the US American professor of international law Andrew T. Guzman on the 'consent problem'. 'We live in a world with nuclear weapons, a warming climate, van-

50   Biermann, Frank, et al. 16 March 2012. 'Navigating the Anthropocene: Improving Earth System Governance'. Science 335 (6074): 1306–1307, p. 1307.

51   Id. Biermann, Frank. 22 April 2014. 'Governance in the Anthropocene: Towards Planetary Stewardship.' Presented at the 4th Interactive Dialogue of the United Nations General Assembly on Harmony with Nature, New York.

52   Goldenberg, Suzanne, Toby Helm, and John Vidal. 20 December 2009. 'Copenhagen: The key players and how they rated'. The Observer (www.guardian.co.uk).

ishing fisheries, grinding poverty, and countless other problems whose solutions require a high level of cooperation among states. Unless we change how we view the role of consent, it will be almost impossible to address these problems.'[53] This expresses a view now held ever more widely. The 'consent principle is undemocratic', is the judgment of Anne Peters, Director at the Max Planck Institute for Comparative Public Law and International Law. 'It is undemocratic because it allows the tyranny of one member of a political community over the others, and allows a small minority to block collective action.'[54] A world parliament serves the key purpose of creating a basis for legitimate, democratic and binding majority decisions at the global level and of overcoming the consensus principle. In doing so, it transcends nation-states as exclusive building blocks of global decision-making and lets elected global representatives, organized in transnational political groups, co-decide across borders and with common interests in mind. Single countries—or their governments, to be more precise—would not be able to veto decisions or to opt out in a world legal order. Nonetheless, qualified majorities will not be easy to come by in a global legislative system and political bargaining will continue. In particular, apart from federalism, qualified majority requirements help limit the potential issue of 'persistent minorities' that 'never participate in winning coalitions in decision-making', a theoretical scenario which the political philosopher Thomas Chiristino highlighted as a challenge to the legitimacy of the democratic process.[55] While majorities will shift depending on the issues at hand, we find it save to assume that most governments and political groups will find themselves part of the majority more often than not. But they will have to accept that sometimes decisions may not go their way. This give and take is part of democracy. At the same time, collectively, all benefit from an effective management of planetary common goods and matters of global concern. Finally, based on an analysis of the distribution of policy values within countries and in the world as a whole, the Oxford University Professor in Global Public Policy Thomas Hale and Mathias Koenig-Archibugi, Lecturer in Global Politics at the London School of Economics, found that the risk of persistent minorities in a hypothetical global democratic policy was not higher than in existing individual states.[56]

53 Guzman, Andrew T. 2012. 'Against Consent'. Virginia Journal of International Law 52 (4): 747–90, p. 749.

54 Peters, Anne. 2009. 'Dual Democracy'. In: The Constitutionalization of International Law, by Jan Klabbers, Anne Peters, and Geir Ulfstein, 263–341. Oxford, New York: Oxford University Press, p. 289.

55 Christiano, Thomas. 2008. The Constitution of Equality: Democratic Authority and Its Limits. Oxford University Press, pp. 104, 288.

56 Hale, Thomas, and Mathias Koenig-Archibugi. 2019. "Could Global Democracy Satisfy Diverse Policy Values? An Empirical Analysis." The Journal of Politics 81 (1): 112–26. See also Koenig-Archibugi, Mathias. 2024. The Universal Republic: A Realistic Utopia?, ch. 6.3, pp. 154-61.

The tragedy of international law

This problem in existing international treaty law is one of a fundamental nature, affecting all regulation concerned with genuinely global issues. 'Because treaties are often ineffective without the participation of certain, and sometimes most, countries', Andrew Strauss, for example, argued, 'a defiant minority can effectively veto the introduction of treaties that are in the vital interest of the world community.'[57] This makes the system of international law dysfunctional. For in order for a treaty to be effective in terms of its *reach*, it usually needs as many states as possible to sign up to it. But in order to achieve this, the *substance* of the agreement has to be subjected to ever lengthier negotiations and ever more compromises. Heinrich pointed out how these conditions lead to international treaties representing no more than the lowest common denominator among the treaty partners.[58] This is the case even for the resolutions of the UN General Assembly, which have no universally binding force under international law. In his report 'In larger freedom', for example, the then UN Secretary-General Kofi Annan lamented the fact that the General Assembly was reaching an increasing number of decisions by consensus. But consensus, he thought, was being interpreted as 'requiring unanimity' and had become an end in itself, yet one which was far from expressing a genuine unity of purpose among the member states. 'Rather', Annan wrote, 'it prompts the Assembly to retreat into generalities, abandoning any serious effort to take action.'[59] It can be concluded as a rule of thumb of international law that a treaty with effective reach will have proportionately less substance, while a treaty with effective substance will have proportionately less reach. This Catch-22 could be termed the tragedy of international law.

Enforcement and its legitimacy

For a treaty to be effective, it not only requires broad reach and strong substance, but it also needs to provide for enforcement mechanisms. Without the possibility of enforcing compliance, even the best treaty substance comes to nothing when it matters most. Overall, intergovernmental treaties are lacking this feature and thus appear to be ineffective. This is one of the conclusions of an assessment carried out, over ten years, of 224 primary studies on treaties'

57   Strauss, Andrew. 1999. 'Overcoming the Dysfunction of the Bifurcated Global System: The Promise of A Peoples Assembly'. Transnational Law & Contemporary Problems 9 (2): 48–70. Reprinted in and citation from: Falk, Richard, and Andrew Strauss. 2011. A Global Parliament: Essays and Articles. Berlin: Committee for a Democratic UN, pp. 107-8.
58   Heinrich, p. 20.
59   United Nations. 2005. 'In larger freedom: towards development, security and human rights for all'. Report of the Secretary-General. A/59/2005, para. 159.

effects. According to this research, 'international treaties have mostly failed to produce their intended effects' with the notable exception of agreements in the field of trade and finance. 'The numerous treaties governing other policy domains have either not worked or have been insufficiently studied', wrote Steven J. Hoffman of the Global Strategy Lab and 30 co-authors. 'For treaties governing environmental, human rights, humanitarian, maritime, and security policy domains, the only modifiable treaty design choice with the potential to improve effectiveness appears to be the inclusion of enforcement mechanisms', they stated. Based on their findings, the researchers believed that new intergovernmental treaties 'are unlikely to be worth their considerable effort' unless enforcement mechanisms are provided for.[60] While arguably it may be better in many cases to have ineffective treaties than none at all, this is a troubling issue that concerns existing agreements as well as important ongoing efforts such as for a Global Forest Convention, a plastics treaty or a potential 'coal elimination treaty', among others.

A recent case concerns ocean governance. After almost two decades of negotiations, the UN in 2023 agreed on a new high seas treaty under the UN Convention on the Law of the Sea that will enter into force once ratified by sixty states. The agreement provides for a framework for the establishment of marine protected areas on the high seas that are outside national jurisdiction. This is one of 'several wins' it represents according to *Nature*. However, the magazine's editors asserted there are 'deficiencies' in the treaty that 'the international community must now work to redress'. Specifically, existing activities and regulations pertaining to fishing, shipping, and deep-sea mining remain unaffected.[61] 'The high seas treaty is an absolute joke,' commented Kieran Kelly, CEO of RIO Ocean's Integrity, in unambiguous terms. Prior to establishing his organization focused on eradicating plastic waste in the oceans, the Irish entrepreneur managed a global fishing enterprise, providing him insight into 'the other side' of the issue. According to Kelly, a complete prohibition on fishing in the high seas is necessary, with enforcement achievable solely through individual criminal prosecution based on global law. As an example, Kelly referenced Interpol's 'Global Fisheries Enforcement team' which supports national agencies in detecting and combating fisheries crime. 'Anything voluntary will not work', he added with a view of treaty-based solutions.[62] In fact, treaty-based enforcement remains subject to the in-built limitations of

60 Hoffman, Steven J., et al. 2022. 'International Treaties Have Mostly Failed to Produce Their Intended Effects.' Proceedings of the National Academy of Sciences 119 (32), p. 5-6.
61 'UN High Seas Treaty Is a Landmark – but Science Needs to Fill the Gaps.' Nature 615, no. 7952 (March 15, 2023): 373–74.
62 Interview on 5 June 2023.

treaty law in a system of nominally sovereign states, in particular voluntarism which enables them to join or withdraw from treaties at will and thus escape any regulation and its enforcement if they wish to.

Nonetheless, if an enforcement capability exists, it obviously increases the authority of a given treaty regime and the body that is managing it. This in turn brings the question of legitimacy to the forefront. The political scientists Jonas Tallberg and Michael Zürn, for instance, argued that authority and legitimacy are linked. Legitimacy in their view addresses the question whether a political institution exercises its authority in an appropriate way. Legitimacy in this sense refers 'to a reservoir of confidence in an institution that is not dependent on short-term satisfaction with its distributional outcomes' because it is perceived to perform its functions for the collective good. Authority creates a demand for legitimacy, Tallberg and Zürn noted. The greater the authority of an institution, the more legitimacy it needs.[63] Binding majority decision-making coupled with enforcement mechanisms requires a high level of legitimacy that a global constitutional order with an elected world parliament at its center can provide best.

---

63   Tallberg, Jonas, and Michael Zürn. 2019. 'The Legitimacy and Legitimation of International Organizations: Introduction and Framework.' The Review of International Organizations 14 (4): 581–606, pp. 585, 587, 593.

12.

Overshoot, the 'Great Transformation', and a global eco-social market economy

Overshoot and ecological footprint

With the spread of industrialization, an economic system based on ever-increasing and ever-accelerating growth and concomitant consumption has become a global phenomenon. This system's functioning is dependent on a perpetual increase in and re-modernization of material prosperity. If economic output fails to grow, or even worse declines, then loss of income, unemployment, corporate bankruptcies and political, social and economic instability loom. Through the worldwide growth in economic activity and in population, the planet's resources are being put under pressure and used up faster than they can renew themselves. There has been intensive discussion of this problem ever since the 1972 report to the Club of Rome on the 'Limits to Growth'. Specialists in the field refer to the transgression of natural ecological regenerative capacity as 'overshoot'. The concept of the 'ecological footprint', as propounded and developed by the researchers Mathis Wackernagel and William Rees since 1990, serves as a way of measuring and depicting overshoot. According to estimates made by the Global Footprint Network, founded by Wackernagel, humankind today is using the equivalent of more than one and half times the biocapacity of the Earth's land and water surface. Thus the ecological footprint of the human race stands at 1.75. In the past ten years, it rose by more than 0.25 points.[1] According to the Footprint Network, in order for every human being today to enjoy the lifestyle of the average US American would require a fivefold increase in the Earth's biocapacity—which is simply not possible. 'If the present growth trends in world population, industrialization, pollution, food production, and resource depletion continue unchanged, the limits to growth on this planet will be reached sometime within the next one hundred years.'[2] This is the core message of the 'Limits to Growth' study, and it remains as valid as ever.

In so far resource use is concerned, the 'Great Acceleration' inevitably will slow down, if not collapse. It is well established that exploitable reserves of oil,

1   See data.footprintnetwork.org.

2   Meadows, Donella, Dennis Meadows, Jorgen Randers, and William W. Behrens III. The Limits to Growth. New York: Universe Books, 1972. p. 23

gas, coal and nuclear fuel are declining and will eventually be exhausted. The question is only how soon. The data available, and their interpretation, are disputed. As regards conventional oil, the maximum global rate of extraction—known as 'peak oil'—may already have been reached. Overall global oil production, including extraction of unconventional oil deposits, so far had an all-time high in 2019. Some studies predicted peak production of coal and gas for as early as 2020.[3] According to the International Energy Agency, however, coal production was to reach an all-time high around 2022.[4] Most of the remaining reserves actually need to stay where they are. For a fifty per cent probability of limiting global warming to the 1.5 °C goal, by 2050 nearly 60 per cent of oil and fossil methane gas, and 90 per cent of coal must remain unextracted and unused.[5] Already producing fields would have to be closed down.[6] 'It is a sad fact that humanity has largely squandered the past 30 years in futile debates and well-intentioned, but half-hearted, responses to the global ecological challenge', wrote Donella and Dennis Meadows with Jørgen Randers in an update of their study. 'Much will have to change if the ongoing overshoot is not to be followed by collapse during the twenty-first century.'[7]

The end of the Utopia of growth

Michael Winter spoke of 'the end of a dream'. In his view, today's highly industrialized countries had largely fulfilled all of the post-Renaissance utopian dreams, namely health, security, prosperity, justice and conviviality.[8] But at what cost? The cost, according to Richard Saage, was equivalent to the failure of the project of modernity. 'The utopian dream of perpetual happiness, guaranteed by the perfect state and the total mastery of nature', this student of utopianism wrote, 'collapsed at the very moment when it seemed to have been realised in the West.'[9] The dream was bought in large part at the expense of the rest of the world, the ecosystem and future generations. 'The Europeans', said Winter, referring to modern affluent societies, 'are to today's world what the aristocracy was to the Ancien régime in France.' This utopia, he thought,

3   Zittel, Werner, Jan Zerhusen, Martin Zerta, and Nikolaus Arnold. 2013. Fossile and Nukleare Brennstoffe – die künftige Versorgungssituation. Ed. by Energy Watch Group. Berlin, p. 14.
4   International Energy Agency. 2021. Coal 2021. Analysis and Forecast to 2024.
5   Welsby, Dan, James Price, Steve Pye, and Paul Ekins. 2021. 'Unextractable Fossil Fuels in a 1.5 °C World.' Nature 597(7875): 230–34.
6   Oil Change International. Sept. 2023. 'Planet Wreckers: How Countries' Oil and Gas Extraction Plans Risk Locking in Climate Chaos.' (priceofoil.org)
7   Meadows, Donella, Jorgen Randers, and Dennis Meadows. 2004. Limits to Growth. The 30-Year Update. 1st ed. White River Junction, VT: Chelsea Green Publishing, p. xvi.
8   Winter, Michael. 1993. Ende eines Traums. Stuttgart: Metzler, p. 298.
9   Saage, Richard. 1997. Utopieforschung. Eine Bilanz. Darmstadt: Wissenschaftliche Buchgesellschaft, p. 96.

cannot last much longer. A point has been reached when the utopian project itself has to be questioned.[10] An economic system geared for maximum profits, material consumption and continuous growth, and the associated values and lifestyles, is subject to ever closer questioning as it becomes ever more apparent that overshoot is a dead end. In view of the growing gulf between the rich and the poor, the fact that the economic benefits of growth accrue disproportionately to certain sections of the population also plays a role here, alongside the ecological question. Moreover, in the light of diseases of affluence like the obesity epidemic, some people speak of 'the curse of overdevelopment' or of 'overdeveloped countries'.[11] Many people are now asking themselves whether the fixation of the economic system on growth, even on what is called 'green growth', makes sense at all. At any event, the fact that economic growth cannot proceed indefinitely and that development too must stagnate at some point was accepted by no less a figure than the liberal pioneer and philosopher John Stuart Mill 150 years ago in his 'Principles of Political Economy'. 'Towards what ultimate point', asked Mill, 'is society tending by its industrial progress? When the progress ceases, in what condition are we to expect that it will leave mankind?'[12] In fact, Mill expressed sympathy for the idea of a world that has escaped the compulsion of ceaseless growth in population and economic activity, has achieved a state of balance and can concentrate on intellectual, social and cultural progress. The motto must be qualitative and not quantitative growth.

Prosperity, happiness and democracy

The US American economist Richard Easterlin carried out an international study in 1974 of the statistical link between subjective life satisfaction and economic growth. He concluded that although people with higher incomes generally report a greater sense of happiness, at the same time a higher per capita national income on average did not indicate a happier society. This 'Easterlin paradox', still debated today, is not necessarily surprising. As US Senator Robert Kennedy already noted in March 1968, shortly before his death, Gross Domestic Product captured cigarette advertising, napalm, nuclear warheads and armoured police cars, but not the immaterial values which

10 Winter, pp. 297-8, 299.
11 Worldwatch Institute (ed.). 2012. State of the World 2012: Moving Toward Sustainable Prosperity. Washington D.C.: Island Press, p. 24.
12 Mill, John Stuart. 1909 [1848]. Principles of Political Economy. Ed. by William J. Ashley. 7th ed. London: Library of Economics and Liberty (www.econlib.org). Book IV, Ch. VI, § 1.

are what make life worth living.[13] An important factor seems to be people's social status relative to one another. Inequality has a detrimental effect on life satisfaction and happiness. These are two different things, though. Even people who are very poor in material terms can experience great emotional happiness. But life satisfaction, which is a thoughtful and measured assessment, indeed grows with increasing material prosperity but it appears only up to a certain point. Tim Jackson, a professor for sustainable development at the University of Surrey in southern England, found that, above a certain threshold, an increase in material prosperity is no longer associated statistically with a significant growth in personal life satisfaction.[14] The lower the income, the greater the measurable increase in life satisfaction and vice versa.

The UN's Development Programme since 1990 measures a Human Development Index, in short HDI, which not only takes into consideration Gross National Income per capita but also education and life expectancy as an indicator for health. The Organisation for Economic Co-operation and Development, OECD, since 2011 measures a 'Better Life Index' in 40 countries which covers 11 topics of well-being. These include indices such as household income, net financial wealth, education or health but also the quality of social support, of the environment, work-life balance, safety or the level of happiness. At the UN, the small South Asian country of Bhutan, a constitutional monarchy with a population of around three quarters of a million, pressed for the adoption of 'gross national happiness' as a measure for the wellbeing of a society. On its initiative, the UN General Assembly passed a resolution in July 2011 which recognised 'that the gross domestic product indicator by nature was not designed to and does not adequately reflect the happiness and wellbeing of people in a country'.[15] A year later there followed in New York the UN Conference on 'Well-Being and Happiness: Defining a New Economic Paradigm'. Since 2012, an annual 'World Happiness Report' is published, put together by a number of institutes and think tanks, which explores how to measure and increase happiness. The first report stated that 'the focused quest for material gain as conventionally measured typically makes a lot of sense' in an impoverished society. But after poverty, what comes next? Endless economic growth is not the answer and 'the lifestyles of the rich imperil the sur-

---

13   Remarks of Robert F. Kennedy at the University of Kansas. 18 March 1968. John F. Kennedy Presidential Library & Museum, 18. März 1968 (www.jfklibrary.org).

14   Jackson, Tim. Prosperity without Growth: Economics for a Finite Planet. Paperback. London; Washington: Earthscan, 2011. p. 5

15   United Nations. 2011. 'Happiness: towards a holistic approach to development.' Resolution of the UN General Assembly 65/309

vival of the poor.'[16] For sure, as proponents of pursuing happiness as a public policy goal such as economist Jeffrey Sachs emphasize, it should be understood as an additional and complementary item in a wider 'program of global aspirations' and not an exclusive one.[17]

Recognizing the importance of happiness is not new. The American Declaration of Independence of 1776 is famous for stating that all people are endowed with unalienable rights, among them 'life, liberty and the pursuit of happiness'.[18] The global analytics firm Gallup has been measuring the perception of happiness at an individual level in over 140 countries since 2006. They draw on five elements of well-being: work, financial, community, physical and social. In the 2022 book 'Blind Spot' Gallup's CEO Jon Clifton provides an overview of their research. Their data confirms that neither GDP nor the HDI measurement necessarily correlates with happiness. It can be quite the opposite. In Egypt and Tunisia, for instance, from 2006 to 2012 GDP per capita and the HDI went up while the share of those who thrived in their own perception dropped significantly. Overall, Gallup data shows a 'global rise of unhappiness' and of 'wellbeing inequality' since they started their surveys. In 15 years, the number of people who reported they are living the best possible life has doubled to 4.7 per cent but those who say it could not be worse has more than quadrupled to 7.6 per cent. According to Gallup, an increasing share of people feels anger, sadness, pain, worry, and stress. On a range from zero to 100, the relevant score rose globally from around 24 in 2006 to around 33 in 2021. Clifton emphasizes that instead of trying to perfect happiness, the priority must be to reduce people's misery. Missing to recognize and address the rise of unhappiness in his opinion helped trigger a majority in the UK to vote for Brexit and the election of Donald Trump in the US, among other things.[19] These events and their connection to unhappiness are a warning. For a long time, researchers have been looking into if and how living in a democracy links to individual well-being. 'Although democracy does not determine a society's level of subjective well-being, other things being equal, democracy does contribute to happiness', the political scientist Ronald F. Inglehart concluded. Citizens of democracies, he said, overall are 'substantially happier' than those of autocracies. Nevertheless, he pointed out that the causal rela-

16   Helliwell, John, Richard Layard, and Jeffrey Sachs, eds. 2012. World Happiness Report. The Earth Institute (worldhappiness.report), p. 3-4.
17   Jeffrey D. Sachs. 2023. 'Three out of Three Is Better.' In: Flanagan, Owen, and et al. Against Happiness, 1st ed. Columbia University Press, pp. 227-234.
18   This is also included in the 1947 Japanese constitution.
19   Clifton, Jon. Blind Spot. The Global Rise of Unhapiness and How Leaders Missed It. Washington, D.C.: Gallup Press, 2022, pp. 5-8. 28-37.

tionship appears to be stronger in the opposite direction. In other words, a happier populace fosters a more conducive environment for democracy to thrive. By implication, a rise in unhappiness can help undermine the foundations of democracy.[20]

The challenge of global eco-social development

The debate over an economically and socially sustainable order that serves human happiness and life satisfaction, and the pathways towards it, one which is so important for the future of humankind, should be brought together at an international level in a democratic world parliament. The great challenge is to move as quickly as possible, and *worldwide*, to an economic system which remains within the parameters set by the Earth system and the natural ecological regenerative capacity of the Earth, and which at the same time enables the best possible development and greatest prosperity for all. In the words of the UN High-level Panel on Global Sustainability, the long-term vision 'is to eradicate poverty, reduce inequality and make growth inclusive, and production and consumption more sustainable, while combating climate change and respecting a range of other planetary boundaries'.[21] In a necessarily *decelerating* world of ever more depleted and scarce natural resources, a global parliament is needed to help bring about legitimate decisions and regulatory frameworks determining how they are to be used in a fair and sustainable way in the best interest of all and future generations.

'Political barriers' as the main obstacle to transformation

The transition to a sustainable global society involves such profound changes that it is often compared to such world-historic shifts as the development of agriculture (the Neolithic revolution) and the Industrial revolution. It is in this sense that the authors of the 'Limits to Growth' speak of the challenge of a 'third revolution' in human history.[22] A fundamental feature of the challenge, one which would in and of itself justify such a comparison, is the shift in energy production to renewable sources accompanied by a simultaneous major increase in energy efficiency. A global energy transition of this kind would transform the existential basis of human civilization and secure it over the long term. Researchers like Ernst Ulrich von Weizsäcker, who was a co-

20 Inglehart, Ronald. 2009. 'Democracy and Happiness: What Causes What?' In: Happiness, Economics and Politics: Towards a Multi-Disciplinary Approach, ed. by Amitava Krishna Dutt and Benjamin Radcliff, 256–70. Edward Elgar, p. 269.

21 United Nations High-level Panel on Global Sustainability (ed.). 2012. 'Resilient people, resilient planet: a future worth choosing. Report of the High-level Panel of the Secretary-General on Global Sustainability'. A/66/700, p. 7.

22 Meadows, Donella, Dennis Meadows, and Jorgen Randers. 1992. Beyond the Limits. Chelsea Green, ch. 7.

president of the Club of Rome for six years until 2018, saw the potential for a five-fold increase in resource productivity.[23] The German Advisory Council on Global Change (WBGU), made up of experts appointed by the German Federal Government and originally established at the time of the UN Environment Conference in Rio in 1992, noted that the greatest obstacles to the transition are not of a technological nature. Rather, according to a significant report from this independent body, at the time led by Hans Joachim Schellnhuber, Director of the Potsdam Institute for Climate Impact Research and Dirk Messner, Director of the German Development Institute, the most difficult challenges include 'a global evolutionary leap towards a greater willingness for global cooperation' and overcoming 'political barriers'.[24] Humanity must 'leave the epoch of nation states behind and foster an unprecedented culture of global cooperation'.[25] The transformation to a post-fossil fuel world society would require a new social contract, enabled by 'a new kind of discourse between governments and citizens, both within and beyond the boundaries of the nation state', a 'Social Contract for Sustainability', as it is called in the subtitle of the report.[26]

The need for a 'Great Transformation' had been mooted already in the concluding declarations of the symposia of Nobel prize winners and other leading figures held in Potsdam, London and Stockholm in 2007, 2009 and 2011, and led by the Potsdam Institute. In the Memorandum of the Potsdam conference, for example, it was stated that humanity was 'standing at a moment in history when a great transformation is needed to respond to the immense threat to our planet'.[27] And a team of scientists linked to the Tellus Institute in Boston and the Stockholm Environment Institute, brought together into the Global Scenario Group, had already presented the scenario of a 'Great Transition' in 2002 in trying to set out a path to a sustainable and solidarity-based world society. The group described two additional classes of scenarios: 'Conventional worlds' assumed an evolution of the global system 'without major surprise, sharp discontinuity, or fundamental transformation' and 'barbarization' in which conventional approaches fail and civilization 'descends

23   von Weizsäcker, Ernst Ulrich, Karlson Hargroves, and Michael Smith. 2009. Faktor Fünf. Die Formel für nachhaltiges Wachstum. München: Droemer Knaur.

24   German Advisory Council on Global Change. 2011. World in Transition: A Social Contract for Sustainability. Berlin: WBGU, pp. 189-90, 203.

25   Ibid., p. 91.

26   Id. 7 May 2011. 'A Social Contract for Sustainability'. Press release (www.wbgu.de).

27   Potsdam-Memorandum. 2007. Conclusions of the sympodium 'Global Sustainability: A Nobel Cause', Potsdam, 8-10 October.

into anarchy and tyranny'.[28] The 'Great Transition' approach has been pursued further by the Tellus Institute under the leadership of the US American physicist and futurologist Paul Raskin. In a brief assessment he published after twenty years, in 2022, Raskin stressed that all their scenarios begin 'with a downward historical spiral rife with conflict and disruption' so a turnaround, in principle, was still in the cards. However, in absence of a 'genuine global movement for systemic transformation', forces of barbarization in his view have become stronger which has made 'breakdown ultimately an ever more plausible scenario'.[29]

The process of state formation and the rise of the market economy

The term of a 'Great Transformation' was originally introduced by the economist and social scientist Karl Polanyi (1886 to 1964) in his 1944 work of the same title. Behind it lies a complex picture of the origins and development of the modern, market economy-based industrial society and of its inherent social, political and economic tensions. In the view of the US American Nobel laureate in economics Joseph Stiglitz, '[e]conomic science and economic history have come to recognize the validity of Polanyi's key contentions'.[30] Polanyi's analysis certainly offers valuable starting points for an understanding of the contemporary situation and for appropriate courses of action.

For Polanyi, born in Vienna but forced into exile in 1933 as a Jew and a socialist, the establishment of the market economy, i.e. the switch from regulated to self-regulating markets at the end of the 18th century, marked the decisive shift in the industrial revolution. Because of the long-term investment needed, the development of mechanized production had only proved economically possible when all the factors involved could be bought and sold as commodities so that it was possible to maintain continuous production. 'The extension of the market mechanism to the elements of industry—labor, land, and money', wrote Polanyi, 'was the inevitable consequence of the introduction of the factory system in a commercial society.' In his view, it has only been possible to speak of the existence of industrial capitalism as a social system since the abolition of the 'Poor Law', and the minimum subsistence for

---

28 Raskin, Paul, Tariq Banuri, Gilberto Gallopín, Pablo Gutman, Al Hammond, Robert Kates, and Rob Swart. 2002. Great Transition. The Promise and Lure of the Times Ahead. A report of the Global Scenario Group. Boston, MA: Stockholm Environment Institute, p. 14-5.

29 Raskin, Paul. November 2022. 'Which Future Are We Living In?' Great Transition Initiative (www.greattransition.org).

30 Stiglitz, Joseph. Foreword in: Polanyi, Karl. 2001. The great transformation: the political and economic origins of our time. Boston, MA: Beacon Press. p. xiii.

existence it provided, in England in 1834.[31] Polanyi's study shows how this social system was established step by step through measures undertaken by the state. The 'invisible hand of the market', as the Scottish political economist Adam Smith described in 1776 the self-regulating equilibrium between supply and demand driven by the individual self-interest of the market participants, does not arise automatically, as if by magic. On the contrary: 'free markets', wrote Polanyi, 'could never have come into being merely by allowing things to take their course. Just as cotton manufactures—the leading free trade industry—were created by the help of protective tariffs, export bounties, and indirect wage subsidies, *laissez-faire* itself was enforced by the state.' Paradoxically, the establishment of free markets required an enormous increase in the administrative functions of the state and the growth of a central bureaucracy working ceaselessly to ensure that the system could function.[32] Even the creation of regulated national domestic markets before the market economy itself arose was achieved by means of similar targeted measures. As Polanyi wrote, internal trade in Western Europe was actually forced through by 'the *deus ex machina* of state intervention' against the opposition of the 'fiercely protectionist towns and principalities'. This 'commercial revolution' was part of the development of competing centralized nation states. 'In external politics, the setting up of sovereign power was the need of the day; accordingly, mercantilist statecraft involved the marshalling of the resources of the whole national territory to the purposes of power in foreign affairs.'[33] The creation of national internal markets and capitalist deregulation in the course of the industrial revolution can therefore be seen as significant stages in the process of state formation. This went hand in hand with a change in value systems at the level of the individual, namely the rise of the so-called 'Homo oeconomicus' in rational pursuit of his economic interests.[34]

The 'double movement' between market fundamentalism and state interventionism

In the 19th century there then arose within society a struggle over the political control of the state powers established for the regulation or deregulation of the markets. Polanyi sets out in his work the concept of a 'double movement' between the forces of market liberalism and those opposing social forces which sought to restrict the market mechanism. This conflict Polanyi saw as

31 Polanyi, Karl. 2001. The Great Transformation: The Political and Economic Origins of Our Time. Boston, MA: Beacon Press, p. 78.
32 Ibid., p. 145.
33 Ibid., pp. 67-8., 69.
34 Ibid., pp. 45-7.

'the one comprehensive feature in the history of the age'.[35] In his view, the First World War, the Great Depression of the 1930s, the rise of fascism and the Second World War were ultimately all symptoms of a single problem: the rise and fall of market fundamentalist capitalism. 'The dissolution of the system of world economy which had been in progress since 1900', wrote Polanyi, referring to the failure of the gold standard and the rise of protectionism, 'was responsible for the political tension that exploded in 1914.'[36] Market fundamentalism, the argument runs, carries within it the seeds of its own failure in the form of the social upheavals it sparks, and at the moment of its collapse it liberates extreme countervailing forces. 'Fascism, like socialism,' wrote Polanyi, 'was rooted in a market society that refused to function.'[37] Fascism and socialism, which both set up a form of state-controlled, centralized command economy, were in Polanyi's reading different examples of an identical countervailing force.

A global eco-social market economy

A prospering and democratic society cannot be maintained at the extreme poles of the double movement described by Polanyi. The art of politics must be that of holding a balance between the forces of free markets and state interventionism. This equilibrium can be achieved by a social market economy of the kind constructed in Western Europe after the Second World War. In the USA, which was badly hit by the Great Depression, a substantial shift was brought about in state welfare and regulation by the economic and social reforms ushered in by President Franklin D. Roosevelt's 'New Deal', beginning in 1933. But the social market economy, which aims at a balance between the forces of laissez-faire and state interventionism, is no longer sufficient today. There is an additional necessity that needs to be integrated: ecological sustainability. The 'Great Transformation' of the 21st century consists in regulating the market economy so that it operates in a manner that is not only socially but also ecologically sustainable. The social concept which emerges from this is that of the 'eco-social market economy'. The economist and mathematician Franz Josef Radermacher and the consultant Estelle Herlyn have summarised this as follows: 'If we want a planet that remains viable for the future, on which people can live prosperously and in peace with nature and with each other, then the human race needs a different model. For this we need to combine the dynamism and innovative power of markets, in the Schumpeterian

35   Ibid., p. 80.
36   Ibid., pp. 42, 22.
37   Ibid., p. 248.

sense, with rigorous protection of the environment and with social equity, above all in terms of promoting universal political participation'—and, as they stress, not merely on a national but on the global level. They believe that the economic model required consists of 'a global extension of an ordoliberal approach in the form of a worldwide eco-social regulated market economy, an eco-social market model.'[38] In essence, this is what a 'Green New Deal' needs to be about.

On account of the intensely competitive international situation and the global common goods involved, the 'eco-social market economy' must of necessity be global. Its chances of success would be small if it were to be implemented via regulation at the nation state level rather than within an international framework. For example, prices in an eco-social economic system would need to include as far as possible all consequential ecological costs, and this in turn would require a functional global taxation system. But the 'tragedy of international law' described before makes precisely that impossible. For a Global Green New Deal to be successful, an evolutionary step forward is required. The Brundtland Report already made the point that the 'traditional forms of national sovereignty are increasingly challenged by the realities of ecological and economic interdependence'.[39] As Stiglitz wrote in his book 'Globalization and Its Discontents', we are dealing today, on account of falling transport and communication costs and the removal of barriers to free trade in goods, services and capital, with 'a process of "globalization" analogous to the earlier processes in which national economics were formed'. 'Unfortunately', as the former World Bank chief economist continued, 'we have no world government, accountable to the people of every country, to oversee the globalization process in a fashion comparable to the way national governments guided the nationalization process.'[40] That, however, is precisely what is needed if we are to have a sustainable civilization on our planet. The *decisive feature* of the new 'Great Transformation' which is on its way must be that the process of state formation described by Polanyi is continued *at the global level*. In the situation that existed after the First World War, Polanyi noted succinctly, the only sensible option would have been 'the establishment of an international order endowed with an organized power which would transcend national sovereignty'.[41] This is still the case today.

38 Herlyn, Estelle L. A., and Franz Josef Radermacher. 2011. 'Ökosoziale Marktwirtschaft: Ideen, Bezüge, Perspektiven'. FAW/n Report, p. 3.
39 World Commission on Environment and Development (ed.). 1987. Our Common Future. Annex to A/42/427. Ch. 10, point 1.
40 Stiglitz, Joseph E. 2003. Globalization and Its Discontents. W. W. Norton & Company, p. 21.
41 Polanyi, p. 43.

13.

Financial crises, countering
global deregulation, and the hidden trillions

The contemporary relevance of the 'double movement' and emancipation

The interest in Karl Polanyi is connected not only to the issue of sustainability, which has now acquired a central importance in the 'double movement' he described. Polanyi's contemporary relevance, in the view of researchers such as the Dublin-based sociologist Ronaldo Munck or the philosopher and feminist Nancy Fraser, who teaches in New York, stems rather from the fact that market forces have once again been released from constraints. The reforms brought in under the British Prime Minister Margaret Thatcher and US President Ronald Reagan in the 1980s were the beginning of a wave of deregulation which led, after the end of the Cold War and the collapse of 'actually existing socialism' in the Soviet bloc, to what has been called globalised 'turbo-capitalism'. A symbolic highpoint was the 1999 abolition in the USA of the Glass–Steagall Act introduced as part of the New Deal in 1933 to maintain a separation between commercial banking and investment banking. According to the US American government adviser Edward Luttwak, who popularised the term 'turbo-capitalism' via his book of the same title, the protests against the WTO meeting in Seattle were a revolt against the 'unfettered market economy'. 'The capitalism of the 1990s', Luttwak summarised, 'is completely different from that of the preceding decades. That is why I came up with the term "turbo-capitalism". It describes a completely deregulated, entirely unfettered market, without any protective barriers.'[1] This characterisation is undoubtedly exaggerated. But it is at least certainly possible to say, using Polanyi's model, that the double movement swung once again in the direction of laissez-faire. 'What we today call "neoliberalism"', wrote Nancy Fraser, 'is nothing but the second coming of the very same nineteenth-century faith in the "self-regulating market" that unleashed the capitalist crisis Polanyi chronicled.'[2] The situation is so similar, she argued, that it is possible to speak of 'a second great transformation'. Fraser emphasized that the contrast Polanyi

---

1   Luttwak, Edward. 9 December 1999. 'Wenige Gewinner, viele Verlierer'. Interviewed by Dietmar H. Lamparter and Fritz Vorholz. Die Zeit (www.zeit.de).

2   Fraser, Nancy. 2011. 'Marketization, Social Protection, Emancipation: Toward a Neo-Polanyian Conception of Capitalist Crisis'. In: Business as Usual. The Roots of the Global Financial Meltdown, ed. by Craig Calhoun and Georgi Derluguian, 137–157, 281/2. New York University Press, p. 139.

draws between 'good embedded markets' and 'bad disembedded markets' is too simple. The point should be to recognize and question *every form of oppression*, regardless of whether its roots are in economics or in society, in market liberalism or in state interventionism. The struggle for emancipation and for a fairer society can therefore not easily be straitjacketed into Polanyi's double movement model. The capitalist crisis, she contended, has to be understood as a three-sided conflict between market forces, social regulation and emancipation. A descent into authoritarianism and totalitarianism is a possibility which, given historical experience, must always be borne in mind and guarded against.

Financial crises and national populism

The tendency of 'disembedded markets' towards self-destruction and associated social breakdown postulated by Polanyi seems to have been confirmed in the course of the global financial crisis 2007-9 and its long-term repercussions. Confronted with the possibility of a collapse of the international financial system, the exact course and results of which were unforeseeable, government and central banks felt themselves compelled to intervene on a massive scale in support of financial institutions and other companies adjudged to be 'too big to fail'. Originally formed to deal with the 1997-98 Asian financial crisis, the G20 forum of the finance ministers of the world's leading economies was upgraded to coordinate the international approach at the level of heads of state and government. The private commercial risks to which financial institutions and their owners were exposed were diverted and passed on to the wider society. Under strict market economy conditions, the institutions concerned would have had to declare insolvency, as Lehman Brothers did. According to figures released by the International Monetary Fund, the G20 countries had promised capital injections totalling 1,160 billion US dollars and given guarantees up to a further 4,638 billion dollars, by August 2009. This equates to 2.2 per cent and 8.8 per cent respectively of GDP for the year 2008 for all G20 member states combined. The IMF figures show furthermore that the sums actually provided up to that point totalled 446 billion dollars in the form of capital injections and 366 billion in the form of credit and equity. Whereas the financial institutions and their owners were rescued, the financial crisis for which they were in part responsible triggered the worst stock market crash and global economic decline since 1929, dubbed the 'Great Recession', a severe dip in the volume of world trade lasting several years, and job losses and continuing unemployment for many millions of people. Denying the G20's legitimacy, Daniele Archibugi commented that 'it is inconceivable that everyman's problems should be addressed in summits held outside the confines of democratic logic', adding that global financial institutions should be placed under the scrutiny of a 'directly elected world parliament' and mentioning the proposal of setting up, at the UN, an 'Economic Security Council'.[3] National populism has risen in many countries following the crisis due to a variety of different factors. Nonetheless, the broad social and economic impact of the financial crisis unquestionably contributed to the erosion of trust in state institutions, rising public dissatisfaction with mainstream political parties and political polarization. Populists managed to exploit the anti-establishment sentiment fuelled by the crisis, particularly in light of government bailouts of financial institutions and because elites were not held accountable for their role in causing the crash in the first place. Those fines and penalties imposed on the financial industry in the US, for instance, were tax deductible and no criminal charges were pushed by the Obama administration.[4] The 'populist wave that swept over the world' was indeed considered by some 'the biggest cost of the crisis'.[5] A study of nearly 100 financial crises and more than 800 national elections in 20 democracies since 1870 found that the largest political beneficiaries of financial crises are far-right parties. Following a crisis, the percentage of votes going to right-wing parties on average increases by over 30 per cent. Government majorities tend to decrease, and governing becomes more challenging as anti-establishment groups and parties gain representation and strength in legislatures.[6] It is clear, the authors note, that another financial crisis would 'likely trigger yet another populist surge' across the world.[7]

Continuing systemic risk

The possibility of another major global financial and economic crisis persists. Then German Federal President Horst Köhler, Director of the International Monetary Fund for four years before he took office, lamented that the international financial markets had become a 'monster that has to be locked away'.[8] Even though many years have passed since then, it is impossible to avoid the impression that the 'monster' has not been successfully bound. There was

3   Archibugi, Daniele. 31 March 2009. 'The G20 Ought to Be Increased to 6 Billion.' OpenDemocracy (www.opendemocracy.net).
4   Baker, Raymond W. 2023. Invisible Trillions. Oakland: Berrett-Koehler, p. 92.
5   Funke, Manuel, Moritz Schularick, and Christoph Trebesch. 13 Sep. 2018. 'The Financial Crisis Is Still Empowering Far-Right Populists.' Foreign Affairs. (www.foreignaffairs.com).
6   Id. 2015. 'Going to Extremes: Politics after Financial Crises, 1870-2014.' CESifo Working Paper No. 5553 (www.ifo.de).
7   Id. (2018), ibid.
8   'Köhler nennt Finanzmärkte Monster', 14 May 2008 (www.stern.de).

some premature talk of a 'renaissance of the state' in the light of the state interventions that took place. But the measures implemented represented mainly emergency responses for the maintenance of the status quo, and not a systematic eradication of the causes of the crisis. Despite all their promises, governments have relied mainly on improving the regulatory oversight of financial markets. But that is not enough. Neil M. Barofsky—who until 2011 had been the independent inspector general of the US government's Troubled Asset Relief Program for the purchase of equity shares to shore up unstable financial institutions—complained that one of the purported main aims of the re-regulation prompted by the financial crisis, namely that of ending the dominance of a small number of 'systemically significant' banks, had not been achieved.[9] On the contrary, the top five US banks, for instance, according to World Bank figures held a share of total commercial banking assets of 43.9 per cent in 2007. This share peaked at 56.3 per cent in 2015 and fell to 49.7 per cent by 2021. Relative to the beginning of the global financial crisis this is still a remarkable increase of 13 per cent. In 2000, the figure stood at 28.1 per cent.[10] If they get into difficulties, these banks are too big to fail, but at the same time may become too big to be rescued. The largest bank failures since the financial crisis indicate a trend towards more concentration and raise concerns over the vulnerability of the financial system after a long period of quantitative easing and low interest rates.[11] After the shutdown of Silicon Valley Bank and Signature Bank following their crash in 2023, JP Morgan, one of the world's largest banks, was allowed to acquire the failed First Republic Bank. As it faced collapse, too, Credit Suisse, which was deemed to be of global systemic relevance, was allowed to be taken over by UBS with the assistance of Swiss government loans and guarantees, making the new conglomerate one of the top 15 largest banks in the world.

The Basel Committee on Banking Supervision, a body of the Bank for International Settlements which is owned by over 60 central banks, drew up the Basel III regulations which are updated continuously and determine minimum capital requirements, among other things. Regardless of how effective these rules might be considered, some believe they are insufficient, speedy and uniform implementation of such international standards has proved difficult. While the 30 governments that make up the Basel Committee pledged to im-

9   Barofsky, Neil M. 22 July 2012. 'Bungled Bank Bailout Leaves Behind Righteous Anger'. Bloomberg (www.bloomberg.com).

10   World Bank Group, Global Financial Development, DataBank, GFDD.OI.06: 5-bank asset concentration (databank.worldbank.org). Accessed 19 June 2024. 2021 latest year available.

11   Archarya, Viral V., and Raghuram Rajam. 2023. 'Quantitative Easing Left the Banking System Vulnerable.' Barron's. March 17, 2023. https://www.barrons.com/articles/sbv-fed-qe-banking-crisis-22175ec0.

plement them in the course of ongoing international negotiations, this is not binding under international law and deadlines have been regularly pushed back. In addition, shadow banks exert a decisive influence on the financial system by virtue of their size alone. These so-called 'non-bank financial intermediaries' are said to either absorb or amplify shocks, depending on their activity and overall market conditions.[12] The extent of those that pose bank-like financial stability risks in the assessment of the G20's Financial Stability Board has grown in the 29 jurisdictions covered from 32.3 trillion US dollars in 2007 to 67.8 trillion in 2021.[13] Relative to the world's gross domestic product, it increased from around 55 to 70 per cent in this timespan. The Argentinian economist Victor Beker noted that most of the post-crisis regulatory efforts have been focused on traditional banks, though, and that 'international regulatory coordination is a big challenge'. In particular, there was a need 'to prevent financial institutions from steering their riskiest operations toward the least regulated jurisdiction. This regulatory arbitrage may end up concentrating the highest risks where regulation is weaker.' He also highlighted that despite their key role in the 'financial meltdown', credit rating agencies emerged 'practically untouched.'[14] On top, crypto-assets markets are developing rapidly and will likely become an additional risk to the stability of the global financial system because of their size, volatility, and growing integration with traditional finance.[15] Numerous bankruptcies in this sector revealed regulators' ignorance, in particular the breakdown of the fraudulent cryptocurrency exchange FTX in 2022. All in all, the systemic traits that led to the global financial crisis appear to be still in place and the conditions may have even worsened. It is probably only a matter of time before the financial systems will be on the brink of collapse again. This is not a good prospect for democracy.

State intervention to stabilize the financial system

State intervention to stabilize the financial sector is not an exceptional phenomenon brought about by the global financial crisis but common practice since decades. The alleged retreat of the state and the advance of the free market are a myth when seen in this light. The state has always intervened in the workings of the market to help investors. Studies show that between 1970 and 2017 there were 151 systemic bank crises, in 118 countries, in which taxpayers have put up on average the incredible figure of 3.3 per cent of GDP for high

---

12 International Monetary Fund. 2023. Global Financial Stability Report, p. 60.
13 Financial Stability Board. 2022. 'Global Monitoring Report on Non-Bank Financial Intermediation', pp. 30, 36.
14 Beker, Victor A. 2021. Preventing the next Financial Crisis. Routledge, pp. 43-44, 85.
15 Cf. Financial Stability Board. 2022. 'Assessment of Risks to Financial Stability from Crypto-Assets.'

income and 9.6 per cent for low- and middle income countries to pay for state interventions to maintain financial stability. Crisis-related increases in public debt on average reach 21.1 per cent of GDP in the latter and 16.4 per cent in the former countries. This contributes to shifting available state resources away from productive use as a larger proportion of revenues needs to be devoted to debt service. Governments on top have also resorted to providing guarantees on bank liabilities in staggering dimensions.[16] As Jeff Faux of the Economic Policy Institute in Washington D.C. emphasized, the great financial crises of the 1990s in Mexico, Thailand, Brazil, Bolivia, South Korea, Indonesia, Russia and Argentina all ended in large investors being protected by public rescue packages while the rest of society was left 'at the mercy of the brutal laws of supply and demand'. This distorted model of the free market economy was in Faux's judgement nothing other than 'socialism for the rich'.[17] But the distinctive feature of the global financial crisis was not only that it began in the USA, a centre of the system, but also that a collapse of the *international* system loomed, requiring simultaneous massive interventions around the world to prevent it. On account of the close global interconnections between financial systems around the world, it is increasingly unlikely that crises can be constrained within local borders. '[I]n the absence of appropriate policies,' the IMF wrote, 'highly integrated economies are still susceptible to harmful cross-border spillovers.'[18] The entire world financial system has become integrated and unstable.

The financial system as a 'priority global public good'

Before the global financial crisis already, the 'International Task Force on Global Public Goods', initiated by Sweden and France and jointly led by the former Mexican President Ernesto Zedillo and Tidjane Thiam from Ivory Coast, numbered 'enhancing international financial stability' among the *priority global public goods*, alongside five others such as tackling climate change and preventing infectious diseases, strengthening the international trading system and achieving peace and security. In contrast to global common goods, which simply exist, 'global public goods' as defined by this task force are important political goals the achievement of which is in the common international interest, will benefit all states and people, and requires effective international cooperation. By definition they cannot be achieved and maintained by

16 Laeven, Luc, and Fabian Valencia. 2020.'Systemic Banking Crises Database II.' IMF Economic Review 68 (2): 307–61, pp. 308, 317, 321.
17 Faux, Jeff. 2006. The Global Class War. Hoboken NJ: John Wiley & Sons, p. 115-7.
18 International Monetary Fund. October 2012. Global Financial Stability Report: Restoring Confidence and Progressing on Reforms. Washington D.C.: IMF. Ch. 3, p. 1.

single countries. The same obstacles that impede the management of global common goods also hinder any attempt to ensure the provision of global public goods such as a stable financial system. Governments find it difficult to agree on far-reaching regulation and measures because of differing national interests. Their willingness to subject themselves to binding rules is limited. Since everyone benefits from a public good, there is an incentive to act as a free rider by deferring or leaving to others the investments and efforts needed to maintain that good. Ensuring compliance with the rules agreed on is difficult. Sometimes the provision or maintenance of a public good can be thwarted if only one of the parties involved, the weakest link, fails to observe the rules. The international Task Force found that adherence to the principle of national sovereignty was the 'basic problem' that 'underlies all the others'. '[T]he major obstacles', the Task Force wrote in its report, 'emerge from the fact that the international sphere is characterized principally by voluntary interaction between sovereign states.'[19] Here, too, it all comes down to the fact that there is no framework of world law that would enable effective and legitimate global regulation and action.

The anarchic system of international law

The entire system of international law can be described in terms analogous to those that characterize a disembedded market. Homo oeconomicus, striving—in the doctrine of laissez-faire—to maximize his benefits, equates in international law to the sovereign state seeking advantage. In the final analysis, what concerns the sovereign state is geopolitical interests, that is, the achievement of a position of power relative to rival states. This includes control over territory and resources enforced by military power—the classic instrument of geopolitics; but it goes beyond that. Rivalry between industrialised countries is no longer played out on the battlefield but on economic territory. In what Luttwak calls the 'geo-economy', states intervene in support of specific industries and companies, be it to further their market dominance, to defend them against unwanted competition or to support their conquest of new markets. 'Even when there is no thought of any military confrontation therefore', according to Luttwak, 'even when they cooperate most amicably in all sorts of ways, states are inherently adversarial.'[20] After the end of the Cold War, the influential political scientist Kenneth Waltz, known in the study of international relations as the founding theorist of neorealism, wrote that in spite of

---

19   International Task Force on Global Public Goods. 'Meeting Global Challenges: International Cooperation in the National Interest. Report of the Intl. Task Force on Global Public Goods'. Stockholm, 2006, pp. 18-9.
20   Luttwak, Edward. 1999. Turbo Capitalism. London: Orion, p. 128

the changes 'the basic structure of international politics continues to be anarchic'. 'Each state', according to Waltz, 'fends for itself with or without the cooperation of others. The leaders of states and their followers are concerned with their standings, that is, with their positions vis-à-vis one another.'[21] George Soros has developed this analogy further. The doctrine of geopolitics, he wrote, 'has some similarity to the doctrine of laissez-faire in that both treat self-interest as the only realistic basis for explaining or predicting the behavior of a subject. For laissez-faire, the subject is the individual market participant; for geopolitics, the state. Closely allied to both is the vulgar version of Darwinism according to which the survival of the fittest is the rule of nature'. In his view, the idea that the state should represent the interests of *its citizens* rather than being an end in itself does not exist in the world of geopolitics. 'Geopolitical realism', according to Soros, 'may be regarded as a translation of the doctrine of laissez faire into international relations with the difference that the actors are states, not individuals or business units.'[22] We would like to take this line of thought one step further. For if in Polanyi's analysis the state has to intervene in order to control the disembedded market, then in our analogy it is precisely the option of intervention on the part of the *world state* which does not exist in international law.

Liberalism, laissez-faire and the question of a world state

However, it should be pointed out here—on behalf of the classical advocates of laissez-faire—that the parallel drawn here with geopolitics and international law distorts and truncates their arguments in important respects. In their doctrine, the point is precisely that the state should *not* get involved in economic affairs, and so for example should not intervene to support specific industries or companies. Moreover, laissez-faire meant for them *not* the *absence* of a superordinate state power, as is the case in the anarchic international order, but precisely its *restriction* to specific tasks. Of course, the state should avoid getting involved in the workings of the market if at all possible, but its active engagement in ensuring peace, liberty and property is taken as given. In their view, the state has to be able to enforce peaceful human cooperation and the observance of common rules when necessary. 'Liberalism is not anarchism, nor has it anything whatsoever to do with anarchism', the influential economist Ludwig von Mises (1881 to 1973) declared in his 1927 work 'Liberalism'. This applies equally to the international order. The international law dogma that 'every single state is sovereign' and represents 'the high-

---

21 Waltz, Kenneth N. 1993. 'The Emerging Structure of International Politics'. Intl. Security 18 (2): 44–79, p. 59.
22 Soros, George. The Crisis of Global Capitalism. New York: PublicAffairs, 1998. p. 215.

est and last instance' was anathema to the proponents of worldwide free trade and movement ('laissez-faire et laissez-passer'). Liberalism is, as Mises attempted to make clear, 'a world-embracing political concept, and the same ideas that it seeks to realize within a limited area it holds to be valid also for the larger sphere of world politics. If the liberal makes a distinction between domestic and foreign policy, he does so solely for purposes of convenience and classification, to subdivide the vast domain of political problems into major types, and not because he is of the opinion that different principles are valid for each'. In the knowledge that it is not enough to ensure peace within the state, liberalism demands 'that the political organization of society be extended until it reaches its culmination in *a world state that unites all nations on an equal basis*' (emphasis added).[23] Friedrich von Hayek (1899 to 1992), a Nobel Prize winner for economics, and together with Mises one of the most important representatives of the Austrian School of economics and for some people a pioneer of neoliberalism, made a clear and simple appeal in his 1944 book 'The Road to Serfdom' for a *world federalist* order with a 'super-national authority'. This international political authority should be endowed with precisely defined but fully enforceable powers, including the power to 'hold the economic interests in check, and in the conflict between them [to] truly hold the scales'. It must have the power vis-à-vis the states to implement a set of rules in order to 'restrain the different nations from action harmful to their neighbours'. Hayek thought federalism was 'nothing but the application to international affairs of democracy, the only method of peaceful change man has yet invented. But it is a democracy with definitely limited powers'. 'Wisely used', he wrote, 'the federal principle of organization may indeed prove the best solution of some of the world's most difficult problems.'[24] So differences of opinion, even with those who represent a properly understood form of Laisser-faire, are to do not so much with *whether* there should be a world state as with what form it should take and what exactly its responsibilities should be.

The global race to deregulate

The fact that countries are in a permanent state of 'unrestrained competition' with one another is a source of great advantage for radical free market forces. Once a deregulation has been implemented in a few countries, then international competition means that this leads to a self-propelling deregulatory race.

23 Mises, Ludwig von. 2002. Liberalism. 3rd ed. Mises.org edition; Cobden Press / The Foundation for Economic Education, Inc., p. 37, 105, 148. He later qualified his position under the influence of the Second World War. See idem. 1944. Omnipotent Government: The Rise of the Total State and Total War. Auburn, Alabama: Liberty Fund / Ludwig von Mises Institute, p. 243.
24 Hayek, Friedrich August von. 2001. The Road to Serfdom. Routledge Classics, pp. 238-9, 243.

What determines this 'race to the bottom' is where companies and capital can find the most favourable conditions. This puts pressure on wages, social security, environmental standards, workers' rights and fiscal policy. The *New York Times* columnist and apostle of globalization Thomas L. Friedman spoke in his bestselling book 'The Lexus and the Olive Tree: Understanding Globalization' of the 'golden straitjacket' created by Thatcher and Reagan. Friedman's metaphor of a straitjacket describes the principles to which a country must adhere in the globalised economy in order to obtain credit and attract capital investment. 'To fit into the Golden Straightjacket a country must either adopt, or be seen as moving toward, the following golden rules: making the private sector the primary engine of its economic growth, maintaining a low rate of inflation and price stability, shrinking the size of its state bureaucracy, maintaining as close to a balanced budget as possible, if not a surplus, eliminating and lowering tariffs on imported goods, removing restrictions on foreign investment, getting rid of quotas and domestic monopolies, increasing exports, privatizing state-owned industries and utilities, deregulating capital markets, making its currency convertible, opening its industries, stock and bond markets to direct foreign ownership and investment, deregulating its economy to promote as much domestic competition as possible, eliminating government corruption, subsidies and kickbacks as much as possible, opening its banking and telecommunications systems to private ownership and competition and allowing its citizens to choose from an array of competing pension options and foreign-run pension and mutual funds.'[25] Friedman calls the straitjacket 'golden' because only this programme, he thought, is now capable of generating growth. Politics, he argued, has become a mere technical skill with the purpose of implementing a programme demanded by the ratings agencies, the investment funds, speculators and other market forces. They are supported in their demands by the International Monetary Fund and the World Bank, which supply credit only subject to the fulfilment of linked conditions. In effect, it is a programme that is weakening, obstructing and degrading democracy in the words of Raymond Baker, the founding president of Global Financial Integrity. That's because in the process, over the last half century, he wrote, 'capitalism has created the means by which trillions upon trillions of dollars, euros, pounds, and other stores of wealth can move and shelter invisibly, out of sight and beyond the control of central bankers, revenue authorities, law enforcement agencies, and international institutions. With this level of financial secrecy now available, to and dominating capitalist operations, riches move inexorably upward, accelerating economic inequality' which in

25   Friedman, Thomas L. 2000. The Lexus and the Olive Tree. New York: Picador, p. 105.

turn undermines the democratic foundations of society and erodes the social contract. 'Rebalancing capitalism and democracy', he goes on, 'is, along with climate change, the most difficult and important challenge facing the world in the twenty-first century.'[26]

Tax havens and anonymous shell companies

As the British journalist Nicholas Shaxson set out in his book 'Treasure Islands', tax havens are a pivot of the unfettered global economic and financial system. Tax havens are sovereign states or territorial jurisdictions under international law which attract businesses by helping people or firms to 'get around the rules, laws and regulations of jurisdictions elsewhere'.[27] What they offer is high levels of discretion and secrecy, low or even no taxation, and a policy of non-intervention on the part of the local authorities. Around two-thirds of world trade is carried out by companies operating internationally. A presence in offshore territories enables such internationally active companies to choose almost at will, by means of nominal internal costing practices, the location where profits and losses become liable or deductible for tax purposes—a trick which is entirely legal. In combination with the use of holding companies registered in tax havens, to which the rights over brands or other forms of intellectual property are assigned, this often succeeds in its aim of reducing tax liabilities to the lowest possible level. The conditions and financial services on offer in many tax havens play an important role, for example through money-laundering and corruption, for criminal enterprises operating at the global level. They service illicit money as a key part of their business. It is even possible that such money flows rescued the financial system during the financial crisis. The head of the UN Office on Drugs and Crime UNODC, the Italian economic expert Antonio Maria Costa, claimed to the *Observer* that at the height of the crisis, money from the drugs trade and other illegal activities totalling nearly 350 billion US dollars was pumped into the financial system and thereby laundered. For some banks on the brink of collapse, he said, that was the only source of liquid capital available at the time.[28]

It is not only isolated territories like the Cayman Islands in the Caribbean (population 50,000), one of fourteen British Overseas Territories and at the same time one of the world's biggest financial centres, which thumb their noses at the rest of the world in this way. 'The world's most important tax

26   Baker, pp. 1, 7.
27   Shaxson, Nicholas. 2012. Treasure Islands: Tax Havens and the Men Who Stole the World. London: Vintage, p. 8.
28   Syal, Rajeev. 13 December 2009. 'Drug money saved banks in global crisis, claims UN advisor'. The Observer (www.guardian.co.uk).

havens are not exotic palm-fringed islands, as many people suppose, but some of the world's most powerful countries', Shaxson reports. The worldwide offshore system involves around sixty shadow finance centres arranged in a network of spheres of influence controlled from Great Britain and the USA. The important roles played by Reagan and Thatcher in the globalization project are well known. Far less attention has been paid to these shadow financial centres, 'the silent warriors of globalization that have been forcing nation states rich and poor to compete through them, and in the process cutting swathes through their tax and regulatory systems and regulations whether they like it or not'.[29] An important study identified 24 so-called 'sink Offshore Financial Centers' (OFCs) which 'attract and retain foreign capital', among them the British Virgin Islands, Cayman Islands, Gibraltar, Hong Kong, Jersey, Liechtenstein, Luxembourg and Malta. In addition, the researchers found a small set of five countries that play a key role as 'conduit OFCs' that 'enable the transfer of capital without taxation': the Netherlands, the United Kingdom, Ireland, Singapore and Switzerland.[30]

The decisive part played by tax havens in this 'damaging tax competition' was clearly identified in 1998 in a ground-breaking OECD report. One problem is tax evasion. In order to track down tax evaders more easily and to increase transparency, a benchmark for bilateral information exchange was developed, to be applied 'on request' and applicable to tax havens. But these efforts, which were taken up by the G20 summit meetings from 2009 onwards, have been ridiculed by many observers despite important efforts such as the OECD's Convention on Mutual Administrative Assistance in Tax Matters which facilitates bilateral treaties. When a tax authority requests information, it usually has to know in advance fairly precisely what information is sought, according to Shaxson. He sees it as window dressing. In any event, when the fox announces that he has improved the security of the henhouse it should always be taken with a large pinch of salt.[31] Several studies agree in concluding that a patchwork of bilateral agreements on information exchange will in the final analysis achieve not much anyway. What is needed instead is a 'big bang': *a watertight global agreement.*[32]In order to successfully close down the offshore system and the associated international money-laundering, corruption

29 Shaxson, pp. 21, 24.
30 Garcia-Bernardo, Javier, et al. 2017. 'Uncovering Offshore Financial Centers: Conduits and Sinks in the Global Corporate Ownership Network'. Scientific Reports 7 (1): 6246.
31 Shaxson, pp. 36, 247-9.
32 Elsayyad, May, and Kai A. Konrad. January 2011. 'Fighting Multiple Tax Havens'. Max Planck Institute for Tax Law and Public Finance, Working Paper 2011-01 (www.tax.mpg.de); Johannesen, Niels, and Gabriel Zucman. 2014. 'The End of Bank Secrecy? An Evaluation of the G20 Tax Haven Crackdown'. American Economic Journal: Economic Policy (6) 1: 65–91.

and tax evasion, the problem of anonymous shell companies must also be addressed. Several massive leaks of internal documents of offshore service providers, in particular the so-called Panama, Paradise and Pandora Papers, published in 2016, 2017 and 2021 respectively, made big waves in the media. Shell companies, meaning companies that cannot be traced back to their true owners, have become one of the most important means of hiding and diverting assets. 'Regulating shell companies', a study found, 'poses a major challenge for many facets of global governance.' While there are international standards, drawn up by the Financial Action Task Force on Money Laundering whose 'essential role' was recognized in a 2019 UN Security Council resolution, these have turned out to be ineffective. The researchers were most surprised by the finding that it is the incorporation providers based in the OECD countries which are the least rigorous in applying the standards intended to combat anonymous shell companies. 'Incorporation providers in the United States, especially in Delaware, Indiana, Wyoming, and Nevada, are among the worst in the world', the report states.[33] In fact, the United States, together with Switzerland and Singapore, is one of the three world's biggest contributors to financial secrecy, according to the 2022 edition of the Tax Justice Network's Financial Secrecy Index. Next on the list are Hong Kong, Luxembourg, Japan and the EU's largest economy, Germany.

The European Parliament immediately created a committee of inquiry to look into the Panama Papers scandal and its implications. The final report concluded among other things that some EU member states are obstructing the fight against money laundering, tax avoidance and evasion and called for a common international definition of what actually constitutes an offshore financial centre, tax haven or secrecy haven.[34] Following the publication of the Paradise Papers connected to the offshore law firm Appleby in November 2017, the Financial Transparency Coalition noted that 'this latest in a succession of leaks demonstrates how the global network of tax havens and the secrecy they enable continue to thrive.'[35]

The hidden trillions

The harm done by the offshore system can barely be quantified. The French economist Gabriel Zucman estimated that 8 per cent of households' financial

---

33 Findley, Michael G. Global Shell Games: Experiments In: Transnational Relations, Crime, And Terrorism. Cambridge University Press, 2014, pp. 168-70.

34 European Parliament. 16 November 2017. 'Report on the inquiry into money laundering, tax avoidance and tax evasion'. A8-0357/2017.

35 Financial Transparency Coalition. 9 November 2017. 'Paradise Papers reiterate need for a truly global response to crack down on tax haven abuses' (financialtransparency.org).

wealth or 7.6 trillion US dollars is held in tax havens.[36] According to a study by Zucman and colleagues based on data leaked from HSBC and Mossack Fonseca in the Panama Papers, the super-rich with a net wealth of above 40 million US dollars on average evade about 30 per cent of personal taxes.[37] Based on macroeconomic data, a more recent paper estimated that 36 per cent of multinational profits are shifted to tax havens globally.[38] In a widely noted assessment commissioned by the Tax Justice Network, James Henry, former chief economist of the business consultancy McKinsey, described the offshore system as 'the black hole of the world economy'. The *purely financial assets* alone stashed away by private individuals in tax havens have been estimated by him at between 21 and 32 trillion US dollars, which is more than the annual GDP of the USA. Roughly half of this is owned by around 100,000 super-rich people from all parts of the world. Since this money cannot as a rule be captured in official statistics, it distorts survey data on the distribution of wealth. Inequality is even greater than the statistics can possibly reflect. With regard to the money that is siphoned into tax havens by the elites from the developing countries, and invested mainly in assets owned by the industrialised countries, the study concludes that the developing countries are in fact net lenders, since the private wealth that has been moved outside their borders far exceeds their public external debt. 'The problem here', wrote Henry, 'is that the assets of these countries are held by a small number of wealthy individuals while the debts are shouldered by the ordinary people of these countries through their governments.' But the super-rich, he adds, are 'one of society's most well-entrenched interest groups'.[39]

The role of a UN Parliamentary Assembly

Below the threshold of a fully-fledged system of world law with a global parliament at its center, a UN Parliamentary Assembly would be an appropriate place to launch investigations into the facilitation of anonymous shell companies, tax evasion, illicit financial flows and similar issues and what to do about it from a global perspective. When it surfaced in 2012, for instance, that leadings banks and traders had been manipulating the Libor interest-rate to their favor, perhaps for longer than two decades, it was suggested that 'a global

36   Zucman, Gabriel. 2015. The Hidden Wealth of Nations. University of Chicago Press, pp. 34-6.
37   Alstadsaeter, Annette, Niels Johannesen, und Gabriel Zucman. 2017. 'Tax Evasion and Inequality'.
38   Tørsløv, Thomas, Ludvig Wier, and Gabriel Zucman. 2022. 'The Missing Profits of Nations.' The Review of Economic Studies 90 (3): 1499–1534.
39   Henry, James S. July 2012. 'The Price of Offshore Revisited'. Tax Justice Network, pp. 3, 5.

independent inquiry' should have been carried out.[40] This is a job that a UN-PA could have taken on. Its role goes beyond being a watchdog that enhances accountability, public attention and political pressure globally. An expert group on 'international financial accountability, transparency and integrity' launched by the presidents of the UN's General Assembly and Economic and Social Council, the so-called FACTI panel, noted in its 2021 final report that international norms in this field need to enjoy 'the highest levels of legitimacy' as they include the possibility of coercive measures. Negotiations of rules on the one hand thus should be based on universal participation of states. But the panel added that legitimacy, on the other hand, 'must not be considered to be only the realm of states, but a matter how of how all citizens of the world find rules and standards to be legitimate.'[41] An obvious way to ensure this is to give them a say, too, in rule-making through an elected representative body.

Global state formation as the goal of the counter-movement

In his book on 'The Strange Non-death of Neo-liberalism', the British political scientist Colin Crouch wrote that the task is not 'to explain why neoliberalism will die following its crisis, but the very opposite: how it comes about that neoliberalism is emerging from the financial collapse more politically powerful than ever'.[42] But this is no longer quite so surprising, given that the counter-movement faces the problem of a lack of world state policy instruments to set against the forces of the market and the global elite. It is effectively neutralised, since there are no global government structures it could use to create globally effective regulation. While initiatives involving a few countries may have some symbolic impact, they cannot achieve much at the level of the system as a whole, and this is even more true of efforts made by states acting unilaterally. 'A third and rather different reason for not seeing the resurgence of the state as a simple strategy for reform', according to Crouch, 'is that political power remains overwhelmingly tied to the level of the nation-state. Not only does this mean that it has problems acting as a truly "public" force on the global stage, but political parties and governments continue to try to define interests in national terms.' In a globalised economy this approach is unrealistic, he argued.[43]

40 Jennings, Philip. 2012. 'Letter to the Editor: Tilting the Power Balance Back towards Fairness.' Financial Times, July 3, 2012. (www.ft.com).
41 United Nations. 2021. 'Financial Integrity for Sustainable Development.' Report of the High Level Panel on International Financial Accountability, Transparency and Integrity for Achieving the 2030 Agenda (www.factipanel.org), p. 17.
42 Crouch, Colin. 2011. The Strange Non-Death of Neo-Liberalism. Cambridge: Polity, p. viii
43 Ibid., p. 173.

In the end, as we have seen already with regard to the transition to a sustainable economy, it comes down to the fact that the counter-movement will have to promote a process of global state formation leading to a system of world law. The fundamental principle on which the offshore system stands, for example, is that of the sovereignty of the states and territorial jurisdictions involved. The freedom that these countries enjoy to undermine at will the global fiscal, economic and financial system must be put into question. The fight against the offshore system, Shaxson wrote, needs 'an international perspective, to build new forms of international cooperation'.[44] 'A constructive counter-movement', in the view of the Canadian economist Myron Frankman in a rewarding book on world federalism, 'must have on its agenda for serious early consideration the building of democratic institutions at the world level as well as building and strengthening systems at lower levels.'[45] Some critics of globalization may find this a difficult step to take, as the movement has foregrounded a broad and fundamental opposition to international organizations such as the WTO or forums such as the G20 and is characterised by a profound distrust of the state. But without realising it, they have thereby accepted as a premise a vulgar neoliberal conception of the international system. In a keynote speech at the fiftieth anniversary conference of the International Studies Association in New York in 2009, the then President of the ISA, political scientist Thomas G. Weiss, asked what had happened to the once prominent notion of a federal world government. He argued passionately that the academic community should give serious consideration to the idea once again. 'The market,' noted Weiss, in a striking observation, 'will not graciously provide global institutions to ensure human survival with dignity. Adam Smith's "invisible hand" does not operate among states to solve problems any more than it does within states.'[46]

44 Shaxson, p. 31.
45 Frankman, Myron J. 2004. World Democratic Federalism. New York: Palgrave Macmillan, pp. 37-8.
46 Weiss, Thomas G. 2009. 'What Happened to the Idea of World Government?' International Studies Quarterly 53: 253–71.

14.

A world currency, global taxation, and fiscal federalism

Potential global solutions to the problems in the fiscal, monetary and finance systems have been pursued and put forward on numerous occasions. This includes proposals for global taxation, international coordination of tax policy (especially with regard to corporations) and the creation of a world currency. Global taxation, in particular, is discussed as an important mechanism to enable global fiscal policy and to finance the provision of global public goods, among other things. A democratic world parliament needs to play a key role in the conception, development and design of these projects.

A world currency and a world central bank

John Stuart Mill famously noted in 1848 that he found it a 'barbarism' that 'all independent countries choose to assert their nationality by having, to their own inconvenience and that of their neighbours, a peculiar currency of their own.'[1] As early as the 1860s there had been a serious French initiative to introduce an international currency, but it was rejected at the time by Great Britain. Then, during the Second World War, the USA and Britain worked on plans for a world currency as part of their post-war planning. In the USA it had the working title of 'Unitas', while in Great Britain John Maynard Keynes worked on a concept named 'Bancor'. As the Nobel laureate in economics Robert Mundell reported, the intention to launch a world currency was then dropped shortly before the decisive conference of the Allies on currency and financial issues in Bretton Woods in 1944. Concerns had arisen in the USA over a possible consequential loss of sovereignty. 'U.S. reluctance to go forward with a global currency', according to Mundell, 'fits the historical pattern that the leading power resist monetary reform that might interfere with the international role of its own currency.'[2] However, the question continues to be raised regularly and prominently. For example, ten weeks after 19 October 1987 saw the biggest stock market crash in post-war history, the *Economist* wrote in its cover story that a world currency, at least between the most important in-

<hr>

1   Mill, John Stuart. Principles of Political Economy. 1909 [1848]. Ed. by William J. Ashley. 7th ed. London: Library of Economics and Liberty (econlib.org), Book III, Ch. XX, §2.
2   Mundell, Robert. 2005. 'The case for a world currency'. Journal of Policy Modeling 27: 465–475, pp. 468, 475.

dustrialised countries, ought to be pursued. The advantages would soon seem 'irresistible to everybody except foreign-exchange traders and governments'.[3] Following the Asian financial crisis ten years later, the former chairman of the US American central bank, the Federal Reserve, Paul Volcker, wrote that 'if we are to have a truly globalized economy, a single world currency makes sense', adding that in his view, 'underlying tendencies are in that direction'.[4] During the global financial crisis, the chief economics editor of *Business Week*, Michael Mandel, asked himself what would happen in the not unlikely event that a dollar crisis were to break out which the Federal Reserve was unable to bring under control. In theory it was clear what the answer ought to be, according to Mandel: 'a global central bank, with the ultimate authority to print money and regulate the financial system around the world'.[5]

External impact of monetary policy: the Triffin dilemma

The necessity and precise design of a world currency and a world central bank continue to be the subject of controversial debates. One thing seems obvious, however: the current system in which a single national currency, the US dollar, effectively serves as the world's reserve currency, is unfair and dysfunctional. The People's Republic of China, for instance, has amassed currency reserves of more than 3 trillion US dollars and potentially another 3 trillion that are hidden from the central bank's balance sheet.[6] The Chinese government fears a severe depreciation of its dollar reserves due to inflation or a possible dollar crash. This concern intensified when the Federal Reserve's 'quantitative easing' program, initially enacted during the financial crisis and later resumed during the COVID-19 pandemic, massively increased the dollar supply. The Governor of the Chinese Central Bank, Zhou Xiaochuan, declared in March 2009, shortly before the G20 summit meeting in London, that the so-called 'Triffin dilemma', described by the economist Robert Triffin in the 1960s, had not gone away. Countries that issue reserve currencies, Xiaochuan said in summarising this dilemma, 'may either fail to adequately meet the demand of a growing global economy for liquidity as they try to ease inflation pressures at home, or create excess liquidity in the global markets by overly

3   'Get ready for the phoenix'. 9 January 1988. The Economist, no. 306: 9–10, p. 9.
4   Volcker, Paul A. 31 January 2000. 'Toward a Single World Currency to Level the Playing Field.' International Herald Tribune.
5   Mandel, Michael. 16 March 2008. 'A Global Bailout?' Businessweek (www.businessweek.com); see also the cover story two years earlier: Mandel, Michael, and Richard S. Dunham. 20 November 2006. 'Can Anyone Steer This Economy?' Businessweek: 57–62.
6   Setser, Brad. 29 June 2023. 'Shadow Reserves. How China Hides Trillions of Dollars of Hard Currency.' The China Project (thechinaproject.com).

stimulating domestic demand'.[7] This demonstrates the strong external impact of monetary policy in those countries with the most important worldwide reserve currencies. This concerns primarily the United States as the dollar, despite a two-decade decline, still accounts for almost 60 per cent of global foreign exchange reserves and is on one side of nearly 90 per cent of foreign exchange trades. Spillover effects will not necessarily be the same everywhere and central banks have little room to take them into consideration to begin with as their mandates are oriented to domestic objectives. The 'dollar is not an impartial means of international exchange since it is a means of issuing credit for one state', French President Charles de Gaulle noted in 1965, frustrated by the 'asymmetries' inherent in the international financial system agreed on in Bretton Woods.[8] Global liquidity ultimately needs to be managed as a global public good which cannot be done properly by means of a national currency.[9] A reform of the international monetary system should therefore have as its goal, according to Xiaochuan and others, an international reserve currency disconnected from individual nations. The President of the 63rd UN General Assembly, the Nicaraguan Miguel d'Escoto Brockmann, in 2008 set up an expert commission on 'reforms of the international monetary and financial system' chaired by Joseph Stiglitz. In a report presented a year later, the commission said that setting up a 'new global reserve currency' was an idea 'whose time has come'.[10]

Currency wars and global fragmentation

The US government at the time responded by accusing China of maintaining an artificially low rate for the renminbi, to the cost of China's trade partners. In fact, monetary policy is an important weapon in geo-economic competition. The American lawyer and investment banker James Rickards, who was jointly responsible for drawing up simulation exercises for economic warfare in the Pentagon, wrote in the *New York Times* bestseller 'Currency Wars' that the Federal Reserve's quantitative easing programme effectively declared a 'currency war' on the world. The flood of dollars, he argued, prompted higher inflation in China, higher food prices in Egypt, speculative bubbles in Brazil,

---

7   Xiaochuan, Zhou. 23 March 2009. 'Statement on Reforming the International Monetary System'. Foreign Affairs Essential Documents (www.cfr.org).

8   Quoted by Gourinchas, Pierre-Olivier, Hélène Rey, and Maxime Sauzet. April 2019. 'The International Monetary and Financial System.' Working Paper Series. National Bureau of Economic Research, p. 2.

9   Bernard Snoy, André Icard, and Philip Turner. 2019. Managing Global Liquidity as a Global Public Good. A Report of an RTI Working Party, Robert Triffin International, pp. 40, 43, 9.

10 United Nations. 2009. 'Report of the Commission of Experts of the President of the United Nations General Assembly on Reforms of the International Monetary and Financial System', para. 7.

and above all a devaluation of US external debt, together with other intended and unintended consequences. High-ranking military and intelligence personnel have recognised, he claimed, that American military dominance is closely linked to the pre-eminent position of the dollar as the *de facto* global reserve currency. The international demand for dollars contributes for example to offsetting the USA's huge external trade deficit and financing the US budget, including its massive military expenditure. According to Rickards, the currency question is therefore now regarded as a 'national security' issue.[11] This assessment was confirmed at a bipartisan hearing in June 2023 organized by the US House of Representatives Financial Services Committee's Subcommittee on National Security, Illicit Finance, and International Financial Institutions which focussed on how the US could preserve the US dollar's 'dominance and supremacy' and retain the 'numerous benefits' that stem from it.[12]

Plans for moving away from the US dollar have been pursued for a long time, in particular by China which increasingly promotes the use of its own renminbi as an international currency. Steep increases in interest rates in the US, a soaring US dollar as well as geopolitical tension and energy and food price shocks in the wake of the attempted invasion of Ukraine by Russia in 2022 once again moved the 'Triffin dilemma' to the center of attention. Sanctions imposed on Russia by the G7 and other countries for its illegal aggression, including a freeze of Russian central bank foreign reserve assets and disconnecting the country's banks from the SWIFT global payment system, has made the Russian government replace the US dollar and euro in foreign settlements, making the renminbi the most traded currency in the country for the first time in April 2023. At the same time, vague talk emerged of the potential creation of a new currency to be used in trade by the BRICS states Brazil, Russia, India, China and South Africa. The Russian war on Ukraine has led to a 'sudden shift' in underlying 'geopolitical tectonic plates' that could fragment the global economy into 'distinct economic blocs with different ideologies, political systems, technology standards, cross border payment and trade systems, and reserve currencies', warned the director of the IMF's research department Pierre-Olivier Gourinchas. Sanctions on central bank assets, in particular, he said, would trigger a move away from the dollar as this possibility posed an additional 'geopolitical Triffin dilemma' for certain countries.[13]

11 Rickards, James. 2011. *Currency wars*. New York: Portfolio/Penguin, pp. xiv f., 223.
12 Norton, Ben. 20 June 2023. 'US Congress Plots to Save Dollar Dominance amid Global De-Dollarization Rebellion.' *Geopolitical Economy Report* (blog) (geopoliticaleconomy.com).
13 Gourinchas, Pierre-Olivier. June 2022. 'Shifting Geopolitical Tectonic Plates.' *Finance & Development* (imf.org).

Building on the IMF's Special Drawing Rights

Enhancing the use of the International Monetary Funds' Special Drawing Rights, in short SDR, is frequently discussed as a potential global approach towards an international reserve system that is not linked to a particular national currency. The commission convened by Brockmann explored how a 'new global reserve system' could be set up, arguing that this could be done either from scratch through a new institution or by 'simply a broadening of existing SDR arrangements, making their issuance automatic and regular'.[14]

SDR were created by the IMF in 1969 as an asset that is supposed to facilitate governments' access to 'freely usable' foreign currency and thus help ensure liquidity. SDR are now valued according to a weighted basket of currencies that includes the US dollar, euro, renminbi, yen, and pound sterling. Governments that wish to exchange SDR for foreign currency or vice versa notify the IMF which makes sure that requests are matched. These exchanges are voluntary. If there are not enough voluntary buyers for SDR, however, a participant whose reserve positions are deemed sufficiently strong theoretically can be obliged by the IMF to provide the currency in question up to a specified amount. This has not happened since 1987.[15] In the most accurate way, Mark Plant, an expert at the Center for Global Development, characterized SDR as a 'reserve sharing mechanism'.[16]

The IMF allocates SDR to its members according to a quota system that is supposed to reflect each country's relative position in the world economy. The IMF's Executive Board that represents member states has decided to do this five times and the latest two allocations were by far the largest: in 2009, to boost liquidity during the financial crisis, SDR equivalent to 250 billion US dollar, and in 2021 an equivalent of 650 billion, in particular to support vulnerable countries in their pandemic recovery. In total, the value of existing SDR equals about one trillion US dollar which means that governments in principle agreed to make around 8 per cent of their collective global reserves pool of nearly the equivalent of 13 trillion US dollar available to each other, if need be.

The allocation of SDR does not create new money and the mechanism is separate from the IMF's lending operations. Nonetheless, if a country trades SDR against hard currency, it can use this at its discretion, including for budgetary use which means crossing the line between fiscal and monetary

---

14   United Nations, 2009, ibid., paras. 32-47. 42.

15   On the functioning of SDRs see International Monetary Fund. IMF Financial Operations. 4th ed. Washington, 2018, pp. 85-105.

16   Plant, Mark. August 2021. 'The Challenge of Reallocating SDRs: A Primer.' Center for Global Development (cgdev.org), p. 3.

purposes.[17] According to the Colombian economist and former minister of finance José Antonio Ocampo, 'perhaps the most important and simplest reform' would be to eliminate the distinction between the IMF's general resources and SDR accounts and 'to finance all IMF lending and conduct all IMF operations with SDRs, thus making global monetary creation similar to domestic money creation by central banks'. This would include departing from the existing quota system, potentially adding more currencies to the basket, allowing broader use of SDR in private transactions, and creating a substitution account that allows countries to transform their existing currency reserves into 'SDR-denominated assets issued by the IMF'.[18] Further, this could go along with periodic allocation of SDR 'in line with the expansion of international commerce' as a 2010 UN report suggested. The expert commission proposed regular or counter-cyclical issuance of SDR.[19] An IMF paper that explored enhanced use of SDR argued that allocation could be 'conditional on policies being deemed appropriate according to benchmarks to be determined'. Among other things, it would also be possible for the IMF to be authorised to market its own SDR-dominated credit instruments. Such securities, the paper said, in the long run could 'constitute an embryo of global currency'.[20]

This 'more ambitious reform option' was explored by the IMF's strategy, policy and review department which pointed out that a limitation of SDR is that they are not a currency. Eventually, SDR or SDR-denominated instruments need to be converted 'to a national currency for most payments or interventions in foreign exchange markets, which adds to cumbersome use in transactions.' Further, the SDR's value would remain linked to the national currencies included in the basket. Instead, a real currency 'sui generis', issued by a global central bank as a lender of last resort and circulating in lieu of national currencies or in parallel with them, could be used as a general medium of exchange.[21]

Such a global currency could be made available as digital cash. The development of central bank digital currency, or CBDC, around the world is facilitating this possibility. According to the Bank for International Settlements 90 per cent of the world's central banks are exploring the introduction of retail

---

17   Id. Oct. 2022. 'Is There a Better Way to Use Global Reserves?' Center for Global Development (cgdev.org), p. 8.
18   Ocampo, José Antonio. 2017. 'Reforming the Global Reserve System.' In: From Great Depression to Great Recession. International Monetary Fund, p. 200-2.
19   UN Department of Economic and Social Affairs. 2010. 'World Economic and Social Survey 2010: Retooling Global Development', p. 128.
20   IMF. 7 January 2011. 'Enhancing International Monetary Stability-A Role for the SDR?', paras. 18, 24.
21   IMF. 2010. 'Reserve Accumulation and International Monetary Stability', paras. 48-51.

CBDCs for use by the general public, with around two thirds of them in the stage of experiments or proof-of-concept.[22] The IMF is concurrently pushing for a common global regulatory framework.

Embedding a world currency

A single world currency would do away with the possibility of geopolitical currency conflicts, and even the more realistic shorter term options of an SDR-based global reserve system or a parallel currency would at least make them much less damaging and help mitigate the Triffin dilemma. According to Robert Mundell, there is 'no need whatsoever' to have a single world currency. 'One world, one currency', he said at an IMF forum in 2000, 'could exist in a dictatorship or a world empire, but I couldn't imagine a world democracy with a single currency'. Possibilities he considered instead included a 'world currency area' as a 'zone of fixed exchange rates', a 'virtual kind of common currency' based on the SDR and 'two or three big currency areas in the world' getting together under a common monetary policy. A single currency would only be possible 'with a complete rupture or change in political circumstances'. After all, a monetary union was impossible unless there was 'an agreed inflation target' and a 'common authority' that determines a coordinated monetary policy.[23] In other words, differing monetary policy interests would have to be discussed and reconciled in an appropriate supranational body, a global central bank. Indeed, one of the lessons of the European debt crisis of 2009-10 is that steps towards a single currency must be seen and implemented within a wider political framework. The US American economist James Tobin pointed this out some time ago. His 1972 proposal for the introduction of a worldwide tax on international currency transactions, aimed at making short-term currency speculation uneconomic, was one of the principal demands of the anti-globalization movement. What is less known is that this transaction tax was for Tobin only 'a realistic second-best option' after a world currency. 'The mobility of financial capital across currencies is a problem whether exchange rates float freely in markets or are pegged by agreements among governments', he wrote in 1994 in the UNDP Human Development Report. No system in which exchange rates are periodically adjusted can eliminate opportunities for speculation or inhibitions on national monetary policy. Only a 'permanent single currency' can do that. However, Tobin stressed that such a currency can only function if it is embedded into appro-

22   Kosse, Anneke, and Ilaria Mattei. 2022. 'Gaining Momentum – Results of the 2021 BIS Survey on Central Bank Digital Currencies.' Bank for International Settlements (bis.org), pp. 3-4.

23   IMF. 8 Nov. 2000. 'Transcript of Economic Forum - One World, One Currency: Destination or Delusion?'

priate political structures. 'The United States example', he wrote, 'shows that a currency union works to great advantage when sustained not only by centralized monetary authorities but *also by other common institutions*' (emphasis added). In the absence of such institutions, he thought, a world currency remained many decades away.[24] In this sense, a world parliament and world law are indispensable prerequisites for a world currency. It is a cause for concern that this broader dimension is basically ignored in debates on the creation of a world currency. With regard to a new SDR-based reserve system, the 2010 UN report noted that 'none of these reforms will work effectively' if the 'democratic deficit undermining the credibility of the Bretton Woods institutions is not repaired'.[25] Primarily, the report had in mind a rebalancing of the voting power and a 'new multilateral agency' to 'enforce the rules to be established for better and more comprehensive international financial regulation and supervision'. While these are important elements, the democratic deficit includes the lack of a global parliamentary body that provides political guidance and supervision.

The fiscal race to the bottom

Together with the currency and the armed forces, the raising of taxes has traditionally been at the core of national sovereignty. International cooperation on tax policy has long been largely restricted to coordinating the taxation of private individuals and companies operating trans-nationally, in order to avoid the duplication of taxation in the different countries concerned. Deregulation and globalization have led to an ever closer interweaving and ever greater mobility of companies, capital and individuals. The associated fiscal race to the bottom is evidenced in the decline in the rates of tax levied on company profits across the world. Since 1980, the statutory corporate tax rate has consistently declined on a global basis. The OECD average has fallen from 48 per cent in 1982 to 23 per cent in 2021.[26] Research suggests that the global effective corporate tax rate declined from 27 per cent in 1965 to 18 in 2018. This average factors in a significant increase in low- to middle income countries from the 1990s on.[27] In the world's largest economy measured by GDP, the United States, the effective tax rate for 'profitable large corporations' fell

24 Tobin, James. 1994. 'A tax on international currency transactions'. In: Human Development Report 1994: New dimensions of human security, ed. by UNDP, Oxford University Press, p. 70.
25 UN Department, 2010, ibid., p. xxii.
26 Id. 29 June 2012. 'OECD Corporate Income Tax Rates, 1981-2012'. For the 2021 figure see id. Nov. 2021. Corporate Tax Rates around the World, 2021. Fiscal Fact 783. (both: (taxfoundation.org).
27 Bachas, Pierre, et al. 2022. 'Globalization and Factor Income Taxation.' National Bureau of Economic Research Working Papier Series, p. 16.

from 16 per cent in 2014 to 9 in 2018. Half of all large corporations had no federal income tax liability at all.[28]

The economists Gabriel Zucman and Ludvig Wier pointed out that the share of corporate profits in global income increased by a third from about 15 per cent to nearly 20 between 1975 and 2019. Had the effective global corporate tax rate remained constant, revenues thus should have *increased* and not *decreased* about a third. More important still than the statutory and effective tax rates is the possibility already mentioned of corporations avoiding tax altogether. According to Zucman and Wier, the fraction of multinational profits shifted to tax havens increased from less than 2 per cent in the 1970s to 37 in 2019. In 2019 alone, this is equivalent to 969 billion US dollars that weren't taxed. Four years into the implementation of the OECD's 'Base Erosion and Profit Shifting' program to curb tax avoidance schemes, BEPS in short, they conclude, 'there was no discernible decline in global profit shifting'.[29] In fact, they say that 'the problem has only gotten worse', casting a dark shadow of doubt on the usefulness of the G20-endorsed OECD efforts so far.[30]

A global minimum corporate tax rate

Following the election of Donald Trump, the US Congress in December 2017 approved a tax bill that was presented by the new US administration which reduced the statutory corporate tax rate in the US from 35 to 21 per cent. According to James Henry, 'the deep corporate tax cuts contained in this bill have already triggered, or at least substantially accelerated, a global tax war.'[31] The statutory tax rate remained unchanged during Biden's presidency which commenced around three years later. However, the Biden administration supported an OECD proposal under discussion since 2019 of introducing a globally coordinated 'minimum tax' on corporations that is supposed to help stop the fiscal race to the bottom and tax avoidance. The complex plan was endorsed by 136 out of 140 members of the OECD's 'inclusive framework' on BEPS and welcomed at a G20 meeting in October 2021.

The complicated scheme in a first pillar addresses the taxation of the digital economy. If a large multinational company has an overall profitability

---

28 United States Government Accountability Office. 2022. 'Corporate Income Tax. Effective Rates before and after 2017 Law Change.' GAO-23-105384 (gao.gov).

29 Wier, Ludvig, and Gabriel Zucman. 2022. 'Global Profit Shifting, 1975–2019.' WIDER Working Paper 2022/121, November.

30 Id. 2023. '$1 Trillion in the Shade – the Annual Profits Multinational Corporations Shift to Tax Havens Continues to Climb and Climb.' The Conversation. February 23 (theconversation.com).

31 Henry, James S. 21 December 2017. 'Ladies and Gentlemen, Take Your Places: The Global Tax Race to the Bottom Is about to Begin'. The American Interest (www.the-american-interest.com).

above 10 per cent and its sales exceed 20 billion euros, then 25 per cent of profit in excess of 10 per cent of revenue are to be taxed in the 'end market jurisdictions' where its products or services are used or consumed. Profits from extractive activities are excluded because they are to be taxed in the source jurisdiction. It is less apparent why financial services—the largest banks in other words—are excluded as well. Initial assessments found that only 78 of the world's biggest 500 companies would fall under these criteria.[32] At the same time, parties are required not to levy any digital services taxes which were subject of political and trade disputes between the US and France in particular.

According to a second pillar, rules are to be implemented that achieve a minimum tax of 15 per cent on profits by corporations with a revenue above 750 million euro. A key mechanism is the so-called 'income inclusion rule' which says that the home country of a multinational group can impose a 'top-up tax' to bring the corporation's overall effective tax rate up to the minimum level. Addressing concerns primarily from developing countries, an additional rule on a 'qualified domestic minimum top-up tax' was included later. This allows low-tax jurisdictions to apply their own 'top-up tax' first so they can collect the relevant revenue instead of a home country government.

The rules and how they came about are subject of ongoing criticism. First of all, a minimum tax rate of 15 per cent is considered too low. Many countries actually have higher rates in place and pressure could persist to lower them. An independent commission on corporate taxation proposed a minimum rate of 25 per cent.[33] The limited scope of both pillars has met with significant doubts, too, as most multinational companies will not be affected. Furthermore, the share of profit to be allocated to market jurisdiction seems very low.[34] The economists José Antonio Ocampo and Tommaso Faccio, head of the independent commission's secretariat, noted that most developing countries only agreed to the plan, despite 'significant reservations', because they were faced with a 'take-it-or-leave-it choice' by the OECD.[35] Experts doubt that an effective implementation of the plan will succeed as they believe this requires a multilateral treaty, in particular with respect to the first pillar, that amends 'articles on physical presence and business profits of all existing

32 Devreux, Michael, and Martin Simmler. 2021. 'Who Will Pay Amount A?' EconPol Policy Brief (econpol.eu).
33 Independent Commission for the Reform of International Corporate Taxation. 2020. 'ICRICT Response to the OECD Consultation on the Pillar One and Pillar Two Blueprints.'
34 See United Nations. 2023. 'Promotion of Inclusive and Effective International Tax Cooperation at the United Nations. Report of the Secretary-General.' Advance unedited version, 8 August, paras. 34-38.
35 Ocampo, José Antonio, and Tommaso Faccio. 2021. 'How to Secure a Fairer Global Tax Deal.' Project Syndicate. July 7. (project-syndicate.org).

bilateral tax treaties'.[36] In the meantime, governments voluntarily implement the rules domestically as far as possible with guidance from the OECD. The EU, Japan, South Korea and others were quick with preparing and adopting legislation while the US lagged behind due to political opposition. Republicans claimed implementation would 'undermine US sovereignty to enact its own tax policy' and harm US interests.[37]

Unitary taxation of multinational corporations

Despite all the difficulties, the agreement represents an important 'shift to a new paradigm' in international corporate taxation that cannot be undone. As the tax law experts Sol Picciotto and Jeffery M. Kadet highlighted, both pillars necessarily build at least partially on the principle of unitary taxation of multinational corporations and the question that remains is not whether but 'how that should occur'. The most desirable and most effective way in their opinion would be 'a comprehensive global convention' even if that was unlikely in an initial stage.[38] Given that the OECD for decades 'has stubbornly refused even to consider the viability of the approach' according to Picciotto, this is a major development.[39] The prevailing international tax practice so far was for profits of a multinational corporation to be split by country and separate entities and then taxed accordingly. What is crucial is where the profit is recorded in accounting terms. Even under the OECD's transfer pricing guidelines corporations can use a variety of strategies to move profits across the entities they control. By contrast, under a system of unitary taxation by formulary apportionment, multinational enterprises and groups of companies are treated as single business units. All companies within a group have to submit a report on the whole of the group, across all countries and companies, detailing assets, turnover and numbers of employees, among other things. The total profits for the group are then divided up and allocated proportionately to the respective countries and notified to their tax authorities, using a specific formula for working out the respective tax bases based on the factors above, so that the appropriate taxes can be levied. Thus the profits are taxed where the group's real business activities take place. This makes tax avoidance strategies much more difficult. A 'High-Level Panel on Financing for Development' convened

36   Avi-Yonah, Reuven, Young Ran (Christine) Kim, and Karen Sam. 2022. 'A New Framework for Digital Taxation." Law & Economics Working Papers, University of Michigan Law School, March, pp. 1, 5.
37   Weil, Julie Zauzmer. 2023. 'Biden Won a Global Tax Rate. Now Americans Wonder If It Was a Good Deal.' Washington Post, July 6 (washingtonpost.com).
38   Picciotto, Sol, and Jeffery M. Kadet. 2022. 'The Transition to Unitary Taxation.' Tax Notes International 108 (4): 453–61.
39   Picciotto, Sol. Nov. 2012. 'Towards Unitary Taxation of Transnational Corporations.' Tax Justice Network, p. 19.

by UN Secretary-General Kofi Annan in 2001 and led by the former Mexican President Ernesto Zedillo suggested already then that a new international organization for tax issues should 'in due course seek to develop and secure international agreement on a formula for the unitary taxation of multinationals'.[40]

The unitary taxation approach has long been applied, in differing variants, in numerous US federal states in order to divide and allocate the tax base for companies active across state lines. When California made unitary taxation calculated on a *worldwide* basis obligatory for multinational companies operating there, governments and companies around the world were up in arms. The US government received over 30 official diplomatic protests, Great Britain threatened counter-measures, and the British Barclays Bank took the issue to the US Supreme Court.[41] According to the Court, a 'battalion of foreign governments' marched to the aid of the bank during the case.[42] These governments stressed that unitary taxation was not compatible with internationally accepted principles of corporate taxation. By this time, California had bowed to the political pressure and made the worldwide calculation optional. In the EU, a step towards unitary taxation was made when in December 2021 the public country-by-country reporting directive entered into force, obliging member states to adopt national legislation by June 2023. Multinational corporations doing business in the EU with a revenue above 750 million euro will have to disclose publicly their income taxes, breakdown of profits, revenues and employees per country, among other things, which will help establish tax transparency and expose profit shifting.

A UN Tax Organization

Ever since the OECD's secretive negotiations on a multilateral agreement on investments in the mid-1990s, if not earlier, the organization has been accused of being too close to multinational corporations and their lobbyists. The OECD's membership in addition excludes developing countries and thus is not properly representative. There have been persistent calls to shift global policy-making in tax matters to the UN as the Zedillo commission did and more recently the FACTI panel appointed by the presidents of the UN's General Assembly and Economic and Social Council. According to FACTI, 'an inclusive intergovernmental body on tax matters under the auspices of a universal membership institution' like the UN could be promptly established. This could be

40   United Nations (ed.). 2001. 'Report of the High-Level Panel on Financing for Development' (Zedillo report), p. 15.
41   See Rixen, Thomas. The political economy of international tax governance. Palgrave Macmillan, 2008, p. 127.
42   Supreme Court of the United States. 20 June 1994. 'Barclays Bank Plc v. Franchise Tax Board of California'. 512 US 298, para. 40.

built upon the existing UN Tax Committee, which has been in operation since 1968. Its task primarily was to help facilitate tax treaties that take into consideration developing countries' interests as opposed to a model set up by the OECD. Among other things, the new body should be a platform to negotiate and implement a UN Tax Convention that provides for 'effective capital gains taxation' and 'taxing multinational corporations based on group global profit'.[43] In the wake of the publication of the Panama Papers, Ecuador launched an initiative for the creation of a UN tax body to deal with the issue of tax avoidance once and for all as the OECD's efforts were perceived as being ineffective. According to the Tax Justice Network, the OECD also opposed country-by-country reporting for years which appeared to confirm its closeness to corporate interests. The OECD nonetheless was mandated by the G20 in 2013 to collect and publish country-by-country data of relevant multinational enterprises. However, the OECD managed to release a first set of data, related to 2016, only seven years later, and another set related to 2017 only in 2022. Following the OECD's failure to release a third set of data on time in 2023, the Tax Justice Network wrote that the organization's performance, if anything, 'has deteriorated over time'. 'It's clear that the mandate for the global public good of tax transparency should be given to the UN instead', they noted.[44] At this point, it seemed that the OECD was losing its firm grip on international tax governance as the UN stepped in. In December 2022, the UN General Assembly decided by consensus that 'the possibility of developing an international tax cooperation framework or instrument' should be evaluated under the UN's auspices.[45] A subsequent report of the UN Secretary-General concluded that existing arrangements, in particular those offered by the OECD, 'do not satisfy the main elements for fully inclusive and more effective international tax cooperation'. The report suggests that negotiations on tax matters *at the UN* should be made a priority with a legally binding treaty or a framework convention among the options.[46]

Global fiscal federalism and the restitution of fiscal sovereignty

In general terms, it is paradoxical that national governments should have concerns over a possible loss of sovereignty due to establishing common taxation.

---

43 United Nations. 2021. 'Financial Integrity for Sustainable Development.' Report of the High Level Panel on International Financial Accountability, Transparency and Integrity for Achieving the 2030 Agenda, pp. 24, 43.

44 Tax Justice Network. 2022. 'State of Tax Justice 2022. Stopgap Edition', pp. 14, 6.

45 United Nations. 2022. 'Promotion of Inclusive and Effective Tax Cooperation at the United Nations.' Adopted on 30 December. UN Doc. A/RES/77/244, no. 2.

46 Id. 2023. 'Promotion of Inclusive and Effective International Tax Cooperation at the United Nations. Report of the Secretary-General.' Advance unedited version, paras. 47, 68.

On the contrary, it effectively strengthens their sovereignty. For although it is correct that it would no longer be possible to regulate autonomously in those areas of tax law—such as corporate taxation—included in common arrangements, on the other hand such arrangements would ensure the full and proper application of the common regulations without offering any loopholes. The political and economic scientist Thomas Rixen, who teaches in Berlin, got to the heart of the matter in a study of the political economy of the international tax system. 'Only if governments come to share their legislative tax sovereignty, which is becoming ever more fictitious', wrote Rixen, 'will they regain de facto sovereignty over their tax systems.'[47]

Global federal institutions will be the decisive factor in the further development of international tax cooperation. In Rixen's view, tax avoidance through the diversion of profits abroad, a result of unregulated tax competition, undermines mutual solidarity within national societies. A fair solution boils down to a 'worldwide social contract' resembling 'a federal system with a vertical dispersion of powers over different levels'. This system could be designed in line with the established principles of fiscal federalism, as set out for example in the classic 1972 basic textbook by the US American economist Wallace E. Oates. In such a system, according to Rixen, it could be expected 'that certain taxing rights would be on the central (global) level and others on decentralized (regional, nation –state, and substate) levels'.[48] The establishment of an UN Tax Organization which negotiates a UN Tax Convention would be a useful step consistent with this long-term goal. The UN Tax Organization could turn out to be the embryo of a future global finance ministry that helps manage global taxation.

Further ideas and attempts for global taxes

As with a world parliament and world currency, there is a long history behind the idea of global taxation. The report of the Brandt Commission in 1980 referred already to a whole series of proposals to raise international revenues which were under discussion at the time. On this list were taxes on 'international trade, on arms trade, on international investment, on hydrocarbons and exhaustible minerals, on durable luxury goods, on military spending, on the consumption of energy, on internationally traded crude oil, on international air travel and freight transport, or on the use of the "international commons"

---

47 Rixen, Thomas. 2008. *The political economy of international tax governance.* Houndmills: Palgrave Macmillan, p. 203.
48 Id. 2011. 'Tax Competition and Inequality: The Case for Global Tax Governance'. *Global Governance* 17: 447–467, p. 457.

ocean fishing, offshore oil and gas, sea-bed mining, the use of space orbits, radio and telecommunication frequencies and channels'.[49] The philosopher Thomas Pogge, whose specialist area is issues of global justice, has been calling since 1994 for the introduction of a 'global resources dividend'. His proposal envisaged 'that states and their governments shall not have full libertarian property rights with respect to the natural resources in their territory, but can be required to share a small part of the value of any resources they decide to use or sell'. The revenues should be used to ensure that all people are able to meet their basic needs in dignity.[50] The French economist Thomas Piketty aroused international interest with his book 'Capital in the Twenty-First Century', which concludes with a recommendation for a 'a progressive global tax on capital, coupled with a very high level of international financial transparency'. Otherwise, he argued, democracy will not be able 'to regain control over the globalized financial capitalism of this century'.[51]

In the international community, proposals for international taxes have always been contentious. On one side of the argument is the belief that the right to raise taxes is an expression of national sovereignty; on the other, the fact that the revenues could be used to finance international organizations and global common goods. At the UN conference in Monterrey on financing for development in 2002, several heads of government, including France's Jacques Chirac, thought that a serious investigation should be carried out into the introduction of global taxes. No specific proposals were made, however. Further assessment had also been suggested by the expert group led by Zedillo, with a focus on taxes on international currency transactions and on CO_2 emissions.

The introduction of an international tax on currency transactions, the so-called Tobin tax mentioned before, served as an initial focal point for the anti-globalization movement during the late 1990s and early 2000s but to no avail. Still, the question of a tax on international financial transactions, a variant on the original Tobin proposal not limited to currency deals, was at some point pursued by the European Union. In December 2009, such a tax was supported by the European Council, on the condition that it had to be worldwide. Some countries, such as Great Britain, then still a EU member, took the position that only worldwide implementation could ensure there would be no distortion of competition. European initiatives to get the G20 summit to adopt the idea have so far been thwarted principally by opposition from the USA. As it has also not been possible to get it adopted in the EU or the Eurozone, ten EU

49	Independent Commission on International Development Issues. 1980. North/South: A Programme for Survival. London: MacMillan, pp. 243-4.
50	Pogge, Thomas. 2008. World Poverty and Human Rights. 2nd ed. Cambridge: Polity, p. 202.
51	Piketty, Thomas. 2014. Capital in the Twenty-First Century. Cambridge: Harvard University Press, p. 515.

countries decided in October 2012 to implement a common financial transaction tax, or FTT, initially by means of an enhanced cooperation procedure, which allows for closer integration within a smaller group of EU member states. Even under this limited scope it is still unclear if and when the plan will actually come to fruition. But the proposal is not forgotten. Speaking at a conference on a 'new global financing pact' hosted by French President Emmanuel Macron in Paris in June 2023, newly elected Kenyan President William Ruto pointed out that a global financial transaction tax was needed. Resources raised by such a levy and contributions made by countries commensurate to the size of their economies should not be managed by the IMF or the World Bank, though, but by a 'new global financial institution of equals'.[52] At an African climate summit held in Nairobi three months later, all African heads of state and government agreed on a joint declaration which urged world leaders, among other things, to 'rally behind the proposal for a global carbon taxation regime including a carbon tax on fossil fuel trade, maritime transport and aviation, that may also be augmented by a global financial transaction tax (FTT) to provide dedicated, affordable, and accessible finance for climate-positive investments at scale, and ringfencing of these resources and decision-making from undue influence from geopolitical and national interests.'[53] A range of proposals or ideas were put on record previously in a 2012 report from the Department of Economic and Social Affairs of the United Nations Secretariat with the caveat that these likely would meet 'intense political resistance on the part of some governments'. Listed there, in addition to an international tax on financial and currency transactions, were taxes on carbon emissions and on personal assets worth over a billion US dollars and an air transport levy. The UN planners speculated that these and other 'innovative financing instruments' such as using IMF Special Drawing Rights could raise up to 400 billion US dollars a year for financing development aid, climate change mitigation or international organizations.[54] Taking inflation into account since that estimate was made, the sum is more than eight times as much as the current budgets of all UN institutions added together, including UN peacekeeping missions, and significantly more than the annual contributions made by the OECD countries to international development work.[55] In fact, the

---

52   Ruto, William S. 22 June 2023. 'Remarks at the Summit of a New Global Financing Pact Round Table in Paris' (video transcript) (youtube.com).

53   'The African Leaders Nairobi Declaration on Climate Change and Call to Action.' 8 Sept. 2023 (africaclimatesummit.org).

54   United Nations Department of Economic and Social Affairs. 2012. World Economic and Social Survey 2012: In Search of New Development Finance. New York: United Nations, pp. 29-30, 98-9.

55   In 2020, the total revenue for the UN system as a whole was US\$ 62.5 billion, see Dag Hammarskjöld Foundation, and The UN Multi-Partner Trust Fund Office. 2022. 'Financing the UN Development System'

sum raised by global levies could be much higher. The model proposed by the Harvard economist Richard N. Cooper for a global CO_2 tax, for example, which is based on a rate of 15 US dollars per tonne of CO_2 equivalent, at the time assumed annual revenues of over 500 billion US dollars.[56] In July 2023, talks at a meeting of the UN's International Maritime Organization in London failed to reach an agreement on a levy on greenhouse gas emissions from international shipping. Countries pushing for the proposal included France, Greece, South Korea and Japan but they met with opposition from over twenty others, among them Australia, Brazil and China. According to observers, it is now unlikely that such a tax could be agreed on 'before 2027 at the earliest'.[57] The World Bank estimated that such a levy alone could raise between 40 to 60 billion US dollars a year until 2050.[58] Talking to the *Financial Times*, William Ruto said that overall 'green taxes and levies applied globally' could generate between 1.5 and 2 trillion US dollars per year.[59] When the proposal of a 'coordinated minimum tax' of two per cent on the wealth of the world's billionaires was investigated during Brazil's G20 presidency in 2024, Gabriel Zucman estimated that this would raise 200 to 250 billion US dollars annually 'from about 3,000 taxpayers'.[60]

References to global taxes can be deceptive. The global corporate minimum tax or the proposed minimum tax on billionaires, for instance, are no global taxes at all. They are cases of internationally coordinated *domestic* taxation, where the generated revenue directly contributes to national income. In the case of actual *global* taxation, revenues are managed and allocated by a collaborative international entity even if it may hold true that technically they are collected with the support of national administrations. No such mechanism exists to date. There is only one interesting example at the regional level. In the EU, a small part of the harmonized value-added tax collected by each member state contributes to the EU budget. According to James Tobin, it is appropriate that the proceeds of an international tax be devoted to interna-

---

(www.daghammarskjold.se); for 2022, the OECD reports net official development assistance of US$ 211 billion but civil society observers say the statistics are inflated and misleading.

56 Cooper, Richard N. October 2008. 'The Case for Charges on Greenhouse Gas Emissions'. Discussion Paper 08-10. Harvard Project on International Climate Agreements, Belfer Center for Science and International Affairs, Harvard Kennedy School, pp. 5, 12.

57 Harvey, Fiona. 7 July 2023. 'Shipping Emissions Levy Delayed but Goals for Greenhouse Gas Cuts Agreed.' The Guardian. (theguardian.com).

58 World Bank. 2022. 'Carbon Revenues from International Shipping: Enabling an Effective and Equitable Energy Transition', p. 13.

59 Mooney, Attracta, and Kenza Bryan. 23 June 2023. 'Kenyan Leader Says World Bank and IMF Are "Hostage" to Rich Nations.' Financial Times(ft.com).

60 Zucman, Gabriel. 25 June 2024. 'A Blueprint for a Coordinated Minimum Effective Taxation Standard for Ultra-High-Net-Worth Individuals.'

tional purposes and be placed at the disposal of international institutions.[61] Only then it is accurate to speak of global taxation.

A framework of institutional reform and democratization

Who manages global tax revenues, who makes the political decisions on how exactly they are allocated, and what control mechanisms exist, are questions of the greatest importance that are not adequately discussed. The existing international institutions and bodies are not fit for that purpose. As Myron Frankman emphasized, the British lawyer James Lorimer clearly pointed out as early as 1884 that global taxes have to be part of a world state structure. 'This is a crucial point', said Frankman. '[O]ne can discuss at length the technicalities of global taxes, a global currency, global competition policy, and progressive global income redistribution, but they cannot exist until we are ready to establish a world government.'[62] It is only when this has been recognised and openly acknowledged that the question of democratic legitimation and accountability acquires the appropriate urgency. Anyone who talks about *genuinely* global taxation, and thus about a world tax authority, must in the same breath mention a world parliament with democratic supervisory powers and a share, at the very least, in decisions over the allocation of funds. In open parliamentary debate within a world parliament, where a broader range of political views would be represented, beyond those of the governments, critical questions could be posed and global political debate could take place. The historian Richard Samuel Deese of Boston University argued that the 'most essential reason for a global democracy' was that a 'supranational carbon tax must not be a form of taxation without representation'. Such a tax, he added, 'cannot be legitimate unless it is levied by a representative assembly'.[63] In the course of a workshop on the idea of a global tax on greenhouse gases held at the University of Helsinki, it was also recognised that such a tax 'could be a fundamental building block for the democratization of global governance', as it would imply the application of the principle of 'no taxation without representation' through parliamentary representation at a *worldwide* level.[64]

The development and improvement of the international currency and finance system and of international tax cooperation, as a corollary of the specific proposals above, has to take place within the framework of an overarching institutional reform and democratization of global public policy, rather than

---

61 Tobin (1994).

62 Frankman, Myron J. 2004. World Democratic Federalism. New York: Palgrave Macmillan, p. 100.

63 Deese, R.S. 2019. Climate Change and the Future of Democracy. Springer, pp. 2-3.

64 Brincat, Shannon. September 2011. 'A Global Greenhouse Tax'. Helsinki Review of Global Governance 2 (2): 42–44, pp. 42-4.

surreptitiously and through the back door because of an erroneous assumption that the existing institutions are adequate to the task. Global taxation, a global currency and a pooling of macroeconomic management at the global level, something desirable in principle, can only be justified if they are prepared, politically managed, supervised and legitimated by a democratic world parliament. There should be a global parliamentary assembly now already with a joint right of decision in the appointment of the executive directors of the IMF, the World Bank and the WTO. The case for such a right would be even stronger with regard to the appointment of board members of a potential world central bank. And who else but a world parliament should negotiate on the details of a worldwide unitary taxation of corporations or a global carbon tax, for instance? Early on, a UN Parliamentary Assembly should be linked to the proposed UN Tax Organization through a portfolio tax committee that provides input and political oversight.

A global regulatory counter-movement with the aim of bringing the disembedded finance, currency and tax systems under control is urgently needed. A merely technocratic approach has *no emancipatory character* and poses grave risks. Ensuring the emancipatory character of this counter-movement through a democratic world parliament has to become a main priority for democratic governments, civil society and social movements.

15.

World domestic policy, trans-sovereign problems, and complex interdependence

'Trans-sovereign problems'

The global civilization of the Anthropocene, which has been developing since the 19th century, has been accompanied by an ever more urgent need for world domestic policy. This need goes well beyond the issues of climate policy and the global economic and financial system addressed above. In addition to the global common goods and matters that touch on the common interests of humanity, world domestic policy covers *all crucial issues and problems with a global dimension*. These are growing rapidly in number and importance on account of the progress of technology and the ever-closer global interconnectedness of all areas of our lives. In an 800-pages textbook on 'theoretical and empirical approaches to global governance', the political scientist Volker Rittberger (1941 to 2011) and his co-authors speak of the increased incidence of 'trans-sovereign problems', which in their definition are 'problems that transgress state borders in a manner over which states have little control, and which cannot be solved through measures taken by states acting alone'.[1] Examples of trans-sovereign problems include the spread of infectious diseases and epidemics, the drugs trade, climate change, weapons of mass destruction and their diffusion, human trafficking, migration and refugee flows, product piracy, terrorism, and 'negative social and ecological externalities of economic globalization' such as 'disparities of wealth and environmental damage'.[2] Furthermore, any problematic situation which initially has no trans-border dimension can quickly escalate and acquire global significance. Thus, in a joint study by the US American National Intelligence Council and the European Union Institute for Security Studies of the long-term challenges for global governance it was stated that on account of rapid globalization 'the risks to the international system have grown to the extent that formerly localized threats are no longer locally containable but are now potentially dangerous to global security and stability'.[3]

1 Rittberger, Volker, Andreas Kruck, and Anne Romund. 2010. Grundzüge der Weltpolitik. Theorie and Empirie des Weltregierens. 1st ed. Wiesbaden: VS Verlag für Sozialwissenschaften, p. 278 with further references (this definition is from Maryann Cusimano).
2 Ibid., pp. 278, 280.
3 National Intelligence Council (ed.). September 2010. 'Global Governance 2025: At a critical juncture', p. iii.

The concept of interdependence

Since the end of the First World War, the term 'interdependence' has been used to describe the underlying conditions of world politics. The most striking feature of the period between 1870 and 1914 was 'an increasing and irrevocable interdependence of nations', wrote James Louis Garvin, the publisher of the *Observer* in Britain, in 1919 in a book which employs this term repeatedly.[4] According to Karl Polanyi, industrialization and urbanization in England and other European countries in the second half of the 18th century went along with instituting free trade and a 'industrial-agricultural division of labor was applied to the planet'. 'With free trade', he wrote, 'the new and tremendous hazards of planetary interdependence sprang into being.'[5] 'The world economically has become an interdependent whole', argued the British politician Philip Kerr in 1935 in a text which is central to the history of the federalist movement.[6] 'Our dependence on each other, which is the essence of society, is increasingly also the rule between states. Society is expanding into the society of states. But this means an indissoluble dependence—the interdependence of states', is how this idea was summarised in 1956 by Wilhelm Wolfgang Schütz, a political scientist and adviser on German politics.[7] With the crises of the 1970s, interdependence became a main theme. For the first time since the War, the industrialised countries were hit by recession, high unemployment and inflation. The US government recorded huge budget deficits, not least on account of the galloping costs of the Vietnam war. The money supply and public debt were both increased. The international system of fixed exchange rates and the convertibility of the US dollar into gold (the 'gold standard') could no longer be maintained. When, in October 1973, in connection with the Arab-Israeli Yom Kippur War, eight OPEC countries drastically cut back oil exports in order to exert political pressure on the West, oil prices increased massively, with severe economic impacts experienced all around the world. US American oil production had peaked in 1970 and it was not possible to increase it to compensate for the OPEC embargo. Wall Street's Dow Jones Index fell by almost a half in less than four years. At that time already, Alvin Toffler spoke about the currency and finance markets as a 'global casino' that was out of control and in need of 'new transnational control mecha-

4   Garvin, James Louis. 1919. The Economic Foundations of Peace: or world partnership as the truer basis of the League of Nations. London: MacMillan & Co., p. 74, see also pp. 13, 72.
5   Polanyi, Karl. 2001 [1957]. The Great Transformation. Boston: Beacon Press, p. 190.
6   Kerr, Philip (Lord Lothian). 28 May 1935. 'Pacifism is not enough nor patriotism either'. Source: Federal Union (www.federalunion.org.uk).
7   Schütz, Wolfgang Wilhelm. 1956. Wir wollen Überleben, Außenpolitik im Atomzeitalter. Stuttgart: DVA, p. 162.

nisms'.[8] Due to insufficient domestic production, the Soviet Union became permanently dependent on grain imports to meet its food supply needs. In spite of the Cold War, it was regularly able to procure huge quantities of grain and animal feeds from the USA and other Western countries for this purpose. The environmental crisis began to enter public consciousness. Against this background, the West German Foreign Minister Hans-Dietrich Genscher chose interdependence as the theme for a speech to the UN General Assembly in 1975. 'The problems', he declared, 'have become global. The unstoppable trend towards ever closer mutual dependence between the states is the hallmark of the new era, it is the direction of World History. For the first time, humanity is travelling together towards a common future: our common survival or our common doom, common prosperity or common decline.'[9] The following year, to mark the 200th anniversary of the American Declaration of Independence, a 'Declaration of Interdependence' was published in the USA, signed by, among others, over 120 Representatives from the US Congress. This remarkable document includes the assertion that 'the economy of all nations is a seamless web', and 'no one nation can any longer effectively maintain its processes of production and monetary systems without recognizing the necessity for collaborative regulation by international authorities'. All people, it states, are part of a global community. If our civilization is to survive, all of mankind must unite.[10]

Transgovernmental networks and the merging of domestic and foreign policy

The American political scientists Robert Keohane and Joseph Nye introduced in their 1977 book 'Power and Interdependence' the concept of 'complex interdependence'. In using this term, they wanted to make clear that states and their governments do not operate in world politics like coherent entities, and also that they are not the only relevant actors. To see interdependence merely as a phenomenon of inter-state relations was therefore inadequate, in their view. Government departments and agencies, individuals and other actors such as banks and corporations create, in many different ways, their own direct cross-border links, and thus themselves become actors in world politics.

8   Toffler, Alvin. 1975. The Eco-Spasm Report. New York: Bantam, pp. 75-6.
9   Genscher, Hans-Dietrich. 1981. 'Außenpolitik im Zeitalter weltweiter Interdependenz. Rede vor der 30. Generalversammlung der Vereinten Nationen am 24. September 1975'. In: Deutsche Aussenpolitik. Ausgewählte Grundsatzreden 1975-1980, 87–104. Stuttgart: Bonn aktuell, pp. 89-91.
10 Steele Commager, Henry. 1976. 'A Declaration of INTERdependence'. In: Third Try at World Order. U.S. Policy for an Interdependent World, ed. by Harlan Cleveland, 107–109. Philadelphia: World Affairs Council of Philadelphia, pp. 109, 107.

The political scientist Anne-Marie Slaughter investigated the trans-governmental networks and institutions that arise from direct international cooperation between such bodies as the staff of government ministries, legal authorities or parliamentarians. Almost every ministry now practises within its own policy domain a form of 'world domestic policy', whether simply through horizontal networks or through formal negotiating processes and inter-governmental organizations. The state and the world order, according to Slaughter, are now 'disaggregated'.[11]

Trans-sovereign problems and interdependence lead to ever more issues being influenced by consultations and decisions that take place at the international level. Keohane and Nye noted already that 'the distinction between domestic and foreign issues becomes blurred'.[12] The political scientist Harlan Cleveland (1918 to 2008), who was involved in the creation of the 'Declaration of Interdependence' at Aspen Institute in Washington D.C., has similarly spoken of the 'melding' of foreign and domestic policy.[13]

The physicist Carl Friedrich von Weizsäcker (1912 to 2007), in his acceptance speech for the Peace Prize of the German Book Trade in 1963, was one of the first to give substance to the concept of world domestic policy. He said that what had previously been considered foreign policy was gradually turning into 'world domestic policy' because of what he called the 'harmonization of the world'. World domestic policy described two phenomena: 'the development of supra-national institutions and the use of analytical concepts taken from domestic policy to investigate problems of world politics'. He argued that from an evolutionist perspective the fact that the 'foreign policy of smaller entities was turning into the domestic policy of bigger entities' was 'a familiar historical phenomenon'.[14] As Ulrich Bartosch underlines, world domestic policy here must be understood as a continuous process. To begin with, the term—as outlined in Bartosch's study of Weizsäcker's concept of peace—denotes the still 'unfinished' attempt to come up with a solution to global political problems under actually existing conditions. Here, particular interests compete to steer the course of events in a favourable direction, while, according to Bartosch, 'not having to submit to a process of conflict resolution managed and imposed by a higher authority'.[15] This is where the critical ele-

11 See Slaughter, Anne-Marie. 2004. A new world order. Princeton University Press.

12 Keohane, Robert, and Joseph S. Nye. 2011 [1977]. Power and interdependence. 4th ed. Boston: Longman, p. 20.

13 Cleveland, Harlan. 1976. Third Try at World Order. U.S. Policy for an Interdependent World. Philadelphia: World Affairs Council of Philadelphia, pp. 83-5.

14 Weizsäcker, Carl Friedrich von. 'Bedingungen des Friedens'. Dankesrede, Friedenspreis des Deutschen Buchhandels, 1963, p. 11.

15 Bartosch, Ulrich. 1995. Weltinnenpolitik. Zur Theorie des Friedens bei Carl Friedrich von Weizsäcker. Berlin: Duncker & Humblot, p. 254.

ment of a 'complete' world domestic policy perspective comes in. For instead of favouring the worldwide implementation of a particularistic solution, such a perspective will foreground the search for *joint* solutions. World domestic policy must enable a *fair and global harmonization of interests* and must steer the existing system towards an optimal outcome for all, and towards their common interests. As Weizsäcker said with regard to the creation of a peaceful world order, this requires the creation of 'solid supra-national institutions' that include 'all countries and have a lifespan measured in generations'.[16] World domestic policy thus points towards the goal of the resolution of global political issues through global political institutions in a process which is as democratic as possible. This does not of course mean the end of conflict, or the abolition of all political differences (a naive idea in any case), but rather the diversion of such differences into 'a dynamic institutional structure with a firm legal basis whose purpose is to pressurize the parties towards a peaceful resolution of conflicts'.[17]

The evolutionary phases of the international order

It is possible to construct a set of sequential phases in the development of inter-state relations based on their degree of interconnectedness. Barry Buzan, for example, an expert on the evolution of the international system who has taught at the London School of Economics among other places, distinguished between six ideal-typical conditions.[18] The first three phases he proposes are characterised by war, enmity and power politics, whereas in the following three it is increasingly shared values, trustful cooperation and solidarity which predominate. At one end of the spectrum is a hypothetical 'asocial condition' in which genocidal wars of extermination are the norm. It continues with an anarchic phase of pure power politics, followed by a state of coexistence. The latter corresponds to the Westphalian System, based on Great Power politics, the balance of powers, sovereignty, territoriality, classical international law and warfare. There follow the phases of cooperation, convergence and confederation, each associated with the strengthening of common institutions and rules. Buzan names the EU as an example of an institution belonging to the 'confederative' phase. 'By this stage', he wrote, 'restraints on the use of force would have to be nearly total, diplomacy largely transformed into something more like the process of domestic politics, and international law transformed

16   Weizsäcker, p. 12.
17   Bartosch, p. 263.
18   See Buzan, Barry. 2004. From International to World Society? English School Theory and the Social Structure of Globalisation. Cambridge University Press, pp. 159-60, 190-3.

into something more like domestic law, with institutions of enforcement to back it up.'[19] We believe, though, that the EU's level of integration is way beyond a confederative model as it includes features such as shared sovereignty, modes of majority decision-making, the principle of primacy of EU law over national law, EU citizenship and monetary union of the eurozone members. The EU is on a path to full political union but has not yet reached this next phase and, meanwhile, lies somewhere in between in an hybrid unstable state. The spectrum thus needs to be extended by a seventh and decisive federal phase: the sphere of inter-state relations is left behind, the participating partners merge in a new common federal order, and constitute a new state unit at a higher level of integration.

A 'comprehensive' world domestic policy amounts—at least in crucial areas—to this kind of programme of federal integration. A world parliament is the most important institutional requirement for a properly functioning world domestic policy, since it offers the best possible democratic and supranational framework for the harmonization and successful management of the particular interests of nation states, for the creation of common rules, and for the representation of the interests of humanity.

The former US American diplomat James R. Huntley spoke in his book 'Pax Democratica' of four phases in the evolution of the international order: imperial subjugation, the state-based balance of power system, organised international cooperation, and supranational community building. In this evolution, the fourth phase institutions are 'as different from empires, nation-states and intergovernmental bodies as modern *Homo sapiens* was from the Neanderthals'.[20] The fact that world domestic politics is only possible in a limited or partial degree within the framework of the classical foreign policy model of sovereign states was pointed out by the philosopher Karl Jaspers (1883 to 1969) in 1953 in his work 'The Origin and Goal of History'. According to Jaspers, technology had brought about 'the unification of the globe'. Humanity now shared a common fate. He proclaimed the start of 'the history of the one human race' and looked forward to the transition to a planetary world order. In the coming 'age of world unity', which he thought would take the form of 'an all-embracing federalism', the *principle of the primacy of foreign over domestic policy would have lost all meaning*. A federal world order, according to Jaspers, would mean not only 'the abolition of absolute sover-

---

19   Ibid., p. 195.
20   Huntley, James Robert. 1998. Pax Democratica: A Strategy for the 21st Century. New York: St. Martin's Press, pp. 21-3, 35.

eignty' but with it 'the abolition of the old concept of the State in favour of mankind'.[21]

Sovereignty and the era of 'implosion'

The influential English political scientist Harold Laski (1893 to 1950), who studied the issue of sovereignty in some depth, pleaded in the 1930s for the term to be banished from the vocabulary of political science. 'It would be of lasting benefit to political science', he wrote, 'if the whole concept of sovereignty were surrendered.' He argued that its roots lay in an era when it could describe an absolute and ultimate authority. But if one looked more closely at state communities it was impossible in reality to find such a 'sovereign' central point. Sovereignty was always restricted and shared. It was therefore even more questionable, and indeed 'morally dangerous', to assume the existence of state sovereignty in international affairs. 'There are problems of which the impact upon humanity is too vital for any State to be left to determine by itself what solution it will adopt', wrote Laski. 'The notion of an independent sovereign State is, on the international side, fatal to the well-being of humanity.'[22]

The dogma of sovereignty dates back to the era when messages were delivered on horseback. Its European genesis is linked to the Reformation and the wars of religion in the rebellion against the rule of kings and popes. The invention of the printing press had a decisive impact. Marshall McLuhan, the theorist of the media, described the 'era of Gutenberg' dominated by the print media as one of *explosion*. From the 16th century onwards, it created the conditions for individualism, nationalism and the fragmentation of the world into sovereign states under international law. Now, however, McLuhan observed with visionary prescience in 1964, 'after more than a century of electric technology, we have extended our central nervous system itself in a global embrace, abolishing both space and time as far as our planet is concerned.' The 'speed-up' set off by electronic technology, and direct access to a global network in real time, have turned this around into an *implosion*. 'Our speed-up today is not a slow explosion outward from center to margins but an instant implosion and an interfusion of space and functions. Our specialist and fragmented civilization of center-margin structure is suddenly experiencing an instantaneous reassembling of all its mechanized bits into an organic whole. This is the new world of the global village.'[23]

21 Jaspers, Karl. 2010. The Origin and Goal of History. Transl. by Michael Bullock. Abingdon, Oxon: Routledge Revivals, pp. 193, 197-8.
22 Laski, Harold J. 1938. A Grammar of Politics. 4th ed. London/New Haven: George Allen & Unwin Ltd./The Yale University Press, pp. 44-6, 65-7.
23 McLuhan, Marshall. 1964. Understanding Media. London: Routledge, pp. 4, 39-41, 101.

The transformation of the world into a 'global village' on the basis of the 'new electronic interdependence' which McLuhan proclaimed in his book 'The Gutenberg Galaxy' has become a reality thanks to intercontinental glass fibre cables, satellite communications and the Internet they have enabled.[24] In the era of the Internet Revolution, and under the conditions prevailing in the Anthropocene, sovereignty is imploding towards a zero point. No-one has a right to unlimited self-determination or to the unlimited exercise of power, or indeed the capacity for either. All states, institutions, bodies and actors are in one way or another accountable to others and bound up with them. None is sovereign over the others in the classical sense, or can act as if they were.

In fact, the sovereignty of nation states is often not as impermeable in constitutional law as a dogmatic interpretation of international law would have us believe. Many national constitutions place limits on state sovereignty and also permit *the transfer of sovereign rights to international organizations*. Joseph Baratta listed 40 national constitutions from Europe, Latin America, Africa and Asia where this was the case.[25] The possibility of the emergence of supra-national political communities was clearly not alien to those who drew up these constitutions.

24 Idem. 1962. The Gutenberg Galaxy. Toronto: University of Toronto Press, p. 21.
25 Baratta, Joseph Preston. 2004. The Politics of World Federation. United Nations, UN Reform, Atomic Control. Vol. 1. Westport, Connecticut; London: Praeger Publishers, p. 255.

16.
The fragility of world civilization,
existential risks and human evolution

The potential for a worldwide collapse

Probably every generation in modern times—indeed, every generation with a consciousness of history—has experienced its own time as a time of decisive radical change. Today however we really are at an unprecedented historical turning point. For the first time in human history there is a single, integrated world civilization that encompasses the whole of the Earth. Not only does human activity now have a significant impact on crucial parameters of the Earth systems, but in addition there is the potential for a *worldwide* collapse of civilization. This stems from the way the potential risks are combined together; that is, the dense interconnectedness and the fragility of the technological, social and economic systems, so that a disruption to one of them can set off a chain reaction with incalculable and unforeseeable consequences. A contribution to a UN report on disaster risk reduction carried out by Thomas Cernev of the Center for the Study of Existential Risk at Oxford University concluded that there was a 'dangerous tendency' of the world towards a 'global collapse scenario' as planetary boundaries are crossed and the Sustainable Development Goals not successfully implemented.[1] In the published proceedings of a major conference on 'global catastrophic risks' at Oxford University the economist and physicist Robin Hanson noted that while humanity could be afflicted by many kinds of catastrophes, 'most of the damage that follows large disruptions may come from the ensuing social collapse, rather than from the direct effects of the disruption'.[2] According to the Fragile State Index that combines assessments of twelve indicators and over 100 sub-indicators, 54 states, home to 27 per cent of the world's population, are in a state of 'high warning' or worse.[3] They are least equipped to withstand the impacts of a potential global calamity.

1   Cernev, Thomas. 2022. 'Global Catastrophic Risk and Planetary Boundaries: The Relationship to Global Targets and Disaster Risk Reduction.' UN Office for Desaster Risk Reduction (undrr.org), pp. 11, 18.

2   Hanson, Robin. 2008. 'Catastrophe, social collapse, and human extinction'. In: Global Catastrophic Risks (ed.). Nick Bostrom and Milan M. Ćirković, 363–377. 1st ed. Oxford, New York: Oxford University Press, p. 375.

3   The Fund for Peace. 2023. Fragile States Index Annual Report 2023.

Global catastrophic risks

A habitable Earth will continue to exist for a very long time yet. It will be about *a billion years* before the radiance and size of the sun have grown so much, and the surface temperature of the Earth has increased so much as a consequence, that life will hardly be possible there any longer. But even from this cosmological perspective, the 21st century could well be 'a decisive moment' according to the British astrophysicist Martin Rees. For the first time in the history of the planet, one species—the human species—is holding the future of the Earth in its hands, and could put at risk not only itself but all of life.[4] In his book 'Our Final Hour', Rees, a former President of the Royal Society, analysed a number of global risks arising predominantly out of modern technological capacity. 'I think', was his dramatic conclusion, 'the odds are no better than fifty-fifty that our present civilization on Earth will survive to the end of the present century without a serious setback.'[5] It is true that humanity has survived natural existential risks for hundreds of thousands of years, as Nick Bostrom of Oxford University notes. However, he wrote, '[c]onsideration of specific existential-risk scenarios bears out the suspicion that the great bulk of existential risk in the foreseeable future consists of *anthropogenic existential risks*—that is, those arising from human activity'. The consequences to be expected from an existential catastrophe of this kind are so enormous that the objective of reducing such risks has to become a 'dominant consideration' for humanity.[6] As Toby Ord, a philosopher researching at Oxford University, pointed out in a noteworthy book on existential risks titled 'The Precipice', anthropogenic risks 'outstrip all natural risks combined' and 'set the clock on how long humanity has left to pull back from the brink' of catastrophe.[7]

Within the broad concept of a world domestic policy for the Anthropocene, long-term solutions are especially needed for those problems which potentially threaten the functional capacity or even the survival of world civilization as a whole, or those which have a massive impact on the wellbeing of large parts of the world population, or which could bring with them irreversible negative consequences for humanity. Securing the stability of the Earth system is a top priority. Further critical goals include maintaining healthy and sustainable economic and financial systems, ensuring food and water supplies, preventing nuclear war as well as the spread of super-viruses and pandemics, and averting potential dangers from advancing technologies like biotech, nanotech, robotics,

---

4   Bostrom and Ćirković (ed.), p. xi.
5   Rees, Martin. 2004. Our Final Century. 1st ed. Arrow Books, p. 8.
6   Bostrom, Nick. Feb. 2013. 'Existential Risk Prevention as Global Priority'. Global Policy (4) 1: 15–31, pp. 16, 19.
7   Ord, Toby. 2020. The Precipice. Existential Risk and the Future of Humanity. London et al.: Bloomsbury, p. 29.

and AI. The emergence of a dystopian totalitarian world state is a potential socio-political long-term threat that needs to be considered and addressed as well.

The genome as the heritage of humanity

The fact that, through genetic engineering and nanotechnology, science is on the verge of endowing us with technical mastery over the fundamental building blocks of life and matter is one of the markers that confirm that this era is a historical turning point. Huge progress in biotechnology, exemplified by the decoding of the human genome in 2003, by cloning technology or genome editing through Crispr and other systems, has enabled fundamental intervention in the essence of human life. The core of a human being is embodied in an individual's DNA sequence. The genome is the construction manual for their entire biological being. The UNESCO General Conference of 1997 stated in the first article of the 'Universal Declaration on the Human Genome and Human Rights' that the human genome 'underlies the fundamental unity of all members of the human family, as well as the recognition of their inherent dignity and diversity', and that in 'a symbolic sense, it is the heritage of humanity'. The text of this ancient book, written by evolution itself, will soon be subject to a thoroughgoing interpretation and manipulation the consequences of which cannot be foreseen. More than twenty years ago, Jeremy Rifkin, from the Foundation of Economic Trends in Washington, spoke of a technological revolution without precedent in all of history. 'Never before in history has humanity been so unprepared for the new technological and economic opportunities, challenges, and risks that lie on the horizon. Our way of life may be more fundamentally transformed in the next several decades than in the previous one thousand years.[8] Unfortunately, we do not seem prepared to steer this development in a proper way.

Gene-editing and reprogenetics

For example, we can expect that 'reprogenetics' will enable specific genes to be either handed on or blocked at will, and will thus enable choice over the genetic characteristics of children. Who would oppose the eradication of hereditary diseases for future generations? Once that line is crossed, the debate will likely shift to why not modify genes to improve human abilities such as vision or memory, if possible? And after this, what comes next?[9] In 2015, more than

8   Rifkin, Jeremy. 1999. The Biotech Century. Trade edition. New York: Tarcher/Putnam, p. 1.
9   Giesen, Klaus-Gerd. 2020. 'The Transhumanist Ideology and the International Political Economy of the Fourth Industrial Revolution.' In: Ideologies in World Politics, ed. by id., 143–56. Wiesbaden: Springer VS, p. 148.

150 experts signed an open letter calling for strengthened prohibitions against heritable human genetic modification. The letter explained that 'genetically modified children who seem healthy at birth could develop serious problems later in life, some perhaps introduced by purported enhancements. Other harmful consequences of germline modification might only present themselves in subsequent generations'.[10] In fact, researchers have already started to experiment with Crispr on human embryos. It was only after a Chinese scientist claimed that he had created the world's first gene-edited babies three years after the letter's publication that the World Health Organization established an expert group on 'developing global standards for governance and oversight of human genome editing'. Upon their recommendation, the WHO established a global registry to track research on human genome editing. Formed at the same time to provide input, another international expert commission with members from 10 countries noted in its final report that 'it is important to recognize that the idea of making intentional modifications to the human germline evokes to the eugenics movements of the late 19th century and first half of the 20th century, which promoted now-discredited theories that led to the persecution of whole groups, based on race, religion, class, and ability.'[11]

In the view of the molecular biologist Lee Silver, who coined the term 're-progenetics', manipulating the human genome offers huge opportunities in the first instance. For example, parents could choose to endow their children with a gene that occurs naturally in one per cent of the population and that provides resistance against infection with the HIV virus. 'Reprogenetics will be used to give children better prospects for their physical and mental development and for a longer life', Silver asserted. The problems, in his view, lie not in the misuse or failure of the technology but rather in the far-reaching social consequences of its application. 'The potential of reprogenetics is so great', argued the Princeton University academic, 'that those families and groups unable to afford it run the risk of being seriously disadvantaged.'[12] The social gulf between the rich and the poor would be genetically entrenched and reproduced. A 'genetocracy' could arise. In his book 'Remaking Eden', Silver described a possible future in which humanity is irrevocably biologically divided into underprivileged 'naturals' and a class of human beings reprogenetically perfected over generations. 'A severed humanity could be the ultimate

10 Center for Genetics and Society. November 2015. 'Open Letter Calls for Prohibition on Reproductive Human Germline Modification' (www.geneticsandsociety.org).
11 International Commission on the Clinical Use of Human Germline Genome Editing, National Academy of Medicine, National Academy of Sciences, and The Royal Society. 2020. Heritable Human Genome Editing. Washington, D.C.: National Academies Press, p. x.
12 Silver, Lee M. 2000. 'Gesündere and glücklichere Kinder mit Reprogenetik'. Novo (44) (www.novo-magazin.de).

legacy of unfettered global capitalism', he wrote.[13] For under current circumstances it is only the market and technological feasibility that will determine developments in this area. Even if a society were to decide to try to regulate reprogenetics, by whatever means, this would not be able to prevent wealthy parents fulfilling their desire for reprogenetic intervention, abroad if necessary. Only a watertight system of world law could hold out the prospect of successful regulation. 'So long as there are still sovereign states', Silver wrote, 'no border will prevent the free movement of cells and genes which are buried deep within a woman's body. Only a world state could control reprogenetics so that its citizens would have access only to what that state allowed.'[14]

Transhumanism

For 'transhumanists' like the computer pioneer Ray Kurzweil, the next logical evolutionary leap forward in human development lies in the fusion of human beings with machine and computer technology.[15] The limitations and defects of the human body will finally be transcended in the posthuman cyborgs which emerge from this fusion, hybrids of biological organisms and machines. Yet here, too, it seems likely that an unavoidable consequence would be the division of humanity into two species: the naturals and the cyborgs. And once again, as David Rotter wrote in an interesting article, 'it would be first and foremost the elites who would have access to these new technologies and who would use the technical advances to become vastly superior to normal people in intelligence, sensory capacity, physical powers, life expectancy and strength'. The 'worker-race', by contrast, would no longer play any significant role in society.[16] The political scientist Klaus-Gerd Giesen cautioned that the political objective of transhumanism is the creation of a new human being and an 'entirely new society', a grand plan that other ideologies such as communism and fascism pursued as well in other but 'ultimately less radical perspectives'.[17] Rotter warns us not to dismiss transhumanism as science fiction. The transhumanist agenda, he said, is dictating scientific activity worldwide and is being pushed forward massively by members of the international elites. An important context is the idea of a fourth industrial revolution which was popularised by the founder of the World Economic Forum, Klaus Schwab. In his view, accelerating technological innovations in artificial intelligence, biotech-

---

13 Id. 6 August 2002. 'Brave New World Dawning'. Project Syndicate (www.project-syndicate.org).
14 Silver (2000), ibid.
15 Kurzweil, Ray. The Age of Spiritual Machines: When Computers Exceed Human Intelligence. New York: Penguin Books, 2000.
16 Rotter, David. 2013. 'Transhumanismus. Die Abschaffung des Menschen'. Tattva Viveka (56): 58–67, p. 64.
17 Giesen, 2020, p. 146.

nology, computing, energy storage, material science, nanotechnology, robotics and others 'inevitably' will lead to a 'convergence of the physical, digital and biological worlds' and will redefine 'what it means to be human'.[18] An effort of this kind is Neuralink, a company started in 2016 by billionaire and businessman Elon Musk that is supposed to develop devices that could merge the human brain with machines and AI. In 2023, the company announced that it had received an approval from the US Food and Drug Administration to launch a first in-human clinical study. 'Not only do the rich seem to get richer, they may get the benefit of having a computer-enhanced brain', *CNBC*'s columnist Dustin McKissen commented earlier. What will inequality look like if only the very wealthy can afford to get an upgrade, he asked.[19] In the opinion of the American writer and scholar Jonathan Taplin, the four billionaires Peter Thiel, Elon Musk, Mark Zuckerberg, and Marc Andreessen have 'long been regarded as technologically progressive heroes, but they are actually part of a broader antidemocratic, authoritarian turn within the tech world'. He believes that their four main projects, the so-called 'metaverse', crypto, interplanetary colonization and transhumanism are 'a lie' that represents 'an existential risk to the world' in political, economic and moral terms. Creating human-machine cyborgs in particular would 'undo the idea at the heart of political liberalism: equal rights for all' because 'whatever problems we currently have with social inequality will be multiplied exponentially by the kinds of biological enhancements' the 'techno-oligarchs' push forward.[20]

Artificial intelligence

In his book 'The Artilect War', the Australian AI researcher Hugo de Garis prophesied that it will be possible to create AI superior to human intelligence by a factor of trillions. Further, that the debate over the direction of human evolution and whether it is acceptable to create machines with such unimaginable artificial intelligence will dominate global politics in the later 21st century, and carries within it serious potential for violent conflict. 'However, once these artificial brains really do start becoming smart and threaten to become a lot smarter and perhaps very quickly (a scenario called "singularity")', wrote Garis, 'then humanity should be ready to take a decision on whether to proceed or not.'[21] Elon Musk believes that the big powers' competition for AI superiority

18   Schwab, Klaus. 2017. The Fourth Industrial Revolution. London et al.: Portfolio Penguin, pp. 23, 64, 98.
19   McKissen, Dustin. 29 March 2017. 'Elon Musk's Neuralink could help rich people get richer'. CNBC.com.
20   Taplin, Jonathan. 22 Aug. 2023. 'How Musk, Thiel, Zuckerberg, and Andreessen - Four Billionaire Techno-Oligarchs - Are Creating an Alternate, Autocratic Reality.' Vanity Fair (vanityfair.com).
21   Garis, Hugo de. 2005. The Artilect War. Palm Springs, Ca.: ETC Publications, p. 19.

may cause a Third World War.[22] According to Stephen Hawking, the development of AI may bring about 'the eventual demise of human beings.'[23] With regard to nuclear and biological warfare, environmental problems and AI, the renowned physicist and cosmologist said in an interview with *The Times* that 'we need to be quicker to identify such threats and act before they get out of control. This might mean some form of world government.'[24]

Following the release of the large language model-based chatbot ChatGPT by OpenAI in November 2022 and similar applications, the issue of AI got more attention. Large language model tools entirely depend on human knowledge, judgement and labor. Drawing on immense data sets, they statistically predict what words should follow one another without any comprehension of their meaning. The AI researcher Kate Crawford argued that AI, as currently known, 'is neither artificial nor intelligent' and builds on 'exploiting energy and mineral resources from the planet, cheap labor, and data at scale'.[25] The impact of AI technology is said to be profound. In May 2023, a group of more than 350 AI executives, researchers and engineers even signed a one-sentence statement saying that 'mitigating the risk of extinction from AI should be a global priority alongside other societal-scale risks, such as pandemics and nuclear war'. Sam Altman, the chief executive of OpenAI warned according to *The New York Times* that the risks of advanced AI systems 'were serious enough to warrant government intervention' and he called for regulation of AI 'for its potential harms'.[26] In July 2023, the UN Security Council held its first-ever briefing on the issue of AI from a peace and security perspective. Among other things, UN chief António Guterres referred to potential harmful malfunctioning of AI systems but also the use of AI tools with malicious intent, including AI-enabled cyberterrorism and cyberwar or systematic disinformation. He stressed that the governance of AI cannot be handled successfully by individual countries and required a 'universal approach' towards 'common measures for the transparency, accountability and oversight' of AI systems.[27] On top, AI poses 'serious risks for democracy', as philosopher of technology Mark Coeckelbergh argued in a book on the subject. In his view, AI 'as it is currently

---

22 Hern, Alex. 4 September 2017. 'Elon Musk Says AI Could Lead to Third World War'. The Guardian (www.theguardian.com).

23 See Caughill, Patrick. 24 Nov. 2017. 'Stephen Hawking believes humankind is in danger of self-destruction due to AI'. Futurism (blog) (futurism.com).

24 Whipple, Tom, and Oliver Moody. 7 March 2017. 'Stephen Hawking on humanity'. The Times.

25 Crawford, Kate. 2021. Atlas of AI: The Real Worlds of Artificial Intelligence. New Haven: Yale University Press, pp. 128, 223.

26 Roose, Kevin. 30 May 2023. 'A.I. Poses "Risk of Extinction," Industry Leaders Warn.' The New York Times (nytimes.com).

27 United Nations. 28 July 2023. 'Secretary-General Urges Security Council to Ensure Transparency, Accountability, Oversight, in First Debate on Artificial Intelligence.' (press.un.org).

developed and used' undermines liberty, maintains or creates economic inequalities, leads to unjust, unfair and biased decisions, increases power asymmetries and erodes knowledge and trust, among other things.[28]

Successful regulation of a AI will have to be done globally instead of
through a patchwork of national or regional approaches, requiring 'the international system' to 'move past traditional concepts of sovereignty', as the political analyst Ian Bremmer and AI researcher Mustafa Suleyman noted. They
suggested a 'minimum of three AI governance regimes' that include a scientific body that evaluates the risk and potential impact of AI on a continuous
basis similar to the existing Intergovernmental Panel on Climate Change in
the environmental field, international monitoring and verification in order to
'prevent the proliferation of dangerous advanced AI systems' and finally a
'technocratic body' that 'can react when dangerous disruptions occur' based
on the example of the Financial Stability Board in the financial sector.[29] When
it comes to global governance of AI, Coeckelbergh found that 'we still find
ourselves in a kind of Hobbesian state of nature' as there is 'no global governance authority'.[30] But how and by whom is the substance of global AI regulation to be discussed and decided? In a joint paper, eleven researchers put forward the idea of an 'intergovernmental or multistakeholder' Advanced AI
Governance Organization, among other things. They found that it is 'unclear
what institutional processes would satisfy the demands of legitimacy and effectiveness, and incentivize the participation of important groups of stakeholders'.[31] On their company's blog, OpenAI executives Sam Altman, Greg
Brockman and Ilya Sutskever wrote that eventually an 'international authority' may be needed that 'can inspect systems, require audits, test for compliance with safety standards, place restrictions on degrees of deployment and
levels of security, etc.' They stressed that 'the governance of the most powerful
systems, as well as decisions regarding their deployment, must have strong
public oversight'. The 'people around the world', they went on, 'should democratically decide on the bounds and defaults for AI systems', adding however,
that they didn't know yet 'how to design such a mechanism'.[32] In his book,
Coeckelbergh too concludes that global democracy is needed but also found 'it
is not clear what that means'. But is it not precisely for the purpose of demo-

---

28   Mark Coeckelbergh. 2024. Why AI Undermines Democracy and What to Do About It. Polity, pp. 6, 45-48, 57.
29   Bremmer, Ian, and Mustafa Suleyman. 2023. 'The AI Power Paradox.' Foreign Affairs 102 (5): 26–43, pp.
      29, 40-43.
30   Coeckelbergh, p. 79.
31   Ho, Lewis, et al. July 2023. 'International Institutions for Advanced AI.' arXiv (arxiv.org), p. 11.
32   Altman, Sam, Greg Brockman, and Ilya Sutskever. 22 May 2023. 'Governance of Superintelligence.' (open-
      ai.com).

cratically determining common rules that parliaments have been established throughout history? Why should this not apply at the global scale as well? In principle, the need for global democratic regulation and oversight of AI leads straight to a global parliament as an obvious solution. For sure, Coecklbergh raises the important practical question whether 'existing non-democracies' can 'even be integrated in a global democratic governance structure' whatever it looks like.[33] Nonetheless, a global parliament would be 'in line' with his thoughts, he told us.

Autonomous weapons

Military application of AI is another field that requires special attention. Leading military planners think that the armed conflicts of the future will be dominated by unmanned battle systems, which are already increasingly taking the place of soldiers. Drones and robots, they believe, will revolutionize warfare, just as tanks once did. Drones have become an essential weapon and reconnaissance tool in the war in Ukraine following the Russian invasion in 2022. Military robotics is an industry that is experiencing exponential growth. One major objective currently being energetically pursued is the development of *fully autonomous* killer robots and battle drones. '[W]e are sleepwalking into a brave new world where robots decide who, where and when to kill', warned the AI researcher Noel Sharkey, co-founder of the International Committee for Robot Arms Control (ICRAC). No computer system, he argued, can reliably distinguish between combatants and innocent people.[34] According to *Science* magazine, computer scientists counter that advanced AI may one day even be superior to human judgement in this area. But Mark Gubrud of the Program on Science and Global Security at Princeton University, another member of ICRAC, believes that this risks human beings 'losing control'. 'Stupid robots are dangerous, but smart robots are even more dangerous', Gubrud told the magazine.[35] One year before the start of a global campaign against autonomous killer robots, the NGO Human Rights Watch called in a 2012 report for a pre-emptive international ban on such weapons. A runaway AI that takes over control of automated weapons and internet-connected systems recalls the dystopian vision of James Cameron's 1984 film 'Terminator'.[36] In this Hollywood blockbuster, intelligent battle robots and information systems have made themselves autonomous and are waging war against humani-

---

33 Coeckelbergh, p. 80.
34 Sharkey, Noel. 18 August 2007. 'Robot wars are a reality'. The Guardian (www.theguardian.com).
35 Citation from Stone, Richard. 20 December 2013. 'Scientists Campaign Against Killer Robots'. Science 342 (6165): 1428–1429, p. 1429.
36 Human Rights Watch. 2012. Losing Humanity. The Case Against Killer Robots (www.hrw.org).

ty. In an open letter to the UN in August 2017, over 100 of the world's leading robotics and AI pioneers, among them Elon Musk and Alphabet's Mustafa Suleyman, backed a ban of autonomous weapons. The campaign aims to achieve this ban by getting it included in the 1980 UN Convention on Certain Conventional Weapons. A step forward was made in this long diplomatic struggle when in November 2023 a UN General Assembly committee stressed in an official resolution 'the urgent need for the international community to address the challenges and concerns raised by autonomous weapons systems.' The technical possibilities now opening up require regulation under binding world law in the longer term, for as soon as one country pulls out of the convention or does not join in the first place and starts to develop autonomous systems, others will feel compelled to follow.

The world-famous science fiction writer Isaac Asimov (1919 to 1992), in his 1950 novel 'I, Robot', was one of the first to address the issues which are raised by robots becoming ever more like humans, and ever more intelligent. There he also set out his famous Three Laws of Robotics. The first of these states that a robot may not injure a human being. A later, 'Zeroth Law' states that robots may not harm humanity. It will be extremely difficult to apply such laws in practise. Asimov held a clear view on dangers that pose a threat to humanity. 'It is important that the world get together and be sufficiently a unit to face the problems which attack us as a unit', he said. '[W]hat we need is some sort of federal world government.'[37]

COVID-19, 'Disease X' and the pandemic threat

Over a decade before the outbreak of the SARS-CoV-2 virus, which causes the respiratory COVID-19 disease, no expert doubted that a global pandemic was one of the greatest worldwide catastrophic risks.[38] Previous disease outbreaks that became pandemics served as warnings including SARS-CoV-1 in 2002, the influenza virus H1N1 in 2009, the Middle East respiratory syndrome (MERS) in 2012, the Ebola virus in 2013 and the Zika virus in 2015. However, effective pandemic preparedness and response is a global public good that has yet to be provided. The COVID-19 pandemic serves as a tragic illustration of the shortcomings and inertia of the international system as well as the challenges of depending on collaboration from a powerful autocratic state like China. COVID-19 was perhaps the final wake-up call to prevent the occur-

37   Asimov, Isaac. 14 January 1989. 'Keynote Address of the Humanist Institute first annual meeting, New York' (www.youtube.com).

38   Bostrom and Ćirković (ed.), p. 16.

rence of a new pathogen that is easily transmissible and multiple times more lethal, the much-dreaded 'Disease X'.

According to the WHO, by May 2023, when the organisation stopped classifying COVID-19 as a global health emergency, more than 760 million confirmed COVID-19 infections and 6.95 million deaths had occurred worldwide. In January 2022, around two years after the pandemic's outbreak in the Chinese megacity of Wuhan, the official death toll had reached 5.5 million. Estimates based on an analysis of excess mortality suggested that the actual figure was between 12 to 22 million at the time.[39] While many countries did not collect reliable data, it appears that authoritarian regimes tended to deliberately provide manipulated lower figures.[40] China's draconian zero COVID policy limited the scope of naturally acquired immunity. In the two months after its abrupt end, in December 2022 and January 2023, researchers estimate that 1.87 million excess deaths occurred throughout the country. This figure stands in contrast to the government's official tally of 60,000 COVID-19 fatalities in the country during that period and merely around double this number for the entire pandemic up until then.[41] In mid-2020, the case fatality rate of COVID-19 varied from 2.2 per cent in South Korea to 14 per cent in Italy. The H5N1 bird flu virus, a mutation of which is a potential candidate for a 'Disease X', by comparison has a case fatality rate that can considerably exceed 50 per cent. What is more, vaccination may not be as quickly available as it was in the case of COVID-19. It is estimated that vaccinations in 2021, the first year of their availability, prevented between 14 and 20 million additional COVID-19 deaths.[42] Distribution of available vaccine was very unequal, however. Rich countries purchased and kept most for themselves, a policy that became known as 'vaccine nationalism'. By mid-2021, high-income countries had a two hundred per cent population coverage of vaccine while in the poorest countries, fewer than 1 per cent had a single dose.[43] From an epidemiological perspective this was counterproductive as it carried the risk of an 'escape mutation' to emerge in unvaccinated populations which would then spread again globally.

39   Adam, David. 2022. 'The Effort to Count the Pandemic's Global Death Toll.' Nature 601 (7893): 312–15.

40   Holleis, Jennifer. 6 Aug. 2021. 'Authoritarian States Obscuring COVID Death Tolls, Study Shows.' Deutsche Welle (www.dw.com).

41   Xiao, Hong, Zhicheng Wang, Fang Liu, and Joseph M. Unger. 2023. 'Excess All-Cause Mortality in China After Ending the Zero COVID Policy." JAMA Network Open 6 (8):

42   Watson, Oliver J., et al. 2022. 'Global Impact of the First Year of COVID-19 Vaccination: A Mathematical Modelling Study.' The Lancet Infectious Diseases 22 (9): 1293–1302.

43   Independent Panel for Pandemic Preparedness and Response. 2021. COVID-19: Make It the Last Pandemic. (theindependentpanel.org), pp. 12, 41-3.

Travel and lockdown restrictions imposed in 150 countries that were supposed to reduce transmission and a subsequent collapse of global trade and supply chains led to a sharp downturn of the global economy with GDP in 2020 declining on average around 3.4 per cent compared to a rise of 2.8 per cent in the previous year. This shock in addition to rising geopolitical tensions made talk of an 'end of globalization' fashionable. Measurements of actual international flows of trade, capital, information, and people by 2021 already rebounded to pre-pandemic levels, however, showing their 'remarkable resilience' and 'no meaningful signs of a wider fragmentation of the world economy into rival blocs or a turn to more regionalized patterns of activity', the DHL Global Interconnectedness Index 2022 reported at the time.[44] In 2021, world GDP was on a growth path again and rose by 6 per cent. But according to an analysis of hundreds of studies across ten categories carried out by Kevin Bardosh, an affiliate assistant professor at the Center for One Health Research at the University of Washington, 'the collateral damage of the pandemic response was substantial, wide-ranging and will leave behind a legacy of harm for hundreds of millions of people in the years ahead'. While the assessment stressed that knowledge gaps exist and further research is needed, it concludes that 'it is likely that many Covid policies caused more harm than benefit', including 'a rise in non-Covid excess mortality, mental health deterioration, child abuse and domestic violence, widening global inequality, food insecurity, lost educational opportunities, unhealthy lifestyle behaviours, social polarization, soaring debt, democratic backsliding and declining human rights.' Bardosh stressed that this does not mean to say that government interventions had no beneficial effects or weren't needed or justified but that a nuanced and broader assessment was necessary. The pandemic was not only a health crisis, he wrote, but a 'whole-of-society crisis'.[45]

The WHO's weakness and the 'sovereignty problem'

A panel set up by the WHO's Director General upon request of the World Health Assembly and chaired by former heads of state Helen Clark and Ellen Johnson Sirleaf pointed out that since the 2009 H1N1 influenza pandemic, 'at least eleven high-level panels and commissions have made specific recommendations in 16 reports to improve global pandemic preparedness' but the majority were never implemented.[46] Changes made to the International Health Regu-

44   Altman, Steven A., and Caroline R. Bastian. 2022. DHL Global Interconnectedness Index 2022. DHL, p. 9.
45   Bardosh, Kevin. 2023. 'How Did the COVID Pandemic Response Harm Society? A Global Evaluation and State of Knowledge Review (2020-21).' SSRN Scholarly Paper.
46   Independent Panel for Pandemic Preparedness and Response. 2021. COVID-19: Make It the Last Pandemic. (theindependentpanel.org), p. 16.

lations, in short IHR, following the 2002 SARS outbreak turned out to be insufficient and difficult to implement. Enshrined in a legally binding treaty accepted by all countries, these regulations ask member states 'to prepare for public health threats according to standards set by the WHO, and to report any outbreaks and all subsequent developments', science writer Stephen Buranyi explained. 'It also allows the WHO to declare a public health emergency of international concern', 'using its own information, over the objection of any single country. During an emergency, countries are expected to take the lead from the WHO's guidelines and report any deviations to the organisation. All of these requirements, bar the reporting of outbreaks, were new', he noted.[47] In reality, however, the WHO's 'coordinating authority and capacity' were 'weak' according to the editor of the medical journal *Lancet*, Richard Horton. In his assessment, the organization's 'ability to direct an international response to a life-threatening epidemic' was 'non-existent'.[48] A COVID-19 commission convened by *Lancet* and chaired by Colombia University economist Jeffrey Sachs noted that the international response was 'a massive global failure at multiple levels'. This included, among other things, 'the lack of timely notification of the initial outbreak of COVID-19' by Chinese authorities, 'costly delays' in acknowledging the airborne exposure pathway of the virus, lack of coordination and implementation of suppression strategies at national and global levels and a failure to ensure an equitable global supply of key medical commodities like protective gear and vaccines in particular. The report pointed out that the WHO in part 'fell victim to the increasing tensions between the United States and China' on the handling of the pandemic which culminated in the Trump administration's decision to withdraw from the organization, a move that was reversed by Biden right after his inauguration.[49]

In December 2021, WHO members decided to launch negotiations on a new binding agreement to strengthen pandemic prevention, preparedness and response and several months later also started a process to consider amendments to the IHR. The *Lancet* and WHO panels were among those that recommended, among other things, the creation of a 'Global Health Board' or a 'Global Health Threats Council' respectively with support from heads of government to 'bolster the authority' of the WHO.[50] But Ilona Kickbusch of the Global Health Centre at the Graduate Institute of International and Develop-

---

47 Buranyi, Stephen. 10 April 2020. 'The WHO v Coronavirus: Why It Can't Handle the Pandemic.' The Guardian (theguardian.com).

48 Quoted in ibid.

49 Sachs, Jeffrey D., et al. 2022. 'The Lancet Commission on Lessons for the Future from the COVID-19 Pandemic.' (thelancet.com), pp. 1, 11.

50 Independent Panel, p. 47; Sachs, p. 41.

ment Studies in Geneva worries that such a body, especially if set up independently from the WHO, would actually achieve the opposite and add 'yet more layers of governance to an already fractured global health system', diluting the goal of 'a coherent and streamlined approach to pandemics.'[51] By mid-2023, international talks on a pandemic treaty have stalled due to disagreements in particular over the licensing of intellectual property rights and the sharing of knowledge needed to decentralize vaccine and drug production globally at a moment of emergency.[52] Observers noted that 'pandemic amnesia' had already set in, political will had ebbed away and an ambitious initial draft thus had been watered down.[53] The WHO panel had originally, with some degree of naivety, called for the adoption of a 'Pandemic Framework Convention' by the end of 2021. An important recommendation the panel made was for the WHO 'to formalize universal periodic peer reviews of national pandemic preparedness and response capacities'.[54]

The Council on Foreign Relations' global health expert and professor emeritus of law David Fidler was right to point out that 'government responses to COVID-19 have purportedly violated or manipulated many treaties' such as the IHR. 'Claims that noncompliance with the IHR' requires 'a pandemic treaty do not explain why a new treaty will generate the commitment that the IHR apparently did not', he rightfully noted.[55] Arguably, however, the process of negotiating a treaty itself involves building political commitment. Mechanisms such as a periodic review or regular laboratory biosafety inspections would enable and require an ongoing engagement. But it remains true, as Fidler wrote, that states rarely accept investigation powers, enforcement provisions or other obligations in treaties in the first place and such may not make it into a pandemic accord either. In 1996 already Fidler described the 'sovereignty problem' in international law in general and in the international efforts against infectious diseases in particular which is still obstructing effective measures. The pandemic threat on the one hand undermines sovereignty because it cannot be dealt with by single states, he argued, but on the other hand, 'the need for international solutions allows sovereignty to frustrate disease control internationally' as states were unwilling to accept restrictions.

51 Kickbusch, Ilona. 23 May 2023. 'The World Won't Be Safer With a Fragmented Global Health System.' Council on Foreign Relations. (thinkglobalhealth.org).

52 'Why the Pandemic Treaty Risks Becoming COVID-19 Groundhog Day.' Editorial. 19 Sept. 2023. Nature 621 (7979): 443–44.

53 Schwalbe, Nina. 31 Aug. 2023. 'We Cannot Give up on the Global Pandemic Treaty.' Financial Times (ft.com).

54 Independent Panel, pp. 47, 51

55 Fidler, David P. 26 Nov. 2021. 'The Case Against a Pandemic Treaty.' Council on Foreign Relations (thinkglobalhealth.org).

Even then, the problem of enforcement remains. 'States often agree to an international legal obligation without any serious intent of fulfilling it', Fidler observed.[56]

The origin of SARS-CoV-2

In the crucial weeks after the outbreak of SARS-CoV-2 became known globally, it seemed that the WHO unquestioningly relied on the information provided by Chinese authorities and reproduced their views without careful scrutiny or analysis. The organization may not have had much of a choice at that point as it lacked the authority and capability to assess the situation on the ground. International and independent probes into the origins of SARS-CoV-2, including those mandated by the WHO, have been met with fierce Chinese resistance and to this day could not be carried out in a meaningful way. 'China prevented a full investigation into the origins of the global pandemic and there was really nothing the rest of the world could do about it', the author and WHO advisor Jamie Metzl, who has been following the matter closely, told us. There has been no proper accountability for this either. However, as the molecular biologist Alina Chan and science writer Matt Ridley rightfully noted in their eye-opening and well-researched book 'Viral' on the 'search for the origin of COVID-19', 'if we do not find out how this pandemic began, we are ill-equipped to know when, where and how the next pandemic may start'.[57] The question of where the virus came from and how it broke out remains muddled by disinformation, lack of transparency, and politicization. Chinese authorities have been attempting to control and suppress information about the virus and the outbreak.[58] Publication of Chinese research into its origins has been restricted and subjected to censorship of central government officials. A joint investigation of the so-called WHO-China study team was discontinued because Chinese authorities did not collaborate and denied access to relevant facilities. The WHO Director-General then established an advisory group which is supposed to provide 'an independent evaluation of all available scientific and technical findings from global studies.'[59]

---

56 Id. 1996. 'Globalization, International Law, and Emerging Infectious Diseases.' Emerging Infectious Diseases 2 (2): 77–84, pp. 79-80, 83.
57 Chan, Alina, and Matt Ridley. 2022. Viral: The Search for the Origin of Covid-19. New York: Harper Perennial, p. 4.
58 Washington Post. 22 Aug. 2023. 'In Wuhan, Doctors Knew the Truth. They Were Told to Keep Quiet.' The Post's View (washingtonpost.com).
59 Scientific Advisory Group for the Origins of Novel Pathogens (SAGO), Terms of Reference. 20 August 2021 (who.int), p. 2.

The spread of SARS-CoV-2 in humans may have been the result of a natural zoonotic spillover from wildlife or a farm animal, as was the case with the 2002 SARS outbreak. Patient zero may also have been a coronavirus researcher who got infected in a laboratory or during field work and then spread it further. SARS-CoV-2 infections can be asymptomatic so this might have gone unnoticed. In the laboratory scenario, SARS-CoV-2 could either be a natural virus that was studied or the result of genetic modification. Neither of these hypotheses can currently be proven or disproven. The Huanan seafood market in Wuhan was the early epicenter of the pandemic but this does not establish that it originated from there.[60] The Chinese government strictly denies the possibility of a laboratory leak, a position which the WHO initially supported, and argues the virus emerged outside China. An animal source for SARS-CoV-2 has not been discovered either in China or elsewhere. But it happens to be the case that after the 2002 SARS outbreak, Wuhan became an international focal point for coronavirus research conducted by a number of institutions with the notorious Wuhan Institute of Virology being only the most important one which hosted China's first biosafety level 4 lab.[61] WIV stored and worked on thousands of animal samples that were collected far away in Southern China and Southeast Asia. From some of these samples, found in a mine shaft in Mojiang in 2013, WIV isolated the genome sequence RaTG13, one of the closest known genetic relatives to SARS-CoV-2.[62] WIV researchers constructed novel chimeric coronaviruses by combining existing genomes. Funding for some of WIV's projects, including on genetically modifying coronaviruses, came from the National Institutes of Health, the US government's main agency for health research, via subgrants of the US-based EcoHealth Alliance. The full extent and scope of this collaboration and research is still not clear. However, following the SARS-CoV-2 outbreak, instead of providing full transparency and pursuing an unconditional investigation, the president of EcoHealth and other scientists involved immediately tried to steer the public narrative away from the possibility of a laboratory leak scenario and toward the natural spillover explanation.[63] The EcoHealth president even served as a member of the WHO's initial team that dismissed the lab scenario. He also chaired the *Lancet* commission's task force on the pandemic's origins. It is remarkable that his significant conflicts of interest apparently

---

60 Worobey, Michael, Joshua I. Levy, et al. 2022. 'The Huanan Seafood Wholesale Market in Wuhan Was the Early Epicenter of the COVID-19 Pandemic.' Science (science.org).

61 Chan and Ridley, p. 158.

62 See ibid., pp. 219-243.

63 Ibid., pp. 151-158. See also Alison Young. 2023. Pandora's Gamble: Lab Leaks, Pandemics, and a World at Risk. Center Street, pp. 222-240.

were not fully understood or acknowledged at first. Sachs dissolved the *Lancet* sub-group when they became evident.[64] Despite efforts to brand it a 'conspiracy theory' not worth exploring, the scenario of a laboratory origin actually has been gaining plausibility over time. A minority interim report of a US Senate committee, for instance, has come to the conclusion that the emergence of SARS-CoV-2 'was most likely the result of a research-related incident'.[65] This view, though with less confidence, by now is shared by the US Department of Energy and the FBI, both of which have institutional expertise in the field. Modern 'seamless' methods leave no trace of genetic intervention. Based on the gene sequence of SARS-CoV-2 alone it is thus impossible to say whether genetic manipulation has occurred or not on the virus that potentially leaked from a Wuhan lab. In any case, the world 'faces the strong possibility that scientific research, intended to avert a pandemic, instead started one' and that 'two decades of research on the genomes of sarbecoviruses had not produced a vaccine but a plague', Chan and Ridley concluded.[66]

The risk of 'gain of function' pathogen research

The origin of SARS-CoV-2 and whether the virus was genetically modified may never be established beyond doubt. Nobody knows if and when a dangerously contagious and lethal natural mutation in a pathogen such as H5N1 will occur and transfer to humans. But such pathogens are being created in laboratories around the world in so-called 'gain of function' experiments. As Chan and Ridley noted in their book, the 'public sees only the research that scientists decide to publish, not the projects that fail, that remain unfinished, or that they choose to keep secret.'[67] The idea usually is to find out which mutations might make particular pathogens more contagious and deadly in order to help develop potential vaccines and other countermeasures. In 2008, for instance, researchers at WIV combined an SARS-like coronavirus with parts of the HIV virus to guess how well it could infect humans. Airborne modified H5N1 bird flu viruses were created in highly controversial laboratory trials in the USA and the Netherlands in 2012. According to a testimony at the US Congress, WIV in 2019 was also working on the Nipah virus which has a 60 per cent lethality rate. If a genetically modified Nipah virus capable of easy

---

64   Robinson, Nathan, and Jeffrey Sachs. 2 Aug. 2022. 'Why the Chair of the Lancet's COVID-19 Commission Thinks The US Government Is Preventing a Real Investigation Into the Pandemic.' Current Affairs (currentaffairs.org).

65   U.S. Senate Committee on Health Education, Labor and Pensions. Oct. 2022. 'An Analysis of the Origins of the COVID-19 Pandemic. Minority Oversight Staff. Interim Report.' (help.senate.gov), p. 4.

66   Chan and Ridley, p. 314.

67   Ibid., p. 197.

airborne transmission were created, it would be one of the most dangerous pathogens in existence, alongside the artificially modified H5N1 equivalent. According to the US-based group Biosafety Now, 'gain of function' research on potential pandemic pathogens creates 'high-potential existential risks' that 'did not exist previously and that might not come to exist by natural means for tens, hundreds, thousands, or tens of thousands of years'.[68] Biosafety Now member and physician Laura Kahn noted that this kind of research receives 'almost no national or international oversight'.[69] A 2022 report of the UN environmental agency on the risk of future pandemics recommended that 'gain of function' pathogen studies should be better regulated or totally banned, a view that Kahn and her group shares. The *Lancet* commission report stated that 'many scientists have warned of the increasing risks of under-supervised and underregulated genetic manipulation of SARS-CoV-like virus-es and other potential pandemic pathogens. There is currently no system for the global monitoring and regulation of gain-of-function research of con-cern.'[70] Experts worry that a fatal 'Disease X' pathogen could accidentally leak from a laboratory and question whether the alleged benefits are worth the risk. Bioterrorists may also manage to obtain specimens or information that ena-bles them to recreate such a pathogen on their own. In fact, it appears that laboratory incidents are not uncommon. According to investigative journalist Alison Young, for instance, over 200 biosafety level 3 and 4 labs in the US alone are studying a wide array of dangerous agents and pathogens, including genetically manipulated strains. From 2006 through 2013, federal regulators were notified about 1,500 incidents. In addition, more than 100 US labora-tories working on 'potential bioterror agents' had been sanctioned for 'serious safety and security failings' since 2003, Young reported.[71] Some with the worst records were run by the same federal agencies that were charged with regulat-ing laboratory safety.[72] Between three and seven US facilities faced enforce-ment actions each year since 2015. In the book 'Pandora's Gamble', the re-porter tells the story of incidents in the US and elsewhere that involved, among others, anthrax bacteria, the infamous modified H5N1 strain, a lab-made SARS virus called MA15 and the smallpox virus, a pathogen declared eradicated in 1980. After the international outbreak of SARS had been

---

68   'Pandemic Pathogens Research.' Biosafety Now (biosafetynow.org).

69   Kahn, Laura. 3 March 2023. 'The Seven Deadly Sins of Biomedical Research.' Georgetown Journal of International Affairs (blog) (gjia.georgetown.edu).

70   Sachs, p. 10.

71   Young, Alison. 28 May 2015. 'Inside America's Secretive Biolabs.' USA TODAY (usatoday.com).

72   Id. 22 March 2021. 'Could an Accident Have Caused COVID-19? Why the Wuhan Lab-Leak Theory Shouldn't Be Dismissed.' USA TODAY (usatoday.com).

brought to a halt in July 2003, the SARS virus actually escaped from labs in China, Singapore and Tawain at least four times due to 'lax safety practices'. These incidents potentially could have reignited the epidemic.[73] There is no official register of relevant laboratories in the world. According to researchers who publish the Global BioLabs Report, the number is increasing substantially. One of them, Gregory Koblentz of George Mason University, told the *New York Times* that in terms of oversight 'barely anyone is doing anything'. He added that in 'a lot of countries', there was 'literally zero' control in place.[74] Biosafety obviously is a matter of global concern. But their report describes a highly fragmented and inefficient landscape of international 'biorisk management efforts' which faces 'constraints imposed by the diverse interests' of governments. Over the 'longer term' it would be 'desirable for an international system to be put in place', run by the WHO, 'to register high-consequence biolabs and provide oversight'.[75] In a report on 'lessons learned and recommendations for the future' related to the COVID-19 pandemic, the European Parliament noted that the WHO should be 'expanded' in order to 'prevent research-related spillovers, by overseeing the biosafety, biosecurity and biorisk management of national and international research programmes that are engaged in the collection, testing, and the genetic manipulation of potentially dangerous pathogens.'[76]

Synthetic pathogens and killer nanobots

Advancements in genetics, biotechnology, AI, computing power, nanotechnology, and robotics give rise to new opportunities but also to amplified future risk scenarios. Yet another example are AI language models for protein design such as ProtGPT2 which are evolving rapidly. Trained on millions of natural protein sequences, they are intended to generate novel proteins tailored for specific purposes. Simultaneously, efforts are underway to develop automated chemical instruments for the rapid manufacturing of peptide chains. In the future, this technology may be capable of producing whole artificial proteins based on AI models. This could be easily misused for malign purposes. Experts fear that synthetic biology could be used to design 'next-generation bio-

---

73 Id. (2023), ch. 9, p. 111.
74 Wallace-Wells, David. 28 Feb. 2023. 'The Lab-Leak Debate Has Left Us No Safer.' The New York Times (nytimes.com).
75 King's Kollege London, and George Mason University. 2023. 'Global BioLabs Report 2023.' (GlobalBioLabs.org), pp. 24, 27.
76 European Parliament. 12 July 2023. 'COVID-19 Pandemic: Lessons Learned and Recommendations for the Future.' Res. P9_TA(2023)0282 (europarl.europa.eu), para. 501.

weapons' that target specific groups of individuals based on ethnic and other gene markers.

Bill Joy, a critic of transhumanism and co-founder of the company Sun Microsystems, which in 2009 was acquired by Oracle Corporation, saw greater dangers ahead in the combined application of genetics, nanotechnology and robotics than those posed by the 'classical weapons of mass destruction'. He pointed out in a dramatic appeal published 2000 in *Wired* magazine that within the next thirty years we must expect it to be technically feasible to construct robotic organisms which self-replicate at the molecular level and which could go out of control, or could even be designed from the outset as 'destruction machines'. In the most extreme case, as postulated in Joy's thesis, such killer nanobots could lead to the extermination of the human species. 'We are on the cusp of the further perfection of extreme evil', wrote Joy, 'an evil whose possibility spreads well beyond that which weapons of mass destruction bequeathed to the nation-states, on to a surprising and terrible empowerment of extreme individuals.'[77] Later on he added that it would not be long before every computer user with a mind to do so would be able to create their own super-viruses using commonly available resources.[78] The only realistic alternative, Joy argued, was to abandon the further development of technologies that are too potentially dangerous and to set limits on the search for certain kinds of knowledge.[79]

Regulation under global law

For a long time, the dangers posed by bioterrorism, and the broader challenge of biotechnology in general, have been judged to be of the greatest significance. It has been emphasized that declining costs will make biotechnology accessible to a wider community, bringing it into reach of 'biohackers', and that an increasing number of laboratories will inadvertently leak expertise and potentially materials.[80] While this scenario is becoming more and more real, efforts toward regulation are not making enough progress. In the book 'Our Posthuman Future', Francis Fukuyama, who was a member of US President's bioethics council, argued that the development and application of biotechnology and medical science need to be politically regulated by new institutions 'that will discriminate between those technological advances that promote human flourishing, and those that pose a threat to human dignity and well-

---

77   Joy, Bill. April 2000. 'Why the Future Doesn't Need Us'. Wired (www.wired.com).

78   Id. 2000. 'Act now to keep new technologies out of destructive hands'. New Perspectives Quarterly 17 (3): 12–14.

79   Id. (April 2000),

80   National Intelligence Council (ed.). September 2010. 'Global Governance 2025: At a critical juncture', p. iii.

being'. These institutions must have 'real enforcement powers' and 'international reach'. Decisions over whether the application of biotechnology in specific cases is legitimate or illegitimate are in essence political rather than technocratic questions, Fukuyama contended. Therefore it is 'the democratically constituted political community, acting chiefly through their elected representatives' that must be responsible for those decisions, he concluded.[81] But Fukuyama was thinking here only of arrangements at the nation state level. These would need to be brought together and harmonised within an international legal regime. As he later made clear, he did not 'see a practical and legitimate means for delegating decision-making power to some kind of a planetary body that stands over the nation-state', adding that he had 'a hard time envisioning a supranational entity that political leaders would be willing to give their authority to.'[82] This view reflects once again the 'sovereignty problem' and a lack of imagination. It means that international collaboration would continue to be voluntary, international enforcement would be impossible and technocrats would remain in charge. Instead, a world parliament, as the political institution representing the world's citizens, should take up the global issues that arise in the fields of advancing technologies, in particular biotechnology and AI, and convene global public debates on them. It is increasingly recognized in the field of genome editing too that 'governance by the few for all is no longer appropriate or acceptable'.[83] Mario Capanna, President of the Rome-based Genetic Rights Foundation, took the view that the human genome must be regarded as a global common good. The time was right, he argued, for a world parliament that would represent effectively all the people of the Earth and 'would concern itself with those great questions with a global impact'.[84] Ultimately, the purpose of a global parliament is to adopt binding global rules to regulate technology, among other things, and to provide political oversight of their implementation through appropriate executive bodies. Institutions with supranational powers are needed, in particular such enabling them to run effective global inspection regimes. In the fields of biosafety and pandemic prevention this includes a significant strengthening and enhancement of the WHO, giving it 'unrestricted access to relevant sites' to investigate disease outbreaks.[85] Even if initially not vested with legislative powers, a global

81 Fukuyama, Francis. 2002. *Our Posthuman Future*. New York: Picador, pp. 182, 204, 211, 186.

82 Fukuyama, Francis, Nils Gilman, and Jonathan S. Blake. 29 April 2021. 'Francis Fukuyama: Will We Ever Get Beyond The Nation-State?' NOEMA (noemamag.com).

83 Yu, Hanzhi, Lan Xue, et al. 2021. 'Toward Inclusive Global Governance of Human Genome Editing.' Proceedings of the National Academy of Sciences 118 (47), p. 4.

84 Capanna, Mario. 2010. 'Towards a World Parliament'. Speech at at the 10th Doha Forum on Democracy and Free Trade (www.fondazionedirittigenetici.org).

85 Independent Panel, p. 53.

parliamentary body has still a crucial contribution to make as an inclusive platform for global deliberation and by providing democratic legitimacy and oversight. In terms of AI governance, a study of the World Federalist Movement recommended the adoption of a UN framework convention drawing on the example of the UN Framework Convention on Climate Change. This could go beyond AI and include 'other disruptive technologies' as well. The study suggests that the convention should set up 'an associated Parliamentary Assembly' to 'provide a democratic input and a constructive monitoring role'.[86] The Princeton-based Australian bioethicist Peter Singer said with regard to global problems that 'a suitable form of government for that single world' would have to be found on the path to a global ethical community. Institutions for global decision-making would need to be strengthened and made more accountable to the people affected by those decisions. 'This line of thought', said Singer, 'leads in the direction of a world community with its own directly elected legislature, perhaps slowly evolving along the lines of the European Union.'[87] Fukuyama noted that neither climate change nor the COVID-19 pandemic thus far made political leaders globally more willing to give up authority. But he contended to be 'open to the possibility or even the likelihood' that things might get so bad 'that at some point it's going to happen, so it's worth thinking now about how to design a new supranational institution', giving special consideration to checks and balances.[88]

86 World Federalist Movement. 2020. 'Effective, Timely and Global: The Urgent Need for Good Global Governance of AI.' Report by the Transnational Working Group on AI and Disruptive Technologies (wfm-igp.org), p. 63.
87 Singer, Peter. 2004. One world: the ethics of globalization. New Haven: Yale University Press, pp. 149, 199-201.
88 Fukuyama, ibid.

17.

The threat of nuclear weapons,
disarmament, and collective security

Nuclear war as the end of all things

The build-up of huge arsenals of nuclear weapons has created the potential to extinguish world civilization and the conditions enabling its existence. The apocalyptic consequences of a nuclear war are well-known. In addition to the direct explosive impact of the nuclear devices themselves, there would be firestorms and radioactive fallout. Large amounts of radioactive dust would be propelled into the atmosphere. Depending on the quantities involved, a protracted reduction in sunlight would follow, and with it a sharp fall in temperature as well as other weather and climatic impacts. A 'nuclear winter' would seriously reduce global food production and lead to worldwide famine. Research suggests that more than 5 billion people could die from a nuclear war between the United States and Russia.[1] 'Although a major nuclear war between the Great Powers would probably not mean the end of humanity', wrote the Dutch social scientist Godfried van Benthem van den Bergh, 'the survivors would probably be catapulted back several thousand years in terms of social and political organization; it is likely that a plethora of armed bands would emerge, who would find themselves forced into a wild struggle of all against all.'[2] This destructive capacity is another thing that distinguishes our time from all the historical epochs of the past. The Greek philosopher Heraclitus thought that war was 'the father of all things'. In the Anthropocene, war has become potentially *the end of all things*.

The world has once before been a hair's breadth away from 'the abyss of nuclear destruction and the end of mankind', as Robert Kennedy wrote in his account of what were perhaps the thirteen most dangerous days in all of history—the Cuba Crisis of October 1962.[3] A few misjudgements could have allowed the conflict between the USA and the Soviet Union to escalate into war. The ex-

---

1   Xia, Lili, Alan Robock, et al. 2022. 'Global Food Insecurity and Famine from Reduced Crop, Marine Fishery and Livestock Production Due to Climate Disruption from Nuclear War Soot Injection.' Nature Food 3 (8): 586–96.

2   Bergh, Godfried van Benthem van den. 1984. 'Dynamik von Rüstung und Staatsbildungsprozessen'. In: Macht and Zivilisation. Materialien zu Norbert Elias' Zivilisationstheorie. Ed. by Peter Gleichmann, Johan Goudsblom, and Hermann Korte, 217–241. Frankfurt: Suhrkamp, p. 217.

3   Kennedy, Robert F. 1999 [1968]. Thirteen Days. A Memoir of the Cuban Missile Crisis. New York and London: W.W. Norton & Company, p. 19.

plosive power of the nuclear weapons in operational readiness spread among the various launch systems is unimaginable. The two hundred intercontinental missiles on the American side alone were apparently armed with 635 megatons of explosive, and the forty on the Soviet side with between 108 and 204 megatons—a combined explosive power more than fifty thousand times greater than the atom bomb dropped on Hiroshima. The other operational warheads, especially those of the USA's strategic bomber fleet, represented an additional destructive capacity greater by several multiples. At that point in time it is believed that the USA had 3,500 operational warheads, and the Soviets perhaps 500.[4] The nuclear arms race reached its peak in 1986, at around 65,000 nuclear weapons and an explosive power of over 20,000 megatons. In the course of disarmament negotiations since then, this arsenal has been reduced significantly. Latest reductions are primarily due to the USA and Russia dismantling retired warheads, however. The number of operational warheads is rising again. Taking all into account, as per 2023, the USA and Russia together had over 11,000 nuclear weapons, and France, China, Great Britain, India, Pakistan and Israel about another 1,500 altogether. North Korea by now is believed to possess up to thirty warheads. China is in the middle of massively expanding its nuclear arsenal and has an inventory of 410. What is more, the USA and the Russian Federation continue to maintain about 2,000 of their nuclear weapons at the highest level of readiness so as to be able to respond in a matter of minutes to any first nuclear strike by the other side.[5] This state of affairs is based on a circular logic, seemingly hard to dispel, according to which one side's nuclear weapons have to be maintained in readiness because those on the other side are as well.[6] 'Nuclear war is seven minutes away, and might be over in an afternoon', the author Martin Amis wrote.[7] In that respect, nothing has changed.

The danger of drifting into nuclear war

The way the states of the world are linked to each other has been fundamentally changed by the existence of nuclear weapons. The possibility of nuclear annihilation has turned potential direct military conflict between the nuclear Great Powers into a form of suicide. They find themselves in an 'interdepend-

---

4   Figures from Dobbs, Rachel. 2011. 'What Was at Stake in 1962?' Foreign Policy (www.foreignpolicy.com). See also Norris, Robert S., and Hans M. Kristensen. 12 October 2012. 'The Cuban Missile Crisis: A nuclear order of battle, October and November 1962'. Bulletin of the Atomic Scientists, Nuclear Notebook.
5   SIPRI Yearbook 2023, p. 247-8.
6   See Kristensen, Hans M., and Matthew McKinzie. 2012. Reducing Alert Rates of Nuclear Weapons. New York and Geneva: United Nations Institute for Disarmament Research (www.unidir.ch), p. viii.
7   Amis, Martin. Einstein's Monsters. London: Vintage, 2003.

ence of destruction', as Wilhelm Wolfgang Schütz called it.[8] However, it would be a fatal error to believe that the obvious insanity of an atomic war makes it impossible. As Norbert Elias pointed out, complex relationships can give rise to an irrational self-perpetuating dynamic from which the partners cannot escape even when they know that it is harmful to them. And it is precisely in a situation of threat that a spiral of escalation can emerge of a kind Elias called a 'double-bind figuration'. In the face of danger, thought and action become increasingly driven by emotion, which in turn leads to an escalation of the danger, and *vice versa*. In fact, Elias thought the 'drift towards atomic war' was a particularly good example of such an 'unplanned social process'.[9] US President Donald Trump was felt to be particularly unfit to hold command responsibility over the US nuclear arsenal but 'no president should have the sole authority to launch nuclear weapons first', former US Secretary of Defense William Perry and nuclear arms expert Tom Collina point out in their book 'The Button'.[10] It is unsettling that unaccountable autocrats such as Russia's Putin, China's Xi Jinping and North Korea's Kim Jong Un also have power over nuclear weapons. It would be difficult to disagree with the view of the US American security and nuclear weapons expert Joseph Cirincione that the danger of a global thermonuclear war most of the time may be close to zero. But *close to zero* is still *not zero*. 'Even a small chance of war each year, for whatever reason, multiplied over a number of years sums to an unacceptable chance of catastrophe', Cirincione pointed out.[11] In the wake of Russia's full-scale invasion of Ukraine in 2022 and Chinese military activity around Taiwan, the global security situation deteriorated significantly and the risk of a nuclear weapon deployment in turn increased. It is of little reassurance that while Russia was massing troops along its border to Ukraine, the US, Russia, China, the United Kingdom and France made a joint statement pledging to work towards 'a world without nuclear weapons' and noting that 'a nuclear war cannot be won and must never be fought.'[12]

8   Schütz, Wolfgang Wilhelm. 1956. Wir wollen Überleben, Außenpolitik im Atomzeitalter. Stuttgart: DVA, p. 162.

9   Elias, Norbert. 1987. Involvement and Detachment. Oxford: Basil Blackwell, pp. 74-5.

10 Perry, William J., and Tom Z. Collina. 2020. The Button: The New Nuclear Arms Race and Presidential Power from Truman to Trump. Dallas: BenBella Books, p. 58.

11 Cirincione, Joseph. 2008. 'The continuing threat of nuclear war'. In: Global Catastrophic Risks (ed.). Nick Bostrom and Milan M. Ćirković, 381–401. 1st ed. Oxford, New York: Oxford University Press, p. 382.

12 3 January 2022. Joint Statement of the Leaders of the Five Nuclear-Weapon States on Preventing Nuclear War and Avoiding Arms Races (whitehouse.gov).

The risk of nuclear accidents

The short response times considerably increase the risk of an order to launch being given on the basis of a misjudgement or human error. Faults can also occur in the command and early warning systems. In a standard work on nuclear safety in the US armed forces, Scott Sagan wrote that '[n]uclear weapons may well have made *deliberate* war less likely, but, the complex and tightly coupled nuclear arsenal we have constructed has simultaneously made *accidental* war more likely'.[13]

Dozens of incidents have come to light. In 1979, for example, the North American Aerospace Defense Command centre (NORAD) mistakenly showed as genuine a simulated attack by over two thousand Soviet rockets which had been entered into the system for test purposes. The mistake was spotted one minute before the US President was due to be informed. In 1995, a sounding rocket (a sub-orbital research rocket) launched in Norway was wrongly identified by the Russian early warning system as a possible US American submarine-launched nuclear attack on Moscow. Its flying time was estimated at five minutes. President Boris Yeltsin placed the Russian nuclear armed forces on battle alert. Fortunately, calculations showed just in time that the rocket would land outside Russian borders. And it is worth noting in this context that according to experts the Russian early warning system is in any event in a dangerously run-down condition. Another significant incident occurred in November 2008. During the extended terrorist attacks and hostage crisis in Mumbai in India, which went on for several days, the Pakistani President received a phone call from the Indian Foreign Minister in which an attack on Pakistan was threatened unless immediate steps were taken against individuals in Pakistan believed to be behind the terrorist attacks. The Pakistani armed forces were placed on the highest level of alert, and planes armed with primed nuclear weapons were sent out on patrol. As it turned out, however, the call was a hoax by an unknown perpetrator. Scientists are convinced that a large-scale nuclear war between India and Pakistan involving the deployment of their one hundred nuclear weapons would result in disastrous worldwide effects over and above the estimated twenty million deaths in the two countries and 'would produce enough smoke to cripple global agriculture'.[14] In the opinion of Tad Daley, a specialist on nuclear disarmament, these and other known incidents are probably only 'the tip of the iceberg'. In his recommended book 'Apocalypse Never', to which we are indebted for a number of ideas

---

13   Sagan, Scott D. 1995. The Limits of Safety. Organizations, Accidents, and Nuclear Weapons. 4th ed. Princeton University Press, p. 264.

14   Robock, Alan, and Brian Toon. Jan. 2010. 'Local Nuclear War, Global Suffering'. Scientific American: 74–81, p. 76.

and references, he asked rhetorically whether we can 'really expect, if we retain nuclear weapons for another twenty or thirty years, that not a single nuclear crisis will ever descend into nuclear war?'[15]

If just a single nuclear warhead were to be detonated, especially in a big city, the consequences would be devastating, possibly leading to a substantial political and economic destabilization of the world. In his book 'Command and Control', the journalist Eric Schlosser detailed numerous, sometimes highly dramatic accidents involving nuclear weapons. In one instance, two W39 hydrogen bombs were released over North Carolina in 1961 following the break-up of a B52 bomber at a height of 3,000 metres. An investigation later uncovered by Schlosser established that the detonation of one of the warheads was prevented only by a simple low-voltage electric switch prone to faults. The explosive power of this bomb was—at four megatons—over three hundred times greater than that of the atom bomb dropped on Hiroshima.[16] Although such a worst-case-scenario accident has fortunately not yet occurred, nobody can give a one hundred per cent guarantee that it will not happen in the future. Moreover, one scenario for nuclear terrorism involves the deliberate detonation of a nuclear weapon which has fallen intact into the wrong hands. It is known that al-Qaida tried to put its hands on a nuclear weapon or on highly enriched uranium for the construction of an atomic bomb. Cyberterrorism against nuclear installations and systems also poses a serious threat. The US American nuclear weapons expert and disarmament campaigner Bruce Blair has pointed out that hackers could try to manipulate early warning systems in such a way as to provoke an atomic war. It is even possible that a fake order to launch could be fed into the chain of command. According to Blair, this is precisely what the Pentagon identified as theoretically feasible during a security review conducted in 1998. Hackers could have gained back-door electronic access to the U.S. naval communications network, seized control electronically of U.S. Navy radio towers and illicitly transmitted a launch order to U.S. Trident ballistic missile submarines armed with 200 nuclear warheads each.[17] A Third World War, as Mikhail Gorbachev

15 Daley, Tad. 2010. Apocalypse never. Forging the path to a nuclear weapon-free world. New Brunswick, N.J.: Rutgers University Press, p. 95.

16 Schlosser, Eric. 2013. Command and control: nuclear weapons, the Damascus Accident, and the illusion of safety. New York: The Penguin Press, pp. 245ff.

17 Blair, Bruce. 19 Sep. 2004. 'The Wrong Deterrence'. Washington Post (www.washingtonpost.com). See also Rosenbaum, Ron. 2011. How the end begins: the road to a nuclear World War III. London: Simon & Schuster, p. 109.

put it in a famous article in *Pravda* in 1987, has been averted not *because of* but *in spite of* the existence of nuclear weapons.[18]

The unfulfilled commitment to general and complete disarmament

As the UN General Assembly has repeatedly and accurately pointed out, 'the only defence against a nuclear catastrophe is the total elimination of nuclear weapons and the certainty that they will never be produced again', as stated in a resolution of 10 December 1996. This view was shared by 'realists' such as the former US State Secretaries Henry Kissinger and George Shultz, William Perry and the former chair of the defence committee of the US Senate Sam Nunn. In one of a series of jointly written articles published in the *Wall Street Journal*, they wrote that the 'risk that deterrence will fail and that nuclear weapons will be used increases dramatically', and that 'the pace of work' on nuclear disarmament 'doesn't now match the urgency of the threat'.[19] In fact, the community of states has been trying to tackle this issue continuously now for more than seventy years. The very first resolution of the UN General Assembly of 24 January 1946 set up a commission to make proposals 'for the elimination from national armaments of atomic weapons'. In the so-called Nuclear Non-Proliferation Treaty, in short NPT, which came into force in 1970 and which almost all the world's states have signed up to, those states without nuclear weapons agreed to forego their acquisition or development and to allow inspections to be carried out by the International Atomic Energy Agency to verify this. This commitment is to be matched, according to Article VI, by a commitment on the part of the five officially recognised nuclear weapons states—the USA, Russia, France, Great Britain and China—to pursue negotiations with all other parties 'on a treaty on general and complete disarmament under strict and effective international control'. When US President Barack Obama announced the aim of 'a world without nuclear weapons' in Prague in 2009, this was celebrated as a huge breakthrough and rewarded with the Nobel Peace Prize. However, it needs to be acknowledged that *a commitment under international law* to realize this very goal by now has been in existence already *for more than five decades*. '[T]he obligation involved here', emphasized the International Court of Justice in an advisory opinion of 1996, 'is an obligation to achieve a precise result—nuclear disarmament in all its aspects' by

18   Gorbachev, Mikhail. 1987. 'Reality and Guarantees for a Secure World'. International Affairs: A Russian Journal of World Politics, Diplomacy and International Relations 33 (11): 3–11, p. 4.
19   Shultz, George P., William J. Perry, Henry A. Kissinger, and Sam Nunn. 5 March 2013. 'Next Steps in Reducing Nuclear Risks: The Pace of Nonproliferation Work Today Doesn't Match the Urgency of the Threat'. The Wall Street Journal (www.nuclearsecurityproject.org).

negotiating and *concluding* a treaty.[20] In spite of this, Obama (who was born in 1961) underlined in Prague that a world free of nuclear weapons would not be achieved quickly—'perhaps not in my lifetime', he said. It appears that the five recognised nuclear weapons states are determined to remain nuclear powers for the indefinite future. Both in the USA and in Russia extensive modernization programmes are under way. More recently, the two nuclear powers accused each other of violating the provisions of the Intermediate-Range Nuclear Forces Treaty concluded in 1987 and it was suspended in 2019. This made the New START Strategic Arms Reduction Treaty, concluded in 2010, the last remaining agreement between the US and Russia on nuclear arms control. It caps the number of strategic nuclear warheads both can deploy at 1,550. In February 2023, Putin announced the end of Russia's participation in the treaty but did not formally withdraw. When 122 UN member states voted in favour of a Treaty on the Prohibition of Nuclear Weapons on 7 July 2017, this was opposed by all nuclear powers and many of their allies, including all NATO member states. From the perspective of India, which—like Pakistan, Israel and North Korea—is not a party to the NPT, the non-proliferation agreement established in practice a permanent system of 'nuclear apartheid'. India cites the fact that the five official nuclear weapons states ignore their commitments under Article VI of the NPT as one of the reasons for not signing up to the treaty. A particularly grotesque moment in the comedy was played out at a meeting of the UN Security Council chaired by Obama on 24 September 2009. In a unanimous resolution celebrated as historic, the five official nuclear weapons states, all of which have a permanent seat on the council, in effect called on themselves to meet their obligations under Article VI. When Ukraine became independent following the dissolution of the Soviet Union, the country had thousands of former Soviet nuclear weapons on its soil. In turn for agreeing to forfeit these weapons and joining the NPT, Russia in the so-called 'Budapest Memorandum' of late 1994 guaranteed to respect Ukraine's sovereignty in the existing borders and to refrain from the threat or use of force against the country, among other things. In view of the Russian aggression since 2014, the uselessness of such security guarantees has become apparent. At the time, US political scientist John Mearsheimer argued that 'Ukrainian nuclear weapons are the only reliable deterrent to Russian aggression'.[21]

20   International Court of Justice. 1996. 'Legality of the Threat or Use of Nuclear Weapons. Advisory Opinion.' ICJ, para. 99, pp. 41-2.

21   Mearsheimer, John J. 1993. 'The Case for a Ukrainian Nuclear Deterrent.' Foreign Affairs 72 (3): 50–66, p. 51.

The architecture of nuclear disarmament

According to Tad Daley, the wording of Article VI of the NPT—'general and complete disarmament under strict and effective international control'—makes it clear that whatever 'nuclear abolitionist architecture might ultimately be created by the conclusion of such negotiations, that architecture must move beyond pure national sovereignty and exclusive national control over nuclear weapons.' States 'must find a way to cede the management, verification, and enforcement of nuclear disarmament to some kind of international institution, global structure, or mechanism of transnational governance'.[22] In this regard, the new Treaty on the Prohibition of Nuclear Weapons does not offer any solution. In Article 4 it vaguely says that the 'States Parties shall designate a competent international authority or authorities to negotiate and verify the irreversible elimination of nuclear-weapons programmes'.

On the initiative of a number of NGOs including the International Physicians for the Prevention of Nuclear War and the International Association Of Lawyers Against Nuclear Arms, a number of experts adopted the roles of the various governments in order to draft—from that assumed perspective—a model nuclear weapons convention, or NWC, that goes into more detail. From a global legal perspective, a significant element of the draft agreement, first published in 1997, is that it includes the possibility of criminal proceedings being taken against individuals in cases of a breach of the provisions of the treaty. If none of the treaty partners is willing or able to instigate such proceedings, then the case becomes the responsibility of the International Criminal Court. In addition, every individual would be obliged under this treaty to report any infringements to the international authority charged with upholding the treaty. It is explicitly stated that this reporting obligation overrides any contradictory national regulations. Whistle-blowers are given international witness protection and where necessary a right of asylum. This makes it clear that there is an assumption that an approach involving the signatory states alone holds out little prospect for success and that the creation of a world free of nuclear weapons requires the citizens of the world themselves to be given direct responsibility. The influential journalist Walter Lippmann had already made the case for such an approach in 1946.[23]

In one other respect, the draft is less innovative. In the course of the START negotiations since 1991, the US and Russia established a wide-ranging bilateral inspections system that is now imperilled by the end of New START.

---

22 Daley, p. 118.
23 Lippmann, Walter. 1946. 'International Control of Atomic Energy'. In: One World Or None, ed. by Dexter Masters and Katharine Way, 180–208. New York: The New Press, pp. 187-9.

It is a prerequisite of complete nuclear disarmament that all countries must submit equally to a thorough *international* inspections system. One problem is how to handle the suspected blocking of inspections or other cases of non-compliance on the part of any state. In the draft NWC, such cases are passed to the UN Security Council for further advice and for decisions on measures to be taken if necessary. This obviously was not an option for the countries that negotiated and adopted the prohibition treaty. It is precisely the five nuclear weapons states whose nuclear disarmament is the objective, but who sit on the council not only as the sole nations with permanent seats but in possession moreover of a right of veto by means of which they can block any decision. They would therefore represent jury, judge and law enforcement at their own hearings. It is clear that such a conflict of interests would make nuclear arms control impossible over the long term. The simple fact of the right of veto of the five permanent members means that the Security Council in its present form cannot play a credible role in the architecture of nuclear disarmament. A multilateral agreement for the abolition of nuclear weapons would either have to involve appropriate reforms to the Security Council or else the creation of a new body better suited to the task. The historical contingency of the special status enjoyed today by the five permanent members of the UN Security Council represents an obstacle to the transition to a world free of nuclear weapons, and will become increasingly hard to justify. We should recall that after the Second World War the US government proposed to renounce nuclear weapons if all other countries would do the same and if at the same time an international inspections system under the control of the UN could be set up to monitor compliance. At that time the USA still had a nuclear monopoly. It was a key element of the US proposal that the right of veto in the Security Council should be abolished in the area of nuclear weapons control. 'There must be no veto to protect those who violate their solemn agreements not to develop or use atomic energy for destructive purposes', explained the US representative Bernard Baruch at a session of the United Nations on 14 June 1946. However, Daley questioned whether it is acceptable at all for the world to be governed by a small group of 'Great Powers', or whether it would not be better if 'our sociopolitical imaginations might someday invent better mechanisms of global governance, and begin to move toward creating something on the world level resembling a parliament of humankind'.[24] 'Unless humanity can someday manage to establish something

---

24　Daley, p. 179.

like a world republic, the logic of anarchy will endure', and with it the danger of self-annihilation.[25]

The link between nuclear and conventional disarmament

The abolition of nuclear weapons once and for all, so important for the survival of world civilization, requires the transformation of the international order into a system of world law. The struggle for political power between the states, which rests ultimately on the institution of war, must be transcended. Although on the one hand the nuclear 'balance of terror' makes military conflict between the nuclear powers impossible as a rational option, on the other hand the danger of drifting into a nuclear war is substantial. But the abolition of nuclear weapons *alone* is not a solution, because then conventional armaments would once again increase in importance in direct proportion. 'Military power would become relative again', argued van den Bergh. Without nuclear deterrence, the likelihood of a military escalation of conflicts, including between great powers, would grow, which would immediately set off in turn a race for nuclear re-armament.[26] Successful nuclear disarmament is therefore directly linked to conventional disarmament and arms control. This became clear already at the tenth special session of the UN General Assembly, on disarmament, which took place in 1978. 'Together with negotiations on nuclear disarmament measures', read the concluding report, agreed by consensus, 'negotiations should be carried out on the balanced reduction of armed forces and of conventional armaments ... These negotiations should be conducted with particular emphasis on armed forces and conventional weapons of nuclear weapons states and other militarily significant countries'.[27] Mikhail Gorbachev highlighted the link at a conference in Rome in 2009, pointing to the US American defence budget, which for a time was equal to those of all the world's other states put together. He said that military predominance such as that enjoyed by the USA represented an 'insurmountable obstacle' to the liberation of the world from nuclear weapons. 'Unless we discuss demilitarization of international politics, the reduction of military budgets, preventing militarization of outer space, talking about a nuclear-free world will be just rhetorical', the former Soviet President declared.[28]

25 Daley, Tad. 25 October 2013. 'Ban the Bomb!' Foreign Policy in Focus (fpif.org).

26 Bergh, Godfried van Benthem van den. 1992. The Nuclear Revolution and the End of the Cold War. Houndsmills: MacMillan Press, p. 211.

27 United Nations. 1978. 'Resolutions and decisions adopted by the General Assembly during its tenth special session'. A/S-10/4, para. 22, p. 5; see also para. 81, p. 10.

28 Hanley, Charles J. 16 April 2009. 'Gorbachev: US military power blocks ‚no nukes". Associated Press.

The problem is closely linked to the origins of modern statehood. As the US American sociologist Charles Tilly (1929 to 2008) emphasized, the process of state formation was marked by war and war preparations, and the modern state and its administrative and enforcement apparatus developed in large part as 'a by-product of rulers' efforts to acquire the means of war'.[29] 'War made the state and the state made war' was his pithy and subsequently frequently-cited formulation.[30] The possibility of military conflict has always been the decisive factor in the competitive relationship between states. Intergroup fighting, killing and warfare in fact have been dominant in the history of the human species from its beginnings hundreds of thousands of years ago as pre-state hunter-gatherers.[31] The ability to dispose over armed forces, the capacity to wage war, and the monopoly on force within a defined territory—historically, these constitute core areas of national sovereignty. Nothing makes it plainer than the continued worldwide existence of national armed forces that the anarchic state of international relations has not in any sense been overcome, but at best overlaid. Even in the European Union, the most advanced example of integration yet, progress towards integrated armed forces, let alone the abolishment of national armies, is painfully slow, despite the lip service paid to a 'common defence policy' and initiatives like Eurocorps since 1992 or the EU Battlegroups which are operational since 2007. In the wake of Brexit, an important milestone may have been reached when in late 2017, 25 EU member states agreed under the EU's enhanced cooperation mechanism on the creation of a new European defence and security cooperation network known as Permanent Structured Cooperation or PESCO. Notwithstanding that, the increasingly multinational composition of armed force units—whether under UN, NATO, EU or AU auspices—reflected a growing acceptance of a general shift in defence policy away from the classical form of defence of the nation and its allies towards global crisis intervention and conflict prevention. The next logical step is fully integrated supra-national armed forces. However, the Russian attack on Ukraine and Russian threats against Europe and the US as well as a potential invasion of Taiwan by China have prompted many states to revert to traditional territorial defence in their military strategies. The Global Peace Index noted a trend reversal towards militarisation affecting over 100 countries.[32]

29   Tilly, Charles. 2010. Coercion, Capital, and European States AD 990 - 1992. Rev. paperback ed. Cambridge, Mass; Oxford, UK: Blackwell, p. 14, see also pp. 67-9.
30   Id. 1975. 'Reflections on the History of European State-Making'. In: The Formation of National States in Western Europe, ed. by Charles Tilly. Princeton University Press, p. 42.
31   See Gat, Azar. 2008. War in Human Civilization. 2nd ed. Oxford: Oxford University Press.
32   Institute for Economics & Peace. 2024. Global Peace Index 2024. (economicsandpeace.org), p. 2.

A sustainable peace order designed to last for generations must consist of more than making war between countries 'unimaginable' and prohibiting it under international law if at the same time the *practical means* of waging war, in the form of national offensive armouries and national decision-making autonomy are *allowed to persist* fundamentally unquestioned. What is needed is a collective security system for the whole of humanity, one that enables the gradual disarmament and ultimately the *total abolition* of national armed forces. There must be a global treaty on nuclear *and* conventional disarmament. This is precisely what is really meant by the phrase 'general and complete disarmament' in Article VI of the Nuclear Non-Proliferation Treaty, which is constantly invoked.

The McCloy-Zorin Accords

It is worth calling to mind how this phrase came to be adopted as the guiding principle on the path to a global peace order. On 20 September 1961, the USA under President John F. Kennedy and the Soviet Union under Premier Nikita Khrushchev reached agreement on a set of 'Agreed Principles for General and Complete Disarmament', also known as the McCloy–Zorin Accords, after the chief negotiators on each side. An international programme for general and complete disarmament is there set out, step by step: the disbanding of all armed forces and the dismantling of all military establishments around the world; the cessation of the production of armaments, as well as their liquidation or conversion to peaceful uses; the elimination of all stockpiles of nuclear, chemical, bacteriological, and other weapons of mass destruction, and cessation of the production of such weapons and of their delivery systems; the cessation of military training, and closing of all military training institutions; and finally the discontinuance of military expenditures. Only those non-nuclear armaments, forces, facilities, and establishments agreed to be necessary to maintain internal order and protect the personal security of citizens would be allowed to continue in existence. In order to ensure the maintenance of international peace, particularly during the changeover period, the text included provision for a UN peace force. Verification of the process of disarmament would be the responsibility of an international authority whose activities would not be subject to veto. Any disputes would be taken before international courts. On 20 December 1961, this programme was unanimously adopted by the UN General Assembly. The programme was intended to ensure that war would no longer be 'an instrument for settling international problems'.[33]

---

33 'Joint Statement of Agreed Principles for Disarmament Negotiations (McCloy-Zorin Accords)'. 20 September 1961. Nuclear Age Peace Foundation (www.nuclearfiles.org).

After the Cuba Crisis, Kennedy was more determined than ever to press forward with it.[34] In an address before the UN he noted that 'the science of weapons and war' has made us all 'one world and one human race, with one common destiny.' Absolute sovereignty no longer assured of absolute security, he argued. The UN needed to be developed into a 'genuine world security system' and its Charter was not intended to be 'frozen in perpetuity'.[35] Two months after this speech, on 22 November 1963, Kennedy was assassinated in Dallas, and the programme sank into oblivion.

The unrealised peace concept of the UN Charter, and UN armed forces

The astoundingly radical, inspirational peace programme embodied in the McCloy-Zorin Accords was not plucked out of thin air, but is in fact simply the practical expression of the peace concept proposed in the UN Charter. According to Article 26, the Security Council shall submit plans 'for the establishment of a system for the regulation of armaments'. Article 43 requires binding agreements to be reached for the provision by member states of armed forces at the request and disposal of the Security Council. Under Article 47, a UN Military Staff Committee will take over the 'strategic direction' of all armed forces placed at the disposal of the Security Council and will advise the Security Council on questions of arms control and disarmament. 'The United Nations Organization must immediately begin to be equipped with an international armed force', demanded the former British Prime Minister Winston Churchill in his famous speech at Fulton, Missouri in the spring of 1946. Such an international force was something he had hoped to see come about after the First World War already.[36] In October 1946, US President Truman pressed for the conclusion of the special agreements required in a speech at the UN. The first UN General Secretary, the Norwegian Trygve Lie, floated several more 'trial balloons' up to 1952, as Oxford professor Adam Roberts reported in an historical overview.[37] The peace concept embodied in the UN Charter has still not been realised today.

As no armed forces have been put at the disposal of the UN, it is basically unable to respond consistently, with its own military measures, to breaches of

---

34 See his speech on peace at the American University Commencement Address, 10 June 1963 in Washington D.C. One month earlier he had also approved a related internal memorandum; see Kennedy, John F. 6 May 1963. 'National Security Action Memorandum Number 239'. John F. Kennedy Presidential Library & Museum.

35 Kennedy, John F. 22 Sept. 1963. Address before the 18th General Assembly of the United Nations.

36 Churchill, Winston. 5 March 1946. 'The Sinews of Peace, Westminster College, Fulton, Missouri'. The Churchill Centre and Museum at the Churchill War Rooms, London.

37 Roberts, Adam. 2008. 'Proposals for UN Standing Forces: A Critical History'. In: The United Nations Security Council and War, 99–130. Ed. by Vaughan Lowe, Adam Roberts, Jennifer Welsh, and Dominik Zaum. Oxford: Oxford University Press.

the peace or to acute conflict situations. However, as UN Secretary-General Boutros-Ghali underlined in the 'Agenda for Peace' in 1992, such a capacity, together with the provision of armed forces in accordance with Article 43 of the Charter, is 'essential to the credibility of the United Nations as a guarantor of international security'. The knowledge of the ready availability of UN armed forces on call could serve, in itself, as a means of deterring potential aggressors.[38] Instead, every UN mission has to be painstakingly and slowly put together ad hoc. For this, what is crucial is whether, and if so when, the member states are willing to provide the necessary resources and troops. Whether the prerequisite political will exists at all is unclear in advance. When between April and July 1994 over 800,000 people were murdered by Hutu extremists in Rwanda and four million more were forced to flee, the Security Council did nothing to intervene in the genocide. It is true that since 1994 there has been a directory where member states can register the availability of troops and equipment for UN peace operations, but it does not represent a fixed commitment and the option of saying 'No' to a specific request always remains open. 'In these circumstances', wrote Boutros-Ghali in 1995 in another report, 'I have come to the conclusion that the United Nations does need to give serious thought to the idea of a rapid reaction force.'[39] A proposal of this kind is the creation of a permanent United Nations Emergency Peace Service that is advocated by the Canadian Peter Langille as a 'first responder for complex emergencies'. 'Aside from providing a military formation to deter aggression and maintain security, there would be sufficient police to restore law and order, as well as an array of civilian teams to provide essential services', he pointed out.[40] A full-scale global army may not be needed and not desirable either.

There is another problem resulting from the limitations on the UN's capacity to act: every UN-led multilateral peace operation since 1990 has had to fall back on private security firms, and this trend has in fact been growing.[41] One of the largest of these firms, the security and military enterprise Blackwater, which later operated under the name Academi and then became part of Constellis Holdings, even 'strives to be an independent army, deploying to

38   United Nations. 1992. 'An Agenda for Peace. Preventive diplomacy, peacemaking and peace-keeping'. Report of the Secretary-General pursuant to the statement adopted by the Summit Meeting of the Security Council on 31 January 1992, A/47/277-S/24111, para. 43.

39   United Nations. 1995. 'Supplement to an Agenda for Peace: Position Paper of the Secretary-General on the Occassion of the Fiftieth Anniversary of the United Nations'. Report of the Secretary-General on the work of the organization, A/50/60-S/1995/1, para. 44.

40   Langille, H. Peter. 2016. Developing a United Nations Emergency Peace Service: Meeting Our Responsibilities to Prevent and Protect. Palgrave Macmillan, pp. 2-3.

41   Avant, Deborah. 2005. The Market for Force: The Consequences of Privatizing Security. Cambridge University Press, p. 7.

conflict zones as an alternative to a NATO or UN force', as the journalist Jeremy Scahill found in a *New York Times* bestseller about the company. However, this army, he adds, would be answerable only to its private owners and not to governments.[42] In view of the fact that the UN does not have its own intervention force at its disposal, the long-serving former UN Deputy Secretary-General Brian Urquhart even opined that private firms could play 'an extremely useful role'. For many tasks, they were better trained and prepared than 'a UN force put together at the last minute'.[43] The idea of the privatization of global security should be met with great scepticism. Indeed, experts from the Global Policy Forum in New York suggested the opposite conclusion: that the UN should cease cooperating with private providers of military services entirely.[44] But if that were to happen, the UN would need a massive upscaling of capacity in order to be able to meet its needs from its own resources.

Moreover, military enforcement measures are often only authorised by the UN Security Council in a legal sense, under international law, and not necessarily carried out under a UN banner. This practice, where the use of armed force by member states is authorised on a case by case basis, again illustrates that in the final analysis governments only generally get involved or provide armed personnel in pursuit of their own core interests. Where their own interests are not involved, Security Council decisions tend to lead nowhere. In addition, the right of veto allows any one of the five permanent members of the Security Council to block the implementation of any measures. Since 2011, Russia, often jointly with China, has cast over 15 vetoes to stop the council from condemning the Syrian regime for its continued systematic human rights violations and mandating measures in this regard. The right of veto needs to be restrained and eventually it needs to be abolished altogether. If the Security Council is unable to meet the international community's responsibility to protect due to the use of the veto, the General Assembly needs to take charge under the 'Uniting for Peace' instrument.[45] Complementing the assembly with a parliamentary body would strengthen its position vis-à-vis the Security Council in such situations. Decisions jointly taken by the General Assembly and a Parliamentary Assembly would enjoy unprecedented global

---

42 Scahill, Jeremy. 2007. Blackwater. The Rise of the World's Most Powerful Mercenary Army. London: Serpent's Tail, p. 345.

43 'Lateline: Dogs of War'. 18 May 2000. Australian Broadcasting Corp (www.abc.net.au). Interview with Brian Urquhart, Tim Spicer and Abdul Musa.

44 Pingeot, Lou. 2012. 'Dangerous Partnership: Private Military & Security Companies and the UN'. Global Policy Forum and Rosa-Luxemburg-Stiftung, p. 8.

45 See p. XXX.

legitimacy.[46] A parliamentary assembly may also be able to help rally international public support for protective measures in the face of massive atrocities like those seen in Rwanda, Darfur, Syria, or Myanmar. This is likely one of the reasons why the UNPA proposal was endorsed by Roméo Dallaire, the former force commander of the UN Assistance Mission for Rwanda who was on the spot during the genocide but unable to stop the mass killings. But to what extent are enforcement measures even possible if it comes to mass atrocities and aggression committed by a nuclear power?

The four pillars of a world peace order

The system of collective security envisaged in the UN Charter has not yet been brought about, and *even if it were*, it would remain only a first step, albeit an important one. The world had to realise, wrote Albert Einstein in 1947, 'that it is merely a transitional system toward the final goal, which is the establishment of a supranational authority vested with sufficient legislative and executive powers to keep the peace'.[47] What he meant by that was above all the establishment of 'a supranational police force, based on world law.[48] The liberal British politician David Davies, whom Einstein cited in support, was an influential champion of this proposal. The elimination of rivalry between the states, Davies argued correctly in his 1930 book 'The Problem of the Twentieth Century', was 'the crux of the disarmament problem'. This could only succeed if ensuring common security were no longer dependent on the whim of one or more Great Powers but had been entrusted to a supranational armed force.[49] And in addition, the jurisdiction of the International Court of Justice in inter-state disputes is not obligatory but optional. An enduring world peace would have to be built on four main pillars: worldwide disarmament and arms control; democratic global institutions that enable a fair reconciliation of interests and can make binding laws with a parliament at the center; obligatory recourse to international courts for the peaceful resolution of conflicts; and supranational powers of enforcement through police and military means. None of these pillars will work in isolation.

46 Bummel, Andreas. 1 Sep. 2014. 'The Failure of the UN: Rebuilding from the Ruins.' OpenDemocracy (opendemocracy.net).

47 Open letter to the United Nations General Assembly. October 1947. Citation from Nathan, Otto, and Heinz Norden (ed.). 1960. Einstein on Peace. New York: Simon and Schuster, p. 440.

48 In a note of May 1947, citation from Nathan and Norden, p. 407. See also pp. 362, 255, 242, 205-6.

49 Davies, David. 1930. The Problem of the Twentieth Century. London: Ernest Benn Limited, p. 271.

The role of a world parliament

The well-known US American astrophysicist Carl Sagan (1934 to 1996) was one of the first people to study the phenomenon of 'nuclear winter'. In view of the threat of an atomic war between the USA and the Soviet Union, he emphasized in his 1982 world bestseller 'Cosmos' that 'the welfare of our civilization and our species is in our hands'. As a supporter of world government, however, he was painfully aware that 'humanity' as a collective is not represented in the political order. 'We know who speaks for the nations', Sagan wrote. 'But who speaks for the human species? Who speaks for Earth?' he asked, unable to answer his own question.[50] Filling this gap would be the task of a world parliament. The worldwide programme of 'general and complete disarmament' must be accompanied by the formation of a democratic political community. Sixty years after the founding of the United Nations and the destruction of Hiroshima by an atom bomb, the Japanese House of Representatives passed a resolution on 2 August 2005 declaring as a long-term goal the creation of 'a world federation for the whole globe'. On the occasion of the 60th anniversary of Japan's membership in the UN, the upper house adopted a similar resolution in May 2016.

Through cosmopolitan institutions such as a global parliamentary assembly, mutual understanding and a sense of shared community across national and cultural borders can gradually be strengthened, leading to growing levels of the cooperation and trust necessary for progress in demilitarization and disarmament. The assembly itself should play a leading role in the development of a 'comprehensive programme for disarmament', as called for already by the tenth special session of the UN General Assembly, and should contribute to mobilising the necessary political will. Government bodies like the Conference on Disarmament in Geneva, which also operates on the principle of consensus, are trapped in a dead end. Not the least important of the arguments for a world parliament is that it would constitute in itself one of the essential core institutions of the emerging system of world law. It should participate in decision-making on coercive measures and on peacekeeping missions and should exercise parliamentary control over international armed forces and their operations. The deployment of supranational global armed forces should not be permissible without the approval of a democratic global parliamentary body.

A comprehensive disarmament and peace programme, politically and institutionally secured through a world parliament and a system of collective securi-

---

50 Sagan, Carl. 2011. Cosmos. Random House, p. 347.

ty, would have a positive impact not only in security policy terms but economically as well. It would lead to more prosperity and to greater social justice simply by virtue of making resources free for other purposes through a progressive reduction in military expenditure—for the improvement and modernization of civil infrastructure, for example, or for civil research or social issues. The opportunity costs of military expenditure are enormous. The economist Seymour Melman illustrated that military expenditure is economically counter-productive and caused the decline of the national industrial and infrastructural base in the US as early as 1970.[51] 'Military goods and services are economically parasitic', he wrote in his critical standard work 'The Permanent War Economy'.[52] Subsequent studies have proven him right. Ludwig von Mises, who had railed against the destructive and unproductive nature of war and the war economy in the aftermath of the First World War already, expressed the overall conclusion in a nutshell: 'peace and not war is the father of all things'.[53] There is no way around the fact that the production of weapons of war and arms trade have to be put under supranational control as part of a programme of complete global disarmament. The Mine Ban Treaty of 1997, the Arms Trade Treaty of 2013 and the 2021 Nuclear Ban Treaty are but small steps in this direction.

51 Melman, Seymour. 1970. Pentagon Capitalism. New York et al.: McGraw-Hill. pp. 2-4, 184-6.
52 Id. 1974. The Permanent War Economy. New York: Simon & Schuster. p. 62.
53 Mises, Ludwig von. 1951 [1922]. Socialism: An Economic and Sociological Analysis. New Haven: Yale University Press, p. 59.

18.
Terrorism, 'blowback',
and surveillance

The terrorist threat and its impact

Terrorism constitutes one of the most serious threats to international peace and security as the UN General Assembly pointed out in 2006 when the world organization started to pursue a system-wide global counter-terrorism strategy. This threat persists and grows as terrorist groups increasingly explore, use and exploit new technologies, in particular to communicate, recruit, spread narratives, finance activities as well as to plan and carry out attacks.[1] Between 2007 and 2022, the researchers of the Global Terrorism Index collected data on 66,000 terrorist incidents which led to 137,000 deaths. The most affected countries at the time of their 2023 report were Afghanistan, Burkina Faso, Somalia, Mali, Syria, Pakistan, Iraq, Nigeria, Myanmar and Niger. Violent conflict, the report noted, 'remains the primary driver of terrorism, with over 88 per cent of attacks and 98 per cent of terrorism deaths in 2022 taking place in countries in conflict'. These are more susceptible to terrorism according to the researchers as there is no fully functioning state and terrorist tactics are used by insurgent and paramilitary groups. The definition used by the Global Terrorism Index only includes terrorism carried out by non-state actors which limits the scope of the assessment. However, they stressed that 'many governments perpetrate state terror against their citizens' and that these acts are tracked instead in the Global Peace Index through the 'Political Terror Scale'.[2] Alex P. Schmid, a leading researcher in terrorism studies who for six years was also working on the subject at the UN, noted that disagreements on defining terrorism have been ongoing ever since the League of Nations made a first attempt in 1937 to the extent that many scholars are now 'sick and tired' of discussing the issue. The matter goes beyond the simplistic and relativistic assertion that 'one man's terrorist is another man's freedom fighter.'[3] A UN Security Council resolution adopted in 2004 with reference to terrorism spoke

---

1   See UN. 2023. 'Activities of the UN System in Implementing the UN Global Counter-Terrorism Strategy. Report of the Secretary-General.' UN Doc. A/77/718, para. 9.
2   Institute for Economics & Peace. 2023. 'Global Terrorism Index 2023: Measuring the Impact of Terrorism.' (www.visionofhumanity.org), pp. 2, 20, 33, 6.
3   Schmid, Alex P. 2011. The Routledge Handbook of Terrorism Research. London and New York: Routledge, pp. 42, 40.

of 'criminal acts, including against civilians, committed with the intent to cause death or serious bodily injury, or taking of hostages, with the purpose to provoke a state of terror in the general public or in a group of persons or particular persons, intimidate a population or compel a government or an international organization to do or to abstain from doing any act.'[4] The impact of terrorism go far beyond the actual terrorist acts. They can generate a lasting atmosphere of fear and insecurity that infiltrates societies, erodes trust and prompts major shifts in public perceptions and policies. A global shift in this regard was triggered by al-Qaeda's terrorist attacks on the United States on 11 September 2001. An authorization passed by the US Congress three days later is still in place that allows the US President to take any action deemed necessary and appropriate, anywhere in the world, to counter terrorist threats against the US. It was the start of the so-called 'war on terror', a term that is officially no longer used, which included the US-led invasions of Afghanistan in 2001 and of Iraq in 2003 and resulted in occupations of these countries for twenty and eight years respectively. The battle zone is the entire world, though, with ongoing violent conflict and drone warfare affecting in particular Pakistan, Syria, Libya, Somalia and Yemen in addition to Iraq and Afghanistan. Researchers of the 'Costs of War' project at Brown University estimated that over 940,000 people, among them 432,000 civilians, died in the post-9/11 wars due to direct war violence. An additional number of an estimated 3.7 million died of indirect causes and 38 million people were displaced. There is a growing recognition that the 'war on terror' has created a cascade of devastation and conflict which feeds terrorism instead of eliminating it. The US is said to have spent eight trillion US dollars on the 'war on terror' from 2001 to 2022.[5] Adjusted for inflation, total Pentagon expenditures rose by over one third in this period, topping 14.1 trillion US dollars. US companies benefited directly big time. One third to one half of the sum went to defence contractors, the largest share to only five of them, Lockheed Martin, Boeing, General Dynamics, Raytheon, and Northrop Grumman.[6] The additional war costs were almost entirely covered by debt, approved as emergency funding outside regular budget procedures for a decade and with no proper legislative or executive oversight.[7]

---

4   Resolution S/RES/1566 (2004).

5   See Watson Institute for International and Public Affairs, Brown University. "Summary of Findings." The Costs of War Project. Accessed 16 Dec. 2023 (watson.brown.edu).

6   Hartung, William D. 2021. 'Profits of War: Corporate Beneficiaries of the Post-9/11 Pentagon Spending Surge.' Watson Institute of International and Public Affairs, Brown University.

7   Bilmes, Linda. 3 Jan. 2024. 'The "Ghost Budget": How America Pays for Endless Wars.' Just Security (justsecurity.org).

Blowback and 'geopolitical black holes'

Chalmers Johnson described the unintended consequences of US foreign policy, and especially of its military and covert operations around the world, as 'blowback'. In his Pulitzer Prize-winning book 'Ghost Wars', the US American journalist Steve Coll set out how US activities in Afghanistan actually created the conditions for the rise of the Taliban and the emergence of al-Qaeda's terrorist network. In this sense, the attacks of 11 September 2001 can be regarded as the most catastrophic backfiring stratagem yet. Nothing can justify terrorist attacks. It goes without saying that they must be defended against. It was important and in the interests of the world community as a whole that a military offensive was undertaken from October 2001 against the Taliban regime, which had for years allowed al-Qaeda to operate on its territory, in contravention of numerous resolutions of the UN Security Council. Lawless territories of this kind, which attract transnationally organised crime and terrorist groups which then practically merge with local structures of government, are very dangerous for the stability of the interdependent world civilization. Moisés Naím, the Venezuelan former editor of the magazine *Foreign Policy*, called them 'geopolitical black holes' in a book on global crime.[8] Still, the so-called 'war on terror' was conducted in a manner that continues to generate further blowback. After the unexpectedly swift overthrow of the Taliban and only few al-Qaeda followers remaining in the country, the US-led operation in Afghanistan proceeded without clear plans or objectives and took a direction that had little to do with 9/11, as detailed by journalist Craig Whitlock in another Pulitzer Prize-winning book. Eventually a nation-building project was attempted, in a country that had been in an armed conflict since 1973, while fighting the Taliban and other militants in an unwinnable guerilla war.[9] But the US occupation ended up radicalizing and strengthening the Pashtun group. In August 2021, the Taliban recaptured Kabul and took control of the country. It is now in a worse state than before the US invasion, observers believe, and the people, women in particular, are at the mercy of unchecked state terrorism and oppression.

In the case of Iraq, the multinational coalition which invaded the oil-rich country, in violation of international law and on the basis of disinformation from the CIA on the alleged existence of hidden weapons of mass destruction, was neither prepared nor able to ensure public order and safety in the coun-

---

8   Naím, Moisés. 2005. Illicit: how smugglers, traffickers and copycats are hijacking the global economy. 1st ed. New York: Doubleday, pp. 261-3.
9   Whitlock, Craig. 2021. The Afghanistan Papers: A Secret History of the War. New York: Simon & Schuster, pp. 20, 26-27, 264.

try. There were no plans for the aftermath of the invasion. The country was plunged into chaos. The journalist Thomas Ricks summarised the totally irresponsible dilettantism of the operation in his book 'Fiasco'.[10] The foreign troops and their private security contractors, at first greeted by the local population as liberators from the despotic regime of Saddam Hussein, soon turned out to be a ruthless and ignorant occupation force, and this gave a decisive additional impetus to the insurgency that followed. The human rights abuses that took place in the Abu Ghraib prison and came to light in May 2004 became a symbol of the arbitrary and uncontrolled violence of the US troops. Similar to Afghanistan, corruption, waste, the disappearance of funds, and overly expensive, pointless and failed projects were familiar features of a difficult and drawn-out reconstruction effort. While the country and its fragile democracy continue to face major obstacles and challenges, the political scientist Marsin Alshamary argued that in the meantime genuine progress had been made and that Iraqi citizens enjoy greater individual rights than almost any of their neighbors. The fate of Iraq was now in the hands of its citizens and that was 'far more than could have been said twenty years ago', she wrote.[11]

In 2014, the extremist terrorist organization 'Islamic State', which had emerged out of the resistance movement, succeeded in taking control of broad swathes of territory in the north of the country, including Mosul, the second-largest city in Iraq. At its height, the organisation was in control of large areas of Syria, almost half of Iraq and its influence extended to Libya. With or without territorial control, the group continues to operate as a transnational terrorist network. Hundreds of terrorist attacks and incidents in dozens of countries across the world have been linked or attributed to IS and still occur. Emma Sky, who from 2007 to 2010 served as political advisor to the commanding general of the US forces in Iraq, believes that Donald Trump's 'tirades against Muslims and immigrants' and his pledges to protect Americans from the IS, the 'bastard child of the Iraq war', helped 'to propel him to the White House'. She argued that 'the faulty intelligence and incompetence that marked the Iraq intervention fuelled a decline in trust in elites, experts, and the establishment, encouraging the rise of populism, polarization, and disinformation'. Thus, the Iraq war in her view 'paved the way to Brexit and Trump.'[12]

11   Alshamary, Marsin. 2023. 'The Iraq Invasion at Twenty: Iraq's Struggle for Democracy.' Journal of Democracy 34 (2): 150–62.
12   Sky, Emma. 2023. 'The Iraq Invasion at Twenty: The Iraq War and Democratic Backsliding.' Journal of Democracy 34 (2): 135–49, pp. 144-5.

Human rights abuses and drone warfare

The United States has lost much of its credibility as a political force for democracy, freedom and human rights as it has been ignoring human rights and international law continuously. From 2001 to 2006, for instance, the CIA maintained a worldwide network of secret jails in which kidnapped terrorism suspects were imprisoned without trial and tortured. The inmates of the Guantanamo Bay detention camp were officially declared 'illegal combatants', people without any legal rights whatsoever. Other supposed combatants or terrorists have been the victims of targeted 'extrajudicial' killings, beyond any parliamentary or judicial accountability, carried out by the US administration on the basis of highly suspect and non-transparent decision-making processes. For these killings, the US armed forces were making extensive use of attacks by unmanned drones. According to estimates from the Bureau of Investigative Journalism, from 2004 to 2020, when they discontinued taking records, a minimum of 14,040 such attacks had been carried out in Afghanistan, Pakistan, Yemen and Somalia, resulting in up to 20,000 deaths, including up to 2,200 civilians and 450 children.[13]

Drone warfare, that peaked during the Obama administration, is a striking example of the counter-productive effect of the so-called 'war on terror'. 'Drones hover twenty-four hours a day over communities in northwest Pakistan, striking homes, vehicles, and public spaces without warning. Their presence terrorizes men, women, and children, giving rise to anxiety and psychological trauma among civilian communities', read a report entitled 'Living under Drones' compiled at the universities of Stanford and New York.[14] Under such circumstances, it is hardly surprising that drone attacks contribute to an anti-American radicalization that in turn creates the conditions that nurture terrorism. In his book 'Dirty Wars', on the USA's secret worldwide 'assassination complex', the journalist Jeremy Scahill interviewed a Yemeni tribal leader in whose region many civilians have died because of drone attacks. 'The drones are flying day and night, frightening women and children, disturbing sleeping people. This is terrorism', Scahill quoted him directly. He believes there should be compensation for the civilian victims. 'The world is one village. The US received compensation from Libya for the Lockerbie bombing, but the Yemenis have not', he complained.[15] As a result of drone warfare, sup-

---

13 Wells, Miriam. 4 Sept. 2020. 'Ten Years Investigating US Covert Warfare.' The Bureau of Investigative Journalism (thebureauinvestigates.com).

14 International Human Rights and Conflict Resolution Clinic at Stanford Law School, and Global Justice Clinic at NYU School of Law. September 2012. 'Living Under Drones. Death, Injury, and Trauma to Civilians From US Drone Practices in Pakistan'.

15 Scahill, Jeremy. 2013. Dirty Wars: The World Is a Battlefield. London: Serpent's Tail, p. 466.

port for groups like al-Qaeda or IS, and the willingness to embrace violent terrorism, are strengthened far beyond the populations directly affected.

Terrorism and the international system

Terrorist organizations, whether driven by political, ideological, or religious motivations, thrive on real or perceived injustices and grievances. They exploit the emotions these grievances evoke to build support and justify their barbaric actions as the sole viable means to attain retribution. Military interventions and covert operations to counter terrorism are only fighting symptoms and immediate threats. To help prevent extremist violence and terrorism from developing, it is necessary to address underlying political, social, cultural and economic conflicts. The international system plays an important role, as it provides a framework that can be conducive or obstructive to solving these problems. Terrorist movements 'typically do rely greatly on a sense of injustice, iniquity, and humiliation that the established world order is seen as having produced', noted Amartya Sen, adding that even though 'poverty and a sense of global injustice may not lead immediately to an eruption of violence, there are certainly connections there, operating over a long period of time, that can have a significant effect on the possibility of violence.' Thus, he thought that 'a more equitable sharing of the benefits of globalization' is a contribution to 'long-run preventive measures.'[16] In his influential 1996 book of that title, the US American political scientist Benjamin Barber spoke of a clash of 'Jihad and McWorld'. The 'commercial imperialism' of a globalization based on a laissez-faire ideology, encapsulated by Barber in the term 'McWorld', in his view fed the forces of Jihad as a 'dialectical response to modernity'. He saw the democratic institutions of the nation state as being undermined equally by both forces. In his analysis, Barber took Jihad to include not just Islamic extremism, as the term suggests, but any form of religious or political fanaticism that makes a dogmatic claim to exclusivity which it is prepared to back with violent means.[17] Richard Falk and Andrew Strauss similarly saw it as an important aspect of transnational terrorism that it also represents a reaction against globalization. Globalization, they argued, increases inequalities within and between societies, and leads to many people feeling that their cultural traditions are under threat. At the same time—and this is the crux of their argument—these people have no opportunity to make their feelings about these impacts and injustices count within the existing international system. 'Present-

<hr>

16   Sen, Amartya. 2007. Identity and Violence: The Illusion of Destiny. London: Penguin Books, p. 145.
17   Barber, Benjamin. 2003. Jihad vs. McWorld. Terrorism's Challenge to Democracy. London: Corgi Books, pp. 219, 157, 31-2.

ly, with trivial exceptions', the two international law specialists wrote in a joint article, 'individuals, groups and their associations are denied an official role in global political institutions where decision-making is dominated by elites who have been officially designated by states.' With 'the possibility of direct and formalized participation in the international system foreclosed, frustrated individuals and groups (especially when their own governments are viewed as illegitimate or hostile) have been turning to various modes of civic resistance, both peaceful and violent.' In their view, global terrorism is at the violent end of a spectrum of transnational protest. Even when it is driven principally by religious, ideological or regional aims, the political extremism at its core is at least in part 'an indirect result of globalizing impacts'.[18] Tad Daley, too, emphasized with regard to the threat of nuclear terrorist attacks that in the medium term 'we need to reduce not just the availability of nuclear weapons and materials, but also the motivations for nuclear terror'. Additionally, he said, we must seriously address as causes the globalization of economic inequality and cultural humiliation. People have to be given the hope and opportunity of genuine participation in a peaceful and prosperous global civilization.[19] From this perspective, exclusion from the relevant international decision-making processes also has to be seen as a form of humiliation. Amartya Sen argued that there is a 'strong case for institutional reforms' in order 'to make globalization a fairer arrangement'. In 2007 he thought that 'in the foreseeable future' a 'democratic global state' was impossible. But if democracy was seen 'in terms of public reasoning, particularly the need for worldwide discussion on global problems', he wrote, 'we need not put the possibility of global democracy in indefinite cold storage'.[20] Israeli world federalists Shimri Zameret and Oded Gilad believe that global democracy will be instrumental in achieving a lasting and peaceful solution of the Israel-Palestine conflict.[21]

In a global parliament, it would be easier for political frustrations to find expression and to be channelled into a democratic and peaceful process capable of exerting a guiding influence on globalization and mitigating conflict. For example, when in May 2013 the highest court of the northern Pakistani

18 Falk, Richard, and Andrew Strauss. 2003. 'The Deeper Challenges of Global Terrorism: A Democratizing Reponse'. In: Debating Cosmopolitics, ed. by Daniele Archibugi, 203–231. London, New York: Verso. Reprinted in and citation from id.: 2011. A Global Parliament: Essays and Articles. Berlin: Committee for a Democratic UN, p. 137.

19 Daley, Tad. 2010. Apocalypse never. Forging the path to a nuclear weapon-free world. New Brunswick, N.J.: Rutgers University Press, pp. 62-4.

20 Sen, pp. 182-4.

21 Zameret, Shimri. 11 Nov. 2023. 'International Democracy as a Solution to the Israeli-Palestinian Conflict' and Gilad, Oded. 14 May 2021. 'World Federation and the Israel-Palestine Conflict', both: Democracy Without Borders (blog) (democracywithoutborders.org).

province of Khyber Pakhtunkhwa classified the US American drone attacks in the region as a violation of Pakistani sovereignty in breach of international law, it called on the Pakistani government to submit a complaint to the UN Security Council seeking political strictures and other possible measures, and to the UN General Assembly in the event of a US veto in the Council. Although the Pakistani government had in fact already made it clear two months previously to Ben Emmerson, the then UN Special Rapporteur on Counter Terrorism and Human Rights, that it did not consent to the drone attacks and saw them as a breach of national sovereignty, cooperation with the USA behind the scenes is probably more complicated than that, and moreover the government has to take into consideration, when taking such steps at the UN, the possible wider ramifications for its international network of relationships. In a world parliament, by contrast, the problem could be raised directly by Pakistani representatives without the need to go through the government or for any special diplomatic considerations to be taken into account, since the members speak as independent parliamentarians for themselves and their constituents, and not in the name or on behalf of the government, which can therefore not be held responsible for what they say.

Falk and Strauss believe that a global parliament, and efforts towards a fairer and more democratic world order, ought to form part of the political response to the challenges of 'megaterrorism' of the kind seen on 11 September 2001. They rightly do not fall victim to the illusion that extremists like 'the Osama bin Ladens of this planet' will engage in a global parliamentary process, but they do believe the ability of such people to attract a substantial following would be considerably weakened by the existence of a global parliament, 'to the extent that such an institution' gave 'the most disadvantaged and aggrieved peoples in the world a sense that their concerns were being meaningfully addressed'.[22] Benjamin Barber also made the point that the forces of Jihad are profoundly undemocratic and can hardly be tamed. He, too, believed that the best prospect for countering the forces of Jihad and 'McWorld' lay in a strengthening of civil society and of democracy at all levels. Barber stressed the importance in this context of a sense of democratic citizenship developed within the framework of a democratic world society. 'If civil society is one key to democracy, then global strong democracy needs and depends on a methodical internationalization of civil society.' A global democratic society was a foundation for 'a global democratic government'. Even though, Barber argued, such a thing might seem no more than 'clever pipe dreams', or 'a distant dream', nonetheless, because international institutions continually came up

---

22 Ibid., p. 140.

against the limits to national sovereignty, he thought the case had to be made for 'a gradualist, voluntary, trust-building strategy of supranationality'.[23] What Barber did not address in his book is the question of how the development of a global civil society and of a democratic global public sphere as prerequisites for such a process of integration could be cultivated at the institutional level, that is, 'systematised'. It is precisely here where we see a crucial role for a world parliament. A world parliament, as the direct representative institution for the world's citizens, would be better able than any previous institution to create a democratic world public sphere and to reflect global public opinion. Ultimately, as an element of a world legislature, a world parliament should be able to go beyond the role of a political forum so as to take decisions with real practical impact and to be involved in the creation of world law and a just global order that guarantees human rights and wellbeing for all.

Global surveillance and data protection

However, instead of being strengthened and protected, civil liberties, basic rights and the rule of law are being undermined under the pretext of fighting terrorism. This applies not only to the direct victims of kidnapping or drone attacks by the United States, but to almost everyone. For example, the partners in the international intelligence agreement UKUSA from the immediate post-war period, the USA, Great Britain, Canada, Australia and New Zealand, employ various covert surveillance programmes that infringe upon the confidential communication, personal data and privacy rights of potentially everyone globally using telecommunications, without any significant constraints. The revelations in 2013 about surveillance programmes like the NSA's Prism, X-Keyscore and Fairview, and the Tempora programme run by the British intelligence service GCHQ, suggest that the accessing of global internet and telecommunications data, carried out through corporate networks and by tapping communications cables, is far more continuous and comprehensive than had previously been thought. Combatting terrorism is the most important reason put forward to justify these measures. Unlike traditional intelligence gathering, which specifically targeted other states and their agencies, all the millions of users of communications systems without exception or distinction are now automatically being eavesdropped. Progress in computer technology has made it possible to handle 'Big Data'. The premise behind this is that it is no longer only states or genuinely suspect individuals who pose a threat, but potentially *everyone*. In the opinion of Alfred McCoy, who teaches history at the Univer-

---

23   Barber, pp. 287-8, 229, 277, 290.

sity of Wisconsin-Madison and studied the history of espionage in the USA, the NSA's global surveillance apparatus exists above all to serve the aims of 'the exercise of global power' and 'global hegemony'. This explains why the NSA has monitored EU institutions, the heads of state or government of at least 35 countries, and delegates at the UN, the G20 summit meetings and international treaty negotiations. According to McCoy, this surveillance not only garners intelligence advantageous to Washington, but occasionally also intimate personal information that can be used to provide leverage.[24] He sees the NSA apparatus as part of 'a powerful, global Panopticon that can surveil domestic dissidents, track terrorists, manipulate allied nations, monitor rival powers, counter hostile cyber strikes, launch pre-emptive cyberattacks, and protect domestic communications'.[25]

Many people outside the immediate conflict zones only realized that they themselves were directly affected by the 'war on terror' through the invasion of their privacy following the revelations about the NSA's Prism programme. It had now become clear, commented journalist Jakob Augstein, that the drone attacks in Pakistan or the camp in Guantanamo were not simply 'unfortunate incidents at the end of the world', as many people liked to think. 'Those who still believed that the torture in Abu Ghraib or the waterboarding in CIA jails had nothing to do with them are now changing their opinions', he wrote.[26] The journalist Thomas Darnstädt spoke of an 'epochal change to international law'. The fact that the people of the world were themselves becoming the objects of US American surveillance threatened to extend the 'erosion of international law which had accompanied the USA's war against people suspected of being terrorists' into the field of espionage.[27] The citizens of other states were being deprived of their legal rights by the governments responsible. Moreover, exactly how which data are being gathered and stored, for what purposes, remains hidden in the fog of secrecy. The fact that the rights to data protection, personal privacy and the confidentiality of personal communications of millions of citizens all around the world are being systematically breached by foreign governments over whom they have no political influence at all highlights the contradiction between the reality of the global communications network and the constriction of democracy and the rule of law within

---

24 McCoy, Alfred W. 19 January 2014. 'Surveillance and Scandal: Time-Tested Weapons for U.S. Global Power'. TomDispatch (www.tomdispatch.com).

25 Id. 14 July 2013. 'Surveillance Blowback: The Making of the U.S. Surveillance State, 1898-2020', TomDispatch (www.tomdispatch.com).

26 Augstein, Jakob. 17 June 2013. 'Obama's Soft Totalitarianism: Europe Must Protect Itself from America'. Spiegel Online (www.spiegel.de).

27 Darnstädt, Thomas. 10 July 2013. 'Amerikas digitaler Großangriff auf das Völkerrecht'. Spiegel Online (www.spiegel.de).

nation state boundaries. On 24 July 2008, in a speech in Berlin during the US Presidential election campaign, Barack Obama addressed 'the peoples of the world' as 'a fellow citizen of the world' and spoke of our common obligations as 'as citizens of Earth'. But this appeal to the 'citizens of the Earth' turns out to be an empty rhetorical device, since as things stand the citizens of the world have neither voice nor rights in that capacity. They can hold neither the US President nor any other foreign government to account for the abuse of their rights and in many cases not even their own. The issue goes far beyond the global mass surveillance programmes of the US and the UKUSA arrangement under the pretext of counter-terrorism. A UN report noted that at least 65 governments have acquired commercial spyware surveillance tools whose capabilities were 'formidable'. Best known is the spyware Pegasus which grants unrestricted access to infected devices. A list of 50,000 phone numbers leaked in 2021 indicated that hundreds of journalists, human rights defenders, politicians and government officials worldwide were affected as targets.[28] The US surveillance programmes are a serious obstacle to data sharing with the EU and there are ongoing negotiations to solve this issue. Ultimately, an enforceable global regulation on data protection and privacy is needed which also restricts questionable practices of data collection by private companies. The firm Cambridge Analytica, for instance, managed to harvest personal data from millions of Facebook users without their consent and misused it to support Donald Trump's election campaign.

---

28 United Nations. 2022. 'The Right to Privacy in the Digital Age.' Report of the Office of the United Nations High Commissioner for Human Rights." UN doc. A/HRC/51/17, paras. 5-7.

19.
Global law enforcement, criminal prosecution, and the post-American era

Global criminal law and a supranational police authority

Transnational terrorism blurs the boundaries between domestic and external security. Within national borders and outside active conflict zones terrorist activities are subject not to military but to police measures, aimed at preventing threats to public safety and pursuing criminal justice. These measures are governed by relevant laws and legal regulations, such as the principle of proportionality, at least in countries where the rule of law prevails. However, addressing terrorist threats originating from abroad poses a more difficult challenge. The comprehensive surveillance of all telecommunications, for example, undoubtedly infringes the principle of proportionality, but this is not applied by governments when dealing with foreign citizens. The targeted 'extrajudicial' killing of alleged 'enemy combatants' by the United States is the most blatant example of a fight against terrorism that has been stripped of all pretence of adherence to the rule of law. 'In the conflicts with terrorism around the world, the unconditional use of violence by the military and the legally constrained enforcement of the law by the police are blurring', wrote journalist Thomas Darnstädt in his book 'The Global Police State'. The instruments available to the United Nations and international law have proved inadequate to the challenge. 'The threats of violence from non-state sources materialising around the world cry out for a world domestic policy that would transcend all state borders', he argued. The 'no man's land' between legal systems that maintain law and order in the domestic realm and the law of war that characterizes the international level must be covered by a 'world police law' which would put 'the whole of the Earth under the jurisdiction of an internal world security order'. This would make it possible to address the source of any and every threat, regardless of state borders, within the framework of a fair and proper legal system.[1]

The idea underlying this is that it must become possible to treat terrorism, one of the most serious forms of crime, principally through police powers and the operation of a criminal justice system, even when it manifests itself in transborder activities or entirely within a foreign state. As the problem is transnational in nature, the solution will also have to be transnational. The

---

1   Darnstädt, Thomas. 2009. Der globale Polizeistaat. 1st ed. München: Goldmann, pp. 294, 46, 326.

implementation and enforcement of global criminal law dealing with very serious criminal threats from non-state sources is precisely one of those tasks which should come under the province of a supranational police force. A supranational police authority should step in where states are too weak or too corrupt to guarantee security. 'Only a power higher than the state', Darnstädt noted, 'can intervene to restore order in the complex affairs of weak, ineffective or dangerously powerful states, in the disputed no man's lands of the squabbling world family of peoples, without being accused of waging war or at least of pursuing political ends.'[2] As we have seen already, a UN intervention force and a supranational police force are among the necessary elements of a properly functioning, de-militarised world peace order and this is a field where they are needed.

The failure of classical sanctions

Law enforcement follows different guiding principles under a world law framework than it does under traditional international law. What counts is not the implementation of sanctions or the use of military force against states that violate the law, but the targeted enforcement of world law *against individuals by the police or through legal action*. More extreme collective security measures are a secondary option, only to be considered if the first approach fails. The wide-ranging economic embargo decided on by the UN Security Council in 1990 in response to the Iraqi invasion of Kuwait destroyed the country's basic infrastructure, brought a humanitarian catastrophe on the general population, led to a drastic rise in infant mortality, and barely impacted on Saddam Hussein's regime. Since then there has been a paradigm shift in favour of so-called 'smart sanctions', which apply only to selected goods and which target specific people and organizations. To combat terrorism, the UN Security Council holds the so-called 1267 list (named after the number of the original 1999 Resolution), on which, as the journalist Victor Kocher put it, it identifies on behalf of the community of states 'the enemies of humanity'. All states are obliged to freeze all property and assets belonging to the roughly 900 (at the present time) people and organizations listed there and to refuse them entry or transit. And we can agree with Kocher that this 'is all right and proper, as long as they really are terrorists'. The problem is that the procedure is untransparent, arbitrary and outside any legal control. If anyone were to end up on the list by mistake, they would have no possibility of defending themselves against the UN through the courts. An Ombudsperson has been ap-

2   Ibid., p. 328.

pointed to whom such people can appeal. But the Security Council still takes the ultimate decisions on recommendations from the Office of the Ombudsperson. 'The Security Council is a political authority which makes political decisions. There is no legal recourse against this. That's the way the UN system was constructed', was the laconic comment from Richard Barrett, a high-ranking official of the UN Sanctions Committee.[3] It was for precisely this reason that the European Court of Justice determined in a judgement of 18 July 2013 that UN procedures do not provide 'the guarantee of effective legal protection', and therefore confirmed the suspension of the EU Directive for the implementation of the UN sanctions on the grounds of an infringement of fundamental rights under European law. The Court ruled that 'a judicial review is indispensable to ensure a fair balance between the maintenance of international peace and security and the protection of the fundamental rights and freedoms of the person concerned'.[4] It can be seen here how the procedural mechanism of classical sanctions has failed to adapt to the new challenges, and thereby also failed to apply in practice those values it is supposed to protect. By contrast, the rule of law, the separation of powers, and independent accountability, in particular adequate judicial review procedures, must be fundamental principles of the enforcement of world law.

The International Criminal Court

The International Criminal Court, or ICC, which took up its work in 2002, is a milestone in the development of such a world law. The court's jurisdiction is unfortunately not universal, as many governments and NGOs had called for. It is complementary to national criminal justice systems and applies only if a crime has been committed by a person or in a place belonging to a state which is a party to the ICC treaty. When Armenia joined as the latest state party so far the number increased to 124 in November 2023. Some important countries such as the USA, Russia, India and China are not among them. They do not want to accept international accountability for the crimes under the ICC statute. The UN Security Council can refer a 'situation' to the court and establish jurisdiction, as has happened in the case of Sudan in 2005 and Libya in 2011. Subject to these conditions, the ICC is responsible for holding individuals to account for charges of war crimes, crimes against humanity, and genocide, irrespective of their official positions and without regard to any immunities granted under international law. After long and bitter negotiations, the ICC's

---

3   Kocher, Victor. Terrorlisten. Die schwarzen Löcher des Völkerrechts. Wien: Promedia, 2011, pp. 13, 139.
4   European Court of Justice. 18 July 2018. 'Judgement of the Court, Kadi v. Council, Joined Cases C 584/10 P, C 593/10 P and C 595/10 P', paras. 133, 131.

jurisdiction over the crime of aggression was activated as of 17 July 2018. Under the agreed rules, a citizen of a non-state party cannot be prosecuted for the war of aggression. In addition, for the jurisdiction over this crime to apply, states individually need to accept it separately in addition to ratifying the ICC's statute. By July 2024, only 45 have done so. Following Russia's full-scale attack on Ukraine, international law experts argued that the ICC's statute could be amended to allow the UN General Assembly, acting under the 'Uniting for Peace' principle, to make referrals to the court as well, a proposal that was already under discussion and supported by numerous states in the early 1990s.[5] This would be an important step to stop impunity for the crimes under the ICC's jurisdiction in view of the P5's veto power in the Security Council's decision-making. Some governments in Africa at hindsight regretted the fact that state leaders can be indicted by the ICC as charges were pressed against Kenya's President Uhuru Kenyatta, among others, for post-election violence in 2007-2008 as Kenya is a state party since 2005. Due to insufficient evidence, the charges were withdrawn, but in response a mass withdrawal from the ICC of the 33 African state parties was discussed at an African Union meeting. This did not materialize though. At this time, Burundi and the Philippines are the only two countries that withdrew from the court. Attempts in this regard in The Gambia and South Africa failed.

Extending the prosecuting powers of the ICC

The jurisdiction of the ICC should not only become universal but also be extended to cover additional crimes with global significance. In fact, a resolution was already passed at the conference of state parties in Rome in 1998 when the ICC Statute was adopted, confirming that the jurisdiction of the court should in the future encompass terrorism and drug offences as well.[6] Lawyers point out that the funding of international terrorism is '[o]ne of today's most pressing issues in international financial crimes'. Many states do not have the resources or are unwilling to take action against money laundering.[7] In Moisés Naím's view, fully-fledged 'Mafia states' have arisen which 'integrate the speed and flexibility of transnational criminal networks with the legal protections and diplomatic privileges enjoyed only by states'. National law enforcement agencies are largely powerless against this new 'hybrid form of international actor',

---

5   Darcy, Shane. 16 March 2022. 'Aggression by P5 Security Council Members: Time for ICC Referrals by the General Assembly.' Just Security (justsecurity.org).

6   Final Act of the International Criminal Court. A/CONF.183/10, 17 July 1998. See resolution E.

7   Anderson, Michael. 2013. 'International Money Laundering: The Need for ICC Investigative and Adjudicative Jurisdiction'. Virginia Journal of International Law (53) 3: 763–786, pp. 764, 771.

and in fact some of them have themselves been infiltrated by criminals.[8] An international form of law enforcement against corruption and money laundering is therefore required. It would be possible to extend the jurisdiction of the ICC to include money-laundering offences on the basis of a convention on money laundering.[9]

In the light of the financial crisis and bearing in mind the status of the financial system as a global public good, it would also be highly advisable to extend the jurisdiction of the court to *economic and financial crimes which affect the financial system as a whole*. The French economist Jacques Attali, regularly numbered among the one hundred leading intellectuals in the world by the magazine *Foreign Policy*, has spoken out in favour of regarding 'very serious violations of social and economic rights with global reach' and associated financial offences as 'crimes against humanity' and of including them within the jurisdiction of the ICC.[10] In view of the dominant role played in such offences by companies and especially by financial institutions, Attali believes it should be possible to prosecute not just individuals but also legal persons in such cases. The US American federal law known as RICO, used to combat criminal associations and their leaders, provides an interesting model for consideration in this context.

Other offences for which international criminal prosecution needs to be considered include ecocide, which has been under discussion in this context since 1970. Ecocide, according to a definition proposed by the British activist Polly Higgins (1968 to 2019), involves 'the extensive destruction, damage to or loss of ecosystem(s) of a given territory' to such an extent 'that peaceful enjoyment by the inhabitants of that territory has been severely diminished'.[11] Additionally, as has already been mentioned, it has been proposed that infringements against bans promulgated by a possible future convention for the abolition of nuclear weapons could be placed under the court's jurisdiction. Global inspection regimes and regulation related to biosafety, genetic engineering or AI could also establish an individual criminal responsibility under the ICC for certain offences.

Of course, it is possible to create separate international tribunals for specific offences not yet covered by the ICC. In particular, support for the creation of an International Anti-Corruption Court, or IACC, first put forward in 2014, has been growing. The court would prosecute the perpetrators of 'grand

---

8　Naím, Moisés. 2012. 'Mafia States'. Foreign Affairs (91) 3: 100–111, p. 109.

9　Anderson, ibid.

10　Attali, Jacques. 16 March 2010. 'For an International Financial Court'. L'Express (www.lexpress.fr).

11　Higgins, Polly. Eradicating ecocide: laws and governance to prevent the destruction of our planet. London: Shepheard-Walwyn, 2010, pp. 62-3.

corruption', defined as 'the abuse of public office for private gain by a nation's leaders'. It has been proposed to link this new judicial body to the UN Convention Against Corruption and giving it authority, as a complementary 'court of last resort', to prosecute bribery, embezzlement of public funds, misappropriation of public property, money laundering, and obstruction of justice.[12] In principle, it appears to be more effective and would help maintain consistency in the development and application of global criminal law to extend and strengthen the ICC and make it the central judicial body in this field. However, changes to the ICC Statute require the consent of seven-eighths of the treaty parties which is a high hurdle to clear. Proponents of the IACC argue that it is too high, pointing out that some of the ICC's member states 'are ruled by kleptocrats who would oppose such an amendment'. Further, they fear that the ICC's prosecutors would have to prioritise other cases over such on 'grand corruption' due to the court's limited resources.[13] It is true that any expansion of the ICC's jurisdiction would have to be accompanied by a corresponding expansion of the means and capacities available to the court. Given the urgency of effective international action against corruption and illicit financial flows, which undermine democracy and the achievement of the Sustainable Development Goals, a pragmatic approach is advisable. If an IACC can be created in a quicker way and endowed with the necessary resources, conceptual considerations related to the ICC should not stand in the way. In the long run, a global constitutional process should nonetheless review and streamline the judicial global architecture, among other things.

A supranational police force to support the ICC

To combat the most serious kinds of transnational crime, a global law enforcement agency is needed, equipped with its own investigative and executive powers, able to support national authorities or to act independently when necessary and appropriate, in particular when national authorities are unwilling or unable to pursue a case. One important task of such a supranational police force is to support the work of the ICC and potentially other international courts. This should include a unit responsible for tracking down, arresting and handing over suspects on behalf of the prosecuting authorities. The formation of such a unit was proposed already in connection with the International Criminal Tribunal for the former Yugoslavia. When, seven years after the establishment of

---

12 Wolf, Mark L., and Robert Rotberg. 2022. 'The International Anti-Corruption Court'. Prepared for the 'Checking Kleptocracy: Creating a New Instrument of World Order' Meeting of the American Academy of Arts and Sciences." Integrity Initiatives International, pp. 14, 10-1.
13 Ibid., pp. 20-1.

the tribunal by the UN Security Council, dozens of those accused of crimes had still not been apprehended, among them Radovan Karadžić and Ratko Mladić, the principal suspects, the Chief Prosecutor Carla del Ponte was at the end of her patience. It was her belief that in spite of numerous opportunities the SFOR military unit for Bosnia-Herzegovina under NATO command and the local authorities had shown themselves to be unwilling or unable ever to carry out many of the arrest warrants.[14] Finally, in 2000, she called for the establishment of a special police unit under the control of the tribunal. 'Such a police force would not be dependent on the support of other states and would not have to worry about political judgements. Today, we issue an arrest warrant and have to wait for SFOR to carry it out', she complained.[15] As things stand, the ICC is also totally dependent on the cooperation of its treaty states. Its statute does not permit it to carry out arrests and the court has no capacity to do so anyway. Nine years after the Security Council referred the situation in Darfur in western Sudan to the ICC, the Chief Prosecutor Fatou Bensouda from Gambia, elected in 2012, complained in strong language that 'no meaningful steps' had been taken by the Security Council to enforce the arrest warrants issued by the court against those accused of crimes in Darfur, including the President of Sudan, Omar Hassan al-Bashir. 'This reflects badly, not just on the international justice system of which the ICC is only a part, but it also greatly undermines the credibility of this Council as an instrument of international peace and security', declared Bensouda. The ICC's judicial process 'cannot take place without arrests', the Chief Prosecutor emphasized.[16] Because of the lack of activity from the Security Council on this issue, she decided in December 2014 to suspend the investigation into the al-Bashir case 'for the time being'. During the Sudanese revolution of 2019, al-Bashir was toppled, and the new transitional government made the decision to 'hand over wanted officials to the ICC,' albeit without providing a specific time frame.[17] As a result, the former President may well face justice in The Hague, a development that few had deemed possible.

14   Karadžić was finally arrested in 2008 and Mladić in 2011.

15   Citation from Bummel, Andreas. 2003. 'Für eine ständige Eingreiftruppe der Vereinten Nationen. Ein Memorandum der Gesellschaft für bedrohte Völker' (in an interview published by Allgemeine Schweizerische Militärzeitschrift, no. 11/2001).

16   'Justice for Darfur's victims mired in political expediency – ICC prosecutor'. 17 June 1014. United Nations News Centre (www.un.org).

17   'Sudan Says Will 'Hand over' al-Bashir to ICC for War Crimes Trial.' 12 Aug. 2021. Al Jazeera (al-jazeera.com).

Sovereignty and law enforcement

Conceptually, the allocation of distinct responsibilities to a global law enforcement agency is entirely feasible along federalist lines. When the FBI, the US American federal law enforcement and investigative agency, was founded in 1908, the aim was to create a police authority with the same geographical horizon as the criminals it was supposed to combat, namely that of the entire US American federal territory. In the opinion of an expert from the Defence Academy of the British armed forces who supports a form of 'global FBI', this 'is a direct parallel to the situation facing the world today'. 'Today's international law-enforcement system', he argued, 'is disjointed, fractious, ineffective and, increasingly, is unfit to tackle the serious emerging threats of transnational organised crime and terrorism.'[18] The first international report on the threat posed by transnational criminal organizations, published by the United Nations Office on Drugs and Crime (UNODC), warned that organized crime—the dark side of globalization—'has diversified, gone global and reached macro-economic proportions'.[19] At the presentation of the report, the then Director of the Office, Antonio Maria Costa, stated that transnational crime had become 'a threat to peace and development, even to the sovereignty of nations'. 'Crime has internationalized faster than law enforcement and world governance', he said.[20] The FBI and over 70 additional federal law enforcement agencies that now exist in the United States complement and assist law enforcement at the state, county and municipal levels. A global agency would add another layer that is still missing today.

One obstacle is that policing and criminal jurisdiction have traditionally been regarded as prominent features of state sovereignty. Domestic security, according to Wilhelm Knelangen, a political scientist based in Kiel, is a 'field of politics laden with sovereignty', in which governments 'jealously defend their formal powers'.[21] But as the UNODC report rightly argued, 'states have to look beyond borders to protect their sovereignty'. 'In the past', the report stated, 'they have jealously guarded their territory. In the contemporary globalized world, this approach makes states more, rather than less vulnerable. If police stop at borders while criminals cross them freely, sovereignty is already

18 Coffey, Stuart. July 2011. 'The Case for the Creation of a "Global FBI"'. Central European Journal of International and Security Studies (5) 2: 23–56, pp. 32, 24.

19 United Nations Office on Drugs and Crime. 2010. The Globalization of Crime: A Transnational Organized Crime Threat Assessment. Vienna: United Nations Office on Drugs and Crime. p. ii.

20 Id. 17 June 2010. 'International criminal markets have become major centres of power, UNODC report shows' (www.unodc.org).

21 Knelangen, Wilhelm. 2008. 'Europäisierung and Globalisierung der Polizei'. Aus Politik and Zeitgeschichte, no. 48 (Beilage) (www.das-parlament.de).

breached—actually, it is surrendered to those who break the law.'[22] Seen in this light, a supranational law enforcement agency would represent a *strengthening* of state sovereignty, even if under shared control. 'We need to consider the possibility that clinging to old ideas about sovereignty may be stunting the evolution of the nation-state and thus weakening the security of its citizens', wrote Moisés Naím.[23]

International criminal prosecution and a world parliament

Experts point out that international cooperation between police and judicial authorities is already increasing continuously. In their book 'Policing the Globe', the US American political scientist Peter Andreas and the Director of the New York-based Drug Policy Alliance, Ethan Nadelmann, noted that 'transgovernmental enforcement networks are more expansive and intensive than ever before, encouraging and facilitating a thickening of cross-border policing relationships'. In their view it is time to abandon the 'popular mythology' of a 'golden age of state control' in the past. On the contrary, the fight against crime is becoming ever more effective, including at the international level. Many of the changes driving the globalization of crime, such as the revolutions in transport and in communications, provide just as much of a boost to globalised crime fighting.[24] Examples of this include the increasingly effective options available for tracking down suspects, for surveillance and for information exchange. The crucial next steps are a world police law with a supranational police force, and a strengthened International Criminal Court with an extended jurisdiction. They are an appropriate and logical response to the global security threats emanating from the 'geopolitical black holes' and to the globalization of organised crime.

However, making international criminal prosecution and global security more effective represents only one side of the coin. These developments need to go hand in hand with an appropriate extension and strengthening of democratic legitimation, oversight and political accountability. Complaints about substantial democratic deficits can be heard already. Although there can be no question, wrote Wilhelm Knelangen, of 'a global Leviathan replacing national security and criminal prosecution systems', it cannot be denied that 'the legal and institutional foundations for the activities of the criminal prosecution authorities are increasingly being located outside the nation state'. The trans-

22 United Nations Office on Drugs and Crime (2010), p. iii.

23 Naím, Moisés. Illicit: How Smugglers, Traffickers and Copycats Are Hijacking the Global Economy. 1st ed. New York: Doubleday, 2005.

24 Andreas, Peter, and Ethan Nadelmann. 2006. Policing the Globe. Criminalization and Crime Control in International Relations. Oxford, New York et. al: Oxford University Press, pp. 232, 246, 248.

fer of decision-making to the regional 'or even the global level' is restricting the scope for democratic accountability. 'The fact that security concerns dominate the political debates about international police cooperation, overshadowing the defence of liberty', according to Knelangen, 'is due not least to the fact that intergovernmental networks are further advanced as yet than their parliamentary or civil society equivalents.'[25] Andreas and Nadelmann spoke of a 'substantial downside' to international crime fighting. This includes 'growing problems of accountability and transparency', 'a widening "democratic deficit" as police functions become more internationalized and privatized', and 'the emergence of an international crime control industrial complex.'[26]

A worldwide parliamentary assembly, by providing a global platform for different political perspectives and critical points of view, would create a counterweight to the governments' one-sided fixation on security issues and their undermining of civil liberties and human rights. The Parliamentary Assembly of the Council of Europe provides an example which demonstrates that initially this is even possible in the absence of specific competences. By means of a Europe-wide investigation, prompted by media reports and beginning in November 2005, into the CIA's secret prisons in the member states of the Council of Europe, the assembly succeeded in building up considerable political pressure on the governments involved. The investigation contributed to the eventual official acknowledgement by President George W. Bush of the existence of the secret CIA prisons abroad on 6 September 2006. A world parliament would have the important task of critically monitoring the activities of and cooperation between police and security authorities, and to this end should establish a committee charged especially with the duty of ensuring that human rights are respected in this regard. A world parliament should be given formal rights of supervision over today's most important existing institution for international police cooperation, Interpol, which was established in 1923, and in the future over any new supranational law enforcement agency. These should include involvement in the selection and appointment of the head of the organization (of the Secretary-General of Interpol, for example) and the right to call leading executive officers to be questioned before parliament.

Interpol and accountability

Interpol, which is based in Lyon and has two further administrative centres in Buenos Aires and Singapore, is not a supranational police force by any stretch of the imagination. It has no investigative or executive powers. It provides

---

25 Knelangen, ibid.
26 Andreas and Nadelmann, pp. 250-1, on securitization see also p. 253.

training, coordination, data collection and information exchange services to the national criminal prosecution authorities, and in addition some operational support services. This is not the place to examine whether it would make more sense to develop Interpol into a supranational criminal police force or whether it might be better to create a new agency for that purpose. But the fact that it is not accountable for its actions, neither legally nor politically, to any independent external authority is certainly a problem that needs to be resolved. Interpol's 'Red Notices', for example, are a core instrument of international criminal prosecution. They are issued at the request of national police authorities or international criminal courts and call on all Interpol members for international help in the arrest and extradition of suspects. Although it remains at the discretion of the national authorities how they react to such requests, suspects then generally have to reckon with arrest and extradition proceedings. This is a legitimate and sensible procedure in the international fight against crime. The problem is that it is misused for the persecution of dissidents, political opponents, business competitors, environmental activists and journalists. Human rights activists have documented countless such cases. The Parliamentary Assembly of the OSCE has repeatedly expressed concern over the misuse of Interpol's Red Notices by 'Mafia' and autocratic states 'whose judicial systems do not meet international standards'.[27] The British *Daily Telegraph* accused Interpol of providing support to the world's most brutal regimes.[28] In a report published in 2013, the London-based NGO Fair Trials International called for a strengthening of Interpol's internal capacity and procedures with regard to checking requests for Red Notices.[29] Four years later they noted that 'there is still a long way to go in ensuring that Interpol has robust procedural safeguards for the human rights of citizens'.[30] Another five years later, the European Parliament stated that 'despite recent reforms, transparency and accountability remain a challenge.'[31] The abuse of Interpol by authoritarian states according to Freedom House is the 'most well-understood form of transnational repression within the international system' and the practice has 'outpaced attempts at oversight'.[32] The proposals by Fair Trials deserve

---

27 See e.g. OSCE Parliamentary Assembly. 2012. Monaco Declaration and Resolutions adopted by the OSCE Parliamentary Assembly at the 21st Annual Session, Monaco, 5-9 July 2012. Para 93 (www.oscepa.org).

28 Oborne, Peter. 22 May 2013. 'Is Interpol fighting for truth and justice, or helping the villains?' The Telegraph (www.telegraph.co.uk).

29 Fair Trials International. November 2013. 'Strengthening respect for human rights, strengthening INTERPOL'.

30 Id. 24 November 2017. 'INTERPOL Four Years On: What's Changed?' (www.fairtrials.org).

31 European Parliament. 5 July 2022. 'Negotiations for a Cooperation Agreement between the EU and Interpol.' Resolution P9_TA(2022)0275, para. 29.

32 Gorokhovskaia, Yana, and Isabel Linzer. 2022. 'Defending Democracy in Exile. Policy Responses to Transnational Repression.' Freedom House, p. 23.

to be fully supported but some observers believe that the ongoing misuse of the red notice system is 'dangerously close to damaging Interpol beyond repair'.[33] The lack of external accountability which is undermining the credibility of the agency must be addressed. At the same time, this case illustrates the limits and risks of international collaboration that involves autocratic governments.

A world parliament as an element of world police law

Another necessary way of establishing democratic legitimation in addition to vesting a world parliament with oversight powers would be to give it a key role in the development of the content and procedures of 'world police law'. One of the main issues would be the question of which offences should be criminalised under world law and how exactly they should be defined. This applies to terrorist offences, as identified already in a number of UN conventions, but also to the definition of terrorism itself, on which it has not yet proved possible to reach agreement at the United Nations. A world parliament should concern itself especially with issues which the governments are inclined to defer; for example, with the definition and criminalization of economic and financial offences of systemic importance. Moreover, a world parliament would serve as a platform where established international law regimes could be called into question. International drugs policy, for example, is firmly in the hands of the UN conventions on narcotics, which establish a comprehensive global prohibition on drugs in line with the logic of the 'war on drugs'. Due to the need to achieve consensus, a historic reform initiative by several Latin-American states failed at a special UN meeting in April 2016. However, the criminalization of intoxicating drugs has proved to be ineffective, counterproductive and self-contradictory. Millions of users and addicts are pursued under criminal law while at the same time, in spite of all the measures taken to suppress it, the market in illegal drugs continues to produce profits in the billions for transnational criminal networks of the worst kind. According to estimates from the UNODC, the illicit drug market yields annual proceeds equivalent to around 0.6 to 0.9 per cent of global GDP.[34] When in 2012 the major British bank HSBC was forced to admit in the course of proceedings brought in the USA to having laundered billions of dollars of drugs profits for Mexican and Columbian cartels over years, the US public prosecutors were satisfied with a fine and did not press for any other form of criminal sanction.

33 Keith, Ben, and Rhys Davies. 6 April 2023. 'Russia and China's Abuse of Red Notices Could Wreck Interpol for Good.' Euronews (euronews.com).
34 United Nations Office on Drugs and Crime. Oct. 2011. Estimating Illicit Financial Flows Resulting from Drug Trafficking and Other Transnational Organized Crimes: Research Report, p. 7.,

Their rationale, astounding as it may seem, was that criminal proceedings would almost certainly have led to the loss of HSBC's US banking licence and that this in turn would have destabilised the banking system.[35] A new and globally coordinated approach to the problem of the drugs trade and money laundering is urgently needed.

Finally, a 'global police law' needs to regulate the responsibilities, powers and limitations of a supranational police force and global law enforcement. This entails drawing a line between routine measures within the purview of relevant agencies taken in collaboration with national law enforcement and extraordinary actions that demand a mandate and legitimization from political bodies. While a world parliament should confine its involvement to a supervisory role in the first category of actions, it needs to play a key role in decision-making in the second category which covers coercive measures. As mentioned before, this is especially the case with regard to employing a potential rapid reaction force or mandating military action. Thomas Darnstädt pointed out that even a hardliner such as George W. Bush's Secretary of Homeland Security Michael Chertoff has spoken out in favour of an international legal regime that allows the world community to take action against transnational threats emanating from the territory of a state unwilling or unable to do so itself. This arises out of the 'modern obligations of reciprocal sovereignty', Chertoff explained in the magazine *Foreign Affairs*. Although every state had the right to autonomy within its own borders with respect to internal security threats, this also entailed a responsibility to 'take reasonable measures to contain the potentially destructive consequences of these security threats to prevent them from spreading and interfering with other states' sovereign right to exclusive authority over their territories'.[36] The problem with this was that it left open the question of who had the authority to decide on such 'peace interventions against terrorists'.[37] A world parliament would have precisely that authority.

The role and significance of the USA

Ultimately, the construction of a world legal order is in the interests of the United States as well. It would be a means of creating stability and security within a legitimate framework the costs of which would be shared on a global basis. The Polish-American political scientist Zbigniew Brzeziński, who was National Security Advisor to US President Jimmy Carter, declared in 1997 in

---

35 Rushe, Dominic, and Jill Treanor. 11 December 2012. 'HSBC's record $1.9bn fine preferable to prosecution, US authorities insist'. The Guardian (www.theguardian.com).
36 Chertoff, Michael. 2009. 'The Responsibility to Contain'. Foreign Affairs (88) 1: 130–147.
37 Darnstädt, p. 334.

his book 'The Grand Chessboard' that in 'the long run, global politics are bound to become increasingly uncongenial to the concentration of hegemonic power in the hands of a single state. Hence', he argued, 'America is not only the first, as well as the only, truly global superpower, but it is also likely to be the very last.'[38] Contrary to the hope of the neoconservatives, the 'unipolar moment' did not become an era, but passed irretrievably. In the long-term perspective, a relative loss of significance for the USA is apparent, one that will lead ultimately to a post-American age in world politics. This development can be seen most clearly in the shift in relative economic power. In the 1960s, the USA's share of global GDP was around 37 per cent on average according to the World Bank; in the 1970s it was around 30 per cent; and since the 1990s it has been around 28 per cent. Since 2008 it has lain below one quarter. The fact that in 2013 the USA was overtaken for the first time as the world's biggest trading nation by China confirms this trend. Of course, the USA still counts as one of the most innovative, productive and competitive economies in the world, one that is also technologically at the leading edge; but the phenomenon of 'imperial overstretch' leading to the implosion of hegemonic great powers, as identified by the historian Paul Kennedy in his well-known bestseller 'The Rise and Fall of the Great Powers', now increasingly seems to be the challenge faced by the USA too. Kennedy wrote that the test will lie in whether the United States can find a sensible balance in the area of military strategy between its defence responsibilities and the resources available, and whether the country will be able to 'preserve the technological and economic bases of its power from relative erosion in the face of the ever-shifting patterns of global production'. In 1987 already, when the book first appeared, the British academic had concluded that the decision-makers in Washington had to face the uncomfortable fact 'that the sum total of the United States' global interests and obligations is nowadays larger than the country's power to defend them all simultaneously'.[39] The USA's enormous public debt fits with the picture of 'imperial overstretch'. In late 2023, it stood at over 33 trillion US dollars, more than 120 per cent of the country's annual GDP. Ironically, a large share of this money is owed by the United States to foreign investors. The US's external trade balance has been in the red since 1976, and the deficit peaked in 2022 at around 102 billion US dollars. This deficit, which is another factor that makes the imperial policies of the US possible, is financed by inward flows of foreign capital.

---

38 Brzezinski, Zbigniew. 1999. The Grand Chessboard. New York: Basic Books, p. 209.
39 Kennedy, Paul. 1989. The Rise and Fall of the Great Powers. New York: Vintage Books, pp. 514-5.

Paul Kennedy emphasized that 'the only serious threat to the real interests of the United States can come from a failure to adjust sensibly to the newer world order'. The United States has to evaluate and recognize the limits and the possibilities of its power.[40] Its striving for global supremacy will not be affordable over the long term and will lead to the social and economic erosion of the nation, provokes anti-hegemonic reaction and anti-Americanism and undermines multilateral cooperation, making the world overall less safe. Unlike the transition from the global predominance of the British Empire to that of the USA, which was concluded by the Second World War, the decline of the USA will not be accompanied by the ascent of a new global hegemon. 'Once American leadership begins to fade', wrote the geostrategist Brzeziński, 'America's current global predominance is unlikely to be replicated by any single state. Thus, the key question for the future is "What will America bequeath to the world as the enduring legacy of its primacy?"'[41] After the First World War, the United States supported a League of Nations, and during the Second World War, the establishment of the United Nations. By contrast, the contribution of the USA to the world order since the end of the Cold War looks very bleak so far. Projects such as the International Criminal Court were initially fiercely opposed. There has not been a 'Third Try at World Order', as called for as early as 1977 by the former US diplomat Harlan Cleveland, along the lines of his 'Declaration of Interdependence'. Even the foreign policy establishment figure Brzeziński believed that 'the U.S. policy goal must be unapologetically twofold: to perpetuate America's own dominant position for at least a generation and preferably longer still; and to create a geopolitical framework that can absorb the inevitable shocks and strains of social-political change while evolving into the geopolitical core of shared responsibility for peaceful global management. A prolonged phase of gradually expanding cooperation with key Eurasian partners,' he continued, 'both stimulated and arbitrated by America, can also help to foster the preconditions for an eventual upgrading of the existing and increasingly antiquated UN structures', adding that a 'functioning structure of global cooperation, based on geopolitical realities, could thus emerge and gradually assume the mantle of the world's current "regent".'[42] In short: the future lies in the creation of a new *global* power centre.

Following the attacks of 11 September, Paul Kennedy, who taught at Yale University, wrote that 'even those Americans hostile to the very notion of the sharing of global power and of the U.S. becoming a "normal" country may

40   Ibid., p. 534.
41   Brzezinski, p. 210.
42   Ibid., p. 215.

sooner or later have to accept that it is unavoidable, and is in fact going to happen because of the sort of liberal nation and open society that we are'. In fact, however, the 'war on terror' and the 'America First' populism of Donald Trump demonstrated an attitude that could hardly be further removed from such acceptance. Kennedy's belief was that a younger generation of Americans in the 2020s or 2030s might come to the conclusion that it would make more sense for the USA to share the 'power and responsibility and burden' with others and to seek 'a voluntary alteration of America's role from being the hegemonic policeman to being the senior partner in a world of democratic states that work out global problems through international structures and shared policies'. Even more: perhaps they could envision 'a future for this planet in which *real democratic representation*, from local government to *world bodies*, exists; human rights are universally respected; a more equitable prosperity is enjoyed; and the "world community" really is that' (emphasis added).[43]

---

43 Kennedy, Paul. 2001. 'Maintaining American Power: From Injury to Recovery'. In: The Age of Terror, ed. by Strobe Talbott and Nayan Chanda, 53–79. New York: Basic Books, pp. 77-8.

20.
Global food security and the political economy of hunger

A sufficient and adequate food supply is the basis for every human existence, whether individually or as a society. 'The history of man from the beginning has been the history of his struggle for daily bread', wrote the Brazilian doctor and diplomat Josué de Castro (1908 to 1973) in an influential book on 'The Geography of Hunger' in 1952.[1] The historian Charles Tilly showed that conflicts over control of the food supply played a decisive role in the process of state formation. As he observed, these constitute 'basic processes of state-making as they touch the everyday lives of ordinary people'. Nation-states began to emerge as 'the organization which had finally assumed the responsibility of keeping its population from starving.' Food riots thereby historically marked 'the most frequent form of collective violence setting ordinary people against governmental authorities.' What lay behind the food riots was the struggle of the nascent states to secure a food supply above all for the people 'most inclined to serve their ends', for example in the administration or in the armed forces, or the inhabitants of the capital cities.[2] Famine has burned itself deep into the collective memory of those societies it affected.

The extent of worldwide hunger and the right to adequate nutrition

The sociologist Jean Ziegler, who was the UN's first Special Rapporteur on the Right to Food from 2000 to 2008, pointed out that hunger 'is by far the leading cause of death and needless suffering on our planet'.[3] Nine million people die from hunger every year according to the World Food Programme.[4] The UN report on 'The State of Food Security and Nutrition in the World', published in 2023, estimated that about 735 million people in the world were still facing hunger. About 29.6 per cent of the world population, or 2.4 billion people, were said to be moderately or severely food insecure. The report attributes a sharp increase of global hunger from affecting 7.9 per cent of the world popu-

1   Castro, Josué de. 1952. The Geography of Hunger. Boston: Little, Brown and Company, p. 4.
2   Tilly, Charles. 1975. 'Food Supply and Public Order in Modern Europe'. In: The Formation of National States in Western Europe, ed. by id., 380–455. Princeton University Press, pp. 455, 431, 385, 392.
3   Ziegler, Jean. 2013. Betting on Famine: Why the World Still Goes Hungry. New York: The New Press, p. 6
4   World Food Programme. 24 Sept. 2021. 'In World of Wealth, 9 Million People Die Every Year from Hunger, WFP Chief Tells Food System Summit.' (wfp.org).

lation in 2019 to 9.2 per cent in 2022 primarily to the impacts of the COVID-19 pandemic and the Russian war against Ukraine.[5]

Adequate nutrition has long been recognised in international law as one of the most fundamental human rights. In the Universal Declaration of Human Rights adopted by the UN General Assembly in 1948 it is stated that everyone 'has the right to a standard of living adequate for the health and well-being of himself and of his family, including food'. The International Covenant on Economic, Social and Cultural Rights, which came into force in 1976, recognises under Article 11 'the right of everyone to an adequate standard of living for himself and his family, including adequate food', and the right 'to be free from hunger'. In the opinion of Jean Ziegler, among all human rights, 'the right to food is certainly one most constantly violated on our planet'. He described hunger as 'organized crime'.[6]

The rhetoric emanating from officialdom on the fight against hunger has declared for over seventy years that the issue has the highest priority and that a solution is imminent. John Shaw, agricultural economist and former UN official, wrote in a historical overview that achieving food security 'has been the subject of countless international conventions, declarations, compacts and resolutions'. Over 120 of them can be listed since the founding of the League of Nations and their number is increasing each year.[7] At the World Food Conference in Rome in 1974, then US Secretary of State Henry Kissinger declared that hunger and malnutrition should and could be overcome 'within a decade'.[8] According to the action plan adopted by the World Food Summit in 1996, food security exists 'when all people, at all times, have physical and economic access to sufficient, safe and nutritious food to meet their dietary needs and food preferences for an active and healthy life'.[9] The summit set a target of reducing the *number* of people suffering from hunger worldwide to around 400 million by 2015, thus halving the figure compared to the reference period of 1990-92.[10] At the UN Millennium Summit in 2000, it was decided for clarification that the actual target was to reduce the *proportion* of people suffering from hunger by half. As the proportion was claimed to have fallen from 23.3 to 12.9 per cent, the report on the Millennium Development Goals in 2015 announced that the goal

5   FAO, IFAD, UNICEF, WFP, and WHO. 2023. The State of Food Security and Nutrition in the World 2023. Rome: FAO, p. xvi.

6   Ziegler, p. 25.

7   Shaw, D. John. 2007. World Food Security: A History Since 1945. Palgrave, p. 388.

8   Kissinger, Henry. 16 December 1974. 'Address at the World Food Conference in Rome'. The Department of State Bulletin (LXXI) 1851: 821–829, p. 829.

9   Food and Agricultural Organization of the United Nations. 13 November 1996. 'Rome Declaration and Plan of Action', para. 1 of the action plan.

10 See id. November 2003. Anti-Hunger Programme. Rome: FAO, para 18.

was almost reached—despite the fact that in *absolute* terms nearly 800 million people still suffered of hunger.[11] As to the second Sustainable Development Goal, worldwide hunger is supposed to vanish completely as part of the 'Agenda 2030' and 'all people' should have access to safe, nutritious and sufficient food. The Global Hunger Index, which provides an independent evaluation, confirms that between 2000 and 2015, the world made 'significant headway against hunger' but since then there was only little progress. The index that measures the level of hunger in the world on a scale from zero to 100 fell from 28.0 in 2000 to 19.1 in 2015 and in 2023 stood at 18.3. In their assessment, 58 countries will not even achieve low levels of hunger by 2030.[12]

According to the United Nations Food and Agriculture Organization (FAO), the minimum energy intake requirement for an adult human being is roughly 1,800 kilocalories per day. The World Health Organization puts the average requirement at a minimum 2,100 kilocalories per day. The FAO estimates that the food available per head of the global population, measured in kilocalories, increased from a worldwide average of 2,200 in the early 1960s to around 3,000 in 2021.[13] Statistically speaking, and despite the rapid increase in the population from around three billion people in 1960 to more than seven billion today, hunger could therefore indeed have been a thing of the past for decades now. But these figures must not be allowed to obscure the fact that mere energy supply is not the whole story. Two billion people also lack the vitamins and minerals essential for good health.[14]

Population growth and food production

The cause of hunger was long considered to be simply a disparity between the size of a population requiring feeding and the available quantity of food. In 'An Essay on the Principle of Population', first published in 1798, the English political economist and Anglican clergyman Thomas Malthus (1766 to 1834) set out his theory that population growth would always outstrip increases in food production, and that as a consequence there must always be shortages in supply and hence hunger. 'Too many people, too little to eat' would be one way to summarize the Malthusian message. It seemed to Malthus that the reduction of 'overpopulation' by hunger, disease and war was a 'law of necessity'. The problem of 'overpopulation' is a constantly recurring theme. At the

11   United Nations. 2015. 'The Millennium Development Goals Report 2015', p. 20.

12   Grebner, Klaus von, and et al. 2023. '2023 Global Hunger Index.' Deutsche Welthungerhilfe and Concern Worldwide. (globalhungerindex.org), p. 7.

13   FAO Statistical Yearbook 2013 (p. 126) and 2023 (p. 277).

14   Schutter, Olivier De. 24 January 2014. 'Final report of the Special Rapporteur on the right to food: The transformative potential of the right to food'. A/HRC/25/57, p. 4.

time of the Roman Empire, the early Christian writer Tertullian (150 to 220 CE) complained that 'our teeming population' is 'burdensome to the world'. 'In very deed, pestilence, and famine, and wars, and earthquakes have to be regarded as a remedy for nations, as the means of pruning the luxuriance of the human race', he wrote.[15] This view enjoyed renewed attention and influence when the biologist Paul Ehrlich warned of 'The Population Bomb' in his eponymous world bestseller of 1968. In the light of a rapidly expanding world population, which had almost tripled since the middle of the 19th century and now stood at 3.5 billion, he declared that 'the battle to feed humanity is already lost'. Massive famines, with hundreds of millions of deaths, were inescapable and imminent, and 'could be one way to reach a death rate solution to the population problem' he added, in the style of a true Malthusian. 'Too many people' wrote Ehrlich '- that is why we are on the verge of the "death rate solution".' 'Rapid improvement in public health, advances in agriculture, and improved transport systems have temporarily reduced the efficacy of pestilence and famine as population regulators', he declared.[16] The misanthropic attitude expressed here is shocking. The British historian David Arnold, who teaches global history at the University of Warwick and studies famines, rightly noted that it expresses 'a deeper repugnance and incomprehension, a failure to understand, even to accept the right to exist, of people of another race and culture'.[17] The right to food is based on the recognition that all people are equal. 'The consciousness of our shared human identity lies also at the foundation of the right to food', as Jean Ziegler made clear. 'No one can tolerate the destruction from hunger of his fellow man or woman without endangering his own humanity, his very identity.'[18]

The unforeseen improvements in agricultural productivity—due to the availability of fossil fuels from the 19th century onwards, for example, and to the use of artificial fertilisers and the 'Green Revolution'—have always kept pace with the rising demand for food from a growing world population and have always forestalled the occurrence of a global Malthusian crisis. However, this must not be allowed to divert attention from the fact that the race is not yet finished. For his contribution to the fight against world hunger through the development of high yield crop varieties that led to the 'Green Revolution', the agricultural scientist Norman Borlaug (1914 to 2009) was awarded the

---

15 Coxe, Cleveland A. (ed.). 1885. The Ante-Nicene Fathers. Translations of the Writings of the Fathers down to A.D. 325, Volume III, Late Christianity: Its Founder, Tertullian. Vol. 3. Buffalo: The Christian literature publishing company.
16 Ehrlich, Paul R. 1968. The Population Bomb. New York: Ballatine, pp. 36, 69.
17 Arnold, David. 1988. Famine: Social Crisis and Historical Change. Oxford et al.: B. Blackwell, p. 41.
18 Ziegler, p. 63.

Nobel Peace Prize. In his acceptance speech he warned against allowing efforts to increase production to slacken. 'We are dealing with two opposing forces', he said, 'the scientific power of food production and the biologic power of human reproduction.'[19] Worldwide population growth, meanwhile, is slowing down, and by the end of the century will in all probability have levelled off. According to United Nations population projections, the world population will increase to 8.5 billion people by 2030, further increase to 9.7 billion by 2050, reach a peak at around 10.4 billion during the 2080s, remain at that level until 2100 and then will start declining. Other studies forecast a peak of around 9.7 billion in 2064 and a decline to 8.7 billion until 2100. By 2050, over three fourths of all countries are projected to have fertility rates lower than the replacement level.[20] The FAO estimated that food production will have to increase by the middle of this century by 60 per cent against 2005/2007 levels to meet the growing demand. FAO experts were confident that 'at the global level there should be no major constraints to increasing agricultural produce by the amounts required to satisfy the additional demand generated by population and income growth to 2050'. In their estimation, in 2050 there will be 3070 kilocalories available in principle per person per day on a worldwide average.[21] In his book 'Feeding the World', the Canadian environmental scientist Vaclav Smil also concluded that there appear to be 'no insurmountable biophysical reasons why we could not feed humanity in decades to come while at the same time easing the burden that modern agriculture puts on the biosphere'.[22]

The fragility of the global food supply

On the other side, Malthusians like Paul Ehrlich do not grow tired of warning of a global hunger crisis. In an article published in 2013, for example, Ehrlich pointed to the fragility of global food supplies and thence to a potential 'collapse of global civilization'. 'Agriculture', wrote Ehrlich, 'has generated miracles of food production. But it has also created serious long-run vulnerabilities, especially in its dependence on stable climates, crop monocultures, industrially produced fertilizers and pesticides, petroleum, antibiotic feed supple-

19   Borlaug, Norman. 10 December 1970. 'Acceptance Speech on the occasion of the award of the Nobel Peace Peace Prize in Oslo' (www.nobelprize.org).

20   Vollset, Stein Emil, et al. 2020. 'Fertility, Mortality, Migration, and Population Scenarios for 195 Countries and Territories from 2017 to 2100: A Forecasting Analysis for the Global Burden of Disease Study.' The Lancet 396 (10258): 1285–1306.

21   Alexandratos, Nikos, and Jelle Bruinsma. 2012. 'World Agriculture Towards 2030/2050: The 2012 Revision'. Food and Agriculture Organization of the United Nations, pp. 7, 17, 23.

22   Smil, Vaclav. Feeding the World: A Challenge for the Twenty-First Century. Cambridge, Mass.: MIT Press, 2001, p. xxvii.

ments and rapid, efficient transportation.' He argued that the foundations of the agricultural system, and thus of world civilization, are under threat, in particular from the effects of climate change and environmental degradation. He believed that global collapse 'could be triggered by anything from a "small" nuclear war, whose ecological effects could quickly end civilization, to a more gradual breakdown because famines, epidemics and resource shortages cause a disintegration of central control within nations, in concert with disruptions of trade and conflicts over increasingly scarce necessities'.[23] The well-known environment expert Lester Brown, founder of the Worldwatch Institute in 1974, also believed that increasingly, 'food is looking like the weak link in our civilization'. If we continue with business as usual, he argued, then a collapse is 'not only possible but likely'. He, too, saw failing states as the likely starting point, where governments lose control and can no longer guarantee the safety of the population and most importantly the security of the food supply. 'If the number of failing states continues to increase', wrote Brown in what was the fourth version of his 'Plan B' to 'save civilization', 'at some point this trend will translate into a failing global civilization.'[24] Rising food prices, he argued, not only lead to protest and revolt, but contribute to the risk of state bankruptcies and thus of failed states.

What is clear is that the ecological challenges posed by global food production are many and complex, including the erosion, degradation and contamination of the soil, water scarcity and falling water tables, temperature rise and the increase in extreme weather conditions, desertification, collapsing fish stocks, and air and water pollution. On the production side, the greatest uncertainty factor seems to be the potential consequences of climate change. The FAO, for example, acknowledges that climate change may 'affect adversely' its projections; and for Vaclav Smil, the possibility of 'a relative rapid global warming induced by higher concentrations of anthropogenic greenhouse gases poses by far the greatest potential threat to future agricultural production'.[25,26] The projected rise in average global temperatures illustrates the problem. Disregarding regional disparities, studies show that higher temperatures have a negative impact on crop yields as a rule.[27] A study in the Philippines, for example, found a ten per cent loss in yield for each degree Celsius of in-

23 Ehrlich, Paul R., and Anne H. Ehrlich. 2013. 'Can a collapse of global civilization be avoided?' Proceedings of the Royal Society B 280, no. 20122845, p. 2.
24 Brown, Lester. 2009. Plan B 4.0. New York and London: W. W. Norton & Company, pp. 3, 4, 185.
25 Alexandratos and Bruinsma, p. 18.
26 Smil, p. xvii.
27 Nelson, Gerald C., et al. 2009. Climate Change: Impact on Agriculture and Costs of Adaptation. Ed. by International Food Policy Research Institute, Washington, D.C.

crease at the lowest temperature range.[28] Studies in Kansas found that every increase of one degree Celsius in average temperatures reduced wheat yields by around 21 per cent.[29] It also appears that a higher concentration of CO_2 in the atmosphere, as anticipated over the coming decades, has a negative impact on the nutritional value of cereals and pulses.[30] Agriculture thus is both, 'a prime driver and first victim of climate change', researchers contend, as it accounts for 12 per cent of greenhouse gas emissions and global demand for agricultural products is projected to increase by 50 per cent by mid-century.[31] It must be put on a new footing. Research found that the required decarbonization of food production and net-zero emissions in agriculture is feasible, in principle, with current technologies.[32] Notwithstanding all the challenges and uncertainties involved, overcoming worldwide hunger, in the foreseeable future as well as the long term, does not appear to be a problem of inadequate food production. This conclusion is supported not least by the fact that substantial improvements and efficiency gains are possible in irrigation, fertilization, storage and the avoidance of food waste. At present, around a third of all food produced for human consumption worldwide is going to waste.[33]

Hunger as a problem of political economy

To regard hunger as a natural catastrophe or as a problem of insufficient food production is in the vast majority of cases mistaken. It was Josué de Castro who established and spread this insight in the years following the Second World War. Just like war, he wrote, hunger is a 'man-made blight' that 'results from grave errors and defects in social organization' and 'always implies society's guilt'.[34] Joseph Collins and Frances Moore Lappé, who founded a think tank on food and development issues in the USA in 1975, pointed out in their bestselling book 'Food First: Beyond the myth of scarcity' that the 'poor do not eat no matter how much food there is'. 'Scarcity', they wrote, 'is not the cause of hunger. A production increase, no matter how great, can never in

28 Peng, Shaobing, et al. 6 July 2004. 'Rice Yields Decline with Higher Night Temperature from Global Warming'. Proceedings of the National Academy of Sciences of the United States of America (101) 27: 9971–75.

29 Barkley, Andrew, et al. 2013. Impact of Climate, Disease, and Wheat Breeding on Wheat Variety Yields in Kansas, 1985-2011. Ed. by Kansas State University Agricultural Experiment Station and Cooperative Extension Service. K-State Research and Extension, p. 27.

30 Myers, Samuel S., et al. 5 June 2014. 'Increasing CO2 Threatens Human Nutrition'. Nature (510) 139-142.

31 Rosa, Lorenzo, and Paolo Gabrielli. 2023. 'Achieving Net-Zero Emissions in Agriculture: A Review.' Environmental Research Letters 18 (6): 063002, p. 1.

32 Rosa and Gabrielli, p. 14.

33 Gustavsson, Jenny, et al. 2011. Global Food Losses and Food Waste. Extent, Causes, and Prevention. Rome: Food and Agriculture Organization of the United Nations, p. 4.

34 Castro, Josué de. 1952. The Geography of Hunger. Boston: Little, Brown and Company, pp. 11, 14, 24

itself solve the problem.'[35] In his influential 1983 study 'Poverty and Famines', the future Nobel Prize winner for economics Amartya Sen showed that famines also occur when there is enough food available. 'Starvation is the characteristic of some people not *having* enough to eat. It is not the characteristic of there *being* not enough to eat', wrote Sen. What mattered, he argued, was not the availability of food in itself but the *access* to it.[36] As Mike Davis underlined in his book on 'Late Victorian Holocausts', during the worst famines of the 19th century, which cost the lives of up to fifty million people in the three extended global droughts between 1876 and 1902 alone, 'there were almost always grain surpluses elsewhere in the nation or empire that could have potentially rescued drought victims'.[37] But the markets, geared for profit maximization, were unable to give food away. It was hoarded, treated as a speculative commodity, and often exported in large quantities. The FAO concluded that 'the issue whether food insecurity will be eliminated by the end of the century is clouded in uncertainty, no matter that from the standpoint of global production potential there should be no insurmountable constraints'.[38] Hunger is a problem of the global political economy.

The relevance of democracy and the international system

Poverty and underdevelopment are the key causes of hunger. Endemic hunger and malnutrition are often the result of civil wars, failed states or bad or autocratic government. Amartya Sen has speculated that 'in the terrible history of famines in the world, no substantial famine has ever occurred in any independent and democratic country with a relatively free press'. Political and civil rights, he argues, give the citizenship means with which to push the government into action.[39] Whereas, by way of illustration, under British rule in India there were countless famines, which caused millions of deaths and which Mike Davis classifies as genocide, in similar situations after independence, the democratic government has intervened, with great success. For decades now there has been a system of broad food support for the poorest, and in 2013 a right to five kilos of grain per person per month was fixed by law, applying to around 70 per cent of the population. If there is a link between democracy and

35 Lappé, Frances Moore, and Joseph Collins. 1977. Food First. Beyond the Myth of Scarcity. Boston: Houghton Mifflin Co., pp. 19, 112.
36 Sen, Amartya Kumar. 1982. Poverty and Famines: An Essay on Entitlement and Deprivation. New York: Clarendon Press/Oxford University Press, 1982, pp. 1, 7.
37 Davis, Mike. 2001. Late Victorian Holocausts: El Niño Famines and the Making of the Third World. Verso, p. 11.
38 Alexandratos and Bruinsma, p. 21.
39 Sen, Amartya. 1999. 'Democracy as a Universal Value'. Journal of Democracy (10) 3: 3–17, pp. 7-8.

success in the fight against hunger, then perhaps the key to overcoming hunger throughout the world lies in the creation of a *global* democracy?

As Thomas Pogge wrote, people like to present poverty and oppression as 'problems whose root causes and possible solutions are domestic to the foreign countries in which they occur'. And the relevant national policies and institutions are indeed often quite bad; 'but the fact that they are', Pogge wrote to underline the key point, 'can be traced to global policies and institutions'.[40] For at the global level we are also dealing with bad or—perhaps even worse—non-existent governance. One factor to which we have already drawn attention is the illegal flows of capital out of the developing countries, facilitated by the existence of tax havens. In addition, Pogge points to the fact that importing natural raw materials from countries with autocratic regimes provides support to those regimes, and that taking part in such business dealings therefore creates a degree of complicity. Two 'core features of our present global order' are especially significant causes of the persistence of serious poverty: 'the international resource privilege' and 'the international borrowing privilege'. 'Whoever can gain effective power by whatever means will have the legal power to incur debts in the country's name and to confer internationally valid ownership rights in the country's resources', is how Pogge summarises the problem. This situation breeds corruption, autocracy, coups d'état and civil war. He therefore proposes 'an international treaty declaring that rulers who hold power contrary to their country's constitution and without democratic legitimation cannot sell their country's resources abroad nor borrow in its name'. Thus, in the event of an unconstitutional putsch, any subsequent democratic government could refuse to pay back loans taken out by the putsch leaders and contest any linked sales of natural resources or of extraction licences. Disputes could be handled by 'a standing Democracy Panel under the auspices of the UN'.[41] It would be even simpler to entrust this task to a *world constitutional court*. And in fact the Tunisian President Moncef Marzouki, elected following the revolution, proposed to the UN General Assembly in September 2012 the establishment of an 'international constitutional court', with the power to decide in cases of doubt whether elections have been conducted democratically and constitutionally.[42]

40 Pogge, Thomas. 2008. World Poverty and Human Rights. 2nd ed. Cambridge: Polity, pp. 147, 149
41 Ibid., pp. 29, 148, 162
42 United Nations. 27 September 2012. 'Statement of H.E. Mr. Moncef Marzouki at the UN General Assembly General Debate of the 67th Session'.

Agricultural subsidies, the WTO, and food security

Agricultural subsidies and protectionism have a direct impact on international trading conditions. The WTO Agreement on Agriculture of 1995 allows the continuation of existing internal price support at a level of 80 per cent, and caps new internal subsidies in developing countries at 10 per cent as a proportion of their total agricultural production. The agreement favours the industrialised countries, as the starting level for them is extremely high. Moreover, they have reformed subsidies in such a way that in strict legal terms they are not classified as a distortion of trade, whereas the developing countries have been persuaded, partly through so-called structural adjustment programmes from the World Bank and the IMF, to reduce import barriers. Producers in the developing countries often cannot compete with the heavily subsidised products from the OECD countries. Where they do have a competitive advantage, they often encounter barriers that make access to the markets in the industrialised countries difficult or impossible. So overall investment in the agricultural sector in developed countries is weak and productivity is low. At the conference of WTO ministers on the Indonesian island of Bali in 2013, the WTO members agreed for the first time on a treaty on trade facilitation. India was able to get an agreement that price support mechanisms and aid in the context of *already existing* public stockholding programmes for food security could exceed the limit set in the Agriculture Agreement. Under a so-called 'peace clause' it is not possible in an interim period to challenge such cases before the WTO's Dispute Settlement Body. However, new programmes could in principle still represent a breach of WTO rules. The fact that the Bali Ministerial Conference prioritised trade concerns over food security 'provides a textbook illustration of the need to improve coherence of global governance for the realization of the right to food', wrote Olivier De Schutter, Jean Ziegler's successor as the UN's Special Rapporteur on the Right to Food, and like him a supporter of a parliamentary assembly at the UN.[43] A decade after Bali and with over 15 negotiating proposals presented by various WTO members, talks for a permanent solution continued.[44] At the WTO, all rules need to be agreed on by consensus. The matter is becoming ever more urgent as the price reference under the Agriculture Agreement are the years 1986-88 and global food prices in the meantime are much higher and subject to considerable volatility. While this and many other issues continue to be pursued within the WTO, the organization's dispute settlement mechanism, the backbone of the

---

43 Schutter, p. 19, para. 48.
44 Glauber, Joe, and Tanvi Sinha. 2021. 'Procuring Food Stocks Under World Trade Organization Farm Subsidy Rules.' IISD, pp. 4-10.

global rules-based trade system, has been paralyzed for years. Since 2016, successive US administrations blocked appointments to the WTO's Appellate Body, which can make binding decisions on trade disputes, and rendered the body dysfunctional. It appears that Washington only wants trade disputes to advance to that stage in the future if both plaintiff and defendant voluntarily agree.[45] This change would undermine the binding nature of multilateral trade rules and potentially destroy the system.

Commodity markets and financial speculation

Prices for agricultural commodities, and hence for staple foods, are set by important commodity markets like those in Chicago, New York and London. Trends in international prices impact especially strongly on low earners and on the poorest people around the world. As a rule, the proportion of household income spent on food goes down as income rises. Whereas expenditure on food accounts for around 150 per cent of the consumer price index for industrialised countries, in the developing countries it is often more than two-thirds. Between 1980 and 2000, food prices on world markets were comparatively low in historical terms. Beginning in 2002, a drastic rise set in, culminating in the food price crisis of 2007 and 2008 which saw at its peak a three-fold increase in the world price of grain. Many millions of people, especially in the global South, were plunged into severe difficulty, and protests and riots broke out in dozens of countries. It is now clear that speculators from the financial sector have long been exerting an increasing influence on the price discovery process in the commodity markets and using the trade in agricultural produce and raw materials for capital investment. This so-called 'financialization' of the commodity markets leads to a de-coupling of prices from the supply and demand of the actual goods. Investors bet on price movements and also consider other factors, such as portfolio distributions and developments in other markets and in monetary policy, which have nothing at all to do with the fundamental data of trading in commodities. There is broad agreement that financial speculation on the commodity markets was a substantial cause of the extreme fluctuations and price increases.[46] According to a study by the United Nations Conference on Trade and Development (UNCTAD), for example, the 'price discovery mechanism is seriously distorted' and leads to an 'increasing

45   Aarup, Sarah Anne. 9 May 2023. 'Reform or Die? If the US Gets Its Way, the WTO Might Do Both.' POLIT-ICO (politico.eu).

46   See the studies in: Institute for Agriculture and Trade Policy (ed.). 2011. Excessive Speculation in Agriculture Commodities. Selected Writings 2008-2011.

risk of price bubbles'.[47] This is not a new discovery. Joseph Collins and Frances Moore Lappé noted in the 1970s with regard to cocoa prices that 'speculative activities are a major cause of extreme fluctuations in price'.[48]

The globalised markets for agricultural commodities result in economies of scale and efficiency gains, and they enable an indispensable international balancing out of supply against demand; but at the same time they lead to a worldwide competition between the basic needs of the poorest and the substantially better resourced needs and wants of the affluent.[49] The growing demand for biofuels and meat, for example, places great demands on available agricultural land. This leads to reductions and price increases in the supply of basic foodstuffs. Energy prices, too, affect the prices of agricultural commodities, mediated via the costs of production and transport. The World Bank estimates the transmission elasticity from world prices for crude oil, natural gas and coal to the price of grain at 0.28.

Food security as a global public good, and the failure of the G20

Global interdependence and interconnectedness are very marked in the food sector. The international trade in food has multiplied by a factor of five since 1960 and has doubled in the period from 2000 to 2010. In the following decade it grew by around one third. Worldwide trade is crucial in overcoming local bottlenecks. Production and supply chains are densely meshed and are largely run by globally operating, vertically integrated corporations able to exploit economies of scale. While these firms managed to increase their influence throughout the supply chains, global trade in food and agricultural products overall has become more decentralized and more equally distributed among countries in the past decades.[50] Because of the complexity and the high level of global interdependence of the food sector, and because of its fundamental importance for humanity and for world civilization, ensuring food security should be regarded as one of the global public goods with the highest priority, as indeed is the case in the report of the International Task Force already referred to.[51] Food security is a normative global responsibility. As researchers pointed out, 'the good cannot be adequately provided by the market, as food security demands that all people, irrespective of purchasing capac-

47 United Nations Conference on Trade and Development. June 2011. 'Price Formation in Financialized Commodity Markets: The Role of Information'. United Nations, p. 55.
48 Lappé and Collins, p. 184.
49 Schutter, p. 11.
50 FAO. 2022. The State of Agricultural Commodity Markets 2022, pp. 8-9.
51 International Task Force on Global Public Goods. 2006. 'Meeting Global Challenges: International Cooperation in the National Interest. Report of the Int. Task Force on Global Public Goods'. Stockholm, Sweden, p. 25.

ity, have the opportunity to cover their nutritional needs'. This makes it necessary to 'centralize the dimension of food as a human right' at the global scale and 'reduce its current role as tradable commodity.'[52] But here too there is a lack of institutions equipped to enact robust global regulations and measures. The stability of agricultural markets as a constituent element of food security provides an illustration. The argument runs that volatility in the markets unsettles farming activities and food security in countries around the world, that farming is linked to other global public goods such as the environment, that important goals of the international community such as the right to food and the fight against poverty are affected by such volatility, and furthermore that 'the stability of agricultural commodities prices assumes a major strategic and geopolitical character'.[53] In order to limit speculative trading, consistent global rules are needed to prevent loopholes and the displacement of trade into less regulated markets. On the initiative of France, the G20 in 2011 placed global food security high on its agenda and adopted an 'action plan on food price volatility and agriculture' that included the creation of a market information system and a 'Rapid Response Forum' tasked to 'prevent and manage market crisis in a coordinated manner', among other things. However, this was a far cry from market regulation. In view of the cost-of-living crisis as the 'hallmark of the post-COVID-19 recovery' that was cascading through the global political economy, UNCTAD in 2023 reported that ongoing 'unregulated activity within the commodities sector' contributed to 'speculative price increases and market instability'. This exacerbated the global food crisis amid a 'period of record profit growth' by global food traders. It was clear, according to UNCTAD, that 'the fragmented and compromised set of regulatory norms governing the financial dimension of the global food trading industry has played a key role in enabling financial speculation, corporate arbitrage and profiteering in the global food industry since 2010'. There was a lack of regulatory oversight and 'a set of market-level, system-level and global governance reforms' were needed.[54] A Foodwatch report in 2011 already characterized the G20 effort as 'global governance at rock bottom'. The G20 was 'nothing more than a kind of discussion group in which decisions could only be reached by a consensus of all members'. The 'global governmental leadership that the

52   Zimmermann, Andrea, and George Rapsomanikis. 2023. 'Trade and Sustainable Food Systems.' In: Science and Innovations for Food Systems Transformation, ed. by Joachim von Braun, et al., 685–709. Cham: Springer, pp. 90-1.
53   Carles, Jacques, and Bastien Gibert. 17 November 2008. 'Financial Stability and Agricultural Markets Stability as Global Public Goods?' (www.momagri.org).
54   UNCTAD. 2023. Trade and Development Report 2023: Growth, Debt, and Climate: Realigning the Global Financial Architecture, pp. 72-5, 84, 93-6.

group is meant to provide', the report noted, 'can therefore only take place at the lowest possible level and via the lowest common denominator'. It was therefore no surprise that the outcomes were weak.[55] The G20, which is an informal group without even a permanent secretariat, is in any event unable to pass binding regulation—not for its own members, and most certainly not for other countries. At best it can achieve agreement on common political goals, which then results in coordinated national policy measures. The decisive factor for the heads of government is what they perceive as their priority national interests. For example, when during the financial crisis the banking sector received state guarantees and injections of capital amounting to billions, at the same time financial aid from the Eurozone countries for the World Food Programme was cut drastically. Jean Ziegler has rightly pointed out that heads of state can hardly be reproached for this, since they 'were not elected to fight world hunger' but to pursue national interests.[56] World parliamentarians, by contrast, would actually have a global mandate, and could be held politically accountable on the issue of world hunger.

The FAO, a World Food Board, and global food reserves

Similarly, the FAO, established in October 1945 as the first UN specialized agency, with responsibility for food and agriculture, has no global powers, and the WTO, the World Bank and the IMF have more influence on agricultural policy. Experts in the field have long complained that the FAO has been downgraded to an 'organ that observes, informs, develops proposals and regularly and repeatedly admonishes'. It would be hard to think of 'a more striking illustration of the deficit in the political management of the world order'.[57] Josué de Castro, who was at one time Chair of the Executive Committee of the FAO, complained that the organization was 'limited to a kind of international consultative function'.[58] The efforts to remedy this made by the first Director-General of the FAO, John Boyd Orr (1880 to 1971), a convinced world federalist, were frustrated by the resistance of the USA and Great Britain. This was the reason he stepped down from the post in April 1948. The following year, he was awarded the Nobel Peace Prize in recognition of his work. The fact that Boyd Orr's concerns continue to be just as relevant and urgent today is underlined by the total lack of progress in international politics over the last dec-

55 Schumann, Harald. 2011. Die Hungermacher. Wie Deutsche Bank, Goldman Sachs & Co. auf Kosten der Ärmsten mit Lebensmitteln spekulieren. Ed. by Foodwatch. Berlin: Foodwatch, pp. 66, 70.
56 Ziegler, p. 154.
57 Donner, Jochen. 2002. 'Ausgegipfelt? FAO: Fünf Jahre nach dem Welternährungsgipfel'. Vereinte Nationen (6): 220–222, p. 222.
58 Castro, p. 306.

ades. At the second FAO conference in Copenhagen in 1946, the Director-General proposed the establishment of a 'World Food Board'. In the opinion of John Shaw, the proposal 'remains one of the boldest and most imaginative plans for international action to achieve world food security'.[59] The Board was to regulate and stabilize prices on the international markets for the most important agricultural commodities by intervening to buy or sell when fixed upper and lower price limits were reached. So it would buy at times when supplies were high, and would sell when supplies were low. It would also build up and manage worldwide food reserves to be able to balance out any production bottlenecks and to ensure food security over the longer term. Excess supplies of basic foods which could not be sold on the markets would be used to feed especially needy people at subsidised prices. And finally the World Food Board would give long-term loans for food purchases and for bringing farming practices up to date, as well as supporting measures to increase production.[60]

In addition to combating purely speculative market participation, strategic worldwide food reserves are also particularly important for stability in the markets, as provision against poor harvests and humanitarian crises, and for maintaining and supporting international trade. The British economist John McClintock, who worked in Brussels for the European Commission, saw the joint management of worldwide food reserves as a potential first step towards worldwide integration. In the book 'The Uniting of Nations', he argued that the management of such reserve provisions is not merely a technical issue but brings with it a transfer of national sovereignty to the international level. If supply bottlenecks and unacceptable price rises occur in any country, one possible counter-measure is to put international reserves on the market there at low prices to take the pressure out of the situation. In order to prevent these goods being bought up cheaply by traders and then exported, export bans would have to apply. Issuing export restrictions of this kind that can be enforced internationally is a supranational matter.[61] In such a system, McClintock explained, there has to be a parliamentary body so that the citizens are democratically represented and proper oversight is provided.

Free trade, food security, and a world peace order

A trade system which is free and open but at the same time fair is very important for global food security. The trade system needs to make sure that

---

59   Shaw, p. xi.
60   See ibid., pp. 24ff;
61   McClintock, John. 2010. The Uniting of Nations: An Essay on Global Governance. 3rd ed., rev. and updated. Brussels et al.: Peter Lang, p. 231.

food can move from surplus to deficit regions globally. Research suggests that agricultural trade openness has, on average, 'a net positive impact on food security'. Trade restrictions imposed by many countries during the food price crisis actually worsened the situation and contributed to food price volatility.[62] A study by the International Food Policy Research Institute based in Washington D.C. identified as one of the main challenges posed by food security the fact that 'perceived national interest too often leads governments to hoard food stocks, artificially encourage production, and limit imports—ostensibly to buffer consumers from food shortages or swings in market prices and to preserve rural traditions'. Even where the international market offers an alternative and cheaper source of food, the study continues, 'the notion of dependence on external sources is anathema to many politicians and their constituents in both North and South. Food self-reliance and independence from foreign interference' are 'extremely popular forms of nationalism'. For the markets and for overall global food security, however, the consequences are counter productive. Although free and open trade will not of itself guarantee food security, since in some cases the necessary purchasing power must be ensured, it remains true that the 'collective consequence of hoarding and protection is actually to destabilize the international market'. In fact, all countries would benefit from open and free trade, but 'a deeper psychological aversion to dependence on foreign sources of goods' stands in its way. Food security, it is argued, is therefore dependent on a psychological question: whether one is prepared to rely on the existence of an open and free market and on supplies from external producers.[63] The world trading system and the institutional and legal arrangements for global food security must be able to ensure both factors. What this comes down to is the need to move beyond internationalism towards a trustworthy and reliable supranational order. Building up mutual trust is closely linked to the establishment of a world peace order, as we sketched out earlier. Fariborz Moshirian, an economic and financial expert who teaches at the Australian University of New South Wales, wrote quite correctly that 'if the UN is not able to establish a global system and a global environment in which all the nations of the world are able to enjoy universal peace and global security, the US, the EU and Japan will continue treating agricultural products as a national security issue and they will keep subsidizing their farmers in order that they do not have to rely on food coming from

---

62 Zimmermann and Rapsomanikis, pp. 687-8.
63 Runge, C. Ford, Benjamin Senauer, Philip G. Pardey, and Mark W. Rosegrant. 2003. Ending Hunger in Our Lifetime: Food Security and Globalization. Baltimore: Johns Hopkins University Press, pp. 105-108.

Africa or Asia, even if these two continents may have natural comparative advantages in agriculture products'.[64]

Concerns over not being able to rely on a free and open market were exacerbated during the food price crisis. Lester Brown identified a newly apparent 'geopolitics of food scarcity'. Exporting countries such as Argentina, Russia and Vietnam, he noted, had restricted or suspended their exports. In response, importing countries increased their efforts to purchase or lease farmland abroad via bilateral agreements to ensure their own food production.[65] During the price crisis, demand for arable land as a global investment and speculation asset grew strongly. Companies and investors are also concerned to ensure access. Since the relevant contracts are not always released into the public domain, it is hard to calculate the extent of what is called 'land grabbing'. Contracts often cover water rights, too, and apply to land that is already being cultivated by local farmers.

The Committee on World Food Security

Global food policy needs not only to be institutionally strengthened but also to be democratised. The interests of those affected by hunger and malnutrition, and of small farmers, must be given more weight. In this spirit, Olivier De Schutter declared at the presentation of his concluding report as UN Special Rapporteur in March 2014 that the 'greatest deficit in the food economy is the democratic one'. The food system, he argued, was efficient only in terms of profit maximization for the agribusiness companies. 'At the local, national and international levels, the policy environment must urgently accommodate alternative, democratically mandated visions.' In the area of global governance, the efforts undertaken by the Committee on World Food Security (CFS) were 'promising', he believed.[66] The CFS was set up at the World Food Conference in 1974 and is an advisory and coordinating body. Reforms in 2009 turned the Committee into a multi-constituency program which includes representatives of UN institutions, NGOs, research institutes, private sector associations and philanthropic foundations. Member governments, however, still have the final say in this arrangement. According to Schutter, perhaps the

64 Moshirian, Fariborz. 2003. 'Globalization and financial market integration'. Journal of Multinational Financial Management, 13: 289–302, p. 293.

65 Brown, Lester R. 2008. 'Jüngstes Gericht. Warum die Nahrungskrise den Anfang vom Ende unserer Kultur markieren könnte'. Internationale Politik, November: 18–35, pp. 20-2 and Brown, Lester R. 2012. Full planet, empty plates: the new geopolitics of food scarcity. 1st ed. New York and London: W.W. Norton & Company, pp. 12-4.

66 Schutter, Olivier De. 10 March 2014. 'Democracy and diversity can mend broken food systems - final diagnosis from UN right to food expert' (www.srfood.org).

most immediate success of CFS 'is the fact that it brings together such a wide variety of stakeholders' which stimulates 'a process of collective learning across different constituencies'.[67] In 2012, in response to land grabbing, the CFS passed 'voluntary guidelines on the responsible governance of tenure of land, fisheries and forests' which are aimed principally at ensuring the observance and protection of 'legitimate' leasehold, freehold and usage rights. Although the drawing up of these guidelines represents an important step, there can be no question of their constituting an effective weapon against land grabs. The implementation of these and other 'voluntary guidelines' is left to the discretion of member states. What is needed instead are sufficiently specific and *binding* global regulations. It has long been recognized, as the agricultural economists Joachim von Braun and Regina Birner noted, that 'in the absence of a global government', 'global action in support of the agricultural and food systems' is subject to the free-rider problem related to the management of public goods.[68]

The issue of multistakeholder governance

The multi-constituency approach of the CFS puts global food policy on a broad foundation and in comparison with the work of other, more insular international bodies it can be considered a step forward. A person familiar with its operations was quoted saying it was a 'debating society' and by design unable to bring about fundamental change.[69] On the other hand, when the CFS was bypassed and not included in the UN's Food Systems Summit first organized by the UN Secretary-General in 2021, this was interpreted by some observers as 'an effort by a powerful alliance of multinational corporations, philanthropies, and export-oriented countries to subvert the growing power' of the body. The observers pointed out that the summit not only evaded existing structures like the CFS but also created new ones in parallel, featuring a 'puzzling combination of top-down closed decision-making' and 'simply opening the door to anyone who wants to participate'. In their view, the UN food systems summit was 'rife with actual and potential conflicts of interest' as its multistakeholder design allowed representatives of profit-oriented agribusiness compa-

---

67 Schutter, 24 January 2014, p. 18.

68 Braun, Joachim von, and Regina Birner. 2017. 'Designing Global Governance for Agricultural Development and Food and Nutrition Security.' Review of Development Economics 21 (2): 265–84, p. 272.

69 Welsh, Teresa. 31 July 2023. 'Is the Committee on World Food Security Fit for Purpose?' Devex. (devex.com).

nies and their associations to take considerable influence.[70] Most civil society groups involved in the CFS and many experts on food policy boycotted the event and its ongoing follow up process.

The UN Food Systems Summit has become an important example of a misguided approach to 'multi-stakeholderism' where very different 'stakeholders' interested in or affected by an issue participate in policy-making processes on an 'imaginary level playing field'.[71] The primary goal is often to involve corporate actors from the private sector based on the claim that they are efficient problem solvers with potentially big impact and considerable resources at their disposal. Governments and international institutions such as the UN supposedly need them to figure out appropriate policies and for implementation. But multistakeholder platforms 'undermine the clear responsibilities of governments and replace political participation with a model that lacks clear rules of participation, subverts traditional means of political representation and erases mechanisms of accountability', the researchers Matthew Canfield, Molly D. Anderson and Philip McMichael noted. Corporations that are 'obliged to maximize profits for its shareholders' should never be allowed to 'usurp the public interest', they believe.[72] According to Harris Gleckman, an associate at the Transnational Institute and former head of UNCTAD's office in New York, the UN, and UN Secretary-General Guterres in particular, have been strongly supportive of the concept nonetheless. A 'strategic partnership' concluded in 2019 between the UN and the World Economic Forum, was denounced by hundreds of civil society organizations, among them the Transnational Institute, as 'a form of corporate capture' of the UN as it would allow corporate leaders private access to 'the heads of UN system departments' and move the world 'toward WEF's aspirations for multistakeholderism becoming the effective replacement of multilateralism.'[73] In fact, a report of the WEF's Global Redesign Initiative one year later not only made proposals on fifty global issues but concluded that 'the time has come for a new stakeholder paradigm of international governance analogous to that embodied in the stakeholder theory of corporate governance'.[74] In connection with the preparations of the UN's 2024 Summit for the Future a group of develop-

---

70 Canfield, Matthew, Molly D. Anderson, and Philip McMichael. 2021. "UN Food Systems Summit 2021: Dismantling Democracy and Resetting Corporate Control of Food Systems." Frontiers in Sustainable Food Systems 5. (frontiersin.org), pp. 2, 9, 11.

71 Ibid., p. 9.

72 Ibid., pp. 10, 11.

73 'End the United Nations/World Economic Forum Partnership Agreement. Open Letter to Mr António Guterres, Secretary General of the United Nations.' 25 Sep. 2019. (tni.org).

74 World Economic Forum. 2010. Everybody's Business: Strengthening International Cooperation in a More Interdependent World Report of the Global Redesign Initiative. Cologny/Geneva, p. 9.

ing countries started pushing back and 'erased the proposed lead role for multistakeholderism' at least in this UN process.[75] In a book on 'Multistakeholder Governance and Democracy', Gleckman emphasized the need to distinguish between *multi-constituency consultations* and *multistakeholder governance* even if in practice the boundaries sometimes were fluid. He explained that a multi-constituency consultative arrangement 'works under the authority of nation-states and takes its frame of reference from a governmental or UN system body' whereas a multistakeholder governance arrangement seeks to set standards and regulations 'largely independent of a public governance system'. While 'soliciting the views of non-state actors from a very wide diversity of constituencies is well within traditional democratic practice', at the domestic level as well as at the UN, 'contemporary multi-stakeholderism, no matter how it is practiced' rests on 'clearly non-democratic features' according to Gleckman. Measured against 'the practices of democracy that currently operate in national democracies and in the multilateral system', multi-stakeholder projects were 'largely retrograde'.[76] While multi-stakeholder discussions certainly may have merit, the approach is not viable as a *governance model*. Ultimately, global rules must have popular legitimacy that is based on the will of the people. It is not acceptable to circumvent this will in vague self-selected multi-stakeholder processes or to degrade elected representatives to one stakeholder group among many, if they are considered at all.

A world parliament and democratizing global food policy

In terms of democratizing global food policy the CFS does not go far enough. According to Hilal Elver, Schutter's successor as special rapporteur on the right to food until 2020, 'an elected UN Parliamentary Assembly' may be a means to give those suffering from hunger, the most vulnerable members of our global community, 'a stronger voice so that the systemic international causes of their misery can be more adequately addressed'. Multi-constituency arrangements such as the CFS ultimately should feed into an inclusive *global parliamentary process* that provides a degree of public deliberation and legitimacy that is required to underpin binding global regulation in the field.

In the area of global food security, a world parliament would represent not only an important supervisory and monitoring authority, with respect for example to the proposed World Food Board, but at the same time it would serve as a body mandated to adopt regulation under world law such as a global

---

75　Gleckman, Harris. 3 Aug. 2023. 'A Corporate Takeover of the UN Must Be Stopped.' Al Jazeera, (aljazeera.com).

76　Id. 2018. Multistakeholder Governance and Democracy: A Global Challenge. Routledge, ch. 1, 6.

convention on food security that supercedes, supplements and goes beyond existing agreements. This should include a restriction of futures markets to producers, dealers and buyers of a commodity and the exclusion of financial speculators. A world parliament would necessarily also deal with world trade issues, and as a first step, until such time as it would have acquired legislative competences under world law, a UN parliamentary body should take part in WTO negotiations in an advisory capacity. A world trade committee of this body should be able to send its own delegation, with full participation rights. As a matter of principle, the promotion of a world trade system which is as free as possible is an important objective. But the world trading regime has to be far better aligned with goals such as global food security, for example with respect to issues such as facilitating local food production, agricultural subsidies, and price dumping. In particular, consideration needs to be given to the concerns expressed in the concept of 'food sovereignty' which farmers' movements and others have been promoting since the 1996 World Food Summit.[77] In 1999, during the protests against the WTO conference in Seattle, Luis Cabrera—at that time an AP reporter, today a professor of political science—was surprised that most of the demonstrators were calling for an end to the word trade negotiations, or even the dissolution of the WTO. 'Why weren't there more groups', he asked in a book on a 'cosmopolitan case for the world state', 'calling for the WTO's supranational powers to be used to help improve the lives of those in less affluent states by linking membership benefits to observance of labor and environmental standards, as well as core human rights?'[78] Members of a UNPA in an initial step would be able to advocate precisely for such an approach. The conference on world trade issues organised by the IPU and the European Parliament since 2003 has proved ineffective and unfit for purpose. No significant initiatives have originated from the event and its influence on global trade discussions is marginal at best. In 2018, attendees called on WTO members to establish 'a formal working relationship' with the conference which indicated that even 15 years after its creation such still did not exist.[79]

---

77 See e.g. Windfuhr, Michael, and Jennie Jonsén. 2005. Food Sovereignty: Towards Democracy in Localized Food Systems. Rugby, Warwickshire: ITDG Publishing and Agarwal, Bina. 2014. 'Food Sovereignty, Food Security and Democratic Choice: Critical Contradictions, Difficult Conciliations.' The Journal of Peasant Studies 41 (6): 1247–68.

78 Cabrera, Luis. 2004. Political Theory of Global Justice: A Cosmopolitan Case for the World State. London: Routledge, p. xiii.

79 IPU, and European Parliament. 7 Dec. 2018. WTO: The Way Forward. Outcome Document. 2018 Annual Session of the Parliamentary Conference on the WTO, item 12.

21.

Global water policy and governance

The state of water supply

Along with food, water is fundamental to human survival and to civilization. Our daily drinking water is our most important nutrient, and water is indispensable for agriculture, industry and energy production. 'Basic access to water', according to the Italian social scientist and water rights activist Ricardo Petrella, 'is a fundamental political, economic and social right for both individuals and collectives, since the biological, economic and social security of every human being and every human community depends upon enjoyment of that right.'[1] The first UN conference on water, in Mar del Plata in Argentina, declared in 1977 that 'all peoples, whatever their stage of development and their social and economic conditions, have the right to have access to drinking water in quantities and of a quality equal to their basic needs', and called in an action plan for national governments to commit to a target of full implementation of this right by 1990.[2] This did not happen though. As part of the Millennium Development Goals the target in 2000 was then set to at least halve the proportion of people in the world without permanent access to hygienic drinking water by 2015 compared to 1990. In 2010, the UN General Assembly recognised the human right 'to safe and clean drinking water and sanitation' and declared that it was 'deeply concerned' that approximately 884 million people, or around 12.7 per cent, lacked access to safe drinking water and that more than 2.6 billion, or around 37 per cent, did not have access to basic sanitation.[3] Nonetheless, these figures, as the UN provided and interpreted them, meant that the 2015 target had already been achieved at that point. But experts expressed scepticism. Most importantly, a realistic estimate should not be based on the condition of the water source, but on the water actually used, which is often contaminated on the way to the user. A study cited by the UN in the 2014 World Water Development Report concluded that the number of people with unreliable access to water in the reference year 2010 actually was

1   Petrella, Riccardo. 2001. The Water Manifesto. Transl. by Patrick Camiller. London: Zed Books, p. 58
2   Report of the United Nations Water Conference. 1977. E/CONF.70/29. New York: United Nations, pp. 66, 68.
3   United Nations. 28 July 2010. 'The human right to water and sanitation'. A/RES/64/292.

about *three billion*—nearly four times as many as previously indicated.[4] This underscores the challenges in collecting, analyzing and interpreting relevant data. According to the sixth Sustainable Development Goal, adopted in 2015, the new agreed global target is to ensure safe drinking water and sanitation for all by 2030. At midpoint in 2023 the UN reported that progress was 'alarmingly off track' and 'well below the pace needed'. In 2022, 2.2 billion people still lacked drinking water services 'that were accessible on premises, available when needed and free from contamination', the UN noted. In addition, only around 57 per cent of the world's population used adequate sanitation in 2022 and approximately 1.5 billion people still lacked 'even basic sanitation services' according to the UN. Rates of progress indicated that by 2030 two billion people would still be left without safe water services and three billion without proper sanitation.[5] Water stress is a measure of the ratio of water demand to renewable supply. According to data from the World Resource Institute, approximately 2.6 billion people in 47 countries, or over a third of the world's population, live under conditions of high or extremely high water stress. In the former case, at least 40 per cent of renewable supply is being used up and in the latter at least 80 per cent. The institute predicts the number living under such extreme stress will increase by one billion by 2050.[6] The Global Commission on the Economics of Water, a group of independent experts and policy makers convened by the government of the Netherlands, believes that the world faces 'the prospect of a 40 per cent shortfall in freshwater supply by 2030'.[7]

Water as a global common good

The use of freshwater resources found in rivers, lakes, reservoirs or aquifers, the so-called 'blue water', is subject to natural limits. In addition, interventions in water cycles, such as those caused by overuse, land degradation or deforestation, have far-reaching consequences for the functioning of terrestrial and aquatic ecosystems. These are essential for storing carbon, growing plants, feeding animals, or sustaining biodiversity as well as natural processes such as evaporation or precipitation. At an aggregate level, they have an impact on global climate regulation and Earth system dynamics. As mentioned

---

4   Onda, Kyle, Joe LoBuglio, and Jamie Bartram. 14 March 2012. 'Global Access to Safe Water: Accounting for
     Water Quality and the Resulting Impact on MDG Progress'. International Journal of Environmental Research and Public Health (9) 3: 880–94, pp. 887, 892.
5   United Nations. 2023. 'Sustainable Development Goal 6 Synthesis Report on Water and Sanitation 2023.'
     (unwater.org), pp. x, xi, 29.
6   Kuzma, Samantha, Liz Saccoccia, and Marlena Chertock. 16 Aug. 2023. '25 Countries, Housing One-
     Quarter of the Population, Face Extremely High Water Stress.' World Resources Institute (wri.org).
7   Global Commission on the Economics of Water. 2023. 'Turning the Tide: A Call to Collective Action'
     (watercommission.org), p. 10.

before, water is considered one of the nine Earth system regulators of the planetary boundaries framework.[8] Under additional consideration of the status of 'green water', which is present in the soil and available to plants, researchers have come to the conclusion that the water-related boundary has already been transgressed.[9] According to Johan Rockström and his co-authors, anthropogenic pressures are pushing Earth's water cycle 'out of balance'. For this reason, they argue, 'a radical shake-up in how water is governed, managed and valued, from local to global scales' is required. The key change is to recast water and the global water cycle as a 'global common good'. That means 'states establishing an obligation under international law to protect the global water cycle for all people and generations, and acknowledging that actions in one place have impacts in another—for instance, that deforestation in Brazil affects rainfall in Peru', Rockström and his colleagues wrote. Interdependence, they noted, goes beyond transboundary issues of 'blue water' governance related to rivers or lakes and extends to the entire water cycle.[10] A report by the Global Commission on the Economics of Water, co-chaired by Rockström, highlighted, for instance, that countries 'are interconnected via atmospheric moisture pathways directing evaporation through the atmosphere to precipitation in downwind areas, creating so-called precipitation sheds (source areas) and evaporation sheds (sink areas) of rainfall'. No country would rely 'on its own territory as the source for more than half its rainfall'.[11]

Water, peace and trade

The Commission found that the water cycle is 'a global common good linking all 17 Sustainable Development Goals' as it is 'one of the essentials for all life on Earth and for a just, sustainable and resilient economy'.[12] Water in particular also concerns peace and security. Increasing water stress in many regions of the world is feeding the fear of escalating conflicts over water and of a destabilising impact on international relations. The Indian geostrategist Brahama Chellaney of the Center for Policy Research in New Delhi argued that this represented one of the most important security policy challenges for the world community. As world water resources become scarcer and the competi-

---

8   See pp. 214-216.
9   Wang-Erlandsson, Lan, Arne Tobian, Ruud J. van der Ent, et al. 2022. 'A Planetary Boundary for Green Water.' Nature Reviews Earth & Environment 3 (6): 380–92.
10   Rockström, Johan, Mariana Mazzucato, Lauren Seaby Andersen, Simon Felix Fahrländer, and Dieter Gerten. 2023. 'Why We Need a New Economics of Water as a Common Good.' Nature 615 (7954): 794–97.
11   Global Commission, Turning the Tide, pp. 11, 14.
12   Id. 2023. 'The What, Why and How of the World Water Crisis', p. 4.

tion between states to control them intensifies, water wars would become more likely, though not necessarily with open resort to force. Instead, the use of 'armed militants or irregular forces' was more likely. It was probably not a coincidence, moreover, that many failing states were among those of the world's countries with the poorest water supply. 'The twenty-first century', wrote Chellaney, 'will be a defining epoch for how humanity manages and addresses its grave water challenges. Ensuring adequate freshwater availability to underpin continued progress has become critical to the future well-being of human civilization.'[13]

The availability of water is not only necessary for agriculture and food processing but directly or indirectly for every good produced. For each good it is possible to calculate a 'water footprint' that measures the water used to produce the good throughout the production chain. This approach ties in with the concept of 'virtual water', first introduced in 1993 by the British geographer John Allan, which highlights that trade in goods results in worldwide 'virtual water flows'. As an example, Allan pointed out that about 1,000 cubic meters of water are required to produce a ton of grain so if a country imports grain, it is spared the stress of mobilizing the equivalent need of water.[14] This demonstrates that world trade issues are also water policy issues, and this is especially the case with regard to water-intensive agricultural products. 'The studies on international virtual water trade show that water should be regarded as a global resource', wrote Arjen Hoekstra, who was a Professor for Water Management at the University of Twente in Enschede in the Netherlands and pioneered the idea of a 'water footprint'. He identified climate change, trade liberalization and privatization in the water sector as the most important factors giving water governance 'a true global dimension'.[15] Among other things, the Global Commission on the Economics of Water recommended that 'mandatory water disclosure requirements' should be adopted in order to achieve transparency of water footprints.[16] In the view of Petra Dobner, a political scientist who teaches in Halle in Germany, another factor arguing for the globalization of water policy is the fact that 'the sustainable management of global water resources is beyond the legal and practical capacities of individual states'. 'This applies not only to water systems that cross state borders', Dob-

13   Chellaney, Brahma. 2013. Water, Peace, and War: Confronting the Global Water Crisis. Lanham: Rowman & Littlefield, pp. 47, 54, xiv, 38.

14   Allan, J. A. (Tony). 2003. 'Virtual Water - the Water, Food, and Trade Nexus. Useful Concept or Misleading Metaphor?' Water International 28 (1): 4–11, p. 5.

15   Hoekstra, A. Y. 2006. The global dimension of water governance: Nine reasons for global arrangements in order to cope with local water problems. Delft: UNESCO-IHE Institute for Water Education, pp. 15, 27.

16   Global Commission, Turning the Tide, p. 22.

ner wrote in a book on global water policy, 'but also to a multiplicity of social, ecological and economic factors which affect either the global water balance or the global management of water.'[17]

The deficits in water governance and a world parliament

Since access to water is not a matter of choice but an existential necessity, Ricardo Petrella, in a 'Water Manifesto' published as early as 1999, called for it to be recognised as 'a common global heritage of humanity'. 'The control of water', he wrote, 'must be given to its true owners, to the inhabitants of planet Earth. It does not belong to nation states, nor to markets, corporations or shareholders. It belongs to human communities, from the smallest (villages) to the largest (the global community).' The water problem is above all a problem of democracy and solidarity, he argued. For that reason, a core demand of the manifesto, in addition to the establishment of an international water tribunal, is for the introduction 'as soon as possible' of a World Water Parliament. In its initial phase, the World Water Parliament could provide a kind of global public hearing to produce a comprehensive review of rights and duties with respect to water and to debate scenarios to drive forward sustainable, equitable and mutually supportive solutions. The manifesto suggests that the members could initially be appointed by national parliaments.[18]

Global water policy is only poorly developed to date, and badly fragmented. There is no competent body within the UN, only the network 'UN Water', formed in 2003 and comprising about 30 UN institutions and around two dozen NGOs. As a group of experts pointed out in a critical review of global water governance, UN Water is not there to make binding decisions. 'Existing global institutions addressing water are very weak in terms of regulation, but they are relatively good at agenda setting, sharing information, mobilizing people, and, to a certain degree, in mobilizing resources', it stated. That, however, is not enough to meet the challenges in their view. 'In fact, today's reluctance to enter into any kind of regulatory framework may generate the need for harsh regulatory measures tomorrow to cope with an aggravated water crisis as the result of present insufficient action.'[19] A decade later, the Global Commission on the Economics of Water confirmed again that 'today's global governance architecture for water is not fit for purpose. It is fragmented, siloed

---

17 Dobner, Petra. Wasserpolitik. Zur politischen Theorie, Praxis and Kritik globaler Governance. Berlin: Suhrkamp, 2010, p. 16.
18 Petrella, pp. 8, 106-109.
19 Dellapenna, Joseph W., Joyeeta Gupta, Wenjing Li, and Falk Schmidt. 2013. 'Thinking about the Future of Global Water Governance'. Ecology and Society (18) 3, p. 3.

and underinvested in'. A dialogue was necessary 'towards the establishment of longer-term structural governance alternatives', the Commission noted.[20]

As Petra Dobner explained in her book, global water policy is 'an object lesson' illustrating 'the lack of forms, institutions and ideas' of global governance that could 'democratically legitimise the transfer of decision-making away from the state level into transnational forums'. Water policy, she believes, is decisively influenced by a shift in the locus of the political debate and in the referential framework from the state to an elite 'global water network' made up of what she calls 'multi-sectoral and multi-level constellations of actors'. Policy fields such as water thereby fall into what she sees as 'the institutional and legitimational black hole of unripe institutions of global democracy'. Her unambiguous conclusion was that the existing global water governance network 'has no democratic legitimacy'. One of the bodies that has stepped in to fill the gap or political vacuum created in part by the UN is the non-governmental World Water Forum, which has met every three years since 1997, operating with a broad, participative multi-stakeholder approach that includes representatives of the water industries. In Dobner's view, the one thousand conference participants principally serve to 'act out a performance that mimics legitimation', as the outcomes have already been decided in advance by a small circle of like-minded leading members of the water network who in her view pursue a privatization agenda as favoured by the water industry. Massive resistance towards this agenda has simply been 'brushed aside'. The claim that a consensus has been reached 'can therefore only be considered valid for the participating elites'. The multi-stakeholder participation is thus a form of 'legitimacy phishing'. Dobner summed it up in a nutshell when she wrote that 'democratic participation and democratic legitimacy cannot consist merely in attending mega-conferences along with 30,000 other interested parties but remaining excluded from the decision-making process'.[21] Privatization of the water supply as a policy aimed at solving the water crisis is in fact highly controversial, and—as we have seen—the global water situation is hardly convincing evidence of good governance. The manifesto of the first 'alternative water forum', held in Florence in 2003, called by contrast for water to be recognised as a global common good and for privatization to be halted. Additionally, it noted that 'citizens must be able to participate directly in the management of water and ecosystems, at local and global levels'. 'Such participation', ran the manifesto, 'could be furthered by the creation of a world wa-

---

20   Global Commission, Turning the Tide, pp. 26-7.
21   Dobner, pp. 28, 348-9, 283, 329-30, 307, 336, 326-7., 351.

ter parliament.'[22] At the time, there appeared to be broad agreement on the need for a world water parliament. At the fifth official World Water Forum, too, in Istanbul in 2009, over two hundred delegates also declared themselves to be in favour.[23] But after this, it seems the proposal vanished from the agenda and no further action was taken. Dobner, however, is not convinced by the argument for a specialized world water parliament. She fears that it would not differ greatly from the format of the World Water Forum, even if its political orientation might well be different. As a matter of principle, she believes that it is problematic for a parliamentary style body to be restricted to a particular sector. One reason for this is the resulting political and institutional fragmentation. By contrast, she saw a UN parliament as an 'excellent' idea.

The proposal for the establishment of a specialized world water parliament should be revived and merged with the wider goal of a world parliament. Given the critical relevance of water governance in numerous policy fields, including climate change mitigation, trade and food security, a broad approach is important. A world parliament could serve as the foundational element for legitimate regulation in the water sector under binding global law. To this end it would establish a dedicated portfolio committee on water to take the lead and to fulfil exactly the deliberative role envisaged for the proposed world water parliament. This committee would interact and consult with other relevant committees set up by the parliament as well as other bodies and stakeholders. Its work would be part of a formal legislative process. If water is to be properly managed as a global common good, a common democratic body of humanity will be needed for this. An initial global parliamentary assembly could build up political pressure for action even as a consultative body and by addressing relevant issues such as the desirability of a UN water organization. However, 'if you are serious about globalising democracy', Dobner said bluntly, 'then the answer can only be to endow the parliament with real powers.'

---

22 'Manifeste du Forum Alternatif Mondial de l'Eau: Pour une autre politique de l'eau'. Magazine H2o, March 2003 (www.h2o.net).
23 5th World Water Forum. 2009. 'Parliamentarians Process: Proposals emerging from Parliaments for Water'.

22.

The elimination of poverty, and social security for all

Poverty as the key problem

The elimination of poverty and of existential misery is the basis for a humane, just, peaceful and safe world, in which all people have the opportunity of education, political participation and self-fulfilment. Poverty is a major cause of hunger and inadequate access to drinking water, poor health care, inadequate education, a lack of family planning, and political instability. As a rule, a higher standard of living is associated with lower birth rates, meaning that overcoming poverty can contribute to slowing down population growth. The political scientist Frank Nuscheler believes that 'the correlation between high population growth and a series of interdependent poverty indicators' suggests strongly that 'poverty is the key problem for population and development policy'.[1] In the view of the Bangladeshi economist Muhammad Yunus, who was awarded the Nobel Peace Prize for his role as a pioneer of microcredit for the poorest, 'poverty is perhaps the most serious threat to world peace, even more dangerous than terrorism, religious fundamentalism, ethnic hatred, political rivalries, or any of the other forces that are often cited as promoting violence and war'. 'Poverty', wrote Yunus, 'leads to hopelessness, which provokes people to desperate acts.'[2] At the top of his wish list was the establishment of a global government to see that 'all parts of the world enjoy the similar quality of life' and to 'protect the interest of all living beings on the planet', among other things.[3]

The state of poverty and its multidimensional nature

Overcoming poverty has been on the international agenda for a long time. At the foundation of the International Labour Organization (ILO) during the Versailles Peace Conference in 1919, it was stated that universal peace 'can be established only if it is based upon social justice'.[4] The Atlantic Charter adopt-

1   Nuscheler, Franz. November 2008. 'Armut'. Online-Handbuch Demografie, Berlin-Institut für Bevölkerung and Entwicklung, November 2008 (www.berlin-institut.org).

2   Yunus, Muhammad. 2007. Creating a world without poverty: social business and the future of capitalism. New York: PublicAffairs, p. 105.

3   'Professor Yunus's Wish List', (muhammadyunus.org). Accessed on 13 Jan. 2018.

4   Versailles Peace Treaty, 28 June 1919, part XIII., ch. 1, before article 387.

ed by the Inter-Allied Council in 1941 declared as one of its goals 'that all the men in all the lands may live out their lives in freedom from fear and want'. The Charter of the United Nations speaks of international cooperation for the solution of economic and social problems, and elaborates on this in the ninth Chapter to say that 'stability and well-being' are prerequisites for peace. The United Nations should therefore work to promote 'higher standards of living, full employment, and conditions of economic and social progress and development'. As already mentioned, Article 25 of the Universal Declaration of Human Rights and Article 11 of the International Covenant on Economic, Social and Cultural Rights include the right to a standard of living adequate for health and well-being. Everybody should be able to meet their basic needs. The first of the Sustainable Development Goals, in short SDGs, included in the Agenda 2030, adopted by the UN in 2015, is the eradication of extreme poverty 'for all people everywhere'.

The international poverty line, as used by the United Nations to track progress, is based on the World Bank definition. It is reached by calculating the median of the absolute poverty thresholds of the world's poorest countries, converted into US dollars. Due to variations in the local purchasing power of the US dollar and to changes in the uniform basket of goods on which the calculations are based, since the method was introduced in 1990 the line has been adjusted upwards from one dollar per day in 1990 to 1.25 dollars in 2008, 1.90 in 2015 and 2.15 in 2022. Since the latest change it is based on the data of 28 countries, before it was 15.At the halfway point of the Agenda 2030, extreme poverty had experienced a strong decline in the past decades. According to World Bank data, the proportion of people in the world living in extreme poverty measured by the 2.15 dollars threshold has fallen from 37.8 per cent in 1990 to 9 per cent in 2019. But there are significant regional differences. In East Asia and the Pacific, for example, the decline was from 65.8 to 1.1 per cent and in Sub-Saharan Africa from 53.8 to 35.4 per cent, much less in comparison. In the Middle East and North Africa, poverty actually has been rising since 2010, from 1.8 to 9.6 per cent in 2018.[5] Even before COVID-19, the speed of extreme poverty reduction was slowing down according to the UN, from an average annual global reduction rate of 1.28 per cent from 2000 to 2014 to 0.54 per cent from 2015 to 2019. In 2020, an increase to 724 million people reversed three years of progress. Projections indicate that in 2030, 575 million people will still live in extreme poverty worldwide.[6] In his conclusive

---

5   World Bank. Poverty and Inequality Platform. Poverty headcount ratio2017 PPP) (pip.worldbank.org). Accessed on 29 Jan. 2024.
6   United Nations Department of Economic and Social Affairs. 2023. The Sustainable Development Goals Report 2023: Special Edition. The Sustainable Development Goals Report, p. 12.

report to the UN, then rapporteur on extreme poverty and human rights, Australian law professor Philip Alston, warned not to celebrate progress in poverty reduction based on the World Bank's international poverty line because those figures would 'underpin a misleading picture'. First of all, he pointed out, this poverty line was well below the national poverty lines of 'most countries' and thus generated 'dramatically lower numbers in poverty'. Further, the international poverty line, at 1.90 dollars at the time of the report, was 'well below any reasonable conception of life with dignity' and this low standard was 'a world apart from the one set by human rights law and embodied in the Charter of the United Nations'. Even meeting food and housing costs under that line could be 'extremely difficult, if not impossible, in certain countries', he wrote. Alston referred to a 'societal poverty line' introduced by the World Bank in 2018 tailored to the level of development in each country. Under this measure, the poverty headcount in absolute terms remained nearly stagnant. In terms of share in world population it declined from 44.5 to 28.5 per cent between 1990 and 2015 but at much slower rates than extreme poverty. All in all, Alston concluded that the world was 'not even close to ending poverty' and climate change would make a 'mockery' of projections that anticipate extreme poverty will stand at 6 per cent in 2030.[7]

Addressing extreme poverty requires a multi-dimensional effort focussing on a simultaneous improvement of numerous development parameters some of which are covered by the SDGs. One such parameter is housing infrastructure. UN-Habitat estimates that over one billion people live in slums with inadequate infrastructure. This includes water supply infrastructure and sanitation facilities, as already discussed. According to UN-Habitat the share of the urban population living in informal settlements decreased at an annual rate of 1.7 per cent from 2008 to 2016. But the trend significantly slowed down to only 0.4 per cent in subsequent years.[8] Access to electricity, banking services, state services as well as the legal system are further examples. The global share of people with access to electricity has improved significantly from nearly 73 per cent in 2000 to almost 90 per cent in 2022. From 2018 onwards, the trend has slowed down, too, and in 2022, the number increased for the first time in decades according to estimates from the International Energy Agency.[9] The share of adults who had an account at a bank or a regulated banking institution increased from 51 per cent in 2011 to 76 per cent in 2021,

7   Alston, Philip. 2020. 'The Parlous State of Poverty Eradication. Report of the Special Rapporteur on Extreme Poverty and Human Rights.' UN Doc. A/HRC/44/40, paras. 8, 10, 12, 14, 23.
8   UN Habitat. 2023. 'Rescuing SDG 11 for a Resilient Urban Planet.' (data.unhabitat.org), p. 19.
9   Cozzi, Laura, and et al. 15 Sept. 2023. 'Access to Electricity Improves Slightly in 2023, but Still Far from the Pace Needed to Meet SDG7.' International Energy Agency. (iea.org).

a trend facilitated by the availability of mobile money services. Nonetheless, this means that 1.4 billion people still have no proper banking access.[10] The OECD reported that around 1.9 billion people, 24 per cent of the world's population and 73 per cent of the very poorest, live in 'fragile contexts', where basic state functions are only poorly developed.[11] For the very poorest, the basic structures of the rule of law are available only to a rudimentary degree, but they are of crucial importance. The international Commission on Legal Empowerment of the Poor supported by UNDP stressed in 2008 that 'four billion people around the world are robbed of the chance to better their lives and climb out of poverty, because they are excluded from the rule of law'. A particular problem is that of weak land property rights which are extremely difficult to enforce. One of the Commission's recommendations was a 'Global Legal Empowerment Compact' that would codify fundamental rights, together with a framework for their enforcement on an international basis.[12] A report of the multistakeholder 'Task Force for Justice' around ten years later found that 5.1 billion people—two thirds of the world's population—lack 'meaningful access to justice'.[13] To the extent that data was available for the indicators tracked in this field, the UN reported in 2023 that 'little or no progress' had been made in 'promoting peaceful and inclusive societies, providing access to justice for all and building effective, accountable and inclusive institutions at all levels' since the SDGs were adopted.[14] A 'multidimensional poverty line' introduced by the World Bank in 2018 includes five indicators of well-being related to education and access to basic infrastructure such as electricity, sanitation and drinking water, in addition to a monetary measure, but available data thus far only covers around half the world's population.[15]

The need for a new approach to development assistance

According to the so-called 'Monterrey Consensus', named after the Mexican city that in 2002 hosted a UN conference on 'financing for development', a

---

10　Demirguc-Kunt, Asli, and Leora Klapper, et al. 2022. 'The Global Findex Database 2021'. World Bank Group, p. 3.

11　Organisation for Economic Cooperation and Development. 2022. States of Fragility 2022. Paris: OECD. Online version. (oecd-ilibrary.org).

12　Commission on Legal Empowerment of the Poor, and United Nations Development Programme (ed.). 2008. Making the Law Work for Everyone. Report of the Commission on Legal Empowerment of the Poor. Vol. I, pp. 1, 10, 34-6, 86.

13　Task Force on Justice. 2019. 'Justice for All - Final Report.' Center on International Cooperation, p. 18.

14　UNODC, OHCHR, and UNDP. 2023. 'Global Progress Report on Sustainable Development Goal 16 Indicators'. (undp.org), p. 10.

15　World Bank Group. 2022. 'Poverty and Shared Prosperity 2022', p. 98.

'substantial increase' in official development assistance is required in order to achieve internationally agreed development goals, among them the eradication of poverty. Developed countries are supposed to mobilize the equivalent of 0.7 per cent of their GDP per year for this purpose. This was confirmed by subsequent UN conferences such as those in Doha in 2008 and Addis Ababa in 2015. The 0.7 per cent target was first mentioned in a UN General Assembly resolution in 1970. The actual sum is equivalent to around 0.2 per cent and there is more and more scepticism. A paradigm shift in development policy and in the battle against poverty may be indispensable if the goal of the total elimination of poverty is to be reached. Consideration must be given to the political lessons to be learned from the fundamental dispute over the benefits and drawbacks of official development assistance, as exemplified by the best-selling book 'Dead Aid' by the Zambian economist Dambisa Moyo. As the decades-long experience with public development aid in Africa convincingly showed, Moyo argued, aid is not part of the solution, but rather a major part of the problem. Her unsparing conclusion was that, in the final analysis, development aid in Africa led to corruption and political dependence, fuelled conflicts over the control of state power, undermined the efficiency of public administration, damaged business, and choked off economic development and growth. The former German diplomat Volker Seitz pointed out that between 1960 and 2006 up to 2.3 trillion US dollars flowed into Sub-Saharan Africa, six times as much per head as went to Europe under the Marshall Plan, without bringing about any discernible improvement in living conditions in his opinion.[16] In the decade between 2010 and 2019, the OECD recorded official aid in the order of 1.4 trillion globally.[17] One step that needs to be done is to bring international anti-poverty campaigns and development policy closer to the people affected. The poor need a voice in international affairs. This means establishing ways of representation and participation that bypass recipient governments that often control the use of development aid. Having impoverished people and communities directly represented in a parliamentary assembly at the world level will help improve their situation and put the debate on a new footing. 'The best way to give the poor a real voice is through a world parliament', argued George Monbiot in the *Guardian*, and he added: 'there is a growing recognition in Africa that a world parliament offers the best chance—perhaps

16 Seitz, Volker. 2009. *Afrika wird armregiert oder wie man Afrika wirklich helfen kann.* 2nd ed. München: dtv, p. 65.
17 OECD Data Explorer. Online. (oecd.org).

the only chance—that the unmediated concerns of the poor will reach the ears of the rich'.[18]

Economic growth is not enough

Traditional thinking holds that economic growth will help lift the poorest out of poverty. Yet, the gains from growth are unevenly distributed in societies and often reach the poorest last and least. Relying on general economic growth and a resultant rise in average incomes to eliminate extreme poverty on its own is not a promising approach. The economist David Woodward extrapolated from the growth figures from 1993 to 2008 that it would take over one hundred years before extreme poverty—even using the income threshold of 1.25 US dollars— would disappear.[19] Not least in view of its ineffectiveness, but also because of the need to reduce CO_2 emissions and to transition to a sustainable economy, he described the idea of relying on general growth as not only unrealistic but 'dangerous and counterproductive'.[20] In this context it is notable that 62 per cent of the poorest people in the world, those with less than around two dollars per day, now live in middle-income countries that are home to 75 per cent of the world's population. In the World Bank's definition, these are countries with an annual GDP per capita between around 1,100 and 13,800 US dollars. As Paul Collier, former head of the research division of the World Bank, emphasized in his book on 'The Bottom Billion', the problem is that growth simply does not benefit the poorest.[21] Research suggests that reaching the 'last 3%' is the hardest.[22] But lowering the number to 3 per cent, the World Bank's own target, is a challenge too as the effect of growth on poverty reduction successively declines. Even achieving the 3 per cent goal by 2030 in Sub-Saharan Africa according to the World Bank would require the region to 'achieve growth rates about eight times higher than historical rates between 2010 and 2019'.[23] Thus, 'growth alone is unlikely to get the world to the 3 per cent target because as extreme poverty declines, growth on its own tends to lift fewer people out of poverty', as the World Bank

18　Monbiot, George. 24 April 2007. 'The best way to give the poor a real voice is through a world parliament'. The Guardian (www.guardian.co.uk).

19　Woodward, David. 2015. 'Incrementum ad Absurdum: Global Growth, Inequality and Poverty Eradication in a Carbon-Constrained World'. World Economic Review, no. 4: 43–62.

20　Woodward, David. 7 July 2013. 'How progressive is the push to eradicate extreme poverty?' The Guardian (www.guardian.co.uk).

21　Collier, Paul. 2008. The Bottom Billion. Oxford University Press.

22　Ravallion, Martin. 2020. 'SDG1: The Last Three Percent.' Center for Global Development. (cgdev.org).

23　World Bank Group, p. 8.

stated. Growth policy, it argued, must be designed to be more inclusive, and more resources must be mobilised for the support of the very poor.[24]

Social security as the foundation of a planetary social contract

The key step towards the elimination of extreme poverty in the world lies in guaranteeing basic social security for everyone. In parallel, consideration should be given to the worldwide introduction of a minimum wage that is adjusted on a country-by-country basis.[25] Kenyan philosopher Henry Odera Oruka (1944 to 1995) rightfully argued that providing a 'human minimum' to all human beings, consisting of unconditional, universal and absolute rights to physical security, health, and subsistence, is a fundamental principle of global justice.[26] This must form the basis for a new planetary social contract and a global ecosocial market economy. The World Commission on the Social Dimension of Globalization set up by the ILO rightly pointed out that 'a certain minimum level of social protection needs to be accepted and undisputed as part of the socio-economic floor of the global economy'. Global engagement in the elimination of social insecurity, it argued, is crucially important for the continuing legitimation of globalization.[27] In fact, 'social security' is already firmly embedded as a human right, in Articles 22 and 25 of the Universal Declaration of Human Rights and in Article 9 of the International Covenant on Economic, Social and Cultural Rights. Numerous recommendations and conventions have emerged from the ambit of the ILO. The ILO Convention 102 of 1952, for example, ratified (though generally only in parts) by only 43 countries, commits them to uphold specified minimum standards in the provision of basic social security benefits. In 1995 the UN held a World Summit for Social Development in Copenhagen. In the 'Declaration on Social Justice for a Fair Globalization' of 2008, unanimously adopted by practically the entire community of states, it is affirmed 'that the ILO has the solemn obligation to further among the nations of the world programmes which will achieve the objectives of full employment and the raising of standards of living, a minimum living wage and the extension of social security measures to provide a basic income to all in need'. The same objective can be found already in the

---

24 World Bank. 2014. Prosperity for All. Ending Extreme Poverty. A Note for the World Bank Group Spring Meetings 2014. Washington D.C.

25 Zervas, Georgios, and Peter Spiegel. 2016. Die 1-Dollar-Revolution. Globaler Mindestlohn Gegen Ausbeutung and Armut. München/Berlin: Piper.

26 Oruka, H. Odera. 1997. Practical Philosophy: In Search of an Ethical Minimum. Nairobi: East African Educational Publishers, p. 84-90.

27 International Labour Organization. 2004. A fair globalization: Creating opportunities for all. Report of the World Commission on the Social Dimension of Globalization. Geneva, para. 491, p. 110.

ILO Declaration of Philadelphia of 1944. Seventy years later, in its first report on social protection, the ILO found to its disappointment that, in spite of notable advances in many countries of the world, 73 per cent of the world population, or 5.2 billion people, had either only partial access to public social security systems or none at all. As of 2020, the figure was 69.4 per cent of the working-age population. Four billion people, or 53.1 per cent of the world population, were left 'wholly unprotected' according to the ILO. In many countries, however, COVID-19 triggered 'an unparalleled social protection policy response' as governments sought to protect 'people's health, jobs and incomes, and to ensure social stability'. Social protection is not only a human right, but plays a key role in the view of the ILO in the reduction of poverty, social inequality and hunger and in the promotion of food security, social cohesion, peaceful communities and political stability. It was found to have a positive impact on health care provision, the education system, job creation, consumer demand and economic growth. 'Investing in social protection is investing in a healthy, productive and equitable society', the ILO stated.[28] The Swedish economist and sociologist Gunnar Myrdal (1898 to 1987), recipient of the Nobel Memorial Prize in Economic Sciences in 1974, argued in 1956 already that the concept of the welfare state, accepted in all advanced nations, had to be 'widened and changed into a concept of a "welfare world"'.[29] A complete realization of the 'moral tenets' of civilization, including liberty, equality of opportunity and universal brotherhood, would mean, among other things, the creation of 'a world without boundaries and without national discrimination.' Politically, Myrdal wrote, it would imply the establishment of a 'world state, democratically ruled by the will of all peoples' even though the 'real world' became less like this ideal 'every day'.[30]

A global basic income

Regular unconditional cash benefits granted to individuals have proven successful in the fight against poverty and in development aid. 'Once a utopian idea, the policy is now widely discussed and piloted throughout the world', the political and moral philosopher Juliana Bidadanure wrote in an article on the subject.[31] Bidadanure, who in 2023 moved to New York University, in 2017

28 International Labour Organization. 2014. World Social Protection Report 2014/15. Geneva: International Labour Office, pp. 2, 154-6; and id. 2021. World Social Protection Report 2020–22, pp. 18, 20.

29 Myrdal, Gunnar. 1956. An International Economy. Problems and Prospects. New York: Harper and Brothers Publishers, pp. 323-4.

30 Id. 1967. Beyond the Welfare State. Bantam, p. 120.

31 Bidadanure, Juliana Uhuru. 2019. 'The Political Theory of Universal Basic Income.' Annual Review of Political Science 22 (1): 481–501, p. 481.

founded the Stanford Basic Income Lab that by now recorded nearly 200 experiments granting a Universal Basic Income, or UBI, in numerous places across the world including in Kenya, Finland, Namibia, India, Canada and the United States. With regard to its use in development assistance, the political scientist Christopher Blattmann and the economist Paul Niehaus noted that 'Western officials and organizations are not the best judges of what poor people in developing countries need to make a better living; the poor people themselves are'.[32] There is no more immediate way of combating poverty than by direct grants. They enable people to decide for themselves which of their needs are the most urgent, from the things needed for day-to-day survival to training and further education or investing in their own small business. Many of the pilot projects thus far confirm that as a rule people are very well able to do this for themselves.

In the EU, the European Parliament confirmed in a resolution on minimum incomes its belief 'that the various experiments with minimum incomes and with a guaranteed basic income for everyone, accompanied by additional social integration and protection measures, show that these are effective ways of combating poverty and social exclusion and providing a decent life for all'.[33] In the USA, the debate around this idea has a long history. It was proposed, in the form of a so-called negative income tax, by the US American economist Milton Friedman in his book 'Capitalism and Freedom' as early as 1962. If earnings are zero, or below a certain threshold, financial support is given by the state at a level up to a basic income. An advisory commission to the US President recommended the introduction of such a system in 1969. Among the supporters of a basic income were the civil rights activist Martin Luther King as well as the economists James Tobin and Kenneth Galbraith. 'I am now convinced', wrote Martin Luther King, 'that the simplest approach will prove to be the most effective — the solution to poverty is to abolish it directly by a now widely discussed measure: the guaranteed income.'[34] Incidentally, this famous fighter against social oppression and recipient of the Nobel Peace Prize also supported the establishment of a world police and a world government. 'There can be a world government where diversity can exist and this would lessen many tensions that we face today,' he noted in 1964.[35]

32 Blattman, Christopher, and Paul Niehaus. 2014. 'Show Them the Money'. Foreign Affairs, no. May/June.

33 European Parliament. 20 October 2010. 'Resolution on the Role of Minimum Income in Combating Poverty and Promoting an Inclusive Society in Europe'. Doc. P7_TA(2010)0375, para. 34, 44.

34 King, Jr., Martin Luther. 1968. Where Do We Go from Here: Chaos or Community? Boston: Beacon Press, p. 162.

35 Id. 1964. 'In a Single Garment of Destiny': A Global Vision of Justice. Ed. by Lewis V. Baldwin. Boston: Beacon Press. Part V: Statements prepared for Redbook Magazine, 5 November 1964, p. 149.

The issue of an UBI has become an indispensable element of discussion on global development and social policy. Götz Werner (1944 to 2022), billionaire and founder of Europe's biggest pharmacy chain, dm, and Adrienne Goehler, former President of the University of Fine Arts in Hamburg, are well-known proponents of the idea in Germany. Citing a successful model project in the Namibian village of Otjivero, they questioned why 'classical development policy, which has deepened corruption and enriched the powerful, the despots, dictators, clans and warlords all around the world, is not radically re-routed towards an unconditional basic income'.[36] Introducing a global UBI also provides an answer to the question that arose earlier about what the money raised by global taxes could be used for. A global basic income is perhaps the most sensible use for the bulk of the income from global taxation. Thomas Pogge, for example, believes that 'something like a Global Basic Income may well be part of the best plan for using funds raised through a Tobin Tax or Global Resources Dividend toward poverty eradication'. Projects for the improvement of public infrastructure, he rightly added, also represent an important component.[37] Werner and Goehler, on the other hand, linked basic income to a global CO_2 emissions tax. 'If emissions rights for CO_2 were auctioned today, and the revenues from that were to be paid out as a basic income', they wrote, 'two fundamental problems of the 21st century would be solved at the same time. CO_2 emissions would be effectively capped, and looming climate change would be slowed down. At the same time, depending on the auction price, everyone would receive between 13 and 14 dollars a month.' This is far below the monetary measure for extreme poverty but other financing sources could be drawn upon to raise the amount. Nonetheless, Werner and Goehler argued that for the poorest of the poor in the world even a sum as low as this could help 'guarantee a minimum subsistence and thus access to clean drinking water and an adequate basic diet.'[38] A UNDP report published at the height of the COVID-19 pandemic calculated that a temporary basic income to protect the most vulnerable 2.78 billion people in 132 developing countries at the time would have cost between 200 and 465 billion US dollar per month depending on the scenario. The most far-reaching of those they examined was a uniform transfer of 5.50 dollar per day and person, equivalent to 0.63 per cent of the combined GDP of the countries in question. The study argued that theoretically this was doable as an emergency measure.

36 Werner, Götz, and Adrienne Goehler. 2011. 1000 € für jeden: Freiheit. Gleichheit. Grundeinkommen. Berlin: Ullstein, p. 218.
37 Pinzani, Alessandro. June 2005. 'Global Justice as Moral Issue'. Interview with Thomas Pogg. Ethic: International Journal for Moral Philosophy (4) 1: 1–6, p. 4.
38 Werner/Goehler, p. 233.

The annual debt service of developing countries would amount to 3.1 trillion US dollar. A debt service standstill alone, the study suggested, would suffice to fund up to 6-7 months of the maximum scenario and 16 months of the minimum one.[39] According to Bidadanure's definition a UBI is supposed to be at 'a sufficiently high level to enable a life free from economic insecurity'. The ILO calculated that providing a global UBI that matches nationally determined poverty lines would cost the equivalent of 39.4 per cent of global GDP.[40] Still it would not be sufficient for all recipients to cover basic needs. For the time being, granting UBI benefits will only be feasible well below these poverty lines. The concept only works complementary and in addition to social safety schemes and the provision of free and adequate public services. Further, as CO_2 emissions phase out successively, so will revenues derived from them. This potential income stream for a global UBI thus is only of a temporary nature and its importance would decrease over time. Another way of granting a UBI could be through so-called 'helicopter money' where central banks directly distribute newly created money to individuals. This could be done as part of an expansionary monetary policy that aims at stimulating economic activity. The concept is the subject of controversial debate. It has been gaining ground, however, since central banks in the wake of the financial crisis and again during the COVID-19 pandemic pursued the policy of 'quantitative easing' and purchased government bonds or other assets from private financial institutions in the order of trillions. Instead, it was argued, this money could be distributed to the people directly. With the introduction of central bank digital currency and the possibility for individuals to open retail accounts with central banks, implementation would become easier at national or Eurozone levels. However, for global payments of this kind, a global central bank and currency would be needed.

Universal ownership of the global commons

The proposal for a basic income is linked to the idea that everyone has a stake in the commons and a right to share the fruits of civilization. As Myron Frankman explains, 'the essential rationale is quite simple: all earned income takes advantage of pre-existing institutions, knowledge, communication, and transportation nets, which are part of what is commonly regarded as social capital. To the extent that each of us is a common beneficiary of the cumula-

---

39   Gray Molina, George, and Eduardo Ortiz-Juarez. 2020. Temporary Basic Income: Protecting Poor and Vulnerable People in Developing Countries. United Nations Development Programme. (undp.org), pp. 7-9, 14.

40   Ortiz, Isabel, Christina Behrendt, et al. 2018. 'Universal Basic Income Proposals in Light of ILO Standards: Key Issues and Global Costing.' International Labour Organization. ESS-Working Paper No. 62. (ilo.org), p. 15.

tive global process of civilization, we are entitled to some reasonable monetary dividend.'[41] Thomas Paine, one of the early proponents of this approach, emphasized in 1797, in connection with the issue of ownership of the land, 'that the earth, in its natural, uncultivated state was, and ever would have continued to be, the common property of the human race', and that all those without property should therefore receive compensation from the propertied classes.[42] Similarly, Odera Oruka based his case for providing a 'human minimum' on the observation, among others, that 'the planet Earth' is 'a common good to all humankind' and that all human beings are equally entitled to its resources. This principle, the philosopher argued, trumps 'territorial sovereignty' of nation states. A world government was required 'with the legitimacy and ability to override, if need be', their 'wills and interests'. Oruka added that the UN General Assembly was a step in this direction but ways needed to be found to 'strengthen the right of the assembly to take precedence over the will of any one nation, however great and wealthy she may be.'[43] The degree of legitimacy required for such an empowerment could be achieved by complementing the General Assembly with a second, elected chamber.

In short, when global common goods are used, all citizens of the Earth have a right to benefit. A global basic income is a way to implement this right and has a strong symbolic dimension. It promotes the idea of the equality of all people and of their global identity. A world parliament, representing all global citizens, should determine the framework for practical implementation, should be the highest budgetary authority, and should exercise democratic control. The practical arrangements might involve several different models, all operating within common global guidelines, to suit differing local conditions. In the developed countries, for example, where there are functioning tax and social welfare systems, it might make sense to implement the basic income in the form of a negative income tax. In other countries it might be better to make cash payments, with the minimum of bureaucracy. In fragile states, and even more so in failing states, there will be severe obstacles to be overcome. While in principle it is intended for everyone, initiating it first in least developed countries as a development aid tool may be a useful way to help eliminate extreme poverty. Indeed it should be unconditional—not subject to any compulsion to work or any kind of means test. The latter not only involves considerable bureaucracy and stigmatises the recipients, but it also contradicts the fundamental rationale for a basic income. Leading experts on taxation and

41 Frankman, Myron J. 2004. World Democratic Federalism. New York: Palgrave Macmillan, p. 150.
42 Paine, Thomas. 1995 [1797]. 'Agrarian Justice'. In: Rights of Man, Common Sense and Other Political Writings. Oxford, New York et al.: Oxford University Press, p. 417.
43 Oruka, pp. 147, 150, 133.

inequality suggested that in order to support development and redistribution, 'it appears logical' that resources derived from global wealth taxes 'could be partly allocated to the Global South'.[44] Whether or not this takes the form of direct cash transfers to the people, a global parliament needs to be at the center of oversight and decision-making.

The dream of a life free from economic compulsion

The social psychologist Erich Fromm pointed out that throughout human history 'man has been limited in his freedom to act by two factors: the use of force on the part of the rulers (essentially their capacity to kill the dissenters), and, more importantly, the threat of starvation against all who were unwilling to accept the conditions of work and social existence that were imposed on them'. In our age of economic abundance, however, when it is actually possible to satisfy the basic needs of all, everyone could for the first time be made free and independent from economic compulsion by means of a guaranteed income. 'Guaranteed income', wrote Fromm, 'would not only establish freedom as a reality rather than a slogan, it would also establish a principle deeply rooted in Western religious and humanist tradition: man has the right to live, regardless! This right to live, to have food, shelter, medical care, education, etc., is an intrinsic human right that cannot be restricted by any condition, not even the one that he must be socially "useful". The shift from a psychology of scarcity to that of abundance is one of the most important steps in human development.'[45] In that sense, a basic income is a step towards what is perhaps the most important of all human dreams: a life without existential fear, with the freedom to do what you want. The humanist ideals of the Enlightenment, and the core demands of the French Revolution for 'liberty, equality, and fraternity', would thereby finally be given a 'real foundation'.[46] Guaranteed basic social security and healthcare for everybody in the world is a human right, and the objective of global social policy. A global basic income can complement national measures and create a financial base that contributes to the elimination of extreme poverty on the planet.

44 Chancel, Lucas, Thomas Piketty, Emmanuel Saez, and Gabriel Zucman. 2021. 'World Inequality Report 2022.' World Inequality Lab, p. 173.
45 Fromm, Erich. 1966. 'The Psychological Aspects of the Guaranteed Income'. In: The Guaranteed Income, ed. by Robert Theobald, 175–84. New York: Doubleday.
46 Werner and Goehler, pp. 11, 25, 265-6.

23.

Global class formation, the 'super class', and global inequality

The emergence of global class conflict and a global middle class

The increasing importance of the developing and emerging countries in the world economy, and the associated growth of their middle classes, renders the concept of the so-called 'Third World' obsolete, notwithstanding the continued existence of extreme poverty. Simultaneously, the long predominance in world systems theory of a division of the world into a 'core', a 'semi-periphery' and a 'periphery' is nearly over. This is evidenced by the increase in direct trade links between countries of the South and by their growing share of worldwide consumption. Michael Hardt and Antonio Negri (1933 to 2023) have encapsulated this well in their description of the 'logic and structure of a new form of sovereignty'. 'If the First World and the Third World, center and periphery, North and South were ever really separated along national lines, today they clearly infuse one another, distributing inequalities and barriers along multiple and fractured lines', they wrote. 'The various nations and regions contain different proportions of what was thought of as First World and Third, center and periphery, North and South. The geography of uneven development and the lines of division and hierarchy will no longer be found along stable national or international boundaries, but in fluid infra- and supranational borders', they further stated in their book 'Empire'.[1] 'There is a "south" in the North and a "north" in the South', as a UNDP report on human development put it.[2] Seen in this light, a crucial conflict of the future lies not between states, neither on a North-South nor an East-West axis, nor on any other such axis, but *within world society*, between the socially disadvantaged classes and a super-rich global elite.

In an article on 'the globalising security environment', the defence expert Tomas Ries wrote that 'the key political fault lines generating violent conflict have shifted from within the elite peer community to the tensions between unequal global socioeconomic classes of society. The drivers of intersocietal violence have shifted from the Westphalian horizontal peer competition to-

---

1   Hardt, Michael, and Antonio Negri. 2000. Empire. Cambridge: Harvard University Press, pp. xi, 335

2   United Nations Development Programme. 2013. Human Development Report 2013. The Rise of the South: Human Progress in a Diverse World. New York: UNDP, p. 2.

wards the vertical asymmetric tensions of the globalised world village, but it is a village on the verge of revolution. While we have an increasingly integrated elite community, we also face increasingly explosive tensions from the poorer strata below'.[3] A study by the UK Ministry of Defence of the strategic defence environment over the next thirty years identified the middle classes as a potential 'revolutionary class'. 'The globalization of labour markets and reducing levels of national welfare provision and employment could reduce peoples' attachment to particular states', the study noted. 'The growing gap between themselves and a small number of highly visible super-rich individuals might fuel disillusion with meritocracy, while the growing urban under-classes are likely to pose an increasing threat to social order and stability, as the burden of acquired debt and the failure of pension provision begins to bite. Faced by these twin challenges, *the world's middle-classes might unite,* using access to knowledge, resources and skills *to shape transnational processes in their own class interest'* (emphasis added).[4] The ambitious middle classes in the developing countries, many of them still living just above the poverty line, demand improved social, political and economic rights, good governance and better public infrastructure, while growing inequality and global structural economic change threaten the grip of the hard-pressed middle classes of the industrialised countries on their precarious relative security. 'The main cause of coming conflicts will not be clashes between civilizations, but the anger generated by the unfulfilled expectations of a middle class, which is declining in rich countries and booming in poor countries', was Moisés Naím's diagnosis.[5]

The economist Branko Milanović, who headed the World Bank's research department for two decades and who is one of the world's leading experts on inequality, at first expressed scepticism about the possibility of global class solidarity in today's world 'because the underlying material conditions of people are simply too different'. The worldwide proletariat, celebrated by Karl Marx in 1867 as the revolutionary class, had already ceased to exist by the end of the 19th century, he argued. At that time, the income differences between workers in Europe and North America, and in the East and the colonies, had 'exploded' and the solidarity that was assumed to exist 'began to fray and eventually evaporated'. The French social philosopher André Gorz thought Marx's proletariat had been no more than a philosophical myth from the be-

---

3   Ries, Tomas. 2009. 'The globalising security environment and the EU'. In: What ambitions for European defence in 2020?, 61–74. Ed. by Álvaro de Vasconcelos. 2nd ed. European Union Institute for Security Studies, pp. 62-3, 67-8.

4   UK Ministry of Defense Development, Concepts and Doctrine Centre. 2007. The DCDC Strategic Trends Programme 2007-2036. 3rd ed. Shrivenham: DCDC, p. 80.

5   Naím, Moisés. 5 August 2011. 'The Clash of the Middle Classes'. Huffington Post (www.huffingtonpost.com).

ginning. 'For over a century the idea of the proletariat has succeeded in masking its own unreality', he wrote in 1980 in his influential book 'Farewell to the Working Class'.[6] Milanović stressed the point in 2011 that even the poorest American was better off than two-thirds of the world population. 'There are many countries in the world', he wrote, 'whose top income classes are poorer than the poorest income classes in rich countries.'[7] But the situation is changing rapidly. Between 2000 and 2022, the share of adults in the global middle class, in this case defined as having an individual net worth between 10,000 and 100,000 US dollars, increased from 13 to 34 per cent.[8] Indeed, Milanović later noted a trend towards 'the convergence of real incomes across vast groups of people' worldwide as China and other populous countries in Asia were catching up with Europe and North America. By 2040, he estimated, 'the world's entire Northern Hemisphere, including North America, Europe (except for Russia), Japan, Korea, and China may have approximately the same income, while South and Southeast Asia will not be far behind'. Perhaps for the first time in history, Milanović concluded, it was possible to 'speak of the emergence of a global middle class'. It was unclear, though, 'what the political consequences of this development will be'. In individual nations the middle class tended to 'prevent the rich from claiming monopoly on governance', among other things, but 'given the lack of a global government' it was likely that the emergence of a global middle class 'will simply mean that more people will share similar patterns of behavior and consumption' on the planet.[9]

As the British study mentioned above suggested, a crucial turning point may occur when parts at least of the global middle class recognize the global dimension to the class conflict and thus their common global interests. All middle classes, whether in Brazil, Germany, India or the USA, suffer in the same way from the tax avoidance practices of the super-rich and their companies, for example. This creates, the study suggested, a powerful popular basis for support for global regulation, in the sense of Karl Polanyi's concept of a double movement. To take the link to the 'Great Transformation' further, one could speak in this context of the creation of a global 'transformative subject'.

6   Gorz, André. 1997 [1980]. Farewell to the Working Class: An Essay on Post-Industrial Socialism. Pluto Press, p. 67.
7   Milanović, Branko. 2011. The Haves and the Have-Nots: A Brief and Idiosyncratic History of Global Inequality. New York: Basic Books, pp. 113, 110-1, 117-8.
8   UBS. 2023. Global Wealth Report 2023, p. 41.
9   Milanović, Branko. 2019. Capitalism, Alone. Cambridge and London: Belknap Press of Harvard University Press, pp. 212-3.

The global precariat

The global middle class is only one of the potential candidates for the role of a 'transformative subject'. The British labour economist Guy Standing, formerly a senior figure at the ILO and now an academic at the University of London, spoke of the need for 'a new vocabulary, one reflecting class relations in the global market system of the twenty-first century'. A proponent of a basic income, Standing sees a 'new dangerous class' materialising—a 'global precariat', which finds itself at the bottom of the emergent global class structure. The contours of what Standing also refers to as a 'class-in-the-making' are as yet very unclear. It belongs to neither the middle class nor the traditional, wage labour-based proletariat. Instead, its members live in precarious circumstances, muddling through on temporary jobs, or unemployed with no prospects of a career or of upward social mobility. His description which is reminiscent of what André Gorz called the 'non-class of post-industrial neo-proletarians', 'all the supernumeraries of present-day social production, who are potentially or actually unemployed, whether permanently or temporarily, partially or completely'.[10] According to Standing, they are the people most directly affected by the flexibilization of the labour markets and by cuts to social welfare systems (insofar as these exist and are accessible), have no employment-related social protection, no income from capital, barely any chance of saving money, and live in permanent uncertainty about what the future might bring. They do not feel represented by either the traditional political parties or the unions, and they are largely alienated from the institutions of the state. The precariat, as outlined here, is very inhomogeneous. According to Standing, the largest and most diverse group consists of well-educated people who cannot find regular work suited to their level of qualifications but often have good networks. This is the group from which youth and student protest movements emerged, and which in Standing's view played a leading role in the Occupy movement in 2011 and subsequent years. Then there are the relatively uneducated former wage labourers, susceptible to populism, who have dropped out of the working class, and the most disadvantaged group, with hardly any rights to fall back on, consisting of migrants (with or without official resident status), asylum seekers and members of ethnic minorities.[11]

---

10   Gorz, pp. 68-9.
11   Standing, Guy. 2011. The precariat: the new dangerous class. London, New York: Bloomsbury Academic, 2011 and id., 2014. A Precariat Charter: From Denizens to Citizens. London, New York: Bloomsbury Academic.

The concept of the Multitude

A different approach is illustrated by the concept of the 'Multitude', which was popularised among a wider audience through the eponymous book by Michael Hardt and Antonio Negri. What they meant by 'Multitude' is a 'multiplicity of singular forms of life', woven together in a kind of network, but demonstrating many and varied differences, and which 'can never be reduced to a unity or a single identity'. The term describes 'all those who labor and produce under the rule of capital' in the broadest sense, so encompassing potentially 'all the diverse figures of social production'. This includes the unemployed, for 'just as social production takes place today equally inside and outside the factory walls, so too it takes place equally inside and outside the wage relationship'.[12] Although 'the common conditions of those who can become the multitude' remain relatively broad and unspecified in Hardt and Negri's description, it can be said of them that this 'emerging global class formation' shares 'a common global existence'.[13] The crucial underlying conception of class here is not empirical but determined by politics. Class, they argued, is defined by class struggle, and 'the task of a theory of class in this respect is to identify the existing *conditions* for potential collective struggle and express them as a political *proposition*'. In this instance, therefore, the project consists in bringing the Multitude to life. 'Class is a political concept, in short, in that a class is and can only be a collectivity that struggles in common.'[14] As the cultural theorist Sylvère Lotringer sarcastically observed, Hardt and Negri's analysis appeared to involve 'an original kind of class struggle', namely 'a struggle looking for a class'.[15]

What is at stake in this struggle, according to Hardt and Negri, is, in short, the resistance to an imperial global apparatus of rule labelled 'Empire', 'composed of a series of national and supranational organisms' including the United Nations, the IMF and the World Bank, which governs the global market and the global circuits of production as a 'sovereign power'. An interesting aspect of this model is that the USA is not regarded as being at its centre. Rather, it is argued that a fundamental principle of the 'Empire' is that its global power has no real centre. The distinction between inner and outer which was so important in world system perspective is increasingly blurred in the 'Empire'. The 'imperial sovereignty' of the 'Empire' spans the entire globe and 'is

---

12   Hardt, Michael, and Antonio Negri. 2004. Multitude: War and Democracy in the Age of Empire. New York: Penguin, pp. 127, xiv, 107, xv, 135.

13   Ibid., pp. 105, xviii, 127.

14   Ibid., p. 104.

15   Lotringer, Sylvère. 2004. 'Foreword: We, the Multitude'. In: Virno, Paolo. 2004. Grammar of the Multitude, 7–19. Los Angeles, CA: Semiotext(e), p. 16.

both everywhere and nowhere' in Hardt and Negri's metaphysically-tinged analysis.[16] An important element of the 'Empire' is formed by a 'global aristocracy' of multinational corporations and industrialists, supranational institutions, dominant industrial states and influential non-state actors. The Multitude 'is and will remain necessarily antagonistic to these aristocracies', they said. Hardt and Negri saw the protests at the WTO summit in Seattle in 1999 as 'the coming-out party of the new cycle of struggles', organised and mobilised now by the Multitude. The aim of the struggles is to 'develop a new framework for the democratic constitution of the world' and to create 'democracy on a global scale'.[17]

The super-rich and global power structures

While it may be difficult to clearly identify a global 'transformative subject' within a traditional class framework, there is on the other hand no problem in establishing that there is a global elite, economically separated by a large gap from the rest, at the very top of the global class structure. This is the super-rich, a group of about 210,000 people each with a fortune worth over 30 million US dollars. The total wealth of the super-rich adds up to over 28 trillion US dollars, or an average of 200 million each.[18] In reality there is no doubt that the sum is higher, as it can be safely assumed, as already outlined, that further sums totalling trillions are hidden away via obscure investments or in tax havens. This also applies to the wealth belonging to the so-called 'shadow elite' of organised crime, which is not captured in the standard statistics. At any rate, according to another conventional estimate, about 243,060 people across the world have fortunes in excess of 50 million US dollars, 79,490 of them with over 100 million, and 7,020 with over 500 million US dollars.[19] Now we are approaching the very pinnacle of this class at the top of the global wealth pyramid. This is formed of a group that *Forbes* magazine calculated in 2023 as comprising 2,640 billionaires with a combined fortune estimated at 12.2 trillion US dollars. The world's richest 25 billionaires according to *Forbes* were worth 2.1 trillion collectively.[20] This represents an extreme degree of concentration of global wealth and it has been increasing for decades. According to the World Inequality Report, the world's bottom 50 per cent in 2021 had a share in total global wealth of 2 per cent whereas the richest 10 per cent a share of 75.6 per cent and the top 1 per cent of nearly 38 per cent. The study

16   Hardt and Negri (Empire), pp. xii, xi, 190.
17   Hardt and Negri (Multitude), pp. 171, 322, 215, 217, 324, xi.
18   Capgemini. 2023. 'World Wealth Report 2023', pp. 6, 9.
19   UBS, pp. 30-1.
20   'World's Billionaires List. The Richest in 2023', Forbes Magazine (forbes.com).

explains that the wealth of the richest individuals on the planet, the top 1 per cent, has grown at rates between 6 per cent to 9 per cent per year from 1995 to 2021, whereas average growth was 3.2 per cent. This means that 38 per cent of all new wealth accumulated in recent decades has been captured by the top of the pyramid whereas the poorest 50 per cent got only 2 per cent. The share in global wealth of the top 0.001 per cent—individuals with assets worth more than 469 million dollars—has almost doubled from 3.5 per cent to 6.5 per cent in 2021 while the share of the bottom 50 per cent has stagnated since the early 2000s. At the same time, the 'squeezed lower and middle classes in industrialized nations' according to the report have been 'largely cut off from economic growth' with the lowest average rates recorded across all wealth groups.[21] Since 1980, the global top one per cent earners captured twice as much of the growth in global *income* as the 50 per cent poorest individuals.[22] In terms of climate responsibility it was calculated that the poorest half of the global population are responsible for only around 7.7 per cent of global emissions yet live overwhelmingly in the countries most vulnerable to climate change. The richest top 10 per cent in the world by contrast account for 50 per cent of emissions. The average carbon footprint of an individual in the top 1 per cent was around 76.6 tons CO_2 according to Oxfam's figures for 2019—over 100 times the average footprint of someone in the poorest half.[23] 'There's class warfare, all right, but it's my class, the rich class, that's making war, and we're winning', the billionaire Warren Buffet told the *New York Times*.[24]

According to Oxfam, the world's richest 1 per cent own 43 per cent of all global financial assets. Billionaires were either the principal shareholder or the CEO of around one third of the 50 biggest corporations in the world, the group noted, adding that they 'use this control to ensure that corporate power is constantly growing through increasing market concentration and monopoly, enabled by government' in order to provide 'ever-greater returns to them, the shareholders, at the expense of everyone else'.[25] It can be assumed that the super-rich are at the center of a dominant global power structure. The German sociologist Jürgen Krysmanski regarded them as the global 'core of power, in the sense of a ruling class', and spoke of a 'power-money-complex' which has become the basis for 'a new form of global sovereignty'.[26] Krysman-

---

21   Chancel, Lucas, et al. 2021. 'World Inequality Report 2022.' World Inequality Lab, pp. 15, 90-2.
22   Alvaredo, Facundo, et al. 2017. World Inequality Report 2018. World Inequality Lab.
23   Oxfam. 2023. 'Climate Equality: A Planet for the 99%', p. xiii. See also related 'Methodology Note', p. 6.
24   Stein, Ben. 26 November 2006. 'In Class Warfare, Guess Which Class Is Winning'. The New York Times (www.nytimes.com).
25   Oxfam. 2024. 'Inequality Inc.', p. 10.
26   Krysmanski, Hans Jürgen. 2012. 0,1 Prozent - Das Imperium der Milliardäre. Frankfurt: Westend, pp. 64-5.

ski pictured the 'new planetary ruling structures' as a 'concentric castle'. 'The centre', he wrote, 'is formed everywhere by the 0.01 per cent that is the super-rich, a social stratum which has been completely cut loose and is capable of anything, and which our knowledge and information society provides with all the means necessary to establish itself as the new centre of society. Around it, and closest to it, the second ring is formed by the business and financial elites, the specialists in the exploitation and securitization of wealth. The next functional ring is composed of the political elites whose job it is, as far as the empire of the billionaires is concerned at least, to arrange for the distribution of the wealth from the bottom to the top, as inconspicuously as possible. The largest group populates the outer ring of the castle: the administrative and knowledge elites of all kinds, from scientists to technocrats and bureaucrats to the feel-good elites of the media, culture and sport.'[27] David Rothkopf, the former managing director of Kissinger Associates and US Under Secretary of Commerce for International Trade, painted a more diffuse picture in his popular book on the so-called 'Superclass'. There, the 'global power elite' is made up of a circle of 6,000 people, linked to each other by innumerable threads, who are distinguished not by their personal wealth but by their 'international influence'. In his view, this means the highest-ranking officials of the internationally most influential states, the commanders of the most powerful armies, the most important board members of the world's largest companies, richest banks and biggest investment firms, the chairpersons of the biggest NGOs and the most important international organizations, and religious leaders, scientists and other thought leaders.[28]

The transnational capitalist class

For a long time, researchers paid little attention to the super-rich and their influence. It has often been rightly pointed out that this reticence is in marked contrast to the intensive research carried out into the living conditions of the poor and the middle classes. In C. Wright Mills and William Domhoff, the USA had two pioneers of serious research into the elites and the global elite by now is also attracting much more attention. The sociologist Leslie Sklair, formerly at the London School of Economics, argued in a 2001 study that the increasing significance of transnational corporations had been accompanied by the rise of a 'transnational capitalist class', or TCC for short, 'that is more or less in control of the processes of globalization' as well as of a large part of the worldwide means of production. In his analysis, the dominant group with-

27   Id. 2013. 'Planetarische Herrschaft'. junge Welt, no. 100.
28   Rothkopf, David. 2008. Superclass: The Global Power Elite and the World They Are Making. London: Abacus.

in the TCC is made up of those in control of the most important transnational companies, that is, their owners (the super-rich) and senior executives. This group is supported by three others, consisting of leading bureaucrats, politicians, experts, scientists and media representatives among others. There are numerous overlaps, interrelationships and switches between these groups. 'They are a *transnationalist capitalist class* in that they operate across state borders to further the interests of global capital rather than of any real or imagined nation-state', Sklair emphasized. Of course there are internal conflicts of interest, but these are 'second order problems'; for 'the global capitalist system as a whole, these intraclass struggles are less important than what binds the members of the class together globally, namely their common interest in the protection of private property and the rights of private individuals to accumulate it with as little interference as possible'.[29]

The sociologist William Robinson of the University of California at Santa Barbara had followed up these studies. In an important work on a 'theory of global capitalism' from 2004, he too emphasized that the formation of a 'transnational capitalist class' is a central aspect of the process of globalization. It is not simply an outcome of the process, but since the 1970s has also been its driving force. The globalization of capitalism, he argued, replicates at the global level the historical 'Great Transformation' depicted by Karl Polanyi. Capital, embodied and controlled by the TCC, has succeeded in setting itself free from the limitations set by nation states. 'This liberation', said Robinson, 'helped free emergent transnational capital from the compromises and commitments placed on it by the social forces in the nation-state phase of capitalism. It dramatically altered the balance of forces among classes and social groups in each nation of the world and at the global level toward an emergent TCC.' The TCC has quite consciously and deliberately circumvented and neutralised at the transnational level those class compromises historically necessitated at the nation-state level by the countervailing movement. As empirical evidence for the rise of the TCC, Robinson cited the growing number and size of transnational corporations, the growth in cross-border mergers and takeovers, rising foreign direct investments, the overlap of personnel on the management boards of transnational corporations, and the evolution of worldwide outsourcing and subcontracting.[30]

29 Sklair, Leslie. 2001. The Transnational Capitalist Class. Oxford, UK; Malden, Mass.: Blackwell, pp. 5, 17, 295, 12.
30 Robinson, William I. 2004. A Theory of Global Capitalism. Production, Class, and State in a Transnational World. Baltimore and London: Johns Hopkins University Press, pp. 41, 54-6.

A transnational state apparatus

Although a later study by the Canadian sociologist William Carroll found that the TCC at the time had developed furthest in geographical terms in the North Atlantic area, it is a phenomenon by no means limited to the West or the global North.[31] In the developing countries, too, the growing numbers of the super-rich and of members of other sections of the national elites are increasingly integrated into the emerging TCC.[32] As Robinson argued, the state can be understood as a manifestation of certain specific, historically contingent class relations which are reflected in the political institutions. Globalization and the emergence of the TCC have been accompanied by a transformation of the character and structures of the state. National elites and functionaries who have been integrated into the TCC tend to act in the interests of their transnational class and to instrumentalize state institutions and their decisions accordingly. Robinson cited the USA as the most important example of a state dominated by the TCC. And he pointed to the number of intergovernmental investment protection agreements designed to protect foreign direct investments, now amounting to several thousand around the world, as evidence of the willingness of governments to accommodate the interests of transnational business. These agreements give companies the right to sue governments for compensation outside the national courts, for example at the International Centre for Settlement of Investment Disputes, part of the World Bank Group in Washington D.C. Robinson believed that the activities of the TCC taken together represent the formation, now proceeding rapidly, of a 'transnational state'. This is a network-like entity, spread over several levels, made up of nation state institutions and the leading international economic and political forums and organizations, linked together by the TCC and without any global institutional centre. The term 'state' applies to a territory and a social system which are subject to rule or domination from a specific source. Using this definition, it is certainly possible to describe the world order dominated by the TCC as a transnational state. 'The TNS comprises those institutions and practices in global society that maintain, defend, and advance the emergent hegemony of this global bourgeoisie', Robinson wrote. The decline of US supremacy is being accompanied by 'the creation of a transnational hegemony through supranational structures'. The fact that the nation states persist as part of this structure serves a number of the interests of the TCC.

---

31 Carroll, William K. 2010. The Making of a Transnational Capitalist Class. Corporate Power in the 21st Century. London and New York: Zed Books.
32 Robinson, William I. 2011. 'Global Capitalism Theory and the Emergence of Transnational Elites'. Critical Sociology (38) 3: 349–63.

The dissolution of the class compromise rooted in the nation state, for example, is based on the power wielded by transnational capital over labour, which has itself essentially also been globalised but remains structurally imprisoned within the nation state system. In short: 'the nation-state system boxes in and controls populations within fixed physical (territorial) boundaries so that their labor can be more efficiently exploited and their resistance contained'.[33] The nation state system thus prevents, or at least makes considerably more difficult, the horizontal, transnational and political coalescence of any kind of 'transformative subject'.

The interconnections between transnational corporations

An extraordinary concentration of power can be seen in the world of transnational corporations, too, whose owners and senior executives form the core of the TCC. Three researchers at the ETH Zurich studied a selection of some 43,000 leading transnational corporations and their interconnecting ownership structures. At the time, they found that almost 40 per cent of the economic value of these firms was under the control of a closely interwoven core group of 147 companies via a complex network of ownership arrangements. On account of the density of the controlling power they called this group the 'super-entity'. A larger core of 737 firms in turn controlled around 80 per cent of the economic value of the transnational companies in the study group. Over and above the question of what this degree of concentration means for global financial stability, the study raised the potential problem of distortion of competition and cartel formation. 'Remarkably', the report stated, 'the existence of such a core in the global market was never documented before and thus, so far, no scientific study demonstrates or excludes that this international "super-entity" has ever acted as a bloc.' The national competition authorities had not yet concerned themselves with the issue.[34] James Glattfelder, one of the co-authors of the study, believed that 'we may need global anti-trust rules, which now exist only at national level, to limit over-connection among TNCs'. The publication of the report prompted the systems science researcher Yaneer Bar-Yam to suggest that 'firms should be taxed for excess interconnectivity to discourage this risk'.[35]

---

33 Robinson (2004), pp. 99, 91, 77, 100, 88, 94, 101, 135, 106.

34 Vitali, Stefania, James B. Glattfelder, and Stefano Battiston. 19 September 2011. 'The network of global corporate control'. PloS One, no. arXiv:1107.5728v2, p. 8.

35 Coghlan, Andy, and Debora MacKenzie. 19 October 2011. 'Revealed – the capitalist network that runs the world'. New Scientist, no. 2835.

The need for a global antitrust authority

The prevention and mitigation of anti-competitive practices is of fundamental importance in the regulation of global markets. By now, over 150 countries have merger control regimes in place. Experts claim that this proliferation benefits consumers through a reduction of anticompetitive mergers.[36] But major sectors such as automotive, pharmaceuticals, finance, agriculture and technology continue to consolidate globally. The IMF reported in a 'discussion note' that in the advanced economies 'industry concentration has increased more than 30 percent since 1980'. A rise in market power was 'concentrated among a small group of firms whose high price markups are increasingly persistent', the document said. These findings would suggest that competition authorities should be 'increasingly vigilant' when enforcing merger control and it was necessary to 'strengthen international cooperation' among them with a view of cross-country mergers.[37] In the meantime, efforts towards global anti-cartel regulation are making only very slow progress. As the Chicago law expert David J. Gerber showed in a book on global competition law, the problem of international cartels was already a dominant issue at the First International Economic Conference of the League of Nations in Geneva in 1927. Following the Second World War, the international community agreed in Havana in 1948 to establish the International Trade Organization (ITO), with a Charter which included competition law provisions for the prevention of 'exclusionary practices'. When the US government under President Harry Truman realised that the initiative had no chance in the US Congress, they dropped it from the legislative agenda in 1950. With that, the ITO was doomed to failure. Gerber stressed that the eventual failure of the ITO project 'was the result of numerous geo-political and national developments, none of which were related directly to the competition law project'.[38] However, it was resistance on the part of the USA which also torpedoed a proposal put forward in 1953 by the Economic and Social Council of the United Nations for a specialised international organization to monitor 'exclusionary practices' which was largely based on the relevant provisions of the Havana Charter. A UN conference in 1980 adopted so-called 'multilaterally agreed equitable principles and rules for the control of restrictive business practices', also dubbed the 'UN set', but those remained non-binding recommendations. An

---

36   Leddy, Mark, et al. 2023. 'The Proliferation of Global Merger Control.' In: Research Handbook on Global Merger Control, ed. by Ioannis Kokkoris and Nicholas Levy, 11–48. Edward Elgar Publishing, pp. 11-

37   Chen, Wenjie, et al. 2021. 'Rising Corporate Market Power: Emerging Policy Issues: Emerging Policy Issues.' International Monetary Fund Staff Discussion Notes 2021 (001), pp. 7-8.

38   See ch. 2 in Gerber, David J. 2010. Global Competition: Law, Markets and Globalization. Oxford, New York: Oxford University Press, pp. 20-54.

attempt to determine international minimum competition law standards and a dispute resolution process was taken up on the WTO agenda after the Cold War was over, as part of the so-called Singapore issues of 1996 but also failed when it proved impossible to reach agreement at the WTO conference in Cancún seven years later. The USA did not see the need for it, and feared a restriction of its national sovereignty. Many developing countries, on the other hand, with little experience of competition law, suspected that in the WTO framework it might be constructed in a way that would serve the interests of the transnational corporations based in the industrialised countries rather than exercising better control over them. Yet all these proposals were in any event a long way from creating an effective world antitrust authority. International competition law regulation applies only unilaterally, and can be enforced extraterritorially only at the nation state level, and in the case of the EU at the regional level too.

In light of the ongoing deepening of globalization, Gerber saw this situation as 'increasingly precarious' and 'frightening'.[39] The German law expert Dietmar Baetge addressed one of the principal issues in his book on the subject: the task of national antitrust legislation, he wrote, 'lies only in protecting national interests, and not the interests of other states or of the international community'. The wellbeing of others is of no consideration. Nearly all countries, for example, exclude export cartels from their competition legislation. In view of the global interconnectedness of the markets, Baetge, called for 'a globally-based welfare paradigm' to underpin antitrust law, one that would take as its benchmark the optimum outcome for *all* countries involved and would aim to ensure that 'a broad spectrum of the world population', and ultimately the individual consumer, would benefit. Industrial policy concerns must be subordinated to those aims, and the interests of the developing countries must also be taken into account. At the same time, the burden placed on business by the patchwork of national regulations must be reduced. The objective of improving the welfare of consumers around the world which should underlie antitrust law, according to Baetge, is a global public good that can only be delivered by a 'central international authority'.[40] The antitrust experts Robert W. Hahn and Anne Layne-Farrar argued that 'a system that acknowledges the primacy of consumer welfare worldwide is the natural extension of a national antitrust authority aimed at promoting domestic welfare'. They saw the international situation as comparable to that in the USA. In antitrust is-

---

39 Ibid., p. vii.
40 Baetge, Dietmar. 2009. Globalisierung des Wettbewerbsrechts. Eine internationale Wettbewerbsordnung zwischen Kartell- and Welthandelsrecht. Tübingen: Mohr Siebeck, pp. 103-4, 108, 112, 471, 476, 109, 467.

sues taken up by the US government, any US federal states involved will tend to pursue their own particularistic state interests rather than those of the federation, and will therefore tend not only to delay and further complicate their resolution but to make the process more expensive. Furthermore, the individual states are much easier prey for lobbyists than the federal authorities. Most experts who have studied the problem, they said, therefore support restricting the role of the states in national antitrust proceedings. At the international level, the crucial difference is of course that there are no global antitrust proceedings. 'The logical solution', the two experts believed, 'would be a global antitrust authority with enforcement powers.'[41] This is not the right place to discuss whether it would be better to establish such an authority as a new and independent organization or as, to take one option, a part of the WTO. It is worth stressing, however, that in any event it would only be possible for it to claim adequate democratic legitimation if it were accountable to a global parliamentary body that is drafting the relevant global antitrust and competition law.

Global inequality and instability

The increasing concentration of power at the very top, the emerging worldwide predominance of a transnational elite class and the unequal distribution of income and wealth in the world are all of central importance for a detailed understanding of the new 'Great Transformation'. Reducing global inequality, within individual countries but also among all the world's people, is an important goal of global policy, and contributes to political, financial and social stability and to the creation of a fairer world order. Wealth distribution across different sectors of the world's population—as outlined before—is an important measure of global inequality. The most frequently used statistical indicator of inequality is the Gini coefficient, which gives a value between zero for a totally equal distribution (everybody has the same) and one for a totally unequal distribution (one person has all). In terms of global income, an estimation of the Gini index suggests that there was little development for almost a century. According to the World Inequality Report, the indicator moved between 0.72 and 0.68 since 1900. In 2000 it stood at 0.72 and fell to 0.67 in 2020. Comparing wealth and income distribution within a population provides more nuanced information. One such measure of inequality is the 'Palma ratio' which captures the relationship between the incomes of the top ten per cent and the bottom forty per cent of a population. A Palma value of 5.0, for example, means that the top ten per cent receive five times more in income than the bottom

---

41 Hahn, Robert W., and Anne Layne-Farrar. 2002. 'Federalism in Antitrust'. Harvard Journal of Law & Public Policy (26) 3: 877–921, p. 917.

forty per cent. Unlike the more abstract Gini index, providing a ratio makes disparities more evident and tangible. The World Inequality Report, for instance, compares the income of the top 10 per cent and the bottom 50 per cent. This measure peaked at 53 in 1980, hovered around 50 until 2008 and then fell to 38 by 2020, returning to levels observed from 1900 to 1960.[42] Whether these declines will persist remains to be seen. COVID-19 and geopolitical conflicts since then had adverse impacts on the development of inequality.

The link between inequality and social instability has preoccupied thinkers and researchers since antiquity. A pioneering study of development in 71 countries between 1960 and 1985 came to the conclusion that income inequality is causally connected to socio-political instability. 'A large group of impoverished citizens', it found, 'facing a small and very rich group of well-off individuals is likely to become dissatisfied with the existing socio-economic status quo and demand radical changes, so that mass violence and illegal seizure of power are more likely than when income distribution is more equitable.'[43] More recently, another study concluded that 'polarized sentiments among the masses are strongly associated with income inequality'.[44] Although these findings may not represent a scientific consensus, Aristotle already regarded the connection as obvious. He put it in a nutshell more than two thousand years ago: 'everywhere inequality is a cause of revolution'.[45] In the view of Branko Milanović, 'locally, high inequality among communities and individuals is associated with political instability'. In turn, 'national instabilities tend to spill over to neighboring countries and even to the rest of the world'. In other words: 'high levels of global inequality make global chaos more likely.'[46] Complexity scientist Peter Turchin historically identified a so-called 'wealth pump' as a destabilizing social mechanism and a primary factor in the breakdown of complex societies. This phenomenon involves the disproportionate redistribution of wealth from a working class to an economic elite, leading not only to a decline in the former's relative wages and living standards but also to increasing popular discontent due to growing inequality. Moreover, according to Turchin, an escalating concentration of wealth and income eventually triggers 'elite overproduction,' which in turn leads to additional, destabilizing intraelite conflict.[47]

42　Chancel et al., pp. 55-6.

43　Alesina, Alberto, and Roberto Perotti. 1996. 'Income distribution, political instability, and investment'. European Economic Review (40) 6: 1203–28.

44　Gu, Yanfeng, and Zhongyuan Wang. 2022. 'Income Inequality and Global Political Polarization: The Economic Origin of Political Polarization in the World.' Journal of Chinese Political Science 27 (2): 375–98, p. 391.

45　Aristotle. 'Politics'. Transl. by Benjamin Jowett. The Internet Classics Archive. Book Five, Part I.

46　Milanović (The Haves and the Have-Nots), p. 161-2.

47　See Turchin, Peter. 2023. End Times: Elites, Counter-Elites, and the Path of Political Disintegration. New York: Penguin Press.

Inequality as the cause of the financial crisis

Inequality, combined with factors such as the deregulation and inadequate supervision of the financial markets and systematic fraud on the part of numerous leading financial institutions such as the Bank of America, JPMorgan Chase and Goldman Sachs, also played a role in the 2008 financial crisis which triggered the 'Great Recession'. The economist James K. Galbraith believed that 'in a deep sense inequality was the heart of the financial crisis'.[48] In the opinion of researchers at the IMF, the crisis was ultimately the result of a growing disparity, over several decades, between the income shares of the top earners and the rest of the population. The background to the crisis was largely given, in this view, by the fact that only a small proportion of the growing incomes of the top earners was spent on higher consumption, whereas the bulk went into savings. On the look-out for investment opportunities, this accumulated wealth flowed in the form of loans from the financial sector to the rest of the population, and especially to the low earners, who in this way were able, in spite of a reduction in their earnings, to maintain or even increase their consumption levels, at least for a while. However, as the IMF economists noted, a 'large and highly persistent rise of workers' debt-to-income ratios generates financial fragility which eventually can lead to a financial crisis.'[49] This is putting it very cautiously. The growth in defaults on subprime mortgage loans in the USA caused a severe downturn in property prices and is thus regarded as one of the most important triggers of the financial crisis. From a macroeconomic perspective, inequality contributes to a decline in consumption and thus to slowing economic growth. 'The real cause of the crisis', according to Branko Milanović, 'lies in huge inequalities in income distribution that generated much larger investable funds than could be profitably employed. The political problem of insufficient economic growth of the middle class was then "solved" by opening the floodgates of cheap credit. And the opening of the credit floodgates, to placate the middle class, was needed because in a democratic system, an excessively unequal model of development cannot coexist with political stability.'[50]

48 Galbraith, James K., Professor. Inequality and Instability: A Study of the World Economy Just Before the Great Crisis. New York: Oxford University Press, 2012, p. 4.

49 Kumhof, Michael, and Romain Rancière. 'Inequality, Leverage and Crises'. IMF Working Paper WP/10/268, November 2010, p. 3, 22.

50 Milanović (2011), p. 196.

The growth of capital investments and a global tax on capital

In the analysis of the economist Thomas Piketty, inequality is a characteristic of every capitalist economic system, and the state has to intervene in order to cushion this tendency. According to his research, which attracted great attention around the world, the rate of return on capital investments over long periods regularly and significantly exceeds the growth rate of general wealth creation in a country. This means that income from capital investments grows faster than that from paid employment. The greater one's wealth, the greater is the growth rate tendency. According to Piketty's data, the income of the top one per cent in the USA more than doubled between 1980 and 2010, while for the top 0.1 per cent it more than tripled, and for the top 0.01 per cent, more than quadrupled. Over the same period, the income of the bottom ninety per cent fell by nearly five per cent.[51] Inequality is thus increasing not only between the wealthy owners of capital and the rest of the population, but within the wealthy class itself. The primary purpose of a global tax on capital that Piketty proposes would be 'not to finance the social state but to regulate capitalism', he noted. 'Without a global tax on capital or some similar policy, there is a substantial risk that the top centile's share of global wealth will continue to grow indefinitely.' The aim of the global tax on capital would be 'first to stop the indefinite increase of inequality of wealth, and second to impose effective regulation on the financial and banking system in order to avoid crises. To achieve these two ends, the capital tax must first promote democratic and financial transparency: there should be clarity about who owns what assets around the world.'[52] When critics of the proposal counter that global capital will simply slip through the fingers of such a tax, they have failed to understand its essential feature, which is precisely the introduction of a global and watertight tax system.[53] A proposal put forward by Gabriel Zucman would make sure that billionaires at least pay a minimum tax rate globally. Their income almost entirely derives from capital but they have 'lower effective capital tax rates than the average person', he explained. According to his plan, countries would agree to implement domestic measures which raise the equivalent amount of taxes that is below the minimum of two per cent of a billionaire's overall wealth in order to 'offset the failure of the income tax, when it fails'. An actual wealth tax, by con-

51 Piketty, Thomas, and Emmanuel Saez. Table A6: Top fractiles income levels (including capital gains) in the United States (elsa.berkeley.edu/~saez/TabFig2010.xls).

52 Piketty, Thomas. 2014. Capital in the Twenty-First Century. Cambridge Massachusetts: Harvard University Press, pp. 518-9.

53 Cowen, Tyler. 2014. 'Capital Punishment. Why a Global Tax on Wealth Won't End Inequality'. Foreign Affairs, May/June.

trast, would come in addition to income taxes already paid.[54]The need for global public policy instruments and a world parliament

Despite good proposals such as this, in the fight against global inequality, it is a key insight that, without the structures of a world state, there are few practical options for addressing the problem effectively. 'The political instruments for reducing income inequality between the richest 10 per cent and the poorest 40 per cent of the world's population do not exist. Progressive taxation, provision of social security, etc. are country-level instruments, and official development assistance comes no way near addressing global inequality', noted Lars Engberg-Pedersen.[55] And Branko Milanović wrote that 'so long as there is no global government, dissatisfaction with the level of inequality cannot be meaningfully expressed or translated into political action, the opinions cannot be conveyed to anyone, and, most important, there is no body who can act upon it'.[56]

A democratic world parliament would enable the discontent over the obscene inequality in the world to be articulated and therefore channelled into constructive pathways. But this can only succeed in defusing global socio-economic conflict if the world parliament is actually equipped with the power to enact serious measures against global inequality, or at least to contribute to enacting them. This category certainly includes measures such as global taxes and a basic income, but also *macroeconomic regulation* at the global level. In an appeal for a 'democratic global Keynesianism', Heikki Patomäki, Professor for World Politics at the University of Helsinki, emphasized that raising the purchasing power of the ordinary population, and thus global aggregate demand, must be a key economic goal. An increase in real wages, above all in the global South, can be achieved by making workers' rights and systematic worker organization 'the central goal of planetary economic policy for states and international organizations'. 'Regulation and maintenance of demand at a universal level', he argued, could be coordinated by a world parliament. 'From the standpoint of regulating global aggregate demand, the key question is how to create the kinds of institutional arrangements that would allow coordination between the economic policymakers of states and international organizations. One possible solution to this is a world parliament.'[57] As mentioned before a global basic income could also serve as a macroeconomic instrument.

---

54 Zucman, Gabriel. 25 June 2024. 'A Blueprint for a Coordinated Minimum Effective Taxation Standard for Ultra-High-Net-Worth Individuals', pp. 15-7.
55 Engberg-Pedersen, Lars. March 2013. 'Development goals post 2015: Reduce inequality'. DIIS Policy Brief, Danish Institute for International Studies, p. 4.
56 Milanović (2011), p. 160.
57 Patomäki, Heikki. 2013. The Great Eurozone Disaster. From Crisis to Global New Deal. Transl. by James O'Connor. London and New York: Zed Books, pp. 179-81.

In addition to a fixed basic sum, Guy Standing argued, a basic income could include a variable element which could be adjusted in a direction counter-cyclical to trends in the overall economy, i.e. increased during recessions and reduced in boom periods.[58] The economist Mark Blyth and the hedge fund manager Eric Lonergan made the point that direct financial grants made to the population can be a suitable means of stimulating the general economy. 'In the short term, such cash transfers could jump-start the economy. Over the long term, they could reduce dependence on the banking system for growth and reverse the trend of rising inequality', they wrote. Instead of seeking to influence aggregate demand via interest rates, central banks could institute direct cash transfers to the population as a monetary policy instrument. This would be especially effective in reducing inequality if the transfers were restricted to the bottom eighty per cent of households on the income scale. 'The transfers wouldn't cause damaging inflation, and few doubt that they would work. The only real question is why no government has tried them', they noted.[59] Money transfers as part of a wider framework including an unconditional global basic income could be part of the macroeconomic toolbox of a world central bank and a tool to help reduce global inequality.

A new global social contract

From a broader perspective, what is needed is the establishment and institutionalization of *a new global social contract*. The path to a fair and social world order will inevitably require reining in the dominance of the global economic elite. A world parliament provides the institutional platform for the ongoing task of organising a new settlement between the global elite and the rest of the world population. David Rothkopf rightly made the point that the answer cannot lie in a world *without* global elites. This is indeed unrealistic. However, a balance needs to be struck. 'Without the emergence of countervailing power centers to represent and ultimately institutionalize the will of the people at large', Rothkopf observed, 'we will continue to get only partial solutions.' He argued that such a development ultimately serves the most fundamental interests of the superclass itself. Otherwise, 'crisis is virtually inevitable' and only in this way might it be possible for the superclass to 'avoid the fate of past elites that were brought down due to their overreaching greed, insensitivity and short-sightedness'.[60]

58 Standing, Guy. 2014. A Precariat Charter: From Denizens to Citizens. London, New York: Bloomsbury Academic, pp. 321-2.
59 Blyth, Mark, and Eric Lonergan. 2014. 'Print Less but Transfer More'. Foreign Affairs (93) 5: 98–109, pp. 99, 103.
60 Rothkopf, David. 2008. Superclass: The Global Power Elite and the World They Are Making. London: Abacus, pp. 321-323.

24.

The debate on world government,
the age of entropy, and federalism

The global elite and the question of a world government

The World Economic Forum in Davos annually publishes a report on global risks based on surveys conducted among the business elite it is associated with. These surveys demonstrate a strong awareness of dozens of global risks in the economic, environmental, geopolitical, societal and technological fields. Failure to mitigate climate change, erosion of social cohesion and societal polarization or geoeconomic confrontation are just a few of them. With regard to most of the risks discussed, the prevailing view is that existing mechanisms for dealing with them are ineffective. For a long time, the ineffectiveness of multilateral institutions and international cooperation and 'global governance failure' themselves have been considered global risks which needed to be countered through 'long-term thinking'.[1] But this does not seem to translate into specific action. It is likely that general opinion in the group is actually closer to what David Rothkopf reported about the attitudes of the global elite. Referring to the idea of 'some global authority' that has 'serious taxing power', he wrote that 'virtually everyone whom I interviewed about the superclass fell in the range of "not in my lifetime" and "never" on the question of progress toward real and effective institutions of international government'.[2] This is linked to the fact that the majority of the elites clearly regard the idea of a global structure of governance not only as something difficult to bring about but as something that is itself *not desirable* whatever the risks may be. A democratic world legal order, with a constitution, a clear structure and division of powers, clear binding rules and decision-making processes, is something that must strike much of the transnational elite as potentially obstructive to their interests. Of all the people on the planet, the members of the super-class are the ones who personally will be affected last and least by a failure of global governance. They have the means to live wherever and however they please, entirely shielded from the existential problems that affect everyone else.

---

1 World Economic Forum. Global Risks 2023, p. 12 and id. Global Risks 2014, p. 9.
2 Rothkopf, David. 2008. Superclass: The Global Power Elite and the World They Are Making. London: Abacus, p. 497.

The economist Jeff Faux accurately described the dilemma faced by the global elite gathered at the World Economic Forum, whom he termed the 'Party of Davos'. 'Having found a way to escape the social contract of the national community through the creation of a global economy, the Party of Davos is confronted with the "catch-22" of how to govern that economy in the absence of a legitimate global government', he wrote. The problem is that promoting the 'freedom of capital' requires global rules, whereas a democratically constituted global government established for that purpose would restrain the 'freedom of capital'. 'So the vacuum created by the absence of global government is being filled by transnational bureaucratic networks aimed at supervising the global market in a way that maximizes corporate investor freedom', Faux wrote.[3]

One example of this is the transgovernmental networks of 'complex interdependence' described by Princeton University Professor Anne-Marie Slaughter, among others. She welcomed the fact that these networks 'perform many of the functions of a world government—legislation, administration, and adjudication—without the form', since a world government is 'both infeasible and undesirable'. 'The size and scope of such a government presents an unavoidable and dangerous threat to individual liberty', she wrote, repeating an argument that has been advanced, in several variants, for over two hundred years. 'Further, the diversity of the peoples to be governed makes it almost impossible to conceive of a global demos. No form of democracy within the current global repertoire seems capable of overcoming these obstacles', she stated. According to Slaughter, 'directly elected legislative assemblies at the regional level may yet have a valuable role to play in the world. Similar bodies on a global scale may also have a future, though it is hard now to imagine any that would be taken seriously.'[4] Apparently this view, expressed twenty years ago, hasn't changed.

One important regular meeting of the transnational class is the annual Bilderberg conference, which began in 1954. The participants always include more than one hundred prominent leading figures from the worlds of finance, business, international organizations, politics and media, mainly from the USA, Canada and Europe. Not much is known about the meetings, since the conferences are not public, no reports are published, and the participants mostly maintain a discreet silence. Speculation about them is therefore all the more rife. In 1976, in one of the first reports published about the Bilderberg conferences in Germany, it was stated that 'the Bilderbergers' discussed 'questions about the state of the international financial system, about the worldwide dismantling and removal of customs barriers and the free movement of

---

3　Faux, Jeff. 2006. The Global Class War. Hoboken NJ: John Wiley & Sons, pp. 169-70.
4　Slaughter, Anne-Marie. 2004. A new world order. Princeton University Press, pp. 4, 8, 124.

capital and labour', and in addition participants allegedly expressed a wish for 'some kind of world police, and also an international parliament'.[5] Whatever is actually discussed at the Bilderberg conferences, it surely is *not* the creation of a world police or a democratic world parliament. What the transnational elite thinks of the project of a world parliament became apparent at a meeting of the Trilateral Commission in London in 2001. This body was founded in 1973 at the instigation of leading Bilderberg participants such as the billionaire banker David Rockefeller. The commission brings together leading representatives of academia, business and politics from North America, Western Europe and Japan. For William Robinson, the establishment of the commission represents a marker of the 'politicization' of the 'transnational bourgeoisie', which ultimately led, through the 'Washington Consensus', to the creation of a programme for global liberalization of the markets.[6] At the core of one of the commission's first reports, in 1975, was a critique of democracy. Its authors bemoaned the fact that an 'excess of democracy' and of political participation, and an accompanying 'delegitimation of authority', was diminishing the governability of the USA, the countries of Europe and Japan.[7] At the conference in London there was agreement that a global parliament was 'quite obviously nonsense', as one of the participants put it. In particular, it was said that the European Parliament was not a suitable model for the global level. The UN, it was argued, was not a supranational project, and governments were of course already under the supervision and control of the national parliaments. It was explicitly stated that 'there is (and should be) room for institutions that are outside the realm of direct popular control'.[8] Joseph Nye, one of the co-chairs of the commission, is one of the originators of the concept of 'complex interdependence' and has done much to popularize it, and it is hardly surprising if he believes that a world government or federal power at the global level is no answer to the problem of how the globalised world ought to be governed. 'Rather than thinking of a hierarchical world government', Nye noted, 'we should think of networks of governance crisscrossing and coexisting with a world divided formally into sovereign states.'[9]

---

5   Wagner, Hans. 1976. 'Internationale Hochfinanz im Zwielicht: Der unheimliche Kreis um Prinz Bernhard'. Quick, no. 9, February, p. 27.

6   Robinson, William I. 2004. A Theory of Global Capitalism. Production, Class, and State in a Transnational World. Baltimore and London: Johns Hopkins University Press, pp. 113-4.

7   Crozier, Michael, Samuel P. Huntington, and Joji Watanuki. 1975. The Crisis of Democracy. Report on the Governability of Democracies to the Trilateral Commission. New York University Press, pp. 113, 161-3.

8   Nye, Joseph S., et al. 2003. The 'Democracy Deficit' in the Global Economy: Enhancing the Legitimacy and Accountability of Global Institutions. Report to the Trilateral Commission, The Triangle Papers Vol. 57. Washington, Paris, Tokyo: Trilateral Commission, pp. 33-5., 37.

9   Nye, Joseph S. 2002. The Paradox of American Power. Oxford, New York et al: Oxford University Press, pp. 104-5.

The specter of a global Leviathan

In a critique of Karl Jaspers' observations on the question of a world state, Hannah Arendt (1906 to 1975), whose own research focus was on totalitarianism, wrote that a sovereign world state would represent the greatest threat to human freedom. She was thinking of sovereignty in the classical sense, which presumes a monopoly on force. 'No matter what form a world government with centralized power over the whole globe might assume', Arendt wrote, 'the very notion of one sovereign force ruling the whole earth, holding the monopoly of all means of violence, unchecked and uncontrolled by other sovereign powers, is not only a forbidding nightmare of tyranny, it would be the end of all political life as we know it.'[10] However, at the same time she acknowledged that simply pointing out the dangers of such a world state was not a solution. Arendt believed that the classical concept of sovereignty had to be abandoned, as she set out in her book 'On Revolution', since 'in the realm of human affairs sovereignty and tyranny are the same'.[11] Like Jaspers, she arrived finally at the conclusion that the solution lay in a *federal world order*. 'Politically, the new fragile unity [of humankind] brought about by technical mastery over the earth can be guaranteed only within a framework of universal mutual agreements, which eventually would lead into a world-wide federated structure.'[12] Corresponding with the economist Bryan Caplan, Nick Bostrom raised the possibility 'that the creation of a democratic world government might provide better protection against the emergence of a totalitarian world government than the status quo does'. While we agree with this view, Caplan warned that 'once a world democratic government exists, there is at least a modest probability that it becomes totalitarian'. This risk should not be taken in his opinion. In consequence, he noted a 'disturbing implication': there may be a trade-off between preventing global totalitarianism and mitigating other global catastrophic risks because a world government may be the most effective way to prevent the latter from materializing. But Caplan highlighted that 'overblown doomsday worries' should not serve as a rationale for world government. However, conversely, he himself drew on a worst-case dystopian scenario of 'an eternity of totalitarianism' on Earth that perhaps would be 'worse than extinction'.[13] History cautions us that democracy is never save but totalitarian regimes have proven unstable as well. Robust constitutional

10   Arendt, Hannah. 1995. Men in Dark Times. San Diego, New York, London: Harcourt Brace & Company, pp. 81-2.
11   Id. 1965. On Revolution. London: Penguin Books.
12   Id. (1995), p. 93.
13   Caplan, Bryan. 2008. 'The Totalitarian Threat.' In: Global Catastrophic Risks, ed. by Nick Bostrom and Milan M. Ćirković, 1st ed., 504–19. Oxford, New York: Oxford University Press, pp. 512 (fn. 3), 514, 517.

systems of checks and balances and separation of powers, in particular strong parliamentary and judicial oversight, in addition to a federal order based on the principle of subsidiarity are among the structural and institutional requirements of global democracy that can help prevent an authoritarian backsliding. What is more, as the political scientist Daniel Deudney, a Professor at Johns Hopkins University, emphasized, a world government would be novel and 'unlike virtually every previous government in human existence' because it would eliminate the anarchic system of sovereign states and thus not face external adversaries. Deudney argued that this facilitates 'federal-republican arrangements' and makes some assumptions underlying the 'totalitarian specter' obsolete. Given that a world government 'would not face the pressures of an interstate anarchy, then it follows that an important set of pressures for hierarchical centralization would be absent', he wrote.[14] In order to estimate 'the risk that, once established, a global polity with democratic features would morph into something else over time', Mathias Koenig-Archibugi used historical data of democratic survival in nearly all countries of the world to construct a statistical model of longevity based on a number of economic, cultural and social variables. He then used the model to predict the longevity of democracy in a hypothetical state that featured the values of the world today for each of the variables. While Koenig-Archibugi stressed a considerable level of uncertainty in his analysis, he found that 'the probability of a world state remaining democratic over time is similar to that of an average country', making it a viable undertaking in structural terms.[15]

Nonetheless, the image of a global Leviathan is often used as a quick and easy way to brush aside the idea of a world state. Nothing is less desirable, wrote UN Secretary-General Kofi Annan in his report to the Millennium Assembly in 2000, than 'images of world government, of centralized bureaucratic behemoths trampling on the rights of people and states'.[16] But this is to attack a straw man, as there is nobody who seriously advocates a global centralized state. 'It is absurd to conceive a world government as a form of state endowed with the same characteristics that the sovereign, independent and mutually competing individual states had', as the federalist and political scientist Lucio Levi pointed out.[17] 'There is wide agreement that any viable world state would

14 Deudney, Daniel. 2007. Bounding Power: Republican Security Theory from the Polis to the Global Village. Princeton University Press, pp. 276-7.
15 Koenig-Archibugi, Mathias. 2024. The Universal Republic: A Realistic Utopia?, p. 61.
16 Annan, Kofi. 2000. We the Peoples. The Role of the United Nations in the 21st Century. Report of the Secretary-General. A/54/2000. New York: United Nations, para. 42, p. 7.
17 Levi, Lucio, Giovanni Finizio, und Nicola Vallinoto (ed.). 2014. The democratization of international institutions: first international democracy report. Milton Park et al.: Routledge, p. 20.

need to have a *federal* structure', Koenig-Archibugi noted.[18] What is really going on here, however, is the rejection of *any form of overarching hierarchical order* at the global level. In response, political scientists like Volker Rittberger spoke of 'heterarchical world governance', meaning something between anarchy and hierarchy. The term describes 'a dense net of institutions of world governance which are created and maintained by public and private actors to deal in a regulated way with trans-sovereign problems by means of *horizontal* political coordination and cooperation' (emphasis added).[19] The 'very notion of centralizing hierarchies', Annan's report continued, 'is itself an anachronism in our fluid, highly dynamic and extensively networked world—an outmoded remnant of nineteenth century mindsets.'[20] In 2021, Slaughter was among twelve individuals selected by UN Secretary-General António Guterres to serve on a panel tasked with the objective of generating 'actionable recommendations that point towards a radical shift in our approach to global governance'. In a report presented a year later, the panel wrote that its thinking was based on the presumption that 'global governance must evolve into a *less hierarchical*, more networked system' (emphasis added). While emphasizing the significance of a 'people-centered' multilateral system that grants 'meaningful opportunities' for the inclusion of various groups, in addition to states, the panel missed to address the fundamental question of how *citizens* and elected representatives can be enabled to participate in international decision-making. Instead, it stressed that it was 'an unavoidable and necessary aspect of more effective multilateralism' to 'directly involve' the *private sector* in 'multilateral processes'. This is a key purpose of the numerous 'multi-stakeholder platforms' the panel suggested should be created. The future of global governance, according to the panel, 'will not be based on worldwide unity or top-down control, but rather on connectivity across distinct domains, communities, and spheres of influence.'[21] In effect, the ideology of 'complex interdependence' and 'less hierarchy' shifts the power balance in global governance further away from citizens and to multinational corporations. Paradoxically, this approach thus creates *more* top-down power domination and not less, the opposite of what it allegedly wishes to achieve.

18 Koenig-Archibugi, p. 37.
19 Rittberger, Volker, Andreas Kruck, and Anne Romund. 2010. Grundzüge der Weltpolitik. Theorie and Empirie des Weltregierens. 1st ed. Wiesbaden: VS Verlag für Sozialwissenschaften, p. 315.
20 Annan, para. 42, p. 7.
21 High-Level Advisory Board on Effective and Multilateralism (HLAB). 2023. A Breakthrough for People and Planet: Effective and Inclusive Global Governance for Today and the Future. New York: United Nations University, 2023, pp. 4, 6, 61, 18, 13.

Hierarchical order and complexity

A key insight offered by the history of evolution is that hierarchies developed as a natural way of *governing complexity*. The influential social scientist and Nobel laureate for economics Herbert A. Simon (1916 to 2001) noted that it 'is a commonplace observation that nature loves hierarchies'.[22] Simon was an early pioneer of the study of the architecture of complex biological, physical and social systems. 'Empirically,' he wrote, 'a large proportion of the complex systems we observe in nature exhibit hierarchic structure. On theoretical grounds we might expect complex systems to be hierarchies in a world in which complexity had to evolve from simplicity. In their dynamics, hierarchies have a property, near decomposability, that greatly simplifies their behavior.'[23] What Simon terms 'near decomposability' indicates that subsystems can be almost independent, and that the interaction of elements within the subsystems is more intensive than that between them. The nub of the matter, however, is that despite this there is an ordered hierarchical nesting of systems and their interactions, as well as an overarching governance.[24]

Different types of hierarchies

The philosopher and author Arthur Koestler suggested in his 1967 book 'The Ghost in the Machine' that the constituent parts of the nested hierarchies found everywhere should be called 'holons'. The term is intended to make it clear that the elements of a hierarchical order are always simultaneously both a part and a whole. 'Organisms and societies', Koestler wrote, 'are multi-levelled hierarchies of semi-autonomous sub-wholes branching into sub-wholes of a lower order, and so on. The term "holon" has been introduced to refer to these intermediary entities which, relative to their subordinates in the hierarchy, function as self-contained wholes; relative to their superordinates as dependent parts. This dichotomy of "wholeness" and "partness", of autonomy and dependence, is inherent in the concept of hierarchic order.'[25] To emphasize this connection, the term 'holarchies' is sometimes used for hierarchies.

The scepticism towards hierarchies derives in part from the experience of higher levels having a tendency to become too dominant or even oppressive towards lower levels. Totalitarian systems are characterised by a monopoly on

22   Simon, Herbert A. 1973. 'The Organization of Complex Systems'. In: Hierarchy Theory. The Challenge of Complex Systems, ed. by Howard H. Pattee, 1–27. New York: George Braziller, p. 5.

23   Id. 1962. 'The Architecture of Complexity'. Proceedings of the American Philosophical Society (106) 6: 467–82, pp. 481-2.

24   Id. 2002. 'Near decomposability and the speed of evolution'. Industrial and corporate change (11) 3: 587–99, pp. 595-6.

25   Koestler, Arthur. 1967. The Ghost in the Machine. London: Pan Books, p. 76.

power at the highest level, meaning that all lower levels are in principle downgraded to mere recipients of orders. The US American author Ken Wilber, however, emphasized that the 'existence of pathological hierarchies does not damn the existence of hierarchies in general'.[26] He cited in support the distinction drawn by the systems scientist and lawyer Riane Eisler between domination and actualization hierarchies. 'The term *domination hierarchies* describes hierarchies based on force or the express or implied threat of force. Such hierarchies are very different from the types of hierarchies found in progressions from lower to higher orderings of functioning—such as the progression from cells to organs in living organisms, for example. These types of hierarchies may be characterized by the term *actualization hierarchies* because their function is to maximize the organism's potentials', Eisler wrote in the book 'Chalice and the Blade'.[27] The challenge thus lies in creating a *planetary actualization hierarchy* with citizens at its core. The key to this is a federal and democratic structure. One organizational principle of the functional relationship between sociopolitical holons on different levels, once again, is that of subsidiarity.

The principle of subsidiarity

According to the principle of subsidiarity tasks and competences of public administration and legislation are required to be located at the lowest possible level of government where they can still be carried out in an effective manner. Guaranteeing 'a degree of independence for a lower authority in relation to a higher body', it is perhaps the most important principle for devolution and empowerment of local government and underlies the organization of federal states.[28] Their constitutions accordingly include legal rules as to how competences and administrative functions are shared across existing levels of government. 'Federalism entails that the constituent units of a world state would retain important constitutionally protected areas of competence. Where opinions diverge is the range of issues over which a world state would have authority', Koenig-Archibugi explained.[29] In terms of the European Union, the most advanced supranational organization, the principle of subsidiarity is enshrined in Article 5 of the Lisbon Treaty which says, among other things, that 'in areas which do not fall within its exclusive competence, the Union shall act only if and in so far as the objectives of the proposed action cannot be sufficiently achieved by the Member States, either at central level or at regional

26   Wilber, Ken. 2000. Sex, Ecology, Spirituality: The Spirit of Evolution. 2nd ed. rev. Boston Mass.: Shambhala, p. 30.
27   Cit. from ibid., pp. 30-1; see also Riane Eisler, 1987. Chalice and the Blade. San Francisco: Harper, p. 205.
28   European Parliament. 2022. 'The Principle of Subsidiarity.' Fact Sheets on the European Union. (europarl.europa.eu).
29   Koenig-Archibugi, ibid.

and local level'. While in the global context the principle in important cases of managing global commons and challenges will prescribe *upward delegation* of competences, from nation-states to a world state, it means at the same time that this needs to be done in a limited and justified way within the framework of a federal global constitution.

Subsidiarity thus plays a key role in conceptualizing a world state. The philosopher Christoph Horn, for instance, who teaches at the University of Bonn, is among those who believe that 'a tiered system of powers based on the principle of subsidiarity' is a 'key means of nullifying the fear that a world state holds for people'. 'Consideration should for example be given to a decentralization arranged in tiers from world state—continental units—national and regional units—finally down to local units. The bulk of current competences could thus remain at the national, regional and even local levels; and thus a considerably stronger degree of delegation of decision-making competences down to small units could be considered than is presently the case in contemporary states. In this way, the structure of a world state—far from requiring a massive bureaucracy—could be precisely what leads to a transformation of political decision-making along participatory and democratic lines', Horn argued. A world state could thus, and perhaps better than any other structure, 'by means of an appropriate division into federal sub-states and the protection of minorities ensure adequate legal protection for group interests and identities'.[30]

The fragmentation of global governance and of international law

The system of global governance and international law is marked by a fragmentation unmitigated by any form of overarching hierarchy, harmonization, governance or coordination. This also applies to the United Nations, with its dozens of programmes, specialised agencies, commissions, secretariats, funds and other 'entities'. Its coherence and governability have always been considered inadequate. As Thomas G. Weiss reported, the UN's development work was described in 1969 already as a 'prehistoric monster' in an official evaluation. Even forty years later, this 'lumbering dinosaur' was no better suited to the conditions prevailing in the 21st century according to Weiss. It would be difficult, he noted, to imagine 'a better design for futile complexity'.[31] The UN High-level Panel on Global Sustainability noted in a report that while 'institutional fragmentation may begin at the national level, it is endemic at the in-

---

30   Horn, Christoph. 1996. 'Philosophische Argumente für einen Weltstaat'. Allgemeine Zeitschrift für Philosophie 21: 229–51, p. 244.

31   Weiss, Thomas G. 2009. 'What Happened to the Idea of World Government?' International Studies Quarterly 53:253–71, p. 255.

ternational level'. In order to achieve sustainable development, the report said, we 'must overcome the legacy of fragmented institutions established around single-issue "silos"'.[32] The German law expert Dieter Grimm, a former member of the constitutional court, gave an accurate description of the characteristics of world governance with regard to the issue of putting the international use of public authority by states on a constitutional footing. 'There is no coherent form for the exercise of public authority by the world community', he wrote. 'Rather, there are individual, functionally specific, publicly authorised bodies which are unconnected to each other and which possess only ad hoc powers. Their legal bases are equally ad hoc and do not add up to a systematic and coherent world legal order. The currently prevailing world order', according to Grimm, 'is instead reminiscent of the medieval order with its widely dispersed forms of ad hoc powers delegated to independent holders, which similarly did not add up to a basis for a constitutional order.'[33]

The fragmentation of the international system of states is mirrored in the system of international law. In an influential report commissioned by the UN International Law Commission, the Austrian international law expert Gerhard Hafner warned in 2000 against its increasing fragmentation. Existing 'international law does not consist of one homogenous legal order, but mostly of different partial systems, producing an "unorganized system"', he wrote, and referred to a 'disintegration of the legal order'. He identified the causes as being specialization in differing autonomous legal regimes, differing norm structures, parallel or competing regulations within the same area of law, the extension of the application of international law to new areas, and overlapping and contradictory subsystems of secondary law. But the first and perhaps most important cause identified by Hafner, at that time a member of the International Law Commission, was *the lack of centralised organs*. 'Fragmentation stems from the nature of international law as a law of coordination instead of subordination as well as from the lack of centralized institutions which would ensure homogeneity and conformity of legal regulations', he wrote.[34] For Tomer Broude, an international law specialist teaching in Jerusalem, the problems of norm fragmentation and authority fragmentation are 'the warp and weft of the complex fabric that is international law'. The goal of normative integration has

32 United Nations High-level Panel on Global Sustainability (ed.). March 2012. 'Resilient people, resilient planet: a future worth choosing. Report of the High-level Panel of the Secretary-General on Global Sustainability'. A/66/700, pp. 8, 74.

33 Grimm, Dieter. 2006. 'Transnationale Macht - konstitutionalisierbar?'. In: Vernunft oder Macht: zum Verhältnis von Philosophie and Politik, ed. by Otfried Höffe, 161–70. Tübingen: Francke, p. 168.

34 Hafner, Gerhard. 2000. 'Risks Ensuing from Fragmentation of International Law'. In: Report of the International Law Commission on the work of its fifty-second session, Official Records of the General Assembly, Fifty-fifth session, suppl. no. 10, A/55/10, 143–50, pp. 143, 147, 145.

'a political meaning for the entire international system's structure of authority and governance', he wrote, because it requires 'greater centralization and/or harmonization of authority.'[35] But the use of the term 'fragmentation' here should not be taken to mean that a once uniform and coherent system is falling apart. International law from the beginning, by its nature, has always been fragmentary and fully intentionally so. Creating hierarchy 'is actively and deliberately avoided' and even faces 'severe resistance', observed Rakhyun E. Kim, Assistant Professor of Global Environmental Governance at Utrecht University, in an article he wrote with four co-authors. One of the reasons is an 'important political consequence' of this non-hierarchical architecture which is characterized by 'conditions of complexity, uncertainty and unpredictability', namely that 'powerful states could take advantage of "chaotic" situations to exert their power and gain more leverage over global governance outcomes at the expense of the less powerful'. In other words, the absence of coherence and hierarchy serves their interests. In view of many far-reaching proposals for better systematization, centralization and prioritization, none of which were implemented in the past four decades, the researchers contended that not only big powers such as China and the United States, but 'many actors within this architecture have an interest in maintaining the status quo', however ineffective it may be. The proposals they refer to have all been well below the threshold of the 'vision of a single global constitutional polity with a global legislature, executive and judiciary' which Kim and his colleagues believe represents 'arguably the most extreme example of hierarchy in the international system'.[36] Arguably, however, it is also the most effective and most democratic option.

One of the issues in international treaty law under conditions of fragmentation is 'problem shifting'. This occurs when an intergovernmental treaty is put into place to solve one issue but, as a side effect, creates new ones. According to Kim, an expert on the subject, treaties 'are often self-interest driven, meaning they compete against each other to achieve their own narrowly-defined goals'. In the process, the big picture gets lost. A well-known example is biofuel policy. 'Because of the incentives given by the UN Climate Change Convention to achieve carbon neutrality, some countries have cut down forests and planted biofuel crops like palm oil. Although these crops remove carbon dioxide from

35   Broude, Tomer. 2008. 'Fragmentation(s) of International Law: On Normative Integration as Authority Allocation'. In: The Shifting Allocation of Authority in International Law, ed. by Tomer Broude and Yuval Shany, 99–120. Oxford and Portland, Oregon: Hart Publishing, pp. 104, 110.
36   Kim, Rakhyun E., Harro van Asselt, Louis J. Kotzé, Marjanneke J. Vijge, and Frank Biermann. 2020. 'Hierarchization.' In: Architectures in Earth System Governance: Institutional Complexity and Structural Transformation, ed. by Frank Biermann and Rakhyun E. Kim, 275–96. Cambridge Univ. Press, pp. 275, 290, 277.

the air as they grow, they also result in biodiversity loss, water scarcity, and have negative consequences for the livelihoods of local communities', Kim noted.[37]

Coherent world law and a world parliament

The international law specialist Wilfred Jenks, later Director-General of the ILO, pointed out as early as 1953 that in 'the absence of a world legislature with a general mandate, law-making treaties are tending to develop in a number of historical, functional and regional groups which are separate from each other and whose mutual relationships are in some respects analogous to those of separate systems of municipal law'.[38] It is precisely a world legislature that must form the starting point and the centre of a coherent and harmonised world legal system which can establish clear and universally binding hierarchies of norms and prioritization rules. A hierarchization into constitutional primary law and secondary or delegated legislation is indispensable. An essential basic principle will be that world law takes precedence over international law. In areas regulated by world law, it must therefore be able to intervene directly in international law. This will involve bringing together in the world legislature hitherto disconnected and divergent political regulation processes within network governance and international institutions, and applying to all of those processes a system of global political balancing, preference-setting and prioritization. This is automatically the result of a parliamentary legislative process based on deliberation and drafting in specialized committees, which interact with each other and finally submit a proposed regulation to the plenary for adoption. Using Anne-Marie Slaughter's terminology, one could speak of a world parliament having the responsibility to 'aggregate' the existing but fragmented elements into a coherent world order. From the elevated vantage point of a historian, Charles Maier of Harvard University attacked the concept of 'governance' as 'a utopia of the academic administrative elite', and emphasized this point in connection with a lack of state control. 'The concept of governance, which enjoyed such popularity at the end of the 20th century and which still today holds such a fascination for social scientists and foundations, was and is testament to the hope for a government without "statehood"—as if politics in future could be relieved of the task of gathering to-

---

37   'Passing the Buck: Getting to the Bottom of Environmental Problem Shifting.' 2022. Utrecht University. October 5, 2022. (www.uu.nl)
38   Jenks, Wilfred. 1953. 'The Conflict of Law-Making Treaties'. Brit. Yearbook of Int. Law 30: 401–53, p. 403.

gether different preferences and finally opting for one or the other, and could instead function via consensus and the power of rational debate.'[39]

The bewildering world order and the 'age of entropy'

Politically, too, the world order is characterised by confusion and complexity. Samuel Huntington wrote in 1999 that global politics 'has thus moved from the bipolar system of the Cold War through a unipolar moment—highlighted by the Gulf War—and is now passing through one or two uni-multipolar decades before it enters a truly multipolar 21st century'.[40] Richard Haass, President of the Council on Foreign Relations, noted ten years later that we would have to *completely abandon* the concept of geopolitical polarity as the main explanatory model for the world order. At first sight, according to Haass, the world may appear to have become multipolar, with China, the EU, India, Japan, Russia and the USA as the most important powers. In fact, however, there are far more centres of power, some of which are not even nation states. The power and predominance of the states is being challenged in the course of globalization by regional and global governmental organizations as well as a multitude of NGOs and companies. 'The principal characteristic of twenty-first-century international relations is turning out to be nonpolarity', wrote Haass. This is 'a world dominated not by one or two or even several states but rather by dozens of actors possessing and exercising various kinds of power.' If left to itself, this 'nonpolar world' would become ever more chaotic over time.[41] As Haas observed, the COVID-19 pandemic did not change the direction of the world but rather accelerated it. The pandemic had brought pre-existing characteristics of the international environment 'into sharper-than-ever relief', he wrote, including waning American leadership, faltering global cooperation, great-power discord and failure of global organizations.[42] The political scientist Ian Bremmer, founder of the Eurasia Group consultancy, spoke of a 'G-Zero world' to describe the disappearance of any single state or even group of states with the capacity to provide effective leadership for the international system. 'Who will lead?' he asked rhetorically, only to immediately provide the answer himself. 'No one.' Neither the G7, nor the G20, nor

---

39 Maier, Charles S. 2012. 'Leviathan 2.0: Die Erfindung moderner Staatlichkeit'. In: Geschichte der Welt. 5, Weltmärkte and Weltkriege 1870-1945, ed. by Akira Iriye and Jürgen Osterhammel, 34–286. München: Beck, p. 285.
40 Huntington, Samuel P. 1999. 'The Lonely Superpower'. Foreign Affairs (78) 2: 35–49, p. 37.
41 Haass, Richard N. 2008. 'The Age of Nonpolarity - What Will Follow U.S. Dominance'. Foreign Affairs (87) 3: 44-56.
42 Id. 7 April 2020. 'The Pandemic Will Accelerate History Rather Than Reshape It.' Foreign Affairs. (foreign-affairs.com).

any other forum.[43] For Stewart Patrick of the Council on Foreign Relations, 'what really marks the contemporary era is not the absence of multilateralism but its astonishing diversity'. In the world of the 'G-X', as Patrick called it, collective action 'is no longer focused solely, or even primarily, on the UN and other universal, treaty-based institutions, nor even on a single apex forum such as the G-20. Rather, governments have taken to operating in many venues simultaneously, participating in a bewildering array of issue-specific networks and partnerships whose membership varies based on situational interests, shared values, and relevant capabilities'.[44]

The US American political scientist Randall L. Schweller believes that the world order is transitioning into an 'age of entropy'. In contrast to Stewart Patrick, however, he found little positive to say about the associated 'multilateralism à la carte' and disaggregated network governance. 'What some call global governance', said Schweller, 'is little more than a spaghetti bowl of clashing agreements brokered within and among thirty thousand or so international organizations of varying significance.' It is practically impossible to find out where international responsibility for any given problem actually lies. The reason for this, according to Schweller, is that as a consequence of growing entropy there is no central international authority over anything any longer. 'No one will know where international authority resides because it will not reside anywhere; and without authority, there can be no governance', Schweller noted. And he complained that 'the labyrinthine structure of global governance is more complex than most of the problems it is supposed to be solving'.[45] As Dirk Messner long ago established, 'it must not be overlooked that the architecture of global governance can itself become a global problem on account of its complexity'.[46] This point has undoubtedly been reached.

The entropic decline of world civilization?

The current system of 'heterarchic' world governance is highly ineffective and inefficient. It adds to the complexity of the world system rather than guiding or reducing it. This could lead to entropic decline, as described by the US American futurologist Hazel Henderson (1933 to 2022) in 1978, writing about industrial societies. She believed that on account of increasing complexity industrial societies could at some point reach an 'entropy state'. 'The entropy

43　Bremmer, Ian. 2012. *Every Nation for Itself: Winners and Losers in a G-Zero World*. London: Portfolio Penguin, p. 4.

44　Patrick, Stewart. 2014. 'The Unruled World'. Foreign Affairs (93) 1: 58–73, p. 62.

45　Schweller, Randall L. 2014. *Maxwell's Demon and the Golden Apple: Global Discord in the New Millennium*. Baltimore, Maryland: Johns Hopkins University Press, pp. 118, 23.

46　Messner, Dirk. 1998. 'Architektur der Weltordnung'. Internationale Politik, November: 17–24, p. 23.

state', she wrote, 'is a society at the stage where complexity and interdependence have reached the point where the transaction costs that are generated equal or exceed the society's productive capabilities. In a manner analogous to the phenomenon that occurs in physical systems, the society slowly winds down of its own weight and complexity.' This is linked in her view to the fact that the unproductive costs of social governance and coordination, and the costs of the externalities arising, become too large. 'We seem unwilling to come to terms with the fact that each increase in the order of magnitude of technological mastery and managerial control requires and inevitably leads to a concomitant order of magnitude of government coordination and control.'[47] This reasoning can be applied to world civilization as a whole. In an influential study of 'The Collapse of Complex Societies', the US American anthropologist and historian Joseph Tainter also came to the conclusion that the growth of complexity brings with it a fundamental problem. According to his analysis, it lies in the nature of human societies that mastering problems inevitably involves an increase in socio-political complexity. This is brought about by the cumulative expansion of bureaucracy and organizational structures, or perhaps by ever-increasing social and hierarchical differentiation. This brings in turn a growing burden of costs and taxes for the productive population. The economic benefits that accompany this growth in complexity steadily decrease, and beyond a certain point of social development they can tip over into the negative. This means that what Henderson described as 'the entropy state' has been reached. In this phase, a collapse in the form of socio-political disintegration is—despite its disastrous consequences—an economically explicable and even inevitable development in Tainter's view, unless new sources of productivity growth can be tapped. A collapse of civilization would consist in a forced return to less complex organizational stages. Tainter emphasized in his study that under the prevailing conditions of a complex world civilization, the isolated collapse of a single society is no longer possible. Should another collapse happen, it will be *on a global scale*. 'World civilization will disintegrate as a whole.' Tainter feared that contemporary world civilization, like earlier societies that did collapse, does not have the capacity to solve its problems. 'If we are to escape nuclear annihilation, if we control pollution and population, and manage to circumvent resource depletion, will our fate then be sealed by the high cost and low marginal return that these things will require?' he asked.[48]

---

47 Henderson, Hazel. 1996 [1978]. Creating Alternative Futures. The End of Economics. First Kumarian Press Printing. West Hartford CT: Kumarian Press, 1996, p. 83-4.

48 Tainter, Joseph A. 1988. The Collapse of Complex Societies. Cambridge University Press, p. 213, see also pp. 118, 123, 127, 195.

World federalism as a means of reducing complexity

However, the question arises whether these costs would really be so over-whelming at a higher socio-political level of organization—that is, at the level of world-state structures—or whether they might not in fact be lower than they are today. One important objective of the global programme of integration that would accompany a world parliament is the harmonization, reorganization and de-fragmentation of today's system of global governance within a democratic world-state framework. A world federal order with a global legislative system would contribute to *a reduction in complexity* and to *lower transaction costs*. It represents a hierarchical consolidation of the civilizational process at a *higher systemic level*. The reason why world civilization is threatening to reach the 'entropy state' is that the current, inter-state based system by its very nature *cannot* deliver efficient global solutions to problems at low transactional cost. The fragmented 'heterarchical' structure of global governance, based on the paradigm of national sovereignty without any central control and authority, is inherently incapable of it. One example of transaction costs that also lower productive capacity is the immense expenditure on the military and on armaments, which arises not least out of the dysfunctional structure of the system. It is a result of the fact that it has not yet proved possible, in spite of all the accretion of subsequent social layers, to entirely move beyond the phase of anarchism. The creation of a world peace order, as sketched out in this book, would make it possible to do without much of this expenditure. The increase in inequality coupled with the growing accumulation of capital by the super-rich, a process facilitated by the system, represents an additional illustration of how productive forces are being held back without any possibility of effective central countervailing policies.

A world state as a taboo topic

Few people are willing to speak openly about the need for world state structures. It is not rare for us to hear from academics and others that, although they find the idea of a world parliament interesting and in principle support it, they don't want to risk opening themselves up to criticism. The horizon of the debate over the form of world governance has narrowed sharply. In the keynote speech already referred to by the political scientist Thomas G. Weiss on the fiftieth anniversary of the International Studies Association, he observed that 'the idea of world government has been banned in sober and sensible discussions of global affairs and certainly is absent from classrooms'. In drastic words, he bemoaned before the assembled representatives of the discipline 'the abject poverty of our current thinking'. Following the Second World War, an intensive engagement with the issue had been part of the mainstream, he argued; however, 'currently a world federal government or even elements of one is not only old-fashioned, it is commonly thought to be the preserve of lunatics'. Yet Weiss reminded his audience that even realists such as Hans Morgenthau and Reinhold Niebuhr believed that a world state was 'logically necessary'.[49] In his 2011 book 'The Realist Case for Global Reform', the political scientist William E. Scheuerman set out the argument that there was an 'important programmatic overlap' between leading representatives of the realist school of international relations and world federalism.[50]

The teetering paradigm of intergovernmentalism

The mainstream suffers from its readiness to content itself with describing the state of things as they are. The modern nation state, and the associated idea of sovereignty, remains the hub around which mainstream thinking revolves. The resulting conception of the necessarily intergovernmental nature of world governance can be classified in line with Thomas S. Kuhn's theory of scientific revolutions as a classical paradigm. Deviations from the paradigm are neither conceived, recognised or desired by the mainstream. Long-term reflection on alternative ways of organising world governance is therefore of no interest. 'It is not a diagnosis which is lacking; what needs to be explained is the timidity towards a perspective which would open up a path, however difficult to pursue, towards a transnational world domestic policy', Jürgen Habermas wrote, referring to the social sciences. 'A discipline of sociology which almost always considers "society" as a unit defined by the nation state, that is, as a national society, will have severe conceptual difficulty in dealing with an entity as weakly structured politically as the "world society".'[51] It may be correct that the 'heterarchical model', as Volker Rittberger and colleagues wrote, 'is best placed to explain many of the empirically observable forms of world governance'.[52] However, the dominant paradigmatic framework will struggle to recognize and explain the characteristic processes of the formation of a global state. Although Rittberger regarded a world state as an unlikely outcome of the socio-evolutionary process, and opposed it anyway, he himself wrote in 1973 that 'the world-state model must be exposed to tentative empirical testing

---

49   Weiss, p. 261-3.
50   Scheuerman, William E. 2011. The realist case for global reform. Cambridge: Polity Press.
51   Habermas, Jürgen. 1998. 'Jenseits des Nationalstaats? Bemerkungen zu Folgeproblemen der wirtschaftlichen Globalisierung'. In: Politik der Globalisierung, ed. by Ulrich Beck, 67–84. Frankfurt: Suhrkamp, p. 79.
52   Rittberger et al., ibid., p. 711.

at least insofar as there may or may not exist discernible trends in present-day world politics that point toward the eventual establishment of a world state'.[53]

In his famous work 'The Civilizing Process', published first in 1939 and then in a revised edition in 1969, Norbert Elias adopted a long-term perspective on the development of the structures of personality and society in Europe since about the 8th century. The 'forces of social interweaving' he described there, which ever since the 'point of utmost feudal disintegration' created pressure for the integration of ever larger socio-political associations, are seen as still operating today and now spanning a system of interdependence 'embracing the entire inhabited earth'. 'The competitive tension between states,' wrote Elias, 'given the pressures which our social structure brings with it, can be resolved only after a long series of violent or non-violent trials of strength have established monopolies of force, and central organizations for larger dominions, within which many of the smaller ones, "states", can grow together in a more balanced unity.' Although it was impossible to foresee the timeframe and the make-up of the 'larger hegemonial units', the direction of the processes of interweaving was clear: the creation of 'a worldwide monopoly of physical force' and 'a single central political institution' for the Earth.[54] Referring to long-term processes of state formation, Elias bemoaned the fact that these were obviously 'developmental processes of such duration as to be beyond the reach of the contemporary sociological imagination, which is focused on much shorter-term perspectives'.[55] Not much has changed with regard to this finding. Yet in view of the ever more apparent failure of global governance, doubts continue to grow over whether the dominant perspective will be adequate. The model of a paradigmatic crisis as described by the philosopher of science Thomas S. Kuhn can be clearly observed. 'Political revolutions', he wrote, 'are inaugurated by a growing sense, often restricted to a segment of the political community, that existing institutions have ceased adequately to meet the problems posed by an environment that they have in part created. In much the same way, scientific revolutions are inaugurated by a growing sense, again often restricted to a narrow subdivision of the scientific community, that an existing paradigm has ceased to function adequately in the exploration of an aspect of nature to which that paradigm itself had previously led the way. In both political and scientific development the sense of

---

53 Rittberger, Volker. 1973. Evolution and International Organization. Toward a New Level of Sociopolitical Integration. Den Haag: Nijhoff, p. 47.

54 Elias, Norbert. 2000. The Civilizing Process: Sociogenetic and Psychogenetic Investigations. Transl. by Edmund Jephcott. Rev. ed. Oxford; Malden, MA: Blackwell, pp. 436-438, 446.

55 Id. 1984. What Is Sociology. Rev. ed. New York: Columbia University Press.

malfunction that can lead to crisis is prerequisite to revolution.'[56] In this instance, modern international law and the existing Westphalian international order are without doubt a product of the idea of the sovereign nation state, of that idea which continues to serve the discourse as paradigm. This paradigm is no longer sufficient for an understanding of the world order or the direction in which it might develop. In addition, the failure of the Westphalian order to meet global challenges is the source of ever growing criticism. In an article published in 1999 already, the British social scientist Susan Strange encapsulated this in the pithy term 'Westfailure System'. 'We have to escape and resist the state-centrism inherent in the analysis of conventional international relations', she wrote. 'It is not our job, in short, to defend or excuse the Westphalian system.'[57]

The standard reactionary arguments

However, the problem is not just academic or intellectual as we have seen. It would be a mistake to believe that the debate over the form that world governance should take is conducted entirely free of influence by interest groups. Rather, the debate reveals distinct traits of what might be termed a *hegemonic discourse.* It is not of course mere coincidence that the paradigm of intergovernmentalism, the notions of multistakeholder and network governance as well as the fiction of the sovereignty of the nation state are defended most vigorously precisely by the members of the transnational elites. The rhetoric that emanates from that quarter against the idea of a world democracy ultimately serves the purpose of making it appear that there is no alternative to the current system and condition of world governance. This is often accompanied by recourse to the perversity thesis and the jeopardy thesis. Fear of the supposed danger of a tyrannical world state is thus instrumentalized and extended to *any* form a world state might take. A democratic, federal world state, so the argument runs, may be a noble aim, but it always bears within it the potential to degenerate into tyranny, which would pose a *much greater threat* to democracy and freedom than existed before. As the sociologist Albert O. Hirschman showed, this line of argumentation—the perversity and jeopardy theses—is among 'the major polemical postures or manoeuvres likely to be engaged in by those who set out to debunk and overturn "progressive" policies and movements of ideas'. Reactionary rhetoric of this kind, according to Hirschman, has been used since the 19th century to oppose individual human rights, the universal franchise and democracy, as well as the development

56   Kuhn, Thomas S. 1970. Structure of Scientific Revolutions. 2nd ed. Chicago: University of Chicago Press, p. 92.
57   Strange, Susan. 1999. 'The Westfailure System'. Review of International Studies (25) 3: 345–54.

of the welfare state. Now it is being directed against a globalization of these hard-won achievements through a democratic world state. In his book 'The Rhetoric of Reaction', Hirschman examined the typical rhetorical devices of reactionary argumentation. 'According to the *perversity* thesis', he explained, 'any purposive action to improve some feature of the political, social, or economic order only serves to exacerbate the condition one wishes to remedy. The *futility* thesis holds that attempts at social transformation will be unavailing, that they will simply fail to "make a dent." Finally, the *jeopardy* thesis argues that the cost of the proposed change or reform is too high as it endangers some previous, precious accomplishment.'[58] The fact that hundreds of millions of people, if not the majority of the world population, are *already now* subjected to structural violence embedded in the global system, and that the failure of global governance puts at risk the existing level of world civilization, is simply disregarded in this line of argument. The concept of structural violence was introduced by Johan Galtung. Following Galtung, structural violence is violence which cannot be attributed directly to one single actor and which, on account of its permanent presence and 'noiselessness', is often not recognised as such even by its victims. This violence, Galtung summed up, 'is built into the system and expresses itself in unequal power relations and consequently in unequal life chances'. When 'people starve at a time when it could objectively be avoided, then violence is being committed, regardless of whether a clear subject-object relation obtains.', he noted. The enabling condition of structural violence, according to Galtung, is social injustice, and particularly the unequal distribution of power.[59] A democratic world state and a world parliament are intended to serve the goal of *eliminating the existing global barbarity*.

58 Hirschman, Albert O. 1991. The Rhetoric of Reaction. Cambridge, London: The Belknap Press of Harvard University Press, pp. 6-7.
59 Galtung, Johan. 1975. Strukturelle Gewalt. Reinbek: Rowohlt, pp. 12-3, 19.

25.

The third democratic transformation and the global democratic deficit

'In perusing the pages of our history', wrote the lawyer and historian Alexis de Tocqueville in the introduction to his 1835 work 'Democracy in America', 'we shall scarcely meet with a single great event, in the lapse of seven hundred years, which has not turned to the advantage of equality.' He saw before his eyes the long arc of history, tracing the continual decline of the aristocracy and the rise of the bourgeoisie from the Crusades via the Reformation to the revolutions of the 18th century. He pointed out how the invention of firearms and the printing press, along with improvements in education, science and literature had contributed to this development. A 'great democratic revolution' was going on, he wrote.[1] At that time, the revolution was just beginning.

The waves of democratization

The spread of democracy around the world, and of the civil and political rights associated with it, is among the most important political trends of the last two centuries. This development can be divided up into historical waves of democratization, as first proposed by the US American political scientist Samuel Huntington. A 'wave of democratization' means that over a given period considerably more non-democratic states become democracies than vice versa. When considering different attempts to capture such developments, it is important to bear in mind that the evaluation of a democracy in a given country is often determined by subjective judgements, starting with the choice of indicators. However, this does not affect the overall picture. The first wave identified by Huntington began in 1828 and lasted until about 1926. It had its roots in the American and French Revolutions and involved a gradual extension of suffrage and the subordination of the executive to parliament. In the one hundred years of the first wave, Huntington reported, over 30 countries established at least a minimum level of democratic institutions.[2] Using the data and definitions of the Polity research programme, at the end of the first wave, 1926, 21 countries, or 30 per cent of all states surveyed, qualified as

---

1   Tocqueville, Alexis de. 1899. Democracy in America. The Colonial Press, pp. 3, 5.
2   Huntington, Samuel. 1991. The Third Wave: Democratization in the late Twentieth Century. Norman: University of Oklahoma Press, pp. 15-7.

democracies.[3] Some 17 per cent of the world population lived in these countries at that time.[4] After the setbacks of the 1920s and 1930s, a second democratization wave took place in the period roughly between 1943 and 1962. By the end of this wave, 35 of the countries analysed for the Polity programme, or one-third of the growing total number of states in the world, holding 36 per cent of the world population, were now classified as democracies. After some further setbacks, in 1974, following Huntington's categorization, the third wave of democratization began with the 'Carnation Revolution' in Portugal. Other researchers place the beginning of the third wave in 1987, as in their view the movements towards more and towards less democracy among states balanced each other out earlier.[5] At any rate, from 1989 onwards, with the onset of the reform programme in the Soviet Union, the peaceful revolutions in Eastern Europe and the end of the Cold War, democratization acquired unprecedented momentum throughout the world. Between 1974 and 1989, the number of democracies counted by the Polity programme grew from 34 to 49, which was an increase from 25 to 35 per cent. Over just the next three years to 1992, the number shot up to 75, representing 47 per cent of all states. Since that point, for the first time ever more than half the world's population was living under democracy. The third wave reached a tentative high point in 2006, when Polity counted 95 democracies around the world, or 57 per cent. According to Polity's latest data, the number of democracies between 2006 and 2015 varied in a range from 92 to 96, and then increased to an all-time high of 99, or 59 per cent of all states analyzed, in 2018.[6]

A global democratic reversal?

The Washington D.C. based NGO Freedom House estimates each year the level of civil and political rights in the world. In 2006, they reported the highest number of free countries and electoral democracies since their assessments began in 1974, with 90 and 123 respectively. This peak was matched in 2013 and 2014, with free countries reaching 90 again, after a slight decline, and electoral democracies increasing to a peak of 125. The drop in electoral democracies from 123 to 116 in the 2018 report was due to the introduction of more stringent criteria. In 2023, the number of free countries according to

---

3   Center for Systemic Peace, Polity IV Annual Time-Series 1800-2010 (www.systemicpeace.org/inscr-data.html).

4   These figures and the ones which follow on population proportions were put together by Max Roser based on Polity IV, US Census and Gapminder (ourworldindata.org).

5   Inglehart, Ronald, and Christian Welzel. 2005. Modernization, cultural change, and democracy: the human development sequence. Cambridge University Press, pp. 176-7.

6   Center for Systemic Peace, Polity5 Annual Time Series 1800-2018.

Freedom House had fallen to 84, and electoral democracies to 110. Two years earlier, the world's largest democracy, India, had been downgraded to 'partly free'. As of 2024, Freedom House had been observing aggregate score declines of freedom for 18 years in a row.[7]

Since the Economist Intelligence Unit initiated its annual global democracy assessment in 2006, by 2023 the count of 'full democracies' slightly decreased from 26 to 24, peaking at 28 in 2008, while 'flawed democracies' dropped from 53 to 50. Conversely, 'hybrid regimes' increased slightly from 33 to 34, and 'authoritarian regimes' rose from 55 to 59, the highest count yet. The Economist's researchers noted a decrease in the average global index they calculate from 5.52 in 2006 to 5.23 in 2023.[8] According to another analysis made by the Varieties of Democracy research project, or V-Dem, in 2024, 'the level of democracy enjoyed by the average person in the world' in the previous year was 'down to 1985-levels; by country-based averages, it is back to 1998'. V-Dem reported an increase in closed autocracies from 22 in 2012 to 33 in 2023, while liberal democracies declined from a peak of 44 in 2009 to 32, with the remainder classified as either electoral autocracies or electoral democracies. The institute observed that autocratization was ongoing in 42 countries, affecting 35 per cent of the world population, while democratization was only taking place in 18, harboring 5 per cent.[9] Their researchers previously already concluded that a third 'wave of autocratization' had set in, the first two having occurred from 1926 to 1942 and 1961 to 1977 after the first and second waves of democratization at the time.[10] However, V-Dem earlier had warned 'that alarmist reports about a global demise of democracy are not warranted' from a long-term perspective.[11] Indeed, other experts argue that the data provided by the different assessments of democracy, like those of V-Dem and Freedom House, do not justify talk of a reversal. They attribute pessimistic interpretations partly to the fact that many observers had been hoping for much clearer progress. The disappointed hopes are perceived as setbacks. 'In effect, nondemocratization in China, the Middle East, or Central Asia is treated as a setback', was the verdict of the professors Steven Levitsky and Lucan Way, for example.[12] They pointed out that Freedom House as well as V-Dem still counted 'many more democracies than there were in 1995, at the height of the

7   Freedom House. 2024. Freedom in the World 2024.

8   Economist Intelligence Unit. 2024. Democracy Index 2023, p. 3 and id. Index of Democracy 2006, p. 7.

9   V-Dem Institute. 2024. Democracy Report 2024: Democracy Losing and Winning at the Ballot, p. 6, 12.

10   Lührmann, Anna, and Staffan I. Lindberg. 2019. 'A Third Wave of Autocratization Is Here: What Is New about It?' Democratization 26 (7): 1095–1113.

11   V-Dem Institute. 2017. Democracy at Dusk? V-Dem Annual Report 2017, pp. 12, 14.

12   Levitsky, Steven, and Lucan Way. 2015. 'The Myth Of Democratic Recession'. Journal of Democracy (26) 1: 45–58, p. 53.

third wave' and that leading indices suggested 'only a modest erosion'. In fact, Levitsky and Way noted that democracy was showing a 'surprising resilience' despite widespread perceptions of decline. Firstly, the election of illiberal or authoritarian leaders as such could not be taken as evidence of democratic backsliding, they advised, as these leaders still 'may govern democratically' or leave office 'with democracy intact'. Further, instances of democratic backsliding 'are frequently short-lived', they noted, followed by a 'slide back' to democracy. Finally, in terms of global assessments, they maintained that 'cases of democratic backsliding have been offset by democratic advances in other countries'. Overall, they believed that a key reason why democracies continued to survive despite being challenged by illiberal and autocratic forces was modernization—a 'robust correlation between economic development and stable democracy'.[13]

Economic development and democracy

Whether there is a link between economic development and democracy has been debated for decades. The debate was set off by the sociologist and political scientist Seymour Lipset (1922 to 2006), who argued in 1959 that 'the more well-to-do a nation, the greater the chances that it will sustain democracy'.[14] A distinction is drawn between the 'endogenous' theory, which holds that the likelihood of democratization in poor countries is increased by development, and the 'exogenous' theory, which holds that development makes it less likely for established democracies to relapse into dictatorship. Recent studies have confirmed these hypotheses. The political scientists Carles Boix and Susan Stokes, for example, demonstrate both effects over the period from 1850 to 1990. In contrast to earlier studies, theirs also covered the first wave of democratization.[15] The political scientists Ronald Inglehart and Christian Welzel, on the other hand, investigated whether economic development brought with it more regime changes to democracy than to autocracy, as might be expected from the assumptions. 'The balance of regime changes shifts strongly and monotonically in favor of democracy as income rises', they reported. With each increase in per capita income of 1,000 US dollars, they found that the relative number of changes to democracy as against autocracy *doubled*. 'Socio-economic development does contribute to the emergence of democracy and it does so dramatically', was their conclusion.[16] Above a per capita income of

13   Id. 2023. 'Democracy's Surprising Resilience.' Journal of Democracy 34 (4): 5–20, pp. 8-10.
14   Lipset, Seymour Martin. 1959. 'Some Social Requisites of Democracy: Economic Development and Political Legitimacy'. The American Political Science Review (53) 1: 69–105, p. 75.
15   Boix, Carles, and Susan C. Stokes. 2003. 'Endogenous Democratization'. World Politics 55: 517–49.
16   Inglehart and Welzel, p. 169.

4,000 US dollars, the likelihood of a democracy collapsing is practically nil.[17] Nonetheless, Steven Levitsky and Lucan Way pointed out that 'wealthy democracies are not immune to backsliding, as recent developments in Hungary, Israel, Turkey, and even the United States make clear. But rich democracies are markedly more robust than poorer ones'.[18] As observed above, economic inequality in particular can contribute to political instability. These results in turn do not mean that poor countries cannot democratise. Economic development only makes democratization *more likely*, and democratic systems more stable. Conversely, the oil states of the Arab world demonstrate that wealth alone is no guarantee of democratization. A crucial factor is *cultural* change linked to economic development.

The post-industrial transformation in values

The worldwide forward march of modernization and the post-industrial structural transformation to an information and knowledge society is being accompanied in the better-off population segments of an increasing number of countries by a shift in values and culture. Continuing economic prosperity and higher levels of literacy and education encourage the turn towards post-material values, which put to the foreground individual self-realization and the search for quality of life, freedom and happiness over issues of economic survival and betterment. This development was captured in the large-scale project World Values Survey, or WVS. Representative survey data on socio-cultural and political views were collected in seven waves between 1981 and 2022 in over ninety countries, covering all regions of the world and almost ninety per cent of the world population. Ronald Inglehart (1934 to 2021), the programme director, concluded that 'rising self-expression values play a central role in the trend toward democracy'. 'Postindustrialization', according to Inglehart and his colleague Welzel, 'brings even more favorable existential conditions than industrialization, making people economically more secure, intellectually more autonomous, and socially more independent than ever. This emancipative process gives people a fundamental sense of human autonomy, leading them to give a higher priority to freedom of choice and making them less inclined to accept authority and dogmatic truths.' They explain that 'the shift from survival to self-expression values linked with postindustrialization brings emancipation from authority' and produces 'increasingly powerful

---

17   Przeworski, Adam, and Fernando Limongi. 1997. 'Modernization: Theories and Facts'. World Politics (49) 2: 155–83, p. 165.
18   Levitsky, Steven, and Lucan A. Way. 2023. 'Democracy's Surprising Resilience.' Journal of Democracy 34 (4): 5–20, p. 15.

mass demands for democracy, the form of government that provides the broadest latitude for individuals to choose how to live their lives.'[19] Not for nothing are the ambitious middle classes regarded as the 'potential revolutionary class'.

Of course, post-industrial structural change is not the only driver of democratization. After the end of communism, democracy is without an ideological competitor as a form of government. Authoritarian and repressive regimes are subject to an ever stronger pressure to justify themselves, one that cannot remain hidden from their own populations. Despite their attempts to control the internet, for example, these regimes can have only limited success in trying to cut their people off from the global flow of information. 'There is hardly a dictatorship in the world', wrote the leading democracy expert Larry Diamond of Stanford University in California, 'that looks stable for the long run. The only truly reliable source of regime stability is legitimacy, and the number of people in the world who believe in the intrinsic legitimacy of any form of authoritarianism is rapidly diminishing. Economic development, globalization, and the information revolution are undermining all forms of authority and empowering individuals. Values are changing, and while we should not assume any teleological path toward a global "enlightenment," generally the movement is toward greater distrust of authority and more desire for accountability, freedom, and political choice.'[20] We see the fact that autocratic regimes are turning the screw as evidence that the desire and pressure for freedom and democracy in their populations is growing ever stronger.

The issue of populism revisited

While Welzel believes that modernization theory in essence is 'proving correct', he also pointed out that this 'long-term process cannot guarantee a transition to democracy at any particular historical juncture, of course.' In fact, reactionary forces have been gaining ground in the form of illiberal and national populism even in mature democracies, as the Professor of Research of Political Culture at Leuphana University of Lüneburg contended. In an effort to bury emancipative values, autocrats and populists according to Welzel 'compose narratives about national destinies and geopolitical missions to breed a "culture of allegiance"' and this strategy pays off to 'some extent'. But ultimately, 'illiberal scripts with their authoritarian versions of modernity can slow but not stop the emancipative effects of modernization', he wrote.[21] Pop-

---

19 Inglehart and Welzel, p. 209, 29, 1.
20 Diamond, pp. 153-4.
21 Welzel, Christian. 2021. 'Why the Future Is Democratic.' Journal of Democracy 32 (2): 132–44, pp. 131-2, 132, 138.

ulism is a global phenomenon that has been observed regularly in countries across all world regions. In particular, leaders of major powers including figures like Donald Trump in the United States, Andrés Manuel López Obrador in Mexico, Jair Bolsonaro in Brazil, Narendra Modi in India or Rodrigo Duterte in the Philippines, to name but a few, have been relying on populist mobilization to greater or lesser degrees. Populism manifests in different forms across the political spectrum and does not necessarily fit into a classic 'left versus right' division.[22] Scholars have described different types depending on the focus of the political message, including national, progressive, authoritarian, redistributive, ethnic, religious or civilizational populism. While each case has its own characteristics, a common thread that defines populism is a claim of political leaders and movements to truly represent the will of the common people. Populist rhetoric is usually directed against an allegedly morally corrupt and self-serving elite, mainstream parties and state institutions that are said to be out of touch with the concerns of a 'silent majority'. Populists often draw on an 'Us' versus 'Them' narrative and portray themselves as the only legitimate political actors, the 'true democrats', while questioning the legitimacy of the 'establishment'. Their claim to a 'exclusive moral representation of the people' makes them inherently dangerous to democracy according to Jan-Werner Müller, a professor on political theory at Princeton University.[23] Scholars explain the success of populist mobilization by economic and socio-cultural grievances that make citizens receptive to simple and polarizing messages. With regard to Western developed countries, Harvard professor Pippa Norris and Ronald Inglehart argued that recent support for populist leaders and movements, particularly in the US and the UK, was part of a 'conservative backlash and authoritarian reflex' triggered by the ongoing 'silent revolution' in which cultures gradually evolve 'from socially conservative to socially liberal and post-material values'. As socially conservatives have become a 'new cultural minority', their feeling of being threatened is exacerbated in particular by growing economic insecurity as a consequence of economic globalization and high rates of immigration.[24] The political scientists Roger Eatwell and Matthew Goodwin pointed out that 'national populism appeals to a broad alliance of different groups in society' that sometimes represents more than half of the populations and not only includes the usual suspects such as uneducated white male workers, older generations or people

22   Eatwell, Roger, and Matthew Goodwin. 2018. National Populism: The Revolt Against Liberal Democracy. Pelican Books, p. 70.
23   Müller, Jan-Werner. 2017. What is Populism? Penguin, pp. 48, 56-7.
24   Norris, Pippa, and Ronald Inglehart. 2019. Cultural Backlash: Trump, Brexit, and Authoritarian Populism. Cambridge University Press, pp. 446, 449.

belonging to the 'squeezed middle classes'. They too believe that the 'national-populist' revolt in Western countries is 'partly linked to the rise of neoliberalism' and a growing sense of relative deprivation that 'unites large numbers of citizens'. In particular, Eatwell and Goodwin emphasised that distrust in the political process and the elite was strengthened by a 'gradual diffusion of power away from democratically elected national governments to transnational organizations, from politicians at the national level who had been elected by citizens to non-elected "expert" policymakers and lobbyists who operated in the international sphere, beyond the realm of democratically accountable politics.' The political scientists warned that those belonging to this complex group should not all simply be dismissed as anti-democrats. Quite the contrary, in what appears to be a paradox, surveys indicated that in several democracies 'national populist voters are actually *more* supportive of representative democracy than the general population'. Rejecting democracy is 'no longer a vote winner', Eatwell and Goodwin observed.[25] It appears that a platform along the lines of 'taking back control' through global democracy could appeal even to some populist voters. But as the political theorist Margaret Canovan (1939 to 2018) argued in a convincing way, populism follows democracy 'like a shadow'. As she explained, populism necessarily appears in the tension that lies between modern democracy's romantic, 'redemptive style' that promises 'salvation through politics' and the sober pragmatism of democracy as a simple form of government characterised by compromise and technicalities that cannot live up to the pure form. In other words, populism exploits the 'gap between promise and performance' that is inherent in democracy. But if populist forces actually get into power, their own inability to deliver on their promises will be revealed—the gap persists and the dynamic continues. 'This ambiguity affects democracies regardless of their scale, and cannot be avoided either by participatory democracy in face-to-face communities or by the global democracy now projected in some quarters', Canovan noted.[26]

Democracy as a universal value

Narratives of democracy are often narrowly focused, giving the impression that its development was exclusively linked to Western culture. But the history of democracy is more nuanced, and the democratic idea has global roots. In fact, most people in the world 'can call on some local tradition on which to

---

25 Eatwell and Goodwin, pp. 1-40, 17, 181, 96-7, 117-20.
26 Canovan, Margaret. 1999. 'Trust the People! Populism and the Two Faces of Democracy.' Political Studies 47 (1): 2–16, pp, 9-10, 13, 12.

build a modern democracy'.[27] There is no doubt that democracy today can be considered a universal value. Representative surveys around the world attest to very high approval rates in the world population. Average worldwide approval rates in each of the three most recent WVS survey waves carried out between 2005 and 2022 stood above 85 per cent. Pippa Norris, concluded, based on the empirical data from the fifth WVS wave and other surveys, that 'overt approval of democratic governance is widespread and universal'. She emphasized that although there is a variety of motivations for the approval for democracy, the respondents' cultural background or region of origin, or the political regime under which they lived, made no real difference. Their level of education had an influence on the attitude of the respondents, but interestingly enough the level of economic development of their country did not play a role. 'No statistically significant contrasts in democratic aspirations or in satisfaction with democratic performance can be observed when comparing affluent post-industrialized societies, emerging manufacturing economies, or poorer developing nations', she reported. Moreover, the empirical data were *not* able to confirm a general trend towards a growing loss of faith in democracy. The widespread theory of a 'democratic crisis' is in her view an 'oversimplification' based on 'over-simple claims' and isolated anecdotes, one which 'needs revising'.[28] The opposite is true, according to Ronald Inglehart and Christian Welzel. 'Contrary to often-repeated claims that social capital and mass participation are eroding, the publics of postindustrial societies are intervening in politics more actively today than ever before', they wrote.[29] Precisely because democracy is held in such high regard, there is also considerable dissatisfaction in some quarters. An important distinction here is that between approval for democracy as an *abstract ideal* and satisfaction with the implementation of democracy *in practice*. Norris saw the democratic deficit as arising from the gap between expectation and reality. In the 2023 edition of the Democracy Perception Index, for instance, 84 per cent of respondents across 53 countries agreed that democracy is important but only 57 per cent said that their country is actually democratic which can be interpreted as a measurable democratic deficit of 27. When it comes to specific elements of democracy such as freedom of speech, fair elections or equal rights, over 90 per cent confirmed they are important.[30]

---

27 Muhlberger, Steven, and Phil Paine. 1993. 'Democracy's Place in World History.' Journal of World History 4 (1): 23–45, p. 26. See also: Isakhan, Benjamin, and Steven Muhlberger, eds. 2011. The Secret History of Democracy. Palgrave Macmillan.

28 Norris, Pippa. 2011. Democratic Deficit: Critical Citizens Revisited. Cambridge Univ. Press, pp. 92, 129, 110, 58, 4.

29 Inglehart and Welzel, pp. 44, 117.

30 Latana, and Alliance of Democracies Foundation. 2023. 'Democracy Perception Index 2023', pp. 8, 10.

At the level of international politics, too, democracy is established as a universal value. Democracy is seen today as the only legitimate form of government. In the Millennium Declaration of the year 2000, adopted by the heads of state and government of the world, for example, the talk is of strengthening democracy, the rule of law and human rights in all countries. At the world summit that followed five years later, it was 'reaffirmed' in the concluding statement 'that democracy is *a universal value* based on the freely expressed will of people to determine their own political, economic, social and cultural systems and their full participation in all aspects of their lives' (emphasis added).[31] When the UN General Assembly in 2007 declared the 15th September as the 'International Day of Democracy', it was emphasized once more that democracy is a universal value, and moreover that it belongs to 'the universal and indivisible core values and principles of the United Nations'.[32] On the 75th anniversary of the UN in 2020, heads of state and government declared in another UN General Assembly resolution that they 'will continue to promote respect for democracy'. As UN Secretary-General, Boutros Boutros-Ghali argued, with the opening words of the UN Charter—'We the peoples'—'the founders invoked the most fundamental principle of democracy, rooting the sovereign authority of the Member States, and thus the legitimacy of the Organization which they were to compose, in the will of their peoples'.[33]

This development is reflected across the world's regions as well. In Europe, promotion of democracy became a key regional concern after the end of the Second World War, especially through the Council of Europe. The European integration process only included democratic countries and according to Article 10 of the Treaty on European Union, last amended in 2009, the EU 'shall be founded on representative democracy' and member states need to be democratic, too. A 'right to democracy' is embedded in the first article of the Inter-American Democratic Charter adopted by the Organization of American States (OAS) in 2001, and the governments of the member states 'have an obligation to promote and defend it'. The Charter pronounces the 'rule of law', the 'separation of powers and independence of the branches of government' essential to democracy. Representative democracy is declared to be fundamental and indispensable. In the 2008 Charter of the Association of Southeast Asian Nations 'strengthening democracy' is named as one of the purposes of the organization. In the Charter of Democracy of the South Asian

---

31   United Nations. 24 Oct. 2005. '2005 World Summit Outcome'. A/RES/60/1, para. 135.
32   Id. 13 December 2007. 'Support by the United Nations system of the efforts of Governments to promote and consolidate new or restored democracies'. A/RES/62/7.
33   Boutros-Ghali, Boutros. 20 Dec. 1996. Supplement to reports on democratization. Report to the 51st Session of the United Nations General Assembly. A/51/761, para. 28.

Association for Regional Cooperation, passed in 2011, the member states undertake to 'promote democracy at all levels of the Government and the society at large' and to 'uphold participatory democracy characterised by free, fair and credible elections, and elected legislatures and local bodies'. And the African Charter on Democracy, Elections and Governance, which entered into force in 2012, commits the treaty partners to adhere to 'the universal values and principles of democracy'.

The right to democracy

There are of course different views as to what exactly defines democracy and a democratic system. There is no universally recognised model that could serve as a yardstick. The propaganda of autocratic governments is seizing upon this in an attempt to redefine the concept of democracy and strip it of any genuine meaning. Nevertheless, certain requirements and elements have clearly been defined by the UN and under international law. The UN's Commission on Human Rights, for instance, established in 1946 and replaced in 2006 by the Human Rights Council, in 2002 declared in a resolution that 'the essential elements of democracy include respect for human rights and fundamental freedoms, freedom of association, freedom of expression and opinion, access to power and its exercise in accordance with the rule of law, the holding of periodic free and fair elections by universal suffrage and by secret ballot as the expression of the will of the people, a pluralistic system of political parties and organizations, the separation of powers, the independence of the judiciary, transparency and accountability in public administration, and free, independent and pluralistic media.'[34] A key provision is Article 21 of the Universal Declaration of Human Rights of 10 December 1948 which stipulates that '[t]he will of the people shall be the basis of the authority of government; this will shall be expressed in periodic and genuine elections which shall be by universal and equal suffrage and shall be held by secret vote or by equivalent free voting procedures'. Most countries were still colonized at the time and their people thus not represented but Latin-American states were there, strongly pushed a human rights agenda at the UN and made crucial contributions.[35] Eight months ahead of the Universal Declaration they already adopted their own American Declaration of the Rights and Duties of Man which in Article 20 states that every person is 'entitled to participate in the government of his

---

34   United Nations. 2002. 'Further Measures to Promote and Consolidate Democracy.' Commission on Human Rights resolution 2002/46 of 23 April 2002.
35   Cardenas, Sonia, and Rebecca K. Root. 2022. Human Rights in Latin America: A Politics of Transformation. University of Pennsylvania Press, pp. 15-7.

country, directly or through his representatives, and to take part in popular elections, which shall be by secret ballot, and shall be honest, periodic and free.' The OAS Charter adopted at the same time proclaims the principle that 'the political organization' of its member states should be based on 'representative democracy.'

The Nepalese international lawyer and professor Surya P. Subedi pointed out that claiming human rights are 'Western' is 'an affront' to the contribution made by developing states to the evolution of international human rights law, the foundations of which, he argued, 'can be found in all major civilisations of the world'. Subedi referred in particular to the International Covenant on Civil and Political Rights and highlights that it was adopted 'after developing countries gained a numerical majority' at the UN.[36] According to Article 25 of the covenant, which entered into force in 1976 and has been ratified as a binding treaty by 173 states, 'every citizen shall have the right and the opportunity' to 'take part in the conduct of public affairs, directly or through freely chosen representatives' and 'to vote and to be elected at genuine periodic elections which shall be by universal and equal suffrage and shall be held by secret ballot'.

In a resolution adopted by consensus, the Human Rights Council as recently as 2021 affirmed the provisions of the Universal Declaration and the covenant that relate to democracy.[37] In 1992 already, the US American lawyer Thomas M. Franck (1931 to 2009) argued in an influential article that democratic governance was becoming an international norm and an entitlement under international law.[38] In essence, the right to democracy means that everyone who is affected by the exercise of public authority must have the right to influence it, at the very least through the free election of representatives.

A right to global democracy

The Universal Declaration, the Covenant on Civil and Political Rights and other UN statements primarily intend to address democratic rights at the level of nation-states. As noted, Article 21 of the declaration, for instance, speaks of 'the authority of government' as reference points for democratic rights. How can this then extend to the global scale since neither the UN or any other global institution is a government? The level at which public authority is exercised cannot play a role though. Joseph Schwartzberg argued that 'many decisions taken by entities comprising the UN system, whether or not they are

36   Subedi, Surya P. 2021. Human Rights in Eastern Civilisations. Edward Elgar Publishing, p-163.
37   United Nations. 2021. 'Equal Participation in Political and Public Affairs.' A/HRC/RES/48/2.
38   Franck, Thomas M. 1992. 'The Emerging Right to Democratic Governance'. The American Journal of International Law 86: 46–91.

regarded as binding, contribute to the governance of masses of citizens of the UN's 193 member states', indicating that the UN indeed exercises public authority, if not in form, then in substance.[39] The output of 'transgovernmental networks' touched on in a previous chapter needs to be considered in a similar way. The right to democracy thus demands the democratization of international decision-making and organizations as well. Article 28 of the Universal Declaration of Human Rights can be read in this light. 'Everyone', it is stated there, 'is entitled to a social and *international order* in which the rights and freedoms set forth in this Declaration can be fully realized' (emphasis added).

The argument does not rely solely on the Universal Declaration. One key question is the meaning and scope of Article 25 of the International Covenant on Civil and Political Rights quoted above. Does the right to take part 'in the conduct of public affairs, directly or through freely chosen representatives' extend beyond the nation-state? According to the UN's Independent Expert on the 'promotion of a democratic and equitable international order', Livingstone Sewanyana, the rights enshrined in Article 21 of the Universal Declaration of Human Rights and Article 25 of the covenant are indeed not restricted to local affairs, but extend to global institutions.[40] He referred to the UN's own interpretation: The Human Rights Council's predecessor Commission agreed in 1996 that 'the conduct of public affairs' covers 'all aspects of public administration, and the formulation and implementation of policy at international, national, regional and local levels'.[41] Without doubt this covers the UN's and other international activities.

Starting in 2004, the UN General Assembly has declared in numerous resolutions, passed annually by now and using identical wording, that a 'democratic and equitable international order' requires the realization of 'the right to equitable participation of all, without any discrimination, in domestic and *global* decision-making' (emphasis added).[42] How that can be institutionally ensured is answered by the right to democracy itself, namely through the involvement of *freely elected representatives of the people*. The democratic exercise of public authority within the framework of the international order is only possible if parliamentary representation is extended to the global level. Only in this way can the 'will of the people'—here, the will of the world popu-

---

39 Schwartzberg, Joseph. 2013. Transforming the United Nations System. Designs for a Workable World. Tokyo, New York, Paris: United Nations University Press, p. 37.

40 Sewanyana, Livingstone. 2019. 'Report of the Independent Expert on the Promotion of a Democratic and Equitable International Order.' UN Doc. A/74/245, para. 31.

41 UN Human Rights Committee. 1996. 'General Comment No. 25: The Right to Participate in Public Affairs, Voting Rights and the Right of Equal Access to Public Service (Art. 25)', para. 5.

42 United Nations. 19 Dec. 2016. 'Promotion of a Democratic and Equitable International Order'. A/RES/71/190.

lation—be given effect as pluralistically as possible. Ultimately, worldwide parliamentary representation must be based on *worldwide elections*. Franck proposed in 1995 a parliament directly elected by the world population, with seats allocated according to population size, in order to institutionalize the 'democratic entitlement'.[43]

The undermining of democracy by intergovernmentalism

Even if all the countries in the world were perfect democracies, that would not alter the fact that the intergovernmental system of international law is undemocratic. The democratic process of policy formulation and promotion has to date been extremely difficult in the international arena. The political scientist Klaus Dieter Wolf posited that the 'de-democratization effect' which has accompanied the internationalization of governance is in fact one which is positively desired. Wolf argued that 'the parallelism of voluntary intergovernmental commitment and structural democratic deficit which is characteristic of governance beyond the state is *the intended result* of strategic interaction between state governments' (emphasis added). The executive, he believed, can strengthen 'its tactical position in the domestic power struggle' by shifting decisions into the intergovernmental arena and thereby 'removing them from domestic political control and accountability'. According to Wolf, what is termed the 'Politics of the new Raison d'état' consists in 'the cartel-like attempt to safeguard state authority by means of intergovernmental ties and reciprocal voluntary commitments. Its purpose is to create a space in which substantive decisions can be made beyond the reach of social disputation and thus also beyond the possibility of domestic political challenge'.[44]

Indeed, intergovernmental treaty negotiations are often conducted by government officials away from public scrutiny, even if related domestic policy matters are touched upon and decided on. The secretive negotiations on the Anti-Counterfeiting Trade Agreement (ACTA) or on the Transatlantic Trade and Investment Partnership (TTIP), treaties both of which failed for a number of reasons, are illustrative cases. The parliaments are seldom involved, and often do not know what their governments are even discussing. Representatives of trade associations and large corporations by contrast are frequently consulted in proactive ways. The principle of the separation of powers is effectively suspended, and the executive promotes itself to the role of legislature. After the conclusion of the negotiations, the parliament is usually only able to

---

43   Franck, Thomas M. 1995. Fairness in International Law and Institutions. Oxford: Clarendon Press, pp. 482-4.
44   Wolf, Klaus Dieter. 2000. Die Neue Staatsräson - Zwischenstaatliche Kooperation als Demokratieproblem in der Weltgesellschaft. 1st ed. Baden-Baden: Nomos, pp. 13, 17-8, 67.

accept or reject the treaties presented to it by the government in their totality. The supervisory rights of the parliament are 'curtailed in the field of foreign policy, or in fact in all cross-departmental areas of international politics, especially when it comes to the specific rules for parliamentary influence on treaties under international law' was a criticism made in the report of the Enquete Commission of the German Bundestag on 'The Globalization of the World Economy' in 2002. Parliamentarians needed to play 'a supervisory as well as a policy-making role also with regard to processes of globalization'.[45] Over twenty years later, these points are still valid. The arbitrary involvement of individual parliamentarians in selected government delegations, as practised by some states, is irrelevant in this context. 'Modern parliamentarism demanded in many states the ratification of foreign policy treaties', wrote Klaus von Beyme. 'But in practice, not even the opposition were prepared to withhold their approval from most treaties so as not to put at risk the continuity of external relations'.[46] This applies all the more to the parliamentary groups of governing parties, who certainly were not willing to stab their own executive in the back. In most cases the parliaments give straightforward majority approval to the international law treaties laid before them, if only not to destabilize their own governments either domestically or in terms of foreign relations. The governments can take the easy position that international guidelines have to be followed—guidelines that they themselves of course have negotiated. In addition, in intergovernmental relations in practice, treaties under international law can be developed and expanded in an organic process without the parliaments being able to have any appreciable influence on them.

The Harvard sociologist and political scientist Robert D. Putnam spoke of 'two-level games'. The first level is that of inter-governmental negotiations, the second that of national approval for the outcomes of those negotiations. 'The motives of the chief negotiator' include shifting 'the balance of power at Level II in favor of domestic policies that he prefers for exogenous reasons', Putnam noted.[47] To strengthen its position, the executive can invoke 'the national interest' or 'national security'. These concepts can be employed repeatedly as rhetorical figures to suggest actions taken for the greater public good, on the basis of broad public consensus, to the point where they lose all substance. 'The pervasive phrase "the national interest" is one of the cloudiest concepts in our political environment', wrote Jeff Faux. 'It hides more than it reveals, and

---

45 Deutscher Bundestag. 16 June 2002. Schlussbericht der Enquete-Kommission 'Globalisierung der Weltwirtschaft - Herausforderungen and Antworten', pp. 446, 445-7.

46 Beyme, Klaus von. 1998. 'Niedergang der Parlamente'. Internationale Politik 4: 21–30, p. 21.

47 Putnam, Robert D. 1988. 'Diplomacy and domestic politics: the logic of two-level games'. International Organization (42) 3: 427–60, pp. 436, 457.

has the effect of giving the ordinary citizen the false impression that a democratic consensus has been reached and therefore no longer has to be debated.'[48]

The example of the Codex Commission

The two level-game not only encompasses intergovernmental treaty negotiations but also includes multistakeholder governance arrangements and arenas of 'networked multilateralism' discussed previously. Transnational corporations, along with the business interests they represent, are skilled at navigating and leveraging the complexities of the international system. The Codex Alimentarius Commission, set up in 1963 by the FAO and WHO, serves as an illustration of the intricate nature global governance can have. While operating in relative obscurity, it attracts significant interest and participation from the global food industry due to its pivotal role in setting international standards in the food sector. These standards cover critical issues directly impacting consumers worldwide, including rules on food labelling, limits on additives and toxins, and safety assessments for feed additives. Originally intended as recommendations, the Codex standards have evolved into de facto binding rules. This shift goes back to the 1994 WTO agreements on food safety and plant protection measures and on technical barriers to trade which stipulate that international standards must be taken into account and that their observance is regarded as evidence of compliance with the agreements. Legal experts consequently consider the Codex rules binding for WTO members as violations indicate an adverse outcome in the WTO trade dispute settlement procedure.[49] There exists a 'de facto compulsion' to adhere to these standards and thus there is a 'hidden supranationality' embedded in the Codex Commission. While international standardization, in principle, is of course reasonable and often necessary, serious concerns persist regarding the legitimacy deficits of the respective organizations and procedures, particularly given that industry interests are often perceived as having a predominant influence.[50] Another pertinent example is the International Accounting Standard Board (IASB) which is entirely in the hands of the private sector. 'The IASB', said the Member of the European Parliament Sven Giegold, 'decides on international accounting regulations without any effective democratic accountability. The Board is dominated by so-called experts from international corpora-

48   Faux, Jeff. 2006. The Global Class War. Hoboken NJ: John Wiley & Sons, p. 50.
49   Pruchniewicz, Karolina, and Tomasz Srogosz. 2020. 'The Codex Alimentarius Standards Decision-Making: Some Critical Remarks on an Ongoing Discussion.' European Food and Feed Law Review 15 (6): 571–78, pp. 573-4.
50   Herrmann, Christoph, Wolfgang Weiß and Christoph Ohler. 2007. Welthandelsrecht. München: C.H. Beck, 2nd ed. §12 no. 591, p. 258.

tions.' The standards drawn up by the IASB are regularly adopted into EU law. While private sector participation in international standard-setting and deliberation is useful, there need to be limits as the inherent conflict of interest is evident. The creation of crucial standards and rules, with legal implication and devoid of parliamentary involvement or accountability, poses significant concerns. It is also characteristic of 'post-democracy' that parliaments and their elected members allow themselves to be sidelined in this way.

Fragmentation as a problem of democracy

In the view of Armin von Bogdandy, Director of the Max Planck Institute for Comparative Public Law and International Law, ensuring the continuing global development of parliamentarism is 'one of the greatest contemporary challenges'. An expert in international law, he noted that 'in the light of the requirement for universality' the fragmentation of the 'international level of policy formation' must be regarded as 'problematic in terms of democratic theory'. The 'requirement for universality' with respect to the process of legislation means that the democratic legislature must be the principal locus of regulation and legitimation, where all possible perspectives are carefully assessed openly and impartially. 'The starting point', according to von Bogdandy, 'is the individual as a whole and multidimensional person, one who is not divisible in accordance with the logic of functionality but instead claims the right to a representational mechanism in which competing perspectives can be weighed up against each other.' The setting of particularistic priorities by international regimes therefore undermines 'the requirement for universality as a core element of the principle of democracy'.[51] According to Mathias Koenig-Archibugi, to 'the extent that making choices is a key aspect of democracy, the absence of international institutions for the comprehensive balancing of multiple social goals is bound to generate a democratic deficit'. It is a purpose of parliamentary institutions to ensure that 'all issues of public concern are deliberated upon and decided in one forum, by representatives who are held accountable for public policy as a whole, rather than for the attainment of specific goals'. This principle would need to be 'transported beyond the national level'.[52] Against this background, the 'aggregating' function of a world parliament assumes a key significance for democracy. A world parliament needs to be directly integrated at the level of international rule-making

51 Bogdandy, Armin von, and Ingo Venzke. 2010. 'Zur Herrschaft internationaler Gerichte: Eine Untersuchung internationaler öffentlicher Gewalt und ihrer demokratischen Rechtfertigung'. Zeitschrift für ausländisches öffentliches Recht and Völkerrecht (70) 1: 1–49, pp. 21, 25-6.

52 Koenig-Archibugi, Mathias. 2024. The Universal Republic: A Realistic Utopia?, p. 183.

and standard-setting. Where necessary or appropriate it must assume the relevant regulatory competences. With such competences pending, a global parliamentary body at least should be linked into existing processes via committees. For example, it should take part in the deliberations of the Codex Commission and ideally sanction their outcomes. The right for a UN Parliamentary Assembly 'to send fully participating parliamentary delegations or representatives to international governmental fora and negotiations' has already been called for.[53] In 1954, the British philosopher, Nobel Prize winner and world federalist Bertrand Russell made the interesting proposal that agreements under international law should require approval by a federal 'Central Authority' within the framework of a constitutional federal world order.[54] Insofar as matters of world law are affected by international law treaties, this is an idea worth considering. In any event, the only institution that ought to come into question here as the relevant responsible authority is a world parliament.

The dilemma of scale

Considerable attention has been given to the view of the political scientist Robert Dahl that an honest acknowledgement and expression is required of the fact that international organizations, institutions and processes simply *cannot be* democratic *when measured by the yardstick of proximity to the citizens*, since of necessity they require the delegation of decision-making powers to international elites who by their very nature are distant from the ordinary citizen. A 'fundamental dilemma' of democratic theory and practice, according to Dahl, is the fact that 'a smaller democratic unit provides an ordinary citizen with greater opportunities to participate in governing than a larger unit. But the smaller the unit the more likely that some matters of importance to the citizen are beyond the capacity of the government to deal with effectively'. Larger units are needed to solve such problems. While the capacity to govern is then improved, the individual's opportunities for influence are conversely reduced. At the international level, the acceptable upper limit for what can still be considered democracy is thereby exceeded.

Nevertheless, it is clear to Dahl that international organizations are indispensable. It might be possible to agree with him that democracy cannot be realised at the international level *in any ideal form* (insofar as this is possible at all). However, that is no reason to give up on the possibility of steady dem-

---

53   Pan-African Parliament. 24 Oct. 2007. 'A United Nations Parliamentary Assembly'. Resolution adopted at the 8th Ordinary Session, Midrand, South Africa, para. 16.
54   Russell, Bertrand. 28 August 1954. 'A Prescription for the World'. The Saturday Review: 9–11, 38–39, p. 10.

ocratic progress towards that objective. 'If we judge that important human needs require an international organization, despite its cost to democracy, we should not only subject its undemocratic aspects to scrutiny and criticism but also try to create proposals for greater democratization and insist that they be adopted', Dahl himself noted. In order for even just an approximation of the level of democratic control that exists in democratic states to be achieved at the international level, 'political institutions that would provide citizens with opportunities for political participation, influence, and control roughly equivalent in effectiveness to those already existing in democratic countries' would be needed.[55] Dahl is thinking here, entirely in line with the 'right to democracy', of an 'international citizen body' with elected representatives and international parties.[56]

The concept of a chain of legitimation

The concept of a chain of legitimation, also referred to as chain of delegation, is often employed as a way of demonstrating that international organizations are democratically accountable. The concept originated with the German lawyers and former constitutional court judges Roman Herzog and Ernst Wolfgang Böckenförde. It posits that democratic legitimation comes from the electorate and is then transferred from one level to the next. In a parliamentary democracy, the chain looks like this: the voters elect the parliament, the parliamentarians of the majority party (or coalition parties) elect the head of government, the latter appoints the ministers, who in turn appoint career diplomats to represent the government In international bodies. These ambassadors and delegates themselves often give proxies to less senior officials who will then sit on given bodies of the relevant organizations or participate in international negotiations. Together with their colleagues from other countries, they collectively are responsible for decision-making and holding the organization's administration and its officials accountable. These diplomats and bureaucrats are not accountable and answerable to voters but to their relevant superiors in the chain. It must be borne in mind that there is therefore not one chain of legitimation, but 193 of such chains running in parallel for all states. However, the less democracy is developed in a given country, the less the concept of a chain of legitimation works in the first place. If free and fair elections and other key elements of democracy are flawed, or even non-existent, there is no democratic electorate and this breaks the whole chain from the start. Even

55　Dahl, Robert. 1999. 'Can international organizations be democratic? A skeptic's view'. In: Democracy's Edges, ed. by Ian Shapiro and Casiano Hacker-Cordón, 19–36. Cambridge University Press, pp. 22, 34, 31.

56　Id. 2000. On democracy. New Haven: Yale University Press, p. 116.

with regard to liberal democracies significant portions of the population do not find representation in intergovernmental bodies. This is because the views of citizens who voted for minority parties, which are not part of the government, typically are not reflected in the executive's policies.

According to Anne Peters, 'the democratic link between international institutions and citizens' it is supposed to supply 'is a legal fiction that has little to do with reality'.[57] With each successive link in the chain, proximity to the citizen and legitimation both become weaker, and the democratic deficit larger. The political scientists Frank Nullmeier and Martin Nonhoff do not believe the theory works at all for inter- and supra-national political constellations. 'As there are no direct electoral relationships between the world population, i.e. a world citizenship, and the ruling bodies of international organizations there can be no question of direct legitimation. From this perspective, talk of a "democratic deficit" is almost an understatement, as these systems are fundamentally democratically illegitimate.'[58] The political scientist Giovanni Sartori, who also speaks of 'macrodemocracies', 'got to the heart of the dilemma when he compared the legitimation chain to a swimmer. Just because he can swim does not automatically mean he is able to cross an ocean'.[59] The gulf that separates the citizens from intergovernmental processes has grown too wide. The metaphorical swimmer is thus destined to drown.

Output legitimation

The idea of the legitimation chain belongs to the field of what political scientists call input legitimation. 'The input-oriented perspective emphasizes "government *by the people*". Political decisions are legitimate if and when they reflect the "will of the people"—that is, if they have their roots in the genuine preferences of the members of a community', wrote the political scientist Fritz Scharpf. With regard to international organizations, where input-legitimation is poorly developed, an 'output perspective' is applied in order to provide legitimation. The 'output-oriented perspective', Scharpf explained, 'places the aspect of "government *for the people*" in the foreground. Political decisions are thereby legitimate if and when they effectively promote the general wellbeing of a community'. But who should judge whether that is the case, using which criteria? Ultimately, the output perspective, too, leads us back to the electorate. 'In all constitutional democracies, output legitimacy is primarily ensured

57   Peters, Anne. 2009. 'Dual Democracy'. In: The Constitutionalization of International Law, by Jan Klabbers, Anne Peters, and Geir Ulfstein, 263–341. Oxford, New York: Oxford University Press, p. 294.
58   Nullmeier, Frank, et al. 2010. Prekäre Legitimitäten: Rechtfertigung von Herrschaft in der postnationalen Konstellation. Frankfurt: Campus Verlag, p. 21.
59   Petersen, Niels. 2008. 'Demokratie and Grundgesetz'. Max Planck Institute for Research on Collective Goods, p. 3.

through universal, free and equal elections', Scharpf noted. Regular elections, he asserted, maintain and strengthen the orientation of the office holders toward the public interest. The anticipation of public debate, and its potential repercussions for the political career of the office holders, creates the conditions for output legitimacy.[60]

The global governance system is increasingly discredited within civil society on account of both inadequate output and the democratic deficit. Year after year, the crisis of global governance and the democratic deficit are emphasised in the report on the state of global civil society published by CIVICUS, a global alliance promoting civic rights. 'Global governance isn't working. Global problems still lack global people-oriented solutions', the 2014 annual report found. 'Many of the institutions and processes by which international decisions are made, and by which norms are set and diffused, are out of date and unable to meet present-day, entrenched challenges', the report said. But the crisis is more than one of efficiency. It is also one of democracy. 'The institutions of international governance are not open enough. It is hard for people to relate to them or indeed to understand them. They are less democratic even than the states that make up their membership, and it is naive to expect citizens' voices to be filtered through their states to be heard at the global level', the report concluded.[61] Ten years later, the situation according to CIVICUS has become worse as authoritarian regimes such as China and Russia seize every opportunity for 'the construction of an even less democratic global order with even fewer barriers to impunity for human rights abuses'. Arguably, the output of the international system is very poor even measured against its own declared goals. Climate emissions continue to increase, for instance, and there is no progress towards the elimination of nuclear weapons, an obligation included in the Non-Proliferation Treaty, as discussed previously. As CIVICUS pointed out in its 2024 report, only 15 per cent of the Sustainable Development Goals were on track at the time, adding that the 'longer-term problem is that the current global governance system isn't set up to deliver' them.[62]

Accountability to the world's citizens

In his book 'Independent Diplomat', the former British diplomat Carne Ross observed that even the connection between the governments in the capitals and their own diplomats sitting on international bodies is often unsatisfacto-

---

60   Scharpf, Fritz W. 1999. Regieren in Europa. Effektiv and demokratisch? Frankfurt: Campus, pp. 16, 22-3.
61   CIVICUS: World Alliance for Citizen Participation 2014. 'Towards a Democratic Multilateralism: Civil Society Perspectives on the State of Global Governance'. In: State of Civil Society Report 2014, 39–69, p. 39.
62   Id. 2024. 'Global Governance: Reform Desparately Needed'. in: 2024 State of Civil Society Report, 35-59, pp. 37, 46.

ry. And indeed, in today's massively networked world it 'is ridiculous to pretend that the wishes and needs of an entire country can be embodied in a single diplomat'.[63] We have already described the disconnection between governments and parliaments on intergovernmental issues and the associated 'de-democratization effect'. Like Ross, Anne Peters pointed out that government representatives in international organizations must be accountable not only to their national electorates but to *the citizenry of the world as a whole*, since their interests must also be taken into account. 'The sum of national constituencies does not make a proper global constituency. Thus the parallel chains of accountability to parallel domestic constituencies do not generate an appropriate accountability to the combined citizenry of all the states involved, the global constituency. This also means that the sum of national mechanisms for monitoring and controlling respective national representatives acting in international bodies does not result in full oversight', she argued.[64] The point here is not how effectively a national parliament can monitor the stance and actions of its own government and officials within international organizations, but the supervision of the international organization itself, and of its bureaucracy. A world parliament charged with this task would create *an additional, significantly shortened and unified* legitimation chain, since there would be no mediation via the government executives and their representatives. The members of the world parliament would in principle be accountable to the entire world citizenry.

Equality and representation in international law and world law

In intergovernmental bodies, all states as a rule have one vote and equal rights, in accordance with the fundamental international law principle of 'sovereign equality'. But the countries of the world are anything but equal. The world's population is divided extremely unequally between the states. Compared with the heavyweights, most countries are tiny dwarfs with respect to their population size. This imbalance, which can also be seen with respect to economic power and to the size of their UN budget contributions, in conjunction with the principle of equality under international law, is a significant problem in the political reality of intergovernmental organizations. According to Mark Malloch Brown, who served as UN Deputy Secretary-General, Chef de Cabinet to the Secretary-General, administrator of the UN Development Programme and since 2021 as President of Open Society Foundations, 'the intergovernmental gridlock between the big contributors and the rest of the membership concern-

---

63　Ross, Carne. 2007. Independent diplomat: dispatches from an unaccountable elite. Ithaca N.Y.: Cornell University Press, p. 210.
64　Peters, p. 295.

ing governance and voting is the core dysfunction'.[65] The sociologists Patrick Nolan and Gerhard Lenski took the same view, and noted that the 'greatest obstacle to the effectiveness of that organization is probably the system of representation in the General Assembly, which provides an equal vote for the People's Republic of China, with its population of 1.3 *billion*, and for Tuvalu with its population of 10 *thousand*'.[66] Pascal Lamy, former EU Commissioner for external trade and at one time Director-General of the WTO, believed that the principle of equal voting rights for the states 'is a long-standing fiction dating back to a distant period when democracies did not exist. It was a useful fiction in its day, but it is completely out of step with contemporary geopolitical realities. It can represent neither the diversity of the world nor the variety of its actors.'[67]

Notwithstanding this, the international law principle of the equality of states is often celebrated as a key element of international democracy. From the perspective of cosmopolitan world law, it is in fact just the opposite—a symptom of the undemocratic nature of the intergovernmental order. The principle of equality underlying international law, which applies to *states* ('one state, one vote'), stands in contrast to the principle of equality underlying world law, in which people as individual world citizens are the key element. Thus, the 100 countries with the smallest population sizes represent about 300 million inhabitants and *3.8 per cent* of the world population, but they make up *more than half* of the total votes in the UN General Assembly with its 193 member states. The 128 least populous countries, which can constitute *a two-thirds majority* in the General Assembly, have 668 million inhabitants, or roughly *8.4 per cent* of the world population. By contrast, the 10 most populous countries, with some *4.5 billion* inhabitants, or 57.5 per cent of the world population, have a voting strength of *5 per cent*. The members of the G20 represent about *two-thirds* of the world population and almost 90 per cent of global GDP, but have a voting strength of only *10 per cent*.[68] In the light of these figures, it is no surprise that the heads of state and government of the biggest industrialised and newly industrialising countries decided to coordinate their response to the global financial crisis within the framework of the G20 summit meetings and not at the UN. As the social scientist Geoffrey McNicoll noted, the powerful states always have an 'exit option'. 'Powerful states', he wrote, 'have a de facto option of exit: they can shrug off Lilliputian

---

65   Malloch Brown, Mark. 2008. 'Can the UN Be Reformed?' Global Governance 14: 1–12, p. 8.
66   Nolan, Patrick, and Gerhard Lenski. 2006. Human societies: an introduction to macrosociology. 10th ed. Boulder Colo.: Paradigm Publishers, p. 352.
67   Lamy, Pascal. 2005. Towards World Democracy. London: policy network, pp. 24-5.
68   Calculations based on World Bank population data as per 2022 (data.worldbank.org).

efforts to trammel them and conduct their business elsewhere.'[69] In reality, the least populous countries do not vote together in blocs. When it really counts, the bigger economic powers are quite prepared to try to influence their votes. But that does not alter the fact that the votes of the world's citizens in the intergovernmental bodies are extremely unequally weighted, subject as they are to their national citizenship.

It must also be considered that the political opposition and (in most cases) ethnic minorities have no voice at all under this system. Although it is true that almost 100 per cent of all states are represented by diplomats in the General Assembly, these do not represent 100 per cent of the world population if domestic national arrangements are taken into account. In democratic states, in addition to the governing majority there is generally a political opposition—which, however, has no access at all to the intergovernmental level. Its voters are not represented there. Further, there are around 5,000 indigenous peoples in the world with an estimated combined population of 476 million people. Although their global population size is much larger than that of the 100 smallest countries, the latter have 100 votes at the UN and the former none at all. Thomas M. Franck explained the situation with regard to minorities as follows: 'there are some fifty nations in which an indigenous minority has identified itself: Hmong, Inuit, Lap, Sorb, Mauri, etc. Nowhere do these indigenous peoples form a majority. Taken together, however, they form a constituency larger than the respective populations of half the states represented at the UN'. Yet, he said, 'the global system as now constituted affords them little opportunity to be heard.'[70] The South Asian ethnic group of the Hmong, for example, numbers four to five million people. That is roughly equivalent to the aggregate total population of the 27 to 30 least populous countries. To be represented under the current Westphalian system, Franck observed, such peoples would have no other choice but to try to establish their own states where they represent a majority.

The principle of equality underlying world law by contrast requires a form of political representation for the world population in which ideally the vote of every person on the planet would have an equal weight. Ultimately, this must be the guiding principle for the design of elections to a world parliament and for the allocation of seats within it. A world parliament would thus be made up of independent members who should reflect the whole spectrum of political opinion of the world citizenry. From the viewpoint of democratic theo-

---

69 McNicoll, Geoffrey. 1999. 'Population weights in the international order'. Population and Development Review (25) 3: 411–42, p. 422.
70 Franck (1995), pp. 480-1.

ry, the best way of allocating seats would be in direct proportion to the respective share of the vote. This would be a means of enabling political and other minorities to be represented who take no part, or only a limited part, in national governments. In several countries across the world there are special procedures in place to guarantee a representation of ethnic and other minorities in the national parliament. In India, for instance, the constitution provides for a proportional number of seats to be reserved for candidates belonging to Scheduled Castes and Scheduled Tribes, better known as Dalits and Adivasis, which represent the country's most disadvantaged groups and make up nearly 25 per cent of the population. Based on an analysis of such precedents, mechanisms for adequate minority representation should also be implemented in a world parliament.

The historic beginnings of democracy

Robert Dahl believes that three 'great transformations' can be observed in the history of democracy.[71] Each of these transformations involves a step up in the *scale* of democratic governance. The first transformation, he observed, began around 500 BCE and consisted in the metamorphosis of the autocratic Greek city states into the first communities with democratic features. Their central institution was the assembly of the people, in which all male citizens who had completed military service could take part. The Australian political scientist John Keane located the roots of 'self-government by assemblies of people who regard each other as equals' two thousand years earlier in the Syrian-Mesopotamian region.[72] According to the political scientist David Stasavage, the first early forms of democracy were characterized by single rulers having to consult with assemblies and councils that constrained their actions. This was 'common in small-scale settings' and in his assessment indeed 'so common in all regions of the globe that we should see it as a naturally occurring condition in human societies.'[73] In parts of classical India, a system of village self-government known as *panchayats* was flourishing within monarchical rule which may have developed over a similarly long time. According to the Indian historian Abraham Eraly these local assemblies were embedded into an ad hoc pyramidal structure of representative bodies. The village organization, said Eraly, 'was essentially democratic, in so far as it could be democratic within

71   Dahl, Robert. 1994. 'A Democratic Dilemma: System Effectiveness versus Citizen Participation'. Political Science Quarterly (109) 1: 23–34, pp. 25-7.
72   Keane, John. 2010. The life and death of democracy. London: Pocket Books, pp. 101-155, 111.
73   Stasavage, David. 2020. The Decline and Rise of Democracy: A Global History from Antiquity to Today. Princeton Oxford: Princeton University Press, 2020, pp. 5, 56.

the ambit of a caste society'.[74] Hereditary monarchy appears to have been the most widespread form of government.[75] Nonetheless, with regard to the period before 400 BCE, historian Steven Muhlberger noted that India was also home 'to a variety of self-governing polities using quasi-democratic institutions comparable with those of the Greek city states of the same era'.[76] Early democracy also emerged prominently in Northern Africa. From the 5th century BCE on, the city state of Carthage, which controlled a vast empire in the region and the western Mediterranean Sea, was administered by magistrates, called *suffetes*, who were elected annually by a 'popular assembly' and consulted a senate composed of influential citizens.[77] In the ancient Roman Kingdom and later during the Roman Republic from 509 BCE on, voting assemblies of citizens existed but gradually declined until Caesar's dictatorship and the establishment of the Romen Empire in 49 BCE.[78] An advisory and governing senate was in place from the beginning and it survived for many centuries even after the division of the Roman Empire in 395.

None of this, of course, represented democracy in any modern sense. Citizenship was strictly limited. Women were excluded. Individual rights were usually not protected. The commonwealth of the Greek polis just like Rome or Carthage, relied heavily on slave labor. More so, as the French philosopher Christian Delacampagne reported in terms of ancient Greece, there arose here 'for the first time in history a society in which slavery was no longer one economic resource among others' but even 'became the most important means of production'.[79] With these and other caveats in mind, it may still be said that the Greek city states were among the first to pursue the idea of rule by the people but they certainly weren't the only ones. 'For the next two thousand years', according to Dahl, 'the idea and practice of democracy were associated almost exclusively with small scale city-states.'[80] This changed in the course of the second democratic transformation. The process of state formation had advanced, and had created relatively large territorial dominions. In the nascent nation states, the idea of representative democracy established itself through resistance to and rebellion against monarchical rule. An exemplary

---

74 Eraly, Abraham. 2011. The First Spring: The Golden Age Of India. New Delhi: Penguin India, Part III, section 7 ('Village democracy').

75 Sharma, J.P. 1968. Republics in Ancient India. Leiden: Brill, p. 15.

76 Stephen Stockwell. 2012. 'Chapter 3: Ancient India', in: The Edinburgh Companion to the History of Democracy, ed. by Benjamin Isakhan and Stephen Stockwell. Edinburgh University Press, 50–59, p. 50.

77 Cartwright, Mark. 2016. "Carthaginian Government." World History Encyclopedia. (www.world-history.org).

78 See Taylor, Lily Ross. 1990. Roman Voting Assemblies from the Hannibalic War to the Dictatorship of Caesar. University of Michigan Press, 1990.

79 Delacampagne, Christian. 2004. Die Geschichte der Sklaverei. Artemis & Winkler, p. 51.

80 Dahl (1994), p. 25.

and revolutionary instance was the federal constitution of the USA adopted on 17 September 1787. In the 19th century other federations to emerge were those in Mexico, Switzerland, Argentina, Bolivia, Canada and Brazil with more to follow later. This went along with the establishment of the nation state system around the world and the waves of democratization described above.

The third democratic transformation

The spread of democracy at the nation state level is not, however, the 'end of history', as Francis Fukuyama suggested. The idea that the territorial state and the system of international law represent the end of ten thousand years of the political development of humanity is an absurd and ahistorical way of looking at things. Just as very few people in the 18th century, before the second democratic transformation, were able to picture representative democracy in the territorial states, so today the idea that there can be democracy at the world level is still beyond many people's imagination. But that is precisely what the *third transformation* is about, and it is already happening. 'Just as earlier city-states lost much of their political, economic, social, and cultural autonomy when they were absorbed into larger national states, so in our time the development of transnational systems reduces the political, economic, social, and cultural autonomy of national states', is how Dahl described the situation.[81] As in the second transformation, the development is part of a process of state formation, but one that now encompasses the entire world system. It is the vehicle for a new 'Great Transformation' in Karl Polanyi's sense, leading towards the establishment of a global eco-social market economy. The future of democracy depends on the success of this third transformation, as it will be increasingly marginalised within the framework of the nation state system. At the same time, continuing democratization within the community of states is an important prerequisite for global democratization. The two processes are intertwined.

The third transformation involves the globalization not only of democracy but also of government. Democracy is a type of government. The history of democracy is a history of the *transformation of government*. Public participation, representation and deliberation are futile unless they feed into government. If the necessary instruments do not exist, as is the case at the global level, then they have to be created. The call for global democracy is thus at the same time a call for global government. As Otfried Höffe argued, the third democratic transformation means 'the formation of a democratic, constitu-

81   Ibid., p. 26.

tional state at the global level, under the rule of law and justice, a world republic based on subsidiarity and federalism'.[82] During the second transformation, the assumption of a right to self-determination for all peoples was of the greatest importance for overcoming foreign rule and oppression and for the development of democracy at the nation state level. The dense interdependence of the world system and the planetary-level tasks and challenges are now insistently raising the question of a *right to self-determination for humanity*. Global democratic structures of government are needed so that the global government vacuum can be ended and foreign rule by an elite, imperial, transnational order—one based paradoxically on the perpetuation of the Westphalian system of states—can be thrown off. Parliament is the core institution of democracy. The creation of a world parliament is thus at the centre of the third transformation. What is needed first is to gradually link the various existing forms and processes of public authority at the global level to a global parliamentary body so that they can be made subject to effective democratic supervision and participation by the world population. The parliament is both the starting point and the engine for the formation of a supra-national community at the global level.

International parliamentary institutions

The growth in the number of international parliamentary institutions, or IPIs, and their development can be considered an indicator of the incipient third transformation and how it is going. They represent a variety of forms of democratic representation and cooperation beyond the nation state not mediated through the governments but delivered by elected representatives. The oldest of these institutions is the Inter-Parliamentary Union, founded in 1889, which paradoxically has so far played an ambivalent role in the efforts to establish a world parliament as the first part of this book demonstrates. The foundation in 1949 of the Council of Europe and its Parliamentary Assembly, PACE for short, represented the creation of an important IPI and was immediately taken as an opportunity to propose a UNPA. As the directly elected legislative organ of the European Union, the European Parliament is the IPI that has evolved the furthest. The Andean Parliament and the Central American Parliament represent two further directly elected IPIs. In 2004, the Pan-African Parliament was established with the goal to make it a continental legislative body but this plan was still pending implementation two decades later. Academic interest in the phenomenon of IPIs remained very weak for a considerable time but this has started to change. Claudia Kissling, an expert in public

---

82　Höffe, Otfried. 2002. Demokratie im Zeitalter der Globalisierung. New ed. Munich: C.H. Beck, p. 428.

administration and law, undertook a survey and legal classification of all IPIs in existence in 2011. She found 40 such institutions in 1990 and counted around 160 twenty years later.[83] Using a more rigorous definition that leaves out networks of individual parliamentarians which are not public bodies, political scientist Frank Schimmelfennig and seven co-authors observed a rapid increase as well but contended that since around 2010, the development had 'stopped altogether'. In their assessment, this is connected to the slowdown of post-Cold war democratization that is giving way to an 'autocratic reverse wave', indicating that 'the prospects of international parliamentarization also depend on the career of democracy as a global legitimacy standard'. According to their count, there are now 25 IPIs that cover a third of what they consider the world's relevant international organizations.[84]Most importantly among them, the UN, the WTO, the World Bank Group and the IMF still do not possess parliamentary bodies. 'Those parliamentary institutions that do exist and relate to the activities of these IGOs, such as the Inter-Parliamentary Union, the Parliamentary Conference on the WTO, or the Parliamentary Network on the World Bank, are not willing—and not legally able—to exert any considerable influence on their agenda and decision-making, let alone exert formal oversight', Kissling remarked. She rightfully emphasized however that not every one of these organizations should have its own separate parliamentary organ. Instead, a UNPA could be created as a *common* parliamentary body with appropriate portfolio committees. 'In any case', Kissling wrote, 'an UNPA would contribute significantly to overcoming an ever-growing legitimacy gap at the international level.[85] To this end, a great deal can be learned from an analysis of existing IPIs. Schimmelfennig and his colleagues came to the conclusion that the 'overwhelming majority' of today's IPIs 'remain weak in their decision-making competences, and their effect on international cooperation is limited'. Governments deliberately establish IPIs in this way because they sense 'legitimation pressures' due to a shift of policymaking from the nation-state to international organizations but they merely wish to benefit from 'the appearance and perception' of international democratic governance that IPIs provide without actually granting them relevant legislative, budgetary or appointment powers nor 'effective channels of political participation'.[86]

---

83 Kissling, Claudia. 2011. The Legal and Political Status of International Parliamentary Institutions, Committee for a Democratic UN.

84 Schimmelfennig, Frank, Thomas Winzen, Tobias Lenz, Jofre Rocabert, Loriana Crasnic, Cristina Gherasimov, Jana Lipps, and Denusa Mumford. 2020. The Rise of International Parliaments: Strategic Legitimation in International Organizations. Oxford University Press, pp. 16, 4, 287-8.

85 Kissing, p. 53.

86 Schimmelfennig et al., pp. 270, 286, 9.

With the most prominent exception of the European Parliament, IPIs thus often represent no more than 'Potemkin villages' that do not change the nature of intergovernmental collaboration. While their very existence is an important step forward in overcoming the Westphalian paradigm, in order to make a real difference they ultimately need to be vested with actual powers which in turn puts direct elections on the agenda.

Complementing representation

From the beginning, representative democracy had its opponents. The history of modern parliamentarism is at the same time a history of its ongoing critique. References to a real or perceived crisis of parliamentarism are a constant companion. They were as fashionable a hundred years ago as they are today in certain quarters. The influential German legal scholar Carl Schmitt (1888 to 1985), for instance, was one of its infamous opponents from the right. In the 1920s he argued that 'compared to a democracy that is direct', parliament 'appears an artificial machinery, produced by liberal reasoning, while dictatorial and Caesaristic methods not only can produce the acclamation of the people but can also be a direct expression of democratic substance and power'.[87] Schmitt intellectually helped pave the ground for Nazi dictatorship which he readily supported after Adolf Hitler's seizure of power in 1933. The events in the aftermath of the October Revolution in Russia in 1917 provide another example. In a historic step, a democratically elected assembly was convened to work out a constitution. But when the Bolsheviks realized that they will not get a majority for a Soviet government in this body, they dismissed the assembly as an expression of 'ordinary bourgeois democracy' and forcibly dissolved it.[88] Not much later they launched a brutal political repression known as the Red Terror, which crushed all opposition. Rosa Luxemburg (1871 to 1919), herself a revolutionary socialist, expressed disapproval and noted that 'without general elections, without unrestricted freedom of the press and of assembly, without a free struggle of opinions, life dies out in every public institution'.[89]

According to the Italian political theorist Norberto Bobbio, democracy is dynamic and constantly in transformation. The process of 'becoming', he said,

87   Schmitt, Carl. 1988 [1923]. The Crisis of Parliamentary Democracy. Translated by Ellen Kennedy. Cambridge, London: MIT Press, p. 17.
88   Lenin, V. I. 1972 [1917]. 'Theses On The Constituent Assembly.' In: Collected Works. Vol. 26, ed. by George Hanna, transl. by Yuri Sdobnikov and id., 379–83. Online Version: Lenin Internet Archive (marxists.org).
89   Luxemburg, Rosa. 1961 [1919]. The Russian Revolution, and Leninism or Marxism? Ann Arbor, p. 71.

is its natural state.[90] The realisation of democracy is a continuous approximation to an ideal that will never be complete. This is even more true for global democracy, given the dilemma of scale. Bringing democracy to the planetary scale, to the best possible degree, will help address critical contemporary challenges and usher in a new era for humanity but the incompleteness of democracy will remain. While we do not know how democracy may evolve over hundreds of years into the future, at this point elections and parliamentary representation are an indispensable element on which others build upon such as separation of powers or checks and balances and those listed in the landmark resolution of the UN's Commission on Human Rights mentioned previously. A concern for democracy and a drive to improve it is inherent in a democratic system. This is a good feature. It is necessary to identify, criticise and address shortcomings constantly. First-past-the-post systems, for instance, are highly problematic, especially when combined with gerrymandering, the manipulation of electoral district boundaries for political gain. This election procedure regularly delivers winners who do not have majority support and leaves large proportions of voters unrepresented. The role of political parties, the degree of their internal democracy, issues of political financing, the effectiveness and independence of parliaments, or the dominance of government bureaucracies over the legislative branch are other examples that require attention.

It is not a new insight that representative democracy, however essential, is not enough. The Universal Declaration of Human Rights and the International Covenant on Civil and Political Rights, for instance, both not only refer to a right of citizens' participation in public affairs through freely chosen representatives, but also in *direct* ways. Benjamin Barber saw the future of democracy in 'strong democracy' with politics in the 'participatory mode', enabling citizens to 'govern themselves directly' as opposed to 'thin democracy' of the representative type where this is done in their name. This strong democracy, he wrote, was based on the 'universality of participation' of every citizen, albeit 'not necessarily at every level and in every instance'.[91] As Jan-Werner Müller, noted, it is 'naïve political solutionism to expect that *one* product of what has become a kind of global democracy innovation industry—be it internet voting, assemblies of randomly chosen citizens, or what have you—will get us out of our difficulties'.[92] While it is easy to point out the imperfections of representative democracy, especially at the global scale, the

---

90   Bobbio, Norberto. 1987. The Future of Democracy. Polity Press, p. 18.

91   Barber, Benjamin. 2003. Strong Democracy: Participatory Politics for a New Age. 20th anniv. ed., Univ. of California Press, pp. 150-3, x, xiii.

92   Müller, Jan-Werner. 2021. Democracy Rules. Allen Lane, p. xiv.

challenges of direct and participative approaches are numerous as well, in practical as well as in theoretical terms. None of them are fully satisfactory either and most importantly, they are not capable of rendering elections 'optional', as some appear to think.[93] This radical view implies a disfranchisement of all citizens, camouflaged by a populist message that is inherent in the deliberative approach as Margaret Canovan observed. It is the faith that the 'transforming power of deliberation' would unearth—and guide into the right direction—the true will of the ordinary people that otherwise cannot find an expression.[94] But such a uniform will of the people exists only in the populist imagination. Apart from that, in a 'lottocracy' of randomly chosen assemblies only the lucky winners have a say and everybody else is shut out. The demos in effect is shrunk to a tiny proportion of the citizenship which is literally selected by chance.[95] The members of a randomly chosen assembly *politically* are accountable to no one, as representative as such a body may be in *statistical* terms. In terms of the technicalities of deliberation this might be an advantage, but it forbids giving such bodies legislative powers. Representativeness, which is hardly ever fully achievable, is not the same as representation, John Parkinson pointed out in a book on the 'problems of legitimacy in deliberative democracy'. According to the professor of social and political philosophy at Maastricht University, randomly chosen participants 'have no formal bonds with any principals, so any decisions they make cannot bind non-participants'.[96] In addition, it remains a mystery how government would be chosen and kept in check. Random assemblies are not designed to form an executive or organize opposition. When it comes to the global scale, even some of the strongest proponents of the deliberative approach doubt that a demographically representative body is doable and believe it would have to 'number more than five thousand' members. Since such a body is unworkable in practice, it was suggested that a smaller 'committee or council' is to be elected 'from its membership'.[97] Thus, we come full circle back to elections but such conducted by a tiny and unaccountable elite only.

Anne Peters in a discussion of 'new types of democracy for the global level' concluded that 'deliberation, participation and contestation are no real substitute for formal democracy.' At some point, these 'mechanisms would ideally

93 Landemore, Hélène. 2020. Open Democracy. Reinventing Popular Rule for the Twenty-First Century. Princeton University Press, p. 19.
94 Canovan, p. 15.
95 Müller, p. 87.
96 Parkinson, John. 2006. Deliberating in the Real World: Problems of Legitimacy in Deliberative Democracy. Oxford University Press, pp. 83-4.
97 Pope, Maurice. 2023. The Keys to Democracy. Sortition as a New Model for Citizen Power. Imprint Academic, p. 174.

have to be linked to voting'. On their own, despite being 'important first steps on the path of democratization', they even may be 'too weak to deserve the label democracy', she wrote.[98] It is a fallacy to assume that deliberative and participatory democracy can substitute electoral representative government. But the tools they offer are still indispensable components. Representation and participation should not be understood as opposites, Müller suggested.[99] According to Benjamin Barber, the aim of his approach 'was not and is not to replace representative with strong democracy but to thicken thin democracy with a critical overlay of participatory institutions'.[100] In a volume on 'complementary democracy', Matt Qvortrup of Coventry University and Daniela Vancic, a pro-democracy activist, rightly concluded that they 'do not think that there is an alternative to a system of government with elected representatives, but neither do we think that this system can stand alone. It needs to be complemented. We need representative government as well as other mechanisms.'[101] At the global scale as well, citizens' assemblies, citizens' initiatives, petition procedures, direct voting and methods of liquid democracy need to be considered and institutionalized. An elected global parliament, nonetheless, will have to be at the centre of any democratic global architecture.

98   Peters, p. 270-1.
99   Müller, p. 88.
100 Barber, p. xvi.
101 Qvortrup, Matt, and Daniela Vancic. 2022. 'Complementary Democracy: Conclusions and the Way Ahead.' In: Complementary Democracy: The Art of Deliberative Listening, ed. by id., 197–201. Berlin, Boston: De Gruyter, p. 197

26.

The development of a planetary conscious-
ness, and a new global enlightenment

The social evolution of the human species can be described as a continual coming together and breaking apart of human communities.[1] Oscillating between cooperation and rivalry, they competed since the dawn of history for settlements, raw materials and food, and finally for geopolitical control. Through technological progress and population expansion, the social units have grown ever more intricate, and their interconnections ever closer and more complex. Within the communities, rules evolved to make living together as free of conflict as possible, albeit that this was primarily serving the interests of a ruling class which controlled the use of force and the distribution of resources. Political violence, rebellion and civil war were common manifestations of their disintegration. Mistrust was the predominant attitude towards other units, and the willingness to use force was high. War, forcible displacement, oppression, slavery and assimilation were universal characteristics under these circumstances. Democracy, human rights and humanitarian international law are in historical perspective very recent developments. Over the long term, the number of autonomous social units steadily decreased. Their maximum size and degree of organization have increased. Hunter-gatherers, nomadic shepherds and settled communities have evolved and merged into city states, principalities, dynastic kingdoms, continental empires and today's territorial states. Based on a collection and analysis of 'Big Data', the field of 'cliodynamics' attempts to identify and draw conclusions from 'cycles of political integration and disintegration' throughout human history.[2] Setbacks such as the fall of the Western Roman Empire were followed eventually by new consolidation processes. Around 1500 BCE, when the world popula-

<hr>

1   See also Bummel, Andreas. 2021. 'Towards a Planetary Polity: The Formation of Global Identity and State Structures.' In: Expanding Worldviews: Astrobiology, Big History and Cosmic Perspectives, ed. by Ian Crawford, 325–40. Astrophysics and Space Science Proceedings. Cham: Springer
2   See Turchin, Peter. 2023. End Times: Elites, Counter-Elites, and the Path of Political Disintegration. New York: Penguin Press; and id. 2015. Ultrasociety: How 10,000 Years of War Made Humans the Greatest Co-operators on Earth. Beresta Books.

tion is estimated to have been 50 million, there were perhaps 600,000 units.[3] Today the 193 states of the world are inhabited by over eight billion people, and it is more than questionable whether any of them can be seen as autonomous units at all. In reality, we are dealing with *one* integrating world system.

War and socio-political evolution

Historically, wars of conquest and the use of force played a key role in the emergence of larger social units and state structures. 'Force, and not enlightened self-interest, is the mechanism by which political evolution has led, step by step, from autonomous villages to the state', wrote the anthropologist Robert Carneiro in an influential essay in 1970. From small villages to great empires, in the whole of history there could not be found 'a single genuine exception' to 'the demonstrated inability of autonomous political units to relinquish their sovereignty in the absence of overriding external constraints', he argued.[4] However, the socio-political dynamic of development is undergoing a fundamental change, one which increasingly excludes the use of force. The English sociologist Herbert Spencer established in 1897 already that wars of conquest had outlived their day as a means of bringing about lasting integration. 'That integration of simple groups into compound ones, and of these into doubly, compound ones, which war has effected, until at length great nations have been produced, is a process already carried as far as seems either practicable or desirable', he wrote. He recognised the human urge to emancipation and opposed imperialism. Rule by oppression would not work any longer. 'Empires formed of alien peoples habitually fall to pieces when the coercive power which holds them together fails; and even could they be held together, would not form harmoniously-working wholes: *peaceful federation* is the only further consolidation to be looked for'[5] (emphasis added). Spencer was one of the first who noted that a social law of 'survival of the fittest' was at play in human history but he did not endorse what he observed, even if he was a proponent of a minimalist state. Instead, he believed this dynamic was undesirable and had to be overcome.[6]

Nevertheless, wars of conquest continue to be pursued to this day. The anthropologist Robert Bates Graber cited the two world wars as the most important examples. Territorial conflicts played a significant part in the outbreak of the First World War, and the Second World War was conducted by Nazi

3   Carneiro, Robert L. 2004. 'The Political Unification of the World: Whether, When, and How—Some Speculations'. Cross-Cultural Research (38) 2: 162–77, p. 175.
4   Id. 1970. 'A Theory of the Origin of the State'. Science 169: 733–38, p. 734.
5   Spencer, Herbert. 1897. The Principles of Sociology. Vol. II, Part 2. New York: D. Appleton and Company, p. 664.
6   Taylor, Michael W. 2014. 'Herbert Spencer: Nineteenth-Century Politics and Twentieth-Century Individualism.' In: Herbert Spencer: Legacies, ed. by Mark Francis and Michael W. Taylor, 40–59. Routledge, p. 57-8.

Germany as a war of annihilation and conquest. As Graber noted however, the final outcome of both wars was an increase, not a decrease, in the total number of states. 'In terms of political evolution, this suggests disintegrative rather than integrative overall effects for conquest warfare', was his summing up for the 20th century.[7] After 1945, maintaining the territorial integrity of states became a key international principle which can be found in Article 2, Paragraph 4 of the UN Charter. This principle was thought to help reduce the resort to inter-state war but on the other hand it is often accompanied by violent suppression of minorities within a state's given borders.[8] Even the artificial colonial borders remained intact in the course of decolonization. While the number of wars overall declined from a long-term perspective, dozens of cases that involved military occupation and takeover of territories by foreign powers continued to occur. Instances of illegal occupation that have been going on for over five decades include Tibet, Palestine territories and Northern Cyprus. One of the few cases of ongoing territorial aggrandizement since 1975 is Morocco's occupation of Western Sahara.[9] The Russian occupation of Georgia's region of South Ossetia since 2008, Russia's illegal takeover of Crimea in 2014 and the full-scale Russian invasion of Ukraine in 2022, with the intention of annexing territory and annihilating Ukraine's independent statehood, represent dramatic steps backwards in the development of the international order.

The prohibition against the use of force in the UN Charter documents that resorting to force actually is no longer acceptable between states under international law. Since 2018, wars of aggression are part of the crimes that can be prosecuted by the ICC, as was originally planned. Jurisdiction, however, is not universal and relies on specific conditions such as ratification or referral of a case by the Security Council, resulting in critical gaps as in the case of the Russian aggression against Ukraine. In the context of holding Russian President Vladimir Putin accountable, references were made to the Nuremberg Principles. These principles, formulated after the Second World War as a manifestation of general rules of international law, provided the foundation for the prosecution of war criminals from the Axis powers Germany and Japan. The principles classify the 'planning, preparation, initiation, or waging of a war of aggression' as an internationally punishable crime and could be used again to

7   Graber, Robert Bates. 2006. Plunging to Leviathan? Exploring the World's Political Future. Boulder Colo.: Paradigm Publishers, p. 67.
8   Waters, Timothy W. 2015. 'Taking the Measure of Nations: Testing the Global Norm of Territorial Integrity.' Wisconsin International Law Journal 33 (3): 563–86, p. 579.
9   Zacher, Mark W. 2001. 'The Territorial Integrity Norm: International Boundaries and the Use of Force'. International Organization (55) 2: 215–50, p. 237.

underpin a special tribunal. As discussed previously, enforcement remains an open question.

Nonetheless, the prohibition of war under international law, as first laid down in the Kellogg–Briand Pact of 1928, reflects a change in attitudes. The desire to wage war or to conquer is a relic of an archaic mentality. The demonstrations against the USA-led Iraq War in 2003, that led to eight years of occupation, were in many countries the biggest in their history. On one day alone, 15 February 2003, more than ten million people are believed to have gone out on the streets in an internationally coordinated protest. The protest was directed not only against the war but against the hegemonic conduct, in defiance of international law, of the USA. The *New York Times* commented apropos of these protests that world public opinion was now a new 'superpower'.[10]

The 'interdependence of destruction' (Schütz) between the nuclear great powers means from a larger geopolitical perspective that the consolidation of the system of states into a single world state entity by the exercise or threat of military force by a hegemonic power is practically impossible. A third world war would destroy world civilization. It is simply wrong to assert, as Rittberger and his co-authors did, that the establishment of a world state 'would require the exercise of military force, in the worst case even a global war of elimination between the states in existence today'.[11] Just like the process of economic and political integration in the regions, the global process of state formation cannot be driven by the use of force between states. Contrary to Carneiro's assumption, the example of European integration demonstrates that it is perfectly possible for states to relinquish their rights of sovereignty in a gradual, peaceful and cooperative process. The formation of the United States of America by the original thirteen founding states is an historic example of a voluntary relinquishment of sovereignty. How else but in this way could a world federation committed to human rights and democratic principles come about? As Jacques Maritain pointed out, 'it is by means of freedom that the peoples of the earth will have been brought to a common will to live together' in a 'world political society'. The time when political societies could be formed by force is past, he remarked.[12] On major issues, sovereignty at the international level has become no more than a façade. A world state framework would offer the possibility of a collective restoration of genuine political control. It may be true, though, that the *rapid* establishment of a global federal

10 Tyler, Patrick E. 17 February 2003. 'A New Power In the Streets'. The New York Times (www.nytimes.com).
11 Rittberger, Volker, Andreas Kruck, and Anne Romund. 2010. Grundzüge der Weltpolitik. Theorie and Empirie des Weltregierens. 1st ed. Wiesbaden: VS Verlag für Sozialwissenschaften, p. 317.
12 Maritain, Jacques. 1998 [1951]. Man and State. Washington D.C.: The Catholic University of America Press, pp. 206, 203.

state under present conditions is unrealistic. We have already pointed out, for example, how the democratization processes at the nation state and global levels are mutually dependent. The sharing of sovereignty appears only possible between states that have reached a certain degree of internal democratic governance. However, as William E. Scheuerman pointed out, this is no reason 'to preclude more or less a priori' (as he accuses those belonging to the contemporary cosmopolitan school of thought of doing) 'that a global federal state might proffer a worthwhile eventual goal, whose bases could potentially be *carefully and gradually constructed via responsible and peaceful political means*' (emphasis added).[13]

The decline of violence

An important precondition and driver of the changing dynamics of socio-political development lies in a changing global mindset. In an influential book the Harvard psychologist Steven Pinker argued with the aid of a multitude of statistics that human recourse to violence had decreased over the centuries: for example, that, *relative to total population*, the numbers of murders, rapes, war deaths and genocide victims had gone down sharply. This development is especially observable in the period since 1945 which involved an exponential growth of the world's population. According to Pinker, the 'decline of violence may be the most significant and least appreciated development in the history of our species', and 'nostalgia for a peaceful past is the biggest delusion of all'. Following Norbert Elias, Pinker believes that the single most important factor in the reduction in violence may be the rise of the state, which 'uses a monopoly on force to protect its citizens from one another'. As bands and tribes came under the control of the state, something Pinker described as a 'pacification process', the rate of violent death fell by a factor of five. As the fiefs of Europe, for instance, coalesced into kingdoms and sovereign states, 'the consolidation of law enforcement eventually brought down the homicide rate another thirtyfold'.[14] Further progress in the 'humanitarian revolution' was brought about by the era of the Enlightenment, the decline in violent conflict between states and the revolution in human rights following the Second World War.

The development of reason, empathy, and morality

Among the *psychological* factors responsible for the declining use and acceptability of force Pinker included the rise of empathy, self-control, morality and rationality. The New Zealand political scientist James R. Flynn found that intel-

---

13   Scheuerman, William E. 2014. 'Cosmopolitanism and the world state'. Rev. of Int. Studies (40) 3: 419–41, p. 425.
14   Pinker, Steven. 2011. The Better Angels of Our Nature. New York: Viking, pp. 692-3, 681.

ligence as measured by IQ tests has increased steadily and significantly over the course of the last century from generation to generation. Flynn admitted that such gains could not go on forever. Research is in fact investigating whether in certain countries a stagnation or reversal can be observed.[15] According to Flynn, 'the greater complexity of everyday life in the modern world' promotes classificatory, logical, abstract and hypothetical thought of a kind which is valorised in intelligence tests.[16] This refers to the 'formal operational' stage of cognitive development as described by the developmental psychologist Jean Piaget (1896 to 1980). According to Piaget's research, human intellectual development from birth to adulthood, in all cultures, can be divided into up to four consecutive stages—the sensorimotor, preoperational, concrete operational and formal operational periods. Extended modern school education is a precondition for a successful formal operational stage, roughly between the eleventh and sixteenth years.[17] 'Thinking now draws the appropriate conclusions from arbitrary assumptions and premises, without necessarily believing in them', is the summary put forward by the sociologist Georg W. Oesterdiekhoff. This is what first enables the formation and testing of hypotheses, for example.[18] He argued that modern culture and modern education have enabled the diffusion of formal operational thinking 'throughout the entire industrial population'. This is how the scientific-technical civilization arose over the course of the 19th and 20th centuries. 'The 20th century can be understood not just as the age of the industrialization and modernization of the world, but also as the epoch of the worldwide expansion of formal operational thinking, or as the era of the maturation of humanity', wrote Oesterdiekhoff.[19]

Advances in cognitive development create the conditions required for a maturation of human empathetic capability and moral judgement. Research shows that the cognitive stages identified by Piaget represent a prerequisite for the parallel development of stages of social perception and role performance, which in turn form a prerequisite for a parallel maturation of moral judgement. While cognitive development leads to a progressively better understanding of the objective world, the development of the capacity to adopt others' perspectives brings with it a progressively better understanding of how

---

15   Dutton, Edward, Dimitri van der Linden, and Richard Lynn. 2016. 'The Negative Flynn Effect: A Systematic Literature Review.' Intelligence, no. 59: 163–69; and Dworak, Elizabeth M., William Revelle, and David M. Condon. 1 May 2023. 'Looking for Flynn Effects in a Recent Online U.S. Adult Sample: Examining Shifts within the SAPA Project.' Intelligence no. 98 (online).

16   Flynn, James R. 2012. Are We Getting Smarter? Rising IQ in the Twenty-First Century. Cambridge Univ. Press, p. 96.

17   Oesterdiekhoff, Georg W. 2006. Kulturelle Evolution des Geistes. Die historische Wechselwirkung von Psyche and Gesellschaft. Münster: LIT, pp. 65-8.

18   Ibid., p. 45.

19   Id., (2012), pp. 324, 59.

and why people as subjects think and behave in certain ways. Moral judgement then represents a further step in which a judgement is made as to how we, and others, *ought to* think and behave.[20] The developmental psychologist Robert Selman distinguished between four stages in the evolution of social perception which relate to Piaget's stages. With regard to individual moral development, the psychologist Lawrence Kohlberg (1927 to 1987) identified three cognitive levels, each with two stages, which are linked to Piaget's and Selman's stages: the preconventional, conventional and postconventional levels.

At the first stage of Kohlberg's preconventional level, morality is situation specific and aligned with punishment and obedience. Whether an act is viewed as right or wrong depends on its consequences. At the second stage, an action is right if it serves to satisfy the self's needs and occasionally others'. Moral evaluation on the conventional level is then aligned with the expectations of others, regardless of consequences. The third stage here is linked to people, while the orientation of the fourth is towards law and authority. 'There is orientation toward authority, fixed rules, and the maintenance of the social order', wrote Kohlberg. 'Right behavior consists of doing one's duty, showing respect for authority and maintaining the given social order for its own sake.'[21] On the postconventional level, moral values and norms are generally applied regardless of the authority of the groups or persons advocating those principles. It is also irrelevant whether one identifies with these groups oneself. At the fifth stage called 'social-contract legalistic orientation', the relativity of one's own behaviour is recognised, and an action is regarded as right if it is in accordance with laws and standards agreed by the whole society following democratic rules and procedures. The sixth stage then involves an orientation towards self-selected ethical and moral principles with the personal conscience as a guiding agent. Kohlberg summed this up as follows: at 'the heart, these are universal principles of *justice*, of the *reciprocity* and *equality* of the human *rights* and of respect for the dignity of human beings as *individual persons*'.[22]

Kohlberg's theory is not good at explaining *why* people decide to take account of others' wellbeing and to act selflessly. As the psychologist Martin Hoffman emphasized, the formation of the relevant cognitive capacities alone is not enough. For him it is the *emotional* aspect of empathy and morality which is the decisive factor. A tendency towards empathising and caring is

---

20 Walker, Lawrence J. 1980. 'Cognitive and Perspective-Taking Prerequisites for Moral Development'. Child Development (51) 1: 131–39, p. 137.
21 Kohlberg, Lawrence, and Richard Kramer. 2009. 'Continuities and Discontinuities in Childhood and Adult Moral Development'. Human Development 12: 93–120, p. 101.
22 Ibid.

innate to human beings, he believed, and can be observed already in small children. On the preconventional level already, children spontaneously demonstrate empathetic reactions and an intuitive, pro-social moral attitude. According to Hoffman, human empathetic maturation develops in five steps, beginning in infancy.[23] It is only at the more advanced stages of empathetic development that emotional reactions are linked to cognitive processes.

The origin of morality in group selection

In evolutionary psychology, a whole branch of research is now focussing on the evolutionary origins of human psychology. The constant and ubiquitous human disposition to empathy seems to be a feature with deep evolutionary roots. The picture of human beings as egotistical and asocial creatures which underlies the thinking of Thomas Hobbes, to name one example, 'is untenable in light of what we know about the evolution of our species', wrote the primatologist Frans de Waal. Human beings 'have been group-living forever' and are 'social to the core'.[24] In his famous work 'The Descent of Man', published in 1871, Charles Darwin (1809 to 1882) asked how social instincts, altruism and actions for the benefit of the community might be explained by his theory of natural selection. The solution, he argued, might lie in prehistoric group selection. Individuals who were prepared to take risks for others and died in the process would on average have fewer descendants, and the leaning towards selflessness should therefore gradually disappear. 'It must not be forgotten', he explained, 'that although a high standard of morality gives but a slight or no advantage to each individual man and his children over the other men of the same tribe, yet that an increase in the number of well-endowed men and an advancement in the standard of morality will certainly give an immense advantage to one tribe over another. A tribe including many members who, from possessing in a high degree the spirit of patriotism, fidelity, obedience, courage and sympathy, were always ready to aid one another, and to sacrifice themselves for the common good, would be victorious over most other tribes; and this would be natural selection. At all times throughout the world tribes have supplanted other tribes; and as morality is one important element in their success, the standard of morality and the number of well-endowed men will thus everywhere tend to rise and increase.'[25]

23 Hoffman, Martin L. 2000. Empathy and Moral Development: Implications for Caring and Justice. Cambridge University Press, pp. 6, 63-5.
24 Waal, Frans de. 2006. Primates and Philosophers and How Morality Evolved. Princeton University Press, pp. 4-5.
25 Darwin, Charles. 1874. The Descent of Man. 2nd ed. New York: Clarke, Given and Hooper, p. 150.

In an important research contribution to this topic, the economists Samuel Bowles and Herbert Gintis confirmed the significance of group selection to the early origins of social behaviour, altruism and morality in the harsh conditions that characterised the Pleistocene, beginning roughly 2.5 million years ago and ending about 10,000 years BCE. In the book 'A Cooperative Species', they explained that 'between-group competition for resources and survival was and remains a decisive force in human evolutionary dynamics'. They ascribed the decisive role to the extremely violent and deadly conflicts between Palaeolithic hunter-gatherers. 'Groups with many cooperative members tended to survive these challenges and to encroach upon the territory of the less cooperative groups, thereby both gaining reproductive advantages and proliferating cooperative behaviors through cultural transmission. The extraordinarily high stakes of intergroup competition and the contribution of altruistic cooperators to success in these contests meant that sacrifice on behalf of others, extending beyond the immediate family and even to virtual strangers, could proliferate.'[26] Since altruism and selfless behaviour are extended to a much wider circle than just direct genetic relatives, the theory of kin selection is not sufficient to explain the phenomenon. Forms of reciprocity on the other hand, which can explain the cooperative behaviour of individuals, are ineffective for larger groups, and apart from that they are not truly altruistic, as they include an expectation of reward in return. Edward O. Wilson also endorsed this school of thought. In his *New York Times* bestseller 'The Social Conquest of Earth', the founder of sociobiology and the world's leading researcher on ants supported a multi-level selection interpretation. 'At the higher level of the two relevant levels of biological organization,' he wrote, 'groups compete with groups, favoring cooperative social traits among members of the same group. At the lower level, members of the same group compete with one another in a manner that leads to self-serving behavior.' Thus, individual selection favours selfishness and group selection favours altruism—the latter, however, not with respect to the members of *other* groups, but only of *one's own*.[27] As Frans de Waal wrote, '[m]orality likely evolved as a *within-group* phenomenon in conjunction with other typical within-group capacities, such as conflict resolution, cooperation, and sharing' (emphasis added). 'In the course of human evolution', he went on, 'out-group hostility enhanced in-group solidarity to the point that morality emerged.'[28]

---

26 Bowles, Samuel, and Herbert Gintis. 2011. A Cooperative Species. Human Reciprocity and its Evolution. Princeton University Press, p. 4.
27 Wilson, Edward O. 2012. The Social Conquest of Earth. New York: Liveright Pub. Corporation, pp. 289, 241.
28 Waal, pp 53-4.

In-group morality and humanity's crisis of adolescence

Not only is it important that the individual's emotional and cognitive moral capacity is able to develop progressively through the different stages; the degree to which the empathy and morality that result are group-oriented or universal is also key. It is routinely the case that a different moral yardstick is applied to members of the same social group from that applied to those outside the group. In-group and out-group morality can differ sharply. Aspects of group identity and group membership therefore play an important role in practical moral assessments. In the most extreme cases, this can go so far that outsiders are denied the status of human beings. Such a dehumanization means that the minimum moral consideration naturally due to every human being is taken away from them. According to Gregory Stanton, an expert on genocide studies who taught in the USA, dehumanization of a previously recognised group of persons is a key precondition for genocide. 'Dehumanization overcomes the normal human revulsion against murder', Professor Stanton explained.[29] The industrialised genocide carried out by Nazi Germany against the Jews was based not only on a 'law and order' morality on the conventional level, in which obedience of authority represents an end in itself, but also on just such a dehumanization.

On the postconventional level, in terms of moral judgement, an emancipation from group memberships takes place as values and norms begin to be guided by principles and to take on a universal character. As Peter Singer argued, in a coherent ethical system the same standards must be applied to everyone—to oneself, one's family, one's own group and to other groups. As a matter of principle, one's own interests cannot be more important than another's simply because they are one's own.[30] A postconventional morality as pure in-group morality is a contradiction in terms. Thus, the German philosopher Karl-Otto Apel pointed out, for instance, that the integration of universalist moral principles into 'European post-Enlightenment morality' cannot be equated with 'the successful transformation of the *purely conventional* in-group morality of the tribes, nations and militant faith communities into a *postconventional* morality that now extends into the institutions and conventions'. Apel saw the 'universalist transcendence of any pure "in-group morality"' as an 'unfinished project of humanity'—'the overcoming of the collective crisis of adolescence of the human race'. The adolescent crisis of the human race is 'a problem on a world-historical scale' that can be observed in the tran-

---

29   Stanton, Gregory H. 2013. 'The Ten Stages of Genocide.' Genocide Watch (www.genocidewatch.org).

30   Singer, Peter. 2011. The Expanding Circle. Princeton University Press, pp. 118-9.

sition from the conventional to the postconventional level of morality.[31] If the ethical principle of impartiality is taken to its logical conclusion, according to Singer, then we would have to treat all people with the same compassion that we extend to our own wider family. 'The ideal of the brotherhood of human beings has now passed into official rhetoric; turning that ideal into reality, however, is another matter. There can be no brotherhood when some nations indulge in previously unheard-of luxuries, while others struggle to stave off famine.'[32] From the perspective of postconventional morality, structural violence and the underlying governance and democracy deficits afflicting the international system cannot be justified.

According to Karl-Otto Apel, modern democracies manifest in their constitutions and their recognition of human and civil rights 'a representation of postconventional morality at the level of law and of cultural revolution'.[33] For Georg W. Oesterdiekhoff, the emergence of formal operations, which is a precondition for postconventional thought, should be regarded as 'the only cause' of the emergence of the democratic state and the rule of law. 'Democratic institutions are direct products of the spirit of liberty and of humanism. These ideas only arise in the formal operational stage', he wrote.[34] The capacity to adopt other social perspectives and for empathy is another precondition. Jeremy Rifkin stressed this aspect in a book on the 'empathic civilization'. 'Empathy', he wrote, 'is the soul of democracy', adding that 'the evolution of empathy and the evolution of democracy have gone hand in hand throughout history. The more empathic the culture, the more democratic its values and governing institutions. The less empathic the culture, the more totalitarian its values and governing institutions. While apparent, it's strange how little attention has been paid to the inextricable relationship between empathic extension and democratic expansion in the study of history and evolution of governance.'[35]

The challenge of 'humanity's crisis of adolescence' lies in giving objective form to the principles of postconventional morality in a *democratic world legal order*. The current international system is the expression of a morality which contains elements from both the preconventional and the conventional levels. On the one side, although the main features of a legal order are absent, at the same time the states are most certainly bound to each other by complex legal

31 Apel, Karl-Otto. 1990. Diskurs and Verantwortung. Das Problem des Übergangs zur postkonventionellen Moral. Frankfurt am Main: Suhrkamp, pp. 410, 429, 474
32 Singer, p. 119.
33 Apel, p. 433.
34 Oesterdiekhoff (2012), pp. 392-3.
35 Rifkin, Jeremy. 2010. The Empathic Civilization: The Race to Global Consciousness in a World in Crisis. Cambridge: Polity Press, p. 161.

ties which make behaviour foreseeable and regulate interactions and which all of them therefore have an interest in maintaining. On the other side, the actions of the governments are largely directed towards the pursuit of their own narrow interests and as far as possible towards the instrumentalization of the system to that purpose.

Sociogenesis and psychogenesis

As Norbert Elias demonstrated, there is an indivisible connection between the development of the human psyche and that of the social institutions, between psychogenesis and sociogenesis. Psychological change and structural change are mutually dependent. It was only after a given level of complex social interdependence was reached, characteristic of the state formation process and modernity, that greater control of the emotions, rationality and a fully developed sense of shame were able to develop. 'Psychological developments contingent on sociogenetic or institutional factors in turn effect institutional transformations', Oesterdiekhoff summarised. 'Civilization and the civilising of human beings is a psychogenetic process which totally transforms the cognitive, emotional and habitual structures of the population. Industrialization, modernization and state formation are the result of this civilising of the population. The civilising of psychological functions is a movement away from "natural", instinctive, egocentric, childish, undifferentiated and primitive states to more differentiated, more rational and more intellectual psychological states. This gradual increase in cognitive sophistication and emotional self-control is what gave rise to nation-building, modernization and industrialization', he explained. In human history, there can thus be observed 'a sequentially proceeding, unilinear and increasing sophistication and integration of *social and psychological structures*' (emphasis added).[36] Reflecting on the development of international law a decade after the Second World War, Gunnar Myrdal observed that there was a connection between 'attitudes and institutions'. Law, he wrote, had 'no independent existence' outside its social context. Moving the international system 'upwards towards cooperation and integration' would require 'fundamental changes of popular attitudes' in the direction of international solidarity, Myrdal noted. The 'gradual realization of a world community' thus had to be in synch with a conducive change in attitudes. Law, and international law in particular, could not be established 'by pronouncements, nor by majority votes in international organizations, nor by writing constitutions of "superstates" which have as yet no basis in inter-

---

36 Oesterdiekhoff, Georg W. 2000. Zivilisation and Strukturgenese. Norbert Elias and Jean Piaget im Vergleich. Frankfurt: Suhrkamp, pp. 48-9, 29.

national solidarity', he wrote.[37] The continuing growth of global interdependence, complexity and modernity should lead us to expect both a deepening psychological transformation and an accompanying transformation of the social structure. As formal operational thinking, empathy, postmaterialist values and postconventional morality spread and deepen through the world population, so the issue of a world legal order and a global state will present itself ever more insistently and inescapably. As Immanuel Kant wrote during the era of the stagecoach already, while 'gradually approaching' the goal of a world state, cosmopolitan law becomes a 'necessary complement' of public and international law as soon as 'a violation of right in *one* part of the world is felt *all over* it.'[38]

The widening circle of empathy

In Peter Singer's view, it is an unavoidable consequence of postconventional rationality that altruistic concern for people's wellbeing will be extended to the entire human race. Ultimately, all living creatures capable of pain and pleasure will be included within this circle.[39] It has been a recurrent observation since the 18th century that, as the size of social units grows, so too does the circle of those to whom feelings of empathy, moral equality and solidarity are extended. Kant's contemporary David Hume (1711 to 1776), for example, pointed in his 'Enquiry Concerning the Principles of Morals' to the 'natural progress of human sentiments', and 'the gradual enlargement of our regards to justice'. Beginning with the family, the circle of those to whom the same rules apply, and thus of those deserving to be treated with justice and fairness, grows steadily and continuously *as interaction with them increases*.[40] 'As man advances in civilization, and small tribes are united into larger communities,' wrote Charles Darwin, 'the simplest reason would tell each individual that he ought to extend his social instincts and sympathies to all the members of the same nation, though personally unknown to him. This point being once reached, there is only an artificial barrier to prevent his sympathies extending to the men of all nations and races.'[41] According to Carl Sagan, human 'history can be viewed as a slowly dawning awareness that we are members of a larger group. Initially our loyalties were to ourselves and our immediate family, next, to bands of wandering hunter-gatherer, then to tribes, small settlements, city-

---

37 Myrdal, Gunnar. 1956. An International Economy. Problems and Prospects. New York: Harper and Brothers Publishers, 43, 51-5.
38 Kant, Immanuel. 1903 [1795]. Perpetual Peace, transl. by Campbell Smith. London: George Allen & Unwin, p. 142.
39 Singer, p. 120.
40 Hume, David. 1912. An Enquiry Concerning the Principles of Morals. Chicago: The Open Court Publ. Co., p. 25.
41 Darwin, p. 138.

states, nations. ... If we are to survive, our loyalties must be broadened further, to include the whole human community, the entire planet Earth'.[42]

Jeremy Rifkin traced this development and saw a link between increasing global interconnectedness and the extension of human 'empathic consciousness'. Globalization has created an 'ever more boundaryless social space', bringing hundreds of millions of people into permanent contact with each other and enabling their empathic capacity to grow and reach beyond national cultures, beyond continents, oceans and other traditional barriers. The 'cosmopolitanization of the human race' has begun, he believed.[43] Over fifty years ago, Marshall McLuhan noted that 'electric speed in bringing all social and political functions together in a sudden implosion has heightened human awareness of responsibility to an intense degree. ... The aspiration of our time for wholeness, empathy and depth of awareness is a natural adjunct of electric technology'.[44] Following McLuhan, who always emphasized the point that the technological medium changes our perception and awareness independently of its content ('the medium is the message'), we should expect the increasing interconnectedness of global communications to lead to a planetary consciousness and ultimately to planetary integration. Rifkin perceived in his fellow human beings 'a journey to mature empathic consciousness' leading to a 'universal consciousness'. This consciousness gives one 'the ability to experience an entire group of people or even other species as if their distress were one's own'. Since in Rifkin's view the empathic circle is widening as the societal structures of world civilization grow ever more complex, and since these in turn entail an ever greater use of resources, he believed the great paradox of human history lies in the fact that the price of our growing empathic consciousness is the ever more piratical plundering of our home planet. Just at the moment when the human race is so close to achieving global empathic consciousness, it stands simultaneously on the brink of self-destruction through climate change or weapons of mass destruction. 'We are at a decisive moment in the human journey', he wrote, 'where the race to global empathic consciousness is running up against global entropic collapse.'[45]

In his 1979 book 'The Imperative of Responsibility', the philosopher Hans Jonas declared global empathy to be the ethical imperative of the technological age. On account of modern technology, he argued, the consequences of individual actions now had the potential to affect every other person on the planet and the survival of the human species. For this reason, there was no longer a

---

42   Sagan, Carl. 2011. Cosmos. Random House, p. 361.
43   Rifkin, ibid., pp. 425, 428.
44   McLuhan, Marshall. 1964. Understanding Media. London: Routledge, p. 5.
45   Rifkin, pp. 127-128, 42.

duty to love only one's neighbour, i.e. those in the immediate vicinity of one's actions, but also to love the most distant strangers, including *all people* and *all life* on Earth, now and in the future. From the responsibility for the survival of the human species Jonas derived the so-called 'ecological imperative': 'Act so that the effects of your action are compatible with the permanence of genuine human life'; and 'do not compromise the conditions for an indefinite continuation of humanity on earth'.[46] Based on his theory of universal stages of evolution, the British author Richard Barrett argued that human evolution 'will only continue to progress if we, the members of the species known as Homo sapiens, can learn how to bond with each other to create human group structures that cooperate with each other to solve the problems of humanity.'[47]

The transition to integral consciousness

There are numerous models for the categorization of human consciousness and its development, under the most diverse aspects. Ken Wilber tried to provide a comparative overview within the theoretical framework of an 'integral psychology'.[48] From the perspective of world history, the description by the philosopher of culture Jean Gebser (1905 to 1973) proved especially influential. He distinguished in his groundbreaking work 'The Ever-Present Origin', the first volume of which appeared in 1949, between four structures of consciousness: the magical, the mythical, the mental and the integral, all of them deriving from an underlying fundamental structure he termed 'archaic'. According to Gebser, humanity finds itself now in a transitional phase in which the integral structure is beginning to form. Each structure of consciousness is characterised by its own perception of time, space, self and external world, by different forms of thinking and feeling, discourse and language, and by certain social and societal features.[49] The integral structure arises out of a holistic realization, perception and integration of the others which according to Gebser still remain 'present in more or less latent and acute form' in every person. If one structure or any element of it begins to predominate, it becomes destructive, or to use Gebser's term 'deficient'.[50] Whereas the magical and mythical structures are associated with clan and tribal consciousness, and the mental with nationalism, the integral structure stands for 'a consciousness of the

46   Jonas, Hans. 1985 [1979]. The Imperative of Responsibility: In Search of an Ethics for the Technological Age. University of Chicago Press, p. 11.
47   Barrett, Richard. 2015. The Metrics of Human Consciousness, p. 34.
48   Wilber, Ken. 2000. Integral Psychology: Consciousness, Spirit, Psychology, Therapy. Shambhala Publications.
49   An English edition of this groundbreaking work finally appeared in 1985: Gebser, Jean. The Ever-Present Origin. Transl. by Noel Barstad. Athens, OH: Ohio University Press, see pp. 51-3.
50   Ibid., pp. 42, 99.

whole, an integral consciousness encompassing all time and embracing both man's distant past and his approaching future as a living present'.[51] The integral consciousness is *planetary and humankind-oriented.*

The third democratic transformation thus also represents an internal revolution of the human mind. With 'the rise of the integral worldview, a world federation becomes realistic and even inevitable', wrote the US American author Steve McIntosh. 'The mechanism of a world federation', he continued, 'is the practical way that integral consciousness can take greater responsibility for the problems of the world.' The link between sociogenesis and psychogenesis can also be found in his work. He argued that every new worldview developed around a political project, and that the integral worldview will not be an exception. The creation of 'a new level of human political organization' will be the political project that enables the integral worldview 'to produce lasting cultural evolution'.[52] As Jürgen Habermas observed, each new evolutionary push is marked by contributing institutions in which the rationality structures of the next higher stage of development are already embodied.[53] An assembly of democratically elected representatives of the world population will be the first political body in the history of humankind to establish a direct connection between every single person and the planet as a social unit. It will be the most powerful symbolic embodiment of a postconventional, integral and planetary consciousness. Two months after his election to the presidency of Czechoslovakia, Václav Havel, a believer in the vision of a world parliament, gave a remarkable speech in Washington D.C. 'Consciousness precedes Being, and not the other way around, as Marxists claim', he declared before the US Congress. 'For this reason', said Havel, 'the salvation of this human world lies nowhere else than in the human heart, in the human power to reflect, in human humbleness and in human responsibility. Without a global revolution in the sphere of human consciousness, nothing will change for the better in the sphere of our Being as humans, and the catastrophe toward which this world is headed, whether it be ecological, social, demographic or a general breakdown of civilization, will be unavoidable.'[54]

Group narcissism and the Promethean gap

More than six decades ago, Jean Gebser wrote that the world was heading for a catastrophe 'of decisive finality for life on earth'. The span of time separating

---

51 Ibid., p. 6.
52 McIntosh, Steve. 2007. Integral Consciousness and the Future of Evolution. St. Paul, Minnesota: Paragon House, pp. 115-6.
53 Habermas, Jürgen. 1976. Zur Rekonstruktion des Historischen Materialismus. Frankfurt: Suhrkamp, p. 37.
54 Havel, Vaclav. 21 February 1990. 'Address to the Joint Session of the U.S. Congress, Washington D.C.'

us from that event, he continued, 'is determined by an increase in technological feasibility inversely proportional to man's sense of responsibility'.[55] Albert Einstein's theory of relativity links space and time in a four-dimensional structure, and is regarded by Gebser as a striking manifestation of integral consciousness. However, it was used to construct the atom bomb. The world crisis is characterised by a destructive excess of rationality and egoism within the framework of the mental structure, combined with the lust for power of the magical level. Humanity and the Earth in their present forms could disappear, and the transition to an integral consciousness could be delayed by 'two millennia', Gebser thought.[56] Nevertheless, he assumed that many people were already capable of developing an integral consciousness, especially as the predominant rationalistic-mental structure proved to be 'no longer adequate for mastering the world.'[57]

The gulf between humankind's emotional-moral maturity and its technological abilities was something that also preoccupied the humanist Erich Fromm. In his book 'The Heart of Man', he investigated the connections between narcissism and destructiveness, nationalism and war. 'We live in a historical period', wrote Fromm, 'characterized by a sharp discrepancy between the intellectual development of man, which has led to the development of the most destructive armaments, and his mental-emotional development, which has left him still in a state of marked narcissism with all its pathological symptoms.'[58] The philosopher Günther Anders (1902 to 1992) spoke of a 'Promethean gap' to describe the 'final rupture', in this technical age, of the link between knowledge, ability and action on the one side and comprehension, feeling and conscience on the other. Human beings, he thought, were not up to the challenge posed by 'their inner Prometheus'. The consequences of this gulf could destroy humanity.[59] Fromm, too, stressed that the contradiction between human intellectual and emotional development could 'easily' lead to a catastrophe.

According to Fromm, it can be assumed that the narcissistic drive, just like the sex drive and the instinct for self-preservation, has an important biological function, since in the interests of their own survival all human beings are bound to treat themselves as more important than anyone else. However, it is only an *optimal* narcissism, not a *maximal* one, that serves the goal of survival. The biologically necessary quantum can only be so great as to remain compat-

55   Gebser, p. xxvii.
56   Ibid., p. 297.
57   Ibid., p. 294.
58   Fromm, Erich. 2010. The Heart of Man. Riverdale NY: American Mental Health Foundation, p. 86.
59   Anders, Günther. 1956. Die Antiquiertheit des Menschen 1: Über die Seele im Zeitalter der zweiten industriellen Revolution. München: Verlag C.H. Beck, pp. 267-9.

ible with social cooperation. Fromm described the process whereby individual narcissism transmutes into group narcissism. In place of the self, the family, the clan, the people or the nation becomes the object of the narcissistic drive. 'Thus, narcissistic energy is maintained but used in the interests of the survival of the group rather than for the survival of the individual', Fromm observed.[60]

Ideally, the solution would lie in a gradual reduction and eventual overcoming of narcissism in every individual human being in the course of *an expansion of consciousness*. In the meantime, however, according to Fromm, the simpler option lay in *at least changing the object* towards which narcissistic energy was directed. Fromm was thinking of an orientation towards the planet and the human race. 'If the individual could experience himself primarily as a citizen of the world and if he could feel pride in mankind and in its achievements, his narcissism would turn toward the human race as an object, rather than to its conflicting components.' And, he added, the 'image of the human race and of its achievements as the object of benign narcissism could be represented by supranational organizations such as the United Nations'. However, Fromm noted, 'it is clear that such a development can occur only inasmuch as many and eventually all nations concur and are willing to reduce their national sovereignty in favor of the sovereignty of mankind; not only in terms of political, but also in terms of emotional, realities. A strengthened United Nations and the reasonable and peaceful solution of group conflicts are the obvious conditions for the possibility that humanity and its common achievements shall become the object of group narcissism'. Among the main preconditions that had to be achieved first before destructive group narcissism could be overcome and Man could 'experience in himself all of humanity' Fromm included the 'subordination of national sovereignties *to the sovereignty of the human race and its chosen organs*' (emphasis added).[61]

The problem of cultural lag

It is notable that the revolutionary developments in technology have had strangely little impact on international political structures. The author and critic of technology Lewis Mumford pointed out this phenomenon in the middle of the 1970s. 'By turns the steamboat, the railroad, the postal system, the electric telegraph, the airplane, have been described as instruments that would transcend local weaknesses, redress inequalities of natural and cultural resources, and lead to a worldwide political unity—"the parliament of man, the federa-

---

60   Fromm, p. 70.
61   Ibid., pp. 87-90.

tion of the world." Once technical unification was established, human solidarity, "progressive" minds believed, would follow. In the course of two centuries, these hopes have been discredited', he noted.[62] This observation likely came with some disappointment, for Mumford was a proponent of world government, which he believed needed to be based on 'universal humanism' and 'a universal spiritual revival'.[63] Clearly, what we are dealing with is the phenomenon of 'cultural lag', as described in 1922 by the sociologist William Ogburn (1886 to 1959). According to this theory, every society requires time to adjust to dealing with new technologies and their applications. Thus the problem is not only the great and ever-increasing speed of change in modernity, but also the differing rates at which cultures manage, to a greater or lesser degree, to come to terms with those changes.[64] The Westphalian international system of sovereign states, which solidified in the 19th century, is in this respect the most extreme anachronism in our time. Ogburn wrote in 1957 that 'the lag in adjusting to the atomic bomb' was 'a lag of great danger'.[65] In fact, there has been no adjustment to this destructive technology. As we have argued, to be successful and sustainable, such an adjustment would have to consist in the establishment of a demilitarised, federal world peace order.

Interestingly, the inter-state rivalry for power inherent in the Westphalian system is an important driver of the dynamic of acceleration. The states system is the calm at the eye of the raging hurricane tearing through the world. The philosopher Paul Virilio, who examined the development of the modern world under the aspect of speed, spoke of 'dromocratic politics', that is, the politics of the race. In an outstanding study of 'time structures in modernity', the sociologist Hartmut Rosa wrote that the unfolding of the modern process of acceleration 'can only be adequately grasped in light of the military and state-centered competition for the conquest, control, and defense of national territories'. Modernization, he continued, 'is an accelerative project of national states that was driven by nothing more than the political striving to preserve and accumulate power within a system of competing national states that took shape after the Treaty of Westphalia.' In his view, the nation states have now mutated in some respects into obstacles to acceleration. 'In a complete inversion of the circumstances of classical modernity, acceleration in late modernity is not achieved by state regulation of social, cultural, and economic process-

62   Mumford, Lewis. 1970. The Myth of the Machine: The Pentagon of Power. Harcourt, Brace & World, p. 296.
63   Rosenboim, Or. 2017. The Emergence of Globalism: Visions of World Order in Britain and the United States, 1939-1950. Princeton University Press, pp. 234-7, 237.
64   Ogburn, William Fielding. 1922. Social Change with Respect to Culture and Original Nature. New York: The Viking Press, pp. 200-2.
65   Id. 1957. 'Cultural Lag as Theory'. Sociology and Social Research XLI: 167–74.

es and relations, but by their *deregulation*', he wrote. However, he conceded that overall they remain 'decisive agents of acceleration'. What has changed is merely the mode. The forces of acceleration have globalised, and compel the states, in a self-reinforcing dynamic, to push forward their own erosion. 'The political project of modernity has perhaps come to its end as a result of the desynchronization of socioeconomic development and political action', Rosa observed.[66] But that would only be the case if the 'cultural lag' were to persist, i.e. if the Westphalian system were to continue and there was therefore no adjustment in the global political structures. The elites are still managing to block the obvious solution, namely *the globalization of state power itself*. Within the world population, meanwhile, the outlines of the necessary change of consciousness are clearly emerging.

For William E. Scheuerman, the question arose whether meaningful democracy is still possible 'amidst a state system whose fundamental temporal dynamics seem fundamentally inconsistent with careful, slow-going democratic deliberation and debate'. He then went on to suggest where a possible solution might lie. 'If social acceleration represents a dangerous yet indispensable facet of the modern state system, how might we reconfigure that system so as to at least minimize the obvious dangers at hand, not the least of which remains the terrible specter of (high-speed) nuclear war? Might an alternative model of interstate relations—some form of transnational democracy, perhaps—at least provide a better starting point than the Westphalian system for doing so?'[67] Democratic decision-making takes time. Paradoxically, a global democratic legislative system based on qualified majority voting might even lead to faster and more effective outcomes than international law, which is extremely slow. And a world parliament is also a political instrument that could be used to delay developments, to speed them up or even to block them entirely. It could serve to contain the self-propelling forces of acceleration.

Global identity and the Other

Late modernity according to Anthony Giddens 'produces a situation in which humankind in some respects becomes a "we", facing problems and opportunities where there are no "others"'.[68] The absence of 'others' is uncharacteristic of the developmental dynamics of human evolution to date. This gives rise to the argument that the emergence of a global government is impossible, since

---

66   Rosa, Hartmut. 2015. Social Acceleration. A New Theory of Modernity. Transl. by Jonathan Trejo-Mathys. New York: Columbia University Press, pp. 311, 204-6, 313.

67   Scheuerman, William E. 2003. 'Speed, States, and Social Theory: A Response to Hartmut Rosa'. Constellations (10) 1: 42–48, p. 47.

68   Giddens, Anthony. 1991. Modernity and Self-Identity. Stanford: Stanford University Press, p. 27.

humanity does not face an external adversary or any kind of external entity that would enable the development of a global identity and in the wake of it political integration on a planetary scale.[69] The anthropologist Richard Adams summed up the identity issue thus: identity 'is fundamentally the binary differentiation of some set of "we" from some set of "other"'.[70] And Volker Rittberger wrote, 'without strong externally generated adaptation pressures there seems little likelihood of a world state'—without, however, wanting to entirely exclude the possibility.[71] US President Ronald Reagan addressed the issue in 1987. 'In our obsession with antagonisms of the moment, we often forget how much unites all the members of humanity', he said in a speech before the UN General Assembly. 'Perhaps we need some outside, universal threat to make us recognize this common bond. I occasionally think how quickly our differences worldwide would vanish if we were facing an alien threat from outside this world.'[72]

The Canadian political scientist Arash Abizadeh pointed out that Georg Friedrich Hegel argued already in his 'The Phenomenology of Spirit' that the emergence of a consciousness of the self, and thus of identity, presupposes the recognition of that self by another. Following on from that, more recently the philosopher Charles Taylor emphasized that identity was always formed in dialogue or in dispute with others. In Abizadeh's view, however, it is a mistake to simply assume that what is true for *individual* identity formation applies equally to *collective* identity formation. Unlike an individual, so the core of the argument runs, a collective can also constitute itself through recognition by its individual members. Recognition by another external collective is also a possibility, but not an absolute precondition.[73] In an influential article on 'why a world state is inevitable', political scientist Alexander Wendt got to the heart of the matter. 'The world state' he wrote, 'would be recognized by the individuals and groups that constitute its parts, and it in turn would constitute and recognize them. This is possible because even though parts and whole are mutually constitutive, they are not identical; there is a boundary or difference between them. The members of a world state have their own subjectivities that constrain its behavior, and the world state has a subjectivity that constrains

---

69   See also Bummel, ibid.

70   Adams, Richard Newbold. 1975. Energy and Structure. A Theory of Social Power. Austin, London: University of Texas Press, pp. 210, 304.

71   Rittberger, Volker. 1973. Evolution and International Organization. Toward a New Level of Sociopolitical Integration. Den Haag: Nijhoff, p. 48.

72   Reagan, Ronald. 21 September 1987. 'Address to the 42nd Session of the United Nations General Assembly in New York'.

73   Abizadeh, Arash. 2005. 'Does Collective Identity Presuppose an Other? On the Alleged Incoherence of Global Solidarity'. American Political Science Review (99) 1: 45–60, pp. 47–9.

their behavior.' Wendt also pointed out that global identity formation in a world state could also be engendered by means of *self-differentiation from a past that has been left behind*, and from its obsolete values.[74] 'In Hegelian terms we could say that 'history' becomes the Other in terms of which the global Self is defined', he explained. Identity is based on stories, which can distinguish between *a past and a present self*, he continues. Germany, for example, draws part of its identity today from the demarcation separating it from the Nazi regime and its crimes. 'Humanity's own past provides a rich and terrifying repository in contrast to which cosmopolitan identity could constitute its "difference"', Abizadeh observed.[75]

The vision of a humanity transformed by history, the promise 'Never again!', is thus a part of the formation of a global identity. In a passionate plea for a planetary perspective, the French philosopher Edgar Morin dated the beginning of the planetary era to around 1500, when the small western European nations began to circumnavigate the world. Morin thought that this ushered in a 'planetary Iron Age', which he also called the 'prehistory of the human spirit'.[76] In this age, in light of the threat posed by war, nuclear weapons, environmental destruction and overshoot, the dangerous 'Other' lies *in humanity itself*. An awareness that human history is actually just beginning, and a determination to finally overcome war, genocide, exploitation and environmental destruction, are important constituent parts of a global identity.

A Global Truth and Reconciliation Commission

Humanity must address the issue of its collective shadow. This includes the structural violence inherent in the international system. A *global truth and reconciliation commission*, following the example of national commissions like that in South Africa, could be helpful in this and could accompany the transition to a democratic world order. An analysis of over fifty such bodies established nationally since the 1980s suggested that they can be understood as 'civic participatory processes within state-building agendas'.[77] In this sense, a global commission could be a helpful contribution to a *global* state-building process. One of the tasks of such a commission might be to investigate from a global perspective and to make public, in a manner as objective and free from ideology as possible, the circumstances surrounding the most serious crimes against

---

74 Wendt, Alexander. 2003. 'Why a World State Is Inevitable.' European Journal of International Relations 9, no. 4: 491–542, pp. 527-8.

75 Abizadeh, p. 58.

76 Morin, Edgar, and Anne Brigitte Kern. 1999. Homeland Earth. Cresskill, NJ: Hampton Press, pp. 8, 58.

77 Ibhawoh, Bonny, Jasper Abembia Ayelazuno, and Sylvia Bawa, eds. Truth Commissions and State Building. McGill-Queen's University Press, 2023, p. 35.

humanity, wars and internal conflicts of past and present times, to identify the culprits, to recognize and honour the victims, and to create a basis for reconciliation. It has been argued that 'planetary truth and reconciliation commissions' on 'such experiences of our common humanity' as annihilation of cultures and people, colonialism, slavery or the Holocaust, among other things, are needed as part of a planetary conversation and 'trans-civilizational dialogue' on what constitutes cosmopolitanism.[78] The scope could also include harms done to the environment in the conceptual framework of the crime of ecocide. The planetary perspective makes this proposal distinct from a permanent international truth commission that 'would be available to countries in the aftermath of situations involving grave humanitarian or human rights crimes'.[79] Both approaches could be combined in one institution, however.

As Heikki Patomäki and Teivo Teivainen emphasized, the moral and political legitimacy of a global commission of this sort is of the utmost importance.[80] A study on the prospects of such a project concluded 'that the objective conditions for the establishment of a global truth commission can only exist after global democratisation has advanced on various fronts.'[81] This suggests that the creation of a UNPA should come first and a truth commission later. Indeed, an independent global truth and reconciliation commission could be set up by a UNPA and continued within the framework of a world parliament. In the opinion of Michael Hardt and Antonio Negri, the work of such commissions is 'an exemplary Enlightenment project of modernist politics, and the critique of it in these contexts could serve only to aid the mystificatory and repressive powers of the regime under attack'.[82]

The 'Overview Effect' and a planetary worldview

Even though there is no extra-terrestrial 'Other', and chances of an encounter are slim, given the vast distances in space and time in the universe, the experience of seeing Earth as an integral entity, from the outside, is one of epochal significance for the self-knowledge and awakening consciousness of humanity. The first two full-face pictures of the Earth are among the most influential and important photographs ever taken. The photos in question are 'Earthrise',

---

78   Giri, Ananta Kumar. 2018. 'Cosmopolitanism and Beyond: Towards Planetary Realizations.' In: Beyond Cosmopolitanism: Towards Planetary Transformations, ed. by id., 13–31. Palgrave Macmillan.

79   Scharf, Michael P. 1997. 'The Case for a Permanent International Truth Commission.' Duke Journal of Comparative & International Law 7 (2): 375–410.

80   Patomäki, Heikki, and Teivo Teivainen. 2004. A possible World: democratic transformation of global institutions. London, New York: Zed Books, p. 136.

81   Teivainen, Teivo, and Tuomas Forsberg. 2004. Past Injustice in World Politics: Prospects of Truth-Commission-Like Global Institutions. Crisis Management Initiative.

82   Hardt, Michael, and Antonio Negri. 2000. Empire. Cambridge: Harvard University Press, p. 156.

taken during the Apollo 8 mission on 24 December 1968, and the famous 'Blue Marble', taken on 7 December 1972 during the Apollo 17 mission. The television coverage of the moon landing in 1969 was followed by hundreds of millions of people, who were confronted with an outside perspective on the planet. The picture of the Earth in its totality is without question *the* symbol of our age. The author Frank White called the impact of the planetary perspective the 'Overview Effect'. It is not necessary to travel into space to experience this effect to some degree. 'Anyone who flies in an airplane and looks out of the window has the opportunity to experience a mild version of it', said White.[83] Satellite and aerial images are now part of everyday media experience. Apps like Google Earth, for instance, make it possible to virtually explore the entire globe from above on mobile phones.

The best descriptions of the 'Overview Effect' come from those who have experienced it themselves—the astronauts. Since the beginning of space travel, they have reported how deeply they were changed by the view of the planet from space. They describe being gripped by a feeling of unity, of home, and of vulnerability. The German astronaut Ulf Merbold, for example, was in space for 40 days in the course of three missions. 'The first sight of the Earth horizon', he reported, 'took my breath away. Not because I was surprised by the curve of the line of the horizon; it was more the royal blue colour of the atmosphere that enchanted me. But how thin this life-preserving layer was! This was the moment that all astronauts had talked of ... The Earth lay spread out below us. Its beauty was captivating—no language can describe it—yet how vulnerable it looked! ... We looked for the dividing border lines that are so clearly present between the countries on all the maps. But they don't exist.' 'When you go around the Earth in an hour and a half,' said the pilot of the Apollo 9 moon landing, Russell Schweickart, 'you begin to recognize that your identity is *with that whole thing*.' (emphasis added) It 'comes through to you so powerfully that you're the sensing element for humankind. You look down and see the surface of that globe that you've lived on all this time, and you know all those people down there and they are like you, they are you—and somehow you represent them.' For Merbold, the greatest significance of space travel may turn out to be the development of '*a global consciousness*'.[84] Ac-

83 White, Frank. 2014. The Overview Effect. 3rd ed. Reston, VA: American Institute of Aeronautics and Astronautics, p. 1.
84 Quotations translated from the preface of the German edition of 'The Overview Effect': White, Frank. 1993. Der Overview-Effekt. München: Goldmann.

cording to retired astronaut Ronald Garan, the overview effect brings about an 'elevated empathy' that helps realize 'that we are all one human family.'[85]

The German-American political scientist John H. Herz, well-known for his theory of the 'security dilemma', argued in a 1980 essay that 'for the first time, a truly planetary worldview seems plausible'. 'It arises out of the view the astronauts had of the small, blueish sphere that is the Earth, the realization of its uniqueness, its limitedness and its vulnerability.' Although this may be only one of many possible worldviews, 'the others are provincial, antagonistic, and under the new conditions of worldwide interdependence they carry within them the risk of the devastation or even the extinction of humanity. And for that reason, the global worldview presents itself even to a moral relativist as more fundamental than all the others, because it gives moral precedence to the survival of humanity, without which all other measures of worth are meaningless'.[86]

The planetary worldview has already had important and direct effects on world politics. Mikhail Gorbachev made a major contribution to the ending of the Cold War through glasnost and perestroika as well as his committed efforts towards détente with the USA and NATO. The inferno of an atomic self-destruction of the human race was averted, for the time being at least. According to Gorbachev's own account, the planetary perspective was of considerable significance for his politics. 'Ultimately, human beings, with the gift of reason, must understand that they are global human beings, individuals who must take responsibility not only for themselves and their own fate, their own community, but also for planet Earth, for the whole of humanity.' This is how Gorbachev sketched out the so-called 'New Thinking' that he claimed served as his political guideline. 'The whole history of thought is a story about pushing back its own limits, expanding its own horizon. The time has now come for this horizon to encompass the entire globe. Already today we can see how humankind is embracing a broader, a global worldview', the former General Secretary of the Communist Party of the Soviet Union and his advisers wrote in a book published in 1997.[87]

Although the 'New Thinking' may have had a considerable influence on world politics and contributed to 'a consolidation of the civilising process' (as Gorbachev himself put it)[88], so long as the switch to a planetary consciousness is

85 Garan, Ron. 2015. The Orbital Perspective: Lessons in Seeing the Big Picture from a Journey of 71 Million Miles. Berrett-Koehler Publishers, p. 65.
86 Herz, John H. 1980. 'Weltbild and Bewußtwerdung - vernachlässigte Faktoren beim Studium der Internationalen Beziehungen'. Aus Politik and Zeitgeschichte 11: 3–17, p. 15.
87 Gorbatschow, Michail, Vadim Sagladin, and Anatoli Tschernjajew. 1997. Das Neue Denken. Politik im Zeitalter der Globalisierung. München: Goldmann, pp. 205-6.
88 Ibid., p. 209.

not reflected in changed institutional global structures the world will remain trapped in a dangerously unstable condition of cultural lag. 'A system which can only maintain the peace of the world so long as it is in the hands of first-rate men', wrote Lionel Curtis, 'is a standing danger to peace. It is self-condemned, for no system has a right to count on an unbroken succession of first-rate leaders to see that it works. The only systems to be trusted are those which continue to maintain peace when run by leaders of average ability.'[89] The only lasting solution lies in overcoming the anarchic structure of the international system.

Identity, demos, and state formation

The emergence of a global identity and the development of global state structures are inextricably intertwined. On the one hand, a planetary perspective is the foundation on which a world parliament will arise. Conversely, a world parliament is perhaps the most important vehicle for the promotion of a planetary perspective. The development of institutions and the growth of solidarity and identity are reciprocal processes—neither can originate or establish itself without the other. This is well illustrated by the emergence of the nation states. In his influential book on nation states as 'Imagined Communities', the political scientist Benedict Anderson described nationality and nationalism as 'cultural artefacts'. In Anderson's view, the nation should be understood in an anthropological sense as 'an imagined political community'. 'It is *imagined*', he elucidated, 'because the members of even the smallest nation will never know most of their fellow-members, meet them, or even hear of them, yet in the minds of each lives the image of their communion.'[90] The idea of such a national community is not innate, or natural, but *historically constructed*. According to Jürgen Osterhammel, there is a growing tendency within the theory of nationalism to see the modern nation state 'not as the almost inevitable result of a mass construction of consciousness and identity from below', but rather as 'the product of a concentrated and deliberate exercise of power from above'. It was a project of powerful elites, or—as Osterhammel stresses—of anticolonial or revolutionary counter-elites.[91] Modern state formation was often not the outcome, but only the beginning—and the most important instrument—of the process of becoming a nation. The Italian politician of the 1860s Massimo d'Azeglio is famously supposed to have said: 'We have made Italy.

89 Curtis, Lionel. 1949. World Revolution in the Cause of Peace. Macmillan Co., p. 42.
90 Anderson, Benedict. 1991. Imagined Communities: Reflections on the Origin and Spread of Nationalism. Verso, pp. 5-7.
91 Osterhammel, Jürgen. 2003. Geschichtswissenschaft jenseits des Nationalstaats. 2nd ed. Göttingen: Vandenhoeck & Ruprecht, p. 325.

Now we must make Italians.'[92] This does not preclude the fact that *premodern* ethnonational identities, political formations and states can be identified 'around the world for millennia', as Azar Gat convincingly argued.[93]

The academic study of history, as it developed in the 19th century, performed an important service as midwife at the birth of the new nation states. It set about constructing continuous ancient national histories. 'Rather than neutral instruments of scholarship, the modern methods of researching and writing history were developed specifically to further nationalist aims', wrote the historian Patrick Geary. Programmes of education were put together to spread the national ideology and the 'national language', usually used initially only by a minority, among the population. Geary rightly cautioned against dismissing national ideologies as trivial only because they were largely products of the imagination.[94] They had a very real impact. Nationalism was able to mobilize the people in their masses and to lead them into war. It is an example of the construction of an in-group morality that shows how significant the division into a 'We' and an 'Other' can be. William E. Scheuerman pointed out that the 'construction of national identities permitted elites, for example, to call on common people to fight against social peers—sometimes living just across the border—chiefly because they saw themselves as French, for example, rather than Dutch or German'.[95]

But what defines a modern nation and a constitutive people—a demos? Eric Hobsbawm pointed out that, historically, ethnic, linguistic or religious criteria were not paramount. 'Indeed, if "the nation" had anything in common from the popular-revolutionary point of view, it was not, in any fundamental sense, ethnicity, language and the like, though these could be indications of collective belonging also. As Pierre Vilar pointed out, what characterized the nation-people as seen from below was precisely that it represented the common interest against particular interests, the common good against privilege ... Ethnic group differences were from this revolutionary-democratic point of view as secondary as they later seemed to socialists.'[96] It was only later that theorists, and nationalist programmes, tried to narrow down the concepts of the people and the nation on the basis of such criteria. In fact, most of the world's states

92   Hom, Stephanie Malia. 2013. 'On the Origins of Making Italy: Massimo D'Azeglio and 'Fatta l'Italia, bisogna fare gli Italiani'. Italian Culture (XXXI) 1: 1–16.

93   Gat, Azar. 2012. Nations: The Long History and Deep Roots of Political Ethnicity and Nationalism. Cambridge: Cambridge University Press, p. 133.

94   Geary, Patrick J. 2003. The Myth of Nations: The Medieval Origins of Europe. Princeton University Press, pp. 16-7.

95   Scheuerman, William E. 2011. The Realist Case for Global Reform. Cambridge: Polity Press, p. 43.

96   Hobsbawm, Eric. 1992. Nations and Nationalism Since 1780: Programme, Myth, Reality. Cambridge University Press, p. 20.

are unquestionably multicultural and have large minorities. The homogenous
'nation state' is largely a fiction. The multi-faith and multi-ethnic state of India, with its 1.4 billion inhabitants and countless language communities, is a
good illustration of the fact that a homogenous culture, a common religion or
a minimum threshold of prosperity do not represent prerequisites for a demos
or a functioning democracy. The French scholar Ernest Rénan recognised in
1882 that ethnic categorizations were fundamentally problematic, and that
membership of a nation cannot be purely dependent on linguistic, religious
and geographical criteria either. In Rénan's view, a nation is 'a great solidarity
constituted by the feeling of sacrifices made and those that one is still disposed
to make. It presupposes a past but is reiterated in the present by a tangible
fact: consent, the clearly expressed desire to continue a common life'. 'A nation's existence', he summed up forcefully, 'is a daily plebiscite.'[97] It is based
on the mutually acknowledged self-identification of its members.

The demos does not exist in isolation, detached from institutions. The demos only comes into being through state formation. The political scientists
Michael Zürn and Gregor Walter-Drop pointed out that 'a demos is never
externally given, but always the result of political institutions and intensified
transactions'. They cited the examples of France and Great Britain to illustrate
that it was primarily the state which, at an early point in its history, created a
symbolic framework supporting the development of an imagined community
and a strong national identity.[98] The demos is a legal entity that arises out of a
political act, namely the founding of the state; its membership is defined by
citizenship of that state. This applies just as much to the world state as to territorial states. The formation of a world demos is similarly not a precondition
for, but a consequence of, global state formation. The difference, however, lies
in the fact that the community of humanity as a collective of all human beings
is natural and innate. From a cosmopolitan perspective, there are no problems
of segregation here, as there are with national citizenship. Everybody is included, and a part of the potential world demos. Homogeneity, in any respect,
is not a requirement. The world society is and will remain multi-cultural, multi-ethnic, multi-faith and multi-lingual. The creation of a world parliament will
call into being a planetary demos. And the demos embodied in the world parliament will represent *the common interests of humanity* and will defend them
against the particularistic interests of the states and the privileges of the transna-

---

97 Rénan, Ernest. 1992. 'What Is a Nation? Text of a Lecture Delivered at the Sorbonne on March 11th, 1882',
    published in: id., Qu'est-Ce Qu'une Nation?, Paris, Presses-Pocket. Transl. by Ethan Rundell.
98 Zürn, Michael, and Gregor Walter-Drop. 2011. 'Democracy and representation beyond the nation state'.
    In: The Future of Representative Democracy, ed. by Sonia Alonso, John Keane, and Wolfgang Merkel, 258–
    81. Cambridge University Press, p. 265.

tional elite. Even though antidemocratic governing elites and antimodern extremists may deny it, the Universal Declaration of Human Rights and the other established treaties on human rights, above all the two Covenants, on Civil and Political Rights and on Economic, Social and Cultural Rights, have already served to bring about a common global set of shared basic values. Surveys document a 'dramatic international consensus' on fundamental human rights among the world population.[99] This provides a broad foundation of shared values on which a world parliament, and with it a world demos, can be built.

The philosopher Peter Singer believes the moral significance of national borders needs to be reconsidered in the context of globalization. 'We need to ask', he wrote, 'whether it will, in the long run, be better if we continue to live in the imagined communities we know as nation-states, or if we begin to consider ourselves *as members of an imagined community of the world*' (emphasis added).[100] National and global identity are not mutually exclusive. The sociologist Georg Simmel (1858 to 1918) described identity as the product of *individually combined affiliations* to social circles and groups.[101] Each group affiliation is accompanied by feelings of solidarity and identity, of varying strength, which if necessary have to be reconciled and balanced off. Ultimately, national citizenship is merely one affiliation among many. The economist and philosopher Amartya Sen emphasized in his book 'Identity and Violence' that people must not be reduced to one identity. Identities are 'robustly plural' and overlap, and 'the importance of one identity need not obliterate the importance of others'. For that reason, he wrote, it is not necessary 'that our national allegiances and local loyalties be altogether *replaced* by a global sense of belonging, to be reflected in the working of a colossal "world state." In fact, global identity can begin to receive its due without eliminating our other loyalties.'[102]

The progressive attitude of the world population

As the spread of postmaterial values and of a planetary perspective might lead us to expect, more and more people already consider themselves to be citizens of the world and as such they feel solidarity with one another. Online platforms and social movements today can quickly mobilize millions of people across the world for global issues. 'Why should women and men from one part of the world worry about the fact that people in other parts of the world

99 Patrick, Stewart M. 8 December 2011. 'Surprising International Human Rights Consensus'. Council on Foreign Relations - The Internationalist (blogs.cfr.org).

100 Singer, Peter. 2004. One World: The Ethics of Globalization. New Haven: Yale University Press, p. 171.

101 Simmel, Georg. 2013. Soziologie. Untersuchungen über die Formen der Vergesellschaftung. Gesamtausgabe Band 11. 7th ed. Frankfurt: Suhrkamp. Ch. 6, Die Kreuzung sozialer Kreise, pp. 456-511.

102 Sen, Amartya. 2007. Identity and Violence: The Illusion of Destiny. London: Penguin Books, pp. 19, 185.

are getting a raw deal if there is no sense of global belonging and no concern about global fairness?' asked Amartya Sen, writing about the anti-globalization protest movement at the time. 'Global discontent, to which the protests give voice, can be seen as evidence of the existence of a sense of global identity and some concerns about global ethics.'[103] This finding is confirmed by international surveys. In the fifth wave of the WVS survey from 2005 to 2009, a global average of 73 per cent of respondents in around 50 countries reported that they regarded themselves as citizens of the world. In the sixth wave from 2010 to 2014, it was 71.3 per cent across nearly 60 countries.[104] In an 8-country-survey conducted in 2017 on behalf of the Global Challenges Foundation, an average of 75 per cent of respondents confirmed the same.[105] Another survey carried out annually in 19 countries from 2014 to 2023 asked whether respondents considered themselves *more* a world citizen than a citizen of the country they lived in. On a scale from 1 for strong disagreement and 5 for strong approval, the average response ranged between 3.08 and 3.16.[106] In 2016, for the first time in 15 years of tracking, a poll on behalf of the BBC World Service that asked the same question found that, on average across 18 countries, more than half—51 per cent—confirmed to identify *more* as a world citizen.[107] Those who think of themselves as global citizens includes the group of the so-called 'cultural creatives' described by the sociologist Paul Ray and the psychologist Ruth Anderson. The authors believed this group represents a new subculture, alongside traditionalists and modernists, one that makes up a third of the population of the industrialised societies. The cultural creatives focus on the things that all people have in common. They think ho-listically, and do not believe in business as usual. They take account of the welfare of future generations in their deliberations. They 'are the people most concerned about the condition of our global ecology and the well-being of the people of the planet', according to Ray and Anderson.[108]

Whether it is measures to lessen the effects of climate change, observance of international law, implementation of human rights, participatory democracy, the abolition of nuclear weapons or the strengthening and democratization of the United Nations: relevant international surveys constantly find majorities

103 Ibid., p. 123.
104 Data available at worldvaluessurvey.org. See responses V210 for wave 5 and V212 for wave 6. In wave 7 the same question was no longer included.
105 Global Challenges Foundation. 2017. Attitudes to Global Risks and Governance, pp. 19, 63.
106 Global Nation. 2023. 'Global Solidarity Report 2023', p. 44.
107 GlobeScan Incorporated. 27 April 2016. 'Global Citizenship: A Growing Sentiment Among Citizens Of Emerging Economies: Global Poll.' (globescan.com).
108 Ray, Paul H., and Sherry Ruth Anderson. 2001. The Cultural Creatives: How 50 Million People Are Chang-ing the World. New York: Broadway Books, p. 11.

across the world in support of all these aims. This is an indication that popular thinking in these areas is much more advanced than that of the government officials who act on the public's behalf in international negotiations and are tasked to pursue narrow national interests. Of the numerous surveys made over time, we only mention a few in the following, quoting the average percentage of approval to a particular question across the number of countries covered in each poll (*not* weighted according to population shares). Does the UN Security Council have the responsibility to authorize the use of military force to protect people from severe human rights violations such as genocide (61 per cent, 20 countries, 2006-8); creating a standing UN peacekeeping force under UN command (66 per cent, 22 countries, 2006-8);[109] changes to individual lifestyles are necessary to reduce climate emissions (83 per cent, 21 countries, 2007); the government is not doing enough to tackle climate change (63 per cent, 16 countries, 2009); government should give a higher priority to combating climate change (60 per cent, 19 countries, 2009);[110] establishing an international agreement for the elimination of all nuclear weapons, including oversight measures to ensure compliance (76 per cent, 21 countries, including majorities in the P5 countries, 2008);[111] do you agree that a new supranational organisation should be created to make enforceable global decisions to address global risks (69 per cent, 10 countries, 2018);[112] international organisations like the UN should be given more power to protect and restore nature at a global level (64 per cent, 20 countries, 2021);[113] for certain problems, like environmental pollution, international bodies should have the right to enforce solutions (59 per cent, 21 countries, 2023).[114] A survey conducted on behalf of the Stimson Center covering the 12 countries that are members of the Group of 7 and the BRICS forum published in 2023 found that there was broad support for strong international responses to aggression, in particular the Russian attack on Ukraine, and for bringing war crimes suspects to the International Criminal Court, among other things. There was a consensus across the respondents 'around peace and security issues, UN reform, international law, climate change, and pandemic protection', the study said. Overall, it was concluded that 'the people are ahead of elites when it comes to fundamental issues of

---

109 Council on Foreign Relations. 2012. 'Chapter 3: World Opinion on Violent Conflict'. In: Public Opinion on Global Issues. New York: id., p. 2.
110 Id. 2011. 'Chapter 5a: World Opinion on the Environment'. In: Public Opinion on Global Issues. New York: id., pp. 6-8.
111 Global Zero. 9 December 2008. 'Launch Press Release' (www.globalzero.org).
112 Global Challenges Foundation. 2018. Attitudes to Global Risk and Governance Survey 2018, p. 38.
113 Gaffney, Owen, and Zoe Tcholak-Antitch. 2021. Global Commons Survey: Attitudes to Planetary Stewardship and Transformation among G20 Countries. Global Commons Alliance. (globalcommonsalliance.org), p. 9.
114 See Global Nation, p. 41.

global governance and concrete ideas for improving it'.[115] The obstacle are the governments, not popular opposition.

Popular support for a world parliament

Surveys indicate public support in many countries for different manifestations of a parliamentary body at the UN, like creating 'a new UN Parliament, made up of representatives directly elected by citizens, having powers equal to the current UN General Assembly that is controlled by national governments' (63 per cent, 18 countries, 2005)[116]; creating a 'UN parliamentary network' to 'keep members of parliament or Congress more engaged with the UN's agenda so they can support it or provide feedback' (62 per cent, 12 countries, 2023);[117] the establishment of a 'global parliament, directly elected by the world population, to recommend policies on global issues' (67 per cent, 5 countries, 2019-20);[118] or 'establishing a global democratic assembly whose role would be to draft international treaties against climate change' while each 'adult across the world would have one vote to elect members of the assembly' (64 per cent, 20 countries, 2021).[119] Majority support for 'a Global Parliament, where votes are based on country population sizes, and the global parliament is able to make *binding policies*' (emphasis added) in a 2007 survey was found in 9 of 15 countries with an international average of 37,3 per cent in favor and 35,6 disapproving.[120] In a 2023 survey, the notion found more support when majorities in 14 of 15 countries, the exception being the United States, leaned towards the founding of a 'World Parliament' where 'every country would be represented based on how many citizens it has' and which 'would be part of a global legislative system that under certain circumstances would pass legally binding laws to govern the world as a whole'. The international average of those strongly supporting it was 24 per cent while only 10 per cent strongly opposed. Overall, 60 per cent leaned towards support while only 21 per cent towards disapproval, with 18 per cent undecided.[121] Further, researchers Farsan Ghassim, Mathias Koenig-Archibugi and Luis Cabrera conducted surveys in

115 Stimson Center. 2023. 'Global Governance Survey 2023: Finding Consensus in a Divided World', pp. 3, 8.

116 Council on Foreign Relations (2012). 'Chapter 2: World Opinion on International Institutions', pp. 7, 45.

117 Stimson, pp. 42-3.

118 Ghassim, Farsan. 2020. Who on Earth Wants Global Democracy – and Why (Not)? A Theoretical and Experimental Study of International Public Opinion. DPhil thesis, University College, Oxford, pp. 148, 298.

119 Douenne, Thomas, Adrien Fabre, and Linus Mattauch. 2023. 'International Attitudes Toward Global Policies.' World Inequality Lab Working Paper 2023/08, pp. 53, 75.

120 Synovate. 2007. 'BBC Poll: Why Democracy', question 6.

121 Conducted as part of the Friedrich-Ebert Foundation Global Census 2023. Results published by Bummel, Andreas. 5 Oct. 2023. 'International Poll: Public Supports a World Parliament and World Law.' Democracy Without Borders (blog). (democracywithoutborders.org)

six countries in 2019 to 'identify public preferences on nine distinct institutional design dimensions figuring prominently in UN reform debates'. Their study showed that 'the general public in several countries prefers certain designs to others, and often the most popular option is not the one represented by the current UN'. Most preferred proposals were such that 'would make the UN more authoritative and reduce global inequalities in representation'. Overall, they found 'public opinion to lean toward the positions of those reformers who have sought to see the UN and related global institutions moving closer to supranationalist and cosmopolitan ideals'. In particular, this included the creation of a directly elected second chamber alongside the UN General Assembly.[122] Finally, Oxford University researcher Farsan Ghassim and Dublin City University assistant Professor Markus Pauli between 2017 and 2021 explored public opinion on world government in 17 countries 'in the global South, North, East, and West'. With the exception of the United States, they found that different specifications of a world government were supported by majorities everywhere. The creation of a world government, for instance, 'which should be democratic in that people worldwide would be represented through free and fair elections or other ways of citizen participation; and which should have the right and the power to deal with global issues like climate change, world poverty, and international peace' was endorsed on average by 69 per cent of respondents. Overall, the researchers found that 'citizens of more populous, less wealthy, less free, and/or less powerful countries are generally even more supportive, all else equal', than respondents elsewhere. 'This indicates', they noted, 'that people may view the idea of a democratic and functionally focused global government as a way of overcoming inequalities in wealth and power, advancing their nation's preferences in world politics, and acquiring greater freedoms.' Ghassim and Pauli concluded that anecdotal references to alleged popular opposition could not be backed up by the evidence. Those who claimed otherwise appear to make their observations based on a perception of the exceptional situation in the United States, ignoring substantial public support everywhere else. As 'media outlets, researchers, and policymakers concentrate on the resurgence of right-wing nationalism, authoritarianism, and populism all over the world', their study reveals 'a largely overlooked side of contemporary global public opinion: majoritarian support for much stronger global governance institutions that currently exist', Ghassim and Pauli wrote.[123] Reflecting on the willingness of governments to join 'a

---

122 Ghassim, Farsan, Mathias Koenig-Archibugi, and Luis Cabrera. 2022. 'Public Opinion on Institutional Designs for the United Nations: An International Survey Experiment.' Int. Studies Quarterly 66 (3), pp. 1, 8, 16.
123 Ghassim, Farsan, and Markus Pauli. 2023. Who on Earth Wants a World Government – and Why? An International Survey Experiment: Paper Presented at the Global Studies Seminar, Shanghai University, pp. 4, 23-4.

process of world state formation' in light of some of these and other studies, Koenig-Archibugi observed that they would only be prevented from doing so if 'the mass of citizens were overwhelmingly opposed to it'. However, quite the opposite, 'a non-negligible share of citizens in multiple countries is already sympathetic towards a democratic world state' and under the right conditions, the 'proportion of supporters would further increase', he noted.[124]

Global history and global citizenship education

The planetary perspective has had an impact on the writing of history, too. Historians observe a veritable global history boom in the academic literature, in research and in teaching. Sebastian Conrad, an academic historian who teaches in Berlin, wrote in an introduction to this approach that 'cross-border processes and exchange relationships, but also comparative studies within the framework of global connections' are at its centre. 'The starting point is always the interconnectedness of the world, and the circulation and exchange of things, people, ideas and institutions are among the most important topics for this approach', he explained. Global history can mean universal history in the tradition of Arnold Toynbee or H.G. Wells, but 'the most interesting questions often arise at the intersection between global processes and their local manifestations'. According to Conrad, three 'ideal-typical forms' of global history can be distinguished: world or universal history with a global horizon, the history of global interdependence, and the history of global integration.[125] Global history represents a decisive turn away from the discipline's previous fixation on the nation state framework, and at the same time it is committed to abandoning all forms of Eurocentrism. 'Following the end of European domination of the world, in an epoch of rapidly advancing intercontinental connections, and in light of growing doubts about the universal normative validity and practical benefits of conceptions of modernity originating from Europe, the discipline of history, too, finds itself confronted with the irrefutable need for all the problems to be seen in a global context', wrote Jürgen Osterhammel, a professor of history in Konstanz regarded as a pioneer and leading figure of global history. It is quite clear that global history is also being seen here as a political project. 'It is time for *a history with a cosmopolitan agenda* to step up alongside history with the self-appointed role of building national historical identity and teaching national values, and that which sees its role as the strengthening of a European historical identity', wrote Osterhammel, who since 2012 has been working together with former Harvard professor Akira

124 Koenig-Archibugi, 2024, p. 97.
125 Conrad, Sebastian. 2013. Globalgeschichte. Eine Einführung. München: C.H. Beck, pp. 9-10.

Iriye and others on a six-volume 'History of the World'.[126] Global history, Sebastian Conrad observed, is 'usually written in a cosmopolitan spirit'. It is 'a political project with emancipatory potential', and 'a step on the path to a global consciousness which opens possibilities for cross-border communication and interaction. Just as the study of history as practised in the 19th century was intended to produce national subjects, so a global perspective is a prerequisite for an understanding of oneself as a citizen of today's world'.[127]

The arrival of global history as an acknowledged school within the discipline serves to create an important foundation for the formation of a global identity and to complement the process of global state formation. Unlike national history writing in the 19th century, which first had to construct a national subject, the history of humanity finds its subject—the human species—ready and waiting. What is more, in the Anthropocene it is clear that the human species *shares a common destiny*, since the wellbeing of all people, including coming generations—indeed, perhaps the very survival of human civilization—is essentially dependent on the management of the world system, of the global common public goods, and of the global existential risks. In schools, and education in general, there is significant potential and need to embrace a global history perspective and to cultivate a cosmopolitan identity. Efforts initiated by the United Nations serve as a solid foundation for this endeavour. Over the years, the UN has advocated for the integration of global citizenship in national school curricula. In 1974, UNESCO adopted a pivotal resolution on education for international understanding, co-operation and peace as well as human rights and fundamental freedoms. The document emphasizes the importance of education encompassing 'an international dimension and a global perspective' as well as fostering an awareness of 'the increasing global interdependence between peoples and nations', among other objectives. The resolution underscores that education should address not only the eradication of conditions perpetuating and exacerbating major problems affecting human survival and well-being but also inequality, injustice, and international relations predicated on the use of force. In the 'Global Education First' initiative set up by then UN General Secretary Ban Ki-moon in 2012, fostering global citizenship in schools was one of three global priorities, along with improving the general quality of learning and enabling every child on the planet to have a school education. In 2015, the importance of global citizenship education was underscored by its inclusion in the Agenda 2030. Target 4.7 of the Sustainable

126 Osterhammel, Jürgen. 2003. Geschichtswissenschaft jenseits des Nationalstaats. 2nd ed. Göttingen: Vandenhoeck & Ruprecht, pp. 47, 9.
127 Conrad, p. 26.

Development Goals articulates the imperative for all learners to acquire the knowledge and skills necessary to advance sustainable development, uphold human rights, advocate for gender equality, foster a culture of peace and non-violence, embrace global citizenship, and appreciate cultural diversity. Progress towards this target is measured by the extent to which global citizenship education and education for sustainable development are integrated into national education policies, curricula, teacher training and student assessment.

'Big History' as a modern creation story

Seeing the human species in its cosmological context is a part of what it means to have a planetary perspective on human history. One's gaze is directed not just backwards from space onto the Earth, but also outwards into the universe. Spectacular images such as those from the Hubble and James Webb space telescopes encourage us to think about life on Earth and existence as a whole. Thus, in the tradition of popular authors such as Carl Sagan, Isaac Asimov and Stephen Hawking, global history becomes a part of what the historian David Christian and the biochemist Fred Spier call 'Big History'. The time horizon of this interdisciplinary field stretches from the Big Bang, which according to current knowledge occurred about 13.8 billion years ago, up to today. The home of the human species, 'Spaceship Earth', is a small planet orbiting one of up to 400 billion stars that form the galaxy we call the Milky Way. The Milky Way in turn is only one of perhaps 200 billion galaxies, grouped in clusters and superclusters, that make up the known universe. The nearest solar system to ours, Alpha Centauri in the Andromeda galaxy, is 4.3 light years or over 40 trillion kilometres away. In between is empty space, traversed by cosmic radiation. In view of these cosmic distances, as things stand it is very unlikely that even the tiniest proportion of the human species will ever live anywhere but on the Earth.

The common denominator in the history of the universe, according to Spier, is 'the emergence and decline of complexity' within the self-regulating systems of the world of inorganic matter, of life and of human culture under conditions of increasing entropy.[128] The perspective of 'Big History', wrote Spier, 'may stimulate another type of identity, namely the idea that all of us belong to one single, rather exceptional, animal species, which emerged on a rather exceptional planet somewhere in the universe; that our closest cousins are the primates; that we are, in fact, related to all life forms and that, seen from a cosmic perspective, our far cousins are the rocks, the water, and even the stars. For if the cur-

---

128 Spier, Fred. 2011. Big History and the Future of Humanity. Malden, MA: Wiley-Blackwell, pp. 24-6.

rent big history account provides a reasonably accurate overview of the past, everything would have descended from the "fire mist" of tiny particles that emerged immediately after the big bang'.[129] 'Big History' provides an account of the origin of all existence and of life on Earth on a strictly scientific basis. The cosmological worldview thus helps us on the path to an integral consciousness and creates an important frame of reference for planetary identity.

One of the leading thinkers in the field of 'Big History' is the US American historian David Christian. At the beginning of his work 'Maps of Time', he observed that every human community tries in one way or another to answer the question of the origins of existence. Creation stories have helped people to see their existence in an overall context, to give it meaning and to develop a sense of belonging within the whole. In the modern world, however, Christian lamented, while there may be more information and knowledge than ever before, it is present only in unrelated fragments and not in the context of a universal story. 'Big History' represents the attempt to bring these fragments together into a 'modern Creation myth'.[130] If it were to address the great questions such as our place in the universe, then history could play just as important a role in modern industrial societies as traditional creation myths did in non-industrial communities, Christian argued.[131]

The continuation of the project of modernity

Advocates of postmodernism, following the path laid out by Jean-François Lyotard, contend it is a defining characteristic of our era that people are no longer able to believe in overarching guiding ideas like progress, enlightenment or socialism. By 2007, with the beginning of the global financial crisis, market fundamentalist neo-liberalism—one of the potential 'Grand Narratives' still remaining following the collapse of 'actually existing socialism'—was also delegitimised. As the German philosopher and authority on Lyotard Wolfgang Welsch emphasized, this strain of postmodernist thought is suffused by the conviction that no narrative able to claim *universal* validity and legitimacy is possible any longer. This version of postmodernism has abandoned all concepts of universality and focuses on the particular. 'This, if you like, is now our meta-narrative', wrote Welsch.[132]

Postmodernist thinking paradoxically presents itself as the new meta-narrative. Its master idea is that there can and should no longer be any univer-

129 Ibid., p. 139.
130 Christian, David. 2011. Maps of Time: An Introduction to Big History. Berkeley: Univ. of California Press, p. 2.
131 Id. 1991. 'The Case for ‚Big History'.' Journal of World History (2) 2: 223–38, p. 227.
132 Welsch, Wolfgang. 2008. Unsere postmoderne Moderne. Berlin: Akademie Verl., pp. 172-3.

sal master ideas. This attempt to provide a post-modernist narrative has itself failed, ironically, and should be regarded as finished. Without a shared sense of self and a common orientation, world civilization will not be able to survive. Even with a post-modernist mindset, it should not be possible to avoid giving serious thought to the need and the necessary conditions for a global form of government as a prerequisite for the survival of humanity in the Anthropocene, if one is not prepared to simply give up on humanity altogether. Welsch emphasized that both the defenders of modernity and the advocates of post-modernism want to 'diagnose and treat the pathologies of modernity'.[133] But post-modernist thinking, at least such in the manner of Lyotard, cannot offer solutions to the global problems. In effect, it inherently excludes global approaches, as the social scientist David Harvey summarized the situation in his book 'The Condition of Postmodernity'.[134] From a post-modernist perspective, the problem, as Welsch put it, lies in the fact that 'totality can only arise from making one particularity into an absolute, which is inevitably linked to the suppression of other particularities'.[135] The totalization of the particular, in the shape of nationalism for example, and the resulting fragmentation of international law and of global governance, is a typical feature of modernity. Since it excludes the possibility of a shared cosmopolitan perspective, post-modernist thinking in the tradition of Lyotard does not overcome this state of affairs but further cements it. But why should a holistic perspective—in the sense of an integral consciousness—not be able to allow room for the particular at the same time?

As Karl-Otto Apel noted, in Lyotard's view not only the 'universal narrative of emancipation' but also the idea of 'humanity as the singular subject of history, to be realised in the future' have foundered. For Lyotard, the reason lay 'in the failure of cosmopolitan solidarity in the modern period, from the nationalism of the French Revolution and Stalinism to the power struggles within the capitalist economic system'.[136] With respect to core concerns of the Enlightenment such as democracy and human rights, the empirical basis for the post-modernist theory of the end of meta-narratives is highly questionable. The enduring aspiration towards democracy and human rights throughout the world demonstrate that the lust for liberty and emancipation remains unbroken. Growing global empathy and the trend towards a planetary perspective are laying the foundations for a cosmopolitan solidarity. Apel pointed out decades

---

133 Ibid., p. 165.
134 Harvey, David. 1990. The Condition of Postmodernity. Malden, MA: Blackwell, p. 52.
135 Welsch, p. 181.
136 Apel, pp. 396-7 with reference to 'Discussion entre Jean-Francois Lyotard et Richard Rorty'. Critique 456: 559–85 (May 1985).

ago that, although the deterministic assumption of a 'fixed path of history' is obsolete, by contrast the belief in 'progress, in the sense of the cosmopolitan unity of human history, which must remain a goal to be pursued and invoked at all times, and resilient against all frustrations, remains more topical and urgent than ever'.[137]

The characteristic feature of our time is not the failure but on the contrary the *continuation* of the modern project of emancipation, albeit focused on the planetary level. Following the argument made by Jürgen Habermas, who has set himself decidedly against the idea of postmodernity, modernity should be seen as an 'unfinished project', one which must be continued in a 'post-national constellation' under the banner of a 'radicalised enlightenment' in order to 'develop new forms of democratic self-control of society'.[138] Habermas has written frequently in more detail about his ideas for the necessary 'constitution of a community of citizens of the world', which include a world parliament made up of representatives of the states and of the world citizenry.[139] If it is considered necessary to speak of an epochal change, then Ulrich Beck's concept of a transition to a *second modernity* offers the most convincing approach. The focus here is on the erosion of the institutions and systems associated with the nation state and on the risks and side-effects engendered by modern industrial societies. Nevertheless, so Beck asserted, the question of what is disintegrating 'is immediately countered by the question of what is coming into being— the meaning of the emergent outlines, principles and opportunities of a second, non-linear, global modernity with a cosmopolitan agenda'.[140] One could also speak of a transition to a *planetary modernity*.

The philosopher Peter Sloterdijk expressed the thought that the 'wretchedness of the conventional forms of grand narrative by no means lies in the fact that they were too great, but that they were *not great enough*' (emphasis added). If the grand narratives known so far 'have been seen through as unsuitable attempts to seize power over the world's complexity', he added, 'this critical realization neither delegitimizes the narration of things past nor exempts thought from striving to cast an intense light on the comprehensible details of the elusive whole.' Accordingly, 'the talk of the end of the grand narratives overshoots the mark as soon as it is no longer content to reject their intolera-

---

137 Apel, pp. 410-1.
138 Habermas, Jürgen. 1998. Die postnationale Konstellation. Frankfurt: Suhrkamp, p. 134.
139 In recent times see for example: Habermas, Jürgen. 2011. Zur Verfassung Europas. Berlin: Suhrkamp, pp. 85-7.
140 Beck, Ulrich, Anthony Giddens, and Scott Lash. 1996. Reflexive Modernisierung. Eine Kontroverse. Frankfurt am Main: Suhrkamp, p. 19.

ble simplifications.'[141] 'Not great enough' for us means not self-reflexive enough and not comprehensive enough. This brings to mind the development of
utopian thinking. Reflections on the ideal form of the state and an ideal society constitute a distinct literary genre, beginning with Plato's 'Republic' around
370 BCE. It is named after the novel 'Utopia', written by Thomas More in 1516,
which laid the foundations for utopian thinking in the modern era. If utopian
literature was at first characterised by static, descriptive models of the state such
as More's, it later produced more reflexive stories. In Ursula K. LeGuin's 1974
utopian novel 'The Dispossessed', for example, the conditions for and the problems with the concept itself are debated and critically analysed.

What is needed is not a closed narrative but rather an inclusive, integral
and vibrant approach. The acknowledgement of it's own limitations and a
self-critical stance, with the aim of steady and constant further development,
are important features of a new grand narrative seeking to claim universal
validity. It is clear that it cannot represent any kind of static and final wisdom.
This resonates with the theory of a 'reflexive modernity' which begins to take
itself as object of critical self-reflection.[142] In a now-famous 1958 lecture on liberty, the Russian-British philosopher Isaiah Berlin (1909 to 1997) identified the
problems with closed worldviews. 'One belief, more than any other', Berlin said,
'is responsible for the slaughter of individuals on the altars of the great historical
ideals—justice or progress or the happiness of future generations, or the sacred
mission or emancipation of a nation or race or class, or even liberty itself, which
demands the sacrifice of individuals for the freedom of society. This is the belief
that somewhere, in the past or in the future, in divine revelation or in the mind
of an individual thinker, in the pronouncements of history or science, or in the
simple heart of an uncorrupted good man, there is a final solution.'[143]

The new 'Grand Narrative' is the story of human history itself, global history embedded in the 'Big History', from the formation of the Earth to its end,
when in a billion years the increase in solar radiation will mean the end of life
on our planet. It is a story in which the human species becomes gradually ever
more aware of itself and its actions. It is the story of the development of a
planetary democracy that ensures the wellbeing and peaceful coexistence of all
people in harmony with all other life on Earth. It is a meta-narrative in that it
draws from the failure of previous narratives claiming exclusivity and truth
the conclusion, in the spirit of Isaiah Berlin, that it is not closed but ever

---

141 Sloterdijk, Peter. 2013. In the World Interior of Capital: Towards a Philosophical Theory of Globalization.
     Transl. by Wieland Hoban. 1st ed. John Wiley & Sons, pp. 5, 4.
142 Lash, Scott. 1994. 'Reflexivity and Its Doubles: Structure, Aesthetics, Community.' In: Reflexive Moderni-
     zation, ed. by Ulrich Beck, Anthony Giddens, and Scott Lash, 110–73. Cambridge: Polity Press, p. 112.
143 Berlin, Isaiah. 1969. Four Essays on Liberty. Oxford University Press, p. 167.

changing and developing in the light of self-criticism and self-reflection. 'We need to try to understand our universe even if we can be certain that our attempts can never fully succeed', is how historian David Christian encapsulated the fundamental approach of 'Big History'. He pointed out how people unfailingly search for stories that give them a sense of purpose and direction. We should therefore not be afraid to offer an enlightened, universal picture of the world. 'Only when a modern creation myth has been teased out into a coherent story will it really be possible to take the next step: of criticizing it, deconstructing it, and perhaps improving it. In history as in building, construction must precede deconstruction.'[144]

The new global enlightenment

With regard to social organization, the new 'Grand Narrative' revolves around the development of democracy and emancipation over the course of human socio-political intellectual and spiritual evolution. There will always be differing opinions on politics and on the associated distribution conflicts. Democracy as a means of making decisions must always remain subject to constant improvement. Under planetary modernity, a world parliament is the principal institution for the preservation and improvement of democracy as a form of government. At the same time, it is the focal point of the new global enlightenment which, following a period of uncertainty and disorientation, goes together with the third democratic transformation. The new global enlightenment does not have to be proclaimed. With advancing human cognitive and moral development and with the spread of a planetary consciousness, it is taking place already. A large proportion of the world's population has understood that humanity has to take responsibility for the actions of the human species in order for life on Earth and humanity itself to have any future. As Edward O. Wilson argued, this knowledge is an important component of 'a new Enlightenment'.[145] The crisis of the early phase of planetary modernity is caused by humanity's inability to live up to this responsibility as a collective. The inspiration and motivation behind the new global enlightenment is to change this and to liberate humanity from its disenfranchisement, through the construction of a planetary democracy.

144 Christian, pp. 10-1.
145 Wilson, p. 294.

PART III

Shaping the future: the design and realization of world democracy

The establishment of a democratic world parliament has been regarded since the beginning as a practical political project. It was not philosophers but revolutionaries like Anacharsis Cloots and social reformers like Constantin Pecqueur who were its early proponents at the end of the 18th and the middle of the 19th centuries. It was they who first spelt out the principles of universal equality and the sovereignty of peoples in a rigorous and cosmopolitan approach. They regarded a world parliament as both goal and product of the democratic self-realization of humanity. This perspective is inseparably connected with the idea. The project is about the institution as well as the profound global change it will bring about.

The creation of a new world organization with a democratic world parliament at its center must be accomplished as soon as possible. The transition from intergovernmental international law to a cosmopolitan world law is an urgent necessity. Worldwide cooperation must become a project that goes beyond economic and financial integration and needs to pursue the goal of democratic political unification. Globalization and global governance must be recognised for what they are, namely a part of an incomplete and fragile process of global state formation. Stagnation and disintegration are both drivers and symptoms of an intensifying global polycrisis. But in the background the energies for an evolutionary leap forward are building up at the same time. The polycrisis is pushing the world towards a critical bifurcation point. The likelihood of either collapse or progress becomes more and more probable. It is crucial to prepare for the possibility of an unexpectedly rapid shift in the global political conditions which will open a historic window of opportunity. Simultaneously, the goal of establishing a world parliament and a new world organization should be pursued persistently, following a gradual and evolutionary approach. We follow the reasoning that such a world parliament needs to consist of two chambers: one representing the people and another representing the states. The key to set the process in motion has long been possible, and indeed overdue. This entails creating a global parliamentary assembly within the existing global system which would then evolve into the citizen chamber of a fully-fledged world parliament. Such an assembly holds the potential to address global democratic deficits and enhance the accountability, legitimacy, and efficacy of both the UN and global governance structures. Crucially, however, it will serve as a vehicle and catalyst for a global constitutional process, ultimately leading to the formation of a democratic world federation. In the spirit of the project of a new global enlightenment, it will foster the growth of a global civil society and cultivate a democratic global public sphere. Building on the observations, analyses and developments presented in the previous parts of this book, in the following we draw conclusions and offer suggestions regarding implementation, structure and design, and reflect on socio-political factors and preconditions of this transformation. This includes developing an understanding of the potential institutional evolution of a global parliamentary assembly and addressing pertinent questions such as how to set it up initially? How to select its members? How to deal with the fact that democratic elections for the time being will not be possible in all countries? How should the seats be allocated? What powers and functions should the assembly be vested with? And finally, how can the outlines of a new world organization, a global constitution and a bicameral world parliament look like? The vision we present for the design of a new world organisation is intended as a contribution to the discussion and to illustrate a scenario.

27.

Evolution and elements of a
global parliamentary assembly

Considerations and plans for a process of global political integration and the development of a global parliamentary assembly should be grounded in real-world experience. This includes examining efforts towards regional integration as well as existing international parliamentary institutions (IPIs) for possible patterns and lessons learned. The European Union by far represents the most advanced project of supranational integration in the world and as such is a natural starting point to look at.

The example of European integration

The European integration process was set in motion with the establishment of the European Coal and Steel Community (ECSC) in 1952 following the Second World War. The idea was to place the production of coal and steel, essential resources for armaments, under common control to prevent the possibility of a new military build-up and confrontation in Europe. From the beginning, the ECSC treaty provided not only for a court to settle disputes, the European Court of Justice, but also for a parliamentary body from which the European Parliament would emerge. This so-called Common Assembly was more than just an advisory body. In line with the treaty, it exercised oversight powers over the executive body of the Community, the High Authority. The treaty left it to the individual states to decide whether their deputies in the Common Assembly were to be representatives selected by and from the national parliament or to be directly elected. However, the latter option was not taken up. The Assembly was initially comprised of 78 delegates sent by the national parliaments of the six founding states of the ECSC. The members organised themselves not in national delegations but in transnational political groupings, a key characteristic that remained in place ever since. The Assembly formed committees corresponding to the areas of responsibility of the High Authority. It debated the annual financial report submitted by the latter, and had the power, with a two-thirds majority vote, to call on the Authority to resign.

The Treaty of Rome in 1957 established the objective of achieving an 'ever closer union among the peoples of Europe'. The European Economic Community (EEC) and the European Atomic Energy Community (Euratom) were created alongside the ECSC as independent organizations. A parliamentary assembly was foreseen as a part of all three communities. To avoid a parallel three-part structure, during the negotiations on the Treaties it was agreed that the Common Assembly was to be transformed into a *joint organ* for all three communities. The clause allowing the option of direct election of the deputies was dropped. However, the EEC Treaty included a provision for the Assembly to submit proposals for direct elections following a common procedure in all member states. The Assembly was now made up of 142 deputies and called itself the European Parliament (EP). Its first meeting in this new configuration took place in 1958. The Merger Treaty which came into force in 1967 completed the joining together of all the remaining community organs. From 1975 onwards, two years after the first enlargement that added three member states to the EEC, the parliament acquired the right of co-decision on the community budgets. As the practical powers and legal significance of the European Communities grew, so too did the need for greater democratic legitimacy. In a landmark ruling in 1964, the European Court of Justice established the primacy of European law over national law as a basic principle, thus determining a hierarchical relationship between the two. Agreement on the introduction of direct elections to the EP was finally reached in 1976, albeit without a common procedural basis, and formally ratified by the member states. Since 1979 the members of the European Parliament have been directly elected. Politically strengthened in this way, the EP rejected the Commission's proposed budget for the first time in 1980.

In the early 1980s, the European institutions became bogged down in a complex of problems due to the requirement for unanimity. The fact that each of the growing number of member state governments could block any decision often meant that no decisions were taken at all. In response to this situation, in 1984 the EP under the leadership of Altiero Spinelli drew up a draft constitution for a federal European Union with a genuine legislature based on the principle of majority rule. This initiative helped gain the support of the governments to drive forward institutional reform of the Communities. It is not necessary here to elaborate in detail on the further development of the European Treaties from the Single European Act (1985) via Maastricht (1992), Amsterdam (1997) and Nice (2000) to the establishment of the European Union as an independent legal personality with the Treaty of Lisbon in 2007. In the process, more and more policy areas were subjected to qualified majority

voting. A few notable exceptions left at this time include taxation, social security as well as common foreign, security and defense policy. After a seventh
enlargement in 2013 and the UK's exit in 2020 the number of member states
stands at 27. Twenty of them by now adopted the Euro as their common currency. The decisive point is that the European Parliament evolved from the
Common Assembly of the ECSC, made up of national parliamentarians, to a
directly elected legislative and supervisory organ of the European Union and
that it played a key role in driving the integration process forward at critical
junctures. Together with the Council of Ministers the EP decides on the Union's
budget, and in most areas of policy it legislates on an equal basis with the Council, albeit *as yet* still without a right of initiative. In the course of European integration, the EP has developed into a centre of power which in the European
landscape wields more influence than national parliaments. The EP arguably is
the most important embodiment of European identity and unification as it represents the EU's citizens. In the EU-wide Eurobarometer surveys, the European
Parliament consistently is the European institution that is most trusted by respondents. On top, it is also considerably more trusted than national parliaments or governments. In 2022, for instance, 34 per cent on average said they
tended to trust their national parliament and government, but 52 per cent expressed trust in the European Parliament.[1]

While recognizing that the European experience is a regional example that
developed under specific circumstances, it offers several lessons for a global
parliamentary body regarding its structural framework and potential developmental stages. These lessons particularly pertain to its remit (which intergovernmental organizations and bodies it should be institutionally linked with
and in which policy areas); the powers it should possess; how its members
should be elected (by national parliaments, directly, or by either method); how
seats should be allocated; and how members should organize internally.

An engine for global transformation

A common starting point suggested for the creation of a global parliamentary
assembly is the UN, the world's most important multilateral organization. At
the time when the idea of a UN Parliamentary Assembly (UNPA) was first put
forward in 1949, it was proposed as a consultative body modelled on the example of PACE, the Parliamentary Assembly of the Council of Europe which
was created in the same year.[2] The Council of Europe is an intergovernmental
organization set up by ten founding member states at the time which was not

---

1   European Commission. 2022. 'Standard Eurobarometer 97 Annex.' (europa.eu/eurobarometer/), pp. T34-5, T55.
2   See also pp. 82ff.

related to the EEC or later to the EU. It does not pursue a program of integration but rather is a platform of today 46 member states for the promotion of common goals and principles such as cooperation, democracy and human rights. The UNPA, made up of members from the national parliaments, was conceived as providing input to the committees of the UN General Assembly. Similarly, PACE interacts with the Council of Europe's Committee of Ministers. Then in 1990, the Parliamentary Assembly of the Organization for Security and Co-operation in Europe (OSCE PA) was established and met for its first formal session two years later. This assembly strengthened the case for a UNPA as it has a wider regional scope, by now bringing together 57 participating states, spanning the whole of the northern hemisphere, including four of the five permanent members of the UN Security Council with China being the only exception. The 320 members of the OSCE PA include parliamentary deputies from all the OSCE member states. The task of the Assembly is to contribute to security and the development of democracy in the OSCE region. It passes resolutions, makes recommendations and is known especially for its electoral observation work. What these and other examples of existing IPIs have in common, however, is their static nature and limited powers. The most important insight from the case of the European Parliament is instead to conceive of a UNPA as an *evolving institution* that is part and engine of a wider framework aimed at achieving global political integration and a transformation of the UN. The international Campaign for a UNPA advocated that the assembly's overriding objective should be 'a reform of the present system of international institutions and global governance'.[3] The Campaign's 2007 appeal, signed by parliamentarians from across the world, called for the assembly to become 'a political catalyst for further development of the international system and of international law'. The ECSC Assembly was tasked already in 1952, its founding year, with drafting a treaty for the establishment of a political Union. A UNPA thus should be set up as an engine and inclusive platform for a review of the UN Charter which is a key element of a global constitutional process.

Growing remit and powers

A UNPA could initially be established in a modest way within the parameters of given political realities. It would then undergo gradual development as circumstances allow. At first vested primarily with advisory and oversight powers, it would later become part of a system of binding global decision-making

---

3   Campaign for a UN Parliamentary Assembly, November 2007. 'Conclusions regarding policies of the Campaign for a UN Parliamentary Assembly' (www.unpacampaign.org).

and ultimately a world parliament. In terms of how its members are selected, the UNPA campaign's statement suggested that the assembly 'could initially be composed of national parliamentarians' and 'in a later stage' could be 'directly elected'. With regard to its powers, the document further echoed language adopted by the European Parliament two years earlier, emphasizing that a UNPA 'should be vested with genuine rights of information, participation and control'.[4] The appeal suggested that these rights could 'step by step' extend to encompass 'the UN and the organizations of the UN system'. There is now broad agreement that confining the assembly to a purely advisory role, even in its initial phase, is inadequate. The example of the Common Assembly of the ECSC, which possessed supervisory powers from its inception and could dismiss the executive, illustrates the importance of granting meaningful authority to a UNPA from the outset. A UNPA should not be allowed to be set up by governments merely as a façade of democratic legitimation. The IPU's lack of influence on the UN and an analysis of other IPIs serve as a warning against accepting token gestures.[5]

Based on the model of the ECSC Assembly the point was made that the first step could consist in the establishment of a parliamentary assembly within an organization with a narrower specialised remit, for example the WTO or the UN Framework Convention on Climate Change. However, instead of creating a specialized parliamentary body of this kind—which bears the risk of stalling further evolution—a UNPA could be set up that is tasked to focus on a particular field *first* but has the discretion to widen its scope *later*, ideally on its own initiative. The next steps in either case would need to involve broadening the assembly's remit and powers. It is impossible on practical grounds alone to equip each of the dozens of different intergovernmental organizations and UN entities with its own parliamentary body. Instead, mirroring the structure of the UN system, the work of the UNPA should be thematically focused through relevant portfolio committees. The UNPA would thus develop gradually and in a natural way into a 'common assembly' for the organizations and programmes of the UN system and beyond, helping counteract the prevalent fragmentation of the global system.

A UNPA is intended to complement, not replace, existing intergovernmental bodies like the UN General Assembly. The underlying idea is to create a *Second Chamber*, with the UN General Assembly, or a successor body, ultimately serving as the other in a bicameral world parliament. A UNPA initially

<hr>

4   European Parliament. 6 June 2005. 'European Parliament Resolution on the Reform of the United Nations.' P6_TA(2005)0237. (europarl.europa.eu), para. 39.
5   See also pp. 427ff.427

could be established by a vote of the UN General Assembly as a subsidiary organ under Article 22 of the UN Charter. Another possibility under discussion is to have it set up through an intergovernmental treaty. But in a second step this latter option would also require a General Assembly vote to affiliate the treaty-based assembly with the UN organization. In either case, however, no amendment of the UN Charter would be needed. This requires the approval and ratification of two-thirds of all UN member states and all five of the veto powers in the Security Council—a difficult hurdle to take. In the treaty approach, ratifications of individual countries would be needed for them to join. A review of the UNPA proposal undertaken by Maja Brauer and Andreas Bummel concluded that making the additional effort required by the treaty approach only makes sense 'if there is widespread support for a global parliamentary assembly endowed with substantial rights and competences among UN members, but not enough to exceed the threshold for a charter amendment'.[6] In this scenario, significant powers and duties of the assembly could be included in a treaty, obligating only the participating state parties—a majority of UN member states but less than two thirds—while other functions related to the UN for the time being would be determined by an affiliation agreement with the UN adopted by a majority vote of General Assembly. The treaty approach in this scenario could establish legislative powers albeit not of a universal nature, only such binding the treaty parties. In terms of functions based on Article 22 or a collaboration agreement, as a matter of principle, the UN General Assembly cannot confer more powers on a UNPA than it has itself. This sets limits on supervisory and co-decision-making powers. But the powers of the General Assembly should not be underestimated. It can exert influence on the programmes and funds it has set up, such as the children's fund UNICEF, the development programme UNDP, the refugees' commission UNHCR or the environment programme UNEP, including their governing regulations. It is feasible for the UN General Assembly to confer on a UNPA questioning, citation and interpellation rights, as well as the right to involvement in the approval of the UN budget or the election of top positions throughout the system, including the election of the UN Secretary-General. In principle a UNPA could be given the same prerogatives by the General Assembly as are enjoyed by the General Assembly itself. This also includes drawing the attention of the Security Council to critical situations or submitting legal questions to the International Court of Justice. The assembly, making use of specialized portfolio committees, could in principle involve itself in all areas

---

6   Brauer, Maja, and Andreas Bummel. 2020. A United Nations Parliamentary Assembly: A Policy Review of Democracy Without Borders. Berlin: Democracy Without Borders, p. 48.

relevant to the UN, from providing advice on moving to a sustainable global economy, investigating the implementation of the Agenda 2030 and a future successor program, to exercising oversight over peacekeeping operations. The assembly should be able to participate in intergovernmental negotiations such as those under the UN Framework Convention on Climate Change (UN-FCCC) or at the UN's Conference on Disarmament.

A Common Assembly for global governance

Former UN Secretary-General Boutros Boutros-Ghali noted in 2007 that the assembly 'should become a force to provide democratic oversight over the World Bank, the IMF and the WTO.'[7] He added later that on 'the economic front, a Parliamentary Assembly at the UN could facilitate the alignment of the Washington-based Bretton Woods Institutions and the World Trade Organization with the policies of the UN'. In particular, it 'could monitor the impact of the policies of the international financial and economic institutions in fields such as sustainable development, food security, education, public health, human rights and the eradication of extreme poverty.'[8] The International Monetary Fund, the World Bank Group and the World Trade Organization are not formally part of the UN System. An affiliation of the assembly with them under international law at first perhaps could be achieved without the necessity for amending each of their treaties by means of cooperation agreements. Later, following the model of the Rome Convention on certain institutions common to the European Communities, we can picture an intergovernmental treaty which amends relevant existing treaties and transforms a UNPA into a common body with extensive rights related to *all relevant institutions* of global governance. This would be a way, for instance, of *legally* establishing the right to be involved in the selection of the Directors of the IMF, the World Bank Group and the WTO and in setting the policies of these organizations. The assembly should also be able to take part in the global setting of norms and standards and to exercise democratic oversight over these procedures. The Climate Governance Commission suggested that a UNPA could provide 'the deliberative and legislative functions of the Global Environmental Agency' they proposed.[9] If it were politically feasible, one could imagine leap-frogging the Article 22 process and establishing the assembly by means of an intergovernmental treaty of this kind. But the thresholds are high and more

---

7   Boutros-Ghali, Boutros. 16 May 2007. 'Message to the Campaign for the Establishment of a UN Parliamentary Assembly.' (www.unpacampaign.org). See also pp. 145, 148.

8   Id. 9 June 2009. 'The Missing Link of Democratization.' OpenDemocracy. (opendemocracy.net).

9   Climate Governance Commission. 2023. 'Governing Our Planetary Emergency.' (stimson.org), p. 77.

creative thinking may be needed. According to the Marrakesh Agreement establishing the WTO, for example, changing the organization's decision-making procedure requires an approval of all members. Amending the procedure for the appointment of the Director-General is possible with a two thirds majority. Amending the IMF treaty requires the approval of three-fifths of the members, having 85 per cent of the total voting power. Giving a parliamentary assembly a formal role in the UNFCCC procedures would require an approval by consensus since states thus far failed to determine general rules of decision-making under the climate framework. In the meantime, even in the absence of such formal affiliations and powers, a UNPA can harness political leverage to influence global policies and decision-making.

Binding decision-making

In line with its conception as a *joint assembly*, a UNPA can be integrated into the decision-making processes of various existing or new intergovernmental treaties and organizations. The most important scenario arises when binding majority decision-making authority is to be established which is fundamental for a development towards a system of world law. Traditional intergovernmental mechanisms and bodies usually lack the necessary level of legitimacy for this and involving the UNPA can address this deficiency. As observed before, it may often be easier to incorporate the UNPA into new treaties rather than amend existing ones and decisions will then only bind the relevant state parties. In this case, the assembly may have to deliberate and make decisions in different configurations. The discussion about a separate parliament for the Eurozone, which does not include all EU countries, is instructive and shows numerous pitfalls in the possible construction of 'differentiated representation'. One conclusion may be generalized and is important for our purposes: the political scientist Ian Cooper suggested there is an 'inverse relation between the magnitude of the powers' a chamber is vested with and 'the number of states who should be represented there'. If the powers are largely advisory and supervisory, an inclusive approach is warranted. If 'by contrast the chamber has substantial power as a regulatory legislator', 'then it may be reasonable to limit the membership to representatives from those states directly subject to—and not just incidentally affected by—the rules that it makes.'[10] In order to cover such cases, the global parliamentary assembly should be enabled to establish committees dedicated to decision-making under given treaties and only members originating from treaty parties would be admitted.

10　Cooper, Ian. 2017. "A Separate Parliament for the Eurozone? Differentiated Representation, Brexit, and the Quandary of Exclusion." Parliamentary Affairs 70 (4): 655–72, pp. 5-7.

Ultimately, however, the objective is a different one: the parliamentary assembly is to become part of a *global legislative system* of a *universal nature* that includes and binds *all states* under certain conditions and within parameters to be discussed later. The obvious starting point for creating such authority is a revision of the UN Charter, as the UN is the world's most universal intergovernmental organization in terms of both its scope and state membership. While the political hurdles are high, amending the UN Charter has the advantage that once the required threshold is reached—ratification by two-thirds of UN member states, including the five permanent members of the Security Council—the new Charter would automatically enter into force for *all* UN members. This would ensure that the new UN has a universal character from the outset, just like the old one. Whether a revision of the UN Charter results from a Charter review conference foreseen in the Charter's Article 109 or a different process is a secondary formality.[11] Given the countless treaty regimes and bodies established over time that have a legal status independent from the UN, the challenge is to build an overarching and coherent world constitutional order. This can happen in successive steps, which suggests the possibility of various revisions of the UN Charter which eventually culminate in its transformation into an actual world constitution with a world parliament at its center. Again, if it were politically feasible and if important preconditions were in place, it is possible to imagine skipping intermediate stages and go for a revision of the UN Charter right away that would incorporate a parliamentary assembly as part of a bicameral decision-making body.

Growing democratic legitimacy

Growing remit and powers need to go along with enhancing the assembly's democratic character and legitimacy. The most important element is putting in place and guaranteeing a democratic process for the selection of its members. As suggested before, there are two primary options for this. Representatives could be either elected from within a national parliament or by popular vote. To be democratically sound, in both cases the underlying elections would have to be direct, competitive, free and fair. From the start, participating states should be able to choose between both options. Progressive countries could opt for direct elections of representatives and others would follow later. Still others will prefer to maintain indirect selection through the national parliament for the longer term. An evolving hybrid membership that includes directly and indirectly elected representatives will likely help create momen-

---

11   On Article 109, see also pp. 80, 97.

tum towards the introduction of popular elections in more and more democratic countries. Directly elected members could form a non-partisan caucus to facilitate this process, among other things. The review undertaken by Brauer and Bummel recommended that 'the objective of general direct elections in all states should be enshrined in the statutes from the outset.' After a designated transitional period, direct elections should become mandatory for all.[12]

Important preconditions for the step to a world parliament are not yet in place and will need to develop over time. In terms of its democratic character and legitimacy, this relates to the level of democratization across the world's states. An important difference from the European example is that not all countries globally are governed democratically. A significant number of them, in particular the nuclear powers Russia and China, are not free and their governments suppress democratic rights. Democratic representation and participation of their citizens in a world parliament is not possible unless national democratization takes place. The European integration process only involved democracies bound together by their support of common basic values. Democratic backsliding in the EU's member states Poland and Hungary in recent times gave rise to serious political, legal and institutional issues in the EU. However, as a matter of fact, global integration without regard to the form of government of the participating countries is quite far advanced already and in consequence there is a global democratic deficit that contributes to an erosion of democracy at the national level too. Whether this is right or wrong, the UN at this time does not make a distinction in terms of how its member states are governed. After all, one of the UN's most important founding members, the Soviet Union, was a totalitarian state. In addition, managing planetary commons and providing global public goods will require universal state participation to avoid weakest link and free rider issues, among other things. In this situation, trade-offs need to be made between the principles of democracy and universality as the assembly evolves. The Campaign for a UNPA advocated that it should be open to delegates from all the UN's member states irrespective of their government type, the same way as it is handled at the UN overall. Only then it will be possible for a UNPA to claim validity as a universal platform for world domestic policy, and for it be integrated into the existing system of global governance. The alternative would be to make participation in a UNPA and its later manifestations dependent on a country's level of democracy. Arguably, at least in theory, a precedent exists. When the UN General Assembly created the Human Rights Council, it decided that in the election of its members, 'the contribution of candidates to the promotion and protection

12 Brauer and Bummel, pp. 5, 74.

of human rights' shall be taken into consideration and that members 'shall uphold the highest standards' in this regard. Unfortunately, these have remained empty words which are not implemented. The Council's membership regularly includes the world's worst human rights violators. While there are solid global assessments of the level of democratic rights accessible and guaranteed in the world's countries, it is hard to imagine how these could be operationalized in a UN setting. In such a scenario, where exactly to draw the line whether a country is sufficiently democratic, or in other words, in or out? Who makes the assessment on what grounds? Ultimately, it would be the UN's member states who decide based on political considerations which are prone to misuse. Furthermore, even if a country's *government* is authoritarian, this does not necessarily exclude the possibility that a democratic opposition exists even in the parliament. Providing the latter with representation in a global assembly arguably would support democracy. All in all, we believe that these issues cannot be solved in a satisfactory manner and going for a universal approach is best. An exclusive assembly of initially twenty or thirty self-selected countries, which is one of the alternative proposals put forward, will likely not be able to achieve recognition from the UN General Assembly that grants it any significant status. With little, if any, direct points of contact with the decision-making centres at the UN and in global governance, it would not be able to take on the roles we envision even for a UNPA and it would not be in a moral position to speak on behalf of humanity either. While a UNPA in conclusion should be open to participation of all states, some qualifications can still be made. As Brauer and Bummel suggested, in the case of serious human rights violations in a given country, the assembly should be able to suspend the voting rights of individual members 'who represent those decision-makers to whom a shared responsibility can be attributed'.[13] Further, members would at least have to be formally elected from the midst of national parliaments, anyone holding a government office at the same time should be barred from membership and governments should not be allowed to give instructions to representatives.

The establishment of a UNPA is also a measure for the promotion of democracy at the national level. It can be expected that many countries in transition to democracy or in a fragile state will benefit in terms of having parliamentarians represented in a UN body. Lessons can be learned in this regard from existing IPIs. As international networks of elected representatives, they are regarded as 'schools for democracy' where learning and persuasion take place.

13 Ibid., p. 59.

The political scientist Beat Habegger spoke of a socialization function.[14] The world's first multinational parliament, the Imperial Council of the Austro-Hungarian Empire, which lasted until 1918 and which comprised deputies from eight nationalities, was seen as a 'recruiting school for the Central and Southeast European democracies' by Karl Renner, one of the founders of the first Austrian republic.[15] Renner, incidentally, advocated a world state composed of autonomous national components following the example of Switzerland and Austria-Hungary.[16] In any event, the socialization effect is another argument for making a UNPA open to all UN member states. Possible 'pseudo-parliamentarians' could come under the positive influence of the democratic representatives and the parliamentary culture of interaction and debate. Actually, this is one of the reasons why it is questionable whether some autocratic governments would even want their country to take part in a UNPA at all and they may opt not to do so. This might be a move to keep the parliamentary opposition away from the assembly but also their own delegates. It is worth consideration if and how members from relevant parliamentary groups could still be represented under such circumstances.

Step by step, the requirements for compliance with democratic norms and procedures will grow. At a meeting of the international Campaign for a UNPA it was clearly stated, with an eye on the future development of the assembly, that 'direct elections of the UNPA's delegates are regarded as a precondition for vesting the body with legislative rights.'[17] The power to adopt binding regulation must go along with strong democratic legitimacy which ultimately derives from popular elections. Still, the threshold perhaps could be set lower at half of its members being directly elected. In any event, such elections must be competitive, free, fair, equal, universal and secret. The linkage between the second and third democratic transformations is apparent. Only if democracy succeeds at the national level, a country will be able to have free elections for a global assembly. Unfortunately, with regard to many states it remains to be seen if and when they will transition towards democracy. But to wait until the community of states has been fully and successfully democratised before even the *first step* is taken is not a viable alternative and not necessary either. This is all the more the

14 Habegger, Beat. 2005. Parlamentarismus in der internationalen Politik: Europarat, OSZE and Interparlamentarische Union. 1st ed. Baden-Baden: Nomos, pp. 34, 228.
15 Cit. from Österreichisches Parlament, Parlamentskorrespondenz Nr. 98, 18 Feb. 2002 (parlament.gv.at).
16 Renner, Karl. 1915. 'Der Krieg und die Wandlungen des nationalen Gedankens'. Der Kampf 8:8–23. See also Riehle, Bert. 2009. Eine neue Ordnung der Welt: föderative Friedenstheorien im deutschsprachigen Raum zwischen 1892 und 1932. V&R unipress, pp. 89-92.
17 Campaign for a UN Parliamentary Assembly, ibid.

case because a UNPA even in its most modest form may help support national democratization.

Transnational groups and global political parties

For a considerable initial period, the members of a UNPA—and a world parliament—will most likely need to be elected within a national framework, either directly or indirectly. This is because nation-states are the most important administrative, political, and identity units in the global order. Using them as the starting point for the allocation of seats and the election of members is a pragmatic approach in line with this reality. This is also how it is still done in the case of the EP. Nonetheless, even if these procedures are located in the world's individual states, the members of a UNPA and the assembly's later manifestations are to represent the world's citizens and not the countries they originate from. If parliamentarians simply repeat government positions and pursue perceived national interests, there is not much added value. In the EP there is a tested method to avoid this and to facilitate a European perspective: members are organized in transnational political groups instead of national delegations and regional geopolitical formations as they are usually found in intergovernmental bodies and many IPIs. One of the latter is the Pan-African Parliament, the only place where opposition parties are supposed to have a say at the level of the African Union. In this case, rivalries between regional blocs within the PAP led to a leadership crisis for years and raised doubts about the utility of the entire institution.[18] Members of the UNPA instead should also be organised in *transnational groups* based on common views in order to support global perspectives and collaboration. This is a crucial way to strengthen the assembly's potential socialization function as members will be required to work very closely with others from across the world. The review undertaken by Brauer and Bummel insisted that such groups are necessary to guarantee a democratic and cosmopolitan character of the assembly. For this reason, the assessment pointed out, the 'UNPA statutes should give transnational groups a central position', adding that they should hold 'key procedural rights' such as 'representation in committees or the ability to table draft resolutions.' Each member would only be able to join one such group. For a group to be accredited, it would need to include a specified minimum number of members from a minimum number of states and world regions and require a 'common ideological orientation'.[19] Such an orientation would need to encompass a set of

---

18   Louw-Vaudran, Liesl. 10 June 2021. 'Pan-African Parliament's Woes Reflect a Crisis in Leadership.' ISS Africa, (issafrica.org).
19   Brauer and Bummel, pp. 3, 64-67.

shared beliefs, values and interests. In the EP, the groups are based on common views related to particular political party ideologies. In all probability, similar political groups across the political spectrum would emerge in a UNPA as well, like conservative, liberal, green, socialist or left groups. As long as the membership criteria can be met that ensure a global character, other groups with shared views and interests could emerge just as well. They do not necessarily need to be connected to existing party lines. Elections will take place regularly in different countries so the composition of the parliamentary assembly will change constantly as long as those elections are not synchronous. This makes transnational groups ever more important as they provide for institutional memory and a continuous framework as the assembly's membership changes.

To date, the political influence of international party associations—such as the conservative Centrist Democrat International, the Socialist International, the Progressive Alliance, the Liberal International or the Global Greens—has been minimal, in particular due to the lack of a global political sphere in which they can engage. As Heikki Patomäki pointed out in a book examining the emergence of 'world statehood', the 'fact that there are no global elections or parliaments means that building party-like transnational organs tends to remain a relatively unattractive idea. If there are no offices to capture, why bother?'[20] This will indeed change with the creation of a global parliamentary body. Party associations will likely affiliate and collaborate with political groups in a UNPA and become increasingly relevant over time. This has a particular value for smaller national parties that may not have a seat in the assembly themselves. Via their international party network and its affiliated transnational group in the assembly they can achieve indirect representation of their interests. It is possible to envision a mutually reinforcing process in which the successive development of a world parliament facilitates the formation of global political parties and vice versa. As sociologist Max Weber noted in a 1918 lecture, modern political parties are 'the children of democracy' and particularly of the mass franchise. The selection of parliamentary candidates was no longer decided by 'local notables' but by 'assemblies of the organized party members,' which Weber considered as a 'fargoing democratization'.[21] While their roles and performance vary across countries and issues such as polarization, party financing and internal democracy need to be addressed, there is no doubt that political parties are a cornerstone of democratic

20 Patomäki, Heikki. 2023. World Statehood: The Future of World Politics. Springer, pp. 213-5.
21 Weber, Max. 1958. From Max Weber: Essays in Sociology. Ed. by H.H. Gerth and C. Wright Mills. Oxford University Press, p. 102.

systems and will likely play a crucial role in global democracy as well. They serve as vital links between citizens, civil society and the state, provide platforms for political participation, accountability, and opposition, and contribute to the formation of public opinion and a public political sphere.

The apportionment of seats

Determining the apportionment of seats is one of the most important elements in designing a UNPA and ultimately the parliamentary chamber of a bicameral world parliament. Over time, various principles and models have been proposed, many of which were mentioned earlier in this book. Although this may change in the long run, using existing states as a framework for seat allocation at this point seems to be the only feasible and politically viable method. While we do not recommend any particular model, we believe that three key principles should be observed.

First, the size of the assembly must be manageable. This suggests that a limit on the total number of seats is determined. A maximum of around 800 seats seems reasonable and a lower figure could be chosen at first.

Secondly, the assembly needs to include members from all countries in order to be representative and universal in this respect. For a plurality of views to be represented, each country in principle should be allocated at least two seats. However, considering their population size, the world's smallest countries with less than one million inhabitants each—37 states with a combined population of around 12 million or 0.15 per cent of the world population—may be allocated only one seat each. In the case of indirect elections, the first seat allocated should be filled by the governing majority in parliament and the second by the largest opposition group.[22] If there is no opposition in parliament, the second seat should remain vacant. In the case of popular elections, the first seat should be allocated to the list or candidate with the most votes and the second to the list or candidate with the second-most votes.

Thirdly, following the idea of democratic representation of the world's citizens, population size needs to be factored in by allocating additional seats beyond the minimum of one or two. Populous countries should be allocated relatively more seats than less populous ones, while smaller countries receive more seats per capita. In other words, the larger the population of a country, the more people each of its assembly members theoretically represent. Given the significant variations in population size among the world's countries, it may be prudent to establish an upper limit on the number of seats allocated

---

22 Also recommended by Sohn, Louis B., ed. 1970. The United Nations: The Next Twenty-Five Years. Twentieth Report of the Commission to Study the Organization of Peace. Dobbs Ferry, NY: Oceana Publications, p. 59.

per country, such as five per cent of the total size. Seat allocations following the approach of degressive proportionality are already implemented most prominently in the European Parliament but also in other IPIs such as the OSCE PA or the Parliament of the Economic Community of West African States. Ultimately, any system designed to balance representation must be *politically* acceptable to both large and small countries. If a country is allocated more than two seats, the additional seats should be filled in a way that reflects either the strength of political groups in the national parliament or the proportion of votes received by lists and candidates as best as possible, depending on whether there are indirect or direct elections.

An apportionment of seats based on these principles can be achieved in many ways and will be the outcome of political deliberations and negotiations. In an example provided by Brauer and Bummel, called model (A), a minimum number of two seats per country is allocated first. Assuming all current 193 UN member states are included, this results in an allocation of 386 seats. Aiming at a total of around 800 seats, 414 additional seats are then allocated among all countries in direct proportion to their share of the world population. The results are rounded to the nearest whole number, leading to a total of 795 seats which are distributed in 16 increments. The minimum allocation of two automatically brings about a system of degressive proportionality. In another model, called (B), the number of seats allocated is initially determined by taking the square root of a country's population in millions and the result is rounded to the nearest whole number. In a second step, 52 countries that do not receive the minimum number of two seats under this formula are each allocated one or two additional seats, 72 in total. This model results in an assembly with a total of 853 seats distributed in 17 increments. Using the square root of the population size in million was originally proposed by Lionel Penrose in 1946 for calculating the voting strengths of countries in a world assembly. Comparing models (A) and (B), the latter results in a more even distribution across countries and therefore seems to be 'more adequate for the goal of balancing'.[23] As Joseph Schwartzberg rightly noted, any root other than the square root can achieve the same purpose.[24] A variation of model (B) based on the 2.2nd root, for instance, yields a total number of 759 seats in 14 increments. Since this remains below the defined maximum of 800 seats, it may actually be a preferred method. In model (A), China and India, the world's most populous countries, would each be allocated 9.6 per cent of the seats, or 76 each,

---

23 See Brauer and Bummel, pp. 80-92.

24 Schwartzberg, Joseph. 2013. Transforming the United Nations System. Designs for a Workable World. Tokyo, New York, Paris: United Nations University Press, p. 50.

together accounting for almost one-fifth of the total seats. This could be reduced to a maximum share of 5 per cent or 38 seats each. The United States, being in the third position, would receive 2.6 per cent or 19 seats. In the original version of model (B), China and India would receive 4.7 per cent or 38 seats each and in the variation 3.6 per cent or 27 seats each whereas the United States would be allocated 2.1 or 1.8 per cent (18 or 14 seats). At the first stage of setting up a UN-PA, models may be considered that aim at a lower total size, for instance at 400 or 500 seats, and the size of the assembly could then be increased over time. According to our calculations, around 70 per cent of the assembly members in the models discussed before would originate from countries rated as free or partly free by Freedom House and around 40 per cent from countries classified as liberal or electoral democracy by V-Dem.[25]

In terms of the apportionment of seats in the European Parliament, the EU Treaty provides that 'representation of citizens shall be degressively proportional', with a minimum of six members and a maximum of 96 per member state.[26] Based on these principles, the precise number of seats per country is determined in negotiations. In the tenth EP elected in 2024, there were 720 seats in total. Malta, the smallest EU member state, was allocated six seats, meaning one member for each 90,000 inhabitants, while Germany, the most populous state, was allocated the possible maximum of 96, equivalent to one member for each 878,000 inhabitants. This type of unequal representation in the EP previously was the subject of constitutional complaints in Germany. Two judgements were made by the Federal Constitutional Court which contain interesting observations. In the first, pertaining to the Maastricht Treaty of 1993, the court noted that in a community of states 'democratic legitimation cannot be established in the same form as it can within a state system uniformly and conclusively regulated by a single state constitution'.[27] In the other judgement pertaining to the Lisbon treaty of 2009, the court again considered the question of the democratic legitimacy of the EU and stated that as 'a representative body of the peoples in a supranational community, characterised as such by a limited willingness to unite, it cannot, and need not, as regards its composition, comply with the requirements that arise at state level from the equal political right to vote of all citizens'[28]; and further, that the 'democratic basic rule of equal opportunities of success ("one person, one vote") only applies within a people, not within a supranational representative body, which re-

---

25 Based on 2024 figures and ratings, see also p. 401.
26 Article 14 para. 2.
27 BVerfG, 2 BvR 2134, 2159/92, 12 October 1993 - Maastricht, para. 93.
28 BVerfG, 2 BvE 2/08, 30 June 2009 - Lisbon, para. 271.

mains a representation of the peoples linked to each other by the treaties albeit now with special emphasis on citizenship of the Union'.[29]

A graduated apportionment of seats is politically imperative and justified for the time being. As the models cited above demonstrate, it is also feasible, even though a careful balance has to be struck between a plethora of mini-states on the one hand—half the world's countries collectively account for only 3.4 per cent of the population—and the population giants China and India on the other, accounting together for over 35 per cent. As Germany's Federal Constitutional Court pointed out, the inequality of democratic representation within the EP is only acceptable if the German Bundestag, the national parliament, 'retains own responsibilities and competences of substantial political importance'.[30] The degree of democratic representativeness and legitimacy required thus corresponds to the depth of supranational integration. Seen from this perspective, a graduated apportionment of seats in a UNPA does not pose a problem, since the legal competences would initially be limited and significantly less developed than those currently held by the EP. Even at the stage of a legislative world parliament, the issue of proportional representation of citizens will only gradually become more prominent with regard to the parliamentary chamber.

In the long term, the apportionment of seats, subject to regular review and revision, will likely tend to increasingly align with the democratic principle of 'one person, one vote'. This evolution can be expected to occur alongside an equalization of economic conditions, increasing democratization, and a growth of political trust and transnational identities worldwide. Eventually, creating constituencies of roughly equal size worldwide for the direct election of global deputies may be considered, resulting in shared parliamentary seats for many smaller countries. Schwartzberg explored this scenario in the third and final stage of a potential evolution of representation in a World Parliamentary Assembly.[31] Looking further into the future, elections could become partially or entirely decoupled from national frameworks. One possibility is electing assembly members through global lists. Another is organizing elections through self-constituted virtual constituencies.[32] After all, the principal purpose of the parliamentary assembly is a democratic representation of the world's *people*. All *states* will continue to have representation in the General

---

29 Ibid., para. 279.

30 Ibid., para. 246. see also para. 263.

31 Schwartzberg, ch. 3, and id., 2012. Creating a World Parliamentary Assembly. An Evolutionary Journey. Berlin: Committee for a Democratic UN.

32 See Pogge, Thomas W. 2002. 'Self-Constituting Constituencies to Enhance Freedom, Equality, and Participation in Democratic Procedures.' Theoria: A Journal of Social and Political Theory, no. 99, 26–54.

Assembly or in the relevant body that will replace it in a bicameral design of a world parliament.

From the outset consideration needs to be given as to how representation of large stateless and dispersed ethnic minorities such as the Kurds, Rohingya or Hmong can be guaranteed in the parliamentary assembly.[33] Initially, a number of additional seats can be allocated for this purpose and candidates representing these groups could be elected by the assembly's plenary upon recommendation of a relevant committee. Furthermore, in order to strengthen the assembly's inclusive and representative character, committees can be enabled to co-opt a number of additional non-voting and advisory members for a limited period of time, enabling them to participate in their work. These members could represent the UN's so-called major groups of stakeholders which include indigenous peoples, women, children and youth, workers and trade unions, farmers, local authorities, the scientific community, business and industry, and NGOs.

---

33 On minority representation, see also p. 423.

28.

Outlines of a new world organization

Reflections on a world constitution

Following the League of Nations and the United Nations, a world parliament would be founded as a main organ of a world organization of the third generation which is based on a universal global constitution. The empirical existence and normative requirements of a global constitutional process constitute a significant area of research to draw upon. As the concept of constitutionalism in the global context 'moves on towards a new historical period', according to the international relations experts Anthony F. Lang and Antje Wiener, it is possible to build on centuries of theory and practice that established four core principles of this 'underlying philosophical ideal of a political order': the rule of law, separation of powers, the people as the constituent power and human rights.[1] A written global constitution first of all must not fall short of the achievements, codifications, and practices already established in international law in this regard while at the same time taking into account the deficits and failures of the Westphalian international system. As argued throughout this book, one of the biggest fallacies in our view is the assumption that human society must be organised fundamentally differently at the global level than it is at the lower levels. The development of a global constitution should be informed by a comparative assessment of principles and designs implemented at national and regional levels, necessitating, in particular, a thorough examination and evaluation of national constitutions and political practices in democratic countries worldwide, with particular attention to federal systems that include subnational component parts. We advise against the idea of using the creation of a global constitution—and a new world organization—as an opportunity for experimenting with untested institutional and political concepts. While incorporating a degree of innovation is important, it should be done bottom-up, in careful doses, and adjusted over time based on accumulated experience. Established methodologies for measuring national democracy provide valuable insights into essential elements and questions that need to be considered. The 'Global State of Democracy' framework of

---

1   Lang, Jr., Anthony F., and Antje Wiener. 2023. 'Introduction to the Handbook on Global Constitutionalism: Protecting Rights and Democracy While Binding Power.' In: Handbook on Global Constitutionalism, ed. by id., 2nd ed., 1–21. Edward Elgar Publishing, pp. 6, 11-3.

International IDEA, for instance, is based on four main attributes of democracy each of which covers three to six subattributes which are operationalized using dozens of indicators. The main attributes, which also reflect the principles of constitutionalism, are representation (free and equal access to power); rights (individual liberties and resources); rule of law (predictable and equal enforcement of the law, and limitation of government power); and participatory engagement (instruments of and for the realization of political involvement). Of course, in line with such attributes, democracy can be realized in many different ways 'with various electoral systems (majoritarian, proportional or mixed), different forms of government (presidentialism, parliamentarian, or mixed), different legal systems (common law, civil law and so on), different types of political parties and party systems and unitary or federal states'.[2] The core of a global constitutional process consists in reaching agreement on the precise global arrangements. With regard to the last point, only a federal system comes into question, composed primarily of states but also of regional blocs and possibly other entities as component parts. How exactly they are constitutionally organized can be left to their own devices, provided it is within democratic attributes. Pockets of authoritarianism or worse cannot be tolerated at this advanced stage of integration. As the 'new Ventotene manifesto' adopted by European federalists in 2022 pointed out, on 'the path towards global political integration, it should be clear that the democratic nature of the resulting global federation as well as its constituent parts is the only option. Federalism and autocracy cannot be reconciled.'[3] The global constitution would sit at the top of a universal global norm hierarchy, followed—in the order of precedence—by global, regional (if applicable) and national law. The creation of international law through intergovernmental treaties would become obsolete, except perhaps for matters that do not fall within global or regional jurisdiction.

International law and world law compared

Following this conceptualization, the global constitution represents primary world law and global legislation secondary world law. In an important study the law expert Angelika Emmerich-Fritsche set out, over 1200 pages, the elements and development of world law. As she explained, the purpose of world law 'is not that of reconciling the diverging interests of states, which is what interna-

---

2   Skaaning, Svend-Erik, and Alexander Hudson. 2023. The Global State of Democracy Indices Methodology. Conceptualization and Measurement Framework, Version 7. International IDEA. (idea.int), pp. 19, 10.

3   'Proposal for a Manifesto for a Federal Europe: Sovereign, Social and Ecological.' 2022. Brussels. (thespinelligroup.eu).

tional law exists to do, but rather that of meeting the elemental needs and interests of the whole of humanity'. The nature and character of a system of world law to be considered in global constitutionalization can be best seen by examining the most significant respects in which it differs from international law:[4]

— In international law, the *state* is the primary unit, while in world law it is the individual as *a citizen of the world*. World law is based on world citizenship. Individuals are innately and directly endowed with rights and duties. They are the constituent subject.

— The central paradigms of international law are *national independence* and the *sovereign equality of states*, whereas the corresponding principles in world law are *global interdependence* and *the equality of all people*.

— The dominant perspective in the intergovernmental system is that of the *national interest*, or Raison d' État, while in world law it is that of the *planetary interest*, or Raison d'Humanité, a term coined by Yehezkel Dror.[5]

— International law is based on the principle of *non-interference* whereas under world law universal standards may imply a *responsibility to interfere*. Political and legal boundaries are *permeable*.

— International law is based primarily on intergovernmental treaties, which states can *voluntarily* choose to ratify or not (ius dispositivum), whereas world law is *universally binding* (ius cogens).[6]

— Whereas international law as a rule applies only *to states* and must be implemented via national law, world law can apply directly *to everyone*, everywhere, not only states but also individuals, companies and other actors.

— The creation of new rules in international law by means of intergovernmental treaties is based on the *consensus principle*, whereas world law is based on democratic *majority decision-making*.[7]

— In intergovernmental negotiations and bodies, representation is generally done through officials *appointed by the executive branch of national governments*, while representatives in the decision-making bodies of world law are *democratically elected by the world's people*.

— As a rule, the guiding principle for representation and decision-making in international law is '*one state, one vote*', whereas in world law it is '*one person, one vote*'.[8]

---

4   Emmerich-Fritsche, Angelika. 2007. Vom Völkerrecht zum Weltrecht. Berlin: Duncker & Humblot, p. 340, see also pp. 1049-50.

5   Dror, Yehezkel. 1995. Ist die Erde noch regierbar? Ein Bericht an den Club of Rome. Transl. by Hans-Jürgen Baron von Koskull. 1st ed. C. Bertelsmann, pp. 116-8.

6   On voluntarism, see pp. 186ff.

7   On majority decison-making, see pp. 193ff.

8   On representation, see pp. 421ff.

- Once negotiated, intergovernmental treaties need to be *signed, ratified and adhered* to by individual states whereas global legislation, in principle, can take *immediate effect.*
- In international law, rules, treaties, regimes and institutions are *disconnected and fragmented* whereas world law is based on the principle of the *unity of the legal and institutional order* and on norm hierarchies.[9]
- By contrast to international law, where the question of precedence is *at the discretion of the states*, world law *always takes precedence* over national law.
- Under international law principles, a state is able to decide whether or not, and under what conditions, to accept external jurisdiction, on a *voluntary* basis. Under world law, submission to external jurisdiction is *obligatory.*
- Enforcement in international law is directed *collectively at states* and *implemented by states* at their discretion, whereas under world law, it targets *individuals* and is carried out by dedicated *global public law institutions.*[10]

World law is concerned not only with the welfare of the world's individual people but simultaneously with the wellbeing and the survival of the entire human species and of its habitat, the Earth. Emmerich-Fritsche noted that some elements and objectives of world law can in principle be realised within the framework of international law. She argued that agreements under international law can be a vehicle for this purpose if and when they are approved and implemented by almost all states, so that they have practically universal applicability. In her view, a world legislature that adopts positive world law is in such cases 'not absolutely imperative'.[11] Traces of world law and its principles are indeed already present in the international law system. This applies for example to the Universal Declaration on Human Rights, in particular its first Article which proclaims 'all human beings are born free and equal in dignity and rights'; the binding nature of UN Security Council decisions under Chapter VII of the UN Charter concerning the maintenance of international peace and security; the concept of the common heritage of humankind in the Convention on the Law of the Sea; the obligatory dispute settlement procedure of the WTO; the power of the International Criminal Court to prosecute individuals; the emergent principle of the Responsibility to Protect which in theory sets limits on sovereignty and non-interference; or the shift from collective coercive measures toward so-called 'smart sanctions' aimed at individuals and specific entities rather than entire states. Such advances within the system of international law represent important stepping stones. They

---

9   On fragmentation, see pp. 388ff; and its effect on democracy, pp. 416ff.
10 On law enforcement, see pp. 304ff.
11 Emmrich-Fritsche, pp. 458, 1036.

must be defended against regression and pursued further. Nonetheless, the imperatives and requirements of a democratic global constitutional order obviously cannot be realised through international law. For over a century the international law system has shown ample evidence of its undemocratic and dysfunctional nature which undermines, in particular, an adequate and timely provision of global public goods[12], including peace and security, and a management of planetary commons.[13] The inherent 'tragedy of international law' delivers lowest common denominator solutions, if any solutions at all.[14] The aim of international law must ultimately be its own abolition, as the philosopher Vittorio Hösle aptly put it.[15] The global constitution will be adopted in the name of humanity, but technically it will be the most significant act ever undertaken by the world's states under international law as it will mark the transition to a world legal order.

A bicameral world legislature

Notwithstanding this, states will remain the most important unit of governance in the world, serving as a crucial point of reference for many people's identities, even as they become global citizens under a global constitution *de lege lata*. In a federal world order guided by the principles of pluralism and subsidiarity, states constitute an indispensable level of government and decision-making.[16] After all, it is the states that will establish this new order in the first place. Following Otfried Höffe, Jürgen Habermas, Václav Havel and others, a third-generation world organization requires institutional representation of both states and the world's people. Therefore, the world parliament should consist of two chambers: a parliamentary assembly and a state assembly.[17] Designing the relationship between these chambers and which powers they should have, either concurrently or individually, requires careful consideration. According to International IDEA, approximately 80 countries worldwide have a bicameral legislature. This provides ample cases for examination. First of all, a popularly elected legislative assembly holds the 'central place' in 'all modern forms of democracy'. In a federal system the second chamber in turn serves 'to protect the right and interests of the territorial units and to give them a say in legislation'. They may have 'fairly extensive veto powers' over all

---

12 On global public goods, see pp. 215ff.
13 On planetary and global commons, see pp. 191ff.
14 On the 'tragedy of international law', see pp. 196ff.
15 Hösle, Vittorio. 1997. Politik und Moral. München: C.H. Beck, p. 933.
16 On subsidiarity, see pp. 387ff.
17 This and the following sections draw partly on Bummel, Andreas. 2018. 'A Renewed World Organization for the 21st Century.' Democracy Without Borders. (democracywithoutborders.org).

or certain classes of legislation.[18] A bicameral parliament enables checks and balances between the chambers. In principle, the parliamentary assembly can be compared with chambers such as the US House of Representatives, the Indian Lok Sabha or the German Bundestag whereas the state assembly is similar to the Senate, the Rajya Sabha or the Bundesrat, respectively. While the parliamentary assembly may evolve from possible preliminary stages discussed above, or otherwise be established from scratch, the state assembly will succeed today's UN General Assembly. To enhance participatory engagement, the constitution should provide for the world parliament to set up the instrument of citizens' initiative, that allows ordinary people to put forward proposals, and make use of advisory citizens' assemblies composed of people selected by lottery from the general population.[19]

Representation in the state chamber

When considering the representation of member states in the state assembly, one might initially think it could remain as it is under the UN Charter: each state having one vote and no more than five representatives. However, it is questionable from the viewpoint of democratic principles whether in the General Assembly's transition to a co-legislative upper chamber it can be justified to give an equal vote to all states irrespective of their population size. In the US Senate, the same is the case with each US state having two senators. This situation is described by Fordham University professor John J. Davenport as 'the largest problem of all in the US Constitution according to virtually every political scientist' who compares the US with other democracies.[20] University of Maryland professor Maxwell L. Stearns found that the US Senate 'is among the most antidemocratic elective bodies in the world'. He noted that California, with almost forty million people, and Wyoming, with 600.000, a ration of 67:1, have the same number of two seats in the Senate. Historically, the argument goes, equal apportionment in the Senate was essential for the founding states to cede sovereignty and accept the US Constitution.[21] A similar situation could arise in the discussion about a world constitution, but today there is an awareness of the problem and at the world level, the disparity is larger by orders of magnitude. Weighted voting has been proposed to reduce the imbalance between small and large countries in a global state chamber. Joseph

---

18 Bulmer, Elliot. 2017. 'Bicameralism.' International IDEA Constitution-Building Primer 2, pp. 3-4, 10, 12.

19 On complementing representative democracy, see pp. 429ff.

20 Davenport, John J. 2023. The Democracy Amendments: Constitutional Reforms to Save the United States. Anthem Press, p. 188.

21 Stearns, Maxwell L. 2024. Parliamentary America: The Least Radical Means of Radically Repairing Our Broken Democracy. Baltimore: Johns Hopkins University Press, p. 247.

Schwartzberg worked out a model for the UN General Assembly, since until 'such time as the United Nations adopts a system of weighted voting that realistically reflects the actual global distribution of power, it seems doubtful that any major state will willingly grant the GA, the most representative organ within the UN system, the authority to make binding decisions'.[22] It is a misconception though to consider the state assembly in isolation. The required level of legitimacy for binding decision-making necessarily derives from its combination with an elected parliamentary body. The implementation of an acceptable system of degressive proportionality in the latter mitigates the issue of representation in the state assembly to a degree but does not solve it. Instead of a granular calculation of voting weights up to the third decimal place, which Schwartzberg and others[23] suggested, coming up with a simple graduation seems advisable at first. There are a variety of ways how this could be done. For example, starting with one vote for each country with a population size below one million, one additional vote could be assigned for each tenfold increase in population: above a population of one million two votes; above ten million three votes; above 100 million four votes; and above one billion, five votes. Compared to the General Assembly today, the combined voting power of the 128 least populous countries in this scenario would decrease from 66.3 per cent to 53.8 per cent, from a 2/3 to a simple majority. Over time, more granular scales could be introduced. In terms of how the member state representatives in the UN General Assembly are determined, it is interesting to note that the UN Charter does not prescribe a modality. They are all government-appointed diplomats, of course, but this is at the discretion of individual states. If they wanted to, they could opt for popular elections or have them selected by national legislatures. For the time being, a global constitution could leave this open as well.

Legislation of world law

In principle, for world law to be enacted, it should require the concurrent approval of both chambers, with each chamber having the power to initiate legislation. Each chamber will have its own portfolio committees but joint committees will be important for harmonising legislative initiatives and drafts. The main governing bodies that exist today across the UN system could be transitioned, as appropriate, into such specialized committees of the world

22 Schwartzberg, Joseph. 2013. Transforming the United Nations System. Designs for a Workable World. Tokyo, New York, Paris: United Nations University Press, p. 17.
23 Lopez-Claros, Augusto, Arthur L. Dahl, and Maja Groff. 2020. Global Governance and the Emergence of Global Institutions for the 21st Century. Cambridge University Press, pp. 91-100.

parliament. Special features can be accommodated. A state assembly committee, for instance, that carries on the rule-making dimension of the ILO should continue to have a tripartite structure that represents governments, employers, and workers. Representation of the parliamentary assembly could be included, making it a joint committee.

To ensure adequate legitimation and acceptance, qualified majorities in both chambers will be necessary for binding legislation for a considerable time. As in the law-making process in the EU, at least two types of universally binding global legislation should be envisaged. Firstly, legislative regulations, which have direct and immediate applicability to their legal addressees. Secondly, framework directives, which establish goals and guidelines, leaving the specifics of implementation to member states who are obligated to transpose them into national law within a given time. This instrument allows for a degree of flexibility and adaptation to local circumstances. If a group of member states transfers relevant competences to a regional organization, as is already the case with regard to the EU, it may be this tier of government that instead is required to implement a directive depending on the matter at hand. The global constitution of course needs to specify in which areas the world parliament has legislative competence and that rules need to comply with the principles of proportionality as well as uniform, equal, and non-discriminatory applicability with regard to their legal addresses. Additionally, only matters that cannot be dealt with effectively at lower levels should be in the legislative scope of the world parliament. Depending on the matter being legislated and the type of legislation, different levels of qualified majority could be required. Regulations might need a higher threshold of votes to pass than directives. In the former case it could be a 3/4 majority and in the latter 2/3, each in both chambers.

Voting requirements in the *state chamber* could additionally be linked to the issue at hand.[24] For illustration purposes, in budgetary matters the required 2/3 majority might also need to represent at least 2/3 of member state contributions if such are affected. Similarly, legislation concerning global climate policy might require that the 2/3 approval also represents at least 2/3 of worldwide CO_2 emissions, and matters relating to world trade or global taxation could necessitate votes also representing at least 2/3 of global GDP. The overall goal, however, should be to ensure broad acceptance, not to give small groups of states a power to block decisions. As an additional means of checks and balances, national parliaments—and regional ones, if applicable—could be granted the ability to delay the entry-into-force of certain legislation. If a

---

24 On differentiated majorities, see p. 194.

certain number, such as 1/4, record an objection within a specified time, a mediation committee could be convened to consider their concerns. The world parliament could then decide whether to confirm, amend or repeal the law in question.[25] This is a space where the IPU, the umbrella organization of national parliaments, could assume an important role. Finally, inspired by EU law, a procedure for enhanced cooperation could be established, permitting a certain minimum number of member states to collaborate within the world organization's framework, including the world parliament, even if not all member states are involved. This would enable member states to progress with global integration at varying paces. Under this system, a given regulation or directive might be adopted by participating member states as an instrument of enhanced cooperation and only apply to them and other states that join later.

A global executive branch

One of the key functions of the world parliament is to oversee the executive branch and its departments and agencies as they implement global legislation and fulfil their constitutional responsibilities. Existing intergovernmental institutions and programs within and outside the UN system already constitute a *de facto* executive structure, albeit a helplessly fragmented one. A renewed world organization should build on these structures and, where appropriate, carry them forward. This needs to go along with a radical consolidation to achieve coherence, harmonization, greater efficiency, less duplication and more transparency. The UN's secretariat with its departments as well as the administrative structures of the UN system's specialized agencies, funds and programs, related organizations, conventions and other entities should be merged and reorganized as departments under the roof of a *World Commission* that functions as a cabinet government. How exactly this is to be done will have to be carefully analysed. It might be considered that UNEP and the Secretariat of the UNFCCC could merge into an environment and climate department, for instance; the FAO could become the core of a department on food and agriculture; UNESCO the core of a department on education, science and culture; the WTO and the UN Conference on Trade and Development could become part of a department on trade; the proposed UN Tax Organization[26] could transition into the Commission's treasury department; and so on. Each department of the Commission could be headed by an individual

25   See also Lange, Christian (ed.). 1911. 'Un Congrès International, Conférence de Bruxelles, 1905'. In: Union interparlementaire: Résolutions des Conférences et Décisions principales du Conseil, 2nd ed., 93–94. Brussels: Misch & Thron, see point 8, p. 94.
26   On a UN Tax Organization, see pp. 237ff.

commissioner who is nominated by the Commission's President and confirmed on an individual basis by majority votes of both chambers of the world parliament. The President of the World Commission could be elected by the parliamentary assembly upon recommendation of the state assembly.

A legislature's capacity to conduct independent investigations of and to replace the executive are considered top indicators in measuring legislative powers.[27] Therefore, the world parliament must have the authority to dismiss the World Commission, which includes its President, or individual commissioners by a no-confidence vote. No consideration should be given to designs where the chief executive is hardly accountable to the legislative branch, for instance if the position is directly elected and can only be removed through cumbersome impeachment procedures. As political scientist Arend Lijphart put it, the 'disadvantages of presidentialism are so overwhelmingly clear that all presidential democracies should be advised to switch to parliamentarism'.[28] Given the perils presidentialism entails—among them majoritarianism, concentration of power, personality politics, institutional stalemate and rigidity— it is not a suitable model for the global scale.[29]

The Commission would draft and propose the world organization's budget for consideration and approval by the world parliament. It may be mandated by either chamber of the parliament to assist in preparing new legislation but should not otherwise participate in the legislative process to maintain the separation of powers. The Commission nonetheless could be entrusted with monitoring implementation of directives through member states and assist them in this regard. The primary responsibility for maintaining international peace and security should be assigned a Joint Security Committee (JSC) of the world parliament which would replace the current UN Security Council. The JSC, comprising members from both chambers, would be responsible for approving and monitoring measures in this field recommended by the Commission or adopting measures on its own initiative, following on lines similar to Chapter VII of the current UN Charter. This includes decisions to use force, in particular the deployment of rapid reaction and peacekeeping forces under the command of the Commission, and other coercive measures.[30] But the world parliament itself would remain the highest authority and could revoke or am-

---

27 Chernykh, Svitlana, David Doyle, and Timothy J. Power. 2017. 'Measuring Legislative Power: An Expert Reweighting of the Fish-Kroenig Parliamentary Powers Index.' Legisl. Studies Quarterly 42 (2): 295–320, p. 8.

28 Lijphart, Arend. 2023. 'The Perils of Presidentialism: Juan Linz's Analysis and Further Reflections.' Revista Chilena de Derecho y Ciencia Política 14 (1): 1–8, p. 7. See also Linz, Juan J. 1990. 'The Perils of Presidentialism.' Journal of Democracy 1 (1): 51–69.

29 On the risk of global autocracy, see also pp. 383ff.

30 On a rapid reaction force, see also pp. 86, 287.

end decisions taken by the JSC. Due to its powers and importance, the JSC would be one of the joint committees regulated by the constitution itself instead of the world parliament's rules of procedure or secondary law.

To help keep the Commission's administration as small and decentralized as possible, states should, where feasible, assume responsibility for the administrative implementation of certain elements of the world law system and global legislation on behalf of the world organization. In Germany, for instance, it is routine for the federal states to carry out federal administration on behalf of the federal government, an arrangement provided for in the German constitution. A number of institutions and agencies can be anticipated that will be largely autonomous from the Commission but part of the executive. This includes a World Central Bank[31], a global antitrust authority[32] or a law enforcement agency that replaces Interpol.[33] For administering global elections, an impartial and independent election management body will be required. In accordance with world law and under the supervision of the world parliament, relevant departments of the Commission will continue to manage existing inspection regimes and manage new ones. This includes, among others, monitoring the reduction and regulation of conventional arms; overseeing the destruction and preventing the proliferation of nuclear, chemical, and biological weapons of mass destruction; verifying that nuclear, chemical, and biological production and research facilities comply with global safety standards and are not used for prohibited activities; as well as monitoring artificial intelligence research and AI systems to prevent harmful use and adherence to ethical, human rights and safety standards.[34]

A world constitutional court and the judiciary

A global constitution must be firmly anchored in and protect fundamental human rights, the rule of law, and democratic principles. A robust global judiciary that enables legal protection and ensures checks and balances is essential for this. Nearly all state constitutions in the world give courts the power to 'supervise implementation of the constitution and to set aside legislation for constitutional incompatibility.'[35] Following the 2011 revolution, the new democratic government of Tunisia at the time proposed the creation of an international constitutional court that could be called upon to rule on the democratic

---

31 On a World Central Bank, see pp. 226ff.
32 On a global antitrust authority, see pp. 372ff.
33 On a global law enforcement agency, see pp. 304ff.
34 On inspection regimes, see pp. 266, 273, 280, 283, 308.
35 Ginsburg, Tom, and Mila Versteeg. 2014. 'Why Do Countries Adopt Constitutional Review?' The Journal of Law, Economics, and Organization 30 (3): 587–622, p. 587.

nature and legality of national elections and changes of government. The responsibilities of such a court, at first established within the international law framework, could later be extended in the course of the transition to a world legal order. At the global level, there are two dimensions to consider: on the one hand, the compliance with global constitutional principles and provisions by individual member states and, on the other, by the bodies and representatives of the world organization itself. Both cases must be subject to judicial review by a *World Constitutional Court.* Based on an analysis of national constitutional courts, vesting such a global court with the following types of power should be considered, among others: reviewing legislative acts in advance or after legislation; initiating or requiring legislation; reviewing executive actions and decisions; impeachment proceedings against holders of public office; adjudication of disputes as to the competence of state organs; adjudication of disputes between state organs; and examination of the legality of elections and election results at any level.[36] Particular areas of concern are safeguarding against potential violations by the global legislative and executive branches of the constitutional allocation of powers between the world organization and its member states as well as safeguarding against democratic backsliding in member states. In particular, bodies of the world organisation could refer cases to the Court, above all the chambers of the world parliament, the Commission and member states. The Constitutional Court will not adjudicate ordinary civil or criminal cases.[37] Rather, it will decide on constitutional questions referred to it by other courts, including a significantly adapted International Court of Justice (ICJ). Currently, the ICJ has jurisdiction over disputes between states and could continue to do so, provided such disputes involve the interpretation and application of secondary public world law rather than their constitutional rights, responsibilities, and relationships, which would be matters for the Constitutional Court to deal with. The ICJ's role could be expanded not only to applying and interpreting secondary public world law but also civil law, where applicable, with specialized chambers for different legal areas. The court could primarily function as an appellate body that ensures a uniform and coherent application of global law. Additionally, the ICJ could serve as an instance for individual legal protection against infringements by global public authorities. Finally, the International Criminal Court would have jurisdiction in criminal matters under world law. As part of the Court, the Prosecutor's Office would be independent of the global executive and

---

36 Harding, Andrew. 2017. 'The Fundamentals of Constitutional Courts.' International IDEA Constitution
      Brief. (idea.int), p. 3.
37 Cf. ibid., p. 5.

could include a special investigation unit that examines serious allegations of corruption, malpractice and maladministration within the world organization.[38] Of course, judges themselves must be subject to accountability and the rule of law as well. This issue is particularly critical and complex concerning the judges of apex courts whose decisions are not subject to review by other courts—such as the proposed World Constitutional Court. An acceptable balance needs to be found in this regard between independence and accountability in judicial systems.[39] As the editors of a volume examining diverse designs across thirteen countries pointed out, the 'question of what to do about (alleged) misconduct by a judge' has 'troubled societies for millennia' and was already addressed in Hammurabi's Code composed at around 1750 BCE. They noted that in recent times, due to 'significant developments in numerous jurisdictions' the issue of 'judicial discipline has taken on a particular urgency'.[40] Considering national models and experiences as well as pertinent international norms, an appropriate mechanism will need to be devised for the global judiciary, particularly for the Constitutional Court.

Finally, the selection of judges and constitutional judges in particular 'is a highly problematic and potentially controversial area'.[41] With regard to international courts, Armin von Bogdandy and Ingo Venzke pointed out that they, too, are 'actors of global governance' and 'somehow require democratic legitimation conveyed by representative institutions'. 'Their establishment and legal basis are mostly enshrined in international treaties that draw their democratic legitimation from the domestic procedure of parliamentary ratification. While we do not question the democratic significance of this parliamentary consent, we see limits to its legitimatory power: limits that render it advisable—given the development of many international courts—to open up additional sources of legitimation.' At the centre of their democratic legitimation, von Bogdandy and Venzke argued, must be 'the individuals whose freedom is shaped by judicial decisions, however indirectly'.[42] Angelika Emmerich-Fritsche noted that 'world courts that make legal decisions with binding effect on the citizens of the world' require, as a matter of fundamental principle, 'deeper democratic legitimation'. What this means in practice is that the judges must be elected by either the citizenry under their jurisdiction, or their parliament, or a

---

38 On the International Criminal Court, see pp. 306ff.
39 Tushnet, Mark. 2013. 'Judicial Accountability in Comparative Perspective.' In: Accountability in the Contemporary Constitution, ed. by Nicholas Bamforth and Peter Leyland, 57–74. Oxford University.
40 Devlin, Richard, and Sheila Wildeman, eds. 2021. Disciplining Judges: Contemporary Challenges and Controversies. Edward Elgar Publishing, pp. 2-3, 10-1.
41 Harding, p. 3.
42 Bogdandy, Armin von, and Ingo Venzke. 2014. In Whose Name? A Public Law Theory of International Adjudication. Oxford University Press, pp. 207, 148, 149, 212.

democratically appointed selection committee. With regard to a world court, it would make 'practical sense' in Emmerich-Fritsche's view, to set up a selection committee 'composed of members drawn from the national parliaments and/or the world parliament and from among the highest judges of state courts'.[43] Their selection should be approved individually by concurrent 2/3 majority votes in both chambers of the world parliament.[44]

43   Emmerich-Fritsche, pp. 651-2.
44   Cf. Harding, p. 4.

29.

Conditions and drivers
for the transformation

The structural conditions for institutional change

A world legal system with a world parliament will not come about simply because it is ethically and morally superior to the present system of international law and because in any rational debate it has the more persuasive arguments. That may be a good starting position, but in and of itself it is of course not sufficient. The international law expert Richard Falk pointed out that in 'world order studies it is traditional to propose a better system of world order and then argue for its adoption. Such an approach tends to be "utopian" or "romantic" in the sense that it overlooks the transition from "here" to "there"'. It was assumed that the better arguments would prevail. However, this dispute will be settled not in the debating clubs but in the political arena. 'Those who benefit from existing arrangements of power and interest', wrote Falk, 'are unlikely to be swayed, except in marginal or cosmetic respects, by appeals based on argument or values.' He argued that power can be transformed only by countervailing power. 'No world order solution which presupposes the substantial modification of the state system can be achieved unless the advocates of the new system are aligned with important social and political forces within the existing world structure.'[1] It is in the nature of the third democratic transformation and the new global enlightenment that their goals, values and perspectives will spread gradually through world society and thereby gain ever more potential. This process will be driven forward by the long-term economic, social and cultural changes associated with global industrialization and post-industrialization. We have already looked, for example, at the signifi-

---

1   Falk, Richard. 1975. A Study of Future Worlds. Amsterdam: North-Holland Publishing Company, p. 277.

cance of sustained prosperity and rising levels of education for an emancipatory shift in values and ultimately for the evolution of a post-conventional morality.[2] The ever more widespread experience of global interconnectedness and the global growth of empathy are other factors we have looked at.[3] The ambitious middle classes in the developing countries on the one side and the squeezed middle classes in the industrialised countries on the other represent—together with the global precariat—the social forces which, as part of a 'transformative subject', may be the principal social agents of the third transformation.[4]

However, this does not mean that these trends will inevitably continue and end in the realization of a world democracy. The powers of persistence within the status quo, and the resistance from its beneficiaries to a new global social contract and a new global class compromise as part of an eco-social and pacifist world legal order, must not be underestimated. In the area of climate policy, for example, representatives of the oil and coal industries work ceaselessly to thwart the international negotiations, to discredit the findings of climate research and to influence public opinion in their favour. During his presidency, Donald Trump was one of their most powerful allies in recent times. Moreover, there is a real danger of a serious setback to civilization, or even of collapse on a global scale. The new precariat and the squeezed middle classes also have an anti-modern, nationalistic-reactionary potential that populists and demagogues mobilize for their purposes.[5]

The challenge of autocratization revisited

The increasing interlinkage between national and global democratization in connection with the pressures of the global polycrisis seems to suggest that the second and third democratic transformations will either succeed or fail together. While it is true that following the Second World War there was widespread public support in many countries for a world parliament and world citizenship, the second democratic transformation was not yet sufficiently far advanced to make it a realistic option at the time. The Soviet Union, for example, the main victorious power alongside the USA, was ruled by the mass murderer and dictator Joseph Stalin, and decolonization was only just beginning. Once again, the rise, consolidation and strengthening of new and existing autocratic regimes is emerging as perhaps the biggest obstacle of all.[6] The suppression of democracy and fundamental human rights by autocratic re-

---

2   On value shifts, see pp. 404ff; on post-conventional morality, see pp. 442ff.
3   On empathy, see pp. 445ff.
4   On middle classes, see pp. 361ff; on precariat, see pp. 364ff.
5   On populism, see pp, 211, 405ff.
6   On autocratization, see also pp. 401ff.

gimes is intolerable and there are also serious international consequences. As the Professor of International Law and Political Science at the University of Chicago, Tom Ginsburg, summarized research in this field, 'as a general matter authoritarian states do not seem to participate in the international legal order to the same degree as democracies.' Democracies, he reported, 'are much more likely than autocracies to conclude treaties, to litigate cases before international tribunals, and to engage in international lawmaking bodies.' Authoritarians, in turn, are unlikely to 'submit to the authority of dispute resolution bodies.' Empirical evidence shows that 'highest-level democracies join more treaties by an order of magnitude.' According to the professor, much of 'what we have come to think of as general international law, it turns out, is the product of democratically elected governments.' Under authoritarian international law, by contrast, 'integration will be shallower, agreements will be thinner, and courts will play a relatively smaller role', Ginsburg explained.[7] While he contended that 'in the long view, international law has always been amenable and even facilitative of authoritarian governance', in the post-World War II era it increasingly became a vehicle for advancing human rights and the rule of law.[8] Embedded into the global economy, the leading autocratic states are interested in enhancing their global regulatory power and market position through international law but they oppose its cosmopolitan dimension. Under the leadership of the so-called 'Big Five'—China, Russia, Iran, Saudi Arabia and Venezuela—authoritarian powers are collaborating ever more closely to push back. They are no longer content to suppress dissent and civil society at home, but determined to contain and reverse progress on a global level.[9] Part of this effort is an attempt to redesign international law and the international system so they serve extending 'the survival and reach of authoritarian rule'.[10] This program of autocracy promotion includes stressing the principle of sovereignty, reasserting norms of non-interference, undermining international human rights regimes, strengthening executive power, neutralizing multilateral promotion of democracy, undermining democratic governance where it exists, closing the space for civil society and enhancing cross-border repression. As a 'well-known example', Ginsberg referred to the 'capture of the Human Rights Council' by authoritarian regimes.[11] A new UN

---

7   Ginsburg, Tom. 2020. 'Authoritarian International Law?' American Journal of International Law 114 (2): 221–60, pp. 227, 235, 258.
8   Id., 2021. Democracies and International Law. Cambridge University Press, p. 190.
9   Diamond, Larry, Marc F. Plattner, and Christopher Walker. 2016. Authoritarianism Goes Global: The Challenge to Democracy. Baltimore: Johns Hopkins University Press, pp. 4-5.
10 Ginsburg, p. 228.
11 Ibid., 255.

convention on combatting cybercrime, pushed by Russia and China, as well as Russia's efforts to move internet governance to the International Telecommunication Union in order to exert state control are other instances that raise deep concern. In a UN committee on reforming the UN Charter and 'strengthening the organization', an axis of the thirteen most autocratic states in the world questioned the benefit of the UN's long-standing involvement of civil society organizations with arguments which appear to be constructed in a way so they appeal to an audience of Southern developing countries and tie in with a Western self-critical post-colonial discourse. Among other things, they claimed that civil society was a Western phenomenon and NGO participation would 'cement historical legacies of colonialism and neocolonial economic structures, contributing to an inherent bias in favour of Western interests'.[12] An important component of the autocratic resurgence involves capturing and dominating narratives, in particular by 'repurposing the language of democracy' as well as abusing democratic forms for antidemocratic aims.[13] With few exceptions, democracies around the world are proving weak and indecisive in countering autocratization even after Russia's full-scale invasion of Ukraine. Economic interdependence, in particular the need for natural resources such as oil and gas, and an associated fear of political confrontation appear to be among the reasons. The Community of Democracies should be transformed into a strong global alliance. But democracy thus far is not proving to be an effective common denominator of global cooperation, as the BRICS alliance illustrates, bringing together the world's leading autocratic states Russia and China with the democracies of Brazil, India, and South Africa. The decades-long refusal of important Western democracies, in particular the US and UK, to help bring about a more democratic and just international order and not merely to pursue their own interests, while misusing democratic rhetoric as well, is taking its revenge. Based on the data of the seventh wave of the World Values Survey, researchers already recognized signs of a 'democratic deconsolidation' that may also be looming in the established Western democracies, and they cautioned against the idea that a breakdown of democracy in these countries is impossible.[14] Democracy supporters fear that this is exactly what could happen, in particular in the United States. The rise of Trump in US politics is an expression of a fundamental political, democratic and constitutional crisis in the country which appears to be heading towards a tipping point. As

12 United Nations. 2024. 'Identification of New Subjects. Special Committee on the Charter of the United Nations and on the Strengthening of the Role of the Organization.' UN Doc. A/AC.182/L.164.
13 Ginsburg, Tom. 2021. Democracies and International Law. Cambridge University Press, pp. 232, 118.
14 Foa, Roberto, and Yascha Mounk. 2016. 'The Democratic Disconnect'. Journal of Democracy (27) 3: 5–17.

Norbert Elias pointed out, the civilizing process 'is never finished and always under threat.'[15]

Long-term value shifts, protests and the elites

Increased repression in autocratic states and their international program of autocracy promotion can be seen as a backlash against a growing desire for emancipation and democracy. A study that analyzed around 2.800 protest events lasting up to one year in the period from 2006 to 2020 in over 100 countries, found that there was a steady rise in their numbers. Over half of them related to 'a failure of political representation and political systems', with democracy being 'the most prevalent protest issue' of all, present in nearly 28 per cent of protest events counted worldwide.[16] At the same time, Erica Chenoweth, a professor of public policy at the Harvard Kennedy School, found that nonviolent protests 'are seeing their lowest success rates in more than a century'.[17] Autocracies 'have learned to undermine mass movements with subtler methods than brute force alone', the *New York Times* summarized.[18] Ronald Inglehart and Christian Welzel described how long-term value shifts in society create the foundation for institutional changes. As an illustration of this, they pointed to the slow but steady trend to greater emphasis on self-determination and self-realization in the populations of the Eastern European countries in the decades preceding 1989. This shift in values built up a pressure for change in society that finally, under specific historical circumstances, quite suddenly and unexpectedly erupted in successful mass protests which resulted in the fall of the Iron Curtain and the collapse of the communist regimes in Eastern Europe. According to Inglehart and Welzel, the exact point in time when a long-term value shift of this kind leads to an institutional breakthrough is usually determined by the removal or overcoming of blocking factors *at the level of the elites*. In their view, the turning point in the revolutions in Eastern Europe was when Mikhail Gorbachev made clear in 1988 that, unlike in 1956 in Hungary or 1968 in Czechoslovakia, the Soviet Union would not support collapsing governments of allied states with military force.[19] An interesting aspect of the example they chose is that, at least accord-

15 Elias, Norbert. 1992 [1989]. Studien über die Deutschen, Frankfurt: Suhrkamp, p. 225.

16 Ortiz, Isabel, Sara Burke, Mohamed Berrada, and Hernán Saenz Cortés. 2022. World Protests: A Study of Key Protest Issues in the 21st Century. Palgrave Macmillan, pp. 112, 20-1.

17 Chenoweth, Erica. 2022. 'Can Nonviolent Resistance Survive COVID-19?' Journal of Human Rights 21 (3): 304–16, p. 305.

18 Fisher, Max. 30 Sept. 2022. 'Even as Iranians Rise Up, Protests Worldwide Are Failing at Record Rates.' The New York Times, (nytimes.com).

19 Inglehart, Ronald, and Christian Welzel. 2005. Modernization, cultural change, and democracy: the human development sequence. Cambridge University Press, pp. 41-3.

ing to Gorbachev's own account, a decisive factor for him personally was a shift to a planetary perspective.[20] In fact, Chenoweth according to the *New York Times* argued that 'the success of protest is no longer determined by crowd size but the most important factor may be a movement's skill at persuading or pressuring key power brokers in a country to break ranks with the government'. This requires 'fissures' among ruling elites which protestors are able to make use of.[21] In the face of sustained blocking at the elite level, tensions can increase to the point when they find release in violent explosions. Unfortunately, the likelihood of this appears to be growing. The success of non-violent protests, for instance, is no longer having a 'statistically significant advantage over armed insurrection', Chenoweth concluded.[22] In an essay on 'a new paradigm of human development', Ivo Šlaus and Garry Jacobs from the World Academy of Art and Science wrote that radical change in history usually comes in the form of violent revolutions. These are directed against elites who doggedly refuse to relinquish any power. Occasionally, however, far-sighted leaders had recognised the urgent need for rapid social evolution to stave off such revolutions. For example, the English elites had consciously sought to prevent a repeat there of the bloodshed of the French Revolution, which had wiped out the French aristocracy, through an opening up towards the middle classes.[23] The situation with regard to the world system is different as there is no clear political power centre to target at the global level. The development of the nation states in the 19th century and later was driven forward by the adoption of ideas of nationhood and state formation at the elite level which supported the emergence of popular movements.[24] At this time, there are few signs that parts of the transnational elite are interested in helping establish a global power centre, let alone a democratic one.[25] Instead, the elite mainstream is promoting diffuse ideas of networked multilateralism and multistakeholder governance.[26] The more difficult it is for counter-movements to get a hold on the machinery of the transnational state, the less popular pressure can be put on the transnational elite.[27] Jean Rossiaud, a sociologist based in Geneva, noted that this is precisely the reason why the efforts of social movements to bring about global change largely come to nothing. 'The lack of

20   On a planetary perspective, see pp. 455ff.
21   Fisher, ibid.
22   Chenoweth, pp. 308-9.
23   Šlaus, Ivo, and Garry Jacobs. 2013. 'In Search of a New Paradigm for Global Development.' Cadmus (6) 1
     (cadmusjournal.org).
24   On nation building, see pp. 458ff.
25   On elite resistance, see pp. 380ff.
26   On multistakeholderism, see pp. 337ff.
27   On the transnational state, see pp. 370ff.

a world state limits social movements to resistance, a repertoire of defensive or reactive actions, at the local or national level', he wrote.[28] In the opinion of the Swedish professor of philosophy Torbjörn Tännsjö, it indeed 'simplifies the task of establishing a global democracy if the relevant political unity, the world state, already exists'—even if it is in a 'form of global despotism', he argued. He noted that it 'is typically through periods of despotism that national democracies have evolved', suggesting that a similar path may be required globally. 'Not only can global despotism save our human civilization and humanity, but such despotism can also provide us with a first step toward global democracy', he wrote. However, there is no reasonable scenario in which states would involuntarily submit to the dictates of a 'world government' jointly set up by the USA and China that would obtain 'a firm grip on national and local political authorities', 'disarm the world' by force and impose an 'immediate end to further emission of greenhouse gases', as Tännsjö imagined. The prerequisite for this would probably be a global catastrophe of unprecedented proportions, indeed a 'situation of utmost emergency', when the world population is 'close to despair', and the global dictate is 'the last hope of survival'.[29]

A cosmopolitan movement

Even though autocratic states and autocratization represent a formidable obstacle and global mobilization faces particular challenges, we certainly prefer pursuing more proactive and positive scenarios. During the COVID-19 lockdowns in 2020, Democracy Without Borders developed a long-term theory of change aimed at establishing a global constitution and a global parliament by 2045, the centenary of the United Nations. In order to have sufficiently broad legitimacy, the constitution will have to be supported by a majority of the world's population. This in turn, it was argued, would require mass support for the ideas of global citizenship and global democracy, which would also help overcome political blockades at the elite level. The vehicle for generating mass support and perhaps its most important manifestation would be a cosmopolitan movement whose primary goal is to push for the establishment of a democratic world state. This world state would provide the institutional foundation for the realization of specific policy objectives in the fields of global peace, security, justice, climate, sustainability and others.[30] But the movement would not need to reach unified positions on each of these second-order ob-

28 Rossiaud, Jean. 2012. 'For a Democratic Cosmopolitan Movement.' Forum for a New World Governance, pp. 11-2. A 'World Democratic Forum' co-founded by Rossiaud discontinued in 2016.

29 Tännsjö, Torbjörn. 2023. From Despotism to Democracy: How a World Government Can Save Humanity. Singapore: Springer, pp. viii, x, 78-81.

30 Cf. Rossiaud, ibid.

jectives. Unity is important only with regard to the goal of establishing a democratic global institutional framework which would enable global politics to be effectively pursued *at all.*

The idea of such a cosmopolitan movement has been nurtured for quite some time. 'The global transformation will require the awakening of a new social actor: a vast movement of global citizens expressing a supranational identity and building new institutions for a planetary age', wrote Paul Raskin of the Tellus Institute.[31] The Institute is working together with others as part of a 'Great Transition Initiative' to bring such a 'global citizens' movement' into being. An Institute paper stated that the establishment of a world parliament should be one of the projects of the movement.[32] In an essay titled 'Journey to Earthland', Raskin imagined a scenario in which after phases of crisis and emergency an 'Earthland Parliamentary Assembly' adopts a world constitution in 2048 that brings a 'Commonwealth of Earthland' into being. At the pinnacle of the formal structure sits a world assembly with regional and at-large members selected by popular vote in world-wide elections.

A cosmopolitan movement of this kind will be decentralized, diverse and dynamic, with support and participation of a wide array of actors from the local to the global levels. It would be a platform for 'existing movements in the fields of climate, environment, peace, disarmament, democracy, social justice and others' to join forces.[33] After all, democratic statehood at the global level is the decisive element that is missing for a breakthrough in all these areas. It seems reasonable to assume that the movements of the *second* democratic transformation, which in many countries continue to fight for democratization at the nation state level, eventually will also see themselves as part of such a cosmopolitan movement as they share a common goal in the establishment and strengthening of democracy—just with a different focus. For them and other actors it will be crucial to realize that a commitment to a cosmopolitan state-building project is not a distraction from the daily struggle on the ground, but will ultimately help it succeed. The World Social Forum, held under the premise of 'another world is possible', is an interesting case to learn from in some respects. In the first years following its inception in 2001, it was 'an apparent success, quickly growing from 15,000 to 50,000 and then more than 100,000 participants from around the world', Heikki Patomäki noted. It became a public counterweight to the elite's World Economic Forum. But in 2005 already it

31   Raskin, Paul. 2010. 'Imagine All the People: Advancing a global citizens movement.' Tellus Institute, pp. 1, 3.
32   Id., Orion Kriegman, and Josep Xercavins. 2010. 'We the People of Earth: Toward Global Democracy.' Tellus Institute.
33   Jositsch, Daniel, and Andreas Bummel. 28 Aug. 2020. 'It Is Time for a Democratic Global Revolution.' Democracy Without Borders (blog). (democracywithoutborders.org).

started losing momentum and by now it has become insignificant. In Patomäki's analysis, a key issue was the forum's conception as a mere open space for discussion. Lacking the ability to establish 'substantial direction', as the participants pursued too different goals and priorities, he found it had no chance to develop political agency and transformative capacity.[34] Instead, Patomäki believes that a *global political party* represents a key agency for a 'global Polanyian movement' and that its main purpose would need to be 'to transform existing global institutions and to create new ones.'[35] As outlined before, the emergence of global political parties and a global state-building process can reinforce each other.[36] Political parties can certainly be considered important potential drivers of a cosmopolitan movement. Existing international party networks at some point indeed already passed resolutions supporting a UNPA, including the Socialist International, the Liberal International and the Global Greens, but this had little influence on their national member parties. In the case of an actual global political party, it is reasonable to assume that political positions arrived at globally would be taken seriously and pursued further by its members. An example for such an approach is Atlas. Originally established as an activist group under the name Now!, the movement in 2024 decided to become a global political party and compete in national elections through national branches. The idea is to enter into national parliaments and build support for global change from there. As Atlas' cofounder Colombe Cahen-Salvador told us, 'we need to bring citizens to the core of global governance. For this, we need global political parties representing the interests of citizens and efforts to democratise global institutions need to be pursued, including the creation of a world parliament for which parties can stand for election'. Forming a new global party may seem like a challenging task. Patomäki rightfully noted that in many countries, the membership numbers of most political parties have been in decline. 'In the perceived absence of alternatives concerning economic policy and globalisation, conventional parties have tended to lose legitimacy among large parts of the citizenry in many countries', the professor wrote.[37] In a recent 24-country survey, for instance, a median of 42 per cent of respondents said that none of the political parties in their countries represented their views well.[38] A global political party might actually tap into this potential as most national mainstream parties

34 Patomäki, Heikki. 2023. World Statehood: The Future of World Politics. Springer, pp. 202, 208, 210-1.
35 Ibid., p. 193.
36 See also p. 489.
37 Ibid., p. 214.
38 Pew Research Center. Feb. 2024. 'Representative Democracy Remains a Popular Ideal, but People Around the World Are Critical of How It's Working.' (pewresearch.org), p. 36.

neglect to address global reforms which enjoy considerable popular support in many countries.[39]

The role of NGOs

The political pressure created by civil society and social movements does not consist only of resistance. But it is directed primarily towards achieving *intra-systemic* change, that is, at achieving specific goals within the continuing framework of the existing system; and this fails to address the root problems arising from the anarchic system of international law, let alone solve them. The growing pressure for change in society must be steered towards a radical transformation of the *institutional and legal basis* of the system itself. Although the big international NGOs could play an important role in this by exerting pressure on the elites, up until now they have not appeared as significant actors in the 'Great Transformation' pressing for a change in the institutional structures of the world system. For a long time, attempts to persuade the biggest NGOs to join together in major shared campaigns for a reform of the United Nations were not very successful. One of the last ones came to a halt around 2010.[40] Like companies who want to focus on their core business, their horizons rarely extend beyond their own immediate concerns. Their activities are largely determined by the shifting concerns of day-to-day politics, and focus on the achievement of short-term goals that are easy to measure and present. Even though a systemic change towards a world legal order will often be the best means of achieving their goals on a lasting basis, this approach strikes them as too distant, if they support it at all. Beyond symbolic actions, they have little inclination to address questions of the world order, which requires an overarching, long-term perspective. Just like the worlds of politics and business, and indeed society as a whole, they are often trapped in what the business consultant Pero Mićić described as 'the short-term trap'.[41]

However, the root causes of their lack of engagement in this respect may lie even deeper. In their book 'Protest Inc.', the political scientists Peter Dauvergne and Genevieve Lebaron described how the big NGOs now increasingly look, think and act like businesses, and are turning into supporting pillars of the system. 'One consequence for world politics', they wrote, 'is that activism is now less "radical" than it was forty or fifty years ago, at least in terms of demanding systemic and far-reaching change.' Only rarely do 'career activists' today call for a world government or a new international economic order.

---

39   On popular support, see again pp. 464ff.
40   See pp. 136f.
41   Mićić, Pero. 2014. Wie wir uns täglich die Zukunft versauen Raus aus der Kurzfristfalle. Berlin: Econ.

They are woven into the existing system, and therefore incline towards a conservative 'realist' position, often in response to large grant-making foundations that require them to seek implementation of short-term 'deliverables'. Dauvergne and Lebaron concluded that the de-radicalization of the professional NGO world, and its increasing pragmatic closeness to government, business and sources of finance, explains why so many people are now seeing signs of a global uprising while at the same time the world order 'remains so immune to demands from below for systemic reforms'.[42] Pressure from the streets is not taken up and channelled in the way it should be.

The growing gulf between the professional NGO world and ordinary people was acknowledged as a problem by representatives of the NGO world themselves in a self-critical open letter published in 2014. Signatories including the then head of Greenpeace, Kumi Naidoo, and the director of Oxfam, Winnie Byanyima, wrote that 'we have watched with increasing anxiety as civil society has been co-opted by processes in which we are outwitted and out manoeuvred', adding that their 'actions are clearly not sufficient to address the mounting anger and demand for systemic political and economic transformation that we see in cities and communities around the world every day'.[43]

However, there are promising new initiatives that have been endorsed by at least some large NGOs or in which some are actively involved. Large organizations and networks such as ActionAid, Greenpeace, Forus International or The Nature Conservancy, for instance, endorsed the platform of the 'We The Peoples' campaign for inclusive global governance in 2021, launched with the co-leadership of CIVICUS.[44] The latter, in particular, has become very active in emphasising the need for global reforms. In addition, Oxfam became a steering committee member of the Coalition for the UN We Need and joined a new Coalition for UN Charter Reform initiated by the Baha'i International Community and others in 2024. NGOs can maximize their impact through cooperation in such joint platforms and coalitions. The Coalition for the International Criminal Court (CICC) is still an outstanding example alongside the International Campaign to Ban Landmines (ICBL) and others. The former's success may also be attributed to its ability to unite the world's largest human rights organizations along with many smaller groups. Focused NGO coalitions like this are a cornerstone of a cosmopolitan movement. However, their success hinges on effective cooperation with the most important players

---

42 Dauvergne, Peter, and Genevieve LeBaron. 2014. Protest Inc. The Corporatization of Activism. Polity Press, pp. 4, 1, 136.
43 'An open letter to our fellow activists across the globe: Building from below and beyond borders.' CIVICUS' Blog, 6 August 2014 (blogs.civicus.org).
44 See pp. 170ff.

in the international arena: governments. As Tom Buitelaar, now at Leiden University, and Richard Ponzio of the Stimson Center noted, major 'global governance innovations ensued when treaty-making processes—traditionally reserved for sovereign states—included NGO representatives.' 'The ICBL and CICC, respectively, played a major role in norm diffusion, pressured reluctant governments, conducted awareness campaigns, suggested treaty text revisions, fulfilled an information function, and sometimes directly influenced the negotiations as a part of state delegations', Buitelaar and Ponzio observed, adding that cooperation with like-minded states 'seems to have been a crucial factor'.[45] No wonder that autocratic states are pushing against NGO involvement at the UN.

A UNPA and global constitutionalization

The more the societal value shift and the new global enlightenment take hold across the world's countries, the greater will be the pressure—and the desire—felt by the big professional international NGOs and smaller groups to see their work in the broader context of the 'Great Transformation' and to actively support aims such as that of a world parliament. And the more likely it is that progress can be made on the gradual path we described. The key milestone is to get the process going by convincing a majority of UN member states to set up a UNPA. In many countries, governments, parties, and political leaders may be inclined to support this once they realize a significant proportion of the electorate is likely to honour it. The aforementioned surveys highlight the substantial potential in this regard. The 2023 survey, for instance, showed significant support for creating a legislative world parliament in a number of countries (not taking into consideration respondents who expressed *somewhat* support or opposition): in Kenya, 52 per cent *strongly* favored the idea, with only 9 per cent *strongly* opposed; in South Africa, it was 43 versus 11 per cent; in India, 38 versus 4 per cent; in Tunisia, 38 versus 5 per cent; and in Turkey, 27 versus 8 per cent. Notably, in this particular 15-country survey, perhaps not surprisingly, only in the USA and the UK it was found that strong opposition outweighed strong support, in case of the USA 29 versus 11 per cent and the UK 19 versus 9 per cent.[46] This poll of course covered the most far-reaching manifestation of the proposal, an assembly with binding decision-making powers. Whilst it is admittedly a long time ago, another survey in

45 Buitelaar, Tom, and Richard Ponzio. 2017. 'Mobilizing Smart Coalitions and Negotiating Global Governance Reform.' Stimson Center, p. 15.
46 Friedrich-Ebert-Stiftung, and YouGov. 2023. 'Global Census. Public Opinions on International Cooperation. Support for a World Parliament', published in: Bummel, Andreas. 5 Oct. 2023. 'International Poll: Public Supports a World Parliament and World Law.' Democracy Without Borders (blog). (democracywithoutborders.org).

2005 found majority support in all 18 countries covered, including the US and UK. In this case, the question related to a directly elected 'UN Parliament' but one with limited competences similar to that of the UN General Assembly.[47] This suggests that a modest first step of creating a UNPA may indeed have popular support everywhere and in quite a number of countries there will be a popular desire to see its powers growing. The crucial hurdle then are *the blocks at the elite level*. Instead of dissipating their energy over too broad an area, the tender green shoots of the 'Great Transformation' should be concentrated mainly at one point, the creation of a UNPA, so as to break through them. According to Democracy Without Borders' theory of change, the instrument of a World Citizens' Initiative might be created by the UN prior to a UNPA because the political hurdles are seen to be much lower. The instrument could then be used to help promote a UNPA. As soon as the assembly is created, even in a modest form, a new dynamic comes into play—or at least that is the expectation. As was recognised by world federalists such as Dieter Heinrich in the early 1990s, such 'an assembly of parliamentarian actors, if we could just get it established, would provide the onward momentum necessary to its further evolution as a house of the people at the UN'.[48] In a mutually reinforcing process, the assembly would contribute to the formation and growth of a cosmopolitan movement, which in turn would mobilize public support for its empowerment and further development. Progressive members of the assembly would be perhaps the most important engine of a cosmopolitan movement. A UNPA could become *the* global vehicle for giving expression to the social forces for systemic change and for concentrating the political pressure for change on governments and the elite. At the same time, it would be the decisive political and institutional fulcrum for the creation of a world state structure on the way to a world parliament. Working with governments, political parties, social movements, NGO coalitions, local authorities, and representatives of other major groups, the UNPA could lay the political and conceptual groundwork for a comprehensive UN Charter review and initiate a process of global constitutionalization. Establishing a global constitution and a global polity is a task that requires the highest possible standards in terms of a broad, public, inclusive, transparent, and legitimate process. Substance and process are thus interrelated. While discussions need to be grounded in rigorous academic analysis, it is imperative to solicit, consider and carefully balance the views of key stakeholders during the drafting process to ensure their interests

---

47 Council on Foreign Relations. 2012. 'Chapter 2: World Opinion on International Institutions', In: Public Opinion on Global Issues. New York: id., pp. 7, 45.

48 Heinrich, Dieter. 2010. The Case for a United Nations Parliamentary Assembly. Extended reprint, originally published 1992. Berlin: Committee for a Democratic UN, p. 42.

are sufficiently reflected. Only then can the resulting outcome garner the necessary level of political and popular support. A global parliamentary assembly needs to play a crucial role in this as a driver and platform for public deliberation and consultation. It should set up a constitutional committee that conducts hearings and produces reports on how a global constitution and a universal system of world law could look like and how both can be implemented, thus helping establish political and popular agreement, support and momentum.

Factors of change

When, under what circumstances and in what form the global values shift will help the efforts for a word parliament to achieve an institutional breakthrough cannot be foreseen. This cannot be considered a surprise. Historic events often arrive suddenly and unexpectedly, even for professional observers. In spite of all the advance signs, almost nobody saw the fall of the Berlin Wall coming when and how it did on 9 November 1989, signalling the end of the Eastern bloc, or more recently the Arab Revolutions of 2011. Few people would have believed it possible that the community of states would be able, only nine years after the fall of the Iron Curtain, to approve the statutes of a permanent International Criminal Court, and that this document would be ratified within four years by 60 states, despite aggressive opposition of the USA, and would enter into force. In any scenarios for the possible realization of a world parliament, four factors are likely to play important roles in one way or another, and in one combination or another: persistent preparation and readiness, revolution from below, revolution from above, and a trigger event.

Persistent preparation and readiness

In the initial phase progress is made mostly in the political background and unremarked in the public sphere. Step by step, support will continue to grow in civil society, in academic and intellectual circles, among experts, politicians and governments. We traced this ongoing process and its prehistory in detail in the first part of this book. Just as international support for the ICC was coordinated and propelled by a coalition of NGOs, so there has been since 2007 an international Campaign for a UNPA. While the CICC enjoyed the support of leading international NGOs and like-minded governments from the beginning, this did not apply to the UNPA campaign. Nonetheless, the creation of a UNPA is now firmly endorsed by large parts of international civil society, and the campaign has demonstrated significant support among parliamentarians. A few foreign ministers and other government officials occasionally endorsed the proposal but this did not result in official government backing or initiatives thus far. Overall, the campaign has remained a shoestring operation, building the groundwork and ready to be ramped up when the time is right. Maintaining this effort, even under difficult circumstances, is crucial. The political environment has become more challenging due to the process of autocratization. At the same time, the global polycrisis, which includes autocratization and a failure of multilateralism, may prompt certain governments to realize that standing still means regressing and that they need to go on the offensive. Creating a UNPA may well become part of their agenda without strong external pressure.

The revolution from below

Nonetheless, the blocks in place at the elite level may only be overcome if the social pressure for change becomes visible as mass support for a world parliament. This factor could be called 'the revolution from below'. Again, the international surveys conducted so far on the issue of a global parliament suggest that the potential for this is indeed present in the world population. Sooner or later, the demand could be taken up not only by leading international NGOs but also by social and political grassroots movements across the world. Protest and resistance against autocratic and corrupt regimes as well as undemocratic global governance institutions, including the UN, would then also embrace the demand for *global* democracy. For the environmental movements this would only be a small step as they are already calling for 'system change, not climate change'. Cities and local authorities could play an important role too. In the view of David Wylie, who was a member of the Cambridge city council, initiatives at the municipal level could be decisive in circumventing the resistance of nation-states.[49] All this would mark the emergence of the new cosmopolitan movement. Through mass protests and demonstrations, with the call for a world parliament being prominent at their centre, the demand for a global constitution and an elected global parliament could take its place on the world stage and on the agenda of day-to-day political debate.

This might happen in the course of a new global wave of protest such as was released by the Arab Revolutions. The Tunisian Revolution of 2011 not only spilled over into Egypt, Libya and Yemen, where the governments were also overthrown, but sparked protests around the world. The anti-austerity movement of 15 May arose in Spain, and its call for 'real democracy now' was taken up by demonstrators in other countries. The occupation of Zucotti Park in New York by the 'Occupy Wall Street' movement in September 2011 was

---

49   Wylie, David A. 2009. City, Save Thyself! Boston: Trueblood Publishing.

inspired by the occupation of Tahrir Square in Cairo. The Occupy protests spread through the USA, Great Britain, Germany and other countries. The commonalities and links between the different movements need to be considered in detail, but it was noted at the time with regard to protests in eleven countries, including Egypt, Brazil, China, Thailand, Turkey and Ukraine, that 'popular discontent with the status quo is already apparent among rising middle classes'.[50] The idea that the establishment of a world parliament could become the central rallying-call for mass protests is not far-fetched. The international network of Occupy groups, for instance, adopted a statement for the globally coordinated day of protest on 15 May 2012 calling for a 'systemic transformation' of the global economic and political system and the democratization of international institutions. In the text published by the *Guardian* it is stated that all 'decisions affecting all mankind should be taken in democratic forums like a participatory and direct UN parliamentary assembly or a UN people's assembly, not rich clubs such as G20 or G8'.[51] This is the 'new cycle of struggles' of which Michael Hardt and Antonio Negri spoke.[52]

The revolution from above

Another important factor for the realization of a world parliament will be support from enlightened elites. This is the 'revolution from above'. Elements of the transnational elite, small at first but then growing larger, will recognize that it lies in their own interests to actively drive forward global democratic reforms. Only in this way will it be possible to ensure the necessary social backing for the continuation of economic integration and global modernization and the stability—even the survival—of world society. World law, on account of its universal validity, can be made to work for all economic actors without distortion of competition. Business people may see advantages in regulation through world law compared with the current international system that is heading towards a breakdown. But support from elite circles will not be motivated by calculated self-interest and social pressure alone. The advance of post-conventional morality, of empathy and of a planetary perspective does not stop when it reaches their doors. This could not have been better illustrated than by Mikhail Gorbachev's 'new thinking'. This example suggests that it could be the determined initiative of one influential head of government that achieves the institutional breakthrough for a 'global perestroika'. 'The path to a world order leads via the voluntary renunciation of advantage by the power-

---

50   World Economic Forum. 2014. Global Risks 2014. Geneva, p. 28.
51   'The GlobalMay manifesto of the Occupy movement'. The Guardian, 11 May 2012 (www.guardian.co.uk).
52   See pp. 365f.

ful, whether because they heed the call of their own humanity or because in their wisdom they foresee the collapse of their own power if they fail to join forces with the others', wrote Karl Jaspers.[53] Moreover, significant support—not least financial—for a cosmopolitan movement and for the push for a world parliament could even come from the circle of the super-rich. Microsoft founder Bill Gates, for example, with a personal fortune of over 130 billion US dollars, is one of the world's top 10 richest people. In an interview with the *Süddeutsche Zeitung* he briefly touched on the issue of a world government. There he bemoaned the lack of 'a form of global governance' for climate change. 'We need a world government?' the interviewers pressed him. 'We have global problems, so it is badly needed', he replied.[54] According to billionaire Mark Zuckerberg, who founded Facebook in 2004, 'our greatest challenges also need global responses—like ending terrorism, fighting climate change, and preventing pandemics. Progress now requires humanity coming together not just as cities or nations, but also as a global community'.[55]

The fallacy of a global shock scenario

Studying the history of the international system tells us that important institutional breakthroughs and paradigm shifts often occurred only after dramatic and decisive events. The Thirty Years' War was an important catalyst in the development of the paradigm of equal sovereignty. The League of Nations, the first intergovernmental organization for collective security, and the international law prohibition against war in the Kellogg–Briand Pact were consequences of the First World War. The replacement of the League of Nations as a universal world organization by the United Nations and the European integration process, with its conceptual basis in shared sovereignty, were consequences of the Second World War. The establishment of the International Criminal Court was a delayed consequence of the Holocaust and the Nuremberg trials. Concrete political trigger events of this kind in the first half of the 1990s were the crimes and genocide on the territory of the former Yugoslavia, and the genocide in Rwanda, for each of which the UN Security Council set up its own tribunal.

One often encounters the idea that the next evolutionary step towards a third-generation federal world organization will not be possible without a similar experience of suffering and shock. 'To create, by anything in the na-

53 Jaspers, Karl. Rechenschaft and Ausblick. München: Piper, 1958, p. 301.
54 Gates, Bill. 28 January 2015. Du darfst keine Zweifel haben. Interview by Michael Bauchmüller and Stefan Braun. Süddeutsche Zeitung.
55 Zuckerberg, Mark. 16 Feb. 2017. 'Building Global Community' (www.facebook.com).

ture of a fresh start, a new world system to avert a third world war', wrote Wilfred Jenks in 1969, 'would be a task requiring political imagination and determination of an order which neither history nor current experience gives us any right to expect.'[56] Randall Schweller wrote that the only solution 'is an enormous shock to the system, a calamity of huge proportions that cracks through the closed system's outer crust and injects the world with new, useful energy to do work again'. He was thinking of 'an appalling natural disaster, global pandemic, or series of coordinated worldwide terrorist attacks against major cities', or a world war. Only such destruction, thought Schweller, could prepare the ground for global renewal.[57] For the physicist Leó Szilárd (1898 to 1964), as for many other scientists involved in the development of the atom bomb, there was no doubting that a world government had to be created, whether in order to control nuclear technology or for the maintenance of peace. As he wrote in 1946, the issue that we have to face is 'whether we can have such a world government without going through a third World War'.[58]

The scenario of a Third World War is one we have no desire to describe. 'This atomic blast', wrote Carl Friedrich von Weizsäcker, 'will never be forgotten while people still tell their children stories. It will be the ultimate symbol of the abyss into which the corruption of the human heart once led us.'[59] If the remnants of human civilization following an atomic war or a similar catastrophe were sufficient to enable the construction of any kind of world government, it will most likely not be a democratic one.[60] After all, in times of emergency, whether the threat is imagined or real, a 'state of exception' usually paves the way for undermining and ignoring the rule of law and not the opposite. Such a scenario as a trigger event for the establishment of a democratic world legal order is not only entirely undesirable, but almost certainly an impossible pathway too. 'The primary purpose in the formation of a democratic cosmopolitarian movement should be to prevent a third World War', Jean Rossiaud rightly noted. The historic task of the movement is to try to ensure a 'gentle transition'. 'The trade union movement and Socialist International failed in this task in 1914', he observed, drawing a historical parallel.[61]

56   Jenks, C. Wilfred. 1969. The World Beyond the Charter. London: George Allen & Unwin Ltd., p. 11.

57   Schweller, Randall L. 2014. Maxwell's Demon and the Golden Apple: Global Discord in the New Millennium. Baltimore, Maryland: Johns Hopkins University Press, p. 140.

58   Szilard, Leo. 1946. 'Can we Avert an Arms Race by an Inspection System?' In: One World Or None, ed. by Dexter Masters and Katharine Way, 167–79. New York: The New Press, p. 178.

59   Weizsäcker, Carl Friedrich von. 1979. Der ungesicherte Friede. 2nd ed. Göttingen: Vandenhoeck & Ruprecht, p. 103.

60   On nuclear war, see p. 275.

61   Rossiaud, p. 19.

Anticipating and averting the horror

The biggest challenge lies once again at the level of consciousness. As Ulrich Bartosch noted, 'the hope that the painful path of experience can be supplanted by the sensible path of rational understanding' was expressed already by Carl Friedrich von Weizsäcker. For if 'the actual experience of a horrific final world war would bring about the change in human consciousness, which means that this change in consciousness is indeed possible, then the anticipatory experience of the horror must be a sufficient condition for the possibility of a change of consciousness without war', Bartosch concluded. Such a change of consciousness 'could empower people to pre-emptively construct a politically underpinned world peace order. All the significant elements of a postwar period can be recognised in the present and can be comprehended, which means they can be reflected upon. The only thing we don't have is the actual experience of pain, of fear and devastation'.[62] To put it in a nutshell, being able to imagine the horrors of a Third World War or Disease X should mobilize the necessary strength to prevent such a future from occurring, and to make it permanently impossible through the creation of a world legal order. But that alone is probably not enough. As Joseph Baratta summed up, 'atomic fear has proven too shallow a motivation for the great work of establishing world government. Humanity will not be frightened into delegating its sovereign powers to a common or federal government. Something like love of country—love of the earth—is needed. People must want a higher level of government to guarantee their liberties, their property, and their security. A positive vision is needed'.[63] The experience of COVID-19 points in a similar direction. Despite the virus making global interconnectedness evident down to an individual, biological level, it didn't immediately trigger global solidarity and political integration. On the contrary, at the height of the pandemic governments failed to collaborate, people were overwhelmed and authoritarian regimes took advantage of the state of emergency as an opportunity to tighten their control and further suppress their populations.[64] The key factor during a global crisis seems to be whether the overall political environment is conducive to enhanced cooperation, and only then can it function as a trigger event.

The establishment of a world legal order needs to be achieved without a shock event on the scale of a third world war, another global pandemic or an

62 Bartosch, Ulrich. 1995. Weltinnenpolitik. Zur Theorie des Friedens bei Carl Friedrich von Weizsäcker. Berlin: Duncker & Humblot, p. 311.

63 Baratta, Joseph Preston. 2004. The Politics of World Federation. From World Federation to Global Governance. Vol. 2. Westport, Connecticut; London: Praeger Publishers, p. 528.

64 On COVID-19, see pp. 262ff.

unprecedented natural disaster. Nevertheless, the revolution from below and the revolution from above may need trigger events to enable them to develop the force needed for a breakthrough. An important spark for the ignition of the 'Occupy' protests was not only the occupation of Tahrir Square but also the global financial crisis of 2007 and the bank bailouts. It is possible to imagine scenarios in which unforeseen but powerful events bring about sudden historic reconfigurations that enable a huge leap forward. A collapse of the international financial and banking system with an accompanying global economic crisis, for instance, is not inconceivable, as undesirable as it may be.[65]

Climate-induced events

What seems certain is the increased incidence and strength of extreme climate-induced events such as storms, floods, heat waves, cold spells and droughts. Climate change will force many millions of people, perhaps hundreds of millions, to become refugees. How exactly this will unfold, and with what consequences, cannot be foreseen. As outlined in the previous part of this book, there is good reason to be worried.[66] In a report to the Club of Rome on forecasts for the year 2052, Jørgen Randers assumed that there was 'no chance' that CO_2 emissions will be reduced far and fast enough to keep global warming below two degrees.[67] With regard to long-term effects, research suggested that with two degrees of warming, a sea level rise of several metres must be anticipated. Moreover, this could happen far faster than has been assumed to date. The ecological and social consequences could be 'devastating'. 'It is not difficult to imagine that conflicts arising from forced migrations and economic collapse might make the planet ungovernable, threatening the fabric of civilization', the study said.[68] Low-lying coastal regions, which include areas like New York and large parts of Bangladesh, would become uninhabitable. In addition, the changes that have already been set into motion will leave at least a quarter of the world's land more arid.[69] An overwhelming number of studies warn against such upheavals. Another study noted that the combustion of all remaining reserves of coal, gas and oil over the coming centuries could mean a

---

65   On financial instability, see pp. 212ff.
66   On climate change, see pp. 184ff.
67   Randers, Jorgen. 2012. 2052. White River Junction, Vt: Chelsea Green Publishing Co, p. 118.
68   Hansen, J., et al. 23 July 2015. 'Ice melt, sea level rise and superstorms: evidence from paleoclimate data, climate modeling, and modern observations that 2 °C global warming is highly dangerous.' Atmos. Chem. Phys. Discuss. (15) 14: 20059–179, pp. 20121, 20119.
69   Park, Chang-Eui, et al. 2018. 'Keeping Global Warming within 1.5 °C Constrains Emergence of Aridification'. Nature Climate Change 8 (1): 70.

rise in sea levels of over 50 metres.[70] As far-reaching and dramatic as these changes will be, their impacts and the effects of countermeasures will unfold over very long periods. While a singular global climate event that will prompt radical immediate action seems unlikely to occur, direct exposure to climate-related disasters will increase and may strengthen the will for change continuously. By all means, in the negotiations over a third generation world organization, the decades-long failure of the world community to halt anthropogenic climate change will serve as a key point of reference. Setting up a federal world order will be inevitable to deal with the consequences in an effective, fair and democratic way.

A democratic China

It is not impossible to imagine that under certain conditions a serious initiative could be instigated by an enlightened US President with a cosmopolitan inclination and enjoying the support of both the House of Representatives and the Senate if the US manages to overcome its internal political polarization and constitutional crisis. But a 'global perestroika' may rather originate from a quarter which today seems unlikely. A decisive development in world politics that would make the third democratic transformation almost impossible to stop would be the democratization of China. The democratization of China would mean that the proportion of the world's population living in democracies would jump in one stroke from 60per cent today to 80 per cent. The remaining autocratic regimes would come under enormous pressure, and the goal of a full democratization of the community of states would be very close. In addition, the democratic legitimation of the great majority of deputies to a world parliament then could hardly be questioned. A democratic China would decisively alter the global political landscape, eliminate dangerous geopolitical conflicts and could throw its economic and demographic weight into the scales so as to finally bring about a democratization and strengthening of global governance. Historically privileged democratic countries will find it increasingly difficult to justify their inaction and lack of support for necessary changes.

A successful democratization in the near future seems unlikely, not least in view of the totalitarian surveillance of Chinese society by the state security services and the suppression of any organised opposition. But history has always been able to surprise us. One aspect of the question that has been much discussed is socio-economic development. Average per capita incomes in China have passed the threshold at which many social scientists believe a pro-

70 Winkelmann, Ricarda, et al. 4 September 2015. 'Combustion of Available Fossil Fuel Resources Sufficient to Eliminate the Antarctic Ice Sheet.' *Science Advances* (1) 8.

cess of democratization is almost inevitable. The political scientist Minxin Pei noted with regard to China that, with the exception of oil-producing countries, hardly any autocratic regimes have been able to survive once per capita income has reached 6,000 US dollars.[71] From 2000 to 2020, this figure jumped tenfold in China from around 1,000 US dollars to more than 10,000, according to World Bank data. According to surveys conducted in 2003, at that time already 72.3 per cent of Chinese respondents said that democracy was desirable for China.[72] Sixty years after the adoption of the Universal Declaration of Human Rights, a 'Charter 08' calling for a new democratic constitution for China was published, and was signed by thousands of courageous Chinese citizens. This document, supported by many prominent Chinese figures, stated that authoritarianism was in decline all around the world, and that this process must not halt at the Chinese border.[73] At the June Fourth Massacre in 1989, pro-democratic protests on Tiananmen Square in Beijing and throughout the country were brutally crushed by the government. In the largest nationwide demonstrations since then, many thousands of people spontaneously took to the streets in the White Paper protests in November 2022 to voice their discontent with the authorities' harsh zero-COVID lockdown policy and increasingly with the regime as such.[74] Before being sentenced to 14 years in prison in a political trial in April 2023, Chinese civic rights activist Xu Zhiyong expressed the dream of 'a democratic China'—based on the rule of law and free elections at all levels of government—'that belongs to the people' and where it is no longer possible that 'a few bureaucrats decide what 1.3 billion people should believe and speak'.[75] As China's population begins to shrink and economic growth slows down, the Communist Party's autocratic rule indeed will come under increasing pressure and ultimately fall apart. The theoretical and ideological foundation on which a cosmopolitan initiative of China's future democratic leadership could be based is already being laid down. It consists in a new interpretation, from the perspective of global modernity, of the concept of 'Tianxia' from the time of the Zhou dynasty. The philosopher Zhao Tingyang believes that through the adoption and implementation of this concept China could become a world power and take on responsibility to the benefit of all—not as an oppressive or aggressive empire,

---

71   Pei, Minxin. 13 February 2013. '5 Ways China Could Become a Democracy.' The Diplomat (thediplomat.com).

72   Chu, Yun-Han, Larry Diamond, Andrew J. Nathan, and Doh Chull Shin (ed.). 2010. How East Asians View Democracy. New York: Columbia University Press, p. 22.

73   'China's Charter 08'. Transl. by Perry Link. The New York Review of Books, 15 Jan. 2009 (nybooks.com).

74   Ong, Lynette H. 2023. 'The CCP After the Zero-Covid Fail.' Journal of Democracy 34(2): 32-46.

75   Xu, Zhiyong. 9 April 2023. '"A Democratic China Must Be Realized in Our Time, We Cannot Saddle the next Generation with This Duty"–Xu Zhiyong's Court Statement', China Change, (chinachange.org).

but as a progressive force contributing to the realization of a Tianxia system in the world. According to Feng Zhang from Tsinghua University in Beijing, the central idea is that of 'transforming the world into a home for all peoples'. The concept goes beyond the nation state as the highest political unit and requires the establishment of a world institution able to deal with all global issues. 'This, in effect, amounts to saying a world government is necessary in the tianxia system', Zhang summed up.[76] It explicitly includes the idea of an inclusive world constitution.[77] With this initiative, in the judgement of Allen Carlson from Cornell University in New York, for the first time in the country's history China's foreign policy elite has begun to question the normative structures of the international system, based as they are on Western thinking; and with that, 'a potentially far-reaching ... reconsideration of international order is underway in China'.[78] Another source of inspiration and mobilization in China with respect to achieving global democracy is a revival of interest in the cosmopolitan philosophy of Kang Youwei that was laid out before.[79] This may turn out to be more important because 'it must be said that Zhao Tingyang's commitment to the ideal of a universal polity is much less detailed than Kang's Utopia: the specific form in which the tianxia will be realized is blurred in Zhao's texts', as the sinologist Federico Brusadelli pointed out.[80] Kang Youwei, by contrast, elaborated in detail on a future world parliament.

In the beginning

At the core of the third democratic transformation is a change in values and consciousness. As Mathias Koenig-Archibugi observed in a valuable essay, the possibility of a global democracy is dependent to some extent on people's belief in the possibility of a global democracy.[81] In this book we have tried to show that global democracy is not only necessary but possible. But it will not come about by itself, but only as a result of our efforts. And we will need staying power. The process of structural transformation into a world democracy will take a long time. Meanwhile there are countless acute problems that require immediate attention. Nevertheless, it would be a fatal error not to put our ener-

---

76 Feng, Zhang. 2009. 'The Tianxia System: World Order in a Chinese Utopia.' GlobalAsia (4) 4: 108–12, pp. 108-9.

77 Zhao, Tingyang. 2012. 'All-Under-Heaven and Methodological Relationism.' In: Contemporary Chinese Political Thought, Ed. by Fred Dallmayr and Zhao Tingyang, 46–66. Lexington: Univ. Press of Kentucky, p. 64.

78 Carlson, Allen. 2011. 'Moving Beyond Sovereignty? A brief consideration of recent changes in China's approach to international order and the emergence of the tianxia concept.' Journal of Contemporary China (20) 68: 89–102.

79 See pp. 49ff.

80 Brusadelli, Federico. 2020. Confucian Concord: Reform, Utopia and Global Teleology in Kang Youwei's Datong Shu. Confucian Concord. Brill, p. 173.

81 Koenig-Archibugi, Mathias. 2011. 'Is global democracy possible?' Europ. Journal of Int. Rel. (17) 3:519–42, p. 523.

gies into the necessary long-term transformation for that reason. Short-term thinking will not bring about an evolutionary leap forward, and will lead us further down a blind alley. A fantastic and fulfilling future for humankind in harmony with nature is possible. As the Anthropocene advances and we continue to master the challenges of our age, so people will increasingly grasp the fact that the last 10,000 years of human history were only *the beginning*.

As H.G. Wells wrote over 100 years ago in 'The Outline of History', history 'is and must always be no more than an account of beginnings. We can venture to prophesy that the next chapters to be written will tell, though perhaps with long interludes of setback and disaster, of the final achievement of worldwide political and social unity. But when that is attained, it will mean no resting stage, nor even a breathing stage, before the development of a new struggle and of new and vaster efforts. Men will unify only to intensify the search for knowledge and power, and live as ever for new occasions'.[82] Humankind will finally be able to develop and deploy to the full its creativity and energy, and in a productive way, for the optimal benefit of all people and of all life on earth. This dream *can* become reality. It *must* become reality, if humankind is to have a future.

---

82   Wells, Herbert George. 1920. The Outline of History. Being a Plain History of Life and Mankind. Vol. II. New York: The MacMillan Company, p. 594.

Index of names

9 783942 282246